The American Civil War, 2nd Edition

The American Civil War: A Literary and Historical Anthology brings together a wide variety of writing from the Civil War and Reconstruction eras, including short fiction, poetry, public addresses, diary entries, and essays, accompanied by concise introductions and explanatory notes.

Now in a thoroughly revised second edition, this slimmer volume has been revamped to:

Emphasize a diversity of perspectives on the war
Include more women writers
Achieve greater North–South balance
Include soldiers' testimony
Provide additional historical context.

With selections from Louisa May Alcott, Walt Whitman, Henry Timrod, Abraham Lincoln, Harriet Martineau, and many more, Ian Finseth's careful selection of texts remains an indispensable resource for readers who seek to understand the impact of the conflict on the culture of the United States. *The American Civil War* reaffirms the complex role that literature, poetry, and the documentation of history played in shaping how the Civil War is remembered.

To provide students with additional resources, the anthology is now accompanied by a companion website which you can find at www.routledge.com/cw/finseth. There you will discover additional primary sources, including photographs, sheet music, and literary texts, and an extensive bibliography.

Ian Frederick Finseth is Associate Professor of English at the University of North Texas. He is the author of *Shades of Green: Visions of Nature in the Literature of American Slavery, 1770–1860.*

The American Civil War

A Literary and Historical Anthology

2nd Edition

Edited by Ian Frederick Finseth

Routledge
Taylor & Francis Group

NEW YORK AND LONDON

Please visit the book's companion website at
www.routledge.com/cw/finseth

Second Edition published 2013
711 Third Avenue, New York, NY 10017

Simultaneously published in the UK
by Routledge
2 Park Square, Milton Park, Abingdon, Oxon OX14 4RN

Routledge is an imprint of the Taylor & Francis Group, an informa business

First published by Routledge in 2006

Library of Congress Cataloging in Publication Data
The American Civil War : a literary and historical anthology / edited by Ian Frederick Finseth. — Second edition.
   p. cm.
   1. American literature—19th century—History and criticism. 2. United States—History—Civil War, 1861–1865—Literature and the war. 3. War and literature—United States—History—19th century. 4. War in literature. I. Finseth, Ian Frederick, editor of compilation.
PS217.C58A43 2013
810.9′358—dc23

ISBN: 978–0–415–53706–3(hbk)
ISBN: 978–0–415–53707–0(pbk)
ISBN: 978–0–203–38779–5(ebk)

Typeset in Minion
by RefineCatch Limited, Bungay, Suffolk, UK

Printed and bound in the United States of America
by Edwards Brothers, Inc.

Contents

Acknowledgments

First, I am grateful for the support and generous assistance of my editor at Routledge, Kimberly Guinta, and for the insightful feedback of the external readers who evaluated my proposal for a second edition of this anthology. In preparing the mansucript, I have also benefited greatly from the scholarly acumen and exemplary work ethic of my graduate editorial assistant, Darcy Lewis. Thanks as well to Nick Brock for his excellent copyediting and to Heather Cushing for overseeing production. My deepest gratitude goes to my partner in all things, Stephanie Hawkins, who bore with me through yet another long project; and to our little one, Audrey, who was not even around when the first edition came out.

Preface to the Second Edition

In the seven years since the first edition of this anthology appeared, interest in the American Civil War has abated not one iota. To the contrary, the ongoing sesquicentennial of the war (2011–2015) has inspired another wave of popular and scholarly books, along with periodical series, television programs, feature films, and Internet resources. To an unprecedented extent, there are new perspectives, new arguments, new information, new texts, and new technologies—all of which are reshaping how the Civil War is understood.

This second edition of *The American Civil War* reflects the changing terrain of Civil War studies in its selection of texts, its editorial apparatus, and in its coordination with a Routledge companion website (discussed in more detail below). Yet the essential aim remains unchanged: to provide readers with an original, dynamic, and wide-ranging collection of primary writings illustrating the war's influence on the literary imagination and cultural politics of nineteenth-century America. In this one volume appear Abraham Lincoln's private jottings and Frederick Douglass's public speeches, Herman Melville's war poetry and Louisa May Alcott's short stories, Mary Chesnut's diary entries and Loreta Velazquez's postwar memoir—among many other writings. Taken singly, these writings do not, and cannot, convey the full measure of the Civil War's psychic and social impact. Taken together, however, they attain something of the effect of a symphony, in which all the instruments contribute to the musical experience. Indeed, it is a central argument of this book that Civil War writings, including those of canonical authors such as Walt Whitman or Stephen Crane, are best understood in relation to one another, and in the context of the full range of literary expression that the war stimulated.

How the Texts Were Chosen

Given the sheer volume of available material—an embarrassment of riches which sometimes made the winnowing process seem like a fool's errand—this anthology represents just one possible configuration of Civil War writings. Yet several important principles guided the selection of texts. First, I have given priority to works of significant literary value, in which the meanings of the war are investigated rather than simplified, explored for their human significance rather than reduced to polemic and posturing. Daniel Aaron may have been correct in arguing that the Civil War produced no undisputed masterpiece of fiction, and that nineteenth-century American writers had trouble assimilating it, but his conclusion that the war was "not so much unfelt as unfaced" does an injustice to the literary record.[1] Certainly the war produced its fair share of self-serving histories, contrived narratives, and mediocre poetry, along with a great deal of ephemeral material. Yet it also called forth an impressive number of creative works that took seriously the job of exploring the moral, emotional, and social complexities of the war. Accordingly, I have emphasized short stories, poetry, essays, and oratory which reflect a committed imaginative engagement with the Civil War, and which illustrate how the conflict was creatively interpreted, and continually reinterpreted, for a variety of audiences.

Second, I have focused on the late nineteenth century; chronologically, the texts range from November 22, 1860 (Harriet Martineau's "Election of Abraham Lincoln") to 1902 (Susie King Taylor's *Reminiscences of My Life in Camp*). Although literary and creative artists even now are producing important works about the Civil War, obviously there are limits on what can be included in a single volume. The principle I observed, therefore, was that of living memory: all the writers represented here lived through the Civil War itself or its long aftermath, as participants or observers or both, and always as commentators. Even if they had no direct experience of combat or of camp life, they saw the impact of the war on politics, psychology, medicine, and philosophy; on families and communities; on race relations and the cultural development of the United States.

These writers' varying backgrounds motivated the third principle of selection: diversity. The works here reflect a range of social perspectives: Southern and Northern, African American and European American, male and female, patrician and plebeian. In the same spirit of inclusiveness, canonical works share these pages with less familiar writings by authors whose renown grows dim. There is a double benefit to this approach. The more famous pieces, such as Walt Whitman's "When Lilacs Last in the Door-Yard Bloom'd," are brought into sharper relief when restored to the full context of Civil War literary interpretation and remembrance. At the same time, the noncanonical works provide a richer sense of the war's impact on American culture, and a fresh perspective on the development of American literature during the crucial decades before the First World War. To the degree possible, the selection process has been ideologically neutral, valuing literary quality over political content, but I am also aware that any anthology represents an implicit thesis about its subject matter—in this case, an implicit narrative of American history. So it is worth observing up front that this book gives weighty emphasis to the conflicts of race and slavery that lay at the heart of the Civil War and that hardly abated in its echoing aftermath. At the same time, the primary goal has been to illuminate rather than adjudicate the conflict between different viewpoints—to convey a sense of the various meanings the Civil War quickly acquired, and of how thoughtful observers both shaped and navigated those meanings.

As for the many necessary exclusions, several considerations prevailed. With a few exceptions of notable merit or cultural importance, such as Ulysses S. Grant and Mary Chesnut, I have avoided memoirs, autobiographies, and diaries, preferring to include works in their entirety whenever possible. Novels, for the same reason, do not appear here, although a number of important ones did emerge from the Civil War—notably, Rebecca Harding Davis's *Waiting for the Verdict* (1867), John W. De Forest's *Miss Ravenel's Conversion from Secession to Loyalty* (1867), Elizabeth Phelps's *The Gates Ajar* (1868), S. Weir Mitchell's *In War Time* (1885), Paul Laurence Dunbar's *The Fanatics* (1901), and, of course, Stephen Crane's *The Red Badge of Courage* (1896). For course purposes, clearly, what makes sense is to assign one or more of these novels in conjunction with the anthology. Other kinds of writing, finally, have been excluded because of the inevitable limitations of space: soldiers' correspondence; polemical literature regarding slavery; and documentary narratives, such as *Battles and Leaders of the Civil War*, a historical series published in *The Century Magazine* in the 1880s.

What this anthology offers, then, is a portrait of war in its broad dimensions. It represents just a fraction of the totality of Civil War literature, but in their psychological, ideological, and stylistic diversity, the writings here should convey something of the scope of the war's influence on American literature and culture.

A Note on Notes

In addition to the primary literary and historical writings, you will find here a variety of supplementary editorial materials intended to provide context and explanation. Historical, biographical, and cultural information appears in a number of different places: section introductions, headnotes and textual notes, biographical sketches of the writers, and a glossary of important battles, historical figures, and terminology. Depending on what information you are looking for, you will most likely find it in one or other of these places.

The section introductions give an overview of the historical and conceptual problems involved in a particular section; the aim is not to resolve those problems but to begin mapping out the terrain in order to suggest points of tension and avenues of inquiry. In each case, the discussion has been informed by recent scholarly work on the Civil War, and although I have not provided lists of "suggested reading," extensive bibliographies appear on the Routledge companion website. The headnotes provide more detailed background information for individual readings—not for every selection, but for those which need additional contextualization, such as speeches or memoirs. In these headnotes, interpretive commentary has been carefully limited so as not to interfere with the reader's own independent engagement and discovery. Footnotes, which appear throughout the primary materials, provide factual information about particular details, references, phrases, and so forth. Important battles, personages, or other proper nouns that come up repeatedly—such as Chancellorsville, John Brown, or the Sanitary Commission—are discussed at somewhat greater length in the glossary toward the back of the book, rather than being footnoted in every instance. Finally, the sketches of the authors provide quick introductions to their lives in relation to the Civil War. In this day and age, of course, ample biographical information about almost anybody is available at our fingertips, and so the sketches here are offered as appetizers, in a sense, which will hopefully encourage further research into authors whom the reader finds particularly compelling.

The Companion Website

In addition to the materials in this printed anthology itself, there are a variety of resources available online for both students and teachers. The Routledge companion website for *The American Civil War*—located at www.routledge.com/cw/finseth—has been designed to support your study of Civil War literature by providing additional primary texts and visual images. The website also features a variety of pedagogical resources intended to augment the book's use in the classroom, including discussion questions and essay topics.

The website more or less mirrors the structure of the printed anthology, with online materials organized according to its five major sections: "Origins," "Battlefields,"

"African American Experience," "The Home Front," and "Reconstructing." Within each division, there are additional literary and historical writings; biographical sketches that do not appear in the book; photographs, political cartoons, and other images related to the war; and links to existing online resources. To the degree possible, these materials on the companion website have been internally linked and cross-referenced in order to illuminate the rich interplay of cultural and literary materials, and to facilitate the process of investigation and discovery. Students are encouraged to follow their impulses and intuitions, and to track down leads and possibilities, when using the website; a little serendipity can go a long way when exploring the universe of primary documents that the Civil War generated.

Note

1 Daniel Aaron, *The Unwritten War: American Writers and the Civil War* (New York: Alfred A. Knopf, 1973), 328.

Introduction
The Written War

Virginia. Newspaper vendor and cart in camp. Photographer: Gardner, Alexander. Library of Congress Prints and Photographs Division, LC-DIG-cwpb-01140

War and Language

Writing about war—about the organized killing of people, the complex forces that go into that killing, and the profound consequences that flow from it—is almost as old as war itself. War fascinates, appalls, and defies those who would put words to it. It stretches the language we have, demanding that we create new language to describe its ever-startling face.

The essential material of writing is language, and the essential material of war is violence, or what Walt Whitman called "the red business." These materials, language and violence, intertwine in complex ways. On the one hand, writing seems the apex of civilization, the triumph of culture over nature, while war seems to confirm the survival of a primal, even animalistic, savagery. Social theorists and philosophers of violence have taught us that physical violence, in its overwhelming literalness, can warp and constrain language, which depends on abstraction and metaphor. The suffering of extreme violence so radically departs from ordinary individual experience that it thwarts the human impulse to give voice to that suffering, whether as participant or observer. And violence thrives on the breakdown of language, erupting at the moment when dialogue, negotiation, and self-expression stumble and fail. In the simplest terms, as long as people are talking they are not fighting. At the same time, words and war have a long and intimate history, and that history has much to do with how language is used in the furtherance of violence. Elementally, the destructive power of language—in war or in daily life—involves the use of dehumanizing epithets that remove a person from the circle of human empathy, and makes them, so to speak, fair game. In a more general sense, language establishes the full conceptual framework within which a conflict proceeds. It sets the terms by which people understand the violence (including, frequently, the contractual terms governing the conduct of participants); it promotes ideological coherence amidst the chaos of violence; and, in a very practical sense, it enables the planning and coordination necessary for organized violence.[1]

For all that, however, the violence of war is one of the most powerful of stimuli to the creative imagination. Even as violence stymies language, it requires that we use language to represent it—and thus is born the literature of war.

Generalizations about war literature are perilous, but we might hazard a few. To write about war is to write about a human experience that is horrific and yet all too routine. It is to try to communicate something of the moral ambiguity of deliberate killing; of the feelings of soldiers and civilians; of the unexpected artistry of war. Writing about war is to heroize a nation or an ethnic group; to absolve oneself of cowardice or incompetence; or to anatomize a socio-historical moment. It means evaluating the social relations between the men (and women) who fight, their changed relations to those left at home, and the transformation of personality that can take place in combat. It means weighing the pain and the horror against the visceral thrill and sense of glory that war can invoke, and making room for the random absurdities that cling to all wars. And, above all, to write about war is to offer some interpretation, implicit or explicit, of what the conflict means for the present. Kate McLoughlin has rightfully observed that war "is the greatest test of a writer's skills of evocation" because it is "huge in scale, devastating in impact and encompassing of human behaviour in its greatest trials and intimacies."[2]

We can approach these issues as they apply to the Civil War by considering two other defining wars in American history. In her study of King Philip's War, a brutal conflict involving English colonists and Algonquian tribes in 1675–1676, Jill Lepore has illuminated the impulse to build language out of the destruction of war:

At first, the pain and violence of war are so extraordinary that language fails us: we cannot name our suffering and, without words to describe it, reality itself becomes confused, even unreal. But we do not remain at a loss for words for long. Out of the chaos we soon make new meanings of our world, finding words to make reality real again . . . . War twice cultivates language: it requires justification, it demands description.[3]

This "cultivation" of language often leads in the direction of propaganda, toward a restricted and manipulative interpretation of what the war entailed. For the Puritans, in this case, writing about King Philip's War became a means of securing their own English identity over and against both the Native Americans and other European societies. Yet the literary response to war can also lead in more creative, open-ended directions—if a writer chooses to explore the deeper, uncertain meanings of the conflict.

Some three centuries after King Philip's War, Tim O'Brien looked back on his experience in Vietnam and described both the need to articulate that experience and the difficulty of doing so:

Partly catharsis, partly communication, [telling stories] was a way of grabbing people by the shirt and explaining exactly what had happened to me, how I'd allowed myself to get dragged into a wrong war, all the mistakes I'd made, all the terrible things I had seen and done . . . . By telling stories, you objectify your own experience. You separate it from yourself. You pin down certain truths. You make up others. You start sometimes with an incident that truly happened . . . and you carry it forward by inventing incidents that did not in fact occur but that nonetheless help to clarify and explain.[4]

Throughout history this blending of imagination and reportage—even when the goal is "objectivity"—has been a universal feature of the literature of war. From the *Iliad* or *Henry V* to *Catch-22* and *The Yellow Birds*, communicating the truths of war has required more than the objective transcription of events and details, if such a thing were even possible. It has required many different voices, and a willingness to bend language and to enlist the imagination in order to get at the deeper nerve centers of human experience.

And yet, it is precisely this imaginative dimension of war literature that raises difficult moral and epistemological questions. Can we rely on the imagination to find the "real story" behind the cold hard facts of war? What do we make of a subjective response to war masquerading as general human truth? Do the aesthetic qualities of literature help to bring home the horrors of war or make them more remote? Is figurative language a path to understanding or a glorified form of escapism?

Literature of the Civil War

In his second inaugural address, given about a month before the peace settlement at Appomattox, Lincoln observed that neither North nor South had expected the Civil War to become the kind of conflict it grew into: "Each looked for an easier triumph, and a result less fundamental and astounding." The war had stunned and transformed the nation, with a force that the imagination found hard to reckon, and at a cost difficult to fathom. In the literature of the Civil War—even the literature produced during the war itself—one can sense the feeling of staggered awe with which American authors contemplated the wreckage of the conflict. Yet one can also detect other strains of feeling: humor, outrage, perplexity, denial, forgiveness, guilt, revenge.

The war was represented and reimagined in every available genre. Many veterans published memoirs focused on their war experience. Literary realists explored the meanings of the war in novels or short fiction. Some authors turned to poetic verse, others to the essay, and others to formal history. And then there was the great outpouring of war writing that was never published at all: the many thousands of letters, diary entries, and journals that soldiers and civilians wrote during and after the conflict. Thematically as well, the Civil War evoked a spectrum of writerly responses. The fantasy of a Southern golden age, before the calamity of defeat, arose during these years, as did the narrative convention in which national reconciliation is symbolized by a North–South romance culminating in marriage. In some works, the social instabilities caused by the war are associated with racial and sexual insecurity, while in others they present unexpected opportunities. A number of writers handled the war analytically, even sociologically, approaching its political and military dimensions with the certitude of positivist science. Many more treated the conflict obliquely, apprehending the war in its fragments rather than its totality, concerned to show its indirect psychological influence rather than its overt historical impact. Some concentrated on its grotesque or gothic qualities, while others thought its truths were best reported straight, in realistic accounts of battles and episodes. The notion that the war represented a collective purgation, national sacrifice, or affirmation of Christian belief was a common theme—but so was the thought that the war had unleashed darker energies in American history.[5]

In these various ways, literature was a mode of both psychological and social reconstruction. As James Dawes has suggested, the Civil War fundamentally "challenged the communicative and deliberative procedures of the republic," so writing about the war represented a means of repairing and reinforcing those traditions. "The struggle to talk during and after violence," Dawes writes, "is language's struggle to regain mastery over violence, whether manifest in the individual's attempt to speak her trauma or a culture's attempt to produce a literary record."[6] For authors whom the war had affected most directly, such as Ambrose Bierce or Oliver Wendell Holmes, Jr., putting language to their experiences could serve as a probing or a bandaging of personal wounds. For authors too young to fight in or remember the Civil War, turning to the war enabled them to write about the society the conflict had created: increasingly consolidated, more economically and politically powerful than ever before, yet still riven by the faultlines of social class and race. The challenge was to discern in the Civil War a source of meaning for the postbellum period, a pattern of cause and effect, right and wrong, that would serve as philosophical and emotional ballast for Americans who lived in its turbulent wake.

This does not mean that writing about the Civil War or its aftermath was simply an exercise in social healing or a good-faith effort to reinvigorate the traditions of American public discourse. In some cases, war literature became a second front on which the festering conflicts could be fought anew, or on which old scores could be settled. The military phase of the conflict had concluded, but the struggle to define American culture had by no means waned—even when it appeared to be submerged under an outpouring of nostalgia and reconciliationist sentiment. The old adage that history is written by the victors was not entirely borne out by the late nineteenth-century American literary scene. Magazines, novels, newspapers, public speeches, autobiographies, historical papers—all formed an interpretive arena in which the meanings of the war, and of the racial, political, and economic conflicts that gave rise to the war, were up for grabs. The stakes were high, for what kind of country the United States would become depended in large measure on what kind of war Americans imagined they had fought.

In wars between different nations or cultures, with different languages and histories, the dynamics of post-war interpretation do not have the same closed, impacted quality as they do after a civil war. In this case, the veterans, partisans, and commentators inhabit the same political territory, speak the same language, share the same cultural reference points, and look back to the same past, all of which are nonetheless fought over. For example, after King Philip's War, the English colonists did not have to compete with or accommodate Native American interpretations of the conflict; they had only to work out amongst themselves how the war would be remembered. After the Civil War, by contrast, writers from a more or less reintegrated nation drew from the same bag of cultural tropes and icons and narratives (the martyrdom of Lincoln, the beckoning frontier, the plantation fallen into disrepair), even if they had very different purposes in doing so—and they had to negotiate the expectations of the same publishing industry and of overlapping, increasingly self-aware reading publics.

That last point deserves emphasis. The production and consumption of Civil War literature between the 1860s and the early 1900s did not take place in a vacuum, but rather in a kind of literary ecosystem involving writers, editors, publishers, distribution syndicates, critics, and readers. It thrived, indeed, in a burgeoning periodical culture in which the number of American newspapers rose from about 4,000 in 1860 to almost 19,000 in 1899, while the number of other periodicals rose from about 700 in 1865 to more than 3,000 in 1885.[7] Newspapers, illustrated weeklies, and monthly magazines regularly published fiction, poetry, commentary, and, in serial form, novels dealing with the war and its legacies—including the work of such major authors as Mark Twain, Kate Chopin, Henry James, and many others. Significantly, not only the newspapers but also the big literary magazines represented a far-reaching geographic diversity: the *Atlantic Monthly* (Boston), *Putnam's Monthly Magazine*, *Harper's Weekly*, the *Century*, and the *Galaxy* (all New York); the *Southern Magazine* (Baltimore), the *Overland Monthly* (San Francisco), and the *Lakeside Monthly* (Chicago), to name just a few of the most prominent. Kathleen Diffley has estimated that between 1861 and 1876, some sixteen literary magazines, representing the Northeast, the South, and the West, printed more than 300 pieces of short fiction about the Civil War.[8] Given the wide circulation of many of these periodicals, and also the relatively high rate of American literacy in the late nineteenth century, writings about the Civil War worked down into the capillary level of American culture, reaching millions of readers, in scores of towns and cities, embodying a wide range of social backgrounds.

By the same token, Civil War writings had to be responsive to the pressures of the literary marketplace. Social values and expectations became business considerations, and business considerations in turn weighed on editorial and authorial decisions. For this reason, the ideological diversity of Civil War literature was to a certain degree constrained by a subtle yet pervasive cultural desire to avoid the most difficult subjects, such as race or war guilt. Yet all writings on the war communicated, perforce, a particular vision of the nation's past and future, whether implicitly or explicitly. They engaged in a titanic, slow-motion struggle with each other to determine how the nation would understand regional identity, civil rights, economic growth, and moral responsibility for the war and its aftermath. Even when it broke into acrimony, however, this struggle went forward on the basis of a shared national identity, against the backdrop of a reconciliationist national mood, and within the same national system of commerce.[9]

At one end of this relatively narrow spectrum, some Civil War writings were openly devoted to national reconciliation. The best example of this may be *Battles and Leaders of the Civil War*, a compendium of generals' and veterans' accounts, representing both Northern and Southern perspectives, published serially in *The Century Magazine* between 1884 and 1887, and issued in book form in 1887–1888. At the other end of the spectrum, some literature was aggressively vindicationist, such as the publications of the Southern Historical Society, the brainchild of Gen. Jubal Early, which was dedicated to keeping the Confederate point of view alive and in the public consciousness.

In the midst of the histories and the memoirs, other American authors turned to a variety of literary modes or forms in an effort to get at the lingering mysteries of the conflict. Frequently they had to navigate the crosscurrents of the literary marketplace in order to find a publisher, let alone a receptive audience, and Civil War literature often reveals how a writer could work both within and against the conventions of any particular genre or tradition. Hence we see Charles Chesnutt, for instance, in response to the popular plantation and dialect fiction of Thomas Nelson Page and Joel Chandler Harris, writing short stories that invoke the antebellum plantation not romantically, but for the purpose of representing slavery's unique fusion of economics and cruelty. Similarly, Sarah Morgan Bryan Piatt turned to the well-worn conventions of sentimental poetry not as a retreat from emotional candor but in order to reimagine the feelings of women whose experiences and loyalties resisted easy classification. In short, much Civil War literature can be read against the grain of dominant literary tastes and cultural values. We should read it with an eye toward the recurrent tensions and omissions in its treatment of national identity, toward the unacknowledged or imperfectly suppressed African American presence in its picture of American life, and toward the psychological tics and conflicts that belie the notion of a hale post-war culture. Much American literature reduced the war to its simplicities—though sometimes in a perversely illuminating way—but many other writings struggled against themselves, and against the cultural tide, in order to come to terms with some piece of the war or with its aftermath.

The Civil War became many civil wars when refracted through the prism of literary style. The war can look very different depending on whether we approach it through Ulysses S. Grant's steady factualism, Oliver Wendell Holmes, Jr.'s heroic romanticism, Lucy Larcom's ironic sentimentalism, or Hamlin Garland's regionalism. Each of these styles brings to the fore different meanings and perspectives; each renders just a single aspect of the war, however sweeping a writer's ambition may be; and our impression of the war will vary from one to the next. Local color, humor, naturalism, historical analysis—all imply certain attitudes toward or perceptions of the war's impact on people. At issue is not only subject matter but the worldview, the moral sense, and the epistemology embodied in different ways of using the language. What distinguishes a tabulation of regimental losses from an elegiac poem, for example, goes beyond genre to embrace a fundamentally different view of human mortality.

The ascendancy of "realism" in late nineteenth-century American culture is of particular significance for the development of Civil War literature. While there were (and are) competing theories of realism, and as many practitioners as there were ideas of what constituted "reality" in the first place, certain consistent patterns emerge across the era's fiction, nonfiction, and visual art. Realism of the nineteenth-century variety is generally oriented less toward the heroic individual than toward the representative type. It concerns itself with the details and material conditions of everyday life—with how people look, sound, interact, entertain themselves, earn a living, face the day—in a carefully wrought social context. The realist novel, painting, or photograph often has political overtones, reflecting a progressive concern with the plight of the "common man" during an era of disconcertingly rapid change. Particularly in its early years, realism expressed a belief in a universal moral order that transcended and compensated for the brutalities of the economic and social order. In its local color or regionalist varieties, realism focused on the lives of unusual people in the less familiar areas of the country—coastal Maine, New Orleans, rural Wisconsin—and on the cultural adhesives that held together a geographically diverse nation. In the strain of realism that evolved into naturalism, we find a concern with the forces working in an individual life, from within and without, as biology or culture. Realism, broadly conceived, was an effort to apprehend the textures and operating principles of a world whose startling complexity both the social scientists and the natural scientists made more evident every day.[10]

Realism in the arts and literature was nurtured by a heightened demand for, and an increased supply of, information, and the Civil War contributed to both. In 1860, the United States was well on its way to becoming an information culture, and the war accelerated that process by stimulating the public's appetite for reliable knowledge about military and political matters, and by encouraging the improvement of communication networks. It quickly became the most visible, accessible war in American history, with commerical photographers, magazine sketch artists, and print journalists recording almost every imaginable fact and facet of the conflict, and distributing their work to a knowledge-hungry public.[11]

The rise of reproducible images and syndicated news reports as dominant modes of public knowledge had profound implications for how nineteenth-century Americans understood the world. Along with the proliferation of news outlets and the increasing professionalization of journalism, improvements in photographic and lithographic technology made the representation of "reality" a matter of course. The photograph, seemingly, could not lie, and it set a standard for reliability that the canons of professional journalism echoed by emphasizing "objectivity" as a core principle of the reporter's craft. More than ever before, information became a commodity, and quick, seemingly accurate knowledge of the world could be had for a penny. Yet both the photograph and the news story can have the strange effect of making the world at once more available and more remote. Photographic images, in John Berger's words, "offer appearances—with all the credibility and gravity we normally lend to appearances—prised away from their meaning." The photograph, he writes, "offers information, but information severed from all lived experience."[12] In similar terms, Alan Trachtenberg has made the same point about newspapers in the Gilded Age: "the dailies dramatized a paradox of metropolitan life itself: the more knowable the world came to seem as information, the more remote and opaque it came to seem as experience."[13]

Writings about the Civil War, "literary" or otherwise, can be read partly for how they respond to these problems of realism and the culture of information. On the one hand, both fiction and nonfiction bear the imprint of the era's photographic and journalistic norms in their concern with detail, panorama, visual impact, and the detached point of view. It is not coincidental that many of the major authors of the late nineteenth century—Crane, Bierce, Frank Norris, Mark Twain, and Harold Frederic, among others—were also professional journalists. This was an age, by and large, when the brooding romances of Hawthorne, the elaborate idealism of Emerson, and the stylistic excesses of Melville seemed less in keeping with the hard-nosed, no-nonsense culture the United States imagined itself becoming. Imaginative symbolism, flights of fancy, and other forms of authorial self-indulgence did not always seem well suited to communicating the difficult truths and social nuances of an increasingly complex culture.

On the other hand, postbellum American literature—both fiction and nonfiction—often reveals an uncertainty about the adequacy of realism, about the capacity of writing to get at the deeper truths of the war, or of society more broadly. The conventions of linear narrative, expository description, rational character development, conflict resolution, and so forth, gave literary texts their form and coherence, but at what cost? The sober factuality of military memoirs, orthodox histories, and occasional speeches was indispensable to capturing the war's meaning, but was it sufficient? These questions hung in the air, and they help to explain why much of the salient literature of the period—from S. Weir Mitchell's medical fiction to Ambrose Bierce's horror stories to Elizabeth Stuart Phelps's spiritualist novels—extravagantly violates the norms of "realistic" representation, even as it borrows freely from the realist palette. If imagination had to supplement or trump reportorial objectivity, so be it.

For the confounding, overpowering reality of the Civil War that realists, indeed all Americans, had to assimilate was the horrific death toll. Indeed, that toll appears to be worse than we have realized. While historians have long agreed that about 620,000 soldiers died in the war, recent demographic statistical work by J. David Hacker suggests that the number might be closer to 750,000.[14] And that does not include the tens or even hundreds of thousands of white civilians and African Americans who perished as a result of the Civil War. Numerical figures can become numbing, however, so what we need to remember is that civil war brought death on a scale, and with a ferocity, wholly new to Americans. It is true, as Lewis Saum writes, that in the antebellum era "death was an ever present fact of life," and that Americans had "an immediate, not a derivative or vicarious, awareness" of it.[15] But the Civil War marked a quantum shift, not only in the numbers of dead, but in its spectacular dispensation of agony and disfigurement. How does one put words to such suffering without either trivializing, heroizing, or otherwise falsifying the experience? Memorial Day tributes to the fallen? Elegiac verse? Earnest personal testimony? Stories of battles, triumphs, hospitals, widows, and reunions? Where the carnage lies raw, unburied and unforgotten, the most effective realism may be one that embodies the failure of words, a realism akin to what Mitchell Breitwieser has discerned in Mary Rowlandson's narrative, which "is a realistic work, not because it faithfully reports real events, but because it is an account of experience that breaks through or outdistances her own and her culture's dominant means of representation."[16]

An ability to hold death at a remove would have helped both soldiers and civilians get through the scenes they encountered, and the war had the paradoxical effect of rendering death both shockingly present and increasingly impersonal, through the statistical banality of the body count and through the accumulation of the "unknown dead." From this perspective, the power and the obligation of American realism might be to startle its audience out of their "seeming insouciance," their "capacity to register without questioning."[17] "Realism," Philip Fisher writes in connection to Baudelaire, "surprises us into unwanted moments or necessary moments of confronted sight. We face [the] carrion, and by means of the object, face what lies behind it, decay and death, the fate of the body in its relation to beauty."[18] It takes a rare art to accomplish that, however. How far does graphic description—"The greater part of the forehead was torn away, and from the jagged hole the brain protruded"—take us? Do the aesthetic symmetries of verse—"Two white roses upon his cheeks, | And one, just over his heart, blood red!"—take us any further? Perhaps the desperation of the living is the most vivid mark of the fearsomeness of mortality: "A hundred ghastly fears and fancies strutted a moment, pecking at the young girl's naked heart, like sandpipers on the weltering beach."[19] The dilemma can be sensed even in these brief passages, and it was essentially this: Even for writers who wanted to confront mortality honestly, writing about death is like chasing one's own shadow, the experience itself always flitting away before the net of words.

Those who wrote about the Civil War wrote about a social earthquake whose after-shocks reverberated through American culture, politics, psychology, and literature. In its technical innovations and its violent reorganization of American society, the war marked the advent of a new age and presented an audacious challenge to Americans' sensibilities and moral certainties. The nation's economic and political life was forever altered, and emancipation hardly solved the grinding conflicts of race in the United States. It is not surprising, perhaps, that many Americans and many writers lapsed into platitudes or silence. Yet others made the effort to rise to the occasion—made the effort, that is, to overcome the shock in order to reach and represent the deeper experiences of war, to find the soft tissue and the hard feelings beneath the banalities of press reportage and gauzy reminiscence. They did so even as the United States had much else to occupy itself with between the 1860s and the 1910s: class antagonism and labor strikes; the final push against Native Americans in the West; a steady influx of European immigrants; the radical expansion of American geopolitical power during the Spanish–American War; an ongoing effort to reconcile religious orthodoxy with new forms of science.

In the midst of such upheaval, Americans did what came naturally: they embraced both tradition and the modern world. Michael D. Clark has written that tradition, especially for the elite, "could be a psychological anodyne offering a sense of stability in the midst of unsettling change and the feeling of time-hallowed certainty in the face of religious or metaphysical doubt." At the same time, "[s]ome Americans came to view tradition as extending rather than merely limiting the possibilities of individual and collective life," and it was therefore "the problem of tradition to find the middle ground, or the linkages, which would plausibly bind immediate to transcendent, past to present, local to imperial."[20] Anne C. Rose, stressing the importance of religious change, has also found in Victorian American culture a capacity for preserving or updating the old ways and the old beliefs in the face of widespread social transformation:

> The Victorians were not unaware of the trials and horrors of war. They felt keen disappointment at the failure of the founder's republicanism and saw clearly the suffering of soldiers and civilians alike. But the war's prospects of personal glory and shared idealism contested their soberer judgment, drew them powerfully toward the conflict, and came to dominate their recollections of war. To the extent that the Victorians' relentless search for meaning in secular activities finally achieved resolution, it was the Civil War, conceived as a struggle over profound issues, that convinced them that human effort even without clear supernatural references still had value.[21]

The literature of the American Civil War did not always reach that same conclusion. But as much as anything else, these writings represented part of the wider cultural effort to come to terms with the changes the United States underwent during the late nineteenth century. That was actually inevitable, for these changes depended, to no small degree, on the conduct and the outcome of the war.

If language and literature are forms of social and personal reconstruction, what they were able to accomplish in the fifty years after the Civil War was precarious, imperfect, and incomplete. Indeed, it is a sign of that incompleteness that Americans are still coming to terms with the Civil War. The war settled the central Constitutional crisis of the country's history, and yet in other respects it seems to have resolved so little. The political tensions involving race and region, federal power and states' rights, modernity and tradition, continue to make themselves felt across the cultural landscape, from presidential campaigns to landscape conservation to civil rights. In its continuing hold on the national psyche, the Civil War has become a touchstone for understanding modern American culture, but it means very different things to different people. An essential part of coming to terms with its unresolved status in the American imagination is to explore how earlier generations came to terms with it—and that is best done through an exploration of the writings they left us.

Notes

1 These issues are treated at greater length in a number of classic theoretical works, including Elaine Scarry, *The Body in Pain: The Making and Unmaking of the World* (New York: Oxford University Press, 1985); Hannah Arendt, *On Violence* (New York: Harvest, 1970); and Jürgen Habermas, *Moral Consciousness and Communicative Action* (Cambridge: MIT Press, 1990).

2 Kate McLoughlin, *Authoring War: The Literary Representation of War from the* Iliad *to Iraq* (Cambridge: Cambridge University Press, 2011), 9.

3 Jill Lepore, *The Name of War: King Philip's War and the Origins of American Identity* (New York: Vintage Books, 1999), x.

4 Tim O'Brien, *The Things They Carried* (New York: Broadway Books, 1998), 157–158.

5 Important studies of the impact of the war on American literature include Faith Barrett, *To Fight Aloud Is Very Brave: American Poetry and the Civil War* (Amherst: University of Massachusetts Press, 2012); Kathleen Diffley, *Where My Heart Is Turning Ever: Civil War Stories and Constitutional Reform, 1861–1876* (Athens: University of Georgia Press, 1992); Alice Fahs, *The Imagined Civil War: Popular Literature of the North and South, 1861–1865* (Chapel Hill: University of North Carolina Press, 2001); Randall Fuller, *From Battlefields Rising: How the Civil War Transformed American Literature* (New York: Oxford University Press, 2011); Eliza Richards, *Correspondent Lines: Poetry and Journalism in the U.S. Civil War* (forthcoming); Edmund Wilson, *Patriotic Gore: Studies in the Literature of the American Civil War* (New York: Farrar, Straus and Giroux, 1962); and Elizabeth Young, *Disarming the Nation: Women's Writing and the American Civil War* (Chicago: University of Chicago Press, 1999). The extent to which the war marks a divide in American literary culture, however, is open to debate; see Cody Marrs, *Transbellum America: Literature, Time, and the Long Civil War* (forthcoming).

6 James Dawes, *The Language of War: Literature and Culture in the U.S. from the Civil War through World War II* (Cambridge: Harvard University Press, 2002), 4, 11.

7 Charles Johanningsmeier, *Fiction and the American Literary Marketplace: The Role of Newspaper Syndicates, 1860–1900* (Cambridge: Cambridge University Press, 1997), 2–3; Patricia Okker, *Social Stories: The Magazine Novel in Nineteenth-Century America* (Charlottesville: University of Virginia Press, 2003), ch. 1, ch. 5.

8 Kathleen Diffley, "Home from the Theatre of War: The *Southern Magazine* and Recollections of the Civil War," in Kenneth M. Price and Susan Belasco Smith, eds., *Periodical Literature in Nineteenth-Century America* (Charlottesville: University of Virginia Press, 1995), 183–201, 184.

9 See Lawrence Buell, "American Civil War Poetry and the Meaning of Literary Commodification: Whitman, Melville, and Others" in Steven Fink and Susan S. Williams, eds., *Reciprocal Influences: Literary Production, Distribution, and Consumption in America* (Columbus: Ohio State University Press, 1999).

10 See Phillip Barrish, *American Literary Realism, Critical Theory, and Intellectual Prestige, 1880–1995* (Cambridge: Cambridge University Press, 2001); Amy Kaplan, *The Social Construction of American Realism* (Chicago: University of Chicago Press, 1998); Augusta Rohrbach, *Truth Stranger than Fiction: Race, Realism, and the U.S. Literary Marketplace* (New York: Palgrave, 2002); and David E. Shi, *Facing Facts: Realism in American Thought and Culture, 1850–1920* (New York: Oxford University Press, 1995).

11 David W. Bulla and Gregory A. Borchard, *Journalism in the Civil War Era* (New York: Peter Lang, 2010); Fletcher Thompson, Jr., *The Image of War: The Pictorial Reporting of the American Civil War* (New York: Thomas Yoseloff, 1959); Alan Trachtenberg, *Reading American Photographs: Images as History, Mathew Brady to Walker Evans* (New York: Hill and Wang, 1989); Bob Zeller, *The Blue and Gray in Black and White: A History of Civil War Photography* (Westport, Conn.: Praeger, 2005).

12 John Berger, "Uses of Photography," in *About Looking* (New York: Pantheon, 1980; New York: Vintage, 1991), 55–56. Susan Sontag reaches similar conclusions in *On Photography* (New York: Farrar, Straus and Giroux, 1977).

13 Alan Trachtenberg, *The Incorporation of America: Culture and Society in the Gilded Age* (New York: Hill and Wang, 1982), 125.

14 J. David Hacker, "A Census-Based Count of the Civil War Dead," *Civil War History* 57:4 (December 2011), 307–348.

15 Lewis O. Saum, "Death in the Popular Mind of Pre-Civil War America," in David E. Stannard, ed., *Death in America* (Philadelphia: University of Pennsylvania Press, 1975), 32.

16 Mitchell Breitwieser, *American Puritanism and the Defense of Mourning: Religion, Grief, and Ethnology in Mary White Rowlandson's Captivity Narrative* (Madison: University of Wisconsin Press, 1990), 10.

17 Saum, 35.

18 Philip Fisher, *Still the New World: American Literature in a Culture of Creative Destruction* (Cambridge: Harvard University Press, 1999), 199.

19 From Ambrose Bierce's "Chickamauga," Henry Wadsworth Longfellow's "Killed at the Ford," and Henry James's "The Story of a Year," respectively.

20 Michael D. Clark, *The American Discovery of Tradition, 1865–1942* (Baton Rouge: Louisiana State University Press, 2005), 16, 17, 20.

21 Anne C. Rose, *Victorian America and the Civil War* (New York: Cambridge University Press, 1992), 5.

I
Origins

THE STARTING POINT OF THE GREAT WAR BETWEEN THE STATES.
INAUGURATION OF JEFFERSON DAVIS

The starting point of the great war between the states. Inauguration of Jefferson Davis. Lithograph by A. Hoen & Co., 1887. Library of Congress Prints and Photographs Division, LC-DIG-pga-01584

Introduction

The American Civil War was caused by the national fight over Southern slavery. We might say that it represented the most cataclysmically violent phase of that fight. The conflict often manifested itself as a constitutional debate over states' rights and federal power, or as a philosophical debate over race and freedom, but the central driving force was the uncertain future of slave-based economics as the country expanded geographically. By the 1840s, slavery was generating both tremendous profits (for a few) and moral outrage (among a growing minority), and although most white Americans would have preferred not to have to think about it, the polarization of aggressive proslavery and aggressive antislavery ideologies steadily eroded the cultural middle ground on which the nation had stood since 1787. The problem refused to go away because the undetermined status of new states and territories—slave or free?—kept the controversy always front and center. As the center crumbled during the 1850s, then, every political compromise only seemed to polarize the country further, until all compromise evaporated with the firing on Fort Sumter in 1861.

Needless to say, this thumbnail sketch only hints at the complexity of the Civil War's origins, and of the questions involved. What leads two societies—or two halves of the same society—to commit themselves to war? In the American case, what interests were so compelling that the escalation to total war seemed a worthwhile price to pay? At which historical junctures were the crucial decisions made, and how were they made? During the war itself, what motivated people to fight and die? How, and to what degree, did the thinking of ordinary civilians and soldiers differ from that of their political and military leaders, and what is the historical significance of that difference? How best to understand the kaleidoscope of American opinion when it came to matters of slavery, economics, and the union?

Two major considerations press forward. First, the Civil War resulted from both proximate and root causes, both immediate events that spurred the conflict forward and underlying forces operating behind the scenes. In the former category stand forth such vivid moments as the *Dred Scott* decision of 1856, John Brown's 1859 raid on Harper's Ferry, and the election of Lincoln in 1860. In the latter we might reckon such historical trends as the gradual divergence of Northern and Southern attitudes toward the family or shifting international market for cotton. Second, while these "causative factors" are certainly important, history is not the same thing as fate, and although the war can seem to have emerged inexorably and inevitably from its historical background, an undeniable contingency—of psychology, of accident and random chance, of unintended consequences—hovers around it. The Civil War had causes, but it did not absolutely *have* to happen, or turn out the way it did. What Winston Churchill observed about the First World War holds equally true for the American conflict: "One rises from the study of the causes of the Great War with a prevailing sense of the defective control of individuals upon world fortunes."[1]

Modern scholarship continues to debate the origins of the war, and different accounts emphasize different forces, processes, and events. While antebellum conflicts over economics and racial slavery still define the field's general outlines, and while broad studies of the causes of the Civil War continue to appear, the newly emerging lines of inquiry are remarkably diverse: the geopolitics of the Southern cotton industry (Brian Schoen); westward expansion and the California gold rush (Steven E. Woodworth, Leonard L. Richards); inflammatory partisan journalism (Lorman A. Ratner and Dwight L. Teeter); the cultural value of "honor" (Wiliam James Hoffer); the role of "secession commissioners" (Charles B. Dew); and the impact of recent British history in the West Indies (Edward B. Rugemer), among others. We can rightfully consider all of these as contributing factors, and all of them revolved in relation to each other, and in relation to the great question of human bondage.

Given that complexity, a responsible view of history obliges us not to reduce these issues to simplistic equations pitting abolitionism against greed, industrialism against agrarianism, or political philosophy against apolitical self-interest. In both the North and South, the cultural and intellectual landscape was crossed and recrossed by unpredictable differences of opinion and commonalities of interest. Political and ethical alignments shifted in response to events, and even as the rhetoric about slavery became more feverish, it is worth remembering that the alignment which held in 1861 was just one possible configuration. As Edward L. Ayers puts it:

> The war came through misunderstanding, confusion, miscalculation. Both sides underestimated the location of fundamental loyalty in the other. Both received incorrect images of the other in the partisan press. Political belief distorted each side's view of the other's economy and class relations . . . . By the time people made up their minds to fight, slavery itself had become obscured. Southern white men did not fight for slavery; they fought for a new nation built on slavery. White Northerners did not fight to end slavery; they fought to defend the integrity of their nation. Yet slavery, as Abraham Lincoln later put it, 'somehow' drove everything.[2]

Despite the almost haphazard way it came about, and despite the "obscuring" of the central issue of slavery, once launched the war quickly escalated, taking on both military momentum and the character of a war of beliefs. "The Civil War," Randall Jimerson observes, "became a total war involving the entire population precisely because both sides fought for ideological principles. Compromise and surrender were unthinkable when so much was at stake."[3]

That the "root" cause of slavery, however, was not always or primarily what partisans and participants invoked as a reason for war raises an interesting possibility: that what people *thought* they fought for, politically or militarily, might not have corresponded fully to what they *actually* fought for. This is the problem of false consciousness, and it puts the historian in the unenviable position of questioning or clarifying dead people's stated reasons for acting as they did. And yet ideological principles such as "states' rights" or "preserving the Union" only motivate people to kill and die when there are more tangible, immediate considerations at work. People do fight for abstractions, but they *really* fight for the deeply personal interests those abstractions articulate: family and social group; self-respect, self-protection, and self-promotion; resources and access to resources; investment in a place and a way of life. In nineteenth-century America, these matters increasingly turned, for both Northerners and Southerners, on the question of whether and in what form slavery would exist in the United States. This question had been building for decades, and the Civil War, at once necessary and astounding, decisively resolved it (at least at the constitutional level).

The writings in this section illuminate the harrowing course of events from 1859 to 1861 that formed the prelude to the Civil War, while revealing how those events were being interpreted—both immediately, in a first draft of history, and later, in cultural retrospect. Given that the war was decades in the making, involving countless individuals and deeply entangled social dynamics, the amount of potentially relevant material is practically infinite. So the selections here are meant to sketch out the main territory and to show how the major issues—legal, cultural, moral, intellectual—were being imagined and debated.

Herman Melville, from *Battle-Pieces and Aspects of the War* (1866)

The Portent

> Hanging from the beam,
>   Slowly swaying (such the law),
> Gaunt the shadow on your green,
>   Shenandoah!
> The cut is on the crown
> (Lo, John Brown),
> And the stabs shall heal no more.
>
> Hidden in the cap
>   Is the anguish none can draw;
> So your future veils its face,
>   Shenandoah!
> But the streaming beard is shown
> (Weird John Brown),
> The meteor of the war.

Misgivings

> When ocean-clouds over inland hills
>   Sweep storming in late autumn brown,
> And horror the sodden valley fills,
>   And the spire falls crashing in the town,
> I muse upon my country's ills –
> The tempest bursting from the waste of Time
> On the world's fairest hope linked with man's foulest crime.
>
> Nature's dark side is heeded now
>   (Ah! optimist-cheer disheartened flown) –
> A child may read the moody brow
>   Of yon black mountain lone.
> With shouts the torrents down the gorges go,
> And storms are formed behind the storm we feel:
> The hemlock shakes in the rafter, the oak in the driving keel.

Harriet Martineau, "Election of Abraham Lincoln" (November 22, 1860)

Culminating the increasingly fierce politics of the 1850s, the election of 1860 was an enormously complex affair that reflected divisions not only between North and South but within each region, and it featured bitter disputes about fundamental questions regarding slavery and national identity. Despite the deliberately cautious platform of the Republican party, the campaign featured anti-Lincoln rhetoric of surprising vitriol, and many proslavery Southerners saw Lincoln's victory as fundamentally incompatible with their interests and "way of life." Reporting on the election for the London *Daily News*, Harriet Martineau captured how its immediate aftermath looked from the perspective of a non-American, at the very moment events were unfolding. Her article is also fascinating because it combines sharp, clear-eyed analysis of the moving parts of the whole situation, particularly in its economic dimensions, with a dramatically overoptimistic view of the near future. Martineau's comments on the unlikelihood of secession, the growth of antislavery opinion in the South, the sympathy between the regions, and the transition from slave to free economics, now read more like wishful thinking than deep analysis – but they point up the fact that nobody really knew what was coming in the wake of Lincoln's election.

The election of Mr. Lincoln to the office of President of the United States is an event of the highest importance. In his own country it is the most important event which has occurred since the organization of the great Republic was first got into regular working order; and to the rest of the world, scarcely anything that could happen in a foreign country could involve interests so grave and so various as a radical change of policy in the American Union. The deeper the interest of the occasion, the more desirable it is that there should be no misunderstanding as to the precise grounds of the importance of the event. The tumult and confusion of mind reflected in the American newspapers from the society around them may well mislead European, as they do many American readers as to the probable results of the election of an Anti-slavery President. Instead of believing the threats, and sympathising in the terrors, of interested or agitated alarmists, it will be wise to look at the matter from a more serviceable point of view than they occupy. The chief considerations we believe to be these.

The New President is neither a Northern nor a Southern man. The election of 1860 is the nineteenth since the establishment of American institutions; and of the eighteen terms now fulfilled only four have been occupied by Northern men,[4] and all the rest by Southern men and slaveholders. No Northern man has been re-elected, while five slaveholders have served twice.[5] Now both sections make way for the great West, which did not exist, except as an unexplored wilderness, when Federal government was erected at Washington. That Western territory has become peopled and improved up to the point of claiming and obtaining the honour of giving a President to the Republic. It need hardly be explained that the co-operation of the North and West in this election secures the overthrow of the peculiar policy of the South. The South, weak in itself, has retained the predominance at Washington thus long by working on the fears and the vanity of the other two sections. Now that they have thrown off its influence, it must give up the game. The South has had its turn, and a very long one, at the head of affairs; and now it must go into opposition, if indeed it cannot participate in the policy of the Republican party. Hence arise two more points of importance. The leaders of Southern policy and their organs declare that the Southern States will not go into opposition.[6] If they cannot rule the Republic they will secede from it. It is necessary to ascertain the probable value of this threat.

It is well known that certain members of the existing government have aided the Disunion cry, and have in some places begun it. This mitigates the alarm at the cry, while increasing the general disgust at it. It was raised to affect the election; and, as it has failed in that direction, it will not be repeated by the same persons. But it is not the less true that there is a very serious agitation in several States in favour of leaving the Union. No man whose opinion is of any value believes that it can be done; but the disposition to attempt it is a grave evil. South Carolina, supported by Mississippi and Alabama, proposed, after Mr. Lincoln's election was certain, to secede before Mr. Buchanan's term expires, in order that the Federal forces might not be held by their new enemy, but by their old friend and nominee. The Southern party in Virginia promised to be ready to join, when the movement is begun, and the actual importation of arms into Virginia is so great as to cause a general expectation of civil war through the State. We hear of an universal arming of the citizens throughout several States; of plans for marching on Washington, to get possession of the departments of the Federal Government; of schemes for preventing the inauguration of Mr. Lincoln in March; and so forth. Everywhere outside the frontier of those angry States men smile at such projects; and it need not be explained that they can never be executed: but it is a melancholy truth that most of the misguided citizens suppose that they can, and that others are "ready to perish in the attempt." They imagine an anti-slavery President a sort of monster, and believe all they are told of an impending destruction of society. A few months will show them, if they will wait, that the laws of the Republic are the protection of the citizens, quite apart from the opinions of the President; and that social changes can be wrought only through legislation, in which they have a much larger share than Northern citizens, by means of their three-fifths suffrage.[7] If they can but be induced to wait a little while, they will cease to talk of secession from the Union. If they continue to propose it, and are seen to take any steps towards it – then certain grave considerations enter into the case. The North has an overwhelming preponderance of population and wealth; and the small force of the Slave States must be so occupied in representing five millions of slaves[8] as to have no means to oppose the authority of Government and the Free States. The plain truth is, it is nonsense talking of resisting the national will: and the menaces of civil war would not deserve notice in Europe but for their operation on commercial credit. The suspension of two or three banks, in consequence of panic about an anti-slavery President, the refusal of the Southern banks generally to discount bills till the effect of the election was seen, the sudden decline in the value of negroes to the extent of 30 per cent, and the inevitable effect on industry of such alarms, are substantial evils which belong to the history of the case.

The second consideration referred to is one of extreme importance – the sudden and open manifestation of republican opinion in the Slave States. If the slaveholders did not before know, they will now see and feel how small a minority they are in the great nation they have till now coerced for their own objects. We need but point to the growth of republican and anti-slavery opinion in Virginia, and especially in the Harper's Ferry region, since this time twelvemonth, to show what is the immediate effect of a free discussion such as was introduced by the raid of John Brown, and will now be every-where created by a reversal of the national policy. Looking, also, at the agitation in Maryland, the demonstrations at Washington, and the undisguised purpose of the non-slaveholding states to resist any reimposition of the oligarchical yoke under which they have sunk to be what they are, there remains no doubt whatever that there is a much stronger and broader sympathy between the Free States and the inhabitants of the Southern States than has been at all supposed till within the last few weeks. If the slave-holders will abstain from meddling with others, others will let them alone; but they had better not refuse to fulfil their share of the republican compact – to abide by the decision of the majority.

The dangers of the Republic are incalculably reduced by the bringing of this great quarrel to a constitutional arbitrament. Whatever changes may occur will be very slow in coming to pass. If Mr. Lincoln were the violent fanatic he is assumed to be, he must wait upon Congress. It will take several years to renew the material of the Senate and the House of Representatives;[9] and, till that is done, the South will have more than its share of influence at Washington. No doubt its policy will be reversed, in regard to the aim of extending the conditions of slavery over the whole country; but there will be plenty of wrangling before it is done, and abundance of delay, through the obstacles which an unreformed Legislature can interpose.

A calm review of the position leaves the result, in the shape of good and evil, something like this. To take the evil first: – The existing panic, during which the citizens are hanging their neighbours, and any stranger who may cross their sight, and suspecting and punishing their slaves, and hoarding their gold, and arming their families, and selling off their property, is an evil; but it is a less evil than the reality, in the place of the panic, would be. The universal expectation of a rising of the slaves, in case of Mr. Lincoln's failure, should almost reconcile the citizens, and their commercial correspondents, to the mischievous agitation they have created, even if it should end in a considerable crash. The negroes are less likely to rise now than at any time these thirty years past; and if there is more or less rebellion, it will be owing to the cruelties which the fears of their owners are now impelling them to inflict. There will be a period of obstructed legislation at Washington, and of virulent party strife, till the hitherto dominant party has learned to show due respect to the national will. There will be disorder and much complaint from the change of officials throughout the whole hierarchy of Government, a change indispensable in this case, on account of the reform in the principle of government, and also of the prevalent official corruption which has been so lately exposed. Finally, it is probable that all parties will complain of Mr. Lincoln. We know no more of Mr. Lincoln than all the rest of the world; but, if he were to turn out a second Washington, he would have no chance of satisfying a community like that of the United States, at the moment of its going over from a corrupt to a regenerate republican system. If it is a mystery how any man can govern, at such a moment, a nation which is living in different stages of civilization, it is no mystery that he must fail in doing at once what the people expect, and what the nation requires. One more evil may be impending – the failure of the cotton supply. It need not be so if the planters were wise; but they are, in this matter, not wise. We can only bear in mind that a servile war[10] would have been worse for the cotton crop than a fanciful political agitation, and meantime, for our own part, make haste to create other sources of supply.[11]

As for the good results: – the great Republic will, as soon as an improved Congress permits, transfer her testimony from the side of slavery to that of free labour and free existence. When Slavery is abolished within the congressional district of Columbia (which the inhabitants of the district are now demanding),[12] Negro Slavery will cease to be an American institution. Any of the States in which it exists may keep it up if they like, and if they can; but it will have ceased to be a national interest. We shall have the nation on our side in our opposition to the slave trade, and in our endeavours to make industrial allies of the inhabitants of Africa. Spain must then give way about her Cuban slave trade.[13] In America, free labour will presently supersede the more extravagant method of production, and the antagonism of race will be much softened.

The liberties of the citizens will be recovered from this day onward, after having been more and more encroached upon for a quarter of a century. The Americans will be again the free people their fathers made them. Best of all, the national character and reputation will improve and rise, as character and reputation do rise after the casting off of a great sin and sore disgrace. Both have suffered grievously; but we may hope now that they have touched their lowest point, and that their present noble awakening to duty, and rejection of the compromises of self-interest, may be in time to secure political regeneration and social peace at home, and the respect of the civilized world to institutions which make the people who live under them really free.

Jefferson Davis, Farewell Address to the U.S. Senate (January 21, 1861)

One month after Harriet Martineau's column on the 1860 election appeared, South Carolina seceded from the Union, followed by Mississippi on January 9, 1861, and from there the whole Confederacy began peeling away, led by the deep South and the cotton states. In some respects secession unfolded haltingly and unpredictably, yet in retrospect, given the historical magnitude of the decision, it seems to have occurred with lightning rapidity. Once Mississippi had cast its lot, Jefferson Davis cast his; although he had argued against actually seceding, the Democratic Senator and former Secretary of War under Franklin Pierce fervently embraced the notion of state sovereignty and, though with sadness, followed his home state out of the Union. In bidding farewell to the institution he first joined in 1847, Davis articulated the secessionist argument in its most compact and public form to date; within three weeks, delegates to the Confederate constitutional convention had chosen him to serve as their president, an office Davis formally assumed on February 18, 1861.

January 21, 1861

I rise, Mr. President, for the purpose of announcing to the Senate that I have satisfactory evidence that the State of Mississippi, by a solemn ordinance of her people in convention assembled, has declared her separation from the United States.[14] Under these circumstances, of course, my functions are terminated here. It has seemed to me proper, however, that I should appear in the Senate to announce that fact to my associates, and I will say but very little more. The occasion does not invite me to go into argument; and my physical condition would not permit me to do so if it were otherwise; and yet it seems to become me to say something on the part of the State I here represent, on an occasion so solemn as this.

It is known to Senators who have served with me here, that I have for many years advocated, as an essential attribute of State sovereignty, the right of a State to secede from the Union. Therefore, if I had not believed there was justifiable cause; if I had thought that Mississippi was acting without sufficient provocation, or without an existing necessity, I should still, under my theory of the Government, because of my allegiance to the State of which I am a citizen, have been bound by her action. I, however, may be permitted to say that I do think she has justifiable cause, and I approve of her act. I conferred with her people before that act was taken, counseled them then that if the state of things which they apprehended should exist when the convention met, they should take the action which they have now adopted.

I hope none who hear me will confound this expression of mine with the advocacy of the right of a State to remain in the Union, and to disregard its constitutional obligations by the nullification of the law. Such is not my theory. Nullification and secession, so often confounded, are indeed antagonistic principles. Nullification is a remedy which it is sought to apply within the Union, and against the agent of the States. It is only to be justified when the agent has violated his constitutional obligation, and a State, assuming to judge for itself, denies the right of the agent thus to act, and appeals to the other States of the Union for a decision; but when the States themselves, and when the people of the States, have so acted as to convince us that they will not regard our constitutional rights, then, and then for the first time, arises the doctrine of secession in its practical application.

A great man who now reposes with his fathers, and who has been often arraigned for a want of fealty to the Union, advocated the doctrine of nullification, because it preserved the Union. It was because of his deep-seated attachment to the Union, his determination to find some remedy for existing ills short of a severance of the ties which bound South Carolina to the other States, that Mr. Calhoun advocated the doctrine of nullification, which he proclaimed to be peaceful, to be within the limits of State power, not to disturb the Union, but only to be a means of bringing the agent before the tribunal of the States for their judgment.

Secession belongs to a different class of remedies. It is to be justified upon the basis that the States are sovereign. There was a time when none denied it. I hope the time may come again, when a better comprehension of the theory of our Government, and the inalienable rights of the people of the States, will prevent any one from denying that each State is a sovereign, and thus may reclaim the grants which it has made to any agent whomsoever.

I therefore say I concur in the action of the people of Mississippi, believing it to be necessary and proper, and should have been bound by their action if my belief had been otherwise; and this brings me to the important point which I wish on this last occasion to present to the Senate. It is by this confounding of nullification and secession that the name of a great man, whose ashes now mingle with his mother earth, has been invoked to justify coercion against a seceded State. The phrase "to execute the laws," was an expression which General Jackson[15] applied to the case of a State refusing to obey the laws while yet a member of the Union. That is not the case which is now presented. The laws are to be executed over the United States, and upon the people of the United States. They have no relation to any foreign country. It is a perversion of terms, at least it is a great misapprehension of the case, which cites that expression for application to a State which has withdrawn from the Union. You may make war on a foreign State. If it be the purpose of gentlemen, they may make war against a State which has withdrawn from the Union; but there are no laws of the United States to be executed within the limits of a seceded State. A State finding herself in the condition in which Mississippi has judged she is, in which her safety requires that she should provide for the maintenance of her rights out of the Union, surrenders all the benefits, (and they are known to be many,) deprives herself of the advantages, (they are known to be great,) severs all the ties of affection, (and they are close and enduring,) which have bound her to the Union; and thus divesting herself of every benefit, taking upon herself every burden, she claims to be exempt from any power to execute the laws of the United States within her limits.

I well remember an occasion when Massachusetts was arraigned before the bar of the Senate, and when then the doctrine of coercion was rife and to be applied against her because of the rescue of a fugitive slave in Boston.[16] My opinion then was the same that it is now. Not in a spirit of egotism, but to show that I am not influenced in my opinion because the case is my own, I refer to that time and that occasion as containing the opinion which I then entertained, and on which my present conduct is based. I then said, if Massachusetts, following her through a stated line of conduct, chooses to take the last step which separates her from the Union, it is her right to go, and I will neither vote one dollar nor one man to coerce her back; but will say to her, God speed, in memory of the kind associations which once existed between her and the other States.

It has been a conviction of pressing necessity, it has been a belief that we are to be deprived in the Union of the rights which our fathers bequeathed to us, which has brought Mississippi into her present decision. She has heard proclaimed the theory that all men are created free and equal, and this made the basis of an attack upon her social institutions; and the sacred Declaration of Independence has been invoked to maintain the position of the equality of the races. That Declaration of Independence is to be construed by the circumstances and purposes for which it was made. The communities were declaring their independence; the people of those communities were asserting that no man was born—to use the language of Mr. Jefferson—booted and spurred to ride over the rest of mankind; that men were created equal—meaning the men of the political community; that there was no divine right to rule; that no man inherited the right to govern; that there were no classes by which power and place descended to families, but that all stations were equally within the grasp of each member of the body-politic. These were the great principles they announced; these were the purposes for which they made their declaration; these were the ends to which their enunciation was directed. They have no reference to the slave; else, how happened it that among the items of arraignment made against George III was that he endeavored to do just what the North has been endeavoring of late to do—to stir up insurrection among our slaves?[17] Had the Declaration announced that the negroes were free and equal, how was the Prince to be arraigned for stirring up insurrection among them? And how was this to be enumerated among the high crimes which caused the colonies to sever their connection with the mother country? When our Constitution was formed, the same idea was rendered more palpable, for there we find provision made for that very class of persons as property; they were not put upon the footing of equality with white men—not even upon that of paupers and convicts; but, so far as representation was concerned, were discriminated against as a lower caste, only to be represented in the numerical proportion of three fifths.[18]

Then, Senators, we recur to the compact which binds us together; we recur to the principles upon which our Government was founded; and when you deny them, and when you deny to us the right to withdraw from a Government which thus perverted threatens to be destructive of our rights, we but tread in the path of our fathers when we proclaim our independence, and take the hazard. This is done not in hostility to others, not to injure any section of the country, not even for our own pecuniary benefit; but from the high and solemn motive of defending and protecting the rights we inherited, and which it is our sacred duty to transmit unshorn to our children.

I find in myself, perhaps, a type of the general feeling of my constituents towards yours. I am sure I feel no hostility to you, Senators from the North. I am sure there is not one of you, whatever sharp discussion there may have been between us, to whom I cannot now say, in the presence of my God, I wish you well; and such, I am sure, is the feeling of the people whom I represent towards those whom you represent. I therefore feel that I but express their desire when I say I hope, and they hope, for peaceful relations with you, though we must part. They may be mutually beneficial to us in the future, as they have been in the past, if you so will it. The reverse may bring disaster on every portion of the country; and if you will have it thus, we will invoke the God of our fathers, who delivered them from the power of the lion, to protect us from the ravages of the bear; and thus, putting our trust in God and in our own firm hearts and strong arms, we will vindicate the right as best we may.

In the course of my service here, associated at different times with a great variety of Senators, I see now around me some with whom I have served long; there have been points of collision; but whatever of offense there has been to me, I leave here; I carry with me no hostile remembrance. Whatever offense I have given which has not been redressed, or for which satisfaction has not been demanded, I have, Senators, in this hour of our parting, to offer you my apology for any pain which, in heat of discussion, I have inflicted. I go hence unencumbered of the remembrance of any injury received, and having discharged the duty of making the only reparation in my power for any injury offered.

Mr. President, and Senators, having made the announcement which the occasion seemed to me to require, it only remains to me to bid you a final adieu.

Henry Timrod, "Ethnogenesis" (February 1861)

At Montgomery, Alabama, from February 4 to February 8, 1861, the week before Lincoln began his journey from Springfield, Illinois, to Washington D.C., forty-three delegates from seven seceding states convened to draft a provisional constitution for the Confederacy (the permanent Confederate constitution was signed on Mar. 11, 1861; by August it had been ratified by eleven Southern states). This poem, published in a Charleston newspaper two weeks after the Confederate Congress, represents Timrod's first burst of enthusiasm for the Confederacy but not his later complex feelings toward the war.

Written during the meeting of the first Southern Congress, at Montgomery, February, 1861

I.

Hath not the morning dawned with added light?
And shall not evening call another star
Out of the infinite regions of the night,
To mark this day in Heaven? At last, we are
A nation among nations; and the world
Shall soon behold in many a distant port
    Another flag unfurled!
Now, come what may, whose favor need we court?
And, under God, whose thunder need we fear?
    Thank Him who placed us here
Beneath so kind a sky – the very sun
Takes part with us; and on our errands run
All breezes of the ocean; dew and rain
Do noiseless battle for us; and the Year,
And all the gentle daughters in her train,
March in our ranks, and in our service wield
    Long spears of golden grain!
A yellow blossom as her fairy shield,
June flings her azure banner to the wind,
    While in the order of their birth
Her sisters pass; and many an ample field
Grows white beneath their steps, till now, behold
    Its endless sheets unfold
THE SNOW OF SOUTHERN SUMMERS! Let the earth
Rejoice! beneath those fleeces soft and warm
    Our happy land shall sleep
    In a repose as deep
  As if we lay intrenched behind
Whole leagues of Russian ice and Arctic storm!

II.

And what if, mad with wrongs themselves have wrought,
    In their own treachery caught,
    By their own fears made bold,
    And leagued with him of old,
Who long since, in the limits of the North,
Set up his evil throne, and warred with God –
What if, both mad and blinded in their rage,
Our foes should fling us down their mortal gage,
And with a hostile step profane our sod!
We shall not shrink, my brothers, but go forth
To meet them, marshalled by the Lord of Hosts,
And overshadowed by the might ghosts
Of Moultrie and of Eutaw[19] – who shall foil
Auxiliars such as these? Nor these alone,
    But every stock and stone
    Shall help us; but the very soil,
And all the generous wealth it gives to toil,
And all for which we love our noble land,
Shall fight beside, and through us, sea and strand,
    The heart of woman, and her hand,
Tree, fruit, and flower, and every influence,
    Gentle, or grave, or grand;
    The winds in our defence
Shall seem to blow; to us the hills shall lend
    Their firmness and their calm;
And in our stiffened sinews we shall blend
    The strength of pine and palm!

III.

Nor would we shun the battle-ground,
    Though weak as we are strong;
Call up the clashing elements around,
    And test the right and wrong!
On one side, creeds that dare to teach
What Christ and Paul refrained to preach;[20]
Codes built upon a broken pledge,
And charity that whets a poniard's edge;
Fair schemes that leave the neighboring poor
To starve and shiver at the schemer's door,
While in the world's most liberal ranks enrolled,
He turns some vast philanthropy to gold;
Religion taking every mortal form
But that a pure and Christian faith makes warm,
Where not to vile fanatic passion urged,
Or not in vague philosophies submerged,
Repulsive with all Pharisaic leaven,

And making laws to stay the laws of Heaven!
And on the other, scorn of sordid gain,
Unblemished honor, truth without a stain,
Faith, justice, reverence, charitable wealth,
And, for the poor and humble, laws which give,
Not the mean right to buy the right to live,
    But life, and home, and health!
To doubt the end were want of trust in God,
    Who, if he has decreed
    That we must pass a redder sea
Than that which rang to Miriam's holy glee,
    Will surely raise at need
    A Moses with his rod!

IV.

But let our fears – if fears we have – be still,
And turn us to the future! Could we climb
Some mighty Alp, and view the coming time,
The rapturous sight would fill
    Our eyes with happy tears!
Not only for the glories which the years
Shall bring us; not for lands from sea to sea,
And wealth, and power, and peace, though these shall be;
But for the distant peoples we shall bless,
And the hushed murmurs of a world's distress:
For, to give labor to the poor,
    The whole sad planet o'er,
And save from want and crime the humblest door,
Is one among the many ends for which
    God makes us great and rich!
The hour perchance is not yet wholly ripe
When all shall own it, but the type
Whereby we shall be known in every land
Is that vast gulf which laves our Southern strand,
And through the cold, untempered ocean pours
Its genial streams, that far-off Arctic shores
May sometimes catch upon the softened breeze
Strange tropic warmth and hints of summer seas.

Abraham Lincoln, Speech from the Balcony of the Bates House, Indianapolis (February 11, 1861)

As the Provisional Confederate Congress hammered out a permanent constitution, the President-Elect was traveling from Springfield, Illinois, to Washington, D.C., for his inauguration. On his first night in Indianapolis, Lincoln spoke to an enthusiastic crowd gathered outside his hotel, the Bates House; forecasting some of the central ideas of his first inaugural address, he was frank, humorous, perhaps too bold in his challenge to the secessionists. The next day, he gave a similar, though less provocative, version of the speech to the Indiana legislature; this one better conveys his distinctive voice.

It is not possible, in my journey to the national capital, to address assemblies like this which may do me the great honor to meet me as you have done, but very briefly. I should be entirely worn out if I were to attempt it. I appear before you now to thank you for this very magnificent welcome which you have given me, and still more for the very generous support which your State recently gave to the political cause of the whole country, and the whole world. [Applause.] Solomon has said, that there is a time to keep silence. [Renewed and deafening applause.]***** We know certain that they mean the same thing while using the same words now, and it perhaps would be as well if they would keep silence.

The words "coercion" and "invasion" are in great use about these days. Suppose we were simply to try if we can, and ascertain what, is the meaning of these words. Let us get, if we can, the exact definitions of these words – not from dictionaries, but from the men who constantly repeat them – what things they mean to express by the words. What, then, is "coercion"? What is "invasion"? Would the marching of an army into South California, for instance, without the consent of her people, and in hostility against them, be coercion or invasion? I very frankly say, I think it would be invasion, and it would be coercion too, if the people of that country were forced to submit. But if the Government, for instance, but simply insists upon holding its own forts, or retaking those forts which belong to it, – [cheers,] – or the enforcement of the laws of the United States in the collection of duties upon foreign importations, – [renewed cheers,] – or even the withdrawal of the mails from those portions of the country where the mails themselves are habitually violated; would any or all of these things be coercion? Do the lovers of the Union contend that they will resist coercion or invasion of any State, understanding that any or all of these would be coercing or invading a State? If they do, then it occurs to me that the means for the preservation of the Union they so greatly love, in their own estimation, is of a very thin and airy character. [Applause.] If sick, they would consider the little pills of the homeopathist as already too large for them to swallow. In their view, the Union, as a family relation, would not be anything like a regular marriage at all, but only as a sort of free-love arrangement, – [laughter,] – to be maintained on what that sect calls passionate attraction. [Continued laughter.] But, my friends, enough of this.

What is the particular sacredness of a State? I speak not of that position which is given to a State in and by the Constitution of the United States, for that all of us agree to – we abide by; but that position assumed, that a State can carry with it out of the Union that which it holds in sacredness by virtue of its connection with the Union. I am speaking of that assumed right of a State, as a primary principle, that the Constitution should rule all that is less than itself, and ruin all that is bigger than itself. [Laughter.] But, I ask, wherein does consist that right? If a State, in one instance, and a county in another, should be equal in extent of territory, and equal in the number of people, wherein is that State any better than the county? Can a change of name change the right? By what principle of original right is it that one-fiftieth or one-ninetieth of a great nation, by calling themselves a State, have the right to break up and ruin that nation as a matter of original principle? Now, I ask the question – I am not deciding anything – [laughter,] – and with the request that you will think somewhat upon that subject and decide for yourselves, if you choose, when you get ready, – where is the mysterious, original right, from principle, for a certain district of country with inhabitants, by merely being called a State, to play tyrant over all its own citizens, and deny the authority of everything greater than itself. [Laughter.] I say I am deciding nothing, but simply giving something for you to reflect upon; and, with having said this much, and having declared, in the start, that I will make no long speeches, I thank you again for this magnificent welcome, and bid you an affectionate farewell. [Cheers.]

Abraham Lincoln, First Inaugural Address (March 4, 1861)

By the time Lincoln took the oath of office, seven states had already declared their intent to break away from the Union and the president-elect had navigated a perilous transitional period in which he enjoyed no real authority yet faced unprecedented political burdens. After weeks of researching, drafting, and revising the speech, with the help of quite a few allies, Lincoln finally spoke, from the steps of the Capitol building, to an audience of more than 25,000 people, including lawmakers, diplomats, justices, and various dignitaries. Lincoln, in Harold Holzer's account, "read slowly, disdaining gesture, enunciating as clearly as he could to make sure his words cut through the chill air and penetrated the huge audience."[21] What he sought, above all, was to preserve the Union symbolized by that audience—through interlaced appeals to logic, national feeling, moral principle, and constitutional duty.

Fellow-citizens of the United States:

In compliance with a custom as old as the government itself, I appear before you to address you briefly, and to take, in your presence, the oath prescribed by the Constitution of the United States, to be taken by the President "before he enters on the execution of his office."

I do not consider it necessary, at present, for me to discuss those matters of administration about which there is no special anxiety, or excitement.

Apprehension seems to exist among the people of the Southern States, that by the accession of a Republican Administration, their property, and their peace, and personal security, are to be endangered. There has never been any reasonable cause for such apprehension. Indeed, the most ample evidence to the contrary has all the while existed, and been open to their inspection. It is found in nearly all the published speeches of him who now addresses you. I do but quote from one of those speeches when I declare that "I have no purpose, directly or indirectly, to interfere with the institution of slavery in the States where it exists. I believe I have no lawful right to do so, and I have no inclination to do so." Those who nominated and elected me did so with full knowledge that I had made this, and many similar declarations, and had never recanted them. And more than this, they placed in the platform, for my acceptance, and as a law to themselves, and to me, the clear and emphatic resolution which I now read:

Resolved, That the maintenance inviolate of the rights of the States, and especially the right of each State to order and control its own domestic institutions according to its own judgment exclusively, is essential to that balance of power on which the perfection and endurance of our political fabric depend; and we denounce the lawless invasion by armed force of the soil of any State or Territory, no matter under what pretext, as among the gravest of crimes.

I now reiterate these sentiments: and in doing so, I only press upon the public atten-tion the most conclusive evidence of which the case is susceptible, that the property, peace and security of no section are to be in anywise endangered by the now incoming Administration. I add too, that all the protection which, consistently with the Constitution and the laws, can be given, will be cheerfully given to all the States when lawfully demanded, for whatever cause—as cheerfully to one section, as to another.

There is much controversy about the delivering up of fugitives from service or labor. The clause I now read is as plainly written in the Constitution as any other of its provisions:

> No person held to service or labor in one State, under the laws thereof, escaping into another, shall, in consequence of any law or regulation therein, be discharged from such service or labor, but shall be delivered up on claim of the party to whom such service or labor may be due.

It is scarcely questioned that this provision was intended by those who made it, for the reclaiming of what we call fugitive slaves; and the intention of the law-giver is the law. All members of Congress swear their support to the whole Constitution—to this provision as much as to any other. To the proposition, then, that slaves whose cases come within the terms of this clause, "shall be delivered up," their oaths are unanimous. Now, if they would make the effort in good temper, could they not, with nearly equal unanimity, frame and pass a law, by means of which to keep good that unanimous oath?

There is some difference of opinion whether this clause should be enforced by national or by state authority; but surely that difference is not a very material one. If the slave is to be surrendered, it can be of but little consequence to him, or to others, by which authority it is done. And should any one, in any case, be content that his oath shall go unkept, on a merely unsubstantial controversy as to how it shall be kept?

Again, in any law upon this subject, ought not all the safeguards of liberty known in civilized and humane jurisprudence to be introduced, so that a free man be not, in any case, surrendered as a slave? And might it not be well, at the same time, to provide by law for the enforcement of that clause in the Constitution which guaranties that "The citi-zens of each State shall be entitled to all privileges and immunities of citizens in the several States?"

I take the official oath to-day, with no mental reservations, and with no purpose to construe the Constitution or laws, by any hyper-critical rules. And while I do not choose now to specify particular acts of Congress as proper to be enforced, I do suggest, that it will be much safer for all, both in official and private stations, to conform to, and abide by, all those acts which stand unrepealed, than to violate any of them, trusting to find impunity in having them held to be unconstitutional.

It is seventy-two years since the first inauguration of a President under our National Constitution. During that period fifteen different and greatly distinguished citizens, have, in succession, administered the executive branch of the government. They have conducted it through many perils; and, generally, with great success. Yet, with all this scope for precedent, I now enter upon the same task for the brief constitutional term of four years, under great and peculiar difficulty. A disruption of the Federal Union, heretofore only menaced, is now formidably attempted.

I hold, that in contemplation of universal law, and of the Constitution, the Union of these States is perpetual. Perpetuity is implied, if not expressed, in the fundamental law of all national governments. It is safe to assert that no government proper, ever had a provision in its organic law for its own termination. Continue to execute all the express provisions of our National Constitution, and the Union will endure forever – it being impossible to destroy it except by some action not provided for in the instrument itself.

Again, if the United States be not a government proper, but an association of States in the nature of contract merely, can it, as a contract, be peaceably unmade, by less than all the parties who made it? One party to a contract may violate it – break it, so to speak; but does it not require all to lawfully rescind it?

Descending from these general principles, we find the proposition that, in legal contemplation, the Union is perpetual, confirmed by the history of the Union itself. The Union is much older than the Constitution. It was formed in fact, by the Articles of Association in 1774. It was matured and continued by the Declaration of Independence in 1776. It was further matured and the faith of all the then thirteen States expressly plighted and engaged that it should be perpetual, by the Articles of Confederation in 1778. And finally, in 1787, one of the declared objects for ordaining and establishing the Constitution, was "to form a more perfect Union."

But if destruction of the Union, by one, or by a part only, of the States, be lawfully possible, the Union is less perfect than before the Constitution, having lost the vital element of perpetuity.

It follows from these views that no State, upon its own mere motion, can lawfully get out of the Union; that resolves and ordinances to that effect are legally void; and that acts of violence, within any State or States, against the authority of the United States, are insurrectionary or revolutionary, according to circumstances.

I therefore consider that, in view of the Constitution and the laws, the Union is unbroken; and, to the extent of my ability, I shall take care, as the Constitution itself expressly enjoins upon me, that the laws of the Union be faithfully executed in all the States. Doing this I deem to be only a simple duty on my part; and I shall perform it, so far as practicable, unless my rightful masters, the American people, shall withhold the requisite means, or, in some authoritative manner, direct the contrary. I trust this will not be regarded as a menace, but only as the declared purpose of the Union that it will constitutionally defend, and maintain itself.

In doing this there needs to be no bloodshed or violence; and there shall be none, unless it be forced upon the national authority. The power confided to me, will be used to hold, occupy, and possess the property, and places belonging to the government, and to collect the duties and imposts; but beyond what may be necessary for these objects, there will be no invasion, no using of force against or among the people anywhere. Where hostility to the United States, in any interior locality, shall be so great and so universal, as to prevent competent resident citizens from holding the Federal offices, there will be no attempt to force obnoxious strangers among the people for that object. While the strict legal right may exist in the government to enforce the exercise of these offices, the attempt to do so would be so irritating, and so nearly impracticable with all, that I deem it better to forego, for the time, the uses of such offices.

The mails, unless repelled, will continue to be furnished in all parts of the Union. So far as possible, the people everywhere shall have that sense of perfect security which is most favorable to calm thought and reflection. The course here indicated will be followed, unless current events, and experience, shall show a modification, or change, to be proper; and in every case and exigency, my best discretion will be exercised, according to circumstances actually existing, and with a view and a hope of a peaceful solution of the national troubles, and the restoration of fraternal sympathies and affections.

That there are persons in one section, or another who seek to destroy the Union at all events, and are glad of any pretext to do it, I will neither affirm or deny; but if there be such, I need address no word to them. To those, however, who really love the Union may I not speak?

Before entering upon so grave a matter as the destruction of our national fabric, with all its benefits, its memories, and its hopes, would it not be wise to ascertain precisely why we do it? Will you hazard so desperate a step, while there is any possibility that any portion of the ills you fly from, have no real existence? Will you, while the certain ills you fly to, are greater than all the real ones you fly from – will you risk the commission of so fearful a mistake?

All profess to be content in the Union, if all constitutional rights can be maintained. Is it true, then, that any right, plainly written in the Constitution, has been denied? I think not. Happily the human mind is so constituted, that no party can reach to the audacity of doing this. Think, if you can, of a single instance in which a plainly written provision of the Constitution has ever been denied. If, by the mere force of numbers, a majority should deprive a minority of any clearly written constitutional right, it might, in a moral point of view, justify revolution – certainly would, if such right were a vital one. But such is not our case. All the vital rights of minorities, and of individuals, are so plainly assured to them, by affirmations and negations, guarranties and prohibitions, in the Constitution, that controversies never arise concerning them. But no organic law can ever be framed with a provision specifically applicable to every question which may occur in practical administration. No foresight can anticipate, nor any document of reasonable length contain express provisions for all possible questions. Shall fugitives from labor be surrendered by national or by State authority? The Constitution does not expressly say. *May* Congress prohibit slavery in the territories? The Constitution does not expressly say. *Must* Congress protect slavery in the territories? The Constitution does not expressly say.

From questions of this class spring all our constitutional controversies, and we divide upon them into majorities and minorities. If the minority will not acquiesce, the majority must, or the government must cease. There is no other alternative; for continuing the government, is acquiescence on one side or the other.

If a minority, in such case, will secede rather than acquiesce, they make a precedent which, in turn, will divide and ruin them; for a minority of their own will secede from them, whenever a majority refuses to be controlled by such minority. For instance, why may not any portion of a new confederacy, a year or two hence, arbitrarily secede again, precisely as portions of the present Union now claim to secede from it? All who cherish disunion sentiments, are now being educated to the exact temper of doing this.

Is there such perfect identity of interests among the States to compose a new Union, as to produce harmony only, and prevent renewed secession?

Plainly, the central idea of secession, is the essence of anarchy. A majority, held in restraint by constitutional checks, and limitations, and always changing easily, with deliberate changes of popular opinions and sentiments, is the only true sovereign of a free people. Whoever rejects it, does, of necessity, fly to anarchy or to despotism. Unanimity is impossible; the rule of a minority, as a permanent arrangement, is wholly inadmissable; so that, rejecting the majority principle, anarchy, or despotism in some form, is all that is left.

I do not forget the position assumed by some, that constitutional questions are to be decided by the Supreme Court; nor do I deny that such decisions must be binding in any case, upon the parties to a suit, as to the object of that suit, while they are also entitled to very high respect and consideration, in all parallel cases, by all other departments of the government. And while it is obviously possible that such decision may be erroneous in any given case, still the evil effect following it, being limited to that particular case, with the chance that it may be over-ruled, and never become a precedent for other cases, can better be borne than could the evils of a different practice. At the same time, the candid citizen must confess that if the policy of the government, upon vital questions affecting the whole people, is to be irrevocably fixed by decisions of the Supreme Court, the instant they are made, in ordinary litigation between parties, in personal actions, the people will have ceased, to be their own rulers, having, to that extent, practically resigned their government, into the hands of that eminent tribunal. Nor is there, in this view, any assault upon the court, or the judges. It is a duty from which they may not shrink to decide cases properly brought before them, and it is no fault of theirs if others seek to turn their decisions to political purposes.

One section of our country believes slavery is right, and ought to be extended, while the other believes it is wrong, and ought not to be extended. This is the only substantial dispute. The fugitive-slave clause of the Constitution, and the law for the suppression of the foreign slave trade, are each as well enforced, perhaps, as any law can ever be in a community where the moral sense of the people imperfectly supports the law itself. The great body of the people abide by the dry legal obligation in both cases, and a few break over in each. This, I think, cannot be perfectly cured; and it would be worse in both cases after the separation of the sections, than before. The foreign slave trade, now imperfectly suppressed, would be ultimately revived, without restriction, in one section; while fugitive slaves, now only partially surrendered, would not be surrendered at all by the other.

Physically speaking, we cannot separate. We cannot remove our respective sections from each other, nor build an impassable wall between them. A husband and wife may be divorced, and go out of the presence, and beyond the reach of each other; but the different parts of our country cannot do this. They cannot but remain face to face; and intercourse, either amicable or hostile, must continue between them. Is it possible then to make that intercourse more advantageous or more satisfactory after separation than before? Can aliens make treaties easier than friends can make laws? Can treaties be more faithfully enforced between aliens than laws can among friends? Suppose you go to war, you cannot fight always; and when, after much loss on both sides, and no gain on either, you cease fighting, the identical old questions as to terms of intercourse are again upon you.

This country, with its institutions, belongs to the people who inhabit it. Whenever they shall grow weary of the existing government, they can exercise their constitutional right of amending it, or their revolutionary right to dismember or overthrow it. I can not be ignorant of the fact that many worthy and patriotic citizens are desirous of having the National Constitution amended. While I make no recommendation of amendments, I fully recognize the rightful authority of the people over the whole subject, to be exercised in either of the modes prescribed in the instrument itself; and I should, under existing circumstances, favor rather than oppose a fair opportunity being afforded the people to act upon it. I will venture to add that to me the convention mode seems preferable, in that it allows amendments to originate with the people themselves, instead of only permitting them to take or reject propositions originated by others not especially chosen for the purpose, and which might not be precisely such as they would wish to either accept or refuse. I understand a proposed amendment to the Constitution – which amendment, however, I have not seen – has passed Congress, to the effect that the federal government shall never interfere with the domestic institutions of the States, including that of persons held to service. To avoid misconstruction of what I have said, I depart from my purpose not to speak of particular amendments so far as to say that, holding such a provision to now be implied constitutional law, I have no objection to its being made express and irrevocable.

The chief magistrate derives all his authority from the people, and they have conferred none upon him to fix terms for the separation of the States. The people themselves can do this also if they choose; but the executive, as such, has nothing to do with it. His duty is to administer the present government, as it came to his hands, and to transmit it, unimpaired by him, to his successor.

Why should there not be a patient confidence in the ultimate justice of the people? Is there any better or equal hope in the world? In our present differences is either party without faith of being in the right? If the Almighty Ruler of nations, with his eternal truth and justice, be on your side of the North, or on yours of the South, that truth and that justice will surely prevail by the judgment of this great tribunal of the American people.

By the frame of the government under which we live, this same people have wisely given their public servants but little power for mischief; and have, with equal wisdom, provided for the return of that little to their own hands at very short intervals. While the people retain their virtue and vigilance, no administration, by any extreme of wickedness or folly, can very seriously injure the government in the short space of four years.

My countrymen, one and all, think calmly and well upon this whole subject. Nothing valuable can be lost by taking time. If there be an object to hurry any of you in hot haste to a step which you would never take deliberately, that object will be frustrated by taking time; but no good object can be frustrated by it. Such of you as are now dissatisfied, still have the old Constitution unimpaired, and, on the sensitive point, the laws of your own framing under it; while the new administration will have no immediate power, if it would, to change either. If it were admitted that you who are dissatisfied hold the right side in the dispute, there still is no single good reason for precipitate action. Intelligence, patriotism, Christianity, and a firm reliance on Him who has never yet forsaken this favored land, are still competent to adjust in the best way all our present difficulty.

In your hands, my dissatisfied fellow countrymen, and not in mine, is the momentous issue of civil war. The government will not assail you. You can have no conflict without being yourselves the aggressors. You have no oath registered in Heaven to destroy the government, while I shall have the most solemn one to "preserve, protect, and defend" it.

I am loath to close. We are not enemies, but friends. We must not be enemies. Though passion may have strained, it must not break our bonds of affection. The mystic chords of memory, stretching from every battle-field and patriot grave to every living heart and hearthstone all over this broad land, will yet swell the chorus of the Union when again touched, as surely they will be, by the better angels of our nature.

Mary Boykin Chesnut, from *A Diary from Dixie* (1905)

Mary Chesnut's husband, James Chesnut, Jr., was a member of the Provisional Confederate Congress and helped draft the Confederate Constitution, before going on to serve as a colonel and then general in the Confederate Army. Mary thus enjoyed unusual access to the thinking and conversation of Confederate decision-makers, and this chapter of her diary (revised in later years) covers the harrowing weeks during which the Confederacy had just come into being, the new president and his aides debated strategy, and the undersupplied Fort Sumter emerged as a major point of crisis.

Chapter 2: Montgomery, Ala., February 19, 1861 — March 11, 1861. Making the Confederate Constitution — Robert Toombs — Anecdote of General Scott — Lincoln's trip through Baltimore — Howell Cobb and Benjamin H. Hill — Hoisting the Confederate flag — Mrs. Lincoln's economy in the White House — Hopes for peace — Despondent talk with anti-secession leaders — The South unprepared — Fort Sumter . . . .

Montgomery, Ala., *February 19*, 1861 — The brand-new Confederacy is making or remodeling its Constitution. Everybody wants Mr. Davis to be General-in-Chief or President. Keitt and Boyce and a party preferred Howell Cobb[22] for President. And the fire-eaters per se wanted Barnwell Rhett.[23]

My brother Stephen brought the officers of the "Montgomery Blues" to dinner. "Very soiled Blues," they said, apologizing for their rough condition. Poor fellows! they had been a month before Fort Pickens and not allowed to attack it. They said Colonel Chase built it, and so were sure it was impregnable. Colonel Lomax telegraphed to Governor Moore[24] if he might try to take it, "Chase or no Chase," and got for his answer, "No." "And now," say the Blues, "we have worked like niggers, and when the fun and fighting begin, they send us home and put regulars there." They have an immense amount of powder. The wheel of the car in which it was carried took fire. There was an escape for you! We are packing a hamper of eatables for them.

I am despondent once more. If I thought them in earnest because at first they put their best in front, what now? We have to meet tremendous odds by pluck, activity, zeal, dash, endurance of the toughest, military instinct. We have had to choose born leaders of men who could attract love and secure trust. Everywhere political intrigue is as rife as in Washington.

Cecil's saying of Sir Walter Raleigh that he could "toil terribly" was an electric touch. Above all, let the men who are to save South Carolina be young and vigorous. While I was reflecting on what kind of men we ought to choose, I fell on Clarendon, and it was easy to construct my man out of his portraits. What has been may be again, so the men need not be purely ideal types.

Mr. Toombs[25] told us a story of General Scott and himself. He said he was dining in Washington with Scott, who seasoned every dish and every glass of wine with the eternal refrain, "Save the Union; the Union must be preserved." Toombs remarked that he knew why the Union was so dear to the General, and illustrated his point by a steamboat anecdote, an explosion, of course. While the passengers were struggling in the water a woman ran up and down the bank crying, "Oh, save the red-headed man!" The red-headed man was saved, and his preserver, after landing him noticed with surprise how little interest in him the woman who had made such moving appeals seemed to feel. He asked her "Why did you make that pathetic outcry?" She answered, "Oh, he owes me ten thousand dollars." "Now General," said Toombs, "the Union owes you seventeen thousand dollars a year!" I can imagine the scorn on old Scott's face.

February 25th — Find every one working very hard here. As I dozed on the sofa last night, could hear the scratch, scratch of my husband's pen as he wrote at the table until midnight.

After church to-day, Captain Ingraham[26] called. He left me so uncomfortable. He dared to express regrets that he had to leave the United States Navy. He had been stationed in the Mediterranean, where he liked to be, and expected to be these two years, and to take those lovely daughters of his to Florence. Then came Abraham Lincoln, and rampant black Republicanism, and he must lay down his life for South Carolina. He, however, does not make any moan. He says we lack everything necessary in naval gear to retake Fort Sumter. Of course, he only expects the navy to take it. He is a fish out of water here. He is one of the finest sea-captains; so I suppose they will soon give him a ship and send him back to his own element.

[handwritten margin note: not that bad of view]

At dinner Judge ------ was loudly abusive of Congress.[27] He said: "They have trampled the Constitution underfoot. They have provided President Davis with a house." He was disgusted with the folly of parading the President at the inauguration in a coach drawn by four white horses. Then some one said Mrs. Fitzpatrick was the only lady who sat with the Congress. After the inaugural she poked Jeff Davis in the back with her parasol that he might turn and speak to her. "I am sure that was democratic enough," said some one.

Governor Moore came in with the latest news – a telegram from Governor Pickens[28] to the President, "that a war steamer is lying off the Charleston bar laden with reenforcements for Fort Sumter, and what must we do?" Answer: "Use your own discretion!" There is faith for you, after all is said and done. It is believed there is still some discretion left in South Carolina fit for use.

Everybody who comes here wants an office, and the many who, of course, are disappointed raise a cry of corruption against the few who are successful. I thought we had left all that in Washington. Nobody is willing to be out of sight, and all will take office.

"Constitution" Browne[29] says he is going to Washington for twenty-four hours. I mean to send by him to Mary Garnett for a bonnet ribbon. If they take him up as a traitor, he may cause a civil war. War is now our dread. Mr. Chesnut told him not to make himself a bone of contention.

Everybody means to go into the army. If Sumter is attacked, then Jeff Davis's troubles will begin. The Judge says a military despotism would be best for us – anything to prevent a triumph of the Yankees. All right, but every man objects to any despot but himself.

Mr. Chesnut, in high spirits, dines to-day with the Louisiana delegation. Breakfasted with "Constitution" Browne, who is appointed Assistant Secretary of State, and so does not go to Washington. There was at table the man who advertised for a wife, with the wife so obtained. She was not pretty. We dine at Mr. Pollard's and go to a ball afterward at Judge Bibb's. The New York *Herald* says Lincoln stood before Washington's picture at his inauguration, which was taken by the country as a good sign. We are always frantic for a good sign. Let us pray that a Caesar or a Napoleon may be sent us. That would be our best sign of success. But they still say, "No war." Peace let it be, kind Heaven!

[handwritten margin note: make people go to war]

Dr. De Leon[30] called, fresh from Washington, and says General Scott is using all his power and influence to prevent officers from the South resigning their commissions, among other things promising that they shall never be sent against us in case of war. Captain Ingraham, in his short, curt way, said: "That will never do. If they take their government's pay they must do its fighting."

A brilliant dinner at the Pollards's. Mr. Barnwell[31] took me down. Came home and found the Judge and Governor Moore waiting to go with me to the Bibbs's. And they say it is dull in Montgomery! Clayton,[32] fresh from Washington, was at the party and told us "there was to be peace."

February 28th — In the drawing-room a literary lady began a violent attack upon this mischief-making South Carolina. She told me she was a successful writer in the magazines of the day, but when I found she used "incredible" for "incredulous," I said not a word in defense of my native land. I left her "incredible." Another person came in, while she was pouring upon me her home troubles, and asked if she did not know I was a Carolinian. Then she gracefully reversed her engine, and took the other tack, sounding our praise, but I left her incredible and I remained incredulous, too.

Brewster[33] says the war specks are growing in size. Nobody at the North, or in Virginia, believes we are in earnest. They think we are sulking and that Jeff Davis and Stephens are getting up a very pretty little comedy. The Virginia delegates were insulted at the peace conference; Brewster said, "kicked out."

The Judge thought Jefferson Davis rude to him when the latter was Secretary of War. Mr. Chesnut persuaded the Judge to forego his private wrong for the public good, and so he voted for him, but now his old grudge has come back with an increased venomousness. What a pity to bring the spites of the old Union into this new one! It seems to me already men are willing to risk an injury to our cause, if they may in so doing hurt Jeff Davis.

March 1st — Dined to-day with Mr. Hill[34] from Georgia, and his wife. After he left us she told me he was the celebrated individual who, for Christian scruples, refused to fight a duel with Stephens.[35] She seemed very proud of him for his conduct in the affair. Ignoramus that I am, I had not heard of it. I am having all kinds of experiences. Drove to-day with a lady who fervently wished her husband would go down to Pensacola and be shot. I was dumb with amazement, of course. Telling my story to one who knew the parties, was informed, "Don't you know he beats her?" So I have seen a man "who lifts his hand against a woman in aught save kindness."

Lincoln

Brewster says Lincoln passed through Baltimore disguised, and at night, and that he did well, for just now Baltimore is dangerous ground. He says that he hears from all quarters that the vulgarity of Lincoln, his wife, and his son is beyond credence, a thing you must see before you can believe it. Senator Stephen A. Douglas told Mr. Chesnut that "Lincoln is awfully clever, and that he had found him a heavy handful."

Went to pay my respects to Mrs. Jefferson Davis. She met me with open arms. We did not allude to anything by which we are surrounded. We eschewed politics and our changed relations.

March 3d — Everybody in fine spirits in my world. They have one and all spoken in the Congress[36] to their own perfect satisfaction. To my amazement the Judge took me aside, and, after delivering a panegyric upon himself (but here, later, comes in the amazement), he praised my husband to the skies, and said he was the fittest man of all for a foreign mission. Aye; and the farther away they send us from this Congress the better I will like it.

Saw Jere Clemens and Nick Davis, social curiosities. They are Anti-Secession leaders; then George Sanders and George Deas.[37] The Georges are of opinion that it is folly to try to take back Fort Sumter from Anderson and the United States; that is, before we are ready. They saw in Charleston the devoted band prepared for the sacrifice; I mean, ready to run their heads against a stone wall. Dare devils they are. They have dash and courage enough, but science only could take that fort. They shook their heads.

March 4th — The Washington Congress has passed peace measures. Glory be to God (as my Irish Margaret used to preface every remark, both great and small).

At last, according to his wish, I was able to introduce Mr. Hill, of Georgia, to Mr. Mallory,[38] and also Governor Moore and Brewster, the latter the only man without a title of some sort that I know in this democratic subdivided republic.

I have seen a negro woman sold on the block at auction. She overtopped the crowd. I was walking and felt faint, seasick. The creature looked so like my good little Nancy, a bright mulatto with a pleasant face. She was magnificently gotten up in silks and satins. She seemed delighted with it all, sometimes ogling the bidders, sometimes looking quiet, coy, and modest, but her mouth never relaxed from its expanded grin of excitement. I dare say the poor thing knew who would buy her. I sat down on a stool in a shop and disciplined my wild thoughts. I tried it Sterne fashion. You know how women sell themselves and are sold in marriage from queens downward, eh? You know what the Bible says about slavery and marriage; poor women! poor slaves! Sterne, with his starling – what did he know? He only thought, he did not feel.

In *Evan Harrington* I read: "Like a true English female, she believed in her own inflexible virtue, but never trusted her husband out of sight."[39]

The New York *Herald* says: "Lincoln's carriage is not bomb-proof; so he does not drive out." Two flags and a bundle of sticks have been sent him as gentle reminders. The sticks are to break our heads with. The English are gushingly unhappy as to our family quarrel. Magnanimous of them, for it is their opportunity.

March 5th — We stood on the balcony to see our Confederate flag go up. Roars of cannon, etc., etc. Miss Sanders complained (so said Captain Ingraham) of the deadness of the mob. "It was utterly spiritless," she said; "no cheering, or so little, and no enthusiasm." Captain Ingraham suggested that gentlemen "are apt to be quiet," and this was "a thoughtful crowd, the true mob element with us just-now is hoeing corn." And yet! It is uncomfortable that the idea has gone abroad that we have no joy, no pride, in this thing. The band was playing "Massa in the cold, cold ground." Miss Tyler, daughter of the former President of the United States, ran up the flag.

Captain Ingraham pulled out of his pocket some verses sent to him by a Boston girl. They were well rhymed and amounted to this: she held a rope ready to hang him, though she shed tears when she remembered his heroic rescue of Koszta. Koszta, the rebel![40] She calls us rebels, too. So it depends upon whom one rebels against – whether to save or not shall be heroic.

I must read Lincoln's inaugural. Oh, "comes he in peace, or comes he in war, or to tread but one measure as Young Lochinvar?" Lincoln's aim is to seduce the border States.

The people, the natives, I mean, are astounded that I calmly affirm, in all truth and candor, that if there were awful things in society in Washington, I did not see or hear of them. One must have been hard to please who did not like the people I knew in Washington.

Mr. Chesnut has gone with a list of names to the President – de Treville, Kershaw, Baker, and Robert Rutledge. They are taking a walk, I see. I hope there will be good places in the army for our list.

March 8th — Judge Campbell,[41] of the United States Supreme Court, has resigned. Lord! how he must have hated to do it. How other men who are resigning high positions must hate to do it.

Now we may be sure the bridge is broken. And yet in the Alabama Convention they say Reconstructionists[42] abound and are busy.

Met a distinguished gentleman that I knew when he was in more affluent circumstances. I was willing enough to speak to him, but when he saw me advancing for that purpose, to avoid me, he suddenly dodged around a corner – William, Mrs. de Saussure's former coachman. I remember him on his box, driving a handsome pair of bays, dressed sumptuously in blue broadcloth and brass buttons; a stout, respectable, fine-looking, middle-aged mulatto. He was very high and mighty.

Night after night we used to meet him as fiddler-in-chief of all our parties. He sat in solemn dignity, making faces over his bow, and patting his foot with an emphasis that shook the floor. We gave him five dollars a night; that was his price. His mistress never refused to let him play for any party. He had stable-boys in abundance. He was far above any physical fear for his sleek and well-fed person. How majestically he scraped his foot as a sign that he was tuned up and ready to begin!

Now he is a shabby creature indeed. He must have felt his fallen fortunes when he met me – one who knew him in his prosperity. He ran away, this stately yellow gentleman, from wife and children, home and comfort. My Molly asked him "Why? Miss Liza was good to you, I know." I wonder who owns him now; he looked forlorn.

Governor Moore brought in, to be presented to me, the President of the Alabama Convention. It seems I had known him before he had danced with me at a dancing-school ball when I was in short frocks, with sash, flounces, and a wreath of roses. He was one of those clever boys of our neighborhood, in whom my father[43] saw promise of better things, and so helped him in every way to rise, with books, counsel, sympathy. I was enjoying his conversation immensely, for he was praising my father I without stint, when the Judge came in, breathing fire and fury. Congress has incurred his displeasure. We are abusing one another as fiercely as ever we have abased Yankees. It is disheartening.

March 10th — Mrs. Childs was here to-night (Mary Anderson, from Statesburg), with several children. She is lovely. Her hair is piled up on the top of her head oddly. [Fashions from France still creep into Texas across Mexican borders.] Mrs. Childs is fresh from Texas. Her husband is an artillery officer, or was. They will be glad to promote him here. Mrs. Childs had the sweetest Southern voice, absolute music. But then, she has all of the high spirit of those sweet-voiced Carolina women, too.

Then Mr. Browne came in with his fine English accent, so pleasant to the ear. He tells us that Washington society is not reconciled to the Yankee régime. Mrs. Lincoln means to economize. She at once informed the majordomo that they were poor and hoped to save twelve thousand dollars every year from their salary of twenty thousand. Mr. Browne said Mr. Buchanan's farewell was far more imposing than Lincoln's inauguration.

The people were so amusing, so full of Western stories. Dr. Boykin behaved strangely. All day he had been gaily driving about with us, and never was man in finer spirits. To-night, in this brilliant company, he sat dead still as if in a trance. Once, he waked somewhat – when a high public functionary came in with a present for me, a miniature gondola, "A perfect Venetian specimen," he assured me again and again. In an under-tone Dr. Boykin muttered: "That fellow has been drinking." "Why do you think so?" "Because he has told you exactly the same thing four times." Wonderful! Some of these great statesmen always tell me the same thing – and have been telling me the same thing ever since we came here.

[A man came in and some one said in an undertone, "The age of chivalry is not past, O ye Americans!" "What do you mean?" "That man was once nominated by President Buchanan for a foreign mission, but some Senator stood up and read a paper printed by this man abusive of a woman, and signed by his name in full. After that the Senate would have none of him; his chance was gone forever."]

March 11th — In full conclave to-night, the drawing-room crowded with Judges, Governors, Senators, Generals, Congressmen. They were exalting John C. Calhoun's hospitality. He allowed everybody to stay all night who chose to stop at his house. An ill-mannered person, on one occasion, refused to attend family prayers. Mr. Calhoun said to the servant, "Saddle that man's horse and let him go." From the traveler Calhoun would take no excuse for the "Deity offended." I believe in Mr. Calhoun's hospitality, but not in his family prayers. Mr. Calhoun's piety was of the most philosophical type, from all accounts.[44]

The latest news is counted good news; that is, the last man who left Washington tells us that Seward is in the ascendancy. He is thought to be the friend of peace. The man did say, however, that "that serpent Seward is in the ascendancy just now."

Harriet Lane has eleven suitors. One is described as likely to win, or he would be likely to win, except that he is too heavily weighted. He has been married before and goes about with children and two mothers. There are limits beyond which! Two mothers-in-law!

Mr. Ledyard spoke to Mrs. Lincoln in behalf of a doorkeeper who almost felt he had a vested right, having been there since Jackson's time; but met with the same answer; she had brought her own girl and must economize. Mr. Ledyard thought the twenty thousand (and little enough it is) was given to the President of these United States to enable him to live in proper style, and to maintain an establishment of such dignity as befits the head of a great nation. It is an infamy to economize with the public money and to put it into one's private purse. Mrs. Browne was walking with me when we were airing our indignation against Mrs. Lincoln and her shabby economy. The *Herald* says three only of the élite Washington families attended the Inauguration Ball.

The Judge has just come in and said: "Last night, after Dr. Boykin left on the cars, there came a telegram that his little daughter, Amanda, had died suddenly." In some way he must have known it beforehand. He changed so suddenly yesterday, and seemed so careworn and unhappy. He believes in clairvoyance, magnetism, and all that. Certainly, there was some terrible foreboding of this kind on his part.

Tuesday — Now this, they say, is positive: "Fort Sumter is to be released and we are to have no war." After all, far too good to be true. Mr. Browne told us that, at one of the peace intervals (I mean intervals in the interest of peace), Lincoln flew through Baltimore, locked up in an express car. He wore a Scotch cap.

We went to the Congress. Governor Cobb, who presides over that august body, put James Chesnut in the chair, and came down to talk to us. He told us why the pay of Congressmen was fixed in secret session, and why the amount of it was never divulged – to prevent the lodginghouse and hotel people from making their bills of a size to cover it all. "The bill would be sure to correspond with the pay," he said.

In the hotel parlor we had a scene. Mrs. Scott was describing Lincoln, who is of the cleverest Yankee type. She said: "Awfully ugly, even grotesque in appearance, the kind who are always at the corner stores, sitting on boxes, whittling sticks, and telling stories as funny as they are vulgar." Here I interposed: "But Stephen A. Douglas said one day to Mr. Chesnut, 'Lincoln is the hardest fellow to handle I have ever encountered yet.'" Mr. Scott is from California, and said Lincoln is "an utter American specimen, coarse, rough, and strong; a good-natured, kind creature; as pleasant-tempered as he is clever, and if this country can be joked and laughed out of its rights he is the kind-hearted fellow to do it. Now if there is a war and it pinches the Yankee pocket instead of filling it—"

Here a shrill voice came from the next room (which opened upon the one we were in by folding doors thrown wide open) and said: "Yankees are no more mean and stingy than you are. People at the North are just as good as people at the South." The speaker advanced upon us in great wrath.

Mrs. Scott apologized and made some smooth, polite remark, though evidently much embarrassed. But the vinegar face and curly pate refused to receive any concessions, and replied: "That comes with a very bad grace after what you were saying," and she harangued us loudly for several minutes. Some one in the other room giggled outright, but we were quiet as mice. Nobody wanted to hurt her feelings. She was one against so many. If I were at the North, I should expect them to belabor us, and should hold my tongue. We separated North from South because of incompatibility of temper. We are divorced because we have hated each other so. If we could only separate, a "separation à l'agréable," as the French say it, and not have a horrid fight for divorce.

The poor exile had already been insulted, she said. She was playing "Yankee Doodle" on the piano before breakfast to soothe her wounded spirit, and the Judge came in and calmly requested her to "leave out the Yankee while she played the Doodle." The Yankee end of it did not suit our climate, he said; was totally out of place and had got out of its latitude.

A man said aloud: "This war talk is nothing. It will soon blow over. Only a fuss gotten up by that Charleston clique." Mr. Toombs asked him to show his passports, for a man who uses such language is a suspicious character.

Alexander Stephens, from the "Cornerstone" Speech (March 21, 1861)

In the two months following Jefferson Davis's farewell to the U.S. Senate, the seven states that had seceded from the Union formed the Confederate States of America, and the question hung in the air as to whether the border states would follow. At this precarious moment for the infant Confederacy, there was a rush to consolidate its government and rally its people, and Stephens, who had taken the oath of office of vice-president on February 11, 1861, quickly found the opportunity to deliver a rousing speech defending the newly adopted Confederate Constitution. On March 21, before a raucous audience at the Athenaeum in Savannah, Stephens argued that slavery was the natural condition of blacks and a cornerstone of the Confederacy. Interrupted intermittently by resounding applause and stomping from the crowd that spilled out onto the surrounding streets, the speech proved a rallying cry for Southerners to unite in support of both slavery and the new Confederate government. Although he later sought to downplay his remarks, Stephens's speech was remarkable in its elevation of white supremacy to an organizing political principle; as war loomed on the horizon, Stephens championed slavery as indispensable to the new country envisioned by himself and those whom Charles B. Dew has called "Apostles of Disunion."

When perfect quiet is restored, I shall proceed. I cannot speak so long as there is any noise or confusion. I shall take my time – I feel quite prepared to spend the night with you if necessary. [Loud applause.] I very much regret that every one who desires cannot hear what I have to say. Not that I have any display to make, or any thing very entertaining to present, but such views as I have to give, I wish *all*, not only in this city, but in this State, and throughout our Confederate Republic, could hear, who have a desire to hear them.

I was remarking, that we are passing through one of the greatest revolutions in the annals of the world. Seven States have within the last three months thrown off an old government and formed a new.[45] This revolution has been signally marked, up to this time, by the fact of its having been accomplished without the loss of a single drop of blood. [Applause.]

This new constitution, or form of government, constitutes the subject to which your attention will be partly invited.[46] In reference to it, I make this first general remark. It amply secures all our ancient rights, franchises, and liberties. All the great principles of Magna Charta are retained in it. No citizen is deprived of life, liberty, or property, but by the judgment of his peers under the laws of the land. The great principle of religious liberty, which was the honor and pride of the old constitution, is still maintained and secured. All the essentials of the old constitution, which have endeared it to the hearts of the American people, have been preserved and perpetuated. [Applause.] Some changes have been made. Of these I shall speak presently. Some of these I should have preferred not to have seen made; but these, perhaps, meet the cordial approbation of a majority of this audience, if not an overwhelming majority of the people of the Confederacy. Of them, therefore, I will not speak. But other important changes do meet my cordial approbation. They form great improvements upon the old constitution. So, taking the whole new constitution, I have no hesitancy in giving it as my judgment that it is decidedly better than the old. [Applause.]

Allow me briefly to allude to some of these improvements. The question of building up class interests, or fostering one branch of industry to the prejudice of another under the exercise of the revenue power, which gave us so much trouble under the old constitution, is put at rest forever under the new. We allow the imposition of no duty with a view of giving advantage to one class of persons, in any trade or business, over those of another. All, under our system, stand upon the same broad principles of perfect equality. Honest labor and enterprise are left free and unrestricted in whatever pursuit they may be engaged. This subject came well nigh causing a rupture of the old Union, under the lead of the gallant Palmetto State, which lies on our border, in 1833. This old thorn of the tariff, which was the cause of so much irritation in the old body politic, is removed forever from the new.[47] [Applause.]

* * * * *

But not to be tedious in enumerating the numerous changes for the better, allow me to allude to one other – though last, not least. The new constitution has put at rest, *forever*, all the agitating questions relating to our peculiar institution – African slavery as it exists amongst us – the proper *status* of the negro in our form of civilization. This was the immediate cause of the late rupture and present revolution. Jefferson in his forecast, had anticipated this, as the "rock upon which the old Union would split."[48] He was right. What was conjecture with him, is now a realized fact. But whether he fully comprehended the great truth upon which that rock *stood* and *stands*, may be doubted. The prevailing ideas entertained by him and most of the leading statesmen at the time of the formation of the old constitution, were that the enslavement of the African was in violation of the laws of nature; that it was wrong in *principle*, socially, morally, and politically. It was an evil they knew not well how to deal with, but the general opinion of the men of that day was that, somehow or other in the order of Providence, the institution would be evanescent and pass away. This idea, though not incorporated in the constitution, was the prevailing idea at that time. The constitution, it is true, secured every essential guarantee to the institution while it should last, and hence no argument can be justly urged against the constitutional guarantees thus secured, because of the common sentiment of the day. Those ideas, however, were fundamentally wrong. They rested upon the assumption of the equality of races. This was an error. It was a sandy foundation, and the government built upon it fell when the "storm came and the wind blew."[49]

Our new government is founded upon exactly the opposite idea; its foundations are laid, its corner-stone rests upon the great truth, that the negro is not equal to the white man; that slavery – subordination to the superior race – is his natural and normal condition. [Applause.]

This, our new government, is the first, in the history of the world, based upon this great physical, philosophical, and moral truth. This truth has been slow in the process of its development, like all other truths in the various departments of science. It has been so even amongst us. Many who hear me, perhaps, can recollect well, that this truth was not generally admitted, even within their day. The errors of the past generation still clung to many as late as twenty years ago. Those at the North, who still cling to these errors, with a zeal above knowledge, we justly denominate fanatics. All fanaticism springs from an aberration of the mind – from a defect in reasoning. It is a species of insanity. One of the most striking characteristics of insanity, in many instances, is forming correct conclusions from fancied or erroneous premises; so with the anti-slavery fanatics; their conclusions are right if their premises were. They assume that the negro is equal, and hence conclude that he is entitled to equal privileges and rights with the white man. If their premises were correct, their conclusions would be logical and just – but their premise being wrong, their whole argument fails. I recollect once of having heard a gentleman from one of the northern States, of great power and ability, announce in the House of Representatives, with imposing effect, that we of the South would be compelled, ultimately, to yield upon this subject of slavery, that it was as impossible to war successfully against a principle in politics, as it was in physics or mechanics. That the principle would ultimately prevail. That we, in maintaining slavery as it exists with us, were warring against a principle, a principle founded in nature, the principle of the equality of men. The reply I made to him was, that upon his own grounds, we should, ultimately, succeed, and that he and his associates, in this crusade against our institutions, would ultimately fail. The truth announced, that it was as impossible to war successfuly against a principle in politics as it was in physics and mechanics, I admitted; but told him that it was he, and those acting with him, who were warring against a principle. They were attempting to make things equal which the Creator had made unequal.

In the conflict thus far, success has been on our side, complete throughout the length and breadth of the Confederate States. It is upon this, as I have stated, our social fabric is firmly planted; and I cannot permit myself to doubt the ultimate success of a full recognition of this principle throughout the civilized and enlightened world.

As I have stated, the truth of this principle may be slow in development, as all truths are and ever have been, in the various branches of science. It was so with the principles announced by Galileo – it was so with Adam Smith and his principles of political economy. It was so with Harvey, and his theory of the circulation of the blood.[50] It is stated that not a single one of the medical profession, living at the time of the announcement of the truths made by him, admitted them. Now, they are universally acknowledged. May we not, therefore, look with confidence to the ultimate universal acknowledgment of the truths upon which our system rests? It is the first government ever instituted upon the principles in strict conformity to nature, and the ordination of Providence, in furnishing the materials of human society. Many governments have been founded upon the principle of the subordination and serfdom of certain classes of the same race; such were and are in violation of the laws of nature. Our system commits no such violation of nature's laws. With us, all of the white race, however high or low, rich or poor, are equal in the eye of the law. Not so with the negro. Subordination is his place. He, by nature, or by the curse against Canaan,[51] is fitted for that condition which he occupies in our system. The architect, in the construction of buildings, lays the foundation with the proper material – the granite; then comes the brick or the marble. The substratum of our society is made of the material fitted by nature for it, and by experience we know that it is best, not only for the superior, but for the inferior race, that it should be so. It is, indeed, in conformity with the ordinance of the Creator. It is not for us to inquire into the wisdom of his ordinances, or to question them. For his own purposes, he has made one race to differ from another, as he has made "one star to differ from another star in glory."[52]

The great objects of humanity are best attained when there is conformity to his laws and decrees, in the formation of governments as well as in all things else. Our confederacy is founded upon principles in strict conformity with these laws. This stone which was rejected by the first builders "is become the chief of the corner"[53] – the real "cornerstone" – in our new edifice. [Applause.]

I have been asked, what of the future? It has been apprehended by some that we would have arrayed against us the civilized world. I care not who or how many they may be against us, when we stand upon the eternal principles of truth, *if we are true to ourselves and the principles for which we contend*, we are obliged to, and must triumph. [Immense applause.]

Thousands of people who begin to understand these truths are not yet completely out of the shell; they do not see them in their length and breadth. We hear much of the civilization and Christianization of the barbarous tribes of Africa. In my judgment, those ends will never be attained, but by first teaching them the lesson taught to Adam, that "in the sweat of his brow he should eat his bread,"[54] [applause,] and teaching them to work, and feed, and clothe themselves.

* * * * *

But to return to the question of the future. What is to be the result of this revolution?

Will every thing, commenced so well, continue as it has begun? In reply to this anxious inquiry, I can only say it all depends upon ourselves. A young man starting out in life on his majority, with health, talent, and ability, under a favoring Providence, may be said to be the architect of his own fortunes. His destinies are in his own hands. He may make for himself a name, of honor or dishonor, according to his own acts. If he plants himself upon truth, integrity, honor and uprightness, with industry, patience and energy, he cannot fail of success. So it is with us. We are a young republic, just entering upon the arena of nations; we will be the architects of our own fortunes. Our destiny, under Providence, is in our own hands. With wisdom, prudence, and statesmanship on the part of our public men, and intelligence, virtue and patriotism on the part of the people, success, to the full measures of our most sanguine hopes, may be looked for. But if unwise counsels prevail – if we become divided – if schisms arise – if dissensions spring up – if factions are engendered – if party spirit, nourished by unholy personal ambition shall rear its hydra head, I have no good to prophesy for you. Without intelligence, virtue, integrity, and patriotism on the part of the people, no republic or representative government can be durable or stable.

We have intelligence, and virtue, and patriotism. All that is required is to cultivate and perpetuate these. Intelligence will not do without virtue. France was a nation of philosophers. These philosophers become Jacobins.[55] They lacked that virtue, that devotion to moral principle, and that patriotism which is essential to good government. Organized upon principles of perfect justice and right – seeking amity and friendship with all other powers – I see no obstacle in the way of our upward and onward progress. Our growth, by accessions from other States, will depend greatly upon whether we present to the world, as I trust we shall, a better government than that to which neighboring States belong. If we do this, North Carolina, Tennessee, and Arkansas cannot hesitate long; neither can Virginia, Kentucky, and Missouri. They will necessarily gravitate to us by an imperious law. We made ample provision in our constitution for the admission of other States;[56] it is more guarded, and wisely so, I think, than the old constitution on the same subject, but not too guarded to receive them as fast as it may be proper. Looking to the distant future, and, perhaps, not very far distant either, it is not beyond the range of possibility, and even probability, that all the great States of the north-west will gravitate this way, as well as Tennessee, Kentucky, Missouri, Arkansas, etc. Should they do so, our doors are wide enough to receive them, but not until they are ready to assimilate with us in principle.

The process of disintegration in the old Union may be expected to go on with almost absolute certainty if we pursue the right course. We are now the nucleus of a growing power which, if we are true to ourselves, our destiny, and high mission, will become the controlling power on this continent. To what extent accessions will go on in the process of time, or where it will end, the future will determine. So far as it concerns States of the old Union, this process will be upon no such principles of *reconstruction* as now spoken of, but upon *reorganization* and new assimilation. [Loud applause.] Such are some of the glimpses of the future as I catch them.

* * * * *

As to whether we shall have war with our late confederates, or whether all matters of differences between us shall be amicably settled, I can only say that the prospect for a peaceful adjustment is better, so far as I am informed, than it has been.

The prospect of war is, at least, not so threatening as it has been. The idea of coercion, shadowed forth in President Lincoln's inaugural, seems not to be followed up thus far so vigorously as was expected. Fort Sumter, it is believed, will soon be evacuated. What course will be pursued toward Fort Pickens,[57] and the other forts on the gulf, is not so well understood. It is to be greatly desired that all of them should be surrendered. Our object is *peace*, not only with the North, but with the world. All matters relating to the public property, public liabilities of the Union when we were members of it, we are ready and willing to adjust and settle upon the principles of right, equity, and good faith. War can be of no more benefit to the North than to us. Whether the intention of evacuating Fort Sumter is to be received as an evidence of a desire for a peaceful solution of our difficulties with the United States, or the result of necessity, I will not undertake to say. I would fain hope the former. Rumors are afloat, however, that it is the result of necessity. All I can say to you, therefore, on that point is, keep your armor bright and your powder dry. [Enthusiastic cheering.]

Walt Whitman, "Origins of Attempted Secession" (1882)

Relatively late in his life, Whitman returned to the Civil War in a series of prose fragments, sketches, and short essays gathered together in a volume titled *Specimen Days and Collect* (1882), in which Whitman struggled to come to terms with his country's, and his own, changing identity. Although much of this material had appeared earlier in periodicals and in Whitman's *Memoranda During the War* (1875–1876), this essay was, in the main, original to *Collect*.

Not the whole matter, but some side facts worth conning to-day and any day.

I consider the war of attempted secession, 1860–65, not as a struggle of two distinct and separate peoples, but a conflict (often happening, and very fierce) between the passions and paradoxes of one and the same identity—perhaps the only terms on which that identity could really become fused, homogeneous and lasting. The origin and conditions out of which it arose, are full of lessons, full of warnings yet to the Republic—and always will be. The underlying and principal of those origins are yet singularly ignored. The Northern States were really just as responsible for that war, (in its precedents, foundations, instigations,) as the South. Let me try to give my view. From the age of 21 to 40, (1840–'60,) I was interested in the political movements of the land, not so much as a participant, but as an observer, and a regular voter at the elections. I think I was conversant with the springs of action, and their workings, not only in New York city and Brooklyn, but understood them in the whole country, as I had made leisurely tours through all the middle States, and partially through the western and southern, and down to New Orleans, in which city I resided for some time. (I was there at the close of the Mexican war—saw and talk'd with General Taylor,[58] and the other generals and officers, who were fêted and detain'd several days on their return victorious from that expedition.)

Of course many and very contradictory things, specialties, developments, constitutional views, &c., went to make up the origin of the war—but the most significant general fact can be best indicated and stated as follows: For twenty-five years previous to the outbreak, the controling "Democratic" nominating conventions of our Republic—starting from their primaries in wards or districts, and so expanding to counties, powerful cities, States, and to the great Presidential nominating conventions—were getting to represent and be composed of more and more putrid and dangerous materials. Let me give a schedule, or list, of one of these representative conventions for a long time before, and inclusive of, that which nominated Buchanan. (Remember they had come to be the fountains and tissues of the American body politic, forming, as it were, the whole blood, legislation, office-holding, &c.) One of these conventions, from 1840 to '60, exhibited a spectacle such as could never be seen except in our own age and in these States. The members who composed it were, seven-eighths of them, the meanest kind of bawling and blowing office-holders, office-seekers, pimps, malignants, conspirators, murderers, fancy-men, custom-house clerks, contractors, kept-editors, spaniels well-train'd to carry and fetch jobbers, infidels, disunionists, terrorists, mail-riflers, slave-catchers, pushers of slavery, creatures of the President, creatures of would-be Presidents, spies, bribers, compromisers, lobbyers, sponges, ruin'd sports, expell'd gamblers, policy-backers, monte-dealers, duellists, carriers of conceal'd weapons, deaf men, pimpled men, scarr'd inside with vile disease, gaudy outside with gold chains made from the people's money and harlots' money twisted together; crawling, serpentine men, the lousy combings and born freedom-sellers of the earth. And whence came they? From back-yards and bar-rooms; from out of the custom-houses, marshals' offices, post-offices, and gambling-hells; from the President's house, the jail, the station-house; from unnamed by-places, where devilish disunion was hatch'd at midnight; from political hearses, and from the coffins inside, and from the shrouds inside of the coffins; from the tumors and abscesses of the land; from the skeletons and skulls in the vaults of the federal alms-houses; and from the running sores of the great cities. Such, I say, form'd, or absolutely control'd the forming of, the entire personnel, the atmosphere, nutriment and chyle; of our municipal, State, and National politics—substantially permeating, handling, deciding, and wielding everything—legislation, nominations, elections, "public sentiment," &c.—while the great masses of the people, farmers, mechanics, and traders, were helpless in their gripe. These conditions were mostly prevalent in the north and west, and especially in New York and Philadelphia cities; and the southern leaders, (bad enough, but of a far higher order,) struck hands and affiliated with, and used them. Is it strange that a thunder-storm follow'd such morbid and stifling cloud-strata?

I say then, that what, as just outlined, heralded, and made the ground ready for secession revolt, ought to be held up, through all the future, as the most instructive lesson in American political history—the most significant warning and beacon-light to coming generations. I say that the sixteenth, seventeenth and eighteenth terms of the American Presidency[59] have shown that the villainy and shallowness of rulers (back'd by the machinery of great parties) are just as eligible to these States as to any foreign despotism, kingdom, or empire—there is not a bit of difference. History is to record those three Presidentiads, and especially the administrations of Fillmore and Buchanan, as so far our topmost warning and shame. Never were publicly display'd more deform'd, mediocre, snivelling, unreliable, false-hearted men. Never were these States so insulted, and attempted to be betray'd. All the main purposes for which the government was establish'd were openly denied. The perfect equality of slavery with freedom was flauntingly preach'd in the north—nay, the superiority of slavery. The slave trade was proposed to be renew'd. Everywhere frowns and misunderstandings—everywhere exasperations and humiliations. (The slavery contest is settled—and the war is long over—yet do not those putrid conditions, too many of them, still exist? still result in diseases, fevers, wounds—not of war and army hospitals—but the wounds and diseases of peace?)

Out of those generic influences, mainly in New York, Pennsylvania, Ohio, &c., arose the attempt at disunion. To philosophical examination, the malignant fever of that war shows its embryonic sources, and the original nourishment of its life and growth, in the north. I say secession, below the surface, originated and was brought to maturity in the free States. I allude to the score of years preceding 1860. My deliberate opinion is now, that if at the opening of the contest the abstract duality-question of *slavery and quiet* could have been submitted to a direct popular vote, as against their opposite, they would have triumphantly carried the day in a majority of the northern States—in the large cities, leading off with New York and Philadelphia, by tremendous majorities. The events of '61 amazed everybody north and south, and burst all prophecies and calculations like bubbles. But even then, and during the whole war, the stern fact remains that (not only did the north put it down, but) the secession cause had numerically just as many sympathizers in the free as in the rebel States.[60]

As to slavery, abstractly and practically, (its idea, and the determination to establish and expand it, especially in the new territories, the future America,) it is too common, I repeat, to identify it exclusively with the south. In fact down to the opening of the war, the whole country had about an equal hand in it. The north had at least been just as guilty, if not more guilty; and the east and west had. The former Presidents and Congresses had been guilty—the governors and legislatures of every northern State had been guilty, and the majors of New York and other northern cities had all been guilty—their hands were all stain'd. And as the conflict took decided shape, it is hard to tell which class, the leading southern or northern disunionists, was more stunn'd and disappointed at the non-action of the free-state secession element, so largely existing and counted on by those leaders, both sections.

So much for that point, and for the north. As to the inception and direct instigation of the war, in the south itself, I shall not attempt interiors or complications. Behind all, the idea that it was from a resolute and arrogant determination on the part of the extreme slaveholders, the Calhounites,[61] to carry the states rights' portion of the constitutional compact to its farthest verge, and nationalize slavery, or else disrupt the Union, and found a new empire, with slavery for its corner-stone, was and is undoubtedly the true theory. (If successful, this attempt might—I am not sure, but it might—have destroy'd not only our American republic, in anything like first-class proportions, in itself and its prestige, but for ages at least, the cause of Liberty and Equality everywhere—and would have been the greatest triumph of reaction, and the severest blow to political and every other freedom, possible to conceive. Its worst result would have inured to the southern States themselves.) That our national democratic experiment, principle, and machinery, could triumphantly sustain such a shock, and that the Constitution could weather it, like a ship a storm, and come out of it as sound and whole as before, is by far the most signal proof yet of the stability of that experiment, Democracy, and of those principles, and that Constitution.

Of the war itself, we know in the ostent what has been done. The numbers of the dead and wounded can be told or approximated, the debt posted and put on record, the material events narrated, &c. Meantime, elections go on, laws are pass'd, political parties struggle, issue their platforms, &c., just the same as before. But immensest result, not only in politics, but in literature, poems, and sociology, are doubtless waiting yet unform'd in the future. How long they will wait I cannot tell. The pageant of history's retrospect shows us, ages since, all Europe marching on the crusades, those arm'd uprisings of the people, stirr'd by a mere idea, to grandest attempt—and, when once baffled in it, returning, at intervals, twice, thrice, and again. An unsurpass'd series of revolutionary events, influences. Yet it took over two hundred years for the seeds of the crusades to germinate, before beginning even to sprout. Two hundred years they lay, sleeping, not dead, but dormant in the ground. Then, out of them, unerringly, arts, travel, navigation, politics, literature, freedom, the spirit of adventure, inquiry, all arose, grew, and steadily sped on to what we see at present. far back there, that huge agitation-struggle of the crusades stands, as undoubtedly the embryo, the start, of the high preëminence of experiment, civilization and enterprise which the European nations have since sustain'd, and of which these States are the heirs.

Another illustration—(history is full of them, although the war itself, the victory of the Union, and the relations of our equal States, present features of which there are no precedents in the past.) The conquest of England eight centuries ago, by the Franco-Normans—the obliteration of the old, (in many respects so needing obliteration)—the Domesday Book,[62] and the repartition of the land—the old impedimenta removed, even by blood and ruthless violence, and a new, progressive genesis establish'd, new seeds sown—time has proved plain enough that, bitter as they were, all these were the most salutary series of revolutions that could possibly have happen'd. Out of them, and by them mainly, have come, out of Albic, Roman and Saxon England—and without them could not have come—not only England of the 500 years down to the present, and of the present—but these States. Nor, except for that terrible dislocation and overturn, would these States, as they are, exist to-day.

It is certain to me that the United States, by virtue of that war and its results, and through that and them only, are now ready to enter, and must certainly enter, upon their genuine career in history, as no more torn and divided in their spinal requisites, but a great homogeneous Nation—free states all—a moral and political unity in variety, such as Nature shows in her grandest physical works, and as much greater than any mere work of Nature, as the moral and political, the work of man, his mind, his soul, are, in their loftiest sense, greater than the merely physical. Out of that war not only has the nationality of the States escaped from being strangled, but more than any of the rest, and, in my opinion, more than the north itself, the vital heart and breath of the south have escaped as from the pressure of a general nightmare, and are henceforth to enter on a life, development, and active freedom, whose realities are certain in the future, notwithstanding all the southern vexations of the hour—a development which could not possibly have been achiev'd on any less terms, or by any other means than that grim lesson, or something equivalent to it. And I predict that the south is yet to outstrip the north.

Ulysses S. Grant, from *Personal Memoirs of U. S. Grant* (1885–1886)

Beyond its insights into his own personality and its candid treatment of the war, Grant's memoir is remarkable for the circumstances under which it was written. Having served two controversial, turbulent terms as president; having lost almost everything in a failed business venture; and then having been diagnosed with terminal throat cancer—Grant undertook to write his memoirs in the hope that they would provide financial support for his family. It worked. Published and marketed by Mark Twain, the *Personal Memoirs* sold tremendously well and helped secure Grant's reputation as a writer and decent human being, if not as a president or businessman.

Chapter 16 – Resignation – Private Life – Life at Galena – The Coming Crisis

My family, all this while,[63] was at the East. It consisted now of a wife and two children. I saw no chance of supporting them on the Pacific coast out of my pay as an army officer. I concluded, therefore, to resign, and in March applied for a leave of absence until the end of the July following, tendering my resignation to take effect at the end of that time. I left the Pacific coast very much attached to it, and with the full expectation of making it my future home. That expectation and that hope remained uppermost in my mind until the Lieutenant-Generalcy bill was introduced into Congress in the winter of 1863–4. The passage of that bill, and my promotion, blasted my last hope of ever becoming a citizen of the further West.[64]

In the late summer of 1854 I rejoined my family, to find in it a son whom I had never seen, born while I was on the Isthmus of Panama.[65] I was now to commence, at the age of thirty-two, a new struggle for our support. My wife had a farm near St. Louis, to which we went, but I had no means to stock it. A house had to be built also. I worked very hard, never losing a day because of bad weather, and accomplished the object in a moderate way. If nothing else could be done I would load a cord of wood on a wagon and take it to the city for sale. I managed to keep along very well until 1858, when I was attacked by fever and ague. I had suffered very severely and for a long time from this disease, while a boy in Ohio. It lasted now over a year, and, while it did not keep me in the house, it did interfere greatly with the amount of work I was able to perform. In the fall of 1858 I sold out my stock, crops and farming utensils at auction, and gave up farming.

In the winter I established a partnership with Harry Boggs, a cousin of Mrs. Grant, in the real estate agency business. I spent that winter at St. Louis myself, but did not take my family into town until the spring. Our business might have become prosperous if I had been able to wait for it to grow. As it was, there was no more than one person could attend to, and not enough to support two families. While a citizen of St. Louis and engaged in the real estate agency business, I was a candidate for the office of county engineer, an office of respectability and emolument which would have been very acceptable to me at that time. The incumbent was appointed by the county court, which consisted of five members. My opponent had the advantage of birth over me (he was a citizen by adoption) and carried off the prize. I now withdrew from the co-partnership with Boggs, and, in May, 1860, removed to Galena, Illinois, and took a clerkship in my father's store.

While a citizen of Missouri, my first opportunity for casting a vote at a Presidential election occurred. I had been in the army from before attaining my majority and had thought but little about politics, although I was a Whig by education and a great admirer of Mr. Clay.[66] But the Whig party had ceased to exist before I had an opportunity of exercising the privilege of casting a ballot; the Know-Nothing party had taken its place, but was on the wane; and the Republican party was in a chaotic state and had not yet received a name. It had no existence in the Slave States except at points on the borders next to Free States. In St. Louis City and County, what afterwards became the Republican party was known as the Free-Soil Democracy, led by the Honorable Frank P. Blair.[67] Most of my neighbors had known me as an officer of the army with Whig proclivities. They had been on the same side, and, on the death of their party, many had become Know-Nothings, or members of the American party. There was a lodge near my new home, and I was invited to join it. I accepted the invitation; was initiated; attended a meeting just one week later, and never went to another afterwards.

I have no apologies to make for having been one week a member of the American party; for I still think native-born citizens of the United States should have as much protection, as many privileges in their native country, as those who voluntarily select it for a home. But all secret, oath-bound political parties are dangerous to any nation, no matter how pure or how patriotic the motives and principles which first bring them together. No political party can or ought to exist when one of its corner-stones is opposition to freedom of thought and to the right to worship God "according to the dictate of one's own conscience,"[68] or according to the creed of any religious denomination whatever. Nevertheless, if a sect sets up its laws as binding above the State laws, wherever the two come in conflict this claim must be resisted and suppressed at whatever cost.

Up to the Mexican war there were a few out and out abolitionists, men who carried their hostility to slavery into all elections, from those for a justice of the peace up to the Presidency of the United States. They were noisy but not numerous. But the great majority of people at the North, where slavery did not exist, were opposed to the institution, and looked upon its existence in any part of the country as unfortunate. They did not hold the States where slavery existed responsible for it; and believed that protection should be given to the right of property in slaves until some satisfactory way could be reached to be rid of the institution. Opposition to slavery was not a creed of either political party. In some sections more anti-slavery men belonged to the Democratic party, and in others to the Whigs. But with the inauguration of the Mexican war, in fact with the annexation of Texas, "the inevitable conflict" commenced.

As the time for the Presidential election of 1856—the first at which I had the opportunity of voting—approached, party feeling began to run high. The Republican party was regarded in the South and the border States not only as opposed to the extension of slavery, but as favoring the compulsory abolition of the institution without compensation to the owners. The most horrible visions seemed to present themselves to the minds of people who, one would suppose, ought to have known better. Many educated and, otherwise, sensible persons appeared to believe that emancipation meant social equality. Treason to the Government was openly advocated and was not rebuked. It was evident to my mind that the election of a Republican President in 1856 meant the secession of all the Slave States, and rebellion. Under these circumstances I preferred the success of a candidate whose election would prevent or postpone secession, to seeing the country plunged into a war the end of which no man could foretell. With a Democrat elected by the unanimous vote of the Slave States, there could be no pretext for secession for four years. I very much hoped that the passions of the people would subside in that time, and the catastrophe be averted altogether; if it was not, I believed the country would be better prepared to receive the shock and to resist it. I therefore voted for James Buchanan for President. Four years later the Republican party was successful in electing its candidate to the Presidency. The civilized world has learned the consequence. Four millions of human beings held as chattels have been liberated; the ballot has been given to them; the free schools of the country have been opened to their children. The nation still lives, and the people are just as free to avoid social intimacy with the blacks as ever they were, or as they are with white people.

While living in Galena I was nominally only a clerk supporting myself and family on a stipulated salary. In reality my position was different. My father had never lived in Galena himself, but had established my two brothers there, the one next younger than myself in charge of the business, assisted by the youngest. When I went there it was my father's intention to give up all connection with the business himself, and to establish his three sons in it: but the brother who had really built up the business was sinking with consumption, and it was not thought best to make any change while he was in this condition. He lived until September, 1861, when he succumbed to that insidious disease which always flatters its victims into the belief that they are growing better up to the close of life. A more honorable man never transacted business. In September, 1861, I was engaged in an employment which required all my attention elsewhere.

During the eleven months that I lived in Galena prior to the first call for volunteers, I had been strictly attentive to my business, and had made but few acquaintances other than customers and people engaged in the same line with myself. When the election took place in November, 1860, I had not been a resident of Illinois long enough to gain citizenship and could not, therefore, vote. I was really glad of this at the time, for my pledges would have compelled me to vote for Stephen A. Douglas, who had no possible chance of election. The contest was really between Mr. Breckinridge[69] and Mr. Lincoln; between minority rule and rule by the majority. I wanted, as between these candidates, to see Mr. Lincoln elected. Excitement ran high during the canvass, and torch-light processions enlivened the scene in the generally quiet streets of Galena many nights during the campaign. I did not parade with either party, but occasionally met with the "wide awakes"—Republicans—in their rooms, and superintended their drill. It was evident, from the time of the Chicago nomination to the close of the canvass, that the election of the Republican candidate would be the signal for some of the Southern States to secede. I still had hopes that the four years which had elapsed since the first nomination of a Presidential candidate by a party distinctly opposed to slavery extension, had given time for the extreme pro-slavery sentiment to cool down; for the Southerners to think well before they took the awful leap which they had so vehemently threatened. But I was mistaken.

The Republican candidate was elected, and solid substantial people of the North-west, and I presume the same order of people throughout the entire North, felt very serious, but determined, after this event. It was very much discussed whether the South would carry out its threat to secede and set up a separate government, the corner-stone of which should be, protection to the "Divine" institution of slavery. For there were people who believed in the "divinity" of human slavery, as there are now people who believe Mormonism and Polygamy to be ordained by the Most High. We forgive them for entertaining such notions, but forbid their practice. It was generally believed that there would be a flurry; that some of the extreme Southern States would go so far as to pass ordinances of secession. But the common impression was that this step was so plainly suicidal for the South, that the movement would not spread over much of the territory and would not last long.

Doubtless the founders of our government, the majority of them at least, regarded the confederation of the colonies as an experiment. Each colony considered itself a separate government; that the confederation was for mutual protection against a foreign foe, and the prevention of strife and war among themselves. If there had been a desire on the part of any single State to withdraw from the compact at any time while the number of States was limited to the original thirteen, I do not suppose there would have been any to contest the right, no matter how much the determination might have been regretted. The problem changed on the ratification of the Constitution by all the colonies; it changed still more when amendments were added; and if the right of any one State to withdraw continued to exist at all after the ratification of the Constitution, it certainly ceased on the formation of new States, at least so far as the new States themselves were concerned. It was never possessed at all by Florida or the States west of the Mississippi, all of which were purchased by the treasury of the entire nation. Texas and the territory brought into the Union in consequence of annexation, were purchased with both blood and treasure; and Texas, with a domain greater than that of any European state except Russia, was permitted to retain as state property all the public lands within its borders. It would have been ingratitude and injustice of the most flagrant sort for this State to withdraw from the Union after all that had been spent and done to introduce her; yet, if separation had actually occurred, Texas must necessarily have gone with the South, both on account of her institutions and her geographical position. Secession was illogical as well as impracticable; it was revolution.

Now, the right of revolution is an inherent one. When people are oppressed by their government, it is a natural right they enjoy to relieve themselves of the oppression, if they are strong enough, either by withdrawal from it, or by over-throwing it and substituting a government more acceptable. But any people or part of a people who resort to this remedy, stake their lives, their property, and every claim for protection given by citizenship—on the issue. Victory, or the conditions imposed by the conqueror—must be the result.

In the case of the war between the States it would have been the exact truth if the South had said,—"We do not want to live with you Northern people any longer; we know our institution of slavery is obnoxious to you, and, as you are growing numerically stronger than we, it may at some time in the future be endangered. So long as you permitted us to control the government, and with the aid of a few friends at the North to enact laws constituting your section a guard against the escape of our property, we were willing to live with you. You have been submissive to our rule heretofore; but it looks now as if you did not intend to continue so, and we will remain in the Union no longer." Instead of this the seceding States cried lustily,—"Let us alone; you have no constitutional power to interfere with us." Newspapers and people at the North reiterated the cry. Individuals might ignore the constitution; but the Nation itself must not only obey it, but must enforce the strictest construction of that instrument; the construction put upon it by the Southerners themselves. The fact is the constitution did not apply to any such contingency as the one existing from 1861 to 1865. Its framers never dreamed of such a contingency occurring. If they had foreseen it, the probabilities are they would have sanctioned the right of a State or States to withdraw rather than that there should be war between brothers.

The framers were wise in their generation and wanted to do the very best possible to secure their own liberty and independence, and that also of their descendants to the latest days. It is preposterous to suppose that the people of one generation can lay down the best and only rules of government for all who are to come after them, and under unforeseen contingencies. At the time of the framing of our constitution the only physical forces that had been subdued and made to serve man and do his labor, were the currents in the streams and in the air we breathe. Rude machinery, propelled by water power, had been invented; sails to propel ships upon the waters had been set to catch the passing breeze—but the application of steam to propel vessels against both wind and current, and machinery to do all manner of work had not been thought of. The instantaneous transmission of messages around the world by means of electricity would probably at that day have been attributed to witchcraft or a league with the Devil. Immaterial circumstances had changed as greatly as material ones. We could not and ought not to be rigidly bound by the rules laid down under circumstances so different for emergencies so utterly unanticipated. The fathers themselves would have been the first to declare that their prerogatives were not irrevocable. They would surely have resisted secession could they have lived to see the shape it assumed.

I travelled through the Northwest considerably during the winter of 1860–1. We had customers in all the little towns in south-west Wisconsin, south-east Minnesota and north-east Iowa. These generally knew I had been a captain in the regular army and had served through the Mexican war. Consequently wherever I stopped at night, some of the people would come to the public-house where I was, and sit till a late hour discussing the probabilities of the future. My own views at that time were like those officially expressed by Mr. Seward at a later day, that "the war would be over in ninety days." I continued to entertain these views until after the battle of Shiloh. I believe now that there would have been no more battles at the West after the capture of Fort Donelson if all the troops in that region had been under a single commander who would have followed up that victory.[70]

There is little doubt in my mind now that the prevailing sentiment of the South would have been opposed to secession in 1860 and 1861, if there had been a fair and calm expression of opinion, unbiased by threats, and if the ballot of one legal voter had counted for as much as that of any other. But there was no calm discussion of the question. Demagogues who were too old to enter the army if there should be a war, others who entertained so high an opinion of their own ability that they did not believe they could be spared from the direction of the affairs of state in such an event, declaimed vehemently and unceasingly against the North; against its aggressions upon the South; its interference with Southern rights, etc., etc. They denounced the Northerners as cowards, poltroons, negro-worshippers; claimed that one Southern man was equal to five Northern men in battle; that if the South would stand up for its rights the North would back down. Mr. Jefferson Davis said in a speech, delivered at La Grange, Mississippi, before the secession of that State, that he would agree to drink all the blood spilled south of Mason and Dixon's line if there should be a war. The young men who would have the fighting to do in case of war, believed all these statements, both in regard to the aggressiveness of the North and its cowardice. They, too, cried out for a separation from such people. The great bulk of the legal voters of the South were men who owned no slaves; their homes were generally in the hills and poor country; their facilities for educating their children, even up to the point of reading and writing, were very limited; their interest in the contest was very meagre—what there was, if they had been capable of seeing it, was with the North; they too needed emancipation. Under the old regime they were looked down upon by those who controlled all the affairs in the interest of slave-owners, as poor white trash who were allowed the ballot so long as they cast it according to direction.[71]

I am aware that this last statement may be disputed and individual testimony perhaps adduced to show that in antebellum days the ballot was as untrammelled in the South as in any section of the country; but in the face of any such contradiction I reassert the statement. The shot-gun was not resorted to. Masked men did not ride over the country at night intimidating voters; but there was a firm feeling that a class existed in every State with a sort of divine right to control public affairs. If they could not get this control by one means they must by another. The end justified the means. The coercion, if mild, was complete.

There were two political parties, it is true, in all the States, both strong in numbers and respectability, but both equally loyal to the institution which stood paramount in Southern eyes to all other institutions in state or nation. The slave-owners were the minority, but governed both parties. Had politics ever divided the slave-holders and the non-slaveholders, the majority would have been obliged to yield, or internecine war would have been the consequence. I do not know that the Southern people were to blame for this condition of affairs. There was a time when slavery was not profitable, and the discussion of the merits of the institution was confined almost exclusively to the territory where it existed. The States of Virginia and Kentucky came near abolishing slavery by their own acts, one State defeating the measure by a tie vote and the other only lacking one. But when the institution became profitable, all talk of its abolition ceased where it existed; and naturally, as human nature is constituted, arguments were adduced in its support. The cotton-gin probably had much to do with the justification of slavery.

The winter of 1860–1 will be remembered by middle-aged people of to-day as one of great excitement. South Carolina promptly seceded after the result of the Presidential election was known.[72] Other Southern States proposed to follow. In some of them the Union sentiment was so strong that it had to be suppressed by force. Maryland, Delaware, Kentucky and Missouri, all Slave States, failed to pass ordinances of secession; but they were all represented in the so-called congress of the so-called Confederate States. The Governor and Lieutenant-Governor of Missouri, in 1861, Jackson and Reynolds, were both supporters of the rebellion and took refuge with the enemy.[73] The governor soon died, and the lieutenant-governor assumed his office; issued proclamations as governor of the State; was recognized as such by the Confederate Government, and continued his pretensions until the collapse of the rebellion. The South claimed the sovereignty of States, but claimed the right to coerce into their confederation such States as they wanted, that is, all the States where slavery existed. They did not seem to think this course inconsistent. The fact is, the Southern slave-owners believed that, in some way, the ownership of slaves conferred a sort of patent of nobility—a right to govern independent of the interest or wishes of those who did not hold such property. They convinced themselves, first, of the divine origin of the institution and, next, that that particular institution was not safe in the hands of any body of legislators but themselves.

Meanwhile the Administration of President Buchanan looked helplessly on and proclaimed that the general government had no power to interfere; that the Nation had no power to save its own life. Mr. Buchanan had in his cabinet two members at least, who were as earnest—to use a mild term—in the cause of secession as Mr. Davis or any Southern statesman. One of them, Floyd, the Secretary of War, scattered the army so that much of it could be captured when hostilities should commence, and distributed the cannon and small arms from Northern arsenals throughout the South so as to be on hand when treason wanted them.[74] The navy was scattered in like manner. The President did not prevent his cabinet preparing for war upon their government, either by destroying its resources or storing them in the South until a de facto government was established with Jefferson Davis as its President, and Montgomery, Alabama, as the Capital.[75] The secessionists had then to leave the cabinet. In their own estimation they were aliens in the country which had given them birth. Loyal men were put into their places. Treason in the executive branch of the government was estopped. But the harm had already been done. The stable door was locked after the horse had been stolen.

During all of the trying winter of 1860–1, when the Southerners were so defiant that they would not allow within their borders the expression of a sentiment hostile to their views, it was a brave man indeed who could stand up and proclaim his loyalty to the Union. On the other hand men at the North—prominent men—proclaimed that the government had no power to coerce the South into submission to the laws of the land; that if the North undertook to raise armies to go south, these armies would have to march over the dead bodies of the speakers. A portion of the press of the North was constantly proclaiming similar views. When the time arrived for the President-elect to go to the capital of the Nation to be sworn into office, it was deemed unsafe for him to travel, not only as a President-elect, but as any private citizen should be allowed to do. Instead of going in a special car, receiving the good wishes of his constituents at all the stations along the road, he was obliged to stop on the way and to be smuggled into the capital. He disappeared from public view on his journey, and the next the country knew, his arrival was announced at the capital. There is little doubt that he would have been assassinated if he had attempted to travel openly throughout his journey.

Notes

1 Winston Churchill, *The World Crisis, 1911–1918* (1931; New York: Free Press, 2005), 6.

2 Edward L. Ayers, *What Caused the Civil War? Reflections on the South and Southern History* (New York: W.W. Norton, 2005), 134.

3 Randall C. Jimerson, *The Private Civil War: Popular Thought during the Sectional Conflict* (Baton Rouge: Louisiana State University Press, 1988), 11.

4 I.e., John Adams (Mass.), John Quincy Adams (Mass.), Martin Van Buren (New York), and Millard Fillmore (New York).

5 I.e., George Washington, Thomas Jefferson, James Madison, James Monroe, and Andrew Jackson.

6 I.e., they will not become the "loyal opposition" working within a single governmental system.

7 Article I, section 2, of the original U.S. Constitution counted "the whole Number of free Persons" and "three fifths of all other Persons" (i.e., slaves) in the apportionment of representatives and taxes, thus strengthening Southern political power while denying citizenship to slaves. This clause was subsequently superseded by the Fourteenth Amendment, section 2.

8 The 1860 U.S. Census actually counted just under 4 million slaves.

9 I.e., through the election of new Congressional representatives.

10 A war or armed conflict between masters and slaves.

11 The degree of British dependence on Southern cotton is a matter of debate, as is the larger role that "cotton diplomacy" played in the Civil War. See, for example, Charles M. Hubbard, in *The Burden of Confederate Diplomacy* (Knoxville: University of Tennessee Press, 1998) and Brian Schoen, *The Fragile Fabric of Union: Cotton, Federal Politics, and the Global Origins of the Civil War* (Baltimore: Johns Hopkins University Press, 2009).

12 Slavery was legal in Washington, D.C., until April 16, 1862, when President Lincoln signed the District of Columbia Emancipation Act.

13 Slavery was legal in Cuba until 1886.

14 Mississippi's legislature passed an Ordinance of Secession on January 9, 1861, making the state the second to secede.

15 I.e., President Andrew Jackson, who through threat of force secured the repeal of South Carolina's 1832 "Ordinance of Nullification," passed in response to the federal tariffs of 1828 and 1832.

16 Davis is apparently referring to the 1851 arrest of Shadrach Minkins, a fugitive slave who had escaped to Boston from Norfolk, Virginia, and his subsequent rescue, from a courtroom, by a group of black activists. Three days after this incident, with national attention focused on Massachusetts, then-Senator Davis argued that "if the people of Massachusetts uniformly resisted, then 'the law is dead' and there was no point in using federal force" (Gary Collison, *Shadrach Minkins: From Fugitive Slave to Citizen* [Cambridge: Harvard Unviersity Press, 1997], 139).

17 Jefferson's original draft of the Declaration of Independence included among its catalogue of complaints against King George III the following: "[H]e has waged cruel war against human nature itself, violating it's [sic] most sacred rights of life and liberty in the persons of a distant people who never offended him, captivating & carrying them into slavery in another hemisphere . . . [A]nd that this assemblage of horrors might want no fact of distinguished die, he is now exciting those very people to rise in arms among us, and to purchase that liberty of which he has deprived them, by murdering the people on whom he also obtruded them." The Continental Congress struck out this clause in preparing the final version of the Declaration.

18 U.S. Constitution Article 1, Section 2, Paragaraph 3, subsequently superseded by the Fourteenth Amendment.

19 The battles of Fort Moultrie and Eutaw Springs, in South Carolina, were Continental victories in the American Revolution.

20 I.e., antislavery. Timrod is referring to those biblical passages, such as Ephesians 6:5, Colossians 3:22, and Paul's letter to Philemon, which were construed by proslavery writers as sanctioning slavery.

21 Harold Holzer, *Lincoln President-Elect: Abraham Lincoln and the Great Secession Winter, 1860–1861* (New York: Simon & Schuster, 2008), 455.

22 A native of Georgia, Howell Cobb had long served in Congress, and in 1849 was elected Speaker. In 1851 he was elected Governor of Georgia, and in 1857 became Secretary of the Treasury in Buchanan's Administration. In 1861 he was a delegate from Georgia to the Provisional Congress which adopted the Constitution of the Confederacy, and presided over each of its four sessions.

23 Lawrence Masillon Keitt (1824–1864) was a South Carolina "fire-eater" who resigned his Congressional seat after the 1860 election. William Waters Boyce (1818–1890) was Keitt's less rabid fellow Representative from South Carolina. Robert Barnwell Rhett, Sr. (1800–1876), was an extreme secessionist who helped shape the Confederate Constitution, but spent much of the war complaining about the leadership of Jefferson Davis.

24 Andrew Bary Moore, elected Governor of Alabama in 1859. In 1861, before Alabama seceded, he directed the seizure of United States forts and arsenals and was active afterward in the equipment of State troops.

25 Robert Toombs, a native of Georgia, who early acquired fame as a lawyer, served in the Creek War under General Scott, became known in 1842 as a "State Rights Whig," being elected to Congress, where he was active in the Compromise measures of 1850. He served in the United States Senate from 1853 to 1861, where he was a pronounced advocate of the sovereignty of States, the extension of slavery, and secession. He was a member of the Confederate Congress at its first session and, by a single vote, failed of election as President of the Confederacy. After the war, he was conspicuous for his hostility to the Union.

26 "Duncan Nathaniel Ingraham of Charleston resigned as a U.S. Navy commander in January 1861 and was commissioned captain in the Confederate States Navy (C.S.N.) in March" (C. Vann Woodward, *Mary Chesnut's Civil War*, 8, n. 2).

27 "Common-law judge Thomas Jefferson Withers of Camden, a delegate to the S.C. secession convention and a member of the Provisional Congress, was M.B.C.'s uncle and former guardian" (Woodward, 8, n. 3).

28 South Carolina Gov. Francis Wilkinson Pickens (1805–1869).

29 "William Montague Browne of Washington, D.C., was the Irish-born editor of the Buchanan administration newspaper, the *Washington Constitution*. His commission as colonel in the C.S.A. and his title, assistant secretary of state, were the result of his friendship with Howell Cobb and Jefferson Davis" (Woodward, 9, n. 9).

30 "David Camden DeLeon, a native of Camden, resigned as a U.S. Army surgeon on February 19 and soon became the first surgeon general of the Confederacy" (Woodward, 11, n. 4).

31 Robert Woodward Barnwell, of South Carolina, a graduate of Harvard, twice a member of Congress and afterward United States Senator. In 1860, after the passage of the Ordinance of Secession, he was one of the Commissioners who went to Washington to treat with the National Government for its property

within the State. He was a member of the Convention at Montgomery and gave the casting vote which made Jefferson Davis President of the Confederacy.

32 "Phillip Clayton of Ga. had resigned as assistant secretary of the U.S. Treasury. He held the same post in the Confederate government" (Woodward, 11, n. 5).

33 "Born in S.C., Henry Percy Brewster became secretary of war of the Texas Republic and a prominent lawyer in Tex. and Washington, D.C." (Woodward, 11, n. 6).

34 Benjamin H. Hill, who had already been active in state and national affairs when the Secession movement was carried through. He had been an earnest advocate of the Union until in Georgia the resolution was passed declaring that the State ought to secede. He then became a prominent supporter of secession. He was a member of the Confederate Congress, which met in Montgomery in 1861, and served in the Confederate Senate until the end of the war. After the war, he was elected to Congress and opposed the Reconstruction policy of that body. In 1877 he was elected United States Senator from Georgia.

35 Governor Herschel V. Johnson also declined, and doubtless for similar reasons, to accept a challenge from Alexander H. Stephens, who, though endowed with the courage of a gladiator, was very small and frail.

36 It was at this Congress that Jefferson Davis, on February 9, 1861, was elected President, and Alexander H. Stephens Vice-President of the Confederacy. The Confederate Congress continued to meet in Montgomery until its removal to Richmond, in July, 1861.

37 Clemens was a former U.S. Senator; Davis was an Alabama planter; Sanders "became a Confederate agent in Canada and Europe"; Deas was "acting adjutant general of the Confederacy" (Woodward, 14).

38 Stephen R. Mallory was the son of a shipmaster of Connecticut, who had settled in Key West in 1820. From 1851 to 1861 Mr. Mallory was United States Senator from Florida, and after the formation of the Confederacy, became its Secretary of the Navy.

39 The idea, but not the direct quote, is from George Meredith's *Evan Harrington* (1860).

40 "Martin Koszta took part in the Hungarian revolution against Austria in 1848 and fled to the U.S. in 1850. Traveling to Turkey three years later, he was kidnapped and held prisoner aboard an Austrian man-of-war off Smyrna. Duncan Ingraham, commander of the USS *St. Louis*, forced Koszta's release with an ultimatum on July 2, 1853. This exploit, occurring at a high point of American sympathy for the revolutionaries of 1848 and dislike for Austria, made Ingraham a national hero" (Woodward, 16, n. 6).

41 John Archibald Campbell, who had settled in Montgomery and was appointed Associate Justice of the United States Supreme Court by President Pierce in 1853. Before he resigned, he exerted all his influence to prevent Civil War and opposed secession, although he believed that States had a right to secede.

42 I.e., those delegates who held out hope that the Union could be reconstructed on terms favorable to the South, without taking the irrevocable step of declaring national sovereignty as the Confederate States of America.

43 Mrs. Chesnut's father was Stephen Decatur Miller, who was born in South Carolina in 1787, and died in Mississippi in 1838. He was elected to Congress in 1816, as an Anti-Calhoun Democrat, and from 1828 to 1830 was Governor of South Carolina. He favored Nullification, and in 1830 was elected United States Senator from South Carolina, but resigned three years afterward in consequence of ill health. In 1835 he removed to Mississippi and engaged in cotton growing.

44 John C. Calhoun had died in March, 1850.

45 Secession from the Union began with South Carolina on December 24, 1860, followed by Mississippi, Florida, Alabama, Georgia, Louisiana, and Texas. On February 4, 1861, these seven states officially declared themselves the Confederate States of America (CSA).

46 The Constitution of the Confederate States of America was adopted on March 11, 1861. Though much of the document was taken word-for-word from the U.S. Constitution, a number key changes were made to the Confederate Constitution, chief among them the legality of slavery. In the interest of space, Stephens's later discussion of the details of the Confederate Constitution has been omitted.

47 The South's opposition to federal tariffs, which were meant to protect American manufacturing and promote internal improvements, was long-standing and first burst into prominence during the Nullification Crisis of 1832.

48 Jefferson himself did not describe slavery as the "rock upon which the old Union would split," but he did express anxiety as to whether the Union could survive the issue, most famously in letters to John Holmes and William Short in 1820.

49 See Matthew 7:27.

50 Italian astronomer Galileo Galilei (1564–1642) met with much resistance to his advocacy of heliocentrism—the theory that the sun is the center of the solar system—from other important Renaissance thinkers. Adam Smith (1723–1790), the great Enlightenment philosopher of capitalism, based his economic theories on the principle of rational self-interest. English physician William Harvey

(1578–1657) generated furious controversy by proposing that blood circulates repeatedly throughout the body and is pumped by the heart.

51 Also called the "Curse of Ham," the Curse of Canaan refers to the episode in Genesis 9:20–27, in which Noah curses his son Ham, Canaan's father, for not averting his eyes from Noah's nakedness. Although the biblical version of the story makes no mention of blackness, this tale was appropriated at some point in the Renaissance to articulate a racial theory of black inferiority that would be often used to justify slavery.

52 I Corinthians 15:41.

53 Psalms 118:22, also repeated by Christ in Matthew 21:42 and Luke 20:17.

54 Genesis 3:19.

55 During the French Revolution, the Jacobins were far-left political revolutionaries who resorted to terrorist violence in their pursuit of egalitarian democracy.

56 Article IV, Section 3, of the Confederate Constitution stipulated that other states could join the Confederacy by a two-thirds majority vote of both houses of the Confederate Congress.

57 Fort Pickens, on Santa Rosa Island near Pensacola, was built in 1834 to help secure the far west end of the Florida panhandle. More easily defended than other Gulf forts, it never fell to Confederate forces.

58 Along with Winfield Scott, Zachary Taylor (1784–1850) helped lead American troops to victory in the Mexican War of 1846–1848, a controversial conflict that intensified the domestic debate over the expansion of slavery. After returning to the U.S. in triumph, Taylor won the Presidency in 1848 as a Whig, revealing itself to be both a staunch unionist and, in James McPherson's words, "a free-soil wolf in the clothing of a state's rights sheep" (*Battle Cry of Freedom*, 66). Taylor's death of gastroenteritis, about 16 months after taking office, brought to the Oval Office Millard Fillmore, also a Whig, who would soon sign into law the five bills making up the fateful Compromise of 1850.

59 I.e., the presidencies of Millard Fillmore (Whig, 1850–1853), Franklin Pierce (Democrat, 1853–1857), and James Buchanan (Democrat, 1857–1861).

60 A highly doubtful claim, but certainly there were many Northerners and Midwesterners who would have welcomed a separation of the states—some, such as radical abolitionists, who wanted nothing to do with slavery, and others out of the simple pragmatic desire to let the Southern states do as they would. Moreover, even if Whitman's claim were true in absolute terms, it would still be the case that the South, proportionately, had a much greater number of secessionists.

61 Adherents of the ideas, and/or supporters of the various candidacies, of John C. Calhoun (1782–1850), the politician from South Carolina, best known for articulating the doctrine of nullification, who spent vast amounts of energy on promoting states' rights, defending the South against antislavery agitation, and seeking ways of preventing the sectional controversy from spinning out of control.

62 The Domesday Book, commissioned by William the Conqueror in 1085, was a comprehensive hand-written survey of English landownership and usage, intended as an assessment of resources and taxable property.

63 From mid-1852 to mid-1854, while Grant served in California.

64 In February, 1864, in order to clarify the Federal army's top command structure, Congress resurrected the post of lieutenant general, previously held by George Washington, and President Lincoln named Grant to the post, with the title of general in chief.

65 In the summer of 1852, the 4th Infantry, including Grant, was redeployed to the Pacific Coast. Sailing from New York, the regiment passed through Panama on its way to San Francisco.

66 Henry Clay (1777–1852), Kentucky's most famous statesman, was, along with John C. Calhoun and Daniel Webster, one of the primary architects of the Compromise of 1850.

67 Francis Preston Blair (1791–1876) had one of the more colorful careers in American history, editing the Jacksonian newspaper *The Globe*, helping to organize both the Democratic and Republican parties, becoming a trusted friend and adviser to President Lincoln, and ultimately advocating a gentle policy of Southern reconstruction.

68 The Virginia Declaration of Rights (1776) held that "all men are equally entitled to the free exercise of religion, according to the dictates of conscience."

69 John C. Breckinridge of Kentucky ran as a Democrat with the support of states'-right forces in the South, winning about 45 percent of the region's popular vote.

70 Grant led the successful attack on Fort Donelson, Tennessee, in February 1862. After the surrender of this outpost on the Cumberland River, however, which gave the Union a crucial foothold, Gen. Henry Halleck, who had overall command in the West, pursued a cautious strategy rather than moving aggressively southward.

71 Consider William L. Barney's discussion of "cooperationist" sentiment among rural whites in Alabama and Mississippi in 1860: "The mountain whites, deeply resentful of the planters' wealth and privileges,

did not hate slavery so much as they did the second-class citizenship to which it relegated them" (*The Secessionist Impulse: Alabama and Mississippi in 1860* [Princeton: Princeton University Press, 1974], 271).

72 The South Carolina legislature voted unanimously to secede on December 20, 1860.

73 Clairborne Fox Jackson (1806–1862) led the secessionist faction in a sharply divided state, taking military steps against federal government after Missouri rejected secession in February, 1861, and prompting unionists to convene a rival state government. After a series of clashes across Missouri in the summer and early fall of 1861, Confederate progress spurred the pro-Southern Missouri legislature to secede, and the state was inducted into the Confederacy in November. Jackson died of pneumonia in December, 1862, as vicious guerrilla warfare raged across the state; he was succeeded by Thomas Reynolds in February, 1863.

74 In 1860, Virginia-born John Buchanan Floyd (1806–1863) ordered the transfer of 125,000 federal fire-arms to Southern arsenals, ostensibly to make room for new inventory; he was investigated for this order, and on suspicion of graft, but to no result. After resigning in December 1860, Floyd became a Confederate general, but served without distinction, and died of ill health in 1863.

75 The first Confederate Cabinet was formed in Montgomery in February, 1861. The Confederacy voted to relocate its capital to Richmond, Virginia, on May 20, 1861.

The Texts

Herman Melville, "The Portent" and "Misgivings." Source: *Battle-Pieces and Aspects of the War* (New York: Harper & Bros., 1866).

Harriet Martineau, "Election of Abraham Lincoln." Source: Harriet Martineau, *Writings on Slavery and the American Civil War*, ed. Deborah Anna Logan (DeKalb: Northern Illinois University Press, 2002). "Election of Abraham Lincoln" originally appeared in London's *Daily News*, November 22, 1860.

Jefferson Davis, "Speech in U.S. Senate (Farewell Address)." Source: *Jefferson Davis: The Essential Writings*, ed. William J. Cooper, Jr. (New York: The Modern Library, 2003).

Henry Timrod, "Ethnogenesis." Source: *War Poetry of the South*, ed. William Gilmore Simms (New York: Richardson & Company, 1866). Originally published in the Charleston *Daily Courier*, on February 23, 1861, as "Ode on Occasion of the Meeting of the Southern Congress."

Abraham Lincoln, Speech from the Bates House Balcony. Source: *The Collected Works of Abraham Lincoln*, ed. Roy P. Basler et al., vol. 4, pp. 194–195. Basler's edition follows the version of the speech reported in the Indiana *Daily Sentinel* of February 12, 1861.

Abraham Lincoln, First Inaugural Address. Source: *Complete Works of Abraham Lincoln, Comprising his Speeches, Letters, State Papers, and Miscellaneous Writings*, ed. John G. Nicolay and John Hay. Vol. 2 (New York: The Century Company, 1920).

Mary Chesnut, from *A Diary from Dixie*. Source: *A Diary from Dixie, as written by Mary Boykin Chesnut, wife of James Chesnut, Jr., United States Senator from South Carolina, 1859–1861, and afterward an Aide to Jefferson Davis and a Brigadier-General in the Confederate Army*, ed. Isabella D. Martin and Myrta Lockett Avary (New York: D. Appleton and Company, 1905). *A Diary from Dixie* represents a redacted version of the text that Chesnut wrote between 1881 and 1884, based primarily on the journal she kept between 1861 and 1865. According to C. Vann Woodward, the 1905 title was originally chosen by *The Saturday Evening Post*, which serialized five installments of the book in 1905, and retained by Appleton. Also, despite the volume's editorial credits, Woodward notes, most of the editorial work, including footnotes, was undertaken by Appleton editor Francis W. Halsey (C. Vann Woodward, ed., *Mary Chesnut's Civil War* [New Haven: Yale University Press, 1981], p. xxviii).

Alexander Stephens, from the "Cornerstone" speech. Source: Henry Cleveland, *Alexander H. Stephens, in Public and Private: With Letters and Speeches, Before, During, and Since the War* (Philadelphia, 1866). Stephens's speech was originally reported in the Savannah *Republican*; Cleveland's text and other versions of the speech follow that original transcription, though with variations in italics and paragraphing.

Walt Whitman, "Origins of Attempted Secession." Source: *Specimen Days & Collect* (Philadelphia: D. McKay, 1882–1883).

Ulysses S. Grant, from *Personal Memoirs*. Source: *Personal Memoirs of U. S. Grant*, Vol. 1 (New York: C. L. Webster & Co., 1885–1886).

II
Battlefields

Antietam, Maryland. Bodies in front of the Dunker church. Sept. 1862. Photographer: Alexander Gardner. Library of Congress Prints and Photographs Division, LC-DIG-cwpb-01099

Introduction

The Civil War was fought in eighteen states (counting West Virginia), in ten territories (not counting "Indian Territory"), on hundreds of battlefields. It was fought amidst heavy forest, on mountainsides and bayous, across open plains, on waves and beaches, in rural hamlets and in major cities. The war left its mark on all these places: left it so firmly that the history can still be imagined in the turn of a road or the crest of a hill. Some Civil War battlefields—Antietam, Shiloh, Gettysburg—have taken on a mythic quality that only seems to deepen with time, like Troy or Agincourt. The very word "battlefield" grows archaic, more akin to the Anglo-Saxon *waelstow* (field of slaughter) than to today's more cryptic, decentralized sites of organized killing.

Yet the Civil War marked a period of rapid advance, if we can call it that, in the history of armed conflict. The changes in military strategy and technology it ushered in greatly increased the number of combat casualties, and as the bodies accumulated on each American *waelstow* the dead seemed to bear collective witness to the sudden arrival of the furious modern world.

In classically American fashion, Civil War commanders, engineers, and innovators placed greater emphasis on the practical than on the theoretical when it came to waging war. Military advances occurred in a rather ad hoc fashion, even haphazardly, as the Union and Confederate war machines tried to adapt to evolving needs and contingencies. Technological, organizational, and strategic adaptations all worked together, and they were all responsive to the particularities of American culture and geography.

First, the pressures of war stimulated the invention of a large number of new military technologies, hundreds of which received patents during the 1860s. Not all of these innovations—such as the submarine or the telescopic sight—were widely adopted at the time, but they set the stage for later refinement. The development of the minié ball, a conical, high-impact bullet; the mass manufacture of the rifled musket, which could shoot much farther and more accurately than traditional smoothbore muskets; and the introduction of the Spencer repeating rifle and the Henry repeater, had the greatest impact on battlefield casualties and, eventually, tactics. In naval warfare, the key breakthrough involved the armoring of ships with metal plates, which spelled the end for traditional wooden vessels. Above all, perhaps, the Civil War highlighted the importance of industrial mass production to the creation of a modern war machine, for a central factor in the North's ultimate victory was its greater manufacturing capacity.

Organizationally, the Civil War required the military—whose last conflict had been the comparatively straightforward Mexican–American War of 1846–1848—to upgrade, across the board, its logistical and command procedures. The necessity, particularly for the North, of waging sustained operations in distant theaters of war called for better coordination up and down the military hierarchy, and for improvements in transportation methods and supply line security. Again, many of these lessons of the Civil War would not be applied until America's next major conflict, the Spanish–American War.

Finally, in strategy and tactics the Civil War marked a decisive turn away from the Napoleonic style of conflict, characterized by marching lines, formal assaults, and occupation of territory. New thinking and new weaponry had rendered that style obsolete, and what emerged, haltingly, was something more familiar to us today. The rifle, in particular, shifted the combat advantage to defensive positions, and in digging and protecting their fortified lines, Civil War units saw some of the world's first trench warfare. At the same time, some Civil War commanders—notably Grant in Mississippi, Lee in Pennsylvania, and Sherman in Georgia and South Carolina—came to see the possibilities in an army living off the land and, in effect, terrorizing the locals. The policy of total war, in which a society's entire infrastructure is deemed fair game, and in which an "enemy" civilian population can be made to feel the bite of war, represents the Civil War's most enduring, and most troubling, military legacy.

These changes in technology, organization, and strategy generated a startling variety of combat experience. The Civil War battlefield could be a place of grinding routine or primal hand-to-hand combat; formal infantry charges or improvised cavalry raids; artillery bombardments or amphibious landings; of guerrilla action or extra-legal reprisals; of scouting, spying, digging, looting, burning, fleeing, and chasing.

The emerging forms of warfare also changed the experience of combat for American soldiers, particularly infantry, who found themselves in battle environments for which they were necessarily ill-prepared (and frequently ill-equipped). The fluidity and intensity of Civil War combat, with its acoustic and visual uncertainties, and unpredictable yet pervasive lethality, is a recurrent theme in soldiers' letters and memoirs. What many soldiers also described, often in graphic detail, was the spectacle of violence and death: mutilations, amputations, bodies abandoned on the field, the groaning of the mortally wounded, the smell of decomposition.

Combatants adapt and harden, of course, because they have to. Simple repetition could dull the horrors of war, as one soldier observed: "The work of removing and burying the dead has become so common and tame that the lifeless body of a man was looked upon as nothing more than that of a brute."[1] Other inner resources also helped to buttress the men psychologically: camaraderie; feelings of excitement and determination; a sense of honor and valor; the conviction of fighting for a good cause. Nonetheless, we should not underestimate the level of psychological stress and emotional trauma that Civil War combat produced.

What heightened its impact was the very personal nature of Civil War battlefield experience. These soldiers faced and killed adversaries who, for the most part, were very much like themselves, culturally, physically, and linguistically. They fought on farms and roads, in woods and towns, that they knew, in terrain charged with personal memories, nationalist and family feeling, even future plans. The Civil War was an intimate war, and its battlefields were close and personal crucibles.

If we think of battlefields broadly, as the locations in which human bodies are vulnerable to the gears of war, then the term also includes places like hospitals and prisons, and the testimony of people in these places becomes important to our understanding of Civil War violence. In the following selections a wide array of Americans—men and women, soldiers and civilians, Northerners and Southerners, doctors and nurses—write about the nature and consequences of Civil War violence, whether experienced, observed, or contemplated. In a variety of genres, from poems and short fiction to autobiography, they testify to the emotional, social, and philosophical problems of what war, at its most elemental level, is all about.

Herman Melville, from *Battle-Pieces and Aspects of the War* (1866)

The March into Virginia

Ending in the First Manassas (July, 1861)

> Did all the lets and bars appear
>   To every just or larger end
> Whence should come the trust and cheer?
>   Youth must its ignorant impulse lend –
> Age finds place in the rear.
>   All wars are boyish, and are fought by boys,
> The champions and enthusiasts of the state:
>   Turbid ardors and vain joins
>   Not barrenly abate –
> Stimulants to the power mature,
>   Preparatives of fate.

> Who here forecasteth the event?
> What heart but spurns at precedent
> And warnings of the wise,
> Contemned foreclosures of surprise?
> The banners play, the bugles call,
> The air is blue and prodigal.
>   No berrying party, pleasure-wooed,
> No picnic party in the May,
> Ever went less loth than they
>   Into that leafy neighborhood.
> In Bacchic glee they file toward Fate,
> Moloch's uninitiate;
> Expectancy, and glad surmise
> Of battle's unknown mysteries.
> All they feel is this: 'tis glory,
> A rapture sharp, though transitory,
> Yet lasting in belaureled story.
> So they gayly go to fight,
> Chatting left and laughing right.

> But some who this blithe mood present,
>   As on in lightsome files they fare,
> Shall die experienced ere three days are spent –
>   Perish, enlightened by the vollied glare;
> Or shame survive, and, like to adamant,
>   The throe of Second Manassas share.

A Utilitarian View of the Monitor's Fight with the Merrimac

Hampton Roads, the main federal blockade base at the entrance to the James River in Virginia, was the site of a battle that marked a new era in naval warfare. Here, on March 8, 1862, the Confederate ironclad *Virginia* (previously the USS *Merrimack*) rammed and sank the wood-sided *Cumberland* (temporarily commanded by Lt. George U. Morris), killing 121 of its crew, and shelled the *Congress* into submission, until being driven off, with minor damage, by the Union ironclad *Monitor*, commanded by John L. Worden. The episode proved a compelling one for the war's poets; in addition to Melville's, see Longfellow's and Larcom's interpretations below.

Plain be the phrase, yet apt the verse,
    More ponderous than nimble;
For since grimed War here laid aside
His Orient pomp, 'twould ill befit
        Overmuch to ply
    The rhyme's barbaric cymbal.

Hail to victory without the gaud
    Of glory; zeal that needs no fans
Of banners; plain mechanic power
Plied cogently in War now place –
        Where War belongs –
    Among the trades and artisans.
Yet this was battle, and intense –
    Beyond the strife of fleets heroic;
Deadlier, closer, calm 'mid storm;
No passion; all went on by crank,
        Pivot, and screw,
    And calculations of caloric.

Needless to dwell; the story's known.
    The ringing of those plates on plates
Still ringeth round the world –
The clangor of that blacksmith's fray.
        The anvil-din
    Resounds this message from the Fates:

War shall yet be, and to the end;
    But war-paint shows the streaks of weather;
War yet shall be, but warriors
Are now but operatives; War's made
        Less grand than Peace,
And a singe runs through lace and feather.

Shiloh

A Requiem (April, 1862)

Skimming lightly, wheeling still,
    The swallows fly low
Over the field in clouded days,
    The forest-field of Shiloh –

Over the field where April rain
Solaced the parched ones stretched in pain
Through the pause of night
That followed the Sunday fight
   Around the church of Shiloh –
The church so lone, the log-built one,
That echoed to many a parting groan
     And natural prayer
   Of dying foemen mingled there –
Foemen at morn, but friends at eve –
   Fame or country least their care:
(What like a bullet can undeceive!)
   But now they lie low,
While over them the swallows skim,
   And all is hushed at Shiloh.

Abraham Lincoln, Meditation on the Divine Will (September 1862)

It is not known exactly when Lincoln penned this private reflection, but he probably wrote it after the Second Battle of Bull Run, a disastrous defeat for the Union, and while he was contemplating a general order of emancipation (Basler, *Collected Works*, 5:404, n. 1). One of Lincoln's personal secretaries, John Hay, reportedly found the paper in Lincoln's office, made a copy of it, and gave it the title by which it has become known.

The will of God prevails. In great contests each party claims to act in accordance with the will of God. Both *may* be, and one *must* be, wrong. God cannot be *for* and *against* the same thing at the same time. In the present civil war it is quite possible that God's purpose is something different from the purpose of either party – and yet the human instrumentalities, working just as they do, are of the best adaptation to effect His purpose. I am almost ready to say this is probably true – that God wills this contest, and wills that it shall not end yet. By his mere quiet power, on the minds of the now contestants, He could have either *saved* or *destroyed* the Union without a human contest. Yet the contest began. And having begun He could give the final victory to either side any day. Yet the contest proceeds.

Abraham Lincoln, Reply to Eliza P. Gurney (October 26, 1862)

Gurney (1801–1881; née Elizabeth Paul Kirkbride) was the widow of the influential English Quaker minister Joseph J. Gurney and a prominent Friend in her own right. On October 26, 1862, about one month after Lincoln signed the Emancipation Proclamation, Gurney and three fellow Quakers attained a meeting with Lincoln at the White House, during which she delivered an impassioned prayer and exhortation meant to encourage and sustain the President during one of the most difficult periods of the war. Lincoln, reportedly with tears running down his cheeks (Mott 308; see textual note), accepted the prayer, and in the next two years exchanged several letters with Gurney.

I am glad of this interview, and glad to know that I have your sympathy and prayers. We are indeed going through a great trial — a fiery trial. In the very responsible position in which I happen to be placed, being a humble instrument in the hands of our Heavenly Father, as I am, and as we all are, to work out his great purposes, I have desired that all my works and acts may be according to his will, and that it might be so, I have sought his aid; but if, after endeavoring to do my best in the light which he affords me, I find my efforts fail, I must believe that for some purpose unknown to me, he wills it otherwise. If I had had my way, this war would never have been commenced. If I had been allowed my way, this war would have been ended before this; but we find it still continues, and we must believe that he permits it for some wise purpose of his own, mysterious and unknown to us; and though with our limited understandings we may not be able to comprehend it, yet we cannot but believe that he who made the world still governs it.

Abraham Lincoln, Address Delivered at the Dedication of the Cemetery at Gettysburg (November 19, 1863)

Four months after the battle, as the bodies from Gettysburg were still in the process of being reburied in proper graves, Lincoln was invited to deliver "a few appropriate remarks" as part of the ceremony consecrating the new national cemetery there. Recognizing the critical importance of the Union victory, and keenly aware of "the power of his rhetoric to define war aims" (Wills, *Lincoln at Gettysburg*, 25), Lincoln leapt at the opportunity. Legendarily concise—particularly in contrast with the long, traditional oration by Edward Everett it followed—Lincoln's address was intended not only for the 15,000 people in attendance, but for a national audience and for posterity. Although debate continues over its exact wording (see textual note), the speech shows Lincoln the wordsmith at his best, forging a new kind of political discourse and brilliantly redefining the meaning of the Civil War.

November 19, 1863

Fourscore and seven years ago our fathers brought forth on this continent a new nation, conceived in liberty, and dedicated to the proposition that all men are created equal.

Now we are engaged in a great civil war, testing whether that nation, or any nation so conceived and so dedicated, can long endure. We are met on a great battle-field of that war. We have come to dedicate a portion of that field as a final resting place for those who here gave their lives that that nation might live. It is altogether fitting and proper that we should do this.

But, in a larger sense, we can not dedicate – we can not consecrate – we can not hallow – this ground. The brave men, living and dead, who struggled here, have conse- crated it far above our poor power to add or detract. The world will little note nor long remember what we say here, but it can never forget what they did here. It is for us, the living, rather, to be dedicated here to the unfinished work which they who fought here have thus far so nobly advanced. It is rather for us to be here dedicated to the great task remaining before us – that from these honored dead we take increased devotion to that cause for which they gave the last full measure of devotion; that we here highly resolve that these dead shall not have died in vain; that this nation, under God, shall have a new birth of freedom; and that government of the people, by the people, for the people, shall not perish from the earth.

Henry Wadsworth Longfellow, "The Cumberland" (1862)

See the headnote for Melville's "A Utilitarian View of the Monitor's Fight with the Merrimac," p. 63.

At anchor in Hampton Roads we lay,
    On board of the Cumberland, sloop-of-war;
And at times from the fortress across the bay
      The alarum of drums swept past,
      Or a bugle blast
    From the camp on the shore.

Then far away to the south uprose
    A little feather of snow-white smoke,
And we knew that the iron ship of our foes
      Was steadily steering its course
      To try the force
    Of our ribs of oak.

Down upon us heavily runs,
    Silent and sullen, the floating fort;
Then comes a puff of smoke from her guns,
      And leaps the terrible death,
      With fiery breath,
    From each open port.

We are not idle, but send her straight
    Defiance back in a full broadside!
As hail rebounds from a roof of slate,
      Rebounds our heavier hail
      From each iron scale
    Of the monster's hide.

"Strike your flag!" the rebel cries,
    In his arrogant old plantation strain.
"Never!" our gallant Morris replies;
      "It is better to sink than to yield!"
      And the whole air pealed
With the cheers of our men.

Then, like a kraken huge and black,
    She crushed our ribs in her iron grasp!
Down went the Cumberland all a wrack,
      With a sudden shudder of death,
      And the cannon's breath
For her dying gasp.

Next morn, as the sun rose over the bay,
    Still floated our flag at the mainmast head.

Lord, how beautiful was Thy day!
  Every waft of the air
  Was a whisper of prayer,
 Or a dirge for the dead.

Ho! brave hearts that went down in the seas!
 Ye are at peace in the troubled stream;
Ho! brave land! with hearts like these,
  Thy flag, that is rent in twain,
  Shall be one again,
 And without a seam!

Henry Wadsworth Longfellow, "Killed at the Ford" (1866)

He is dead, the beautiful youth,
The heart of honor, the tongue of truth,
He, the life and light of us all,
Whose voice was blithe as a bugle-call,
Whom all eyes followed with one consent,
The cheer of whose laugh, and whose pleasant word,
Hushed all murmurs of discontent.

Only last night, as we rode along,
Down the dark of the mountain gap,
To visit the picket-guard at the ford,
Little dreaming of any mishap,
He was humming the words of some old song:
"Two red roses he had on his cap
And another he bore at the point of his sword."

Sudden and swift a whistling ball
Came out of a wood, and the voice was still;
Something I heard in the darkness fall,
And for a moment my blood grew chill;
I spake in a whisper, as he who speaks
In a room where some one is lying dead;
But he made no answer to what I said.

We lifted him up to his saddle again,
And through the mire and the mist and the rain
Carried him back to the silent camp,
And laid him as if asleep on his bed;
And I saw by the light of the surgeon's lamp
Two white roses upon his cheeks,
And one, just over his heart, blood-red!

And I saw in a vision how far and fleet
That fatal bullet went speeding forth,

Till it reached a town in the distant North,
Till it reached a house in a sunny street,
Till it reached a heart that ceased to beat,
Without a murmur, without a cry;
And a bell was tolled, in that far-off town,
For one who had passed from cross to crown
And the neighbors wondered that she should die.

Lucy Larcom, "The Sinking of the Merrimack" (1863)

See the headnote for Melville's "A Utilitarian View of the Monitor's Fight with the Merrimac,"
p. 63.

May, 1862.

Gone down in the flood, and gone out in the flame!
What else could she do, with her fair Northern name?
Her font was a river whose last drop is free:
That river ran boiling with wrath to the sea,
To hear of her baptismal blessing profaned:
A name that was Freedom's, by treachery stained.

'T was the voice of our free Northern mountains that broke
In the sound of her guns, from her stout ribs of oak:
'T was the might of the free Northern hand you could feel
In her sweep and her moulding, from topmast to keel:
When they made her speak treason, (does Hell know of worse?)
How her strong timbers shook with the shame of her curse!

Let her go! Should a deck so polluted again
Ever ring to the tread of our true Northern men?
Let the suicide-ship thunder forth, to the air
And the sea she has blotted, her groan of despair!
Let her last heat of anguish throb out into flame!
Then sink them together,—the ship and the name!

Sarah Morgan Bryan Piatt, "Hearing the Battle – July 21, 1861" (1864)

The battle Piatt refers to is the first battle of Bull Run, the first major engagement of the
Civil War, fought near Manassas, Virginia, about 30 miles west of Washington D.C. "Hearing
the battle" would certainly have been possible for many civilians, particularly if, as many
did in their initial naïve enthusiasm for the war, they rode out to observe the scene.

One day in the dreamy summer,
   On the Sabbath hills, from afar

We heard the solemn echoes
    Of the first fierce words of war.

Ah, tell me, thou veilèd Watcher
    Of the storm and the calm to come,
How long by the sun or shadow
    Till these noises again are dumb.

And soon in a hush and glimmer
    We thought of the dark, strange fight,
Whose close in a ghastly quiet
    Lay dim the beautiful night.

Then we talk'd of coldness and pallor,
    And of things with blinded eyes
That stared at the golden stillness
    Of the moon in those lighted skies;

And of souls, at morning wrestling
    In the dust with passion and moan,
So far away at evening
    In the silence of worlds unknown.

But a delicate wind beside us
    Was rustling the dusky hours,
As it gather'd the dewy odors
    Of the snowy jessamine-flowers.

And I gave you a spray of blossoms,
    And said: "I shall never know
How the hearts in the land are breaking,
    My dearest, unless you go."

Louisa May Alcott, from *Hospital Sketches* (1863)

Alcott worked as a volunteer nurse at the Union Hospital in Georgetown from December, 1862, to January, 1863, and during that relatively brief stint (cut short by her own bout with typhoid and pneumonia) she wrote a series of letters to her family that would eventually be gathered together and recast as the lightly fictionalized *Hospital Sketches*. The first two chapters follow "Tribulation Periwinkle" (Alcott's authorial alter ego) as she gets inspired to do something for the Union war effort, enlists as a nurse, and then travels from Massachusetts to the D.C. hospital she nicknames the "Hurly-burly House." Chapter Three picks up a few days later, after the Battle of Fredericksburg.

Chapter Three: A Day

    "They've come! they've come! hurry up, ladies—you're wanted."
    "Who have come? the rebels?"

This sudden summons in the gray dawn was somewhat startling to a three days' nurse like myself, and, as the thundering knock came at our door, I sprang up in my bed, prepared

> "To gird my woman's form,
> And on the ramparts die,"

if necessary; but my room-mate took it more coolly, and, as she began a rapid toilet, answered my bewildered question,—

"Bless you, no child; it's the wounded from Fredericksburg; forty ambulances are at the door, and we shall have our hands full in fifteen minutes."

"What shall we have to do?"

"Wash, dress, feed, warm and nurse them for the next three months, I dare say. Eighty beds are ready, and we were getting impatient for the men to come. Now you will begin to see hospital life in earnest, for you won't probably find time to sit down all day, and may think yourself fortunate if you get to bed by midnight. Come to me in the ball-room when you are ready; the worst cases are always carried there, and I shall need your help."

So saying, the energetic little woman twirled her hair into a button at the back of her head, in a "cleared for action" sort of style, and vanished, wrestling her way into a feminine kind of pea-jacket as she went.

I am free to confess that I had a realizing sense of the fact that my hospital bed was not a bed of roses just then, or the prospect before me one of unmingled rapture. My three days' experiences had begun with a death, and, owing to the defalcation of another nurse, a somewhat abrupt plunge into the superintendence of a ward containing forty beds, where I spent my shining hours washing faces, serving rations, giving medicine, and sitting in a very hard chair, with pneumonia on one side, diptheria on the other, five typhoids on the opposite, and a dozen dilapidated patriots, hopping, lying, and lounging about, all staring more or less at the new "nuss," who suffered untold agonies, but concealed them under as matronly an aspect as a spinster could assume, and blundered through her trying labors with a Spartan firmness, which I hope they appreciated, but am afraid they didn't. Having a taste for "ghastliness," I had rather longed for the wounded to arrive, for rheumatism was n't heroic, neither was liver complaint, or measles; even fever had lost its charms since "bathing burning brows" had been used up in romances, real and ideal; but when I peeped into the dusky street lined with what I at first had innocently called market carts, now unloading their sad freight at our door, I recalled sundry reminiscences I had heard from nurses of longer standing, my ardor experienced a sudden chill, and I indulged in a most unpatriotic wish that I was safe at home again, with a quiet day before me, and no necessity for being hustled up, as if I were a hen and had only to hop off my roost, give my plumage a peck, and be ready for action. A second bang at the door sent this recreant desire to the right about, as a little woolly head popped in, and Joey, (a six years' old contraband,) announced—

"Miss Blank is jes' wild fer ye, and says fly round right away. They's comin' in, I tell yer, heaps on 'em—one was took out dead, and I see him,—hi! warn't he a goner!"

With which cheerful intelligence the imp scuttled away, singing like a blackbird, and I followed, feeling that Richard was *not* himself again, and wouldn't be for a long time to come.[2]

The first thing I met was a regiment of the vilest odors that ever assaulted the human nose, and took it by storm. Cologne, with its seven and seventy evil savors, was a posy-bed to it; and the worst of this affliction was, every one had assured me that it was a chronic weakness of all hospitals, and I must bear it. I did, armed with lavender water, with which I so besprinkled myself and premises, that, like my friend Sairy,[3] I was soon known among my patients as "the nurse with the bottle." Having been run over by three excited surgeons, bumped against by migratory coal-hods, water-pails, and small boys, nearly scalded by an avalanche of newly-filled tea-pots, and hopelessly entangled in a knot of colored sisters coming to wash, I progressed by slow stages up stairs and down, till the main hall was reached, and I paused to take breath and a survey. There they were! "our brave boys," as the papers justly call them, for cowards could hardly have been so riddled with shot and shell, so torn and shattered, nor have borne suffering for which we have no name, with an uncomplaining fortitude, which made one glad to cherish each as a brother. In they came, some on stretchers, some in men's arms, some feebly staggering along propped on rude crutches, and one lay stark and still with covered face, as a comrade gave his name to be recorded before they carried him away to the dead house. All was hurry and confusion; the hall was full of these wrecks of humanity, for the most exhausted could not reach a bed till duly ticketed and registered; the walls were lined with rows of such as could sit, the floor covered with the more disabled, the steps and doorways filled with helpers and lookers on; the sound of many feet and voices made that usually quiet hour as noisy as noon; and, in the midst of it all, the matron's motherly face brought more comfort to many a poor soul, than the cordial draughts she administered, or the cheery words that welcomed all, making of the hospital a home.

The sight of several stretchers, each with its legless, armless, or desperately wounded occupant, entering my ward, admonished me that I was there to work, not to wonder or weep; so I corked up my feelings, and returned to the path of duty, which was rather "a hard road to travel" just then. The house had been a hotel before hospitals were needed, and many of the doors still bore their old names; some not so inappropriate as might be imagined, for my ward was in truth a *ball-room*, if gun-shot wounds could christen it. Forty beds were prepared, many already tenanted by tired men who fell down anywhere, and drowsed till the smell of food roused them. Round the great stove was gathered the dreariest group I ever saw—ragged, gaunt and pale, mud to the knees, with bloody bandages untouched since put on days before; many bundled up in blankets, coats being lost or useless; and all wearing that disheartened look which proclaimed defeat, more plainly than any telegram of the Burnside blunder. I pitied them so much, I dared not speak to them, though, remembering all they had been through since the route at Fredericksburg, I yearned to serve the dreariest of them all. Presently, Miss Blank tore me from my refuge behind piles of one-sleeved shirts, odd socks, bandages and lint; put basin, sponge, towels, and a block of brown soap into my hands, with these appalling directions:

"Come, my dear, begin to wash as fast as you can. Tell them to take off socks, coats and shirts, scrub them well, put on clean shirts, and the attendants will finish them off, and lay them in bed."

If she had requested me to shave them all, or dance a hornpipe on the stove funnel, I should have been less staggered; but to scrub some dozen lords of creation at a moment's notice, was really—really—. However, there was no time for nonsense, and, having resolved when I came to do everything I was bid, I drowned my scruples in my wash-bowl, clutched my soap manfully, and, assuming a business-like air, made a dab at the first dirty specimen I saw, bent on performing my task *vi et armis*[4] if necessary. I chanced to light on a withered old Irishman, wounded in the head, which caused that portion of his frame to be tastefully laid out like a garden, the bandages being the walks, his hair the shrubbery. He was so overpowered by the honor of having a lady wash him, as he expressed it, that he did nothing but roll up his eyes, and bless me, in an irresistible style which was too much for my sense of the ludicrous; so we laughed together, and when I knelt down to take off his shoes, he "flopped" also, and wouldn't hear of my touching "them dirty craters. May your bed above be aisy darlin', for the day's work ye ar doon!—Whoosh! there ye are, and bedad, it's hard tellin' which is the dirtiest, the fut or the shoe." It was; and if he hadn't been to the fore, I should have gone on pulling, under the impression that the "fut" was a boot, for trousers, socks, shoes and legs were a mass of mud. This comical tableau produced a general grin, at which propitious beginning I took heart and scrubbed away like any tidy parent on a Saturday night. Some of them took the performance like sleepy children, leaning their tired heads against me as I worked, others looked grimly scandalized, and several of the roughest colored like bashful girls. One wore a soiled little bag about his neck, and, as I moved it, to bathe his wounded breast, I said,

"Your talisman didn't save you, did it?"

"Well, I reckon it did, marm, for that shot would a gone a couple a inches deeper but for my old mammy's camphor bag," answered the cheerful philosopher.

Another, with a gun-shot wound through the cheek, asked for a looking-glass, and when I brought one, regarded his swollen face with a dolorous expression, as he muttered—

"I vow to gosh, that's too bad! I warn't a bad looking chap before, and now I'm done for; won't there be a thunderin' scar? and what on earth will Josephine Skinner say?"

He looked up at me with his one eye so appealingly, that I controlled my risibles, and assured him that if Josephine was a girl of sense, she would admire the honorable scar, as a lasting proof that he had faced the enemy, for all women thought a wound the best decoration a brave soldier could wear. I hope Miss Skinner verified the good opinion I so rashly expressed of her, but I shall never know.

The next scrubbee was a nice looking lad, with a curly brown mane, and a budding trace of gingerbread over the lip, which he called his beard, and defended stoutly, when the barber jocosely suggested its immolation. He lay on a bed, with one leg gone, and the right arm so shattered that it must evidently follow: yet the little Sergeant was as merry as if his afflictions were not worth lamenting over; and when a drop or two of salt water mingled with my suds at the sight of this strong young body, so marred and maimed, the boy looked up, with a brave smile, though there was a little quiver of the lips, as he said,

"Now don't you fret yourself about me, miss; I'm first rate here, for it's nuts to lie still on this bed, after knocking about in those confounded ambulances, that shake what there is left of a fellow to jelly. I never was in one of these places before, and think this cleaning up a jolly thing for us, though I'm afraid it isn't for you ladies."

"Is this your first battle, Sergeant?"

"No, miss; I've been in six scrimmages, and never got a scratch till this last one; but it's done the business pretty thoroughly for me, I should say. Lord! what a scramble there'll be for arms and legs, when we old boys come out of our graves, on the Judgment Day: wonder if we shall get our own again? If we do, my leg will have to tramp from Fredericksburg, my arm from here, I suppose, and meet my body, wherever it may be."

The fancy seemed to tickle him mightily, for he laughed blithely, and so did I; which, no doubt, caused the new nurse to be regarded as a light-minded sinner by the Chaplain, who roamed vaguely about, informing the men that they were all worms, corrupt of heart, with perishable bodies, and souls only to be saved by a diligent perusal of certain tracts, and other equally cheering bits of spiritual consolation, when spirituous ditto would have been preferred.

"I say, Mrs.!" called a voice behind me; and, turning, I saw a rough Michigander, with an arm blown off at the shoulder, and two or three bullets still in him—as he afterwards mentioned, as carelessly as if gentlemen were in the habit of carrying such trifles about with them. I went to him, and, while administering a dose of soap and water, he whispered, irefully:

"That red-headed devil, over yonder, is a reb, damn him! You'll agree to that, I'll bet? He's got shet of a foot, or he'd a cut like the rest of the lot. Don't you wash him, nor feed him, but jest let him holler till he's tired. It's a blasted shame to fetch them fellers in here, along side of us; and so I'll tell the chap that bosses this concern; cuss me if I don't."

I regret to say that I did not deliver a moral sermon upon the duty of forgiving our enemies, and the sin of profanity, then and there; but, being a red-hot Abolitionist, stared fixedly at the tall rebel, who was a copperhead, in every sense of the word, and privately resolved to put soap in his eyes, rub his nose the wrong way, and excoriate his cuticle generally, if I had the washing of him.

My amiable intentions, however, were frustrated; for, when I approached, with as Christian an expression as my principles would allow, and asked the question—"Shall I try to make you more comfortable, sir?" all I got for my pains was a gruff—

"No; I'll do it myself."

"Here's your Southern chivalry, with a witness," thought I, dumping the basin down before him, thereby quenching a strong desire to give him a summary baptism, in return for his ungraciousness; for my angry passions rose, at this rebuff, in a way that would have scandalized good Dr. Watts. He was a disappointment in all respects, (the rebel, not the blessed Doctor,) for he was neither fiendish, romantic, pathetic, or anything interesting; but a long, fat man, with a head like a burning bush, and a perfectly expressionless face: so I could dislike him without the slightest drawback, and ignored his existence from that day forth. One redeeming trait he certainly did possess, as the floor speedily testified; for his ablutions were so vigorously performed, that his bed soon stood like an isolated island, in a sea of soap-suds, and he resembled a dripping merman, suffering from the loss of a fin. If cleanliness is a near neighbor to godliness, then was the big rebel the godliest man in my ward that day.

Having done up our human wash, and laid it out to dry, the second syllable of our version of the word war-fare was enacted with much success. Great trays of bread, meat, soup and coffee appeared; and both nurses and attendants turned waiters, serving bountiful rations to all who could eat. I can call my pinafore to testify to my good will in the work, for in ten minutes it was reduced to a perambulating bill of fare, presenting samples of all the refreshments going or gone. It was a lively scene; the long room lined with rows of beds, each filled by an occupant, whom water, shears, and clean raiment, had transformed from a dismal ragamuffin into a recumbent hero, with a cropped head. To and fro rushed matrons, maids, and convalescent "boys," skirmishing with knives and forks; retreating with empty plates; marching and counter-marching, with unvaried success, while the clash of busy spoons made most inspiring music for the charge of our Light Brigade:[5]

"Beds to the front of them,
Beds to the right of them,

Beds to the left of them,
    Nobody blundered.
Beamed at by hungry souls,
Screamed at with brimming bowls,
Steamed at by army rolls,
    Buttered and sundered.
With coffee not cannon plied,
Each must be satisfied,
Whether they lived or died;
    All the men wondered."

Very welcome seemed the generous meal, after a week of suffering, exposure, and short commons; soon the brown faces began to smile, as food, warmth, and rest, did their pleasant work; and the grateful "Thankee's" were followed by more graphic accounts of the battle and retreat, than any paid reporter could have given us. Curious contrasts of the tragic and comic met one everywhere; and some touching as well as ludicrous episodes, might have been recorded that day. A six foot New Hampshire man, with a leg broken and perforated by a piece of shell, so large that, had I not seen the wound, I should have regarded the story as a Munchausenism,[6] beckoned me to come and help him, as he could not sit up, and both his bed and beard were getting plentifully anointed with soup. As I fed my big nestling with corresponding mouthfuls, I asked him how he felt during the battle.

"Well, 'twas my fust, you see, so I aint ashamed to say I was a trifle flustered in the beginnin', there was such an allfired racket; for ef there's anything I do spleen agin, it's noise. But when my mate, Eph Sylvester, caved, with a bullet through his head, I got mad, and pitched in, licketty cut. Our part of the fight didn't last long; so a lot of us larked round Fredericksburg, and give some of them houses a pretty consid'able of a rummage, till we was ordered out of the mess. Some of our fellows cut like time; but I warn't a-goin' to run for nobody; and, fust thing I knew, a shell bust, right in front of us, and I keeled over, feelin' as if I was blowed higher'n a kite. I sung out, and the boys come back for me, double quick; but the way they chucked me over them fences was a caution, I tell you. Next day I was most as black as that darkey yonder, lickin' plates on the sly. This is bully coffee, ain't it? Give us another pull at it, and I'll be obleeged to you."

I did; and, as the last gulp subsided, he said, with a rub of his old handkerchief over eyes as well as mouth:

"Look a here; I've got a pair a earbobs and a handkercher pin I'm a goin' to give you, if you'll have them; for you're the very moral o' Lizy Sylvester, poor Eph's wife: that's why I signalled you to come over here. They aint much, I guess, but they'll do to memorize the rebs by."

Burrowing under his pillow, he produced a little bundle of what he called "truck," and gallantly presented me with a pair of earrings, each representing a cluster of corpulent grapes, and the pin a basket of astonishing fruit, the whole large and coppery enough for a small warming-pan. Feeling delicate about depriving him of such valuable relics, I accepted the earrings alone, and was obliged to depart, somewhat abruptly, when my friend stuck the warming-pan in the bosom of his night-gown, viewing it with much complacency, and, perhaps, some tender memory, in that rough heart of his, for the comrade he had lost.

Observing that the man next him had left his meal untouched, I offered the same service I had performed for his neighbor, but he shook his head.

"Thank you, ma'am; I don't think I'll ever eat again, for I'm shot in the stomach. But I'd like a drink of water, if you aint too busy."

I rushed away, but the water-pails were gone to be refilled, and it was some time before they reappeared. I did not forget my patient patient, meanwhile, and, with the first mugful, hurried back to him. He seemed asleep; but something in the tired white face caused me to listen at his lips for a breath. None came. I touched his forehead; it was cold: and then I knew that, while he waited, a better nurse than I had given him a cooler draught, and healed him with a touch. I laid the sheet over the quiet sleeper, whom no noise could now disturb; and, half an hour later, the bed was empty. It seemed a poor requital for all he had sacrificed and suffered,—that hospital bed, lonely even in a crowd; for there was no familiar face for him to look his last upon; no friendly voice to say, Good bye; no hand to lead him gently down into the Valley of the Shadow; and he vanished, like a drop in that red sea upon whose shores so many women stand lamenting. For a moment I felt bitterly indignant at this seeming carelessness of the value of life, the sanctity of death; then consoled myself with the thought that, when the great muster roll was called, these nameless men might be promoted above many whose tall monuments record the barren honors they have won.

All having eaten, drank, and rested, the surgeons began their rounds; and I took my first lesson in the art of dressing wounds. It wasn't a festive scene, by any means; for Dr. P., whose Aid I constituted myself, fell to work with a vigor which soon convinced me that I was a weaker vessel, though nothing would have induced me to confess it then. He had served in the Crimea, and seemed to regard a dilapidated body very much as I should have regarded a damaged garment; and, turning up his cuffs, whipped out a very unpleasant looking housewife, cutting, sawing, patching and piecing, with the enthusiasm of an accomplished surgical seamstress; explaining the process, in scientific terms, to the patient, meantime; which, of course, was immensely cheering and comfortable. There was an uncanny sort of fascination in watching him, as he peered and probed into the mechanism of those wonderful bodies, whose mysteries he understood so well. The more intricate the wound, the better he liked it. A poor private, with both legs off, and shot through the lungs, possessed more attractions for him than a dozen generals, slightly scratched in some "masterly retreat;" and had any one appeared in small pieces, requesting to be put together again, he would have considered it a special dispensation.

The amputations were reserved till the morrow, and the merciful magic of ether was not thought necessary that day, so the poor souls had to bear their pains as best they might. It is all very well to talk of the patience of woman; and far be it from me to pluck that feather from her cap, for, heaven knows, she isn't allowed to wear many; but the patient endurance of these men, under trials of the flesh, was truly wonderful. Their fortitude seemed contagious, and scarcely a cry escaped them, though I often longed to groan for them, when pride kept their white lips shut, while great drops stood upon their foreheads, and the bed shook with the irrepressible tremor of their tortured bodies. One or two Irishmen anathematized the doctors with the frankness of their nation, and ordered the Virgin to stand by them, as if she had been the wedded Biddy[7] to whom they could administer the poker, if she didn't; but, as a general thing, the work went on in silence, broken only by some quiet request for roller, instruments, or plaster, a sigh from the patient, or a sympathizing murmur from the nurse.

It was long past noon before these repairs were even partially made; and, having got the bodies of my boys into something like order, the next task was to minister to their minds, by writing letters to the anxious souls at home; answering questions, reading papers, taking possession of money and valuables; for the eighth commandment was reduced to a very fragmentary condition, both by the blacks and whites, who ornamented our hospital with their presence. Pocket books, purses, miniatures, and watches, were sealed up, labelled, and handed over to the matron, till such times as the owners thereof were ready to depart homeward or campward again. The letters dictated to me, and revised by me, that afternoon, would have made an excellent chapter for some future history of the war; for, like that which Thackeray's "Ensign Spooney" wrote his mother just before Waterloo, they were "full of affection, pluck, and bad spelling;"[8] nearly all giving lively accounts of the battle, and ending with a somewhat sudden plunge from patriotism to provender, desiring "Marm," "Mary Ann," or "Aunt Peters," to send along some pies, pickles, sweet stuff, and apples, "to yourn in haste," Joe, Sam, or Ned, as the case might be.

My little Sergeant insisted on trying to scribble something with his left hand, and patiently accomplished some half dozen lines of hieroglyphics, which he gave me to fold and direct, with a boyish blush, that rendered a glimpse of "My Dearest Jane," unnecessary, to assure me that the heroic lad had been more successful in the service of Commander-in-Chief Cupid than that of Gen. Mars; and a charming little romance blossomed instanter in Nurse Periwinkle's romantic fancy, though no further confidences were made that day, for Sergeant fell asleep, and, judging from his tranquil face, visited his absent sweetheart in the pleasant land of dreams.

At five o'clock a great bell rang, and the attendants flew, not to arms, but to their trays, to bring up supper, when a second uproar announced that it was ready. The new comers woke at the sound; and I presently discovered that it took a very bad wound to incapacitate the defenders of the faith for the consumption of their rations; the amount that some of them sequestered was amazing; but when I suggested the probability of a famine hereafter, to the matron, that motherly lady cried out: "Bless their hearts, why shouldn't they eat? It's their only amusement; so fill every one, and, if there's not enough ready to-night, I'll lend my share to the Lord by giving it to the boys." And, whipping up her coffee-pot and plate of toast, she gladdened the eyes and stomachs of two or three dissatisfied heroes, by serving them with a liberal hand; and I haven't the slightest doubt that, having cast her bread upon the waters, it came back buttered, as another large-hearted old lady was wont to say.

Then came the doctor's evening visit; the administration of medicines; washing feverish faces; smoothing tumbled beds; wetting wounds; singing lullabies; and preparations for the night. By twelve, the last labor of love was done; the last "good night" spoken; and, if any needed a reward for that day's work, they surely received it, in the silent eloquence of those long lines of faces, showing pale and peaceful in the shaded rooms, as we quitted them, followed by grateful glances that lighted us to bed, where rest, the sweetest, made our pillows soft, while Night and Nature took our places, filling that great house of pain with the healing miracles of Sleep, and his diviner brother, Death.

Walt Whitman, from *Drum-Taps* (1865)

By the Bivouac's Fitful Flame

By the bivouac's fitful flame,
A procession winding around me, solemn and sweet and slow;—but first I note,

The tents of the sleeping army, the fields' and woods' dim outline,
The darkness lit by spots of kindled fire—the silence;
Like a phantom far or near an occasional figure moving;
The shrubs and trees, (as I left [lift] my eyes they seem to be stealthily watching me;)
While wind in procession thoughts, O tender and wond'rous thoughts,
Of life and death—of home and the past and loved, and of those that are far away;
A solemn and slow procession there as I sit on the ground,
By the bivouac's fitful flame.

The Dresser

An old man bending, I come, among new faces,
Years looking backward, resuming, in answer to children,
Come tell us old man, as from young men and maidens that love me;
Years hence of these scenes, of these furious passions, these chances,
Of unsurpass'd heroes, (was one side so brave? the other was equally brave;)
Now be witness again—paint the mightiest armies of earth;
Of those armies so rapid so wondrous what saw you to tell us?
What stays with you latest and deepest? of curious panics,
Of hard-fought engagements, or sieges tremendous, what deepest remains?

O maidens and young men I love, and that love me,
What you ask of my days, those the strangest and sudden your talking recals; [sic]
Soldier alert I arrive, after a long march, cover'd with sweat and dust;
In the nick of time I come, plunge in the fight, loudly shout in the rush of
    successful charge;
Enter the captur'd works . . . yet lo! like a swift-running river, they fade;
Pass and are gone, they fade—I dwell not on soldiers' perils or soldiers' joys;
(Both I remember well—many the hardships, few the joys, yet I was content.)

But in silence, in dreams' projections,
While the world of gain and appearance and mirth goes on,
So soon what is over forgotten, and waves wash the imprints off the sand,
In nature's reverie sad, with hinged knees returning, I enter the doors—(while for
    you up there,
Whoever you are, follow without noise, and be of strong heart.)

Bearing the bandages, water and sponge,
Straight and swift to my wounded I go,
Where they lie on the ground after the battle brought in;
Where their priceless blood reddens the grass, the ground;
Or to the rows of the hospital tent, or under the roof'd hospital;
To the long rows of cots, up and down, each side, I return;
To each and all, one after another, I draw near—not one do I miss;
An attendant follows, holding a tray—he carries a refuse pail,
Soon to be fill'd with clotted rags and blood, emptied, and fill'd again.

I onward go, I stop,
With hinged knees and steady hand, to dress wounds;

I am firm with each—the pangs are sharp, yet unavoidable;
One turns to me his appealing eyes—(poor boy! I never knew you,
Yet I think I could not refuse this moment to die for you, if that would save you.)

On, on I go—(open, doors of time! open, hospital doors!)
The crush'd head I dress, (poor crazed hand, tear not the bandage away;)
The neck of the cavalry-man with the bullet through and through, I examine;
Hard the breathing rattles, quite glazed already the eye, yet life struggles hard;
(Come sweet death! be persuaded, O beautiful death!
In mercy come quickly.)

From the stump of the arm, the amputated hand,
I undo the clotted lint, remove the slough, wash off the matter and blood;
Back on his pillow the soldier bends, with curv'd neck, and side-falling head;
His eyes are closed, his face is pale, he dares not look on the bloody stump,
And has not yet look'd on it.

I dress a wound in the side, deep, deep;
But a day or two more—for see, the frame all wasted and sinking,
And the yellow-blue countenance see.

I dress the perforated shoulder, the foot with the bullet-wound,
Cleanse the one with a gnawing and putrid gangrene, so sickening, so offensive,
While the attendant stands behind aside me, holding the tray and pail.

I am faithful, I do not give out;
The fractur'd thigh, the knee, the wound in the abdomen,
These and more I dress with impassive hand—(yet deep in my breast a fire, a
    burning flame.)

Thus in silence, in dreams' projections,
Returning, resuming, I thread my way through the hospitals;
The hurt and the wounded I pacify with soothing hand,
I sit by the restless all the dark night—some are so young;
Some suffer so much—I recall the experience sweet and sad;
(Many a soldier's loving arms about this neck have cross'd and rested,
Many a soldier's kiss dwells on these bearded lips.)

Vigil Strange I Kept on the Field One Night

Vigil strange I kept on the field one night,
When you, my son and my comrade, dropt at my side that day,
One look I but gave, which your dear eyes return'd, with a look I shall never forget;
One touch of your hand to mine, O boy, reach'd up as you lay on the ground;
Then onward I sped in the battle, the even-contested battle;
Till late in the night reliev'd, to the place at last again I made my way;
Found you in death so cold, dear comrade—found your body, son of responding
    kisses, (never again on earth responding;)

Bared your face in the starlight—curious the scene—cool blew the moderate night-
    wind;
Long there and then in vigil I stood, dimly around me the battle-field spreading;
Vigil wondrous and vigil sweet, there in the fragrant silent night;
But not a tear fell, not even a long-drawn sigh—Long, long I gazed;
Then on the earth partially reclining, sat by your side, leaning my chin in my hands;
Passing sweet hours, immortal and mystic hours with you, dearest comrade—Not a
    tear, not a word;
Vigil of silence, love and death—vigil for you, my son and my soldier,
As onward silently stars aloft, eastward new ones upward stole;
Vigil final for you, brave boy, (I could not save you, swift was your death,
I faithfully loved you and cared for you living—I think we shall surely meet again;)
Till at latest lingering of the night, indeed just as the dawn appear'd,
My comrade I wrapt in his blanket, envelop'd well his form,
Folded the blanket well, tucking it carefully over head, and carefully under feet;
And there and then, and bathed by the rising sun, my son in his grave, in his
    rude-dug grave I deposited;
Ending my vigil strange with that—vigil of night and battle-field dim;
Vigil for boy of responding kisses, (never again on earth responding;)
Vigil for comrade swiftly slain—vigil I never forget, how as day brighten'd,
I rose from the chill ground, and folded my soldier well in his blanket,
And buried him where he fell.

Walt Whitman, from *Memoranda during the War* (1875–1876)

Whitman had extensive experience in Civil War hospitals, serving as a volunteer nurse in and around Washington D.C., and the journals he kept of that transformative experience he revised and published as *Memoranda during the War*. His short essays and sketches on ministering to and conversing with many hundreds of wounded or dying patients are justly celebrated. Yet Whitman also wrote about scenes of battle far removed from his own direct experience, and for all his desire to capture the elusive reality of the war, he was not above engaging in a bit of poetic license. When it comes to war, writing from the imagination rather than memory can open one to criticism, and Whitman has certainly received his share. His essay "A Night Battle," for example, has been denounced as a "literary fraud" that "substitutes well-worn literary conventions for the authenticity of personally witnessed scenes."[9] Nonetheless, we have to exercise our own judgment about whether a deeper truth is actually served by such liberty-taking; whether it takes us closer to, or further from, the reality of war.

Fifty Hours Left Wounded on the Field

Here is a case of a soldier I found among the crowded cots in the Patent Office.[10] He likes to have some one to talk to, and we will listen to him. He got badly hit in his leg and side at Fredericksburgh that eventful Saturday, 13th of December. He lay the succeeding two days and nights helpless on the field, between the city and those grim terraces of batteries; his company and regiment had been compell'd to leave him to his fate. To make matters worse, it happen'd he lay with his head slightly down hill, and could not help himself. At the end of some fifty hours he was brought off, with other wounded, under a flag of truce. . . . I ask him how the rebels treated him as he lay during those two days and nights within reach of them — whether they came to him — whether they abused him? He answers that several of the rebels, soldiers and others, came to him, at one time and another. A couple of them, who were together, spoke roughly and sarcastically, but nothing worse. One middle-aged man, however, who seem'd to be moving around the field, among the dead and wounded, for benevolent purposes, came to him in a way he will never forget; treated our soldier kindly, bound up his wounds, cheer'd him, gave him a couple of biscuits, and a drink of whiskey and water; ask'd him if he could eat some beef. This good Secesh, however, did not change our soldier's position, for it might have caused the blood to burst from the wounds, clotted and stagnated. Our soldier is from Pennsylvania; has had a pretty severe time; the wounds proved to be bad ones. But he retains a good heart, and is at present on the gain. . . . . (It is not uncommon for the men to remain on the field this way, one, two, or even four or five days.)

The Wounded from Chancellorsville, May, '63

As I write this, the wounded have begun to arrive from Hooker's command from bloody Chancellorsville. I was down among the first arrivals. The men in charge of them told me the bad cases were yet to come. If that is so I pity them, for these are bad enough. You ought to see the scene of the wounded arriving at the landing here foot of Sixth street, at night. Two boat loads came about half-past seven last night. A little after eight it rain'd a long and violent shower. The poor, pale, helpless soldiers had been debark'd, and lay around on the wharf and neighborhood anywhere. The rain was, probably, grateful to them; at any rate they were exposed to it. The few torches light up the spectacle. All around — on the wharf, on the ground, out on side places — the men are lying on blankets, old quilts, &c., with bloody rags bound round heads, arms, and legs. The attendants are few, and at night few outsiders also — only a few hard-work'd transportation men and drivers. (The wounded are getting to be common, and people grow callous.) The men, whatever their condition, lie there, and patiently wait till their turn comes to be taken up. Near by, the ambulances are now arriving clusters, and one after another is call'd to back up and take its load. Extreme cases are sent off on stretehers. The men generally make little or no ado, whatever their sufferings. A few groans that cannot be suppress'd, and occasionally a scream of pain as they lift a man into the ambulance. . . . To day, as I write, hundreds more are expected, and to-morrow and the next day more, and so on for many days. Quite often they arrive at the rate of 1000 a day.

A Night Battle, Over a Week Since

May 12 – We already talk of Histories of the War, (presently to accumulate) — yes — technical histories of some things, statistics, official reports, and so on — but shall we ever get histories of the *real* things? . . . There was part of the late battle at Chancellorsville, (second Fredericksburgh,) a little over a week ago. Saturday, Saturday night and Sunday, under Gen. Joe Hooker, I would like to give just a glimpse of — (a moment's look in a terrible storm at sea — of which a few suggestions are enough, and full details impossible.) The fighting had been very hot during the day, and after an intermission the latter part, was resumed at night, and kept up with furious energy till 3 o'clock in the morning. That afternoon (Saturday) an attack sudden and strong by Stonewall Jackson had gain'd a great advantage to the Southern army, and broken our lines, entering us like a wedge, and leaving things in that position at dark. But Hooker at 11 at night made a desperate push, drove the Secesh forces back, restored his original lines, and resumed his plans. This night scrimmage was very exciting, and afforded countless strange and fearful pictures. The fighting had been general both at Chancellorsville and northeast at Fredericksburgh. (We hear of some poor fighting, episodes, skedaddling on our part. I think not of it. I think of the fierce bravery, the general rule.) One Corps, the 6th, Sedgewick's,[11] fights four dashing and bloody battles in 36 hours, retreating in great jeopardy, losing largely and maintaining itself, fighting with the sternest desperation under all circumstances, getting over the Rappahannock only by the skin of its teeth, yet getting over. It lost many, many brave men, yet it took vengeance, ample vengeance.

But it was the tug of Saturday evening, and through the night and Sunday morning, I wanted to make a special note of. It was largely in the woods, and quite a general engagement. The night was very pleasant, at times the moon shining out full and clear, all Nature so calm in itself, the early summer grass so rich, and foliage of the trees — yet there the battle raging, and many good fellows lying helpless, with new accessions to them, and every minute amid the rattle of muskets and crash of cannon, (for there was an artillery contest too,) the red life-blood oozing out from heads or trunks or limbs upon that green and dew-cool grass. The woods take fire, and many of the wounded, unable to move, (especially some of the divisions in the Sixth Corps,) are consumed — quite large spaces are swept over, burning the dead also — some of the men have their hair and beards singed — some, splatches of burns on their faces and hands — others holes burnt in their clothing. . . . The flashes of fire from the cannon, the quick flaring flames and smoke, and the immense roar — the musketry so general, the light nearly bright enough for each side to see one another — the crashing, tramping of men — the yelling — close quarters — we hear the Secesh yells — our men cheer loudly back, especially if Hooker is in sight — hand to hand conflicts, each side stands to it, brave, determin'd as demons, they often charge upon us — a thousand deeds are done worth to write newer greater poems on — and still the woods on fire — still many are not only scorch'd — too many, unable to move, are burn'd to death. . . . Then the camp of the wounded — O heavens, what scene is this? — is this indeed *humanity* — these butchers' shambles? There are several of them. There they lie, in the largest, in an open space in the woods, from 500 to 600 poor fellows — the groans and screams — the odor of blood, mixed with the fresh scent of the night, the grass, the trees — that Slaughter-house! — O well is it their mothers, their sisters cannot see them — cannot conceive, and never conceiv'd, these things. . . . One man is shot by a shell, both in the arm and leg — both are amputated — there lie the rejected members. Some have their legs blown off — some bullets through the breast — some indescribably horrid wounds in the face or head, all mutilated, sickening, torn, gouged out — some in the abdomen — some mere boys — here is one his face colorless as chalk, lying perfectly still, a bullet has perforated the abdomen — life is ebbing fast, there is no help for him. In the camp of the wounded are many rebels, badly hurt — they take their regular turns with the rest, just the same as any — the surgeons use them just the same. . . . Such is the camp of the wounded — such a fragment, a reflection afar off of the bloody scene — while over all the clear, large moon comes out at times softly, quietly shining.

Such, amid the woods, that scene of flitting souls — amid the crack and crash and yelling sounds — the impalpable perfume of the woods — and yet the pungent, stifling smoke — shed with the radiance of the moon, the round, maternal queen, looking from heaven at intervals so placid — the sky so heavenly — the clear-obscure up there, those buoyant upper oceans — a few large placid stars beyond, coming out and then disappearing — the melancholy, draperied night above, around. . . . And there, upon the roads, the fields, and in those woods, that contest, never one more desperate in any age or land — both parties now in force — masses — no fancy battle, no semi-play, but fierce and savage demons fighting there — courage and scorn of death the rule, exceptions almost none.

What history, again I say, can ever give — for who can know, the mad, determin'd tussle of the armies, in all their separate large and little squads — as this — each steep'd from crown to toe in desperate, mortal purports? Who know the conflict hand-to-hand — the many conflicts in the dark, those shadowy-tangled, flashing-moonbeam'd woods — the writhing groups and squads — hear through the woods the cries, the din, the cracking guns and pistols — the distant cannon — the cheers and calls, and threats and awful music of the oaths — the indiscribable mix — the officers' orders, persuasions, encouragements — the devils fully rous'd in human hearts — the strong word, *Charge, men, charge* — the flash of the naked sword, and many a flame and smoke — And still the broken, clear and clouded heaven — and still again the moonlight pouring silvery soft its radiant patches over all? . . . Who paint the scene, the sudden partial panic of the afternoon, at dusk? Who paint the irrepressible advance of the Second Division of the Third Corps, under Hooker himself, suddenly order'd up — those rapid-filing phantoms through the woods? Who show what moves there in the shadows, fluid and firm — to save, (and it did save,) the Army's name, perhaps the Nation? And there the veterans hold the field. (Brave Berry[12] falls not yet — but Death has mark'd him — soon he falls.)

Of scenes like these, I say, who writes — who e'er can write, the story? Of many a score — aye, thousands, North and South, of unwrit heroes, unknown heroisms, incredible, impromptu, first-class desperations — who tells? No history, ever — No poem sings, nor music sounds, those bravest men of all — those deeds. No formal General's report, nor print, nor book in the library, nor column in the paper, embalms the bravest, North or South, East or West. Unnamed, unknown, remain, and still remain, the bravest soldiers. Our manliest — our boys — our hardy darlings. Indeed no picture gives them. Likely their very names are lost. Likely, the typic one of them, (standing, no doubt, for hundreds, thousands,) crawls aside to some bush-clump, or ferny tuft, on receiving his death-shot — there, sheltering a little while, soaking roots, grass and soil with red blood — the battle advances, retreats, flits from the scene, sweeps by — and there, haply with pain and suffering, (yet less, far less, than is supposed,) the last lethargy winds like a serpent round him — the eyes glaze in death — none recks — Perhaps the burial-squads, in truce, a week afterwards, search not the secluded spot — And there, at last, the Bravest Soldier crumbles in the soil of mother earth, unburied and unknown.

A Glimpse of War's Hell-Scenes

In one of the late movements of our troops in the Valley, (near Upperville, I think,) a strong force of Moseby's[13] mounted guerillas attack'd a train of wounded, and the guard of cavalry convoying them. The ambulances contain'd about 60 wounded, quite a number of them officers of rank. The rebels were in strength, and the capture of the train and its partial guard after a short snap was effectually accomplish'd.

No sooner had our men surrender'd, the rebels instantly commenced robbing the train, and murdering their prisoners, even the wounded. Here is the scene, or a sample of it, ten minutes after. Among the wounded officers in the ambulances were one, a Lieutenant of regulars, and another of higher rank. These two were dragg'd out on the ground on their backs, and were now surrounded by the guerillas, a demoniac crowd, each member of which was stabbing them in different parts of their bodies. One of the officers had his feet pinn'd firmly to the ground by bayonets stuck through them and thrust into the ground. These two officers, as afterwards found on examination, had receiv'd about twenty such thrusts, some of them through the mouth, face, &c. The wounded had all been dragg'd (to give a better chance also for plunder,) out of their wagons; some had been effectually dispatch'd, and their bodies lying there lifeless and bloody. Others, not yet dead, but horribly mutilated, were moaning or groaning. Of our men who surrender'd, most had been thus maim'd or slaughter'd.

At this instant a force of our cavalry, who had been following the train at some interval, charged suddenly upon the Secesh captors, who proceeded at once to make the best escape they could. Most of them got away, but we gobbled two officers and seventeen men, as it were in the very acts just described. The sight was one which admitted of little discussion, as may be imagined. The seventeen captured men and two officers were put under guard for the night, but it was decided there and then that they should die.

The next morning the two officers were taken in the town, separate places, put in the centre of the street, and shot. The seventeen men were taken to an open ground, a little to one side. They were placed in a hollow square, encompass'd by two of our cavalry regiments, one of which regiments had three days before found the bloody corpses of three of their men hamstrung and hung up by the heels to limbs of trees by Moseby's guerillas, and the other had not long before had twelve men, after surrendering, shot and then hung by the neck to limbs of trees, and jeering inscriptions pinn'd to the breast of one of the corpses, who had been a sergeant. Those three, and those twelve, had been found, I say, by these environing regiments. Now, with revolvers, they form'd the grim cordon of their seventeen prisoners. The latter were placed in the midst of the hollow square, were unfasten'd, and the ironical remark made to them that they were now to be given "a chance for themselves." A few ran for it. But what use? From every side the deadly pills came. In a few minutes the seventeen corpses strew'd the hollow square . . . I was curious to know whether some of the Union soldiers, some few, (some one or two at least of the youngsters,) did not abstain from shooting on the helpless men. Not one. There was no exultation, very little said; almost nothing, yet every man there contributed his shot.

(Multiply the above by scores, aye hundreds — varify it in all the forms that different circumstances, individuals, places, &c., could afford — light it with every lurid passion, the wolf's, the lion's lapping thirst for blood, the passionate, boiling volcanoes of human revenge for comrades, brothers slain — with the light of burning farms, and heaps of smutting, smouldering black embers — and in the human heart everywhere black, worse embers — and you have an inkling of this War.)

Federico Cavada, from *Libby Life: Experiences of a Prisoner of War* (1864)

While serving as a lieutenant colonel for the Union at the Battle of Gettysburg, Cavada was captured and taken to Libby Prison in the Confederate capital of Richmond, Virginia.

Originally a tobacco factory on the James River, by July of 1863 Libby Prison had been converted to a detainment center for prisoners of war, primarily Union officers. Although overshadowed in popular memory by Andersonville Prison in Georgia, Libby Prison was notorious for its dismal conditions and abusive treatment of prisoners. Dark, overcrowded, sparsely furnished, lacking in food, the facility was also open to the elements, and malnutrition and disease were rampant. Such conditions led to numerous attempts at escape, several of which were successful, including the "grand escapade" described here, in which 109 Union prisoners escaped by a tunnel. As Cavada's *Libby Life* reveals—along with other veterans' correspondence and memoirs—Civil War prisons were their own unique battlefields, involving struggles for both physical and psychological survival.

Chapter 5: *Various Forms of Melancholy – Confederate Wails – Surgeons and Chaplains – Supplies from the North – The Great Conspiracy*

While some of the prisoners endeavor by all sorts of ingenious stratagems to divert their minds from the ennui and monotony of captivity, others give up to their sorrows and pine away in the midst of morbid reflections and dismal forebodings. There is a pale, sallow, resurrected-looking youth whom I see wandering like an ill-fed spectre from room to room; he has been a prisoner during many months, and is reduced to the narrowest possible limits of anatomical contraction. He has large eyes which brighten, at times, when you address him kindly or jocosely; but they are eyes which brighten, not with intellectual sunshine, but rather with the weird radiance of moon-light.

This youth has a hobby. — That hobby is, to make his escape from the prison. He dreams of impracticable rope ladders to be manufactured surreptitiously out of blankets, and to be ingeniously concealed from the keen eye of the Inspector, — perhaps of being lowered from the windows in a basket, like Saul from the walls of Damascus.[14] Over his soup, over his coffee, over his stewed apples, over his huckleberries, that one deep and mysterious scheme absorbs all his faculties; at all hours that restless incubus, urged on by an enraged and merciless rider, gallops fiercely to and fro through the bewildering mazes of his brain, — especially during those periods of fearful tedium when he gazes out through the barred windows at the green fields and forests beyond the swift waters of the James.

One stormy night he resolved to carry his long projected plan into execution, by lowering himself from one of the windows. Already his hands resolutely clutched the bars and his foot actually projected beyond the sill, when upon looking more intently at the pavement below to reassure himself before the final spring, he discovered that he was about to alight upon a Confederate hat; now, it so happened that this hat contained a head, and that this head was an indispensable portion of the anatomy of a Confederate sentinel. The lamentable results which would have attended his descent under such adverse circumstances were sufficient to deter him from bringing about so fatal a catastrophe, and he sullenly relinquished his purpose, with a dark and secret vow, the realization of which, if more bloody and terrible than would have been a desperate encounter with a Rebel guard, will not, I dare say, be attended with the same amount of personal peril.

This morbid misanthropy assumes many different forms; it is always melancholy, though variously expressed.

There is a gaunt, sandy-haired individual who may always be seen seated on a *brick*, — why on a brick, I cannot conceive — with his elbows on his knees, and his head between his hands, moaning continually from morning till night, with a pitiable expression of countenance: silent, uncommunicative, and morose. He evidently pets up his grief; I am persuaded that he loves it, and would feel provoked at any one who should cause him to smile. They say he is a Scotchman.

Another eccentric mortal is one whose aberrations follow an entirely different channel. This one has always a black streak somewhere on his face: no wonder, — he is continually in the cook-house, boiling, frying, or stewing something. I do not know when he eats, for I have never seen him yet that he was not cooking: it seems to be his only solace, and his only occupation. I never pass him that some rare and pleasant odor does not greet my olfactories: sometimes of fried eggs, or onions, or nutmeg. He evidently loves to envelope himself in a perpetual atmosphere of culinary fragrances. It is, I dare say, *his* plan, to cook up his melancholy into all sorts of delicious concoctions, and to feed upon it in a substantial and rational manner. I am informed that he is a Frenchman.

Then there is that quiet, reserved, and portly body, who is seldom out of his corner, unless for an evening walk, and who reclines so comfortably in his capacious box-arm-chair, with a huge double-barrelled pipe in his mouth. He envelopes himself in an impenetrable atmosphere of tobacco smoke, puffing it out like a steam-engine, and smacking his lips after every discharge, as though he had just sipped of the exhilarating contents of an invisible glass of Lager. This one *smokes up* his melancholy; he consumes it; he sends it curling upward out of the prison window in huge, serpentine coils of odorous vapor; he puffs out around him a tempestuous little firmament, in the midst of which his incandescent pipe-bowl, like an ominous sun, looms red through the infuriated swirls of stormy smoke-cloud! He smokes, not with ordinary gusto, but with the violence and ferocity of despair; he *must* do it; it is his only hope; take his pipe from him, and in less than twenty-four hours he will be in a strait-jacket in the Insane Asylum; suggest it to him and you will hear him reply: "Gott bewahre! Nicht um die ganze welt! Sie ist mir lieber als das Leben!"[15]

There is yet another: a singularly contradictory specimen of the morbid. He is constantly singing, dancing, or sleeping. His irresistible merriment wrings an echo even from the sober prison walls; he shakes the very bars in the windows, as he leaps about in his jolly dance ; he convulses the whole prison with his laughter. He is always ready with a song, a jig, or a joke. And yet I know he is very miserable; I am positively sure that he is racked nearly to death with ennui, weary in mind, and sick at heart. He hails from the Emerald Isle.

There is a great outcry in the Confederacy about the exorbitant prices which have to be paid for articles of first necessity.[16] Truly do they say:

"The question of high prices is, perhaps, the one now most urgent. How are the people — the soldiers — their wives and children to live — how is the Government to get along — with the enormous and increasing prices required for all necessaries? This is a matter which must press upon the heart and mind of every thinking man and lover of the country. The first step towards solving the problem, is to ascertain the chief cause of this depreciation of the value of our money. Extortioners are a curse to our country. As an affair of equity, if prices must advance, all prices should advance simultaneously, and none should receive more justice in this respect than the defenders of the country. — The value of our currency is not fixed and stable, and therefore no change of wages will remedy the injustice, or meet the difficulty. The principal cause of our monetary troubles is the inflation of our currency. — Energy and wisdom in the

Government alone can furnish an adequate remedy for the evils of our disordered country."

Lieutenant Skelton of the 17th Iowa, and a fellow patient, escaped yesterday from the Hospital by bribing one of the sentinels.[17] Lieutenant Skelton had been lying in the Hospital a long time, severely wounded. *escaped*

The Federal surgeons confined here since the suspension of the cartel are, at last, to be sent North. There is great rejoicing among the Faculty in view of their joyous deliverance from thralldom; we join them heartily in their self-congratulation, for there are noble fellows in the number of these ingenious menders of earthen-ware, who go once more into the field to cement together, as best they can, the human pottery cracked in the shock of armies.

The chaplains, detained on either side notwithstanding the non-combatting sanctity of their office, were sent away more than a month ago. Thus deprived of the medical advice of the one class of Doctors, and of the spiritual comfort to be derived from the other, we feel the loss to be a severe one, both to our bodies and our minds. In a *social* point of view we must regret their absence, however much we may philanthropically rejoice at their deliverance from this abnormal little world of ours, in which the body is always ailing and the mind is never at rest.

A number of boats laden with clothing and commissary stores from our Government are lying in the canal, fronting the prison. These are intended to relieve the needy condition of the Federal prisoners here and on Belle Isle.[18] There are also contributions from various Northern Sanitary Commissions, and other charitable Societies; also generous donations from private individuals, and boxes from the families of prisoners.

A monster plan for the deliverance of all the Federal prisoners in Richmond, and for the capture and destruction of the city, has lately come to light.[19] The plan was more or less as follows:

The officers confined in the Libby, headed by the most determined and desperate of their number, were to break out of the prison by force, overpower the sentries, and seize the arms stacked at the Head-quarters of the guard on the opposite corner of the street; the prisoners on Belle Isle, and in the various prisons in Richmond, were then to be liberated, the arsenal seized, and all the insurgents armed; the garrisons in the fortifications having been driven out, or overpowered, the city was to be held. The conspirators were to be aided by numerous Union Sympathizers. The time appointed for the explosion of this insurrectionary bomb-shell was the first day of the meeting of the Rebel Congress. Jefferson Davis, and as many of the leading legislators as possible were to be secured, and sent prisoners into our lines.

This movement was to be seconded by a force of cavalry and infantry which was to make a dash upon the Rebel capital from the direction of the Peninsula.

The discovery of this huge plot might have led to serious uneasiness on the part of the Rebel Government, on the score of future attempts of the same sort; but the fact that not only the whole plan, but even a detailed and "reliable" account, in one of our leading Northern Journals of the *actual occurrence* of these events, while they, as yet, existed only in the visionary minds of the conspirators, must have had the effect of setting the fears of the Rebel authorities completely at rest on the score of such future attempts; the aforesaid newspaper, a co-conspirator, and fully informed of all the most secret plans, would, no doubt, anticipate the actual explosion, and thus afford the Confederacy ample time to guard against the emergency. The first and most vital requisite for the success of conspiracies, is secrecy: a secret, connected with a conspiracy for the capture of Richmond, and shared with a newspaper, might as well have been shared at once with Secretary Benjamin himself.[20]

Notwithstanding the self-complacency of the Richmond authorities after the revelation of this grand conspiracy, it is a historical fact, that a few days ago, several pieces of Confederate cannon were planted near the prison so as to command the streets leading to and from it, and that the guards have been doubled and paraded in unusual numbers before us. Whether by this display of Rebel strength and vigilance, it is intended to intimidate the most desperate, or appeal to the self-preservative instincts of the more timid, I cannot say; but, from what I see and hear around me, the vital points in question among the prisoners, just now, appear to be — the stewing of rations, and the scouring of cook-pots; from which I gather that most of them are of opinion that, under the present unpromising circumstances, it would be far more philosophical to continue to live uncomfortably, than to attempt to die uselessly.

Chapter 8: A Sermon from a Candle – The Prison World – Crowded Condition of the Prison – Cooking Experiences – Letters – The Grand Escapade

It is a wondrously pleasant thing to sit, on a winter evening, in one's comfortable room, leaning lazily back in a cushioned arm-chair, one's feet propped up by the burnished fender and warmed by the glow of the crackling anthracite. The wind howls without, and drives the cutting sleet against the window panes, with a sound which serves marvellously to increase our sense of comfort, and our store of thankfulness. Ah, how pleasantly we ruminate then, as we watch the gleaming jets of ruby and of azure darting and winding among the glowing coals! Those may, indeed, be grateful and pleasing thoughts of happy morning hours, fresh and green, islanded here and there along the downward current of life's river; of present noon-day hopes sailing calmly onward to peaceful havens; of a tranquil, bright horizon, gleaming down the stream, under an evening sky of violet and of gold!

But, alas! it is quite another affair to sit in your stiff-backed, hard-seated flour-barrel-arm-chair, in a cheerless prison, with the winter wind blowing polar needles in your face through the paneless, shutterless windows, — your hat slouched down on the windward side of your head for a shield, — and to behold around you your shivering fellow-prisoners, blowing their fingers to keep them warm, and all muffled up in their gray blankets, as if they were so many uneasy Rebel ghosts stalking about in Confederate winding-sheets; to have no letters to write, and no book to read, and to sit there staring at your one yellow Confederate tallow candle, stuck in an impracticable cake of corn bread for a candle-stick—staring at it as though you might, by some hitherto unsuspected optical process, extract, for your own bodily comfort, the meagre caloric of its flickering flame, — then from the candle passing your eye to the candle-stick, and staring at that, as though you were speculating upon the frightful probability of having to devour it for your breakfast tomorrow, tallow-drippings and all.

This, I repeat, is quite another case, and the ruminations which occupy your brain are of a correspondingly diverse character. It is all very well to recollect that you once read a beautiful and instructive lecture by Doctor Farraday on the wonderful chemical processes which take place in a burning candle;[21] it may have interested you hugely at the time to read about oxygen and hydrogen, and the many extraordinary antics which these gases play in the blaze of your tallow-dip, and how if it were not for the nitrogen in the air, it would burn itself up in a snap of your fingers. Your thoughts do not flow in this channel just now — unless, indeed, the alarming rapidity with which your candle uses itself up, notwithstanding the charitable assistance of the nitrogen, should suggest the melancholy reflection that this distressed, bilious-looking taper has cost you the round sum of one dollar!

Your thoughts are resolutely cast in the rigid mould of that gloomy philosophy which teaches you, not so much to endeavor to fly from the evils which beset you, but rather to grapple with them, and trample them under foot. But this admirable system of ethics it is not always easy to put into practice; so you continue to stare at your candle, and you stare so intensely and so long, that if you are a hypochondriac (and of course you *are* one) you may readily be led into the suicidal hallucination that you also are made of tallow, and have a' burning wick protruding from the top of your head, and that, after all, you are only two candles staring blankly at one another, and watching each other melt away, inch by inch, with a sort of silent, demoniacal satisfaction!

Finally, you arrive at one, and only one conclusion, which is, that if there be any one thing in this world more utterly unsatisfactory than any other, it is to be a prisoner of war. He who is imprisoned for the commission of a crime, has at least the consolation of knowing that he deserves the punishment he suffers. But the idea of being shut up in a dreary and loathsome tomb, for weeks and months — to be tortured, and pinched, and starved — merely for serving your country, and endeavoring, through it, to serve humanity! Had you failed to answer at your country's call, such tortures might be fully merited. Stop! you must call your moral ethics here to your aid, for you feel that the burning wick in your head is playing the deuce with your cerebral tallow. You moralize for a while, and you finally arrive at the conclusion, (you could not very well arrive at any other,) that it is *all for the best*. Now, with Portia you exclaim:

"How far that little candle throws his beams!
So shines a good deed in a naughty world!"[22]

Then you fall to making a series of quaint, but wholesome similes, and you begin by considering that after all, if you *are* a hypochondriac, and have conceived yourself to be even that most disgraceful of cereous concoctions, a Confederate candle, there is some analogy and truth in the illusion; for, is it not thus our fleeting life melts away in this rude world? — and if you are righteous adamantine, and not impure tallow, will you not burn the brighter, and shine the farther for it? — if the rude winds of sorrow assail you, will you not flicker, and gutter, and melt away the sooner? — if you do not trim your wick, now and then with a pair of moral snuffers, will you not run, and drip, and splutter, and become an abomination in the eyes of all good people? — and are there not moments in your weary captivity, oh, *wicked* prisoner! when you wish some merciful gush of the winter wind through the iron bars would *blow you out*, and be done with it!

The sentinel under my window is crying out at the top of his voice: "Nine o'clock! lights out!"

As I creep in between my blankets I feel that I owe something to that poor candle for the little sermon it has preached to me. I shall wander off now into the empyrean fields of a pre-slumberous reverie — a sort of nocturnal campaign against the evils of discontent, with my dollar's worth of morality in my haversack — and ere I fall asleep I shall be sure to — from the daily intercourse of friends — from the habitual avocations of life — shut out from social pleasures — doomed to the tedium of a solitude which is the heaviest to bear: the solitude of the heart; and to a melancholy which is the saddest:

in which day after day, and month after month, the same gloomy scenes are contemplated, the same cold faces beheld, the same narrow circle walked, — he is lost indeed, who loses hope.

Imprisonment generally renders men serious — with that seriousness of the heart which lifts it to purer thoughts, and to better actions. No place, surely, is better adapted than the prison-house for the study of human nature. Suffering develops the real character. It is in the midst of bodily or mental anguish that we are apt to cast off the mask unreservedly, and indeed, unawares. This is a crucible to the heart. In such an imprisonment as ours, there is no privacy; there are no moments of truce for hypocrisy — of rest for the daily wearing of the mask; we live continually as if in the midst of a crowded street — held up to the observation of the curious — always under the eye of some one. Under such circumstances, that goodness must indeed be sterling which never forgets itself, and that merit genuine which stands firmly upon its pedestal to the last.

Captivity is a flail which threshes the chaff out of human pride. Men are not apt to be supercilious when they are starving; they suffer, and must bow; they are tortured, and must yield. They must battle against idleness, and they become diligent; they must elude their implacable foe, ennui, every hour of the day and every day of the month, and when their resources are exhausted they must stoop to trivial pursuits and pastimes to baffle their enemy, — being no longer able to amuse themselves as men, they remember how they used to amuse themselves when they were children. They are surprised to find that the whittling of toy-boats and playing at jack-straws, and romping like school-boys, can afford even a passing occupation.

All silly pride and squeamishness must be set aside: the future brigadier must sit, barefoot, with a bucket between his legs, while he washes his own stockings; the dashing cavalry officer, who led that glorious charge of which the newspapers were so full, must inevitably serve his turn at cooking and scouring, like a good patriotic cook and scullion that he is, — he must accommodate his genius to circumstances, and display as much gallantry in charging a row of cookpots as he did in scattering a battalion of the enemy's cavalry.

It is curious to see with what earnestness and alacrity every branch of learning is undertaken. There have been at different times in the prison, classes of French, German, Spanish, Italian, Latin and Greek, English Grammar, Phonography, Fencing, Dancing, Military Tactics and a Bible Class. Of course this educational enthusiasm is very ephemeral; these studies are taken up with avidity, to be dropped in disgust at an early day. What the prisoner seeks, in most cases, is not so much instruction as novelty — not so much information as amusement; — much good is no doubt derived from this morbid thirst, for here and there a good seed takes root in a fruitful brain, and glimpses are afforded into the rich arcana of science which may, at some future period, lead to more substantial results. The prison-world must have its educational system; the student turns down the leaf of his Natural Philosophy to set to work at chopping his hash; he lays down his Logic or his Rhetoric to go to the trough to wash his shirt. This is a capital system — for it renders the student humble, while it makes him learned — and this humility will in after life, rather add to than detract from the merit of his wisdom. He is compelled to learn something of housekeeping also — which will prove of great benefit to him in matrimony, and which will be considered by his wife decidedly charming and economical. Indeed, no system of training could be better adapted to prepare a young man for the duties, the responsibilities, the vicissitudes, and may I with all deference be permitted to add, the little counter-revolutions of married life.

He learns something of the real world too: he studies it by contrast; he learns properly to appreciate the evils of idleness, the blessings of freedom, the sympathy of friends, the necessity of social communion; he learns, by sad experience, how many blessings there are in the world, which he had ignored. If gratitude be indeed the memory of the heart, he feels how bright that memory should be ever kept by those who have never read their own names written in the book of suffering, as well as by those who have thumbed its dreary pages in the prison-house.

Most people's notions about imprisonment are connected with the idea of an unbroken solitude; of that constant association with self, which no heart, however gifted and pure, and no mind, however fruitful in resources and rich in lore, can long withstand without drooping into weariness, and languishing into melancholy. With us, here, the case is in many respects different. More than a thousand human beings crowded into the narrow limits of the prison, subjected to the same trials and privations, forced constantly into one another's society, and continually under each other's eyes, we suffer intensely from the want of that very privacy of which the victim of solitary confinement has too much.

This forcing together of spirits often uncongenial, of diverse tastes, and antagonistical ideas, is a curse to the mind.

This jamming together of hapless mortality, this endless "crush of matter," and ceaseless shock of tortured humanity, is a curse to the body.

The prison is crowded to its utmost capacity; every nook and corner is occupied; we jostle each other at the hydrants, on the stairs, around the cooking stoves; at night we must calculate closely the horizontal space required on the floor for the proper distribution of our recumbent anatomy. Everywhere there is crowding, wrangling and confusion.

"If there is society where none intrudes," there is surely very little of it where the intruders are so numerous. As to being exclusive — the attempt would be preposterous; — as to living secluded — that is out of the question. You are in a whirlpool, and you must keep whirling round daily with the merciless eddy in a sort of diabolical gyration. This is apt to render one irascible and crabbed, and sometimes even unjust, — which horribly jangles that precious little silver bell in the human heart — *good nature*, wont at times to ring out, amid the wilder chimes, such pleasant music!

To add to the unwholesomeness, and to the inconveniences of such a mode of life, we are allowed no out-door exercise. The prison is too much crowded to admit of our walking about with any degree of comfort. Some of the prisoners now here, have not once stepped outside the prison door during more than eight months!

The 8th of this month has been one of the most eventful in the history of our prison-life. It will be long remembered on account of the escape of more than a hundred of our number from bondage; some, destined to reach the Federal lines in safety; others, less fortunate, doomed to be recaptured, and to suffer additional tortures at the hands of our keepers.[23]

As far back as last fall, various attempts had been made by officers confined in the prison, under the direction of Colonel Rose of the 77th Pennsylvania,[24] to excavate a tunnel, through which they might hope to effect their escape. To Colonel Rose is chiefly due the credit of these explorations. Animated by an unflinching earnestness of purpose, unwearying perseverance, and no ordinary engineering abilities, he organized, at different times, working parties of ten or fifteen officers, whom he conducted every night into the cellars of the prison. These cellars were very dark, and entirely unguarded, being seldom visited, even in the day time. To these they descended through an opening in the flooring of the room above them used as a kitchen for the prisoners; this opening was carefully concealed by a well-fitted board during the day.

The earliest excavation made led directly into a stratum of rock, and was soon abandoned as impracticable. The next attempt was made in the direction of the main sewer, which runs under the street between the prison and the canal. The plan was to dig from the cellar into this sewer, and by creeping through it, to gain the street at a safe distance from the prison, by means of one of the inlets. After many nights of labor, performed under the most trying circumstances, water began to filter into the excavation, and finally poured in so rapidly that it was impossible to continue the work. This tunnel was abandoned with the greatest reluctance; it was admirably planned, and had it proved successful, would no doubt have emptied the prison of its inmates in a few hours. Several thrilling incidents occurred in connection with it. The cellar from which it was started was sometimes used as a workshop, and a carpenter's table stood directly under the aperture through which the nocturnal diggers dropped down nightly from the kitchen above. The descent and ascent were made by means of a rope or blanket. One night, as one of the officers was being drawn up, the rope broke and he fell from a height of several feet upon the table. His fall made a fearful racket. A sentry whose beat was within a few yards of the locality of this untoward accident, immediately called out for the corporal of the guard. After a lengthy and profound discussion as to what might have occasioned this unusual noise, both the corporal and the sentry ascribed it to some trifling cause, and no further notice was taken of it.

Another night Colonel Rose was digging under the very beat of a sentinel, when a small portion of the earth and pavement caved in. The sentinel, attracted by the circumstance, ran immediately to the spot. "What is it?" asked the soldier at the next post. "A thundering big rat," cried the first one, running his bayonet into the hole. The point of the bayonet grazed the Colonel's cheek. He remained for a long time motionless and almost breathless, until the unsuspecting sentinel resumed his beat, little dreaming what were the real proportions of this Federal *rat*!

After many fruitless attempts to penetrate into the sewers, it was resolved to make an effort to tunnel under the street east of the prison, and to reach the yard of a ware-house opposite. This street was paced day and night by sentinels. Early in January, Colonel Rose organized a working party of fourteen officers, who were to relieve each other regularly in the work, one always remaining on guard near the excavation to prevent a trap being set for the capture of the remainder of the party, in case of discovery by the prison officials. Having succeeded in lifting out the bottom of the fire-place in the cook-room, they removed the bricks from the back of the flue, and penetrated between the floor joists into the cellar, under the end room used as a hospital. Passing through this aperture, they could with facility lower each other down into the cellar. An opening was commenced in the wall near the northeast corner of the cellar. This opening was about two feet by eighteen inches. It was found necessary to cut through the piles on which the building was supported, and this tedious labor was at length successfully completed with no other tools but pocket knives. As they penetrated into the earth, great difficulty was experienced on account of the candles, which refused to burn in the close air of the tunnel. One of the party was compelled to stand constantly at the opening, fanning air into it with his hat. The tunnel fell with a slight depression for a distance of about twelve feet, then continued slightly ascending for about the same distance, and was nearly level the remainder of its length. It was about fifty-three feet long. The first depression was rendered necessary by the fall of the ground towards the ware-house.

The tunnel, at its entrance, was about two feet by eighteen inches, and for some six feet of its length ran at right angles with the street, it then turned a few degrees to the right with a diameter of only sixteen inches, and continued at this angle increasing gradually to a diameter of about two feet to its exit. In order to pass through, it was necessary, of course, to lie flat on one's face, propelling oneself with the hands and feet, as the space was not sufficient to allow of creeping on hands and knees.

As they approached the yard of the warehouse, a slight error in the computation of the distance nearly proved fatal to the enterprise. Thinking they had reached the enclosure, they dug up to the surface and upon breaking through discovered that they had come out in the street, outside the fence, and within a few yards of the sentinels. This hole was quickly filled up with a pair of old pants and some straw, and the digging was continued a few feet further to the desired point under a shed in the yard. An empty hogshead was drawn over the opening to conceal it in the daytime. During more than three weeks this severe labor had been perseveringly carried on. The only implements used were a large chisel furnished with a long handle, and a wooden spit-box brought down from one of the rooms above; to each end of this box a cord was attached, by which it could be drawn into the tunnel and filled with the removed earth by the digger, and drawn out by his assistant. The earth and gravel thus taken out was carefully concealed under some straw and rubbish in the cellar.

On the night of the 8th, the tunnel was finally pronounced practicable for the proposed escape of the party. About twenty-five of the prisoners are said to have been in the secret; these were to make their escape early in the evening, and were to have two hours start; after that, the rest of the prisoners were to be informed, and all who were strong enough to make the attempt were to be allowed to go out.

Colonel Streight[25] and his party were the first to go, and succeeded in making their way out undetected. Once in the yard of the warehouse, they had but to pass out through a gate into the street, between the two lines of guards, and walk boldly away along the canal. During the night one hundred and nine of the officers thus made their escape. Of these only fifty-three have succeeded in reaching the Federal lines. The remainder have been recaptured at different points along the roads leading down to the Peninsula, and are now in the dungeons under the prison, on corn-bread and water. Colonel Rose, to whose protracted labors and untiring zeal, the final success of the plan of escape was mainly due, is unfortunately among the recaptured. After a series of thrilling adventures and narrow escapes, he had succeeded in approaching within a mile or two of Williamsburg, where he deemed himself safe from further pursuit. While resting by the roadside, he was approached by two soldiers dressed in the Federal uniform; convinced that they were Union soldiers, he did not hesitate, in answer to their questions, to state who he was. They proved to be Rebel scouts. After they had taken him at a full run more than a mile out of the way of the Federal scouts and pickets who were close by, one of the Rebels left. Colonel Rose, though well nigh overcome with exhaustion, and fainting from hunger, made one last desperate effort for his liberty. Springing suddenly upon the remaining Rebel, he clutched him by the throat, and endeavored to throw him to the ground and disarm him; he was so feeble, however, that after a brief struggle his strength entirely deserted him. He had contrived to get his finger on the trigger of his opponent's musket, and had discharged the piece during the struggle. The report of the gun having brought back the other scout, Colonel Rose was then secured and brought once more into the Confederate lines.

We are now subjected, in the prison, to an endless ordeal of roll calls, and every precaution is being taken by Major Turner[26] to prevent any further attempts at escape. This rigid exercise of vigilance comes, of course, a day too late, and will not make up for the late laxity of discipline about the prison. Indeed it is wonderful how the grand escapade could have been effected without detection. During the exodus, at about midnight, a sudden panic seized the crowd of prisoners who were gathered about the fireplace in the cook-room, all endeavoring to be the first to get out through the tunnel. Some one said the guard was coming, and a general stampede took place up the stairways to the rooms above, with a frightful noise of feet, and oversetting of boxes and barrels, that must have been heard a square off. But the guards did not suspect what was in progress; one of them, indeed, was heard to call out jocosely to a companion on the next beat "Halloa, Bill — there's somebody's coffee-pot upset, sure!"

The recaptured officers give many thrilling accounts of their adventures. One party got into a boat on the James River, and followed the stream in the hope of reaching Hampton Roads. Unfortunately they got into the Appomattox River by mistake, where their little craft was upset in the darkness of the night, and they were compelled to take to the shore, nearly frozen to death. The next morning they were discovered by some Rebel soldiers and recaptured. Another party had concealed themselves in the swamps near the Chickahominy, where they were hunted out by the aid of dogs and finally secured.

The recaptured officers state that they were treated with kindness by those who retook them, — especially by the officers and soldiers on duty in the neighborhood of the Chickahominy. Indeed, it was not until their return to the prison, where they were locked up in the cells on bread and water, that they experienced any harsh or unsoldier-like treatment.

Sarah Emma Edmonds, from *Nurse and Spy in the Union Army* (1865)

Civil War battlefields were not the exclusive domain of men. Edmonds was just one of a number of women—hundreds, perhaps thousands[27]—who participated actively in the war by posing as male soldiers, working as couriers, or engaging in espionage. Edmonds's narrative stands out not only for its wide popularity, but, not coincidentally, for her zesty adventures in disguise, as Edmonds assumes various combinations of black and white, free and slave, male and female, soldier and civilian, Northern and Southern. In the process, the book becomes "an extended study of omissions, ironies, and double-bluffs."[28] This chapter describes the denouement of the Siege of Yorktown in late April and early May of 1862, in which the Army of the Potomac under Gen. George McClellan, while advancing toward Richmond during the Peninsula Campaign, got temporarily bogged down by a much smaller Confederate forced holed up at Yorktown. Rather than attack, the over-cautious McClellan decided to dig in for a siege, gather more intelligence about the Confederate position, and build up his artillery batteries for a decisive assault. Before that could happen, however, the rebels—under cover of a deceptive artillery barrage of their own—managed to evacuate in order to fight another day.

*Chapter 9: Evacuation of Yorktown – Our Army on the Double Quick – Pursuit of the
Fugitives – The Enemy's Works – A Battle – On the Field – A "Wounded," and Not
Injured Colonel – Carrying the Wounded – Fort Magruder Silenced – The Victory
Won – Burying the Dead – Story of a Ring – Wounded Rebels – A Brave Young
Sergeant – Christian Soldiers – A Soldier's Deathbed – Closing Scenes – Last Words*

The next day[29] the continuous roar of cannon all along the lines of the enemy was kept
up incessantly. "Nor did it cease at night, for when darkness settled over the encampment, from the ramparts that stretched away from Yorktown there were constant gushes
of flame, while the heavy thunder rolled far away in the gloom."[30] A little after midnight
the cannonading ceased, and a strange silence rested upon hill and valley. The first dawn
of day which broke peacefully over the landscape discovered to the practiced eye of
Professor Lowe[31] that the entrenchments of the enemy were deserted; the rebels had
abandoned their stronghold during the night and had fled toward Richmond.

The news spread throughout the Federal army like lightning; from right to left and
from center to circumference the entire encampment was one wild scene of joy. Music
and cheering were the first items in the programme, and then came the following order:
"Commandants of regiments will prepare to march with two days' rations, with the
utmost dispatch. Leave, not to return." At about eight o'clock in the morning our
advance guard entered Yorktown. There were nearly one hundred guns of different
kinds and calibers and a large quantity of ammunition. The road over which the fugitive
army passed during the night was beat up into mortar, knee deep, and was strewn with
fragments of army wagons, tents and baggage.

The Federal troops were in excellent spirits, and pushed on after the retreating army
almost on the double quick. In this manner they kept up the pursuit until toward
evening, when the cavalry came up with the rear-guard of the enemy about two miles
from Williamsburg, where a sharp skirmish followed. Night came on and firing ceased;
the rebels were behind their entrenchments, and our army bivouaced for the night. The
cavalry and artillery forces were under command of General Stoneman; Generals
Heintzelman, Hooker and Smith were in command of the advance column of infantry,
while Generals Kearney, Couch and Casey brought up the rear.[32]

The enemy's works were four miles in extent, nearly three-fourths of their front being
covered by the tributaries of Queen's Creek and College Creek. The main works were a
large fortification, called Fort Magruder,[33] and twelve redoubts for field guns. The woods
around and inside of those works were felled, and the ground was thickly dotted with
rifle pits. The battle commenced the next morning at half-past seven o'clock. General
Hooker began the attack. The enemy were heavily reinforced, and made a desperate
resistance. Hooker lost a great number of men and five pieces of artillery before Kearney,
Couch or Casey came up. The roads were a perfect sea of mud, and now it was raining
in torrents. The roar of battle sounded all along the lines; the thunder of cannon and the
crash of musketry reverberated through the woods and over the plain, assuring the
advancing troops that their companions were engaged in deadly strife.

The thick growth of heavy timber was felled in all directions, forming a splendid
ambush for the rebel sharpshooters. The Federals moved forward in the direction of the
enemy's works, steadily, firmly, through ditch and swamp, mud and mire, loading and
firing as they went, and from every tree, bush and covert, which could conceal a man,
the rebels poured a deadly fire into the ranks of our advancing troops. I was glad now
that I had postponed my second visit to the enemy,[34] for there was plenty of work for me
to do here, as the ghastly faces of the wounded and dying testified. I was subject to all
kinds of orders. One moment I was ordered to the front with a musket in my hands; the

next to mount a horse and carry an order to some general, and very often to take hold of a stretcher with some strong man and carry the wounded from the field.

I remember one little incident in connection with my experience that day which I shall never forget, viz.: Colonel —— fell, and I ran to help put him on a stretcher and carry him to a place of safety, or where the surgeons were, which was more than I was able to do without overtaxing my strength, for he was a very heavy man. A poor little stripling of a soldier and myself carried him about a quarter of a mile through a terrific storm of bullets, and he groaning in a most piteous manner. We laid him down carefully at the surgeon's feet, and raised him tenderly from the stretcher, spread a blanket and laid him upon it, then lingered just a moment to see whether the wound was mortal. The surgeon commenced to examine the case; there was no blood to indicate where the wound was, and the poor sufferer was in such agony that he could not tell where it was. So the surgeon examined by piecemeal until he had gone through with a thorough examination, and there was not even a scratch to be seen. Doctor E.[35] straightened himself up and said, "Colonel, you are not wounded at all; you had better let these boys carry you back again." The Colonel became indignant, and rose to his feet with the air of an insulted hero and said: "Doctor, if I live to get out of this battle I'll call you to account for those words;" to which Doctor E. replied with decision, "Sir, if you are not with your regiment in fifteen minutes I shall report you to General H."[36]

I turned and left the spot in disgust, mentally regretting that the lead or steel of the enemy had not entered the breast of one who seemed so ambitious of the honor without the effect. As I returned to my post I made up my mind in future to ascertain whether a man was wounded or not before I did anything for him. The next I came to was Captain Wm. R. M., of the — Michigan. His leg was broken and shattered from the ankle to the knee. As we went to lift him on a stretcher he said: "Just carry me out of range of the guns, and then go back and look after the boys. Mc—— and L. have fallen, and perhaps they are worse off than I am." Oh how glad I was to hear those words from his lips. It confirmed the opinion I had formed of him long before; he was one of my first acquaintances in the army, and, though he was a strict disciplinarian, I had watched his christian deportment and kind and affectionate manner toward his men with admiration and interest. I believed him noble and brave, and those few words on the battle-field at such a moment spoke volumes for that faithful captain's heroism and love for his men.

The battle was raging fiercely, the men were almost exhausted, the rebels were fighting like demons, and were driving our troops back step by step, while the space between the two lines was literally covered with dead and wounded men and horses. One tremendous shout from the Federals rent the air and fairly shook the earth. We all knew in an instant, as if by intuition, what called forth such wild cheers from that weary and almost overpowered army. "Kearney!" was shouted enthusiastically along the Federal lines, while the fresh troops were hurled like thunderbolts upon the foe. One battery after another was taken from the enemy, and charge after charge was made upon their works, until the tide of battle was turned, Fort Magruder silenced, and the stars and stripes were floating in triumph over the rebel works.

The battle was won, and victory crowned the Union arms. The rebels were flying precipitately from the field, and showers of bullets thick as hail followed the retreating fugitives. Night closed around us, and a darkness which almost equaled that of "Egypt" settled over the battle-field, and the pitiless rain came down in torrents, drenching alike the living and the dead. There lay upon that crimson field two thousand two hundred and twenty-eight of our own men, and more than that number of the enemy. It was indescribably sad to see our weary, exhausted men, with torches, wading through mud to their knees piloting the ambulances over the field, lest they should trample upon the bodies of their fallen comrades.

All night long we toiled in this manner, and when morning came still there were hundreds found upon the field. Those of the enemy were found in heaps, both dead and wounded piled together in ravines, among the felled timber, and in rifle pits half covered with mud. Now the mournful duty came of identifying and burying the dead. Oh, what a day was that in the history of my life, as well as of thousands both North and South. It makes me shudder now while I recall its scenes.

> To see those fair young forms
>   Crushed by the war-horse tread,
> The dear and bleeding ones
>   Stretched by the piled-up dead.[37]

Oh, war, cruel war! Thou dost pierce the soul with untold sorrows, as well as thy bleeding victims with death. How many joyous hopes and bright prospects hast thou blasted; and how many hearts and homes hast thou made desolate! "As we think of the great wave of woe and misery surging over the land, we could cry out in very bitterness of soul—Oh God! how long, how long!"[38]

The dead lay in long rows on the field, their ghastly faces hid from view by handkerchiefs or the capes of their overcoats, while the faithful soldiers were digging trenches in which to bury the mangled bodies of the slain. I passed along the entire line and uncovered every face, in search of one who had given me a small package the day before when going into battle, telling me that if he should be killed to send it home; and, said he, "here is a ring on my finger which I want you to send to ——. It has never been off my finger since she placed it there the morning I started for Washington. If I am killed please take it off and send it to her." I was now in search of him, but could find nothing of the missing one. At last I saw a group of men nearly half a mile distant, who also seemed to be engaged in burying the dead. I made my way toward them as fast as I could, but when I reached them the bodies had all been lowered into the trench, and they were already filling it up.

I begged them to let me go down and see if my friend was among the dead, to which the kind hearted boys consented. His body lay there partially covered with earth; I uncovered his face; he was so changed I should not have recognized him, but the ring told me that it was he. I tried with all my might to remove the ring, but could not. The fingers were so swollen that it was impossible to get it off. In life it was a pledge of faithfulness from one he loved, "and in death they were not divided."

The dead having been buried and the wounded removed to the churches and college buildings in Williamsburg, the fatigued troops sought repose. Upon visiting the wounded rebels I saw several whom I had met in Yorktown,[39] among them the sergeant of the picket post who had given me a friendly shake and told me if I slept on my post he would shoot me like a dog. He was pretty badly wounded, and did not seem to remember me. A little farther on a young darkie lay groaning upon the floor. I went to look at him, and asked if I could do anything for him. I recognized in the distorted face before me the same darkie who had befriended me at Yorktown, and to whom I had offered the five dollar greenback. I assure my friends that I repaid that boy's kindness with double interest; I told Doctor E. what he had done for me when my "hands" turned traitors.[40] He was made an especial object of interest and care.

Some few of the rebel prisoners were gentlemanly and intelligent, and their countenances betokened a high state of moral culture. Many were low, insolent, bloodthirsty creatures, who "neither feared God nor regarded man;"[41] while others there were who seemed not to know enough to be either one thing or the other, but were simply living, breathing animals, subject to any order, and who would just as soon retreat as advance, so long as they did not have to fight. They did not care which way the battle went. On the whole there was a vast contrast between the northern and southern soldiers as they appeared in the hospitals, but perhaps prejudice had something to do in making the rebels appear so much inferior to our men.

In passing through the college building I noticed a young sergeant, a mere boy, who was shot in the temple. He attracted my attention, and I made some inquiry concerning him. He was a Federal, and belonged to the — Massachusetts regiment. An old soldier sitting by him told me the following: "That boy is not sixteen yet; he enlisted as a private, and has, by his bravery and good conduct, earned the three stripes which you see on his arm. He fought all day yesterday like a young lion, leading charges again and again upon the enemy. After we lost our captain and lieutenants he took command of the company, and led it through the battle with the skill and courage of a young brigadier, until he fell stunned and bleeding. I carried him off the field, but could not tell whether he was dead or alive. I washed the blood from his face; the cold water had a salutary effect upon him, for when Hancock and Kearney had completed their work, and the cheers of victory rang over the bloody field, he was sufficiently revived to hear the inspiring tones of triumph. Leaping to his feet, faint and sick as he was, he took up the shout of victory in unison with the conquerers on the field. But he had scarcely uttered the notes of victory and glory when his strength deserted him and he fell insensible to the ground." The old man added: "General —— says if he lives through this he will go into the next battle with shoulder straps on." I went up to him, took his feverish hand, and told him that I was glad that his wound was not mortal. He thanked me, and said with enthusiasm, "I would rather have been killed than to have lost the battle."

There is one thing that I have noticed on the field in every battle that I have witnessed, viz.: that the christian man is the best soldier. Says a minister of the Gospel, writing upon this subject: "It is a common saying among the officers that, as a class, the men who stand foremost when the battle rages are the christian men. Many a time I have talked with them about such scenes, and they have told me that their souls have stood firm in that hour of strife, and that they have been perfectly calm. I have had christian generals tell me this. I have heard General Howard often say that in the midst of the most terrific portion of the battle, when his heart for a moment quailed, he would pause, and lift up his soul to God and receive strength. 'And,' said he, 'I have gone through battles without a particle of fear. I have thought that God sent me to defend my country. I believed it was a christian duty to stand in the foremost of the fight, and why should I be afraid?'"[42]

I once heard an eminently pious lady say that she never could reconcile the idea in her mind of a christian going into the army to fight; it was so inconsistent with the christian character that she was tempted to doubt the piety of all fighting men. I respect the lady's views upon the subject, but beg leave to differ from her; for I believe that a man can serve God just as acceptably in fighting the enemies of liberty, truth and righteousness with the musket down South, as he can in the quiet pulpits of the North; in fact I am inclined to think he can do so a little more effectually in the former place. I only wish that there were more of our holy men willing to take up the carnal weapons of warfare, forego the luxuries of home, and, by setting examples worthy of emulation, both in camp and on the battle field, thus strike a fatal blow at this unholy rebellion.

Silas Weir Mitchell, "The Case of George Dedlow" (1866)

In the immediate aftermath of the war, Mitchell, who had extensive experience as a contract army surgeon in Philadelphia, published his first, and ultimately most influential, literary work. Presented as the first-person account of a veteran and multiple amputee, the story was taken by many readers as a true case – a mistake that testifies to the still-visible carnage of the war, with its routine mutilations and amputations, and to the ongoing suffering of the war's veterans. Not only is the story important to our understanding of these men's experience, but it has been taken seriously for what it reveals about the medical dimension of the Civil War, particularly its groundbreaking clinical description of "phantom limb" syndrome.

The following notes of my own case have been declined on various pretexts by every medical journal to which I have offered them. There was, perhaps, some reason in this, because many of the medical facts which they record are not altogether new, and because the psychical deductions to which they have led me are not in themselves of medical interest. I ought to add that a great deal of what is here related is not of any scientific value whatsoever; but as one or two people on whose judgment I rely have advised me to print my narrative with all the personal details, rather than in the dry shape in which, as a psychological statement, I shall publish it elsewhere, I have yielded to their views. I suspect, however, that the very character of my record will, in the eyes of some of my readers, tend to lessen the value of the metaphysical discoveries which it sets forth.

I am the son of a physician, still in large practice, in the village of Abington, Scofield County, Indiana. Expecting to act as his future partner, I studied medicine in his office, and in 1859 and 1860 attended lectures at the Jefferson Medical College in Philadelphia. My second course should have been in the following year, but the outbreak of the Rebellion so crippled my father's means that I was forced to abandon my intention. The demand for army surgeons at this time became very great; and although not a graduate, I found no difficulty in getting the place of assistant surgeon to the Tenth Indiana Volunteers. In the subsequent Western campaigns this organization suffered so severely that before the term of its service was over it was merged in the Twenty-first Indiana Volunteers; and I, as an extra surgeon, ranked by the medical officers of the latter regiment, was transferred to the Fifteenth Indiana Cavalry. Like many physicians, I had contracted a strong taste for army life, and, disliking cavalry service, sought and obtained the position of first lieutenant in the Seventy-ninth Indiana Volunteers, an infantry regiment of excellent character.[43]

On the day after I assumed command of my company, which had no captain, we were sent to garrison a part of a line of blockhouses stretching along the Cumberland River below Nashville, then occupied by a portion of the command of General Rosecrans.

The life we led while on this duty was tedious and at the same time dangerous in the extreme. Food was scarce and bad, the water horrible, and we had no cavalry to forage for us. If, as infantry, we attempted to levy supplies upon the scattered farms around us, the population seemed suddenly to double, and in the shape of guerrillas "potted" us industriously from behind distant trees, rocks, or fences. Under these various and unpleasant influences, combined with a fair infusion of malaria, our men rapidly lost health and spirits.[44] Unfortunately, no proper medical supplies had been forwarded with our small force (two companies), and, as the fall advanced, the want of quinine and stimulants became a serious annoyance. Moreover, our rations were running low; we had been three weeks without a new supply; and our commanding officer, Major Henry L. Terrill, began to be uneasy as to the safety of his men. About this time it was supposed that a train with rations would be due from the post twenty miles to the north of us; yet it was quite possible that it would bring us food, but no medicines, which were what we most needed. The command was too small to detach any part of it, and the major therefore resolved to send an officer alone to the post above us, where the rest of the Seventy-ninth lay, and whence they could easily forward quinine and stimulants by the train, if it had not left, or, if it had, by a small cavalry escort.

It so happened, to my cost, as it turned out, that I was the only officer fit to make the journey, and I was accordingly ordered to proceed to Blockhouse No. 3 and make the required arrangements. I started alone just after dusk the next night, and during the darkness succeeded in getting within three miles of my destination. At this time I found that I had lost my way, and, although aware of the danger of my act, was forced to turn aside and ask at a log cabin for directions. The house contained a dried-up old woman and four white-headed, half-naked children. The woman was either stone-deaf or pretended to be so; but, at all events, she gave me no satisfaction, and I remounted and rode away. On coming to the end of a lane, into which I had turned to seek the cabin, I found to my surprise that the bars had been put up during my brief parley. They were too high to leap, and I therefore dismounted to pull them down. As I touched the top rail, I heard a rifle, and at the same instant felt a blow on both arms, which fell helpless. I staggered to my horse and tried to mount; but, as I could use neither arm, the effort was vain, and I therefore stood still, awaiting my fate. I am only conscious that I saw about me several graybacks, for I must have fallen fainting almost immediately.

When I awoke I was lying in the cabin near by, upon a pile of rubbish. Ten or twelve guerrillas were gathered about the fire, apparently drawing lots for my watch, boots, hat, etc. I now made an effort to find out how far I was hurt. I discovered that I could use the left forearm and hand pretty well, and with this hand I felt the right limb all over until I touched the wound. The ball had passed from left to right through the left biceps, and directly through the right arm just below the shoulder, emerging behind. The right arm and forearm were cold and perfectly insensible. I pinched them as well as I could, to test the amount of sensation remaining; but the hand might as well have been that of a dead man. I began to understand that the nerves had been wounded, and that the part was utterly powerless. By this time my friends had pretty well divided the spoils, and, rising together, went out. The old woman then came to me, and said: "Reckon you'd best git up. They-'uns is a-goin' to take you away." To this I only answered, "Water, water." I had a grim sense of amusement on finding that the old woman was not deaf, for she went out, and presently came back with a gourdful, which I eagerly drank. An hour later the graybacks returned, and finding that I was too weak to walk, carried me out and laid me on the bottom of a common cart, with which they set off on a trot. The jolting was horrible, but within an hour I began to have in my dead right hand a strange burning, which was rather a relief to me. It increased as the sun rose and the day grew warm, until I felt as if the hand was caught and pinched in a red-hot vise. Then in my agony I begged my guard for water to wet it with, but for some reason they desired silence, and at every noise threatened me with a revolver. At length the pain became absolutely unendurable, and I grew what it is the fashion to call demoralized. I screamed, cried, and yelled in my torture, until, as I suppose, my captors became alarmed, and, stopping, gave me a handkerchief, — my own, I fancy, — and a canteen of water, with which I wetted the hand, to my unspeakable relief.

It is unnecessary to detail the events by which, finally, I found myself in one of the rebel hospitals near Atlanta. Here, for the first time, my wounds were properly cleansed and dressed by a Dr. Oliver T. Wilson, who treated me throughout with great kindness. I told him I had been a doctor, which, perhaps, may have been in part the cause of the unusual tenderness with which I was managed. The left arm was now quite easy, although, as will be seen, it never entirely healed. The right arm was worse than ever— the humerus broken, the nerves wounded, and the hand alive only to pain. I use this phrase because it is connected in my mind with a visit from a local visitor, — I am not sure he was a preacher, — who used to go daily through the wards, and talk to us or write our letters. One morning he stopped at my bed, when this little talk occurred:

"How are you, lieutenant?"

"Oh," said I, "as usual. All right but this hand, which is dead except to pain."

"Ah," said he, "such and thus will the wicked be—such will you be if you die in your sins: you will go where only pain can be felt. For all eternity, all of you will be just like that hand—knowing pain only."

I suppose I was very weak, but somehow I felt a sudden and chilling horror of possible universal pain, and suddenly fainted. When I awoke the hand was worse, if that could be. It was red, shining, aching, burning, and, as it seemed to me, perpetually rasped with hot files. When the doctor came I begged for morphia. He said gravely: "We have none. You know you don't allow it to pass the lines." It was sadly true.

I turned to the wall, and wetted the hand again, my sole relief. In about an hour Dr. Wilson came back with two aids, and explained to me that the bone was so crushed as to make it hopeless to save it, and that, besides, amputation offered some chance of arresting the pain. I had thought of this before, and the anguish I felt—I cannot say endured—was so awful that I made no more of losing the limb than of parting with a tooth on account of toothache. Accordingly, brief preparations were made, which I watched with a sort of eagerness such as must forever be inexplicable to any one who has not passed six weeks of torture like that which I had suffered.

I had but one pang before the operation. As I arranged myself on the left side, so as to make it convenient for the operator to use the knife, I asked: "Who is to give me the ether?" "We have none," said the person questioned. I set my teeth, and said no more.

I need not describe the operation. The pain felt was severe, but it was insignificant as compared with that of any other minute of the past six weeks. The limb was removed very near to the shoulder-joint. As the second incision was made, I felt a strange flash of pain play through the limb, as if it were in every minutest fibril of nerve. This was followed by instant, unspeakable relief, and before the flaps were brought together I was sound asleep. I dimly remember saying, as I pointed to the arm which lay on the floor: "There is the pain, and here am I. How queer!" Then I slept—slept the sleep of the just, or, better, of the painless. From this time forward I was free from neuralgia. At a subsequent period I saw a number of cases similar to mine in a hospital in Philadelphia.

It is no part of my plan to detail my weary months of monotonous prison life in the South. In the early part of April, 1863, I was exchanged, and after the usual thirty days' furlough returned to my regiment a captain.[45]

On the 19th of September, 1863, occurred the battle of Chickamauga, in which my regiment took a conspicuous part.[46] The close of our own share in this contest is, as it were, burned into my memory with every least detail. It was about 6 P.M., when we found ourselves in line, under cover of a long, thin row of scrubby trees, beyond which lay a gentle slope, from which, again, rose a hill rather more abrupt, and crowned with an earthwork. We received orders to cross this space and take the fort in front, while a brigade on our right was to make a like movement on its flank.

Just before we emerged into the open ground, we noticed what, I think, was common in many fights—that the enemy had begun to bowl round shot at us, probably from failure of shell. We passed across the valley in good order, although the men fell rapidly all along the line. As we climbed the hill, our pace slackened, and the fire grew heavier. At this moment a battery opened on our left, the shots crossing our heads obliquely. It is this moment which is so printed on my recollection. I can see now, as if through a window, the gray smoke, lit with red flashes, the long, wavering line, the sky blue above, the trodden furrows, blotted with blue blouses. Then it was as if the window closed, and I knew and saw no more. No other scene in my life is thus scarred, if I may say so, into my memory. I have a fancy that the horrible shock which suddenly fell upon me must have had something to do with thus intensifying the momentary image then before my eyes.

When I awakened, I was lying under a tree somewhere at the rear. The ground was covered with wounded, and the doctors were busy at an operating-table, improvised from two barrels and a plank. At length two of them who were examining the wounded about me came up to where I lay. A hospital steward raised my head and poured down some brandy and water, while another cut loose my pantaloons. The doctors exchanged looks and walked away. I asked the steward where I was hit.

"Both thighs," said he; "the doctors won't do nothing."

"No use?" said I.

"Not much," said he.

"Not much means none at all," I answered.

When he had gone I set myself to thinking about a good many things I had better have thought of before, but which in no way concern the history of my case. A half-hour went by. I had no pain, and did not get weaker. At last, I cannot explain why, I began to look about me. At first things appeared a little hazy. I remember one thing which thrilled me a little, even then.

A tall, blond-bearded major walked up to a doctor near me, saying, "When you've a little leisure, just take a look at my side."

"Do it now," said the doctor.

The officer exposed his wound. "Ball went in here, and out there."

The doctor looked up at him—half pity, half amazement. "If you've got any message, you'd best send it by me."

"Why, you don't say it's serious?" was the reply.

"Serious! Why, you're shot through the stomach. You won't live over the day."

Then the man did what struck me as a very odd thing. He said, "Anybody got a pipe?" Some one gave him a pipe. He filled it deliberately, struck a light with a flint, and sat down against a tree near to me. Presently the doctor came to him again, and asked him what he could do for him.

"Send me a drink of Bourbon."

"Anything else?"

"No."

As the doctor left him, he called him back. "It's a little rough, doc, is n't it?"

No more passed, and I saw this man no longer. Another set of doctors were handling my legs, for the first time causing pain. A moment after, a steward put a towel over my mouth, and I smelled the familiar odor of chloroform, which I was glad enough to breathe. In a moment the trees began to move around from left to right, faster and faster; then a universal grayness came before me, and I recall nothing further until I awoke to consciousness in a hospital-tent. I got hold of my own identity in a moment or two, and was suddenly aware of a sharp cramp in my left leg. I tried to get at it to rub it with my single arm, but, finding myself too weak, hailed an attendant. "Just rub my left calf," said I, "if you please."

"Calf?" said he. "You ain't none. It's took off."

"I know better," said I. "I have pain in both legs."

"Wall, [sic] I never!" said he. "You ain't got nary leg." [sic]

As I did not believe him, he threw off the covers, and, to my horror, showed me that I had suffered amputation of both thighs, very high up.

"That will do," said I, faintly.

A month later, to the amazement of every one, I was so well as to be moved from the crowded hospital at Chattanooga to Nashville, where I filled one of the ten thousand beds of that vast metropolis of hospitals.[47] Of the sufferings which then began I shall presently speak. It will be best just now to detail the final misfortune which here fell upon me. Hospital No. 2, in which I lay, was inconveniently crowded with severely wounded officers. After my third week an epidemic of hospital gangrene broke out in my ward. In three days it attacked twenty persons. Then an inspector came, and we were transferred at once to the open air, and placed in tents. Strangely enough, the wound in my remaining arm, which still suppurated, was seized with gangrene. The usual remedy, bromine, was used locally, but the main artery opened, was tied, bled again and again, and at last, as a final resort, the remaining arm was amputated at the shoulder-joint. Against all chances I recovered, to find myself a useless torso, more like some strange larval creature than anything of human shape. Of my anguish and horror of myself I dare not speak. I have dictated these pages, not to shock my readers, but to possess them with facts in regard to the relation of the mind to the body; and I hasten, therefore, to such portions of my case as best illustrate these views.

In January, 1864, I was forwarded to Philadelphia, in order to enter what was known as the Stump Hospital, South Street, then in charge of Dr. Hopkinson. This favor was obtained through the influence of my father's friend, the late Governor Anderson, who had always manifested an interest in my case, for which I am deeply grateful. It was thought, at the time, that Mr. Palmer, the leg-maker,[48] might be able to adapt some form of arm to my left shoulder, as on that side there remained five inches of the arm-bone, which I could move to a moderate extent. The hope proved illusory, as the stump was always too tender to bear any pressure. The hospital referred to was in charge of several surgeons while I was an inmate, and was at all times a clean and pleasant home. It was filled with men who had lost one arm or leg, or one of each, as happened now and then. I saw one man who had lost both legs, and one who had parted with both arms; but none, like myself, stripped of every limb. There were collected in this place hundreds of these cases, which gave to it, with reason enough, the not very pleasing title of Stump Hospital.

I spent here three and a half months, before my transfer to the United States Army Hospital for Injuries and Diseases of the Nervous System.[49] Every morning I was carried out in an arm-chair and placed in the library, where some one was always ready to write or read for me, or to fill my pipe. The doctors lent me medical books; the ladies brought me luxuries and fed me; and, save that I was helpless to a degree which was humiliating, I was as comfortable as kindness could make me.

I amused myself at this time by noting in my mind all that I could learn from other limbless folk, and from myself, as to the peculiar feelings which were noticed in regard to lost members. I found that the great mass of men who had undergone amputations for many months felt the usual consciousness that they still had the lost limb. It itched or pained, or was cramped, but never felt hot or cold. If they had painful sensations referred to it, the conviction of its existence continued unaltered for long periods; but where no pain was felt in it, then by degrees the sense of having that limb faded away entirely. I think we may to some extent explain this. The knowledge we possess of any part is made up of the numberless impressions from without which affect its sensitive surfaces, and which are transmitted through its nerves to the spinal nerve-cells, and through them, again, to the brain. We are thus kept endlessly informed as to the existence of parts, because the impressions which reach the brain are, by a law of our being, referred by us to the part from which they come. Now, when the part is cut off, the nerve-trunks which led to it and from it, remaining capable of being impressed by irritations, are made to convey to the brain from the stump impressions which are, as usual, referred by the brain to the lost parts to which these nerve-threads belonged. In other words, the nerve is like a bell-wire. You may pull it at any part of its course, and thus ring the bell as well as if you pulled at the end of the wire; but, in any case, the intelligent servant will refer the pull to the front door, and obey it accordingly. The impressions made on the severed ends of the nerve are due often to changes in the stump during healing, and consequently cease when it has healed, so that finally, in a very healthy stump, no such impressions arise; the brain ceases to correspond with the lost leg, and, as *les absents ont toujours tort*,[50] it is no longer remembered or recognized. But in some cases, such as mine proved at last to my sorrow, the ends of the nerves undergo a curious alteration, and get to be enlarged and altered. This change, as I have seen in my practice of medicine, sometimes passes up the nerves toward the centers, and occasions a more or less constant irritation of the nerve-fibers, producing neuralgia, which is usually referred by the brain to that part of the lost limb to which the affected nerve belonged. This pain keeps the brain ever mindful of the missing part, and, imperfectly at least, preserves to the man a consciousness of possessing that which he has not.

Where the pains come and go, as they do in certain cases, the subjective sensations thus occasioned are very curious, since in such cases the man loses and gains, and loses and regains, the consciousness of the presence of the lost parts, so that he will tell you, "Now I feel my thumb, now I feel my little finger." I should also add that nearly every person who has lost an arm above the elbow feels as though the lost member were bent at the elbow, and at times is vividly impressed with the notion that his fingers are strongly flexed.

Other persons present a peculiarity which I am at a loss to account for. Where the leg, for instance, has been lost, they feel as if the foot were present, but as though the leg were shortened. Thus, if the thigh has been taken off, there seems to them to be a foot at the knee; if the arm, a hand seems to be at the elbow, or attached to the stump itself.

Before leaving Nashville I had begun to suffer the most acute pain in my left hand, especially the little finger; and so perfect was the idea which was thus kept up of the real presence of these missing parts that I found it hard at times to believe them absent. Often at night I would try with one lost hand to grope for the other. As, however, I had no pain in the right arm, the sense of the existence of that limb gradually disappeared, as did that of my legs also.

Everything was done for my neuralgia which the doctors could think of; and at length, at my suggestion, I was removed, as I have said, from the Stump Hospital to the United States Army Hospital for Injuries and Diseases of the Nervous System. It was a pleasant, suburban, old-fashioned country-seat, its gardens surrounded by a circle of wooden, one-story wards, shaded by fine trees. There were some three hundred cases of epilepsy, paralysis, St. Vitus's dance, and wounds of nerves. On one side of me lay a poor fellow, a Dane, who had the same burning neuralgia with which I once suffered, and which I now learned was only too common. This man had become hysterical from pain. He carried a sponge in his pocket, and a bottle of water in one hand, with which he constantly wetted the burning hand. Every sound increased his torture, and he even poured water into his boots to keep himself from feeling too sensibly the rough friction of his soles when walking. Like him, I was greatly eased by having small doses of morphia injected under the skin of my shoulder with a hollow needle fitted to a syringe.

As I improved under the morphia treatment, I began to be disturbed by the horrible variety of suffering about me. One man walked sideways; there was one who could not smell; another was dumb from an explosion. In fact, every one had his own abnormal peculiarity. Near me was a strange case of palsy of the muscles called rhomboids, whose office it is to hold down the shoulder-blades flat on the back during the motions of the arms, which, in themselves, were strong enough. When, however, he lifted these members, the shoulder-blades stood out from the back like wings, and got him the sobriquet of the "Angel." In my ward were also the cases of fits, which very much annoyed me, as upon any great change in the weather it was common to have a dozen convulsions in view at once. Dr. Neek, one of our physicians, told me that on one occasion a hundred and fifty fits took place within thirty-six hours. On my complaining of these sights, whence I alone could not fly, I was placed in the paralytic and wound ward, which I found much more pleasant.

A month of skilful treatment eased me entirely of my aches, and I then began to experience certain curious feelings, upon which, having nothing to do and nothing to do anything with, I reflected a good deal. It was a good while before I could correctly explain to my own satisfaction the phenomena which at this time I was called upon to observe. By the various operations already described I had lost about four fifths of my weight. As a consequence of this I ate much less than usual, and could scarcely have consumed the ration of a soldier. I slept also but little; for, as sleep is the repose of the brain, made necessary by the waste of its tissues during thought and voluntary movement, and as this latter did not exist in my case, I needed only that rest which was necessary to repair such exhaustion of the nerve-centers as was induced by thinking and the automatic movements of the viscera.

I observed at this time also that my heart, in place of beating, as it once did, seventy-eight in the minute, pulsated only forty-five times in this interval—a fact to be easily explained by the perfect quiescence to which I was reduced, and the consequent absence of that healthy and constant stimulus to the muscles of the heart which exercise occasions.

Notwithstanding these drawbacks, my physical health was good, which, I confess, surprised me, for this among other reasons: It is said that a burn of two thirds of the surface destroys life, because then all the excretory matters which this portion of the glands of the skin evolved are thrown upon the blood, and poison the man, just as happens in an animal whose skin the physiologist has varnished, so as in this way to destroy its function. Yet here was I, having lost at least a third of my skin, and apparently none the worse for it.

Still more remarkable, however, were the psychical changes which I now began to perceive. I found to my horror that at times I was less conscious of myself, of my own existence, than used to be the case. This sensation was so novel that at first it quite bewildered me. I felt like asking some one constantly if I were really George Dedlow or not; but, well aware how absurd I should seem after such a question, I refrained from speaking of my case, and strove more keenly to analyze my feelings. At times the conviction of my want of being myself was overwhelming and most painful. It was, as well as I can describe it, a deficiency in the egoistic sentiment of individuality. About one half of the sensitive surface of my skin was gone, and thus much of relation to the outer world destroyed. As a consequence, a large part of the receptive central organs must be out of employ, and, like other idle things, degenerating rapidly. Moreover, all the great central ganglia, which give rise to movements in the limbs, were also eternally at rest. Thus one half of me was absent or functionally dead. This set me to thinking how much a man might lose and yet live. If I were unhappy enough to survive, I might part with my spleen at least, as many a dog has done, and grow fat afterwards. The other organs with which we breathe and circulate the blood would be essential; so also would the liver; but at least half of the intestines might be dispensed with, and of course all of the limbs. And as to the nervous system, the only parts really necessary to life are a few small ganglia. Were the rest absent or inactive, we should have a man reduced, as it were, to the lowest terms, and leading an almost vegetative existence. Would such a being, I asked myself, possess the sense of individuality in its usual completeness, even if his organs of sensation remained, and he were capable of consciousness? Of course, without them, he could not have it any more than a dahlia or a tulip. But with them—how then? I concluded that it would be at a minimum, and that, if utter loss of relation to the outer world were capable of destroying a man's consciousness of himself, the destruction of half of his sensitive surfaces might well occasion, in a less degree, a like result, and so diminish his sense of individual existence.

I thus reached the conclusion that a man is not his brain, or any one part of it, but all of his economy, and that to lose any part must lessen this sense of his own existence. I found but one person who properly appreciated this great truth. She was a New England lady, from Hartford—an agent, I think, for some commission, perhaps the Sanitary. After I had told her my views and feelings, she said: "Yes, I comprehend. The fractional entities of vitality are embraced in the oneness of the unitary Ego. Life," she added, "is the garnered condensation of objective impressions; and as the objective is the remote father of the subjective, so must individuality, which is but focused subjectivity, suffer and fade when the sensation lenses, by which the rays of impression are condensed, become destroyed." I am not quite clear that I fully understood her, but I think she appreciated my ideas, and I felt grateful for her kindly interest.

The strange want I have spoken of now haunted and perplexed me so constantly that I became moody and wretched. While in this state, a man from a neighboring ward fell one morning into conversation with the chaplain, within ear-shot of my chair. Some of their words arrested my attention, and I turned my head to see and listen. The speaker, who wore a sergeant's chevron and carried one arm in a sling, was a tall, loosely made person, with a pale face, light eyes of a washed-out blue tint, and very sparse yellow whiskers. His mouth was weak, both lips being almost alike, so that the organ might have been turned upside down without affecting its expression. His forehead, however, was high and thinly covered with sandy hair. I should have said, as a phrenologist, will feeble; emotional, but not passionate; likely to be an enthusiast or a weakly bigot.

I caught enough of what passed to make me call to the sergeant when the chaplain left him.

"Good morning," said he. "How do you get on?"

"Not at all," I replied. "Where were you hit?"

"Oh, at Chancellorsville. I was shot in the shoulder. I have what the doctors call paralysis of the median nerve, but I guess Dr. Neek and the lightnin' battery will fix it. When my time's out I'll go back to Kearsarge and try on the school-teaching again. I've done my share."

"Well," said I, "you're better off than I."

"Yes," he answered, "in more ways than one. I belong to the New Church. It's a great comfort for a plain man like me, when he's weary and sick, to be able to turn away from earthly things and hold converse daily with the great and good who have left this here world. We have a circle in Coates Street. If it wa'n't for the consoling I get there, I'd of wished myself dead many a time. I ain't got kith or kin on earth; but this matters little, when one can just talk to them daily and know that they are in the spheres above us."

"It must be a great comfort," I replied, "if only one could believe it."

"Believe!" he repeated. "How can you help it? Do you suppose anything dies?"

"No," I said. "The soul does not, I am sure; and as to matter, it merely changes form."

"But why, then," said he, "should not the dead soul talk to the living? In space, no doubt, exist all forms of matter, merely in finer, more ethereal being. You can't suppose a naked soul moving about without a bodily garment—no creed teaches that; and if its new clothing be of like substance to ours, only of ethereal fineness, — a more delicate recrystallization about the eternal spiritual nucleus, must it not then possess powers as much more delicate and refined as is the new material in which it is reclad?"

"Not very clear," I answered; "but, after all, the thing should be susceptible of some form of proof to our present senses."

"And so it is," said he. "Come to-morrow with me, and you shall see and hear for yourself."

"I will," said I, "if the doctor will lend me the ambulance."

It was so arranged, as the surgeon in charge was kind enough, as usual, to oblige me with the loan of his wagon, and two orderlies to lift my useless trunk.

On the day following I found myself, with my new comrade, in a house in Coates Street, where a "circle" was in the daily habit of meeting. So soon as I had been comfortably deposited in an armchair, beside a large pine table, the rest of those assembled seated themselves, and for some time preserved an unbroken silence. During this pause I scrutinized the persons present. Next to me, on my right, sat a flabby man, with ill-marked, baggy features and injected eyes. He was, as I learned afterwards, an eclectic doctor, who had tried his hand at medicine and several of its quackish variations, finally settling down on eclecticism, which I believe professes to be to scientific medicine what vegetarianism is to common-sense, every-day dietetics. Next to him sat a female—authoress, I think, of two somewhat feeble novels, and much pleasanter to look at than her books. She was, I thought, a good deal excited at the prospect of spiritual revelations. Her neighbor was a pallid, care-worn young woman, with very red lips, and large brown eyes of great beauty. She was, as I learned afterwards, a magnetic patient of the doctor, and had deserted her husband, a master mechanic, to follow this new light. The others were, like myself, strangers brought hither by mere curiosity. One of them was a lady in deep black, closely veiled. Beyond her, and opposite to me, sat the sergeant, and next to him the medium, a man named Brink. He wore a good deal of jewelry, and had large black side-whiskers—a shrewd-visaged, large-nosed, full-lipped man, formed by nature to appreciate the pleasant things of sensual existence.

Before I had ended my survey, he turned to the lady in black, and asked if she wished to see any one in the spirit-world.

She said, "Yes," rather feebly.

"Is the spirit present?" he asked. Upon which two knocks were heard in affirmation. "Ah!" said the medium, "the name is—it is the name of a child. It is a male child. It is—"

"Alfred!" she cried. "Great Heaven! My child! My boy!"

On this the medium arose, and became strangely convulsed. "I see," he said — "I see—a fair-haired boy. I see blue eyes—I see above you, beyond you—" at the same time pointing fixedly over her head.

She turned with a wild start. "Where—whereabouts?"

"A blue-eyed boy," he continued, "over your head. He cries—he says, 'Mama, mama!' "

The effect of this on the woman was unpleasant. She stared about her for a moment, and exclaiming, "I come—I am coming, Alfy!" fell in hysterics on the floor.

Two or three persons raised her, and aided her into an adjoining room; but the rest remained at the table, as though well accustomed to like scenes.

After this several of the strangers were called upon to write the names of the dead with whom they wished to communicate. The names were spelled out by the agency of affirmative knocks when the correct letters were touched by the applicant, who was furnished with an alphabet-card upon which he tapped the letters in turn, the medium, meanwhile, scanning his face very keenly. With some, the names were readily made out. With one, a stolid personage of disbelieving type, every attempt failed, until at last the spirits signified by knocks that he was a disturbing agency, and that while he remained all our efforts would fail. Upon this some of the company proposed that he should leave, of which invitation he took advantage, with a skeptical sneer at the whole performance.

As he left us, the sergeant leaned over and whispered to the medium, who next addressed himself to me. "Sister Euphemia," he said, indicating the lady with large eyes, "will act as your medium. I am unable to do more. These things exhaust my nervous system."

"Sister Euphemia," said the doctor, "will aid us. Think, if you please, sir, of a spirit, and she will endeavor to summon it to our circle."

Upon this a wild idea came into my head. I answered: "I am thinking as you directed me to do."

The medium sat with her arms folded, looking steadily at the center of the table. For a few moments there was silence. Then a series of irregular knocks began. "Are you present?" said the medium.

The affirmative raps were twice given.

"I should think," said the doctor, "that there were two spirits present."

His words sent a thrill through my heart. "Are there two?" he questioned.

A double rap.

"Yes, two," said the medium. "Will it please the spirits to make us conscious of their names in this world?"

A single knock. " No."

"Will it please them to say how they are called in the world of spirits?"

Again came the irregular raps—3, 4, 8, 6; then a pause, and 3, 4, 8, 7.

"I think," said the authoress, "they must be numbers. Will the spirits," she said, "be good enough to aid us? Shall we use the alphabet?"

"Yes," was rapped very quickly.

"Are these numbers?"

"Yes," again.

"I will write them," she added, and, doing so, took up the card and tapped the letters. The spelling was pretty rapid, and ran thus as she tapped, in turn, first the letters, and last the numbers she had already set down:

"UNITED STATES ARMY MEDICAL MUSEUM, Nos. 3486, 3487."[51]

The medium looked up with a puzzled expression.

"Good gracious!" said I, "they are *my legs—my legs!*"

What followed, I ask no one to believe except those who, like myself, have communed with the things of another sphere. Suddenly I felt a strange return of my self-consciousness. I was reindividualized, so to speak. A strange wonder filled me, and, to the amazement of every one, I arose, and, staggering a little, walked across the room on limbs invisible to them or me. It was no wonder I staggered, for, as I briefly reflected, my legs had been nine months in the strongest alcohol. At this instant all my new friends crowded around me in astonishment. Presently, however, I felt myself sinking slowly. My legs were going, and in a moment I was resting feebly on my two stumps upon the floor. It was too much. All that was left of me fainted and rolled over senseless.

I have little to add. I am now at home in the West, surrounded by every form of kindness and every possible comfort; but alas! I have so little surety of being myself that I doubt my own honesty in drawing my pension, and feel absolved from gratitude to those who are kind to a being who is uncertain of being enough of himself to be conscientiously responsible. It is needless to add that I am not a happy fraction of a man, and that I am eager for the day when I shall rejoin the lost members of my corporeal family in another and a happier world.

Loreta J. Velazquez, from *The Woman in Battle* (1876)

Like Sarah Edmonds's *Nurse and Spy*, Velazquez's *The Woman in Battle* is a rollicking narrative of cross-dressing during wartime. It is presented as the authentic memoir of a Cuban-born Southern loyalist, but suspicions of its fictionality arose from the beginning and have never been dispelled. Velazquez, claiming that she posed as Lt. Harry T. Buford of the Confederate Army, recounts a dizzying series of adventures ranging from her family's upheaval during the Mexican–American war, through the major events of the Civil War, to her postwar prospecting in the American West. Along the way Velazquez fights at Shiloh, runs blockades, carries messages behind enemy lines, switches costumes as the occasion requires, and, amidst everything, acquires four husbands. Published one year before the formal end of Reconstruction, as the South was struggling to rebuild itself, *The Woman in Battle* is dedicated "to my comrades of the Confederate armies, who, although they fought in a losing cause, succeeded by their valor in winning the admiration of the world." Yet in its flamboyant treatment of gender confusion, racial border-crossing, and renegade sexual energies, Velazquez's narrative implicitly calls into question the stability of white male Southern identity.

Chapter 10 – First Experiences as a Spy

Of too restless and impulsive a disposition to endure patiently the prolonged inaction which seemed inevitable after a battle, it fretted me to be obliged to lounge about camp, or to participate in the too often most demoralizing amusements of the city, as I had been compelled to do for many weeks after the fight at Bull Run. I was disgusted, too, at the difficulties which presented themselves at every step whenever I attempted to get myself attached to a regular command, or to be assigned for the kind of service which I felt best qualified to perform, and which was most in accordance with my tastes. It was an absolute necessity for me to be in motion, to be doing something, and the slow and inconclusive progress of the military movements annoyed me beyond expression. The inevitable reaction, after the intense excitements of the battle of Ball's Bluff, caused a depression of spirits which I felt I must do something to shake off. The terrible sights and sounds of that battle haunted me night and day, for I could not help thinking of them, and the more I thought of them the more horrible they appeared.

I determined, therefore, very shortly after the battle, to put into execution a project I had for some time been meditating, which would require the exercise of all my faculties, and which would give me constant employment for mind and body, such as the routine of camp life did not afford, and which would compel me to concentrate my mind on the invention and execution of plans for the achievement of definite results for the cause of Southern independence.

Before entering upon the career of a soldier, I of course knew a great deal about military life, having been the wife of an army officer,[52] and having resided at frontier stations, but I had nevertheless very crude and superficial notions about the exigencies of warfare. My ideas, however, were no cruder than those of thousands of others, for it is very doubtful whether any but a few veterans understood what would have to be gone through with by soldiers in the field, especially when large armies were operating against each other over an immense stretch of country.

The books I had read, in which the doings of heroes and heroines were recorded, devoted a large space to the description of battles, and these, as a matter of course, being more interesting and exciting than the other portions, it was only natural, perhaps, that the notion should become fixed in my mind that fighting was a soldier's chief, if not only employment.

Romance and Reality

I was soon disillusioned on these points, and, after a very brief experience, discovered that actual warfare was far different from what I had supposed it would be. Neither of the battles in which I had thus far been engaged impressed me at all as I had expected they would, although, in some particulars, they were agreeable disappointments; for there was an exhilaration in an actual, hotly-contested fight that far surpassed anything my imagination had pictured. Battles, however, I found were likely to be few and far between, while there were thousands of disagreeable incidents connected with military life which I had never suspected, and of which my husband's warnings had scarcely given me the slightest hint. The inaction of the camp, when one is day after day hoping and half expecting something startling will happen, only to be subjected to perpetual disappointment, and the dull round of camp duties, and the trivial devices adopted to kill time, after a very brief period become most oppressive.

Not only did I discover that fighting was not the only, or the most frequent, employment of the soldier, but I soon awakened to the fact that, in a great war, like the one in which I was now taking part, it was not always the men who wore the uniforms and handled the muskets who performed the most efficient services. As there were other things besides fighting to do, so there must be other than soldiers to perform necessary portions of the work, and to aid in advancing the interests of the cause.

Dreams of Delusion

Many of our hopes, anticipations, and aspirations are mere dreams of delusion, which can have no practical fulfilment in this working-day world, and it sometimes costs a pang to dismiss forever a cherished but mistaken idea, and to weave our own web of romance from the parti-colored threads of commonplace reality; it is like parting with a portion of our own being. But, the illusion once dispelled, we are able to step forward more firmly and more resolutely, to act the part which the will of Providence assigns us to play in the great drama of life.

We may regret that the dreams of our youth do not come true, just as we once loved to hope that they would, almost without endeavor on our part; but who shall say that our own life romances, woven out of the tissues of events from day to day, with much labor, doubt, and pain, are not fairer and brighter than any imagination could create? It is good to do one's duty quietly amid the rush of great events, even when the path of duty lies in hidden places, where the gaze of the crowd penetrates not, where applause cannot follow; and one's own satisfaction at duty well and nobly performed, is, after all, the best recompense that can be had.

To be a second Joan of Arc was a mere girlish fancy, which my very first experiences as a soldier dissipated forever; and it did not take me long to discover that I needed no model, but that, to win success in the career I had chosen, I must be simply myself, and not a copy, even in the remotest particular, of anybody else; and that the secret of success consisted in watching the current of events, and in taking advantage of circumstances as they arose.

In a life so novel as that I was now leading, however, it took me some time to become sufficiently informed to be able to do anything effective in the way of shaping my career; I was, of necessity, obliged to go ahead somewhat at random, and to wait and learn, not only what I could do with the best effect, but what there was for me to do. In assuming the garb of a soldier, I had no other idea than to do a soldier's duty: this was my ambition, and I scarcely gave thought to anything else. The experiences of actual warfare, however, soon had the effect of convincing me that a woman like myself, who had a talent for assuming disguises, and who, like me, was possessed of courage, resolution, and energy, backed up by a ready wit, a plausible address, and attractive manners, had it in her power to perform many services of the most vital importance, which it would be impossible for a man to even attempt.

Difficulties in Obtaining Information

The difficulty which our commander experienced in gaining accurate and thoroughly reliable information with regard to the movements of the enemy, the rumors that prevailed of the enormous preparations being made by the Federal government to crush the South, an insatiable desire to see and to hear for myself what was going on within the enemy's lines, all stimulated me to make an attempt, the hazardous character of which I well knew; but, trusting to my woman's wit to see me safely through, I resolved that the attempt should be made.

My plans were tolerably well matured when the battle of Ball's Bluff took place, and I should probably have put them in execution before I did, had it not been for the insatiate desire I had to take part in another fight. After that battle, I more than ever felt the necessity for some constant, active employment, for I chafed under the *ennui* of the camp, and felt irresistibly impelled to be moving about and doing something. I accordingly was not long in resolving that the time had now arrived for me to attempt something more than I had yet done, and for me to effect a *coup* that might either make or mar my fortunes, but that, whatever its result might be, would give me the excitement I craved, and demonstrate my abilities, and my disposition to serve the Confederacy in such a signal manner that it would be impossible for those in authority any longer to ignore me.

A Woman's Advantages and Disadvantages

A woman labors under some disadvantages in an attempt to fight her own way in the world, and at the same time, from the mere fact that she is a woman, she can often do things that a man cannot. I have no hesitation in saying that I wish I had been created a man instead of a woman. This is what is the matter with nearly all the women who go about complaining of the wrongs of our sex. But, being a woman, I was bent on making the best of it; and having for some time now figured successfully in the garments of the other sex, I resolved upon resuming those of my own for a season, for the accomplishment of a purpose I had in my mind. This purpose I felt sure I could accomplish as a woman; and although I had a tolerably good appreciation of the perils I should run, I had confidence in my abilities to see myself through, and the perils attending my enterprise were incentives, rather than otherwise, for me to attempt it.

Having obtained a letter of introduction to General Leonidas Polk,[53] and my transportation papers, – for it was my intention, after making the trip I had immediately in view, to visit the part of the country in which his army was operating, as it was more familiar to me, and I thought that I could perform more efficient service there than in Virginia, – I turned in my camp equipage to the quartermaster, and bidding farewell to my friends, started off in search of new adventures.

Stopping in Leesburg, I went, in company with a couple of other officers, to pay a visit to Mrs. Tyree, a brave and true-hearted Virginia lady, who, with her interesting family, had suffered greatly through the devastation of her property by the enemy. We tried, by every argument we could imagine, to persuade her to remove to some safer locality, representing that the Federals, though defeated at Ball's Bluff, were likely to repeat the attack at any time, and to march on Leesburg with a large force. Our appeals were in vain, however, and she answered every argument, by saying, "This is my home, and I will perish in it, if necessary." I heartily wished that I had a force of soldiers under my command at the moment, so that I could compel her to remove for her own sake and that of her family; and when I said adieu to her, it was with the sincerest admiration for her inflexible courage and her devotion to the cause of the South.

The Way to Keep a Secret

Leaving my boy where he would be taken care of, I stated to my acquaintances that I intended to make a journey, and that I expected to be gone about ten days, but did not tell any one where I was going, or what my plans were. No one but myself had the slightest notion as to what project I had on foot, for I felt that success would very largely depend upon my secret being kept to myself, at least until I had accomplished, or had tried to accomplish, what I proposed. What I dreaded more than any dangers I was likely to be exposed to was the ridicule that would probably meet me in case of failure, to say nothing of the probabilities in favor of my sex being discovered, or at least suspected. But ridicule, as well as danger, was what I resolved to brave when putting on male attire, and I really dreaded it less than I did my own heart-burnings in the event of my not winning the desperate game I was playing. The way to keep a secret, as I had long since found out, is not to tell it to anybody; and acting upon this very excellent principle, I have generally succeeded in keeping my secrets – and I have, in my time, had some important ones – until the proper moment for revealing them came. Some people are never happy when possessed of a secret until they have told it to somebody else, of course in the strictest confidence. My experience is that this is a sure way to get the matter, whatever it may be, put into circulation as a bit of general information.

Assuming a New Disguise

It was necessary, however, for me to have some assistance in getting my enterprise started, just as it had been for me to select a confidant when I first assumed the uniform of an officer; and I would say here that, to the infinite honor of the friend whose aid I sought on that occasion, the secret of my transformation was as faithfully kept as if it were his own; but, as the circumstances were different, a different kind of an agent was in this case selected. My appeal, this time, was to the strongest sentiments of self-interest, and even then my confidant was only intrusted with the knowledge of a change of apparel.

Going to an old negro woman who had washed for me, and who had shown considerable fondness for me, I told her that I intended visiting the Yankees for the purpose of seeing them about coming and freeing the colored folk, and asked her to let me have a suit of woman's clothes, so that I could get through the lines without being stopped. I made up quite a long yarn about what I proposed to do, and the poor old soul, believing all I told her without a moment's hesitation, consented to aid me in every way she could, her ardor being materially quickened by a twenty dollar Confederate note which I handed her.

She was not long in having me attired in the best she had, – a calico dress, a woollen shawl, a sun-bonnet, and a pair of shoes much too large for me, – and hiding away my uniform where it would be safe during my absence, she started me off with a full expectation that I would be back in a couple of weeks, with the whole Yankee army at my back, for the purpose of liberating all the slaves. The old woman put such implicit faith in me that I really felt sorry at deceiving her, but quieted my conscience with the thought that lying was as necessary as fighting in warfare, and that the prospects were that I would be compelled to do much more fibbing than this before the errand upon which I was about starting would be achieved.

Crossing the Potomac

Managing to make my way to the river without attracting any particular attention, I found an old negro who had a boat, and making up a story that I fancied would answer the purpose, I struck a bargain with him to take me across to the Maryland shore for twenty-five dollars. He was eager to get the money, probably never having handled so much before in his life at any one time, but warned me that it would be a risky piece of business, for the weather was very cold, the river broad and deep, and the current strong, and there was considerable danger of my being fired at by the pickets on either bank. I told him that I was not afraid to take all the risks, and that I thought I could stand the cold. I accordingly concealed myself in his cabin until the time for commencing the crossing arrived, neither of us deeming it prudent to start before midnight.

It was after midnight before we were launched in our little craft on the black, swift-running water of the Potomac, and it was quite three hours before we reached the opposite shore. My old ferryman pulled lustily, but it was hard work for him, although the handsome fee he was to receive when his task was accomplished was a decided stimulant. He really had the best of it, however, in having some work to do, for the night air was bitter cold, and I was thinly clad. I would have been glad to have taken a turn at the oars, just for the sake of warming myself, had I believed myself possessed of the physical strength to wield them with efficiency. I was too eager to get over this unpleasant and hazardous part of my journey, however, to incur any delay by attempting to pull an oar, and bore the sharp winds that swept over the water, and at times seemed to cut me to the bones, with what equanimity I could command.

At length we reached the Maryland side of the river, to my infinite satisfaction, for I was numb with the cold, and stiff in all my limbs, from the cramped position in which I had been obliged to sit in the boat, and was heartily glad of an opportunity to tread dry land once more. Dismissing the boatman, and enjoining him not to say anything, I made my way to a farm-house which I espied a short distance from the place of landing, and about four o'clock in the morning, finding no better place to rest my weary limbs, I crept into a wheat-stack, and slept there until daylight.

I scarcely know whether to say that I enjoyed this sort of thing or not. For a thinly clad woman to find no better place for repose during a chilly night in the latter part of October, after having endured the cutting blasts for three hours while crossing the Potomac in an open boat, was certainly hard lines. It is true that, for some months, I had accustomed myself to tolerably rough living, but this was a trifle rougher than anything I had as yet experienced. As there was no one but myself to applaud my heroism, this particular episode did not, and could not, have the same attraction that some even more perilous ones had; and yet, despite the discomforts of the situation, I had a certain amount of satisfaction, and even of pleasure, in going through with it. My enjoyment – if I can designate my peculiar emotions by such a word – I can only attribute to my insatiable love for adventure; to the same overmastering desire to do difficult, dangerous, and exciting things, and to accomplish hazardous enterprises, that had induced me to assume the dress of the other sex, and to figure as a soldier on the battle-field.

When I crept into that wheat-stack, however, I was not in a mood to indulge in any philosophical reflections on the situation, or on my own motives or feelings; I was simply in search of a reasonably sheltered place where I could repose until morning; and having found one, I was not long in closing my eyes, and lapsing into temporary oblivion of the cares and trials of this wicked world.

I managed to get a nap of a couple of hours' duration, when I was awakened by the increasing light, and by the noises of the farm-yard. Adjusting my clothing as well as I could, and shaking off the straw that clung to me, I approached the house, a little dubious with regard to the kind of reception I should get, but trusting to luck to be able to obtain what I wanted. A man came out to meet me, and looked rather sullenly at me, as if he thought me a suspicious character, whom it would be well to have cautious dealings with. My appearance was such that there was certainly good cause for his distrust. The old colored woman's calico dress, woollen shawl, sun-bonnet, and shoes did not come near fitting me, while my slumbers in the wheat-stack had not tended to make me a particularly attractive object. I had no difficulty in believing that I was a perfect fright, and was amused, rather than displeased, at the rather discourteous reception I met with.

Plucking up courage, however, I advanced, and told him that I had been driven out of Virginia, and was trying to get back to my people in Tennessee. I did not give any hint of my political predilections, thinking it more prudent to find how he and his folk stood first. I then asked him if I could not go into the house and warm myself, and get some breakfast, as I was both cold and hungry, and I suppose must have looked so pitiable that he felt compelled to grant my request, if only for charity's sake. He accordingly invited me into the dining-room, and called his wife.

When the woman came, I told a long rigmarole, taking pains to show that I had some money, with which I could, if necessary, pay for what I ate and drank. My story, I saw plainly, did not take very well, and the man was evidently afraid to say much. The woman, however, soon let out on the Yankees with such fiery energy that I understood at once how matters stood, and consequently began to feel more at my ease.

I now began to embellish my story with plenty of abuse of the Yankees, and with such details of the sufferings I had endured on account of my having sided with the South, that their sympathies were at once aroused, and I felt certain that I could easily get all the assistance from them that I wished. Both of them – but the man especially – were eager to know all about the battle. I had told them that I had just come from the neighborhood of Leesburg, and I accordingly gave them an account of the affair, dilating particularly upon the magnificent manner in which the Confederates had whipped the Yankees, and prophesying that, with a little more of this kind of fighting, there would soon be an end of the war.

The woman now invited me to a nice, warm breakfast, which I enjoyed immensely, for I was desperately hungry after my night's adventure. During the meal I showed them a letter, written by myself, for use in such an emergency as this, which, of course, tended to confirm the story I told, and treated them to the style of conversation they evidently liked to hear. After breakfast was over, the woman, taking pity upon my mean attire, insisted upon dressing me in some of her own clothing. I was soon, there-fore, in a somewhat more presentable condition than I had been, and, having obtained such information as they were able to give in regard to the best method of proceeding in order speedily to reach my destination, I bade them good-by, sincerely grateful for their kindness, and started for Washington, where I hoped to be able to pick up some useful bits of information, – in fact, to make what the soldiers would call, a reconnoissance in force.

Samuel R. Watkins, from *Co. Aytch* (1882)

In its humor, verve, and self-deprecation, Watkins's *Co. Aytch* stands out from the enor-mous crop of veterans' memoirs published in the decades after the Civil War. His account here of the bloodbath at Shiloh, which the Confederates just barely lost, and which heralded more bloodbaths to come, conveys some of the horror of the battle, but it also bears the stamp of bemused reminiscence.

Chapter 2: Shiloh

This was the first big battle in which our regiment had ever been engaged. I do not pretend to tell of what command distinguished itself; of heroes; of blood and wounds; of shrieks and groans; of brilliant charges; of cannon captured, etc. I was but a private soldier, and if I happened to look to see if I could find out anything, "Eyes right, guide center," was the order. "Close up, guide right, halt, forward, right oblique, left oblique, halt, forward, guide center, eyes right, dress up promptly in the rear, steady, double quick, charge bayonets, fire at will," is about all that a private soldier ever knows of a battle. He can see the smoke rise and the flash of the enemy's guns, and he can hear the whistle of the minnie and cannon balls, but he has got to load and shoot as hard as he can tear and ram cartridge, or he will soon find out, like the Irishman who had been shooting blank cartridges, when a ball happened to strike him, and he hallooed out, "Faith, Pat, and be jabbers, them fellows are shooting bullets." But I nevertheless remember many things that came under my observation in this battle. I remember a man by the name of Smith stepping deliberately out of the ranks and shooting his finger off to keep out of the fight; of another poor fellow who was accidentally shot and killed by the discharge of another person's gun, and of others suddenly taken sick with colic.

Our regiment was the advance guard on Saturday evening, and did a little skirmishing; but General Gladden's brigade passed us and assumed a position in our immediate front. About daylight on Sunday morning, Chalmers' brigade relieved Gladden's. As Gladden rode by us, a courier rode up and told him something. I do not know what it was, but I heard Gladden say, "Tell General Bragg that I have as keen a scent for Yankees as General Chalmers has."[54]

On Sunday morning, a clear, beautiful, and still day, the order was given for the whole army to advance, and to attack immediately.[55] We were supporting an Alabama brigade. The fire opened—bang, bang, bang, a rattle de bang, bang, bang, a boom, de bang, bang, bang, boom, bang, boom, bang, boom, bang, boom, bang, boom, whirr-siz-siz-siz—a ripping, roaring boom, bang! The air was full of balls and deadly missiles. The litter corps was carrying off the dying and wounded. We could hear the shout of the charge and the incessant roar of the guns, the rattle of the musketry, and knew that the contending forces were engaged in a breast to breast struggle. But cheering news continued to come back. Every one who passed would be hailed with, "Well, what news from the front?" "Well, boys, we are driving 'em. We have captured all their encampments, everything that they had, and all their provisions and army stores, and everything."

As we were advancing to the attack and to support the Alabama brigade in our front, and which had given way and were stricken with fear, some of the boys of our regiment would laugh at them, and ask what they were running for, and would commence to say "Flicker! flicker! flicker!" like the bird called the yellowhammer, "Flicker! flicker! flicker!" As we advanced, on the edge of the battlefield, we saw a big fat colonel of the 23rd Tennessee regiment badly wounded, whose name, if I remember correctly, was Matt. Martin. He said to us, "Give 'em goss, boys. That's right, my brave First Tennessee. Give 'em Hail Columbia!" We halted but a moment, and said I, "Colonel, where are you wounded?" He answered in a deep bass voice, "My son, I am wounded in the arm, in the leg, in the head, in the body, and in another place which I have a delicacy in mentioning." That is what the gallant old colonel said. Advancing a little further on, we saw General Albert Sidney Johnson[56] surrounded by his staff and Governor Harris,[57] of Tennessee. We saw some little commotion among those who surrounded him, but we did not know at the time that he was dead. The fact was kept from the troops.

About noon a courier dashed up and ordered us to go forward and support General Bragg's center. We had to pass over the ground where troops had been fighting all day.

I had heard and read of battlefields, seen pictures of battlefields, of horses and men, of cannon and wagons, all jumbled together, while the ground was strewn with dead and dying and wounded, but I must confess that I never realized the "pomp and circumstance" of the thing called glorious war until I saw this. Men were lying in every conceivable position; the dead lying with their eyes wide open, the wounded begging piteously for help, and some waving their hats and shouting to us to go forward. It all seemed to me a dream; I seemed to be in a sort of haze, when siz, siz, siz, the minnie balls from the Yankee line began to whistle around our ears, and I thought of the Irishman when he said, "Sure enough, those fellows are shooting bullets!"

Down would drop first one fellow and then another, either killed or wounded, when we were ordered to charge bayonets. I had been feeling mean all the morning as if I had stolen a sheep, but when the order to charge was given, I got happy. I felt happier than a fellow does when he professes religion at a big Methodist camp-meeting. I shouted. It was fun then. Everybody looked happy. We were crowding them. One more charge, then their lines waver and break. They retreat in wild confusion. We were jubilant; we were triumphant. Officers could not curb the men to keep in line. Discharge after discharge was poured into the retreating line. The Federal dead and wounded covered the ground.

When in the very midst of our victory, here comes an order to halt. What! halt after to-day's victory? Sidney Johnson killed, General Gladden killed, and a host of generals and other brave men killed, and the whole Yankee army in full retreat.

These four letters, h-a-l-t, O, how harsh they did break upon our ears. The victory was complete, but the word "halt" turned victory into defeat.

The soldiers had passed through the Yankee camps and saw all the good things that they had to eat in their sutlers' stores and officers' marquees, and it was but a short time before every soldier was rummaging to see what he could find.

The harvest was great and the laborers were not few.

The negro boys, who were with their young masters as servants, got rich. Greenbacks were plentiful, good clothes were plentiful, rations were not in demand. The boys were in clover.

This was Sunday.

On Monday the tide was reversed.

Now, those Yankees were whipped, fairly whipped, and according to all the rules of war they ought to have retreated. But they didn't. Flushed with their victories at Fort Henry and Fort Donelson and the capture of Nashville, and the whole State of Tennessee having fallen into their hands, victory was again to perch upon their banners, for Buell's army, by forced marches, had come to Grant's assistance at the eleventh hour.[58]

Gunboats and transports were busily crossing Buell's army all of Sunday night. We could hear their boats ringing their bells, and hear the puff of smoke and steam from their boilers. Our regiment was the advance outpost, and we saw the skirmish line of the Federals advancing and then their main line and then their artillery. We made a good fight on Monday morning, and I was taken by surprise when the order came for us to retreat instead of advance. But as I said before, reader, a private soldier is but an automaton, and knows nothing of what is going on among the Generals, and I am only giving the chronicles of little things and events that came under my own observation as I saw them then and remember them now. Should you desire to find out more about the battle, I refer you to history.

One incident I recollect very well. A Yankee colonel, riding a fine gray mare, was sitting on his horse looking at our advance as if we were on review. W. H. rushed forward and grabbed his horse by the bridle, telling him at the same time to surrender. The Yankee seized the reins, set himself back in the saddle, put the muzzle of his pistol in W. H.'s face and fired. About the time he pulled trigger, a stray ball from some direction struck him in the side and he fell off dead, and his horse becoming frightened, galloped off, dragging him through the Confederate lines. His pistol had missed its aim.

I have heard hundreds of old soldiers tell of the amount of greenback money they saw and picked up on the battlefield of Shiloh, but they thought it valueless and did not trouble themselves with bringing it off with them.

One fellow, a courier, who had had his horse killed, got on a mule he had captured, and in the last charge, before the final and fatal halt was made, just charged right ahead by his lone self, and the soldiers said, "Just look at that brave man, charging right in the jaws of death." He began to seesaw the mule and grit his teeth, and finally yelled out, "It arn't me, boys, it's this blarsted old mule. Whoa! Whoa!"

On Monday morning I too captured me a mule. He was not a fast mule, and I soon found out that he thought he knew as much as I did. He was wise in his own conceit. He had a propensity to take every hog path he came to. All the bombasting that I could give him would not make him accelerate his speed. If blood makes speed, I do not suppose he had a drop of any kind in him. If I wanted him to go on one side of the road he was sure to be possessed of an equal desire to go on the other side. Finally I and my mule fell out. I got a big hickory and would frail him over the head, and he would only shake his head and flop his ears, and seem to say, "Well, now, you think you are smart, don't you?" He was a resolute mule, slow to anger, and would have made an excellent merchant to refuse bad pay, or I will pay your credit, for his whole composition seemed to be made up of the one word— no. I frequently thought it would be pleasant to split the difference with that mule, and I would gladly have done so if I could have gotten one-half of his no. Me and mule worried along until we came to a creek. Mule did not desire to cross, while I was trying to persuade him with a big stick, a rock in his ear, and a twister on his nose. The caisson of a battery was about to cross. The driver said, "I'll take your mule over for you." So he got a large two-inch rope, tied one end around the mule's neck and the other to the caisson, and ordered the driver to whip up. The mule was loth to take to the water. He was no Baptist, and did not believe in immersion, and had his views about crossing streams, but the rope began to tighten, the mule to squeal out his protestations against such villainous proceedings. The rope, however, was stronger than the mule's "no," and he was finally prevailed upon by the strength of the rope to cross the creek. On my taking the rope off he shook himself and seemed to say, "You think that you are mighty smart folks, but you are a leetle too smart." I gave it up that that mule's "no" was a little stronger than my determination. He seemed to be in deep meditation. I got on him again, when all of a sudden he lifted his head, pricked up his ears, began to champ his bit, gave a little squeal, got a little faster, and finally into a gallop and then a run. He seemed all at once to have remembered or to have forgotten something, and was now making up for lost time. With all my pulling and seesawing and strength I could not stop him until he brought up with me at Corinth, Mississippi.[59]

Ambrose Bierce, from *Tales of Soldiers and Civilians* (1891)

"The Coup de Grâce"

The fighting had been hard and continuous, that was attested by all the senses. The very taste of battle was in the air. All was now over; it remained only to succor the wounded and bury the dead—to "tidy up a bit," as the humorist of a burying squad put it. A good deal of "tidying up" was required. As far as one could see through the forest, between the splintered trees, lay wrecks of men and horses. Among them moved the stretcher-bearers, gathering and carrying away the few who showed signs of life. Most of the wounded had died of exposure while the right to minister to their wants was in dispute. It is an army regulation that the wounded must wait; the best way to care for them is to win the battle. It must be confessed that victory is a distinct advantage to a man requiring attention, but many do not live to avail themselves of it.

The dead were collected in groups of a dozen or a score and laid side by side in rows while the trenches were dug to receive them. Some, found at too great a distance from these rallying points, were buried where they lay. There was little attempt at identification, though in most cases, the burying parties being detailed to glean the same ground which they had assisted to reap, the names of the victorious dead were known and listed. The enemy's fallen had to be content with counting. But of that they got enough: many of them were counted several times, and the total, as given in the official report of the victorious commander, denoted rather a hope than a result.

At some little distance from the spot where one of the burying parties had established its "bivouac of the dead," a man in the uniform of a Federal officer stood leaning against a tree. From his feet upward to his neck his attitude was that of weariness reposing; but he turned his head uneasily from side to side; his mind was apparently not at rest. He was perhaps uncertain in what direction to go; he was not likely to remain long where he was, for already the level rays of the setting sun struggled redly through the open spaces of the wood, and the weary soldiers were quitting their task for the day. He would hardly make a night of it alone there among the dead. Nine men in ten whom you meet after a battle inquire the way to some fraction of the army—as if anyone could know. Doubtless this officer was lost. After resting himself a moment, he would follow one of the retiring burial squads.

When all were gone, he walked straight away into the forest toward the red west, its light staining his face like blood. The air of confidence with which he now strode along showed that he was on familiar ground; he had recovered his bearings. The dead on his right and on his left were unregarded as he passed. An occasional low moan from some sorely-stricken wretch whom the relief parties had not reached, and who would have to pass a comfortless night beneath the stars with his thirst to keep him company, was equally unheeded. What, indeed, could the officer have done, being no surgeon and having no water?

At the head of a shallow ravine, a mere depression of the ground, lay a small group of bodies. He saw, and, swerving suddenly from his course, walked rapidly toward them. Scanning each one sharply as he passed, he stopped at last above one which lay at a slight remove from the others, near a clump of small trees. He looked at it narrowly. It seemed to stir. He stooped and laid his hand upon its face. It screamed.

The officer was Captain Downing Madwell, of a Massachusetts regiment of infantry, a daring and intelligent soldier, an honorable man.

In the regiment were two brothers named Halcrow—Caffal and Creede Halcrow. Caffal Halcrow was a sergeant in Captain Madwell's company, and these two men, the sergeant and the captain, were devoted friends. In so far as disparity of rank, difference in duties, and considerations of military discipline would permit, they were commonly together. They had, indeed, grown up together from childhood. A habit of the heart is not easily broken off. Caffal Halcrow had nothing military in his taste or disposition, but the thought of separation from his friend was disagreeable; he enlisted in the company in which Madwell was second lieutenant. Each had taken two steps upward in rank, but between the highest non-commissioned and the lowest commissioned officer the social gulf is deep and wide, and the old relation was maintained with difficulty and a difference.

Creede Halcrow, the brother of Caffal, was the major of the regiment—a cynical, saturnine man, between whom and Captain Madwell there was a natural antipathy which circumstances had nourished and strengthened to an active animosity. But for the restraining influence of their mutual relation to Caffal, these two patriots would doubtless have endeavored to deprive their country of one another's services.

At the opening of the battle that morning, the regiment was performing outpost duty a mile away from the main army. It was attacked and nearly surrounded in the forest, but stubbornly held its ground. During a lull in the fighting, Major Halcrow came to Captain Madwell. The two exchanged formal salutes, and the major said: "Captain, the colonel directs that you push your company to the head of this ravine and hold your place there until recalled. I need hardly apprise you of the dangerous character of the movement, but if you wish, you can, I suppose, turn over the command to your first lieutenant. I was not, however, directed to authorize the substitution; it is merely a suggestion of my own, unofficially made."

To this deadly insult Captain Madwell coolly replied:—"Sir, I invite you to accompany the movement. A mounted officer would be a conspicuous mark, and I have long held the opinion that it would be better if you were dead."

The art of repartee was cultivated in military circles as early as 1862.

A half hour later Captain Madwell's company was driven from its position at the head of the ravine, with a loss of one-third its number. Among the fallen was Sergeant Halcrow. The regiment was soon afterward forced back to the main line, and at the close of the battle was miles away. The captain was now standing at the side of his subordinate and friend.

Sergeant Halcrow was mortally hurt. His clothing was deranged; it seemed to have been violently torn apart, exposing the abdomen. Some of the buttons of his jacket had been pulled off and lay on the ground beside him, and fragments of his other garments were strewn about. His leather belt was parted, and had apparently been dragged from beneath him as he lay. There had been no very great effusion of blood. The only visible wound was a wide, ragged opening in the abdomen. It was defiled with earth and dead leaves. Protruding from it was a lacerated end of the small intestine. In all his experience Captain Madwell had not seen a wound like this. He could neither conjecture how it was made nor explain the attendant circumstances—the strangely torn clothing, the parted belt, the besmirching of the white skin. He knelt and made a closer examination. When he rose to his feet, he turned his eyes in various directions as if looking for an enemy. Fifty yards away, on the crest of a low, thinly-wooded hill, he saw several dark objects moving about among the fallen men—a herd of swine. One stood with its back to him, its shoulders sharply elevated. Its forefeet were upon a human body, its head was depressed and invisible. The bristly ridge of its chine showed black against the red west. Captain Madwell drew away his eyes and fixed them again upon the thing which had been his friend.

The man who had suffered these monstrous mutilations was alive. At intervals he moved his limbs; he moaned at every breath. He stared blankly into the face of his friend, and if touched screamed. In his giant agony he had torn up the ground on which he lay; his clenched hands were full of leaves and twigs and earth. Articulate speech was, beyond his power; it was impossible to know if he were sensible to anything but pain. The expression of his face was an appeal; his eyes were full of prayer. For what?

There was no misreading that look; the captain had too frequently seen it in eyes of those whose lips had still the power to formulate it by an entreaty for death. Consciously or unconsciously, this writhing fragment of humanity, this type and example of acute sensation, this handiwork of man and beast, this humble, unheroic Prometheus, was imploring everything, all, the whole non-*ego*, for the boon of oblivion. To the earth and the sky alike, to the trees, to the man, to whatever took form in sense or consciousness, this incarnate suffering addressed its silent plea.

For what, indeed?—For that which we accord to even the meanest creature without sense to demand it, denying it only to the wretched of our own race: for the blessed release, the rite of uttermost compassion, the *coup de grâce*.

Captain Madwell spoke the name of his friend. He repeated it over and over without effect until emotion choked his utterance. His tears plashed upon the livid face beneath his own and blinded himself. He saw nothing but a blurred and moving object, but the moans were more distinct than ever, interrupted at briefer intervals by sharper shrieks. He turned away, struck his hand upon his forehead, and strode from the spot. The swine, catching sight of him, threw up their crimson muzzles, regarding him suspiciously a second, and then, with a gruff, concerted grunt, raced away out of sight. A horse, its fore-leg splintered horribly by a cannon shot, lifted its head sidewise from the ground and neighed piteously. Madwell stepped forward, drew his revolver and shot the poor beast between the eyes, narrowly observing its death struggle, which, contrary to his expectation, was violent and long; but at last it lay still. The tense muscles of its lips, which had uncovered the teeth in a horrible grin, relaxed; the sharp, clean-cut profile took on a look of profound peace and rest.

Along the distant thinly-wooded crest to westward the fringe of sunset fire had now nearly burned itself out. The light upon the trunks of the trees had faded to a tender gray; the shadows were in their tops, like great dark birds aperch. The night was coming and there were miles of haunted forest between Captain Madwell and camp. Yet he stood there at the side of the dead animal, apparently lost to all sense of his surroundings. His eyes were bent upon the earth at his feet; his left hand hung loosely at his side, his right still held the pistol. Suddenly he lifted his face, turned it toward his dying friend, and walked rapidly back to his side. He knelt upon one knee, cocked the weapon, placed the muzzle against the man's forehead, turned away his eyes and pulled the trigger. There was no report. He had used his last cartridge for the horse. The sufferer moaned and his lips moved convulsively. The froth that ran from them had a tinge of blood.

Captain Madwell rose to his feet and drew his sword from the scabbard. He passed the fingers of his left hand along the edge from hilt to point. He held it out straight before him, as if to test his nerves. There was no visible tremor of the blade; the ray of bleak skylight that it reflected was steady and true. He stooped, and with his left hand tore away the dying man's shirt, rose, and placed the point of the sword just over the heart. This time he did not withdraw his eyes. Grasping the hilt with both hands, he thrust downward with all his strength and weight. The blade sank into the man's body— through his body into the earth; Captain Madwell came near falling forward upon his work. The dying man drew up his knees and at the same time threw his right arm across his breast and grasped the steel so tightly that the knuckles of the hand visibly whitened. By a violent but vain effort to withdraw the blade, the wound was enlarged; a rill of blood escaped, running sinuously down into the deranged clothing. At that moment three men stepped silently forward from behind the clump of young trees which had concealed their approach. Two were hospital attendants and carried a stretcher.

The third was Major Creede Halcrow.

Stephen Crane, "An Episode of War" (1896)

The lieutenant's rubber blanket lay on the ground, and upon it he had poured the company's supply of coffee. Corporals and other representatives of the grimy and hot-throated men who lined the breast-work had come for each squad's portion.

The lieutenant was frowning and serious at this task of division. His lips pursed as he drew with his sword various crevices in the heap until brown squares of coffee, astound-ingly equal in size, appeared on the blanket. He was on the verge of a great triumph in mathematics and the corporals were thronging forward, each to reap a little square, when suddenly the lieutenant cried out and looked quickly at a man near him as if he suspected it was a case of personal assault. The others cried out also when they saw blood upon the lieutenant's sleeve.

He had winced like a man stung, swayed dangerously, and then straightened. The sound of his hoarse breathing was plainly audible. He looked sadly, mystically, over the breast-work at the green face of a wood where now were many little puffs of white smoke. During this moment, the men about him gazed statue-like and silent, astonished and awed by this catastrophe which had happened when catastrophes were not expected—when they had leisure to observe it.

As the lieutenant stared at the wood, they too swung their heads so that for another moment all hands, still silent, contemplated the distant forest as if their minds were fixed upon the mystery of a bullet's journey.

The officer had, of course, been compelled to take his sword at once into his left hand. He did not hold it by the hilt. He gripped it at the middle of the blade, awkwardly. Turning his eyes from the hostile wood, he looked at the sword as he held it there, and seemed puzzled as to what to do with it, where to put it. In short this weapon had of a sudden become a strange thing to him. He looked at it in a kind of stupefaction, as if he had been miraculously endowed with a trident, a sceptre, or a spade.

Finally, he tried to sheath it. To sheath a sword held by the left hand, at the middle of the blade, in a scabbard hung at the left hip, is a feat worthy of a sawdust ring. This wounded officer engaged in a desperate struggle with the sword and the wobbling scabbard, and during the time of it, he breathed like a wrestler.

But at this instant the men, the spectators, awoke from their stone-like poses and crowded forward sympathetically. The orderly-sergeant took the sword and tenderly placed it in the scabbard. At the time, he leaned nervously backward, and did not allow even his finger to brush the body of the lieutenant. A wound gives strange dignity to him who bears it. Well men shy from this new and terrible majesty. It is as if the wounded man's hand is upon the curtain which hangs before the revelations of all existence—the meaning of ants, potentates, wars, cities, sunshine, snow, a feather dropped from a bird's wing; and the power of it sheds radiance upon a bloody form, and makes the other men understand sometimes that they are little. His comrades look at him with large eyes thoughtfully. Moreover, they fear vaguely that the weight of a finger upon him might send him headlong, precipitate the tragedy, hurl him at once into the dim, grey unknown. And so the orderly-sergeant, while sheathing the sword, leaned nervously backward.

There were others who proffered assistance. One timidly presented his shoulder and asked the lieutenant if he cared to lean upon it, but the latter waved them away mournfully. He wore the look of one who knows he is the victim of a terrible disease and understands his helplessness. He again stared over the breast-work at the forest, and then turning went slowly rearward. He held his right wrist tenderly in his left hand, as if the wounded arm was made of very brittle glass.

And the men in silence stared at the wood, then at the departing lieutenant; then at the wood, then at the lieutenant.

As the wounded officer passed from the line of battle, he was enabled to see many things which as a participant in the fight were unknown to him. He saw a general on a black horse gazing over the lines of blue infantry at the green woods which veiled his problems. An aide galloped furiously, dragged his horse suddenly to a halt, saluted, and presented a paper. It was, for a wonder, precisely like a historical painting.

To the rear of the general and his staff, a group, composed of a bugler, two or three orderlies, and the bearer of the corps standard, all upon maniacal horses, were working like slaves to hold their ground, preserve their respectful interval, while the shells bloomed in the air about them, and caused their chargers to make furious quivering leaps.

A battery, a tumultuous and shining mass, was swirling toward the right. The wild thud of hoofs, the cries of the riders shouting blame and praise, menace and encouragement, and, last, the roar of the wheels, the slant of the glistening guns, brought the lieutenant to an intent pause. The battery swept in curves that stirred the heart; it made halts as dramatic as the crash of a wave on the rocks, and when it fled onward, this aggregation of wheels, levers, motors, had a beautiful unity, as if it were a missile. The sound of it was a war-chorus that reached into the depths of man's emotion.

The lieutenant, still holding his arm as if it were of glass, stood watching this battery until all detail of it was lost, save the figures of the riders, which rose and fell and waved lashes over the black mass.

Later, he turned his eyes toward the battle, where the shooting sometimes crackled like bush-fires, sometimes sputtered with exasperating irregularity, and sometimes reverberated like the thunder. He saw the smoke rolling upward and saw crowds of men who ran and cheered, or stood and blazed away at the inscrutable distance.

He came upon some stragglers and they told him how to find the field hospital. They described its exact location. In fact, these men, no longer having part in the battle, knew more of it than others. They told the performance of every corps, every division, the opinion of every general. The lieutenant, carrying his wounded arm rearward, looked upon them with wonder.

At the roadside a brigade was making coffee and buzzing with talk like a girls' boarding-school. Several officers came out to him and inquired concerning things of which he knew nothing. One, seeing his arm, began to scold. "Why, man, that's no way to do. You want to fix that thing." He appropriated the lieutenant and the lieutenant's wound. He cut the sleeve and laid bare the arm, every nerve of which softly fluttered under his touch. He bound his handkerchief over the wound, scolding away in the meantime. His tone allowed one to think that he was in the habit of being wounded every day. The lieutenant hung his head, feeling, in this presence, that he did not know how to be correctly wounded.

The low white tents of the hospital were grouped around an old schoolhouse. There was here a singular commotion. In the foreground two ambulances interlocked wheels in the deep mud. The drivers were tossing the blame of it back and forth, gesticulating and berating, while from the ambulances, both crammed with wounded, there came an occasional groan. An interminable crowd of bandaged men were coming and going. Great numbers sat under the trees nursing heads or arms or legs. There was a dispute of some kind raging on the steps of the school-house. Sitting with his back against a tree a man with a face as grey as a new army blanket was serenely smoking a corn-cob pipe. The lieutenant wished to rush forward and inform him that he was dying.

A busy surgeon was passing near the lieutenant. "Good-morning," he said, with a friendly smile. Then he caught sight of the lieutenant's arm, and his face at once changed. "Well, let's have a look at it." He seemed possessed suddenly of a great contempt for the lieutenant. This wound evidently placed the latter on a very low social plane. The doctor cried out impatiently: "What mutton-head had tied it up that way anyhow." The lieutenant answered: "Oh, a man."

When the wound was disclosed the doctor fingered it disdainfully. "Humph," he said. "You come along with me and I'll 'tend to you." His voice contained the same scorn as if he were saying: "You will have to go to jail."

The lieutenant had been very meek, but now his face flushed, and he looked into the doctor's eyes. "I guess I won't have it amputated," he said.

"Nonsense, man! Nonsense! Nonsense!" cried the doctor. "Come along, now. I won't amputate it. Come along. Don't be a baby."

"Let go of me," said the lieutenant, holding back wrathfully. His glance fixed upon the door of the old schoolhouse, as sinister to him as the portals of death.

And this is the story of how the lieutenant lost his arm. When he reached home, his sisters, his mother, his wife, sobbed for a long time at the sight of the flat sleeve. "Oh, well," he said, standing shamefaced amid these tears, "I don't suppose it matters so much as all that."

Notes

1 Donald Yacovone, ed., *A Voice of Thunder: The Civil War Letters of George E. Stephens* (Urbana: University of Illinois Press, 1997), 214.

2 Shakespeare, *Richard III*, Act V, scene iii, line xxx: "Conscience avaunt, Richard's himself again." (Bessie Z. Jones, editor of the 1960 edition by the Belknap Press of Harvard University Press.)

3 Sairey Gamp is the drunken nurse and midwife from Charles Dickens's *Martin Chuzzlewit* (1844).

4 "By force and arms" (Cicero, "Pro Caecina").

5 Alfred Lord Tennyson's "The Charge of the Light Brigade," written in 1854 and published in 1855 in *Maud, and Other Poems*, memorialized a heroically disastrous attack by a British cavalry unit in the Battle of Balaclava in the Crimean War (1854–1856). The original stanza Alcott parodies reads: "Cannon to right of them, / Cannon to left of them, / Cannon behind them / Volley'd and thunder'd; / Storm'd at with shot and shell, / While horse and hero fell, / They that had fought so well / Came thro' the jaws of Death, / Back from the mouth of Hell, / All that was left of them, / Left of six hundred." Florence Nightingale, an inspiration and legend among American Civil War nurses, served in the Crimea.

6 I.e., an extravagant tale of adventure, from Baron Munchausen.

7 "Biddy" was a common nickname for Irish servant girls.

8 Slightly misquoted from William Thackeray's *Vanity Fair* (1847), vol. 1, ch. 24. The young ensign's letters, Thackeray writes, were "full of love and heartiness, and pluck and bad spelling. Ah! there were many anxious hearts beating through England at that time; and mothers' prayers and tears flowing in many homesteads."

9 Stephen Cushman, "Walt Whitman's Real Wars," in *Wars within a War: Controversy and Conflict over the American Civil War*, ed. Joan Waugh and Gary W. Gallagher (Chapel Hill: University of North Carolina Press, 2009), 137–156, 147, 145.

10 Along with other government buildings, the U.S. Patent Office served temporarily as a Union hospital during the war.

11 Union Gen. John Sedgwick (1813–1864), fondly nicknamed "Uncle John" by his men, killed at Spotsylvania.

12 Union Gen. Hiram Gregory Berry (1824–1863), fatally shot during a counter-charge at Chancellorsville.

13 John Singleton Mosby (1833–1916), Confederate cavalry leader. After resigning from service under Jeb Stuart, Mosby formed and led a semi-autonomous cavalry group, "Mosby's Rangers," that gained fame leading raids against Union troops and capturing federal resources. Upperville, in northern Virginia, was the scene of a minor battle on June 21, 1863.

14 In Acts 9:20–25, a newly converted Saul angered the Jews of Damascus by proclaiming the divinity of Christ in the city's synagogues. Learning of a murder plot against him, Saul's followers helped him escape by lowering him outside the wall in a basket.

15 "God forbid! Not for the whole world! She is dearer to me than life!" (German).

16 Monetary inflation and the scarcity of basic goods were chronic problems for the Confederacy. Strained by the devaluation of its treasury notes, the Confederate government instituted the policy of impressment in March, 1863, which allowed the government to seize the commodities of its people—from food, crops, and fuel to cattle and slaves—in order to support the Confederate army. The price of goods inflated, and a rash of hoarding, theft, and looting soon followed.

17 Lieutenant (later Captain) John F. Skelton was wounded and captured in the siege at Jackson, Mississippi, then sent to Libby Prison, from which he escaped in December of 1863. The *Richmond Examiner* described him as a "red-headed, bullet-eyed, pestilential abolitionist," and reported that the bribe was

400 dollars (*The Rebellion Record: A Diary of American Events*, vol. 8, ed. Frank Moore [New York, 1865], 22).

18 Belle Isle, a small island on the James River in Richmond, was also used as a prison for Union soldiers during the war. Conditions there were at least as bad as they were at Libby Prison, with high rates of disease and mortality caused by chronic exposure to the elements.

19 For further details of this "[g]randiosely conceived" conspiracy, led by four Union colonels at the prison, see Joseph Wheelan, *Libby Prison Breakout: The Daring Escape from the Notorious Civil War Prison* (New York: Public Affairs, 2010), 123–124.

20 Judah Philip Benjamin (1811–1884) held three different cabinet positions in the Confederacy: Attorney General in 1861, Secretary of War from 1861 to 1862, and Secretary of State from 1862 to 1865.

21 Michael Faraday (1791–1867) was a British scientist and philosopher. While at the Royal Institution of Great Britain, Faraday delivered a series of lectures entitled *The Chemical History of a Candle* describing the chemistry and physics of flames.

22 Shakespeare, *The Merchant of Venice* (*c.*1596–1597), 5.1.90–91.

23 Though Cavada gives February 8 as the date, the escape actually took place overnight between February 9 and 10, 1864. On the long-in-the-making and oft-thwarted planning for this escape, and on its aftermath, see Wheelan, *Libby Prison Breakout*, especially chapters 9–13.

24 Union Colonel Thomas Ellwood Rose (1830–1907), a schoolteacher from Pittsburgh prior to the war, came to Libby after being captured at Chickamauga in September, 1863. Though he successfully led the escape, Rose was recaptured days later and sent back, only to be exchanged the following July. Rose returned to battle, continued his service after the war's end, and retired from the army as a major in 1894.

25 Colonel Abel D. Streight (1828–1892), a midwestern businessman and publisher by trade, was captured by Lt.-Gen. Nathan Bedford Forrest in the spring of 1863 at the disastrous Union campaign known as Streight's Raid in northern Alabama. After his escape from Libby, Streight returned to duty and participated in the battles of Franklin and Nashville before resigning in March of 1865. Postwar, Streight had a successful career as a politician in Indiana, where he continued his publishing business until his death in 1892.

26 Thomas P. Turner (??–1901), a Virginian, served as commandant of both Libby Prison and Belle Isle. At war's end, Turner effected his own escape, travelling to the Bahamas, Cuba, and Canada to elude the postwar manhunt for Confederate officers. Ten years later, Turner returned to the U.S. to practice dentistry in Tennessee (Wheelan, *Libby Prison Breakout*, pp. 221–222).

27 See DeAnne Blanton and Lauren M. Cook, *They Fought Like Demons: Women Soldiers in the American Civil War* (Baton Rouge: Louisiana State University Press, 2002) and Richard Hall, *Women on the Civil War Battlefront* (Lawrence: University Press of Kansas, 2006).

28 Elizabeth Young, *Disarming the Nation: Women's Writing and the American Civil War* (Chicago: University of Chicago Press, 1999), 153.

29 In the previous chapter, Edmonds describes infiltrating the Confederate fortifications at Yorktown diguised as a contraband and, over three days, gathering information about the rebels' artillery and their plans to evacuate. The chapter closes with Edmonds making her report at McClellan's headquarters and then spending a few days talking with "Nellie," a former Confederate sympathizer turned Union nurse after being captured.

30 Quoted, almost verbatim, from Joel Tyler Headley's *The Great Rebellion: A History of the Civil War in the United States*, Volume 1 (1863), 404.

31 Thaddeus S. C. Lowe, Chief Aeronaut of the Union Army Balloon Corps, conducted aerial reconnaissance for the Army of the Potomac from hot air balloons; he was a well-known scientist and inventor but not actually a "professor." Lowe was accompanied by Brig. Gen. Samuel P. Heintzelman in the balloon trip which discovered that the Confederate army had evacuated Yorktown.

32 Cavalry Gen. George Stoneman, Jr. (1822–1894); Brig. Gen. Samuel P. Heintzelman (1805–1880); Brig. Gen. (later Major Gen.) Joseph Hooker; Brig. Gen. William F. "Baldy" Smith (1824–1903); Brig. Gen. Philip Kearney (1815–1862); Brig. Gen. Darius N. Couch (1822–1897); Brig. Gen. Silas Casey (1807–1882).

33 Named for Confederate Brig. Gen. John B. Magruder, who had successfully stalled McClellan at Yorktown, Fort Magruder was a key part of the "Williamsburg Line," a chain of defensive fortifications protecting the Virginia Peninsula.

34 As she relates in the previous chapter, Edmonds had contemplated another "adventure" (i.e., reconnaissance mission) behind Confederate lines.

35 A physician for the Union forces who appears at several places in Edmonds's narrative.

36 This episode returns in Chapter 18, when the "pusillanimous" colonel tries to get Edmonds (still in disguise) to sign a paper attesting to the colonel's (non-existent) wounds and to Doctor E.'s "cruel treatment and insulting language."

37 Possibly taken from Horatio Hackett's *Christian Memorials of the War* (1864), which includes a longer version but does not identify the poet. Edmonds quote three other stanzas of this poem in Chapter 3.

38 This whole paragraph, not just the quoted material, is taken from an essay titled "Sacrifice for Country," by Emilie Mozart, which appeared in *The Ladies' Repository* vol. 24 (Feb. 1864), 68–70.

39 In the previous chapter, Edmonds had reconnoitered the Confederate position at Yorktown disguised as a male slave.

40 While disguised as a slave in Chapter 8, Edmonds is put to work digging fortifications; her hands cannot tolerate the heavy labor and she offers five dollars to another slave who had agreed to exchange work duties with her.

41 See Luke 18:2.

42 From Horatio B. Hackett, *Christian Memorials of the War; or, Scenes and Incidents Illustrative of Religious Faith and Principle, Patriotism and Bravery in Our Army* (Boston, 1864), 78.

43 The 79th Indiana was organized in late summer, 1862, and served in both the Army of the Ohio and the Army of the Cumberland.

44 "Regiment lost during service 3 Officers and 50 Enlisted men killed and mortally wounded and 2 Officers and 147 Enlisted men by disease. Total 202" (Frederick H. Dyer, *A Compendium of the War of the Rebellion* [New York: Thomas Yoseloff, 1959; orig. 1908], Vol. 3, 1147).

45 The system of such prisoner exchanges broke down in the summer of 1863 over the South's refusal to treat captured black soldiers as prisoners of war on an equal basis with whites.

46 The 79th Indiana contributed to the battle of Chickamauga by capturing, with heavy losses, a Confederate artillery battery.

47 Glenna R. Schroeder-Lein writes that Dr. David Wendel Yandell, medical director to Gen. Albert Sidney Johnston, "set up thirteen hospitals in Nashville during the fall of 1861," which ultimately "had beds for about 13,000" (*Confederate Hospitals on the Move: Samuel H. Stout and the Army of Tennessee*. Columbia: University of South Carolina Press [1994], pp. 45–46). The Confederates began vacating Nashville in February 1862.

48 Presumably Benjamin F. Palmer, who developed a prosthetic leg of relatively high mobility which was honored at the World's Fair in London in 1851.

49 Also known as Turner's Lane Hospital, this clinical research facility in north Philadelphia closed in fall 1864 (Ira M. Rutkow, *Bleeding Blue and Gray: Civil War Surgery and the Evolution of American Medicine* [New York: Random House, 2005], pp. 252–254).

50 "The absent ones are always wrong."

51 U.S. Surgeon General William Hammond established the Army Medical Museum in 1862 in order to collect specimens from wounded soldiers for research purposes; it also archived photographs and case histories. The AMM is now the National Museum of Health and Medicine of the Armed Forces Institute of Pathology.

52 Velazquez's first husband reluctantly serves in the Confederate Army, and is killed (off) early in the war.

53 Polk (1806–1864) was a popular, though not terribly successful, commander in the Army of Missisippi and the Army of Tennessee, killed in action at Pine Mountain, Georgia. During this phase of Velazquez's narrative, Polk would have been commanding in the state of Kentucky.

54 Bragg commanded one of the four Confederate corps at Shiloh; his forces were involved in the initial Confederate assault on Sunday, April 6, the first day of the battle. James R. Chalmers (1831–1898) commanded the Second Brigade in the division of Gen. Jones M. Withers, under Bragg. Adley Hogan Gladden commanded the First Brigade under Withers; he was killed at Shiloh by a cannon ball.

55 The Confederate assault on the morning of April 6 came as a surprise to Union forces under Grant and Sherman, and almost succeeded at breaking through their lines. Although the assalt was fierce, it was badly organized and by evening had stalled out, paving the way for a Union counterattack the next day.

56 Watkins means Gen. Albert Sidney Johnston (1803–1862), who along with Gen. P. G. T. Beauregard had overall command of the Confederate forces at Shiloh, commanding the Army of Mississippi. Johnston bled to death after being shot behind the right knee, despite the efforts of staff officers to fashion a torniquet.

57 Isham G. Harris (1818–1897) was Governor of Tennesssee until early 1862, when Lincoln appointed Andrew Johnson military governor of the recalcitrant state; as governor, Harris had refused Lincoln's

call for troops to suppress the Confederate rebellion in Tennessee. At Shiloh he served as staff officer to Johnston and helped the general from his horse after he was shot.

58 Maj. Gen. Don Carlos Buell (1818–1898) commanded the Army of the Ohio, several divisions of which had to march from Nashville to reinforce Grant's Army of West Tennessee, not arriving until the evening of the first day. Fort Henry and Fort Donelson had fallen to Grant in February, opening the Tennessee and Cumberland rivers, respectively, to advancing Union forces. Nashville fell to Buell shortly thereafter.

59 In the next chapter, Watkins describes the siege and fall of Corinth to Union forces as they pressed on after their victory at Shiloh.

60 William Henry Furness (1802–1896) was a liberal Unitarian minister whose theological work *Remarks on the Four Gospels* (1836) was an important early text in the emergence of Transcendentalism. In 1866, Furness was pastor of the First Unitarian Church in Philadelphia. Edward Everett Hale (1822–1909), another liberal Unitarian clergyman, was also a journalist, editor, and author of fiction and nonfiction.

The Texts

Herman Melville, selections from *Battle-Pieces and Aspects of the War*. Source: *The Works of Herman Melville*. Vol. 16 (London: Constable and Company Ltd., 1924). Originally published in *Battle-Pieces and Aspects of the War* (New York: Harper & Bros., 1866).

Abraham Lincoln, Reply to Eliza P. Gurney and Meditation on the Divine Will. Source: *The Collected Works of Abraham Lincoln*, Vol. 5, ed. Roy P. Basler (New Brunswick, N.J: Rutgers University Press, 1953). Two slightly different versions of Lincoln's reply to Gurney exist: the one which appears in *Memoir and Correspondence of Eliza P. Gurney*, ed. Richard F. Mott (Philadelphia, 1884), 313, which is attributed to an unnamed member of Gurney's party, and the one which appears in both Basler's *Collected Works* and (John Nicolay and John Hay's *Complete Works*); this latter document, Basler reports, "is in an unknown handwriting" (*CW* 5:478, n.1). The origin and authority of each text are therefore somewhat murky.

Abraham Lincoln, Address Delivered at the Dedication of the Cemetery at Gettysburg. The textual history of the Gettsyburg Address is complex, involving five manuscript copies of the speech that Lincoln gave to several associates, three of which were written down after he gave the speech, along with differing accounts that appeared in contemporary news reports. It is also unclear which manuscript he actually held in his hand on that day. This anthology follows the judgment of Garry Wills and Gabor Borritt in reprinting the so-called Bliss copy, the fifth draft Lincoln wrote, and the only one that bears his signature and given title. See Garry Wills, *Lincoln at Gettysburg: The Words That Remade America* (New York: Touchstone, 1992), and Gabor Borritt, *The Gettysburg Gospel: The Lincoln Speech That Nobody Knows* (New York: Simon and Schuster, 2006).

Henry Wadsworth Longfellow, "The Cumberland" and "Killed at the Ford." Source: *The Complete Poetical Works of Longfellow* (Cambridge, Mass.: Riverside Press, 1922). Originally published, respectively, in *The Atlantic Monthly*, vol. 10, no. 62 (December 1862) and *The Atlantic Monthly*, vol. 17, no. 102 (April 1866).

Lucy Larcom, "The Sinking of the Merrimack." Source: *The Poetical Works of Lucy Larcom. Household Edition. With Illustrations* (Boston and New York: Houghton, Mifflin and Company, 1890).

Sarah Morgan Piatt, "Hearing the Battle." Source: John James Piatt and Sarah M. B. Piatt, *The Nests at Washington, and Other Poems* (New York: W. Low; London: S. Low, Son & Co., 1864), pp. 103–104.

Louisa May Alcott, *Hospital Sketches*, Chapter 3 ("A Day"). Source: *Hospital Sketches* (Boston: James Redpath, 1863), pp. 31–45. Much of the book had been published earlier in 1863 in *The Commonwealth*, an abolitionist Boston newspaper.

Walt Whitman, selections from *Drum-Taps*. Source: *Walt Whitman's Drum-Taps* (New York: s.n., 1865). In *Leaves of Grass*, Whitman retitled "The Dresser" "The Wound-Dresser" and made two significant revisions to the poem. The first was to add, as lines 4–6, the following: "(Arous'd and angry, I'd thought to beat the alarum, and urge relentless war, / But soon my fingers fail'd me, my face droop'd and I resign'd myself, / To sit by the wounded and soothe them, or silently watch the dead;)". The second was to delete the phrase "In nature's reverie sad" from the start of line 20 (before "With hinged knees").

Walt Whitman, selections from *Memoranda during the War*. Source: *Walt Whitman's Memoranda During the War: Written on the Spot in 1863–'65*, ed. Peter Coviello (New York: Oxford University Press, 2004).

Federico Cavada, *Libby Life*, Chapter 5 ("Various Forms of Melancholy") and Chapter 8 ("A Sermon from a Candle"). Source: *Libby Life: Experiences of a Prisoner of War in Richmond, Va., 1863–64* (Philadelphia: King & Baird, 1864).

Sarah Emma Edmonds, *Nurse and Spy in the Union Army*, Chapter 9 ("Evacuation of Yorktown"). Source: *Nurse and Spy in the Union Army: Comprising the Adventures and Experiences of a Woman in Hospitals, Camps, and Battle-Fields* (Hartford, Conn.: W. S. Williams & Co, 1865). Previously published both as *The Female Spy of the Union Army: The Thrilling Adventures, Experiences and Escapes of a Woman as Nurse, Spy, and Scout, in Hospitals, Camps, and Battle-Fields* (Boston: De Wolfe, Fiske, 1864), and as *Unsexed; or, The Female Soldier: The Thrilling Adventures, Experiences and Escapes of a Woman, as Nurse, Spy and Scout, in Hospitals, Camps and Battle-Fields* (Philadelphia: Philadelphia Pub. Co., 1864).

Silas Weir Mitchell, "The Case of George Dedlow." Source: *The Autobiography of a Quack and Other Stories.* Author's Definitive Edition (New York: The Century Co., 1905). Originally published in *The Atlantic Monthly*, vol. 18, no. 105 (July 1866). Mitchell included the following "Introduction" in his 1905 collection:

"The first two tales in this little volume ['The Autobiography of a Quack' and 'The Case of George Dedlow'] appeared originally in the 'Atlantic Monthly' as anonymous contributions. I owe to the present owners of that journal pemission to use them. 'The Autobiography of a Quack' has been recast with large additions.

" 'The Case of George Dedlow' was not written with any intention that it should appear in print. I lent the manuscript to the Rev. Dr. Furness and forgot it. This gentleman sent it to the Rev. Edward Everett Hale.[60] He, presuming, I fancy, that every one desired to appear in the 'Atlantic,' offered it to that journal. To my surprise, soon afterwards I received a proof and a check. The story was inserted as a leading article without my name. It was at once accepted by many as the description of a real case. Money was collected in several places to assist the unfortunate man, and benevolent persons went to see the 'Stump Hospital,' in Philadelphia, to see the sufferer and to offer him aid. The spiritual incident at the end of the story was received with joy by the spiritualists as a valuable proof of the truth of their beliefs."

Loreta J. Velazquez, *The Woman in Battle*, Chapter 10 ("First Experiences as a Spy"). Source: *The Woman in Battle: A Narrative of the Exploits, Adventures, and Travels of Madame Loreta Janeta Velazquez, Otherwise Known as Lieutenant Harry T. Buford, Confederate States Army* (Richmond, Va.: Dustin, Gilman & Co., 1876).

Samuel R. Watkins, from *Co. Aytch*. Source: *1861 vs. 1882, "Co. Aytch," Maury Grays, First Tennessee Regiment; or, A Side Show of the Big Show* (Nashville: Cumberland Presbyterian Pub. House, 1882). Originally serialized in the Columbia (Tenn.) *Herald*, 1881–1882.

Ambrose Bierce, "The Coup de Grâce." Source: *Tales of Soldiers and Civilians* (New York: Lovell, Coryell, & Co., 1891).

Stephen Crane, "An Episode of War." Source: *The Work of Stephen Crane.* Vol. 9 ("Wounds in the Rain, and Other Impressions of War"), ed. Wilson Follett (New York: Alfred A. Knopf, 1925). Originally published in the British magazine *The Gentlewoman* (Dec. 1899), pp. 24–25. Probably sold to the *Youth's Companion* as "The Loss of an Arm" in late 1896, but never published there. See Fredson Bowers, textual introduction to *The Works of Stephen Crane*. Vol. 6 ("Tales of War") (Charlottesville: University of Virginia Press, 1970), pp. lxxx–lxxxii.

III
African American Experience

Two brothers in arms (1860–1870). Unknown photographer. Library of Congress Prints and Photographs Division, LC-USZ62-132208

Introduction

In 1860, almost 4 million African Americans were held as slaves in the United States. The Emancipation Proclamation, which came into force on January 1, 1863, declared those slaves in rebellious states "forever free," and the Thirteenth Amendment, certified December 18, 1865, declared that "neither slavery nor involuntary servitude . . . . shall exist" in the United States. Whatever else might be said about the Civil War, therefore, it stands next to the emancipation of Russian serfs in 1861 as the single most concentrated moment of legal liberation in human history.

Genuine freedom was another matter, of course. The inability of postwar Reconstruction to secure African American civil rights, indeed survival, in more than a theoretical sense meant that the long, hard struggle for practical liberty and equal citizenship had only just begun. It is also important to remember that the Civil War was not originally, and arguably not ever primarily, a war of liberation; that racism was common among Union soldiers, many of whom bristled at the notion that they risked their lives for "niggers"; and that officially sanctioned unequal treatment of black soldiers persisted in the federal military. Moreover, as historian Jim Downs has recently shown, emancipation was accompanied by rampant physical suffering and death, as newly freed slaves—dislocated, denied adequate medical care, and largely ignored by the government—"struggled to survive in a region torn apart by disease and destruction." Their experience, however, did not fit into "a liberation narrative that heroically described the abolition of slavery" and was thus routinely underestimated.[1] For all of these reasons, African American emancipation is a story of great hope and great accomplishment clouded by disappointment, violence, and hatred.

As the war took hold in the South, siphoning off adult white men and disrupting civil order and the plantation system, slaves began to escape in greater numbers, and the Union soon discovered that it had a problem on its hands: what to do with those who ended up in federally held territory. The solution that emerged—one which African American leaders had been calling for all along—was to employ escaped slaves and freedmen in the war effort. The pivotal year was 1862, which saw an early attempt by Gen. David Hunter to organize a black regiment; Gen. Benjamin Butler's designation of ex-slaves as "contrabands of war"; and the preliminary emancipation proclamation of September 22, which Lincoln justified as "a fit and necessary war measure." The Congressional militia act of July 1862 authorized the enlistment of black soldiers, and in August, the first official black regiment, the First South Carolina Volunteers, was formed. Although resistance accompanied all of these developments, the moral and military arguments in favor of raising African American troops proved irresistible, and in May 1863, the War Department established a Bureau of Colored Troops. Recruitment quickly accelerated, and by the end of the war, on the order of 180,000 to 200,000 African Americans had served as enlisted men, and about 100 as officers.

Their service was not easy. Black soldiers faced an array of difficulties: lower pay than their white counterparts ($10.00 per month instead of $13.00); inferior supplies and medical care; much higher rates of fatal disease and combat casualties; harassment by white soldiers; and reprisals at the hands of Confederate captors. Even so, African American troops—along with many blacks serving in unofficial capacities such as reconnaissance and construction—made significant contributions to the Union war effort, particularly along the coastal regions of the Confederacy, and their performance cured many Northerners of their skepticism about the value of black citizenship.

African American troops saw significant action during the siege of Port Hudson, Louisiana, during the late spring and summer of 1863. The 1st Louisiana Native Guards (later the First

Corps de Afrique and then the 73rd United States Colored Troops) and the 3rd Louisiana Native Guards sustained heavy casualties here but proved their combat mettle.

It was in the Sea Islands area of South Carolina, however, that black regiments would gain their fame. The Union bases at Port Royal and Beaufort—central to the overall strategy of taking advantage of Northern naval superiority, blockading the South, and moving against Charleston—were in an area inhabited by large communities of former slaves. In the so-called "Port Royal Experiment," the U.S. military, with the help of Northern abolitionists, began organizing African American units and deploying them in raids along the coast and upriver. In November, 1862, Rufus Saxton, brigadier general in the Department of the South, asked Thomas Wentworth Higginson to take command of the recently formed 1st South Carolina Volunteers at Beaufort River. The regiment participated in various military expeditions and in the temporary occupation of Jacksonville, Florida, but its main significance consisted in the unprecedented cross-cultural contact between Northern whites and Southern blacks living together and fighting, literally, for the same goal. This remarkable collaboration is recorded in postwar memoirs by both Higginson and Susie King Taylor, a former slave who volunteered as a general aide for the 1st South Carolina, whose autobiography is excerpted here. The educational side of the Port Royal Experiment is described in an 1864 essay by Charlotte Forten (later Grimké), "Life on the Sea Islands," written while Forten worked as a teacher to freedmen on St. Helena Island.

In the summer of 1863, in the wake of a failed assault on Charleston, Gen. Quincy Gillmore replaced Gen. David Hunter as commander of the Department of the South and prepared for further operations against the iconic Confederate city, which was under the command of Gen. P. G. T. Beauregard. After taking Morris Island, near the Charleston Harbor, Gillmore then moved against the Confederate battery at Fort Wagner. On July 18, 1863, a major charge on the fort, led by the 54th Massachusetts Infantry, a black regiment under the command of Col. Robert Gould Shaw, was a disaster in military terms but burned the image of African American heroism into the Northern imagination. Although Fort Wagner and Fort Sumter capitulated in the autumn, Charleston would hold out against Union pressure until February 1865, when the fall of Columbia to William T. Sherman's marauding army put the writing on the wall. Throughout this period, the interaction of whites and blacks was one of the war's vital but largely unremarked themes.

In March 1865, anticipating the need for major postwar assistance for Southern blacks, the United States created the Bureau of Refugees, Freedmen, and Abandoned Lands, under the command of Maj. Gen. Oliver Otis Howard. The Freedmen's Bureau was intended to provide education, legal advice, property assistance, and material goods to newly liberated slaves, but insufficient funding, tepid executive support, and fierce Southern resistance hampered what would have been exceedingly difficult work in the best of circumstances. Having compiled a record much less impressive than its ideals, the Bureau had run its course by 1872, when Congress pulled the plug on the agency, leaving Southern blacks effectively alone for the hard and bloody climb to follow. Many simply moved North, where the economic opportunities were greater and the racism less violent. Others, for a variety of reasons, stayed in the South and made a go of it, in spite of their second-class citizenship and physical and economic vulnerability. Some chose to write, if they had the means, and their collective work—in autobiography, personal journals, correspondence, fiction, speeches, and essays—forms a vital record of those who had arguably the most at stake in the Civil War.

Representing the war and its aftermath posed a challenge for any American writer, but more so for African American authors, whose efforts to record their experience faithfully ran into social and institutional resistance on all sides. Foremost among these was the widespread national desire to move beyond the conflict, and the concomitant desire of

American publishers to print literature that declined to dwell on problems of race. Maintaining a focus on the racial dimensions of the war, and on the postwar struggles of African Americans, thus required of black writers careful strategies of representational parry and thrust; of subtle acquiescence to some, but not all, of the publishing industry's expectations; of rendering individual experience so as to affirm, or to seem to affirm, the national story. Such experience, in the war and after, was incredibly varied, and the title of this section—"African American Experience"—means no more than to suggest a few tiles of the larger mosaic. Taken together, the following selections should convey something of the sweeping range of feeling, action, and attitude with which black Americans responded to the Civil War, and to the complex fugue of possibility and peril that it inaugurated.

Abraham Lincoln, Final Emancipation Proclamation (January 1, 1863)

Lincoln was not the "Great Emancipator" when he took office, for freeing Southern slaves was among neither the political priorities nor the early war aims of his administration. Lincoln and most of the Republican Party meant, rather, to preserve the Union by all means, even if slavery had to be tolerated in one region. But as Union losses mounted in 1862, he came to see the value of depriving Southerners of property and gaining the advantage of the labor or military participation of blacks. In September, 1862, after gaining momentum from the successful Battle of Antietam, Lincoln issued a preliminary proclamation, effectively giving rebellious states one last chance to rejoin the Union, and then issued the final order on January 1, 1863. The Proclamation was immediately controversial, not only among Southerners but among abolitionists who thought it too timid; after all, the order was justified by military necessity rather than philosophical idealism, and was limited in its scope (only states or districts "in rebellion" were affected). Its political meaning is complex, and remains controversial, but it seems hard to deny that the Emancipation Proclamation transformed the meaning of the Civil War, elevating and broadening the Northern war effort, and setting the stage for the long postwar struggle for African American civil rights.

January 1, 1863

By the President of the United States of America:

A Proclamation

Whereas, on the twenty-second day of September, in the year of our Lord one thousand eight hundred and sixty-two, a proclamation was issued by the President of the United States, containing, among other things, the following, to wit:

"That on the first day of January, in the year of our Lord one thousand eight hundred and sixty-three, all persons held as slaves within any State, or designated part of a State, the people whereof shall then be in rebellion against the United States, shall be then, thenceforward, and forever free; and the Executive Government of the United States, including the military and naval authority thereof, will recognize and maintain the freedom of such persons, and will do no act or acts to repress such persons, or any of them, in any efforts they may make for their actual freedom.

"That the Executive will, on the first day of January aforesaid, by proclamation, designate the States and parts of States, if any, in which the people thereof, respectively, shall then be in rebellion against the United States; and the fact that any State, or the people thereof, shall on that day be in good faith represented in the Congress of the United States by members chosen thereto at elections wherein a majority of the qualified voters of such State shall have participated, shall in the absence of strong countervailing testimony be deemed conclusive evidence that such State and the people thereof are not then in rebellion against the United States."

Now, therefore, I, Abraham Lincoln, President of the United States, by virtue of the power in me vested as commander-in-chief of the army and navy of the United States, in time of actual armed rebellion against authority and government of the United States, and as a fit and necessary war measure for suppressing said rebellion, do, on this first day of January, in the year of our Lord one thousand eight hundred and sixty-three, and in accordance with my purpose so to do, publicly proclaimed for the full period of

100 days, from the day first above mentioned, order and designate as the States and parts of States wherein the people thereof, respectively, are this day in rebellion against the United States, the following, to wit:

Arkansas, Texas, Louisiana, (except the Parishes of St. Bernard; Plaquemines, Jefferson, St. Johns, St. Charles, St. James, Ascension, Assumption, Terre Bonne, Lafourche, St. Mary, St. Martin, and Orleans, including the city of New Orleans), Mississippi, Alabama, Florida, Georgia, South Carolina, North Carolina, and Virginia (except the forty-eight counties designated as West Virginia, and also the counties of Berkley, Accomac, Northampton, Elizabeth City, York, Princess Ann, and Norfolk, including the cities of Norfolk and Portsmouth), and which excepted parts are for the present left precisely as if this proclamation were not issued.

And by virtue of the power and for the purpose aforesaid, I do order and declare that all persons held as slaves within said designated States and parts of States are, and henceforward shall be, free; and that the Executive Government of the United States, including the military and naval authorities thereof, will recognize and maintain the freedom of said persons.

And I hereby enjoin upon the people so declared to be free to abstain from all violence, unless in necessary self-defense; and I recommend to them that, in all cases when allowed, they labor faithfully for reasonable wages.

And I further declare and make known that such persons of suitable condition will be received into the armed service of the United States to garrison forts, positions, stations, and other places, and to man vessels of all sorts in said service.

And upon this act, sincerely believed to be an act of justice, warranted by the Constitution upon military necessity, I invoke the considerate judgment of mankind and the gracious favor of Almighty God.

In witness whereof, I have hereunto set my hand, and caused the seal of the United States to be affixed.

> Done at the city of Washington, this first day of January, in the year of our Lord one thousand eight hundred and sixty-three, and of the independence of the United States of America the eighty-seventh.
>
> ABRAHAM LINCOLN

By the President: WILLIAM H. SEWARD, Secretary of State.

Frederick Douglass, "Men of Color, to Arms!" (1863)

Building on the momentum of the Emancipation Proclamation, Massachusetts Governor John Andrew in March 1863 authorized the formation of the state's first African American regiment, the 54th Volunteer Infantry, and abolitionists cheered the move as a defining moment in the war. Douglass, who had been calling for aggressive resistance to slavery ever since his first autobiography appeared in 1845, and had pressed the Lincoln administration to enlist blacks in the war effort, proved an ardent and effective recruiter for the 54th, which quickly reached capacity (including two of Douglass's own sons). His promise that black troops would be treated fairly and respectfully was not exactly borne out by the facts, particularly in other "colored" regiments, but the immediate need was to encourage African Americans to take up arms against the South.

When first the Rebel cannon shattered the walls of Sumter, and drove away its starving garrison, I predicted that the war then and there inaugurated would not be fought out entirely by white men. Every month's experience during these dreary years has confirmed that opinion. A war undertaken and brazenly carried on for the perpetual enslavement of colored men, calls logically and loudly for colored men to help suppress it. Only a moderate share of sagacity was needed to see that the arm of the slave was the best defence against the arm of the slaveholder. Hence with every reverse to the national arms, with every exulting shout of victory raised by the slaveholding rebels, I have implored the imperilled nation to unchain against her foes her powerful black hand. Slowly and reluctantly that appeal is beginning to be heeded. Stop not now to complain that it was not heeded sooner. It may, or it may not have been best – that it should not. This is not the time to discuss that question. Leave it to the future. When the war is over, the country is saved, peace is established, and the black man's rights are secured, as they will be, history with an impartial hand, will dispose of that and sundry other questions. Action! action! not criticism, is the plain duty of this hour. Words are now useful only as they stimulate to blows. The office of speech now is only to point out when, where, and how to strike to the best advantage. There is no time to delay. The tide is at its flood that leads on to fortune. From east to west, from north to south, the sky is written all over with "now or never." Liberty won by white men would lack half its lustre. Who would be free themselves must strike the blow. Better even die free, than to live slaves. This is the sentiment of every brave colored man among us. There are weak and cowardly men in all nations. We have them among us. They will tell you that this is the "white man's war"; that you will be "[no] better off after than before the war"; that the getting of you into the army is to "sacrifice you on the first opportunity." Believe them not – cowards themselves, they do not wish to have their cowardice shamed by your brave example. Leave them to their timidity, or to whatever motive may hold them back.

I have not thought lightly of the words I am now addressing to you. The counsel I give comes of close observation of the great struggle now in progress – and of the deep conviction that this is your hour and mine.

In good earnest, then, and after the best deliberation, I, now, for the first time during this war, feel at liberty to call and counsel you to arms. By every consideration which binds you to your enslaved fellow countrymen, and the peace and welfare of your country; by every aspiration which you cherish for the freedom and equality of yourselves and your children; by all the ties of blood and identity which make us one with the brave black men now fighting our battles in Louisiana, in South Carolina,[2] I urge you to fly to arms, and smite with death the power that would bury the Government and your liberty in the same hopeless grave. I wish I could tell you that the State of New York calls you to this high honor. For the moment her constituted authorities are silent on the subject. They will speak by and by, and doubtless on the right side; but we are not compelled to wait for her. We can get at the throat of treason and Slavery through the State of Massachusetts.

She was first in the war of Independence; first to break the chains of her slaves; first to make the black man equal before the law; first to admit colored children to her common schools, and she was first to answer with her blood the alarm cry of the nation – when its capital was menaced by rebels. You know her patriotic Governor, and you know Charles Sumner – I need add no more.[3]

Massachusetts now welcomes you to arms as her soldiers. She has but a small colored population from which to recruit. She has full leave of the General Government to send one regiment to the war, and she has undertaken to do it. Go quickly and help fill up this first colored regiment from the North. I am authorized to assure you that you will receive the same wages, the same rations, the same equipments, the same protection, the same treatment and the same bounty secured to white soldiers. You will be led by able and skillful officers – men who will take especial pride in your efficiency and success. They will be quick to accord to you all the honor you shall merit by your valor – and see that your rights and feelings are respected by other soldiers. I have assured myself on these points – and can speak with authority. More than twenty years unswerving devotion to our common cause, may give me some humble claim to be trusted at this momentous crisis.

I will not argue. To do so implies hesitation and doubt, and you do not hesitate. You do not doubt. The day dawns – the morning star is bright upon the horizon! The iron gate of our prison stands half open. One gallant rush from the North will fling it wide open, while four millions of our brothers and sisters shall march out into Liberty! The chance is now given you to end in a day the bondage of centuries, and to rise in one bound from social degradation to the plane of common equality with all other varieties of men. Remember Denmark Vesey of Charleston.[4] Remember Nathaniel Turner of South Hampton;[5] remember Shields Green and Copeland, who followed noble John Brown, and fell as glorious martyrs for the cause of the slaves.[6] Remember that in a contest with oppression, the Almighty has no attribute which can take sides with oppressors.[7] The case is before you. This is our golden opportunity – let us accept it – and forever wipe out the dark reproaches unsparingly hurled against us by our enemies. Win for ourselves the gratitude of our country – and the best blessings of our posterity through all time. The nucleus of this first regiment is now in camp at Readville, a short distance from Boston.[8] I will undertake to forward to Boston all persons adjudged fit to be mustered into this regiment, who shall apply to me at any time within the next two weeks.

FREDERICK DOUGLASS
Rochester, March 2, 1863

Frances Ellen Watkins Harper, "The Massachusetts Fifty-Fourth" (1863)

Where storms of death were sweeping,
    Wildly through the darkened sky,
Stood the bold but fated column,
    Brave to do, to dare, and die.

With cheeks that knew no blanching,
    And brows that would not pale;
Where the bloody rain fell thickest,
    Mingled with the fiery hail.

Bearers of a high commission
    To break each brother's chain;
With hearts aglow for freedom,
    They bore the toil and pain.

And onward pressed though shot and shell
    Swept fiercely round their path;
While batteries hissed with tongues of flame,
    And bayonets flashed with wrath.

Oh! not in vain those heros fell,
    Amid those hours of fearful strife;
Each dying heart poured out a balm
    To heal the wounded nation's life.

And from the soil drenched with their blood,
    The fairest flowers of peace shall bloom;
And history cull rich laurels there,
    To deck each martyr hero's tomb.

And ages yet uncrossed with life,
    As sacred urns, do hold each mound
Where sleep the loyal, true, and brave
    In freedom's consecrated ground.

Harriet Jacobs and Louisa M. Jacobs, Letter to Lydia Maria Child (1864)

Within months of the Emancipation Proclamation, abolitionists had ventured into Union-occupied areas of the South to establish "freedmen's schools": hard work in hard circumstances. From late 1863 until the end of the war, Harriet Jacobs, accompanied by her daughter Louisa, undertook such work in Alexandria, Virginia, helping the freed men and women there through her efforts at educational and social uplift. Jacobs wrote often to her abolitionist friends in the North to keep them apprised of the successes and struggles from the front lines of the educational efforts of the antislavery movement. One particularly strong ally was Lydia Maria Child, a prominent member of the American Anti-Slavery Society, one of the founders of the *National Anti-Slavery Standard*, and editor of Jacobs's popular slave narrative *Incidents in the Life of a Slave Girl* (1861). The following letter was published in the *Standard* on April 16, 1864.

Dear Mrs. Child: When I went to the North, last Fall, the Freedmen here were building a school-house, and I expected it would have been finished by the time I returned. But when we arrived, we found it uncompleted. Their funds had got exhausted, and the work was at a stand-still for several weeks. This was a disappointment; but the time did not hang idle on our hands, I assure you. We went round visiting the new homes of the Freedmen, which now dot the landscape, built with their first earnings as free laborers. Within the last eight months seven hundred little cabins have been built, containing from two to four rooms. The average cost from one hundred to two hundred and fifty dollars. In building school-houses, or shelters for the old and decrepid, they have received but little assistance. They have had to struggle along and help themselves as they could. But though this has been discouraging, at times, it teaches them self-reliance; and that is good for them, as it is for everybody. We have over seven thousand colored refugees in this place, and, including the hospitals, less than four hundred rations are given out. This shows that they are willing to earn their own way, and generally capable of it. Indeed, when I look back on the condition in which I first found them, and compare it with their condition now, I am convinced they are not so far behind other races as some people represent them. The two rooms we occupy were given to me by the Military Governor,[9] to be appropriated to the use of decrepid women, when we leave them.

When we went round visiting the homes of these people, we found much to commend them for. Many of them showed marks of industry, neatness, and natural refinement. In others, chaos reigned supreme. There was nothing about them to indicate the presence of a wifely wife, or a motherly mother. They bore abundant marks of the half-barbarous, miserable condition of Slavery, from which the inmates had lately come. It made me sad to see their shiftlessness and discomfort; but I was hopeful for the future. The consciousness of working for themselves, and of having a character to gain, will inspire them with energy and enterprise, and a higher civilization will gradually come.

Children abounded in these cabins. They peeped out from every nook and corner. Many of them were extremely pretty and bright-looking. Some had features and complexions purely Anglo-Saxon; showing plainly enough the slaveholder's horror of amalgamation. Some smiled upon us, and were very ready to be friends. Others regarded us with shy, suspicious looks, as is apt to be the case with children who have had a cramped childhood. But they all wanted to accept our invitation to go to school, and so did all the parents for them.

In the course of our rounds, we visited a settlement which had received no name. We suggested to the settlers that it would be proper to name it for some champion of Liberty. We told them of the Hon. Chas. Sumner,[10] whose large heart and great mind had for years been devoted to the cause of the poor slaves. We told how violent and cruel slaveholders had nearly murdered him for standing up so manfully in defence of Freedom. His claim to their gratitude was at once recognized, and the settlement was called Sumnerville.

Before we came here, a white lady, from Chelsea, Mass., was laboring as a missionary among the Refugees; and a white teacher, sent by the Educational Commission of Boston,[11] accompanied us. One of the freedmen, whose cabin consisted of two rooms, gave it up to us for our school. We soon found that the clamor of little voices begging for admittance far exceeded the narrow limits of this establishment.

Friends at the North had given us some articles left from one of the Fairs.[12] To these we added what we could, and got up a little Fair here, to help them in the completion of the school-house. By this means we raised one hundred and fifty dollars, and they were much gratified by the result. With the completion of the school-house our field of labor widened, and we were joyful over the prospect of extended usefulness. But some difficulties occurred, as there always do in the settlement of such affairs. A question arose whether the white teachers or the colored teachers should be superintendents. The freedmen had built the schoolhouse for their children, and were Trustees of the school. So, after some discussion, it was decided that it would be best for them to hold a meeting, and settle the question for themselves. I wish you could have been at that meeting. Most of the people were slaves, until quite recently, but they talked sensibly, and I assure you that they put the question to vote in quite parliamentary style. The result was a decision that the colored teachers should have charge of the school. We were gratified by this result, because our sympathies are closely linked with our oppressed race. These people, born and bred in slavery, had always been so accustomed to look upon the white race as their natural superiors and masters, that we had some doubts whether they could easily throw off the habit; and the fact of their giving preference to colored teachers, as managers of the establishment, seemed to us to indicate that even their brief possession of freedom had begun to inspire them with respect for their race.

On the 11th of January we opened school in the new school-house, with seventy-five scholars. Now, we have two-hundred and twenty-five. Slavery had not crushed out the animal spirits of these children. Fun lurks in the corners of their eyes, dimples their mouths, tingles at their fingers' ends, and is, like a torpedo, ready to explode at the slightest touch. The war-spirit has a powerful hold upon them. No one turns the other cheek for a second blow. But they evince a generous nature. They never allow an older and stronger scholar to impose upon a younger and weaker one; and when they happen to have any little delicacies, they are very ready to share them with others. The task of regulating them is by no means an easy one; but we put heart, mind, and strength freely into the work, and only regreat that we have not more physical strength. Their ardent desire to learn is very encouraging, and the improvement they make consoles us for many trials. You would be astonished at the progress many of them have made in this short time. Many who less than three months ago scarcely knew the A.B.C. are now reading and spelling in words of two or three syllables. When I look at these bright little boys, I often wonder whether there is not some Frederick Douglass among them, destined to do honor to his race in the future. No one can predict, now-a-days, how rapidly the wheels of progress will move on.

There is also an evening-school here, chiefly consisting of adults and largely attended; but with that I am not connected.

On the 10th of this month, there was considerable excitement here. The bells were rung in honor of the vote to abolish slavery in Virginia.[13] Many did not know what was the cause of such a demonstration. Some thought it was an alarm of fire; others supposed the rebels had made a raid, and were marching down King St. We were, at first, inclined to the latter opinion; for, looking up that street we saw a company of the most woe-begone looking horsemen. It was raining hard, and some of them had dismounted, leading their poor jaded skeletons of horses. We soon learned that they were a portion of Kilpatrick's cavalry,[14] on their way to Culpepper. Poor fellows! they had had a weary tramp, and must still tramp on, through mud and rain, till they reached their journey's end. What hopeless despondency would take possession of our hearts, if we looked only on the suffering occasioned by this war, and not on the good already accomplished, and the still grander results shadowed forth in the future. The slowly-moving ambulance often passes by, with low beat of the drum, as the soldiers convey some comrade to his last resting-place. Buried on strange soil, far away from mother, wife, and children! Poor fellows! But they die the death of brave men in a noble cause. The Soldier's Burying Ground here is well cared for, and is a beautiful place.[15]

How nobly are the colored soldiers fighting and dying in the cause of Freedom! Our hearts are proud of the manhood they evince, in spite of the indignities heaped upon them. They are kept constantly on fatigue duty, digging trenches, and unloading vessels. Look at the Massachusetts Fifty-Fourth! Every man of them a hero! marching so boldly and steadily to victory or death, for the freedom of their race, and the salvation of their country! *Their* country! It makes my blood run warm to think how that country treats her colored sons, even the bravest and the best. If merit deserves reward, surely the 54th regiment is worthy of shoulder-straps. I have lately heard, from a friend in Boston, that the rank of second-lieutenant has been conferred.[16] I am thankful there is a beginning. I am full of hope for the future. A Power mightier than man is guiding this revolution; and though justice moves slowly, it will come at last. The American people will outlive this mean prejudice against complexion. Sooner or later, they will learn that "a man's a man for a' that."

We went to the wharf last Tuesday, to welcome the emigrants returned from Hayti. It was a bitter cold day, the snow was falling, and they were barefooted and bareheaded, with scarcely rags enough to cover them. They were put in wagons and carried to Green Heights. We did what we could for them. I went to see them next day, and found that three had died during the night. I was grieved for their hard lot; but I comforted myself with the idea that this would put an end to colonization projects.[17] They are eight miles from here, but I shall go to see them again to-morrow. I hope to obtain among them some recruits for the Massachusetts Cavalry.[18] I am trying to help Mr. Downing and Mr. Remond;[19] not for money, but because I want to do all I can to strengthen the hands of those who are battling for Freedom.

Thank you for your letter. I wish you could have seen the happy group of faces round me, at our little Fair, while I read it to them. The memory of the grateful hearts I have found among these freed men and women, will cheer me all my life.

Yours truly,
H. Jacobs and L. Jacobs

George Moses Horton, from *Naked Genius* (1865)

The Use of Liberty

With liberty simply all nations are blest,
  To wander creation all over,
And toil for eternity there is their rest,
  The right of all things first discover;
But learn in the ramble yourself to control,
And strictly take care of both body and soul,
For peace with our Maker and law is the whole,
  The pride and the crown of a nation.

But man in a nation without a true wife,
  Had better continue without one,
To live in contention forever in strife,
  Why should I be crazy about one?
Whoever endeavors to keep one in pain,
Your liberty thus is wound up in a chain,
For why should one ever be free to complain,
  The disgust and mock of his nation?

But freedom is not what some take it to be,
  A boon which we never should trifle,
A man may be turned loose and find himself free,
  To ramble the woods with his rifle,
He oft leaves behind him a hut of disgrace,
Without a rough servant to dig in his place,
He's not calculated to prowl thro' the chase,
  But rather to rob his own nation.

Take care recent free men what you are about,
  You are not aware of your danger,
This never should make you too selfish and stout,
  Be never to business a stranger,

Be careful to gather what wisdom you can,
Acknowledge yourself to be only a man;
To undermine others avoid such a plan,
    And shine like a star in your nation.

Whatever your life's occupation may be,
    A teacher, a ploughman or student,
Be never too selfish because you are free,
    To learn in your course to be prudent,
The spring's little streamlet must swell as it flows,
The more runs into it the larger it grows,
Till into the ocean a river it flows,
    And mingles the flood of a nation.

A man never should boast that he lives at his ease,
    Because he is free from his master,
Because I can ramble wherever I please;
    At nothing I strive none the faster,
I have not a servant, I have not a horse,
And have not the power to take one by force,
If nothing to keep one it makes it still worse,
    And poverty takes the plantation.

Mattie Jackson and L. S. Thompson, from *The Story of Mattie Jackson* (1866)

Narrated to her stepmother, Dr. L. S. Thompson, who had married her mother's second husband George Brown (such familial complexities are symptomatic), Jackson's memoir provides a slave's remarkable perspective on the turbulence of the Civil War. Beginning with an account of her ancestors and immediate family and concluding with her free life after the war in Lawrence, Mass., the narrative describes Jackson's experience of enslavement in St. Louis by a "very severe" William Lewis, her personal observations during the war years, her escape to Indianapolis, and her postwar reunion with her mother and half-brother. Beyond shedding light on such matters as the controversial Camp Jackson Affair and the hopeful yet precarious position of slaves in a federal-occupied city, Jackson's memoir can be seen as a vital contribution to the developing tradition of female slave narratives in the late nineteenth century. This excerpt opens with the early days of the war, after Jackson has been caught trying to escape and been purchased by Lewis, and closes with a chance encounter, after the war, between Jackson and her humbled former master.

The Soldiers, and Our Treatment During the War

Soon after the war commenced the rebel soldiers encamped near Mr. Lewis' residence, and remained there one week. They were then ordered by General Lyons[20] to surrender, but they refused. There were seven thousand Union and seven hundred rebel soldiers. The Union soldiers surrounded the camp and took them and exhibited them through the city and then confined them in prison.[21] I told my mistress that the Union soldiers were coming to take the camp. She replied that it was false, that it was General Kelly coming to re-enforce Gen. Frost.[22] In a few moments the alarm was heard. I told Mrs. L. the Unionists had fired upon the rebels. She replied it was only the salute of Gen. Kelley. At night her husband came home with the news that Camp Jackson was taken and all the soldiers prisoners. Mrs. Lewis asked how the Union soldiers could take seven hundred men when they only numbered the same. Mr. L. replied they had seven thousand. She was much astonished, and cast her eye around to us for fear we might hear her. Her suspicion was correct; there was not a word passed that escaped our listening ears. My mother and myself could read enough to make out the news in the papers. The Union soldiers took much delight in tossing a paper over the fence to us. It aggravated my mistress very much. My mother used to sit up nights and read to keep posted about the war. In a few days my mistress came down to the kitchen again with another bitter complaint that it was a sad affair that the Unionists had taken their delicate citizens who had enlisted and made prisoners of them – that they were babes. My mother reminded her of taking Fort Sumpter and Major Anderson[23] and serving them the same and that turn about was fair play. She then hastened to her room with the speed of a deer, nearly unhinging every door in her flight, replying as she went that the Niggers and Yankees were seeking to take the country. One day, after she had visited the kitchen to superintend some domestic affairs, as she pretended, she became very angry without a word being passed, and said – "I think it has come to a pretty pass, that old Lincoln, with his long legs, an old rail splitter, wishes to put the Niggers on an equality with the whites; that her children should never be on an equal footing with a Nigger. She had rather see them dead." As my mother made no reply to her remarks, she stopped talking, and commenced venting her spite on my companion servant. On one occasion Mr. Lewis searched my mother's room and found a picture of President Lincoln, cut from a newspaper, hanging in her room. He asked her what she was doing with old Lincoln's picture. She replied it was there because she liked it. He then knocked her down three times, and sent her to the trader's yard for a month as punishment. My mistress indulged some hopes till the victory of New Orleans,[24] when she heard the famous Union song sang to the tune of Yankee Doodle:[25]

The rebels swore that New Orleans never should be taken,
But if the Yankees came so near they should not save their bacon.
That's the way they blustered when they thought they were so handy,
But Farragut steamed up one day and gave them Doodle Dandy

Ben. Butler then was ordered down to regulate the city;
He made the rebels walk a chalk,[26] and was not that a pity?
That's the way to serve them out – that's the way to treat them,
They must not go and put on airs after we have beat them.

He made the rebel banks shell out and pay the loyal people,
He made them keep the city clean from pig's sty to church steeple.
That's the way Columbia[27] speaks, let all men believe her;
That's the way Columbia speaks instead of yellow fever.

He sent the saucy women up and made them treat us well
He helped the poor and snubbed the rich; they thought he was the devil.
Bully for Ben. Butler, then, they thought he was so handy;
Bully for Ben Butler then, – Yankee Doodle Dandy.

The days of sadness for mistress were days of joy for us. We shouted and laughed to the top of our voices. My mistress was more enraged than ever – nothing pleased her. One evening, after I had attended to my usual duties, and I supposed all was complete, she, in a terrible rage, declared I should be punished that night. I did not know the cause, neither did she. She went immediately and selected a switch. She placed it in the corner of the room to await the return of her husband at night for him to whip me. As I was not pleased with the idea of a whipping I bent the switch in the shape of W, which was the first letter of his name, and after I had attended to the dining room my fellow servant and myself walked away and stopped with an aunt of mine during the night. In the morning we made our way to the Arsenal, but could gain no admission. While we were wandering about seeking protection, the girl's father overtook us and persuaded us to return home. We finally complied. All was quiet. Not a word was spoken respecting our sudden departure. All went on as usual. I was permitted to attend to my work without interruption until three weeks after. One morning I entered Mrs. Lewis' room, and she was in a room adjoining, complaining of something I had neglected. Mr. L. then enquired if I had done my work. I told him I had. She then flew into a rage and told him I was saucy, and to strike me, and he immediately gave me a severe blow with a stick of wood, which inflicted a deep wound upon my head. The blood ran over my clothing, which gave me a frightful appearance. Mr. Lewis then ordered me to change my clothing immediately. As I did not obey he became more enraged, and pulled me into another room and threw me on the floor, placed his knee on my stomach, slapped me on the face and beat me with his fist, and would have punished me more had not my mother interfered. He then told her to go away or he would compel her to, but she remained until he left me. I struggled mightily, and stood him a good test for a while, but he was fast conquering me when my mother came. He was aware my mother could usually defend herself against one man, and both of us would overpower him, so after giving his wife strict orders to take me up stairs and keep me there, he took his carriage and drove away. But she forgot it, as usual. She was highly gratified with my appropriate treatment, as she called it, and retired to her room, leaving me to myself. I then went to my mother and told her I was going away. She bid me go, and added "May the Lord help you." I started for the Arsenal again and succeeded in gaining admittance and seeing the Adjutant. He ordered me to go to another tent, where there was a woman in similar circumstances, cooking. When the General found I was there he sent me to the boarding house. I remained there three weeks, and when I went I wore the same stained clothing as when I was so severely punished, which has left a mark on my head which will ever remind me of my treatment while in slavery. Thanks be to God, though tortured by wrong and goaded by oppression, the hearts that would madden with misery have broken the iron yoke.

Mr. Lewis Calls at the Boarding House

At the expiration of three weeks Mr. Lewis called at my boarding house, accompanied by his brother-in-law, and enquired for me, and the General informed him where I was. He then told me my mother was very anxious for me to come home, and I returned. The General had ordered Mr. Lewis to call at headquarters, when he told him if he had treated me right I would not have been compelled to seek protection of him; that my first appearance was sufficient proof of his cruelty. Mr. L. promised to take me home and treat me kindly. Instead of fulfilling his promise he carried me to the trader's yard, where, to my great surprise, I found my mother. She had been there during my absence, where she was kept for fear she would find me and take my brother and sister and make her escape. There was so much excitement at that time, (1861), by the Union soldiers rendering the fugitives shelter and protection, he was aware that if she applied to them, as he did not fulfill his promise in my case, he would stand a poor chance. If my mother made application to them for protection they would learn that he did not return me home and immediately detect the intrigue. After I was safely secured in the trader's yard, Mr. L. took my mother home. I remained in the yard three months. Near the termination of the time of my confinement I was passing by the office when the cook of the Arsenal saw and recognized me and informed the General that Mr. L. had disobeyed his orders, and had put me in the trader's yard instead of taking me home. The General immediately arrested Mr. L and gave him one hundred lashes with the cow-hide, so that they might identify him by a scarred back, as well as his slaves. My mother had the pleasure of washing his stained clothes, otherwise it would not have been known. My master was compelled to pay three thousand dollars and let me out. He then put me to service, where I remained seven months, after which he came in great haste and took me into the city and put me into the trader's yard again. After he received the punishment he treated my mother and the children worse than ever, which caused her to take her children and secrete themselves in the city, and would have remained undetected had it not been for a traitor who pledged himself to keep the secret. But King Whiskey fired up his brain one evening, and out popped the secret. My mother and sister were consequently taken and committed to the trader's yard. My little brother was then eight years of age, my sister sixteen, and myself eighteen. We remained there two weeks, when a rough looking man, called Capt. Tirrell, came to the yard and enquired for our family. After he had examined us he remarked that we were a fine looking family, and bid us retire. In about two hours he returned, at the edge of the evening, with a covered wagon, and took my mother and brother and sister and left me. My mother refused to go without me, and told him she would raise an alarm. He advised her to remain as quiet as possible. At length she was compelled to go. When she entered the wagon there was a man standing behind with his hands on each side of the wagon to prevent her from making her escape. She sprang to her feet and gave this man a desperate blow, and leaping to the ground she made an alarm. The watchmen came to her assistance immediately, and there was quite a number of Union policemen guarding the city at that time, who rendered her due justice as far as possible. This was before the emancipation proclamation was issued. After she leaped from the wagon they drove on, taking her children to the boat. The police questioned my mother. She told them that Capt. Tirrell had put her children on board the boat, and was going to take them to Memphis and sell them into hard slavery. They accompanied her to the boat, and arrived just as they were casting off. The police ordered them to stop and immediately deliver up the children, who had been secreted in the Captain's private apartment. They were brought forth and returned. Slave speculation was forbidden in St. Louis at that time. The Union soldiers had possession of the city, but their power was limited to the suppression of the selling of slaves to go out of the city. Considerable smuggling was done, however, by pretending Unionism, which was the case with our family.

Released from the Trader's Yard and Taken to Her New Master

Immediately after dinner my mother called for me to accompany her to our new home, the residence of the Captain, together with my brother and sister. We fared very well while we were there. Mrs. Tirrell was insane, and my mother had charge of the house. We remained there four months. The Captain came home only once a week, and he never troubled us for fear we might desert him. His intention was to smuggle us away before the State became free. That was the understanding when he bought us of Mr. Lewis, as it was not much of an object to purchase slaves while the proclamation was pending, and they likely to lose all their property; but they would, for a trifle purchase a whole family of four or five persons to send out of the State. Kentucky paid as much, or more than ever, for slaves. As they pretended to take no part in the rebellion they supposed they would be allowed to keep them without interference. Consequently the Captain's intention was to keep as quiet as possible till the excitement concerning us was over, and he could get us off without detection. Mr. Lewis would rather have disposed of us for nothing than have seen us free. He hated my mother in consequence of her desire for freedom, and her endeavors to teach her children the right way as far as her ability would allow. He also held a charge against her for reading the papers and understanding political affairs. When he found he was to lose his slaves he could not bear the idea of her being free. He thought it too hard, as she had raised so many tempests for him, to see her free and under her own control. He had tantalized her in every possible way to humiliate and annoy her; yet while he could demand her services he appreciated and placed perfect confidence in mother and family. None but a fiendish slaveholder could have rended an honest Christian heart in such a manner as this.

> Though it was her sad and weary lot to toil in slavery
> But one thing cheered her weary soul
> When almost in despair
> That she could gain a sure relief in attitude of prayer

Capt. Tirrell Removes the Family—Another Strategy

One day the Captain commenced complaining of the expense of so large a family, and proposed to my mother that we should work out and he take part of the pay. My mother told him she would need what she earned for my little brother's support. Finally the Captain consented, and I was the first to be disposed of. The Captain took me in his buggy and carried me to the Depot, and I was put into a Union family, where I remained five months. Previous to my leaving, however, my mother and the Captain entered into a contract – he agreeing not to sell us, and mother agreeing not to make her escape. While she was carrying out her promise in good faith, he was plotting to separate us. We were all divided except mother and my little brother, who remained together. My sister remained with one of the rebels, but was tolerably treated. We all fared very well; but it was only the calm before the rending tornado. Captain T. was Captain of the boat to Memphis, from which the Union soldiers had rescued us. He commenced as a deck hand on the boat, then attained a higher position, and continued to advance until he became her Captain. At length he came in possession of slaves. Then his accomplishments were complete. He was a very severe slave master. Those mushroon slaveholders are much dreaded, as their severity knows no bounds.

> Bondage and torture, scourges and chains
> Placed on our backs indelible stains.

I stated previously, in relating a sketch of my mother's history, that she was married twice, and both husbands were to be sold and made their escape. They both gained their freedom. One was living, – the other died before the war. Both made every effort to find us, but to no purpose. It was some years before we got a correct account of her second husband, and he had no account of her, except once he heard that mother and children had perished in the woods while endeavoring to make their escape. In a few years after his arrival in the free States he married again.

When about sixteen years of age, while residing with her original master, my mother became acquainted with a young man, Mr. Adams, residing in a neighboring family, whom she much respected; but he was soon sold, and she lost trace of him entirely, as was the common occurrence with friends and companions though united by the nearest ties. When my mother arrived at Captain Tirrell's, after leaving the boat, in her excitement she scarce observed anything except her little group so miraculously saved from perhaps a final separation in this world. She at length observed that the servant who was waiting to take her to the Captain's residence in the country was the same man with whom she formed the acquaintance when sixteen years old, and they again renewed their acquaintance. He had been married and buried his wife. It appeared that his wife had been in Captain Tirrell's family many years, and he also, for some time. They had a number of children, and Capt. Tirrell had sold them down South. This cruel blow, assisted by severe flogging and other ill treatment, rendered the mother insane, and finally caused her death.

> In agony close to her bosom she pressed,
> The life of her heart, the child of her breast —
> Oh love from its tenderness gathering might
> Had strengthed her soul for declining age.
>
> But she is free. Yes, she has gone from the land of the slave;
> The hand of oppression must rest in the grave.
> The blood hounds have missed the scent of her way,
> The hunter is rifled and foiled of his prey.

After my mother had left the Captain to take care of herself and child, according to agreement with the Captain, she became engaged to Mr. Adams. He had bought himself previously for a large price. After they became acquainted, the Captain had an excellent opportunity of carrying out his stratagem. He commenced bestowing charity upon Mr. Adams. As he had purchased himself, and Capt. T. had agreed not to sell my mother, they had decided to marry at an early day. They hired a house in the city and were to commence housekeeping immediately. The Captain made him a number of presents and seemed much pleased with the arrangement. The day previous to the one set for the marriage, while they were setting their house in order, a man called and enquired for a nurse, pretending he wanted one of us. Mother was absent; he said he would call again, but he never came. On Wednesday evening we attended a protracted meeting. After we had returned home and retired, a loud rap was heard at the door. My Aunt enquired who was there. The reply was, "Open the door or I will break it down." In a moment in rushed seven men, four watchmen and three traders, and ordered mother to take my brother and me and follow them, which she hastened to do as fast as possible, but we were not allowed time to put on our usual attire. They thrust us into a close carriage. For fear of my mother alarming the citizens they threw her to the ground and choked her until she was nearly strangled, then pushed her into a coach. The night was dark and dreary; the stars refused to shine, the moon to shed her light.

'Tis not strange the heavenly orbs
In silence blushed 'neath Nature's sable garb
When woman's gagged and rashly torn away
Without blemish and without crime.
Unheeded by God's holy word: –
Unloose the fetters, break the chain,
And make my people free again,
And let them breath pure freedom's air
And her rich bounty freely share.
Let Eutopia stretch her bleeding hands abroad;
Her cry of anguish finds redress from God.

We were hurried along the streets. The inhabitants heard our cries and rushed to their doors, but our carriage being perfectly tight and the alarm so sudden, that we were at the jail before they could give us any relief. There were strong Union men and officers in the city, and if they could have been informed of the human smuggling they would have released us. But oh, that horrid, dilapidated prison, with its dim lights and dingy walls, again presented itself to our view. My sister was there first, and we were thrust in and remained there until three o'clock the following afternoon. Could we have notified the police we should have been released, but, no opportunity was given us. It appears that this kidnapping had been in contemplation from the time we were before taken and returned; and Captain Tirrell's kindness to mother, – his benevolence towards Mr. Adams in assisting him to furnish his house, – his generosity in letting us work for ourselves, – his approbation in regard to the contemplated marriage was only a trap. Thus instead of a wedding Thursday evening, we were hurled across the ferry to Albany Court House and to Kentucky through the rain and without our outer garments. My mother had lost her bonnet and shawl in the struggle while being thrust in the coach, consequently she had no protection from the storm, and the rest of us were in similar circumstances. I believe we passed through Springfield. I think it was the first stopping place after we left East St. Louis, and we were put on board the cars and secreted in the gentlemen's smoking car, in which there were only a few rebels. We arrived in Springfield about twelve o'clock at night. When we took the cars it was dark, bleak and cold. It was the 18th of March, and as we were without bonnets and clothing to shield us from the sleet and wind, we suffered intensely. The old trader, for fear that mother might make her escape, carried my brother, nine years of age, from one train to the other. We then took the cars for Albany, and arrived at eight o'clock in the morning. We were then carried on the ferry in a wagon. There was another family in the wagon, in the same condition. We landed at Portland, from thence to Louisville, and were put into John Clark's trader's yard, and sold out separately, except my mother and little brother, who were sold together. Mother remained in the trader's yard two weeks, my sister six, myself four.

The Fare at Their New Homes

Mother was sold to Captain Plasio, my sister to Benj. Board, and myself to Capt. Ephraim Frisbee. The man who bought my mother was a Spaniard. After she had been there a short time he tried to have my mother let my brother stop at his saloon, a very dissipated place; to wait upon his miserable crew, but my mother objected. In spite of her objections he took him down to try him, but some Union soldiers called at the saloon, and noticing that he was very small, they questioned him, and my brother, child like, divulged the whole matter. The Captain, fearful of being betrayed and losing his property, let him continue with my mother. The Captain paid eight hundred dollars for my mother and brother. We were all sold for extravagant prices. My sister, aged sixteen, was sold for eight hundred and fifty dollars; I was sold for nine hundred dollars. This was in 1863. My mother was cook and fared very well. My sister was sold to a single gentleman, whose intended took charge of her until they were married, after which they took her to her home. She was her waiter, and fared as well as could be expected. I fared worse than either of the family. I was not allowed enough to eat, exposed to the cold, and not allowed through the cold winter to thoroughly warm myself once a month. The house was very large, and I could gain no access to the fire. I was kept constantly at work of the heaviest kind, – compelled to move heavy trunks and boxes, – many times to wash till ten and twelve o'clock at night. There were three deaths in the family while I remained there, and the entire burden was put upon me. I often felt to exclaim as the Children of Israel did: "O Lord, my burden is greater than I can bear." I was then seventeen years of age. My health has been impaired from that time to the present. I have a severe pain in my side by the slightest over exertion. In the Winter I suffer intensely with cold, and cannot get warm unless in a room heated to eighty degrees. I am infirm and burdened with the influence of slavery, whose impress will ever remain on my mind and body. For six months I tried to make my escape. I used to rise at four o'clock in the morning to find some one to assist me, and at last I succeeded. I was allowed two hours once in two weeks to go and return three miles. I could contrive no other way than to improve one of those opportunities, in which I was finally successful. I became acquainted with some persons who assisted slaves to escape by the underground railroad. They were colored people. I was to pretend going to church, and the man who was to assist and introduce me to the proper parties was to linger on the street opposite the house, and I was to follow at a short distance. On Sunday evening I begged leave to attend church, which was reluctantly granted if I completed all my work, which was no easy task. It appeared as if my mistress used every possible exertion to delay me from church, and I concluded that her old cloven-footed companion had impressed his intentions on her mind. Finally, when I was ready to start, my mistress took a notion to go out to ride, and desired me to dress her little boy, and then get ready for church. Extensive hoops were then worn, and as I had attached my whole wardrobe under mine by a cord around my waist, it required considerable dexterity and no small amount of maneuvering to hide the fact from my mistress. While attending to the child I had managed to stand in one corner of the room, for fear she might come in contact with me, and thus discover that my hoops were not so elastic as they usually are. I endeavored to conceal my excitement by backing and edging very genteelly out of the door. I had nine pieces of clothing thus concealed on my person, and as the string which fastened them was small it caused me considerable discomfort. To my great satisfaction I at last passed into the street, and my master and mistress drove down the street in great haste and were soon out of sight. I saw my guide patiently awaiting me. I followed him at a distance until we arrived at the church, and there met two young ladies, one of whom handed me a pass and told me to follow them at a square's distance. It was now twilight. There was a company of soldiers about to take passage across the ferry, and I followed. I showed my pass, and proceeded up the stairs on the boat. While thus ascending the stairs, the cord which held my bundle of clothing broke, and my feet became entangled in my wardrobe, but by proceeding, the first step released one foot and the next the other. This was observed only by a few soldiers, who were too deeply engaged in their own affairs to interfere with mine. I seated myself in a remote corner of the boat, and in a few moments I landed on free soil for the first time in my life, except when hurled through Albany and Springfield at the time of our capture. I was now under my own control. The cars were waiting in Jefferson City for the passengers for Indianapolis, where we arrived about nine o'clock.

Mattie in Indianapolis—The Glory of Freedom—President Lincoln's Remains Exhibited

My first business, after my arrival at Indianapolis, was to find a boarding place in which I at once succeeded, and in a few hours thereafter was at a place of service of my own choice. I had always been under the yoke of oppression, compelled to submit to its laws, and not allowed to advance a rod from the house, or even out of call, without a severe punishment. Now this constant fear and restless yearning was over. It appeared as though I had emerged into a new world, or had never lived in the old one before. The people I lived with were Unionists, and became immediately interested in teaching and encouraging me in my literary advancement and all other important improvements, which precisely met the natural desires for which my soul had ever yearned since my earliest recollection. I could read a little, but was not allowed to learn in slavery. I was obliged to pay twenty-five cents for every letter written for me. I now began to feel that as I was free I could learn to write, as well as others; consequently Mrs. Harris, the lady with whom I lived, volunteered to assist me. I was soon enabled to write quite a legible hand, which I find a great convenience. I would advise all, young, middle aged or old, in a free country, to learn to read and write. If this little book should fall into the hands of one deficient of the important knowledge of writing I hope they will remember the old maxim: – "Never too old to learn." Manage your own secrets, and divulge them by the silent language of your own pen. Had our blessed President considered it too humiliating to learn in advanced years, our race would yet have remained under the galling yoke of oppression. After I had been with Mrs. Harris seven months, the joyful news came of the surrender of Lee's army and the capture of Richmond.[28]

> Whilst the country's hearts were throbbing,
>   Filled with joy for victories won;
> Whilst the stars and stripes were waving
>   O'er each cottage, ship and dome,
> Came upon like winged lightning
>   Words that turned each joy to dread,
> Froze with horror as we listened:
>   Our beloved chieftain, Lincoln's dead.
>
> War's dark clouds has long held o'er us,
>   They have rolled their gloomy folds away,
> And all the world is anxious, waiting
>   For that promised peaceful day.
> But that fearful blow inflicted,
>   Fell on his devoted head,
> And from every town and hamlet
>   Came the cry our Chieftain's dead.
>
> Weep, weep, O bleeding nation
>   For the patriot spirit fled,
> All untold our century's future –
>   Buried with the silent dead.

God of battles, God of nations to our country send relief
Turn each lamentation into joy whilst we mourn our murdered chief.

On the Saturday after the assassination of the President there was a meeting held on the Common, and a vote taken to have the President's body brought through Indianapolis, for the people to see his dear dead face. The vote was taken by raising the hands, and when the question was put in favor of it a thousand black hands were extended in the air, seemingly higher and more visible than all the rest. Nor were their hands alone raised, for in their deep sorrow and gloom they raised their hearts to God, for well they knew that He, through martyred blood, had made them free. It was some time before the remains reached Indianapolis, as it was near the last of the route.[29] The body was placed in the centre of the hall of the State House, and we marched in by fours, and divided into twos on each side of the casket, and passed directly through the Hall. It was very rainy, – nothing but umbrellas were to be seen in any direction. The multitude were passing in and out from eight o'clock in the morning till four o'clock in the afternoon. His body remained until twelve o'clock in the evening, many distinguished persons visiting it, when amid the booming of cannon, it moved on its way to Springfield, its final resting-place. The death of the President was like an electric shock to my soul. I could not feel convinced of his death until I gazed upon his remains, and heard the last roll of the muffled drum and the farewell boom of the cannon. I was then convinced that though we were left to the tender mercies of God, we were without a leader.

Gone, gone is our chieftain,
The tried and the true;
The grief of our nation the world never knew.
We mourn as a nation has never yet mourned;
The foe to our freedom more deeply has scorned.

In the height of his glory in manhood's full prime,
Our country's preserver through darkest of time;
A merciful being, whose kindness all shared
Shown mercy to others. Why was he not spared?

The lover of Justice, the friend of the slave,
He struck at oppression and made it a grave;
He spoke for our bond-men, and chains from them fell,
By making them soldiers they served our land well.

Because he had spoken from sea unto sea
Glad tidings go heavenward, our country is free,
And angels I'm thinking looked down from above,
With sweet smiles approving his great works of love.

His name with the honor forever will live,
And time to his laurels new lustre will give;
He lived so unselfish, so loyal and true,
That his deeds will shine brighter at every view.

Then honor and cherish the name of the brave,
The champion of freedom, the friend to the slave,
The far-sighted statesman who saw a fair end,
When north land and south land one flag shall defend.

Rest, rest, fallen chieftain, thy labors are o'er,
For thee mourns a nation as never before;
Farewell honored chieftain whom millions adore,
Farewell gentle spirit, whom heaven has won.

Sister Lost—Mother's Escape

In two or three weeks after the body of the President was carried through, my sister made her escape, but by some means we entirely lost trace of her. We heard she was in a free State. In three months my mother also escaped. She rose quite early in the morning, took my little brother, and arrived at my place of service in the afternoon. I was much surprised, and asked my mother how she came there. She could scarcely tell me for weeping, but I soon found out the mystery. After so many long years and so many attempts, for this was her seventh, she at last succeeded, and we were now all free. My mother had been a slave for more than forty-three years, and liberty was very sweet to her. The sound of freedom was music in our ears; the air was pure and fragrant; the genial rays of the glorious sun burst forth with a new lustre upon us, and all creation resounded in responses of praise to the author and creator of him who proclaimed life and freedom to the slave. I was overjoyed with my personal freedom, but the joy at my mother's escape was greater than anything I had ever known. It was a joy that reaches beyond the tide and anchors in the harbor of eternal rest. While in oppression, this eternal life-preserver had continually wafted her toward the land of freedom, which she was confident of gaining, whatever might betide. Our joy that we were permitted to mingle together our earthly bliss in glorious strains of freedom was indescribable. My mother responded with the children of Israel, – "The Lord is my strength and my song. The Lord is a man of war, and the Lord is his name."[30] We left Indianapolis the day after my mother arrived, and took the cars at eleven o'clock the following evening for St. Louis, my native State. We were then free, and instead of being hurried along, bare headed and half naked, through cars and boats, by a brutal master with a bill of sale in his pocket, we were our own, comfortably clothed, and having the true emblems of freedom.

Summary

On my return to St. Louis I met my old master, Lewis, who strove so hard to sell us away that he might avoid seeing us free, on the street. He was so surprised that before he was aware of it he dropped a bow. My mother met Mrs. Lewis, her old mistress, with a large basket on her arm, trudging to market. It appeared she had lived to see the day when her children had to wait upon themselves, and she likewise. The Yankees had taken possession, and her posterity were on an equality with the black man. Mr. Lewis despised the Irish, and often declared he would board at the hotel before he would employ Irish help, but he now has a dissipated Irish cook. When I was his slave I was obliged to keep away every fly from the table, and not allow one to light on a person. They are now compelled to brush their own flies and dress themselves and children. Mr. Lewis' brother Benjamin was a more severe slave master than the one who owned me. He was a tobacconist and very wealthy. As soon as the war commenced he turned Unionist to save his property. He was very severe in his punishments. He used to extend his victim, fastened to a beam, with hands and feet tied, and inflict from fifty to three hundred lashes, laying their flesh entirely open, then bathe their quivering wounds with brine, and, through his nose, in a slow rebel tone he would tell them "You'd better walk a fair chalk line or else I'll give yer twice as much." His former friends, the guerrillas, were aware he only turned Union to save his cash, and they gave those persons he had abused a large share of his luxury. They then, in the presence of his wife and another distinguished lady, tortured him in a most inhuman manner. For pretending Unionism they placed him on a table and threatened to dissect him alive if he did not tell them where he kept his gold. He immediately informed them. They then stood him against the house and fired over his head. From that, they changed his position by turning him upside down, and raising him two feet from the floor, letting him dash his head against the floor until his skull was fractured, after which he lingered awhile and finally died. There was a long piece published in the paper respecting his repentance, benevolence, &c. All the slaves who ever lived in his family admit the Lord is able to save to the uttermost. He saved the thief on the cross, and perhaps he saved him.

When I made my escape from slavery I was in a query how I was to raise funds to bear my expenses. I finally came to the conclusion that as the laborer was worthy of his hire, I thought my wages should come from my master's pocket. Accordingly I took twenty-five dollars. After I was safe and had learned to write, I sent him a nice letter, thanking him for the kindness his pocket bestowed to me in time of need. I have never received any answer to it.

When I complete my education, if my life is spared, I shall endeavor to publish further details of our history in another volume from my own pen.

Mark Twain, "A True Story, Repeated Word for Word as I Heard It" (1874)

Twain based the narrator of this story, Aunt Rachel, on Mary Ann "Auntie" Cord, the cook at his sister-in-law's farm in Elmira, New York, where Twain regularly retreated for the summer to write. The "African American experience" here is artfully retold by a white author, but it telescopes a wide swath of African American history, from the 1850s through emancipation to the Reconstruction years. The story is also significant because it launched the major phase of Twain's career, both by establishing him as a writer for the influential *Atlantic Monthly* and by anticipating his work in *Adventures of Huckleberry Finn*. When he sent it to Howells, Twain wrote that the story "has no humor in it. You can pay as you choose for that, if you want it, for its rather out of my line." In fact, considering the totality of his career as a critical surveyor of American society, it was very much in Twain's line – and in the end Howells paid 20 dollars a page for it, an unprecedented rate for the *Atlantic Monthly*.[31]

It was summer time, and twilight. We were sitting on the porch of the farm-house, on the summit of the hill, and "Aunt Rachel" was sitting respectfully below our level, on the steps, – for she was our servant, and colored. She was of mighty frame and stature; she was sixty years old, but her eye was undimmed and her strength unabated. She was a cheerful, hearty soul, and it was no more trouble for her to laugh than it is for a bird to sing. She was under fire, now, as usual when the day was done. That is to say, she was being chaffed without mercy, and was enjoying it. She would let off peal after peal of laughter, and then sit with her face in her hands and shake with throes of enjoyment which she could no longer get breath enough to express. At such a moment as this a thought occurred to me, and I said: –

"Aunt Rachel, how is it that you've lived sixty years and never had any trouble?"

She stopped quaking. She paused, and there was a moment of silence. She turned her face over her shoulder toward me, and said, without even a smile in her voice: –

"Misto C----, is you in 'arnest?"

It surprised me a good deal; and it sobered my manner and my speech, too. I said: –

"Why, I thought – that is, I meant – why, you *can't* have had any trouble. I've never heard you sigh, and never seen your eye when there was n't a laugh in it."

She faced fairly around, now, and was full of earnestness.

"Has I had any trouble? Misto C----, I's gwyne to tell you, den I leave it to you. I was bawn down 'mongst de slaves; I knows all 'bout slavery, 'case I been one of 'em my own se'f. Well, sah, my ole man – dat's my husban' – he was lovin' an' kind to me, jist as kind as you is to yo' own wife. An' we had chil'en – seven chil'en – an' we loved dem chil'en jist de same as you loves yo' chil'en. Dey was black, but de Lord can't make no chil'en so black but what dey mother love 'em an' wouldn't give 'em up, no, not for anything dat's in dis whole world.

"Well, sah, I was raised in ole Fo'ginny, but my mother she was raised in Maryland; an' my *souls!* she was turrible when she'd git started! My *lan'!* but she'd make de fur fly! When she'd git into dem tantrums, she always had one word dat she said. She'd straighten herse'f up an' put her fists in her hips an' say, 'I want you to understan' dat I wa' n't bawn in de mash to be fool' by trash! I's one o' de ole Blue Hen's Chickens,[32] *I* is!' 'Ca'se, you see, dat's what folks dat's bawn in Maryland calls deyselves, an' dey's proud of it. Well, dat was her word. I don't ever forgit it, beca'se she said it so much, an' beca'se she said it one day when my little Henry tore his wris' awful, an' most busted his head, right up at de top of his forehead, an' de niggers did n't fly aroun' fas' enough to 'tend to him. An' when dey talk' back at her, she up an' she says, 'Look-a-heah!' she says, 'I want you niggers to understan' dat I wa' n't bawn in de mash to be fool' by trash! I's one o' de ole Blue Hen's Chickens, *I* is!' an' den she clar' dat kitchen an' bandage' up de chile herse'f. So I says dat word, too, when I's riled.

"Well, bymeby my ole mistis say she's broke, an' she got to sell all de niggers on de place. An' when I heah dat dey gwyne to sell us all off at oction in Richmon', oh de good gracious! I know what dat mean!"

Aunt Rachel had gradually risen, while she warmed to her subject, and now she towered above us, black against the stars.

"Dey put chains on us an' put us on a stan' as high as dis po'ch, – twenty foot high, – an' all de people stood aroun', crowds an' crowds. An' dey'd come up dah an' look at us all roun', an' squeeze our arm, an' make us git up an' walk, an' den say, 'Dis one too ole,' or 'Dis one lame,' or 'Dis one don't 'mount to much.' An' dey sole my ole man, an' took him away, an' dey began to sell my chil'en an' take *dem* away, an' I begin to cry; an' de man say, 'Shet up yo' dam blubberin','' an' hit me on de mouf wid his han'. An' when de las' one was gone but my little Henry, I grab' *him* clost up to my breas' so, an' I ris up an' says, 'You shan't take him away,' I says; 'I'll kill de man dat tetches him!' I says. But my little Henry whisper an' say, 'I gwyne to run away, an' den I work an' buy yo' freedom.' Oh, bless de chile, he always so good! But dey got him – dey got him, de men did; but I took and tear de clo'es mos' off of 'em, an' beat 'em over de head wid my chain; an' *dey* give it to *me*, too, but I did n't mine dat.

"Well, dah was my ole man gone, an' all my chil'en, all my seven chil'en – an' six of 'em I hain't set eyes on ag'in to dis day, an' dat's twenty-two year ago las' Easter. De man dat bought me b'long' in Newbern, an' he took me dah. Well, bymeby de years roll on an' de waw come. My marster he was a Confedrit colonel, an' I was his family's cook. So when de Unions took dat town, dey all run away an' lef' me all by myse'f wid de other niggers in dat mons'us big house. So de big Union officers move in dah, an' dey ask me would I cook for *dem*. 'Lord bless you,' says I, 'dat's what I's *for*.'

"Dey wa'n't no small-fry officers, mine you, dey was de biggest dey *is*; an' de way dey made dem sojers mosey roun'! De Gen'l he tole me to boss dat kitchen; an' he say, 'If anybody come meddlin' wid you, you jist make 'em walk chalk; don't you be afeard,' he say; 'you's 'mong frens, now.'

"Well, I thinks to myse'f, if my little Henry ever got a chance to run away, he'd make to de Norf, o' course. So one day I comes in dah whah de big officers was, in de parlor, an' I drops a kurtchy, so, an' I up an' tole 'em 'bout my Henry, dey a-listenin' to my troubles jist de same as if I was white folks; an' I says, 'What I come for is beca'se if he got away and got up Norf whah you gemmen comes from, you might 'a' seen him, maybe, an' could tell me so as I could fine him ag'in; he was very little, an' he had a sk-yar on his lef' wris', an' at de top of his forehead.' Den dey look mournful, an' de Gen'l say, 'How long sence you los' him?' an' I say, 'Thirteen year.' Den de Gen'l say, 'He would n't be little no mo', now – he's a man!'

"I never thought o' dat befo'! He was only dat little feller to *me*, yit. I never thought 'bout him growin' up an' bein' big. But I see it den. None o' de gemmen had run acrost him, so dey could n't do nothin' for me. But all dat time, do' *I* did n't know it, my Henry *was* run off to de Norf, years an' years, an' he was a barber, too, an' worked for hisse'f. An' bymeby, when de waw come, he ups an' he says, 'I's done barberin',' he says; 'I's gwyne to fine my ole mammy, less'n she's dead.' So he sole out an' went to whah dey was recruitin', an' hired hisse'f out to de colonel for his servant; an' den he went all froo de battles everywhah, huntin' for his ole mammy; yes indeedy, he'd hire to fust one officer an' den another, tell he'd ransacked de whole Souf; but you see *I* did n't know nuffin 'bout *dis*. How was *I* gwyne to know it?

"Well, one night we had a big sojer ball; de sojers dah at Newbern was always havin' balls an' carryin' on. Dey had 'em in my kitchen, heaps o' times, 'ca'se it was so big. Mine you, I was *down* on sich doin's; beca'se my place was wid de officers, an' it rasp' me to have dem common sojers cavortin' roun' my kitchen like dat. But I alway' stood aroun' an' kep' things straight, I did; an' sometimes dey'd git my dander up, an' den I'd make 'em clar dat kitchen, mine I *tell* you!

"Well, one night – it was a Friday night – dey comes a whole plattoon f'm a *nigger* ridgment dat was on guard at de house, – de house was head-quarters, you know, – an' den I was jist a-*bilin*'! Mad? I was jist a-*boomin*'! I swelled aroun', an' swelled aroun'; I jist was a-itchin' for 'em to do somefin for to start me. *An*' dey was a-waltzin' an a-dancin'! *my!* but dey was havin' a time! an' I jist a-swellin' an' a-swellin' up! Pooty soon, 'long comes *sich* a spruce young nigger a-sailin' down de room wid a yaller wench roun' de wais'; an' roun' an' roun' an roun' dey went, enough to make a body drunk to look at 'em; an' when dey got abreas' o' me, dey went to kin' o' balancin' aroun', fust on one leg an' den on t'other, an' smilin' at my big red turban, an' makin' fun, an' I ups an' says, '*Git* along wid you! – rubbage!' De young man's face kin' o' changed, all of a sudden, for 'bout a second, but den he went to smilin' ag'in, same as he was befo'. Well, 'bout dis time, in comes some niggers dat played music an' b'long' to de ban', an' dey *never* could git along widout puttin' on airs. An' de very fust air dey put on dat night, I lit into 'em! Dey laughed, an' dat made me wuss. De res' o' de niggers got to laughin', an' den my soul *alive* but I was hot! My eye was jist a-blazin'! I jist straightened myself up, so, – jist as I is now, plum to de ceilin', mos', – an' I digs my fists into my hips, an' I says, 'Look-a-heah!' I says, 'I want you niggers to understan' dat I wa' n't bawn in de mash to be fool' by trash! I's one o' de ole Blue Hen's Chickens, *I* is!' an' den I see dat young man stan' a-starin' an' stiff, lookin' kin' o' up at de ceilin' like he fo'got somefin, an' could n't 'member it no mo'. Well, I jist march' on dem niggers, – so, lookin' like a gen'l, – an' dey jist cave' away befo' me an' out at de do'. An' as dis young man was a-goin' out, I heah him say to another nigger, 'Jim,' he says, 'you go 'long an' tell de cap'n I be on han' 'bout eight o'clock in de mawnin'; dey's somefin on my mine,' he says; 'I don't sleep no mo' dis night. You go 'long,' he says, 'an' leave me by my own se'f.'

"Dis was 'bout one o'clock in de mawnin'. Well, 'bout seven, I was up an' on han', gettin' de officers' breakfast. I was a-stoopin' down by de stove, – jist so, same as if yo' foot was de stove, – an' I'd opened de stove do wid my right han', – so, pushin' it back, jist as I pushes yo' foot, – an' I'd jist got de pan o' hot biscuits in my han' an' was 'bout to raise up, when I see a black face come aroun' under mine, an' de eyes a-lookin' up into mine, jist as I's a-lookin' up clost under yo' face now; an' I jist stopped *right dah*, an' never budged! jist gazed, an' gazed, so; an' de pan begin to tremble, an' all of a sudden *I knowed!* De pan drop' on de flo' an' I grab his lef' han' an' shove back his sleeve, – jist so, as I's doin' to you, an' den I goes for his forehead an' push de hair back, so, an' 'Boy!' I says, 'if you an't my Henry, what is you doin' wid dis welt on yo' wris' an' dat sk-yar on yo' forehead? De Lord God ob heaven be praise', I got my own ag'in!'

"Oh, no, Misto C----, I hain't had no trouble. An' no *joy!*"

Susie King Taylor, from *Reminiscences of My Life in Camp . . .* (1902)

Taylor, a young but literate escaped slave, was working as a teacher on Union-occupied St. Simon's Island off the coast of Georgia when Capt. Charles Trowbridge, organizing one of the Union's first black regiments, the First South Carolina Volunteers, came to the island seeking recruits. Along with a number of new black soldiers, Taylor joined a transport for Beaufort, South Carolina, where she began work as a laundress, cook, nurse, and teacher for the regiment, based at Old Fort Plantation, or "Camp Saxton," after Brig. Gen. Rufus Saxton. There, she both witnessed and made history, contributing to the war effort in indirect but important ways, and recording her impressions of life in a mixed military camp and of such major events as the capture of Charleston.

IV—Camp Saxton—Proclamation and Barbecue, 1863

On the first of January, 1863, we held services for the purpose of listening to the reading of President Lincoln's proclamation by Dr. W. H. Brisbane,[33] and the presentation of two beautiful stands of colors, one from a lady in Connecticut, and the other from Rev. Mr. Cheever.[34] The presentation speech was made by Chaplain French. It was a glorious day for us all, and we enjoyed every minute of it, and as a fitting close and the crowning event of this occasion we had a grand barbecue. A number of oxen were roasted whole, and we had a fine feast. Although not served as tastily or correctly as it would have been at home, yet it was enjoyed with keen appetites and relish. The soldiers had a good time. They sang or shouted "Hurrah!" all through the camp, and seemed overflowing with fun and frolic until taps were sounded, when many, no doubt, dreamt of this memorable day.

I had rather an amusing experience; that is, it seems amusing now, as I look back, but at the time it occurred it was a most serious one to me. When our regiment left Beaufort for Seabrooke, I left some of my things with a neighbor who lived outside of the camp. After I had been at Seabrooke about a week, I decided to return to Camp Saxton and get them. So one morning, with Mary Shaw, a friend who was in the company at that time, I started off. There was no way for us to get to Beaufort other than to walk, except we rode on the commissary wagon. This we did, and reached Beaufort about one o'clock. We then had more than two miles to walk before reaching our old camp, and expected to be able to accomplish this and return in time to meet the wagon again by three o'clock that afternoon, and so be taken back. We failed to do this, however, for when we got to Beaufort the wagon was gone. We did not know what to do. I did not wish to remain overnight, neither did my friend, although we might easily have stayed, as both had relatives in the town.

It was in the springtime, and the days were long, and as the sun looked so bright, we concluded to walk back, thinking we should reach camp before dark. So off we started on our ten-mile tramp. We had not gone many miles, however, before we were all tired out and began to regret our undertaking. The sun was getting low, and we grew more frightened, fearful of meeting some animal or of treading on a snake on our way. We did not meet a person, and we were frightened almost to death. Our feet were so sore we could hardly walk. Finally we took off our shoes and tried walking in our stocking feet, but this made them worse. We had gone about six miles when night overtook us. There we were, nothing around us but dense woods, and as there was no house or any place to stop at, there was nothing for us to do but continue on. We were afraid to speak to each other.

Meantime at the camp, seeing no signs of us by dusk, they concluded we had decided to remain over until next day, and so had no idea of our plight. Imagine their surprise when we reached camp about eleven P. M. The guard challenged us, "Who comes there?" My answer was, "A friend without a countersign." He approached and saw who it was, reported, and we were admitted into the lines. They had the joke on us that night, and for a long time after would tease us; and sometimes some of the men who were on guard that night would call us deserters. They used to laugh at us, but we joined with them too, especially when we would tell them our experience on our way to camp. I did not undertake that trip again, as there was no way of getting in or out except one took the provision wagon, and there was not much dependence to be put in that returning to camp. Perhaps the driver would say one hour and he might be there earlier or later. Of course it was not his fault, as it depended when the order was filled at the Commissary Department; therefore I did not go any more until the regiment was ordered to our new camp, which was named after our hero, Colonel Shaw, who at that time was at Beaufort with his regiment, the 54th Massachusetts.[35]

I taught a great many of the comrades in Company E to read and write, when they were off duty. Nearly all were anxious to learn. My husband taught some also when it was convenient for him. I was very happy to know my efforts were successful in camp, and also felt grateful for the appreciation of my services. I gave my services willingly for four years and three months without receiving a dollar. I was glad, however, to be allowed to go with the regiment, to care for the sick and afflicted comrades.

V—Military Expeditions, and Life in Camp

In the latter part of 1862 the regiment made an expedition into Darien, Georgia, and up the Ridge, and on January 23, 1863, another up St. Mary's River, capturing a number of stores for the government; then on to Fernandina, Florida. They were gone ten or twelve days, at the end of which time they returned to camp.

March 10, 1863, we were ordered to Jacksonville, Florida. Leaving Camp Saxton between four and five o'clock, we arrived at Jacksonville about eight o'clock next morning, accompanied by three or four gunboats. When the rebels saw these boats, they ran out of the city, leaving the women behind, and we found out afterwards that they thought we had a much larger fleet than we really had. Our regiment was kept out of sight until we made fast at the wharf where it landed, and while the gunboats were shelling up the river and as far inland as possible, the regiment landed and marched up the street, where they spied the rebels who had fled from the city. They were hiding behind a house about a mile or so away, their faces blackened to disguise themselves as negroes, and our boys, as they advanced toward them, halted a second, saying, "They are black men! Let them come to us, or we will make them know who we are." With this, the firing was opened and several of our men were wounded and killed. The rebels had a number wounded and killed. It was through this way the discovery was made that they were white men. Our men drove them some distance in retreat and then threw out their pickets.

While the fighting was on, a friend, Lizzie Lancaster, and I stopped at several of the rebel homes, and after talking with some of the women and children we asked them if they had any food. They claimed to have only some hard-tack, and evidently did not care to give us anything to eat, but this was not surprising. They were bitterly against our people and had no mercy or sympathy for us.

The second day, our boys were reinforced by a regiment of white soldiers, a Maine regiment, and by cavalry, and had quite a fight. On the third day, Edward Herron, who was a fine gunner on the steamer John Adams, came on shore, bringing a small cannon, which the men pulled along for more than five miles. This cannon was the only piece for shelling. On coming upon the enemy, all secured their places, and they had a lively fight, which lasted several hours, and our boys were nearly captured by the Confederates; but the Union boys carried out all their plans that day, and succeeded in driving the enemy back. After this skirmish, every afternoon between four and five o'clock the Confederate General Finegan[36] would send a flag of truce to Colonel Higginson,[37] warning him to send all women and children out of the city, and threatening to bombard it if this was not done. Our colonel allowed all to go who wished, at first, but as General Finegan grew more hostile and kept sending these communications for nearly a week, Colonel Higginson thought it not best or necessary to send any more out of the city, and so informed General Finegan. This angered the general, for that night the rebels shelled directly toward Colonel Higginson's headquarters. The shelling was so heavy that the colonel told my captain to have me taken up into the town to a hotel, which was used as a hospital. As my quarters were just in the rear of the colonel's, he was compelled to leave his also before the night was over. I expected every moment to be killed by a shell, but on arriving at the hospital I knew I was safe, for the shells could not reach us there. It was plainly to be seen now, the ruse of the flag of truce coming so often to us. The bearer was evidently a spy getting the location of the headquarters, etc., for the shells were sent too accurately to be at random.

Next morning Colonel Higginson took the cavalry and a regiment on another tramp after the rebels. They were gone several days and had the hardest fight they had had, for they wanted to go as far as a station which was some distance from the city. The gunboats were of little assistance to them, yet notwithstanding this drawback our boys returned with only a few killed and wounded, and after this we were not troubled with General Finegan.

We remained here a few weeks longer, when, about April first, the regiment was ordered back to Camp Saxton, where it stayed a week, when the order came to go to Port Royal Ferry on picket duty. It was a gay day for the boys. By seven o'clock all tents were down, and each company, with a commissary wagon, marched up the shell road, which is a beautiful avenue ten or twelve miles out of Beaufort. We arrived at Seabrooke at about four o'clock, where our tents were pitched and the men put on duty. We were here a few weeks, when Company E was ordered to Barnwell plantation[38] for picket duty.

Some mornings I would go along the picket line, and I could see the rebels on the opposite side of the river. Sometimes as they were changing pickets they would call over to our men and ask for something to eat, or for tobacco, and our men would tell them to come over. Sometimes one or two would desert to us, saying, they "had no negroes to fight for." Others would shoot across at our picket, but as the river was so wide there was never any damage done, and the Confederates never attempted to shell us while we were there.

I learned to handle a musket very well while in the regiment, and could shoot straight and often hit the target. I assisted in cleaning the guns and used to fire them off, to see if the cartridges were dry, before cleaning and reloading, each day. I thought this great fun. I was also able to take a gun all apart, and put it together again.

Between Barnwell and the mainland was Hall Island. I went over there several times with Sergeant King and other comrades. One night there was a stir in camp when it was found that the rebels were trying to cross, and next morning Lieutenant Parker told me he thought they were on Hall Island; so after that I did not go over again.

While planning for the expedition up the Edisto River, Colonel Higginson was a whole night in the water, trying to locate the rebels and where their picket lines were situated. About July the boys went up the Edisto to destroy a bridge on the Charleston and Savannah road. This expedition was twenty or more miles into the mainland. Colonel Higginson was wounded in this fight and the regiment nearly captured. The steamboat John Adams always assisted us, carrying soldiers, provisions, etc. She carried several guns and a good gunner, Edward Herron. Henry Batchlott, a relative of mine, was a steward on this boat. There were two smaller boats, Governor Milton and the Enoch Dean, in the fleet, as these could go up the river better than the larger ones could. I often went aboard the John Adams. It went with us into Jacksonville, to Cole and Folly Island, and Gunner Herron was always ready to send a shell at the enemy.

One night, Companies K and E, on their way to Pocotaligo to destroy a battery that was situated down the river, captured several prisoners. The rebels nearly captured Sergeant King, who, as he sprang and caught a "reb," fell over an embankment. In falling he did not release his hold on his prisoner. Although his hip was severely injured, he held fast until some of his comrades came to his aid and pulled them up. These expeditions were very dangerous. Sometimes the men had to go five or ten miles during the night over on the rebel side and capture or destroy whatever they could find.

While at Camp Shaw, there was a deserter who came into Beaufort. He was allowed his freedom about the city and was not molested. He remained about the place a little while and returned to the rebels again. On his return to Beaufort a second time, he was held as a spy, tried, and sentenced to death, for he was a traitor. The day he was shot, he was placed on a hearse with his coffin inside, a guard was placed either side of the hearse, and he was driven through the town. All the soldiers and people in town were out, as this was to be a warning to the soldiers. Our regiment was in line on dress parade. They drove with him to the rear of our camp, where he was shot. I shall never forget this scene.

While at Camp Shaw, Chaplain Fowler, Robert Defoe, and several of our boys were captured while tapping some telegraph wires. Robert Defoe was confined in the jail at Walterborough, S. C., for about twenty months. When Sherman's army reached Pocotaligo he made his escape and joined his company (Company G). He had not been paid, as he had refused the reduced pay offered by the government. Before we got to camp, where the pay-rolls could be made out, he sickened and died of small-pox, and was buried at Savannah, never having been paid one cent for nearly three years of service. He left no heirs and his account was never settled.

In winter, when it was very cold, I would take a mess-pan, put a little earth in the bottom, and go to the cook-shed and fill it nearly full of coals, carry it back to my tent and put another pan over it; so when the provost guard went through camp after taps, they would not see the light, as it was against the rules to have a light after taps. In this way I was heated and kept very warm.

A mess-pan is made of sheet iron, something like our roasting pans, only they are nearly as large round as a peck measure, but not so deep. We had fresh beef once in awhile, and we would have soup, and the vegetables they put in this soup were dried and pressed. They looked like hops. Salt beef was our stand-by. Sometimes the men would have what we called slap-jacks. This was flour, made into bread and spread thin on the bottom of the mess-pan to cook. Each man had one of them, with a pint of tea, for his supper, or a pint of tea and five or six hard-tack. I often got my own meals, and would fix some dishes for the non-commissioned officers also.

Mrs. Chamberlain, our quartermaster's wife, was with us here. She was a beautiful woman; I can see her pleasant face before me now, as she, with Captain Trowbridge, would sit and converse with me in my tent two or three hours at a time. She was also with me on Cole Island, and I think we were the only women with the regiment while there. I remember well how, when she first came into camp, Captain Trowbridge brought her to my tent and introduced her to me. I found her then, as she remained ever after, a lovely person, and I always admired her cordial and friendly ways.

Our boys would say to me sometimes "Mrs. King, why is it you are so kind to us? you treat us just as you do the boys in your own company." I replied, "Well, you know, all the boys in other companies are the same to me as those in my Company E; you are all doing the same duty, and I will do just the same for you." "Yes," they would say, "we know that, because you were the first woman we saw when we came into camp, and you took an interest in us boys ever since we have been here, and we are very grateful for all you do for us."

When at Camp Shaw, I visited the hospital in Beaufort, where I met Clara Barton.[39] There were a number of sick and wounded soldiers there, and I went often to see the comrades. Miss Barton was always very cordial toward me, and I honored her for her devotion and care of those men.

There was a man, John Johnson, who with his family was taken by our regiment at Edisto. This man afterwards worked in the hospital and was well known to Miss Barton. I have been told since that when she went South, in 1883, she tried to look this man up, but learned he was dead. His son is living in Edisto, Rev. J. J. Johnson, and is the president of an industrial school on that island and a very intelligent man. He was a small child when his father and family were captured by our regiment at Edisto.

VI—On Morris and Other Islands

Fort Wagner being only a mile from our camp, I went there two or three times a week, and would go up on the ramparts to watch the gunners send their shells into Charleston (which they did every fifteen minutes), and had a full view of the city from that point. Outside of the fort were many skulls lying about; I have often moved them one side [sic] out of the path. The comrades and I would have quite a debate as to which side the men fought on. Some thought they were the skulls of our boys; others thought they were the enemy's; but as there was no definite way to know, it was never decided which could lay claim to them. They were a gruesome sight, those fleshless heads and grinning jaws, but by this time I had become accustomed to worse things and did not feel as I might have earlier in my camp life.

It seems strange how our aversion to seeing suffering is overcome in war,— how we are able to see the most sickening sights, such as men with their limbs blown off and mangled by the deadly shells, without a shudder; and instead of turning away, how we hurry to assist in alleviating their pain, bind up their wounds, and press the cool water to their parched lips, with feelings only of sympathy and pity.

About the first of June, 1864, the regiment was ordered to Folly Island, staying there until the latter part of the month, when it was ordered to Morris Island.[40] We landed on Morris Island between June and July, 1864. This island was a narrow strip of sandy soil, nothing growing on it but a few bushes and shrubs. The camp was one mile from the boat landing, called Pawnell Landing, and the landing one mile from Fort Wagner.

Colonel Higginson had left us in May of this year, on account of wounds received at Edisto. All the men were sorry to lose him. They did not want him to go, they loved him so. He was kind and devoted to his men, thoughtful for their comfort, and we missed his genial presence from the camp.

The regiment under Colonel Trowbridge did garrison duty, but they had troublesome times from Fort Gregg, on James Island,[41] for the rebels would throw a shell over on our island every now and then. Finally orders were received for the boys to prepare to take Fort Gregg, each man to take 150 rounds of cartridges, canteens of water, hardtack, and salt beef. This order was sent three days prior to starting, to allow them to be in readiness. I helped as many as I could to pack haversacks and cartridge boxes.

The fourth day, about five o'clock in the afternoon, the call was sounded, and I heard the first sergeant say, "Fall in, boys, fall in," and they were not long obeying the command. Each company marched out of its street, in front of their colonel's headquarters, where they rested for half an hour, as it was not dark enough, and they did not want the enemy to have a chance to spy their movements. At the end of this time the line was formed with the 103d New York (white) in the rear, and off they started, eager to get to work. It was quite dark by the time they reached Pawnell Landing. I have never forgotten the good-bys of that day, as they left camp. Colonel Trowbridge said to me as he left, "Good-by, Mrs. King, take care of yourself if you don't see us again." I went with them as far as the landing, and watched them until they got out of sight, and then I returned to the camp. There was no one at camp but those left on picket and a few disabled soldiers, and one woman, a friend of mine, Mary Shaw, and it was lonesome and sad, now that the boys were gone, some never to return.

Mary Shaw shared my tent that night, and we went to bed, but not to sleep, for the fleas nearly ate us alive. We caught a few, but it did seem, now that the men were gone, that every flea in camp had located my tent, and caused us to vacate. Sleep being out of the question, we sat up the remainder of the night.

About four o'clock, July 2, the charge was made. The firing could be plainly heard in camp. I hastened down to the landing and remained there until eight o'clock that morning. When the wounded arrived, or rather began to arrive, the first one brought in was Samuel Anderson of our company. He was badly wounded. Then others of our boys, some with their legs off, arm gone, foot off, and wounds of all kinds imaginable. They had to wade through creeks and marshes, as they were discovered by the enemy and shelled very badly. A number of the men were lost, some got fastened in the mud and had to cut off the legs of their pants, to free themselves. The 103d New York suffered the most, as their men were very badly wounded.

My work now began. I gave my assistance to try to alleviate their sufferings. I asked the doctor at the hospital what I could get for them to eat. They wanted soup, but that I could not get; but I had a few cans of condensed milk and some turtle eggs, so I thought I would try to make some custard. I had doubts as to my success, for cooking with turtle eggs was something new to me, but the adage has it, "Nothing ventured, nothing done," so I made a venture and the result was a very delicious custard. This I carried to the men, who enjoyed it very much. My services were given at all times for the comfort of these men. I was on hand to assist whenever needed. I was enrolled as company laundress, but I did very little of it, because I was always busy doing other things through camp, and was employed all the time doing something for the officers and comrades.

After this fight, the regiment did not return to the camp for one month. They were ordered to Cole Island in September, where they remained until October. About November 1, 1864, six companies were detailed to go to Gregg Landing, Port Royal Ferry, and the rebels in some way found out some of our forces had been removed and gave our boys in camp a hard time of it, for several nights. In fact, one night it was thought the boys would have to retreat. The colonel told me to go down to the landing, and if they were obliged to retreat, I could go aboard one of our gunboats. One of the gunboats got in the rear, and began to shell General Beauregard's force, which helped our boys retain their possession.

About November 15, I received a letter from Sergeant King, saying the boys were still lying three miles from Gregg Landing and had not had a fight yet; that the rebels were waiting on them and they on the rebels, and each were holding their own; also that General Sherman had taken Fort McAllister, eight miles from Savannah.[42] After receiving this letter I wanted to get to Beaufort, so I could be near to them and so be able to get news from my husband. November 23 I got a pass for Beaufort. I arrived at Hilton Head about three o'clock next day, but there had been a battle, and a steamer arrived with a number of wounded men; so I could not get a transfer to Beaufort. The doctor wished me to remain over until Monday. I did not want to stay. I was anxious to get off, as I knew no one at Hilton Head.

I must mention a pet pig we had on Cole Island. Colonel Trowbridge brought into camp, one day, a poor, thin little pig, which a German soldier brought back with him on his return from a furlough. His regiment, the 74th Pennsylvania, was just embarking for the North, where it was ordered to join the 10th corps, and he could not take the pig back with him, so he gave it to our colonel. That pig grew to be the pet of the camp, and was the special care of the drummer boys, who taught him many tricks; and so well did they train him that every day at practice and dress parade, his pigship would march out with them, keeping perfect time with their music. The drummers would often disturb the devotions by riding this pig into the midst of evening praise meeting, and many were the complaints made to the colonel, but he was always very lenient towards the boys, for he knew they only did this for mischief. I shall never forget the fun we had in camp with "Piggie."

James Lindsay Smith, from the *Autobiography of James L. Smith* (1881)

Along with Mattie Jackson, Elizabeth Keckley, and Susie King Taylor, Smith provided one of our best records of what the Civil War looked like from the perspective of an African American. Smith did not actually fight in the war – he was a family man running a shoe-shop in Norwich, Connecticut – and so in describing its major battles and events, and particularly the participation of black soldiers, he generally writes impersonally, from a distance. (His narrative grows more direct and personal in Chapter 8, in his remarkable portrayal of the aftermath of the war and the plight of the South.) Yet even his narration of matters that fell outside his own experience is significant: it shows a former slave defining the meaning of the war, intervening in the public debate, and helping to shape a collective cultural memory.

Chapter 8 – After the War
Fear of capture – A visit to Heathsville – Father Christmas, and a children's festival – Preaching at Washington – My first visit to my old home – Joy and rejoicing – Meeting my old mistress – My old cabin home – The old spring – Change of situations – The old doctor – Improvement in the condition of the colored people – Buying homes – Industry

After the Fugitive Slave Law[43] was passed, terror struck the hearts of those who had escaped to the free States, as no earthly power could prevent them from being returned to their masters. Very many were taken back. For my part, I was very much frightened, and was continually haunted by dreams which were so vivid as to appear really true. One night I dreamt my master had come for me, and, as he proved property, I was delivered up to him by the United States Marshal. In the morning I told the dream to my wife. She said she "believed it would come true," and was very much worried.

I went down to my shop, and, in the course of the morning, while looking out of my window I noticed a number of persons who had just come in on the train, and among them I was sure I saw my master.[44] You may rest assured I was pretty well frightened out of my wits. What to do I did not know. This man did certainly walk like him, had whiskers like him; in fact his whole general appearance resembled his so much that I was sure that he had been put on my track. I peeped out at him as he passed my door and saw him go up the steps leading to the office of the U. S. Marshal, then I was sure he had come for me. I could do no more work that day.

As my friends came in I told them of what I had seen, my fears, etc.; and they assured me they would be on the look-out and see if such a man was in town, find out his errand, etc. Accordingly one of them who was a town crier, Dunton by name, went to the hotels and searched the registers to see if a man by the name of Lackey[45] was registered there. At night he reported that no such name could be found. My friends declared that I should not leave this town. One even went so far as to go to the U. S. Marshal and ask if "anyone should come, looking for me, what he would do; would he give me up?" He replied: "No, he'd resign his position first." Another bought a revolver, and told me that "if they had me up that, by some means, he would manage it so as to get it into my hands that I might in some way defend myself." I had determined never to be taken back alive.

Death was preferable to slavery, now that I had tasted the sweets of liberty. As it was, dreams of this kind ceased to trouble me, and the effects and fear wore off.

It was not till after the Emancipation Proclamation, that a man who is living in Norwich to-day, told me that after I left the South, and had settled here, he went to Heathsville, to the very place where I used to live, saw my master, who asked him whether, in his travels North, he had ever come across a man who was lame, shoemaker by trade; that he would give him two hundred dollars, cash, for any information which would lead to his discovery. He returned home, said nothing whatever to me, for fear I would be alarmed, sell out and leave the place; said nothing to any one about it till after January 1st, 1863, when freedom was proclaimed throughout the land.

During one of my visits to Heathsville, on which I always carried a large stock of clothing, shoes, etc., I formed a plan for some amusement among the young people. On Sunday it was announced that on a certain evening during the week there would be a Christmas tree. All were invited to come; accordingly when the time arrived, the church was packed; many came from miles away. I selected a young man who I intended should represent Father Christmas, as he is called there. I put on him a long swallow tail coat, the ends of which almost touched the floor, then he was filled out so as to be very large; he had on an extremely sharp pointed collar, which extended far out from his face, which was hidden behind a mask. I opened with an address, and at a given signal, Father Christmas made his first appearance. Many of the children, even some of the old people were frightened nearly out of their wits; one child ran forward, crying to his Uncle John to save him; some fell over each other to get out of the way. Well, I laughed till I could laugh no longer, and finally I was obliged to dispense with Father Christmas before anything like order could be obtained. Then the different articles were distributed, and if you could have heard the many prayers that went up from thankful hearts for the gifts received, no one would tire of this good work. General satisfaction reigned, and after a hymn of thanksgiving they dispersed to their homes.

January, 1867, I was called to visit Washington, to see about a school for my daughter. While there I was invited by the pastor of Israel Church[46] to preach on the Sabbath. At the close of the service many of my former friends came forward to greet me, and informed me of the old plantation where my brother and two sisters still resided. I immediately wrote to my brother to let him know that I was still alive, and that I should visit Heathsville at such a time, and asked him if "he thought there would be any danger in coming." He informed me that "there was no danger, for Virginia was free." When he received the letter it seemed as from one risen from the dead. My sister took the letter and went round amongst her friends, wild with joy.

A few weeks after this I made preparations to start on my long-premeditated journey, in the middle of June, 1867. I went by way of Washington. As I was proceeding down the old Potomac River her red banks looked natural to me, so much so that I could hardly suppress the feeling of joy which arose in my heart. That night the boat stopped about forty miles from Heathsville. The next morning, about light, I went ashore, as I was very anxious to tread once more on the old Virginia soil. Very soon the bell rang for the boat to start; I hastened on board again. By this time she had got underway, and I reached Cone Wharf at six o'clock – the very spot from where I started thirty years before.[47] It seemed to me more like a dream than a reality. No one can imagine how I felt; I could not believe that it was possible that I was going home to tread on free soil. I asked myself the question: "Can it be possible that Virginia is free?" I looked ashore before the boat reached the landing, and saw those old ex-slave-holders standing on the dock, which sent a thrill all over me. But soon the boat rounded up to the dock, and as soon as the gang-plank was put out there were some white young men who came aboard and stepped up to the bar and began drinking. A colored man, also, went up to get something to drink. There was a row that commenced with the white men and the colored man, and came very near ending in a fight. Here I saw the old spirit of slavery exhibited by the whites. This somewhat increased my fears; but quiet was soon restored, and I stepped ashore almost on the same spot where I was thirty years before.

Things looked changed somewhat since I left, but after awhile I came to myself and found that I was really home again, unmolested where I was once a slave, and my joy knew no bounds. I was soon discovered by some of my friends, and we congratulated one another like old friends, for I seemed to them like one risen from the grave. I felt as though I wanted to get down and kiss the free ground upon which I stood. I could hardly restrain my feelings, for it was a new day with me. This visit was fraught with many sad reminiscences of the past.

After looking about and seeing the many changes that had been wrought in thirty years, I was taken by my friends and conveyed to my brother's house. On my way, I came to the old mill, gray with age, where I used to work. In the mill was a little room partitioned off where I had in former days done shoe-making. We stopped, and I went into the little room and saw where my bench used to stand, and the old, quaint fireplace where I used to make my fire. While I was there I remembered the joys and sorrows that I had passed through during the time I occupied that room. I then went to look for the old spring where I used to get water; I found it and knelt down by the side of it and drank therefrom. No language could express my feelings while I knelt over that spring. I then arose and continued my journey till I came to a cross-path, which I traveled in my former days. I asked the driver if "he would halt and let me get out of the wagon," and told him that "he could drive around and I would go across." As I viewed the place, old scenes seemed so natural to me that I could not help praising God in the highest for bringing me back to the place of my birth. I waited a few minutes, and then proceeded on. We then came to the old Heathsville spring, here I got out also and stooped to drink. We then came to the village of Heathsville, and as soon as I entered it, I was recognized by old friends who knew me in former days. I alighted from the wagon and we clasped each other, and a full tide of joy rushed over our souls. Here I found my brother's wife, he having been sold years before. After looking around at the different places where I had lived, and the different shops where I had worked, I started for my brother's house, located about two miles out of the village of Heathsville. When I was within half-a-mile of his house, I met my brother coming out of the house of a friend, and as soon as I saw him I knew him, although I had not seen him for years.

Dear reader, you should have been there in order to have realized the scene of our meeting. We got hold of each other and put our arms around each other's neck without speaking for some minutes; the silence was broken, and I exclaimed: "Dear brother, is it possible that we are standing on Virginia's free soil, and we are free?" My brother replied, "yes, dear brother, and you too have been living in the 'land of the free and the home of the brave.'" We wept and rejoiced, and praised God for his goodness in bringing us together once more on free soil. For a short time all was excitement and confusion. When it had subsided we started for the house, where I met my eldest sister. She pressed eagerly forward to greet me, and we seemed to each other as one risen from the dead. We, too, fell on each other's neck and clasped each other and wept. News spread like wild-fire that Lindsey Payne (for that was my name before I escaped from slavery,) had returned home again. Many of my old friends who once knew me, came flocking in to see me. My listeners were never weary, as I related to them the history of my life at the

North, and described the varied scenes through which I had passed. My joy and excitement rose to such a height, that I scarcely knew whether I was in the body or out.

In the afternoon I went down to the "great house," so-called in the days of slavery, where Mrs. Sarah Winsted lived, who was formerly my mistress. She was the second wife of my former master, Mr. Langsdon. She survived him, and afterwards married a Mr. Winsted, who died before her. When I got within two hundred yards of the house she saw me coming, and knew me. It being warm weather she threw on her sun bonnet and came to meet me, and was so glad that she wept and grasped my hand for a minute before either spoke. At last she broke the silence by saying: "Oh! Lindsey, is this you?" I replied: "This is me, what there is left of me." Says Mrs. Winsted: "Let us go to the house." Mrs. Winsted then introduced me to her daughter, who had been born since I left, and then set the table and would have me take dinner with her. Although I had ate dinner, I accepted her cordial invitation as an appreciation of her kindness.

After dinner she told me "to relate to her the narrative of my escape from slavery; how I got away, and how the Yankees had treated me since I had been up amongst them?" I set my chair back, and told her the whole story of my escape. When I told her how frightened I was by seeing the cars,[48] and thought the engine was the devil coming after me, she really did shake with laughter. I also informed her of our sail up the Chesapeake Bay in a small boat, and how we were overtaken by the storm of wind and came very near being lost, but we reached the land of freedom in safety; that the Northern people had treated me comparatively well; and that I had bought me a comfortable home. She seemed to be very much pleased with my recital. I gave her a nice pair of shoes, for which she was very thankful.

While on this visit I saw a great many places of my childhood; among them were Hog Point, where I spent many of my boyhood days; and, also, the very spot where I was made lame.[49] I saw the old oak tree that stood near my mother's cabin home, which I have mentioned in the first part of this work, on a limb of which Mr. Haney[50] hung one of his slaves, and whipped him till the ground beneath him was stained with his blood. I tried to find the same limb, but although the tree appeared to be in perfect health and strength, that limb seemed to have withered and dropped off. While I was meditating under this tree, many scenes of my boyhood came vividly to my recollection. I then searched for my mother's cabin home, but no humble cabin, like the one in my memory, met my eye; it had given place to a dense pine forest. The logs of the cabin had either been burned, or rotted with the dust of the earth. All was desolate in the extreme. I called, but there was no response; no voice of a kind mother greeted my ear; no welcome of the eleven brothers and sisters greeted my approach; all was speechless as the grave. Nothing occupied that sacred spot but the reptile and the owl. As I gazed and thought, I became faint and sorrowful. I turned from here in pursuit of the spring from which I had carried so many buckets of water. After much search and labor, crawling through the bushes and fallen trees, I found the old spring and drank therefrom. The old gum tree that was near this spring in my childhood days, I found there still, being bent with age; its branches hung over this spring. It was once noted for its healing properties, the berries of which were used for medicinal purposes.

These three springs that I have mentioned, have served to quench the thirst of many a weary soldier as he stooped to drink, at the time of the great rebellion. I knelt, and offered my heart in prayer and thanksgiving to "God, who doeth all things well." I thought how often my brothers and sisters with myself, came to and from that spring, but now we were separated, nearly all of us, never more to meet, till we meet in that heavenly land where father, mother and children shall never part, "where the wicked cease from troubling, and the weary are at rest." From there, with a heavy heart, I went in search of our neighbors; they, too, like the cabin, were gone; they had been committed to the dust, and their spirits had returned to "God, who gave them." Their houses were occupied by others; with a sad heart I retraced my steps to the home of Mrs. Winsted, and then to my brother's.

I spent three or four weeks in Heathsville, and while I was on this visit I went a second time to see Mrs. Winsted, and found her in the garden, in the hot sun, hoeing. Said I, "is it possible that you can work out in the hot sun?" She replied, "Lindsey, we can do a great many things when we are obliged to, that we once thought we could not do." I saw the changes that freedom had wrought, and I thought, "how people can accommodate themselves to circumstances." When we were on the plantation together she would not allow herself even to walk out doors in the hottest part of the day, without a servant to hold an umbrella over her.

Many a man who was very rich, has been reduced to beggary. Many of those negro traders, who used to buy up a large number of slaves and carry them down to the lower States and sell them, have become so poor that they have not clothes to hide their nakedness. They go around among the freedmen and beg for something to eat. I know a man who was once very rich, worth about half-a-million, who has since been reduced to such poverty that he has been obliged to hire himself out under the United States service to work on a mud machine,[51] as a common day laborer, and is not allowed to go and see his family but once in three months, he being in Norfolk and his family in Baltimore. Others, who were rich, are even worse off than he. This description does not include all the slaveholders, for those who were kind and humane towards their slaves are far better off in circumstances than the others. The slaves, as a general thing, did not leave them in the time of the war, but stayed with them to protect their property, while their masters were on the battle field. Those who brutalized their victims seem to be marked by the vengeance of the Almighty; they are wasting away like the early dew, for many have nowhere to lay their heads, except among those whom they have abused.

The colored people, unlike all other nations on the face of the earth, are ready to fulfill that passage of Scripture: "Therefore, if thine enemy hunger, feed him; if he thirst, give him drink; for in so doing thou shalt heap coals of fire on his head." Many of them, when bleeding from the effects of the knotted whips applied by their cruel task masters, could have risen and made the land knee deep with the blood of their oppressors, and thus avenged themselves of the host of cruel wrongs which they have suffered; but, instead of raising an insurrection, they calmly left the plantations without injuring a hair of the heads of their masters, and went on the Union side; and not till the United States put arms into their hands, and bade them go forward in the defence of their country, did they attempt to show any signs of revenge.

During my first visit I noticed that very many of the houses looked very ancient and dilapidated. The old slave pens, and the whipping posts, stood just as they were when I left. The fertile soil which once brought forth in abundance, and the cotton and corn, presented an unbroken scene of barrenness and desolation. The place was almost depopulated – plantations forsaken.

The South has been subjected to a fearful waste of population. Thousands of the colored people during the war, and many thousands of whites also left, to say nothing of those who have been killed. I only found one brother and two sisters living. Since that time my eldest sister has died, leaving four or five children, three of whom had been torn from her, and sold into slavery, and she never heard from them again. She was a great sufferer, owing to the want of proper care, and sorrow reigned in her inmost soul. Finally the Angel of Death came and severed her from her sufferings. Her husband survives her, as I write, "The fountains of bitter sorrow are stirred by the healing branch that God can cast." As soon as I struck the Virginia wharf, the words of the aged colored doctor[52] came vividly to my mind, who told me my future destiny: "that in the course of time I would return to my native land." Sure enough I had returned after thirty years' absence.

A day or two after I had made my escape from slavery, Thomas Langsdon, supposing that the old doctor was accessory to my running away, fell on the man and beat him in a brutal manner, most shocking to behold. The doctor never recovered from his injuries; being a free man he did not have any one to intercede for him. After I had been home a few days, I inquired after the doctor, and found, to my great sorrow, that he had gone to his long home, where no foe nor hostile hands will ever enter its peaceful inclosure. In my repeated visits to Heathsville, I observed but little improvement since the great rebellion; there have been but few houses built for the last thirty years. The condition of the colored people is improving very fast, for many of them are buying lands and building, and thus preparing homes for themselves. Their condition is much better than those who once owned them. The old ex-slave holders are dying off very fast. As they have no one to cultivate their large plantations, and can not do it themselves, they are obliged to divide them up and sell them to the freedmen, as they are growing over with dense forests.[53] I think that eventually, Virginia will be in as flourishing a condition as any section of the United States.

The Northern people are beginning to emigrate there. The steam whistle from the factory and sawmill, which serve for the employment of many, is beginning to be heard morning, noon, and night. Things begin to wear a Northern aspect considerably. The log-cabin begins to disappear in some places, giving way to houses of modern construction. The broad long handle Southern hoe is giving place to a more modern make. This improvement is more or less seen, except among the class that bought and sold human flesh, and obtained their living from the bones and sinews of others. But how have the ex-slave holders – that is including all of them in the South – treated the freed people since the great rebellion of 1861? The colored people of the South have suffered every thing, even death itself. Some were violently beaten, or rudely scourged; many were deliberately shot down in open day, on the public streets; others were way-laid and cruelly butchered, and some, God only knows the fate they have suffered. There has been an awful destruction of human life. The streets have been drenched with their blood, for it has flown freely. Many worthy and willing hands were left without employment, while others worked for a mere pittance to get their living, while still others toiled on as formerly, without any agreement or probability of due return. When the civil rights bill was passed, April 9th, 1866, the condition of the colored people was ameliorated in many instances.[54]

During the rebellion some were driven from their cabins during the absence of their owners, who were on the battle field. The cabins, many of them, were stripped of all their contents, leaving the occupants nothing. Oh! how many have suffered malice and revenge, the bitter wrath and vengeance of those who justly shared the disappointments and misfortunes attending the overthrow of slavery and rebellion.

My brother is doing well, and has bought himself a nice farm, from which he raises crops every year. He is a Baptist preacher; and, besides presiding over his own church, he has the oversight of the Lancaster Baptist Church, in Lancaster County; thus supplying two churches, the Northumberland, and the Lancaster churches. My younger sister, who resides in Wycomco, in Northumberland County, Va., has four or five children;

and, through her and her husband's industry have procured a small farm, from which they have obtained principally the support of their family.

During my repeated visits to Heathsville I have carried boxes of clothing and a large trunk closely packed, for the benefit of the freedmen and their families. The little sacks and other children's clothes were presented to mothers whose little children stood in great need of them, and were very thankfully received. "God bless the friends of the North," was the hearty exclamation of many. I found the colored people industriously employed in doing something, and thus they seemed contented and happy.

In December, 1879, during my visit, I went down to Fairfield, some five or six miles from Heathsville, where I had learned my trade, and found the old place much dilapidated. The fields from which were raised corn and wheat were all grown over with thick forests. The "great house" had been burned to the ground. Mrs. Winsted had passed from time into eternity to try the realities of the other world. The old shop that I used to work in had been torn down, and desolation seemed to mark the place. The foot of the war horse had been there. I tender my thanks to the kind friends of Norwich for their generous gifts.

Chapter 11 – Recollections of the War
The spirit of the South – Delaware – Kentucky – Meetings – Conventions – Gen. Wild's raid – Slave heroism – A reminiscence of 1863 – Sherman's march through Georgia – Arming the slave.

The spirit of the rebellion still shows itself in many of the States. Its influences are plainly manifested in the State of Delaware. In my escape from the South I passed through this State. How I ever succeeded, without being detected, I can not tell to this day. Nothing but the mercy of the Lord ever carried me through. Here, in the height of slavery, I went on board the boat at New Castle,[55] and no white man questioned me as to my where-abouts, or asked for my pass. As for the town of New Castle, the very atmosphere seemed tainted with slavery.

The feeling was most bitter in Odessa, during 1865, against persons of color from the North giving lectures in the town. On one occasion a mob of white ruffians surrounded a colored church, showering stones and bricks at the doors and windows, swearing that the meeting should be dismissed. One of the local laws of the State says that: "Any negro or mulatto coming into the State, who is a non-resident of the locality he may visit, is liable to a fine of fifty dollars, six month's imprisonment, and twenty-five lashes."[56] Learning of this, they concluded to dismiss the meeting.

March 4th, 1865, Maj. Gen. Palmer issued an order that: "All slave pens, and other private establishments for confining persons in Louisville, be suppressed; and all confined persons discharged, except such as have committed crimes."[57] A colored police officer brought out many an innocent man and woman. Some had iron bars on their legs, reaching from the hip to the ankle and fastened on with iron straps.

There was a time in the history of Kentucky when colored men, women and children found upon the highways after dark were surrounded by the city guard, and flogged by them in the public streets. In Louisville the Rev. Mr. James[58] called a meeting at which delegates were appointed to hold an interview with the President, calling his attention to a few of the laws which bore so heavily on our race: First, they had no oath; second, they had no right of domicile; third, no right of locomotion; fourth, no right of self-defense; fifth, a statute of Kentucky makes it a penal crime, with imprisonment in the peniten-tiary for one year, for any freeman of color, under any circumstances, to pass into a free

State, even for a moment. Any freeman, not a native, found within her borders is subject to the same penalty; and for the second offense shall be a slave for life.

In 1865 the first delegation of colored men that ever left Kentucky, on a mission of liberty, started for Washington to accomplish the noble work entrusted to their hands. The interview was satisfactory, the President assuring them that the government would yield them every protection, and that the martial law would continue till the Kentuckians should learn more truly their position, and their duty to the nation.

The first free convention in the State of Virginia, during a period of two hundred and fifty-five years, was held in Alexandria, at the Lyceum Building. Fifty delegates were present. Addresses were made by Geo. W. Cook, of Norfolk; Peter R. Jones, of Petersburg; and Nicholas Richmond, of Charlottesville.[59]

The Celebration of the Fourth of July in Louisville, Kentucky

For the first time the people celebrated this day as a free people. Extensive preparations were made. There was a great out-pouring of people. They came from the factories, the work-shops and the fields to enjoy themselves in the pure, fresh air of freedom.

Fully ten thousand persons marched in the procession, and ten thousand more assembled on the ground. A sumptuous dinner was prepared for the soldiers, after which the speaking began. Addresses were made by David Jenkins, J. M. Langston, Chaplain Collins and Lieut. Ward.[60] When Gen. Palmer appeared such a shout as went up was enough to bring all the invisible sprites and spirits from their hiding places. As soon as it became quiet he began. His speech was continually applauded. He finished amid rounds of applause, banners waving, and the band playing the "Star Spangled Banner." That night the heavens were ablaze with rockets, fiery serpents and blue lights.

Gen. Wild's Raid[61]

During a march, when our troops neared a plantation, the slaves would eagerly join them. In many instances in plundering the houses slaves were found locked up. Continually during this raiding expedition, slaves came pouring in from the country in every direction, with their household furniture, thronging the lately deserted streets. This expedition was to search out guerrillas, lurking about the neighborhood of Elizabeth City and firing on our pickets. A force of colored men fell on their camp. There was a hasty escapade, and the soldiers came in possession of fire-arms and horses. Leaving Elizabeth City, they passed by vast fields of corn a mile in extent, commodious looking buildings and magnificent plantations. Here the troops commenced to work in earnest, and became an army of liberation.

On the first plantation they found fourteen slaves, who gladly joined them. An old wagon was found, to which a horse was harnessed. Such furniture as the slaves needed was placed in it, and the women and children on top. And so they went from house to house, gathering together the slaves, and whatever teams and horses could be found. Meanwhile, foraging went on, as there was an abundance of geese, chickens and turkeys. All the planters were "Secesh," so no restrictions were placed on the troops. The line of march continued, the contraband train continually growing in length.

At Indian Town bridge Gen. Wild came upon a guerrilla camp. His men started upon the "double quick," and pursued them through woods, across corn fields, until they came to a swamp. Here no path whatever could be seen, and how the guerrillas succeeded in covering their flight was, at first, a mystery; but our men were in for it now, and did not intend to turn back before ferreting out the matter. They began a careful search, and soon found the trunk of a felled tree, well-worn with footsteps. Near by was another, then another till they made quite a zig-zag footpath across the swamp. This solved the mystery. This, without doubt, led to the guerrilla quarters. Going single file they came upon a small island, which had been hastily evacuated – every thing was lying about in great confusion. According to orders, the soldiers burned the huts and took possession of whatever was worth keeping. The slaves on the plantations, ahead of the line, were notified by scouts to be ready to join the train when it should pass. By the time it reached Currituck Court House it was a mile in length. After three weeks the entire expedition returned to Norfolk. The raid was considered a very important one.

The tables were now turned. Those proud-hearted planters, who claimed such strict obedience from their slaves, now actually fell down on their knees before these armed blacks and begged for their lives. The great cry among them was: "What shall I do to be saved?" Yes, now they were ready to take the oath of allegiance, give up their slaves; any thing "to be saved." Whole families ran to the swamps when they heard that the raiders were near.

This raid put at rest forever the question as to whether the negro troops were efficient in any part of the service. They performed all the duties of white soldiers – scouting, skirmishing, picket duty, guard duty; and, lastly, fighting. Gen. Wild had decided at one time to attack a guerrilla camp. With the exception of thirty-five men, who were too lame to march, every man wanted to go and fight the guerrillas, notwithstanding those could remain back who wished to do so. A hundred men, however, were needed to guard the camp. No persuasions could induce them to volunteer to remain; so at last Gen. Wild was obliged to detail the required number for this duty. Did any one ever think that the men who had been accustomed to hunt runaway slaves in the swamps of the South would now be hiding there themselves, be hunted by them? Mysterious are thy ways, Oh, Lord!

When the rebellion first broke out a great many people thought "now the slaves will make a grand rush for the Northern side." They had prayed so long for liberty. Here it was, right in their hand; but the slaves did n't do any such thing. Remaining quiet, and looking about to see how things on both sides were moving, was the very means that saved them. How were they to contend with their masters? They had no arms, nothing to fight with; their masters had been collecting implements of war for some time and the slaves knew it; knew where they were hid; knew all the lines of fortification which they had been compelled to construct. Ah, the slaves were too wise to run any risk, with nothing but hoes in their hands. They said nothing, saw every thing, and at the right time they would give the Union valuable information. The Rebels lost their cause, and why? Because the slaves were loyal to the government. If they had been disloyal, the Confederates would no doubt have won, or else some foreign power might have intervened and made trouble. As it is, the Rebs. owe an old grudge to the freedman, as much as to say: "Its your fault we did'nt win."

Heroism of a Contraband

It was just after the victory of the Excelsior Brigade at Fair Oaks, when Gen. Sickels received word that the enemy were advancing.[62] Orders for preparation for battle were given. At last all was in readiness for the advance; but only a few shots were to be heard in the distance, otherwise every thing was quiet. What did it mean? The General asked Lieutenant Palmer to take a squad of men with him and ride cautiously to the first bend in the road, but he, too impetuous, rushed daringly ahead till he was within range of the enemy.

He fell, pierced with bullets. His soldiers hastily retreated to their camp and told their news. Among the listeners was a negro servant of Lieut. Palmer, who quietly withdrew and walked down that road – that road of death – for after passing our picket guard he was openly exposed to the Rebel sharpshooters. When our soldiers came up, the faithful servant was found by the side of his dead master. I regret that the name of this heroic soul remains unknown to the world – a name worthy to be emblazoned on the pages of history.

We used often to hear the question asked, can the negro take care of himself? If he is set free, to rely on his own resources, will he not die of starvation? Let us see. At Pine Bluffs there was a full black, known as Uncle Reuben. He was born in Georgia, and displayed such energy, tact, and devotion to his master's interest that he was left in full charge of every thing on the plantation. The slave raised his master from poverty to wealth. At last his master died, and his widow depended still more upon Uncle Reuben, placing all in his hands. He became more ambitious, and succeeded so well that the number of cotton bales increased every year. The children were sent North to school. The white overseers became jealous of him, and compelled his mistress to place a white, nominally, over him. However, he was not interfered with and his mistress treated him as kindly as she dared. Then the sons returned from the North, with no feelings of gratitude to one who by his industry and prudence had educated them, and amassed a fortune of one hundred and fifty thousand dollars. Thank God, he lived to see freedom's light, and after being assured that the Proclamation was a fact, he came over to us.

A Reminiscence of 1863

Probably no act – the Ku Klux system excepted – was more distressing than the ever to-be-remembered riot which occurred in New York city during the year of 1863.[63] (The mob spirit first manifested itself at a meeting held in Boston, December 3d, 1860, in observance of the anniversary of the death of John Brown.)[64] I can but look back and shudder at that great carnival of blood. The mob commenced on the 10th of July, and continued day and night for more than a week. My heart aches when memory recalls that awful day, when the whole city was in a state of insurrection. The full force of the infuriated mob fell upon the black man, the harmless, unpretending black man, whose only crime was that his skin was of a darker hue than his white brethren; that he came of a race which for more than two hundred years has felt the sting of slavery in its very soul. I know of no race that has undergone more sufferings than the black race in America.

Brought here from our mother country, we have bedewed the soil with our blood and tears. Unlike the Indian, we leave vengeance to the Lord. "He will repay." In this riot hundreds of colored people were driven from their homes, hunted and chased through the streets like wild beasts. A sweet babe was brained while holding up his little arms, and smiling upon his murderers. Many little children were killed in this manner. Strong men were dragged from their homes and left dangling from some lamp post or tree, or else slaughtered on the streets – their blood flowing in streams down the pavements. Able-bodied men, whose mangled bodies hung up to lamp posts, were in a great many instances burned to cinders. The colored people were panic stricken and sought shelter in out-of-the-way nooks and places; but even then some were discovered by the mob on their way to a retreat and quickly dispatched; hundreds flocked to the doors of police stations, prisons and jails, and begged admittance. No colored man, woman or child was spared if found. As a general thing, colored tenants occupy whole streets, so the mob knew pretty well what localities to plunder. Pistol shots were fired through the windows, murdering many at their homes and by their firesides. This accounts for the great loss of life, greater than if the people lived more scattered. The police were not able to cope with the murderers, though it is believed they did what they could, going in companies of two or three hundred to such parts of the city as needed their protection most. A most heartless transaction committed by these fiends, was the destruction of the colored Orphan Asylum, after first robbing the little children of their clothing.[65] These helpless lambs were driven friendless upon the world from the burning Asylum, which had been their abode. The mob went on at a terrible rate.

My family were quietly seated at the table one bright July morning when we were startled by the sudden ringing of the door bell. Upon responding, we found that a family with whom we were well acquainted had succeeded in escaping from the city, and sought refuge in our quiet suburb until quietness and peace should reign, so as to enable them to return to their own home. Oh! ye people of the North, before you censure too strongly the actions of the South, rid your own soil of that fiendish element which makes it an opprobrium to call America "the land of the free and the home of the brave."

Sherman's March through Georgia

During Sherman's march from Atlanta to Savannah,[66] many thousands of slaves came into the ranks, all of whom appeared overjoyed that "de Yanks had come." It would often happen that he would encamp on the plantations that planters had deserted. Here would be found an abundance of the good things of this life, of which the soldiers would readily partake. At one place only the old, decrepit slaves were left. These were half naked, and nearly starved; they had been told frightful stories about the cruelties of the Yankee soldiers, and were as frightened as could be when the army arrived. Upon being reassured that no harm would be done them, they were overwhelming in their thanks to Gen. Sherman for clothing and feeding them.

And thus it was; all along the march the most pathetic scenes would occur. Thousands of women, carrying household goods, some with children in their arms, all anxious to join the column. When refused, some most heart-rending scenes would take place; such begging to be allowed to go on to Savannah, where, says one: "My chillens done been sold dese four years;" or to Macon to "see my boy." Gen. Sherman, with great tact, succeeded in quieting them, telling them they would return for them some day and they must be patient. An aged couple had been waiting sixty years for deliverance. No one to see them at work on the plantation would suppose that they were any thing but satisfied with their condition. No murmur, no words of discontent ever passed their lips; they made no comments on the actions of runaway slaves; their master had no fears for them; yet, could he have seen the face of the woman when she heard that the Yankees had come, he would have seen that he had not read her heart aright. Such an expression as her countenance assumed was terrible to behold. "Bress de Lord," she exclaimed, "I expects to follow them till I drop in my tracks." As her husband did not see the situation of things as quickly as she did, she angrily said: "What are you sitting dar fur, don't yer see de door open? I'se not waited sixty years for nuttin'." It is said that no persuasions would prevail upon her to remain where she had suffered so much, and old as she was she would follow the army. This is only one of the many hundred cases which constantly occurred during the war. This poorly enlightened people all seemed to think that the Yankees would come some time or other, and that their freedom was the object of the war. This notion, I suppose, they got from bearing their masters talk.

The Rebel leaders had their attention completely absorbed by the vast preparations they were making for carrying on the war, by the increasing of State debts, etc.[67] The question of arming the slaves, which had been warmly debated at Richmond, was overlooked.[68] The governors of the several Southern States had also pondered this question as the only means to save the Confederacy, which under its various reverses, was slowly but surely dying. The South knew it could not hold out much longer. An intelligent mulatto in Macon, Ga., who used to attend his master's store would often make mention of such conversation as he overheard between his master and some of the first men of the city. They used to get together in the counting room and say: "It was no use to fight the North any longer, the South would surely be whipped in the end, and the best thing that could be done, would be to fix up the old Union." When asked if these men talked so on the public street, he replied: "No sir," these very men would go out on the street and talk wild about "whipping the Yankees, the South never giving up, and a lot of other trash." It is said that the Rebels so frightened their slaves, telling them stories of the cruelties which would be practiced upon them if ever they put themselves in the power of the Yankees that the most ignorant knew scarcely which way to turn, when the question of arming the slaves was discussed. There was nothing said by the South about the reward for their services. It rather looked upon them in the same light as when they worked in the field; neither was it prepared to meet the various objections raised by the white soldiers, if compelled to fight with them, side by side. So, as all parties could not be satisfied, the matter was allowed to drop, though I have no doubt but that to save herself, a few would have been willing to have increased their forces, by accepting the assistance of the slave.

Chapter 12 – The Exodus
Arrival of negroes in Washington – Hospitality of Washington people – Suffering and privation – Education of the freedmen – Causes of emigration – Cruelty at the South – Prejudice at the North – Hopes for the future.

The Rebellion at length closed after a bloody carnage of about four years. The manacles of the slave had been burst asunder. Left in abject poverty, he is suddenly thrown upon his own resources for support. In many instances the ex-slaveholder employed his former slaves on his plantation, paying them certain wages; others hired their own ground, and being perfectly familiar with the raising of cotton, sugar, corn and other grain, succeeded in making quite a comfortable living and having something laid by "for a rainy day." But this was not to last long. The peace of the quiet villages and towns was soon disturbed by night-raiders. Law-abiding citizens were torn from their beds at midnight, hung, robbed and flogged. This was not alone confined to black men, but white men also suffered. The cruelties inflicted upon both races during this "reign of terror" are almost indescribable.

This, together with the unjust treatment by the planters in relation to paying wages, renting land, etc., forms the cause of the exodus. We read accounts of where hundreds are leaving their native soil and beginning life anew in another clime. Whether they will be able to withstand the rigorous winters of the West remains to be seen. Already many have perished from exhaustion and cold, not being sufficiently clad, and being wholly without means to procure articles necessary to their comfort. Yet when we look back and see the wrongs heaped upon a poor, downtrodden race we can not but cry: "On with the Exodus!"

I had read of hundreds of freedmen leaving their homes and starting for the West, but I never expected to be an eye witness of such a scene. In December, 1879, while visiting Washington, preparatory to going further South, there arrived at the depot from two to three hundred freed people, among which were a number of children. It seems their money gave out as they reached Washington, and here they must remain until means could be obtained to send them further on. Here they were strangers; no where to go, near the edge of evening, yet no where to lay their heads. At this crisis the Rev. Mr. Draper hearing of their situation kindly offered them his church, (St. Paul, 8th St., South Washington), till other arrangements could be made. Here they were made as comfortable as possible, and seemed pleased that they were under shelter. I was told that quite a number had gone on some weeks before, and that they were mostly men. This last party had a majority of women, many of them going on to meet their husbands. The people of Washington were very kind to the strangers, giving them food and clothing in abundance. On the Sunday following their arrival, the pavements were blockaded for squares, all anxious to get a peep at them. The church was not a large one, so to prevent confusion, visitors were requested to pass in one door and out of the other.

Within, a novel sight presented itself; the gallery in the rear of the church had the appearance of a nursery. Children, from a two months' babe upwards, were lying here and there upon the benches, or under them fast asleep. Others were busily engaged in satisfying the inner man. The day I was present there was a reporter gathering scraps of information for his paper. It was really interesting to hear some of them converse. Many appeared to be quite intelligent; says one: "Do you suppose I'd leave my little home, which I owned, and go to a place I know nothing of unless I was compelled to. 'Taint natur. We heard dey killed a man the day we left, dey was so mad, and in some places dey tore up de track to keep us from leaving." Says the reporter: "Suppose you get to Indiana and you find no work there?" Answered: "Den I keeps going till I finds it." They all seemed willing to work if they could only find it to do.

Visitors, as they passed around, on coming to the altar found two small baskets into which they could drop as much money as they felt disposed. This was to assist in defraying the expenses the rest of the journey. As often as a certain amount was made up, they would send away so many at a time.

There was among the company a white woman, whom at first I took to be a leader, as she seemed so energetic, going out and begging proper clothing for the most destitute, distributing food, among them, etc. But upon conversing with her I found I was mistaken. She assured me she was as much a part of the "Exodus," as the rest. That she received no better treatment at her home than the rest did, and she was glad to get away. Some of the prominent lady members of St. Paul's Chapel were most kind in their attentions to the wanderers, leaving their own duties at home to spend days in administering to their comfort; and often were the expressions, "God bless you, de Lord will pay you back, honey," heard on all sides. I did not have an opportunity to see them but once, for when I went again I found they had gone; and it is hoped they have all found good, comfortable homes, in that land towards which their hearts had turned with so much faith and hope.

Terrible Suffering of the Freedmen at Washington

A host of miserable women with children, besides old, crippled and sick persons were driven out of Maryland and sought refuge here. Those who were able to work went out by the day to earn money with which to pay a rent of from five to six dollars for some old shanty, garret, cellar or stable. Hundreds of old persons and children were without shoes and stockings, and were badly frost-bitten. Infants, only a few days old, without a garment, perished with cold. Very few of the older persons had any undergarments, for they came from Maryland and Virginia clothed in rags; very few had comfortable beds and household utensils. The children died off rapidly. During the hot weather the quartermaster's department furnished about eighty coffins per week, mostly for children. "In slavery," the mothers say, "our children never dies; it 'pears like they all dies here." One family lost five out of ten children; another, three out of seven. Sleeping on the shanty and stable floors during the winter brought on colds and pulmonary diseases which terminated the lives of hundreds. The ladies of the District were indefatigable in their efforts to relieve them. Those in Springfield, Mass., kindly solicited aid for these distressed people, gathering clothing of every kind, and were quite successful in sending something to their afflicted brethren.[69]

Educating the Freedmen

This is a matter which absorbed the minds of the North: whether the negro would learn, and eagerly improve the facilities opened to him through his liberation. Almost immediately after the close of the war barracks used by the soldiers were turned into schoolhouses, and it was no rare sight to see a number of these freedmen crowded into them, over whom presided some noble-hearted lady engaged in her duties as school-marm. Would they learn? Let the record of the last fourteen or fifteen years testify.

I can not let this opportunity pass without paying a tribute of respect to the memory of Miss Stebbins,[70] who died while devoting her life to this cause. When I last saw her she was in Washington, D. C., at the barracks on the corner of Seventh and O Streets. She lived in one portion of the building, and, although school hours were over, she was instructing two bright, interesting girls in the mysteries of the alphabet. In one corner of the room were boxes of clothing which she distributed among the most needy of her pupils, that they might look presentable day after day. Not only children, but adults attended school, and it was not unusual to see a father and son, a mother and daughter in the same class, eager and anxious to learn. Says one teacher, who kept a night school for the benefit of those who were not able, on account of their work, to attend during the day: "I had a boy present himself as wishing to become a member of the school. After examining him, I found he was pretty well up in all the first principles of arithmetic, except long division; of this he knew nothing. I was astonished to find, after going over a few examples, explaining carefully as I went along, that when the pencil was put in his hand he worked as well as I could." From that night he had no more trouble with long division. That boy was afterwards a hard student at Howard University, and learned to read Latin with ease.

What nation, after years of servitude, has made such rapid strides of improvement? All over the South we find schools with efficient teachers, many of whom were formerly pupils, now going over the same ground others had taken them. The barracks have given way to school buildings of the most modern designs. The schools are all graded, the scholars advancing step by step till they reach the topmost round. Perhaps no better examples can be furnished than the District of Columbia, where the school system is fixed upon a firmer and better basis than elsewhere.

The Beginning of the End

The emigration of my people from the Southern States has engaged my attention for some time. In Heathsville, Va., the place of my birth, the colored people are not treated with such severity as in the States further South, for in Heathsville, they have more privileges than they have in Western Virginia. I think the cause of this great emigration is owing to the fact of ill treatment, equal almost to slavery; because of cruelties heaped upon them in the South, and because of the hopelessness of obtaining an education for their children. It was the burden of their complaint; their political rights had been denied them, and every possible advantage had been taken from them, and feeling aggrieved they had looked around for relief, and the only solace offered was to emigrate. In some parts of the South our people labor without hardly wages enough to get them food, which places many of them in a starving condition, and without sufficient clothing. Twenty-five cents a day is considered great wages, taking part corn for pay. My heart has been drawn out for them in sympathy, knowing myself what it was to want, even in Virginia, a meal of victuals.

The emigrants adopted a plan of action to appeal to President Hayes, for him to enforce the laws to protect their rights. Then they appealed to Congress to set apart a territory, or aid them to emigrate to Liberia.[71] Our people lost all hope of bettering their condition at that time. In 1877 they petitioned Congress and President Hayes.[72] Not hearing from this petition, the colored emigrants became exasperated, saying, "let us go any where in God's world to get away from these men who once enslaved us." Many of the white republicans of the South are treated not much better than the colored people, because they are republicans. Since they have emigrated many children, fathers and mothers have died from starvation and exposure, for they were without shelter and nothing to wear, lying on the cold ground, exposed to the winter blasts with only the sky for a covering.

The number of those who poured in upon the State of Kansas, early in the spring of 1879, is known to have been four or five thousand. Steadily has been the flow of the small stream which attracted so little attention, and by the opening of the spring of 1880 over ten thousand arrived, and probably since the spring of 1880 twice the number have emigrated. I think that something must be the cause for their great emigration more than common, for my people are a home-like people; they would never leave the Southern soil if properly treated, or had wages enough to make them comfortable; as a general thing they are home-loving and law abiding citizens. While living South they felt they had "no rights that the white man was bound to respect."[73]

All praise is due to Mrs. Comstock,[74] for her self-denying philanthropy exhibited towards my people, for they must have suffered more had it not been for her endeavors, in writing all over the United States to our most prominent citizens for help to relieve their sufferings. The people in many places have responded to her call. Here, in Norwich, the ladies have come up to the work as they always do where assistance is needed among my people. God bless them for what they have done; hoping that they will think of them in the future, as they are still leaving their land of slavery, as they expect the freedom which they have fought for and hoped for. In their going away their places can not be filled, for they were the bone and sinew of the South.

While I write, there are fifty thousand pounds of clothing, sent on in 1879 from England, held at the New York Custom House for duty to be paid on them. They were sent for my people in Kansas. It is wicked to deprive these poor, suffering people of comfortable clothing while so many are dying for the want of it. I trust that the hearts of the people everywhere will be so softened towards my injured people that they will be induced to send them on, even if obliged to pay the duty on them, and not wait for Congress to decide. Shall this people die, who have stood by us in sunshine and storm? Shall we let them suffer for the want of bread, for the want of corn, for the want of clothing? God forbid it! As they stood by the flag once, they stand by it still, because it bespeaks freedom to them and their posterity.

When the Rebel army was five miles from the Capital, and the skirmishers were three miles from Georgetown, when it was conjectured that the assault would take place the next morning, it was then our colored soldiers met the waves of conflict; it was then the bone and sinews of the South saved the Capital of the United States. Aye; my soul listens already to the glad prelude of the song of triumph, welling up from myriads of hearts, and swelling into a pæan that fills the vast concave of heaven itself with the deep-toned melodies of an universal jubilee: "Washington is saved!" Then our colored soldiers came up to its rescue, which contradicts the saying, that colored men will not fight. Well did they do their duty, and proved their manhood at Fort Wagner, Fort Moultrie, Petersburg, Milliken's Bend, Fort Fisher, and other places, while their families were left starving at home. We all know that these things are so, although they are not recorded in history with other events of the war.

We hope the time will come when our children, attending white seminaries of learning, may receive medals the same as white students. In Connecticut, and elsewhere, prizes and medals have been, and are withheld from our most brilliant scholars of color. In one of our Eastern colleges a colored student was robbed of his essay, and had recourse to a law-suit to have justice done him; but was obliged to write another, and received the prize at his graduation, after the lawsuit was ended. He was obliged to go another year in order to accomplish it. The wrongs of this system will go up before the Throne of Infinite Justice.

The United States ought to be strong enough in intellect, in moral sensibility and Christian feeling, to conquer her prejudices. Until she does, the poet's tribute to "Columbia" as "the land of the free and home of the brave," will be a satire that shall provoke a reproachful smile – attesting her fidelity to justice and liberty, God and man.

The leading question of to-day is, why do the colored people emigrate? Almost every day and week during the spring of 1880, it was discussed among the senators and representatives in Congress, the argument having taken up most of the time; the question also created quite a discussion in 1879; the Southern senators, who were the majority in the Senate, were loath to drop the question.

In conclusion, I must say that the more I contemplate the condition of my people, the more I am convinced that this is only the beginning of the end; but the end is not yet.

Paul Laurence Dunbar, from *Lyrics of Lowly Life* (1895)

The Deserted Plantation

Oh, de grubbin'-hoe 's a-rustin' in de co'nah,
    An' de plow 's a-tumblin' down in de fiel',
While de whippo'will 's a-wailin' lak a mou'nah
    When his stubbo'n hea't is tryin' ha'd to yiel'.

In de furrers whah de co'n was allus wavin',
    Now de weeds is grown' green an' rank an' tall;
An' de swallers roun' de whole place is a-bravin'
    Lak dey thought deir folks had allus owned it all.

An' de big house stan's all quiet lak an' solemn,
    Not a blessed soul in pa'lor, po'ch, er lawn;
Not a guest, ner not a ca'iage lef' to haul 'em,
    Fu' de ones dat tu'ned de latch-string out air gone.

An' de banjo's voice is silent in de qua'ters,
    D' ain't a hymn ner co'n-song ringin' in de air;
But de murmur of a branch's passin' waters
    Is de only soun' dat breks de stillness dere.

Whah 's de da'kies, dem dat used to be a-dancin'
    Evry night befo' de ole cabin do'?
Whah 's de chillun, dem dat used to be a-prancin'
    Er a-rollin' in de san' er on de flo'?

Whah 's ole Uncle Mordecai an' Uncle Aaron?
    Whah 's Aunt Doshy, Sam, an' Kit, an' all de res'?
Whah 's ole Tom de da'ky fiddlah, how 's he farin'?
    Whah 's de gals dat used to sing an' dance de bes'?

Gone! not one o' dem is lef' to tell de story;
    Dey have lef' de deah ole place to fall away.
Could n't one o' dem dat seed it in its glory
    Stay to watch it in de hour of decay?

Dey have lef' de ole plantation to de swallers,
    But it ho's in me a lover till de las';
Fu' I fin' hyeah in de memory dat follers
    All dat loved me an' dat I loved in de pas'.

So I 'll stay an' watch de deah ole place an' tend it
    Ez I used to in de happy days gone by.
'Twell de othah Mastah thinks it 's time to end it,
    An' calls me to my qua'ters in de sky.

Paul Laurence Dunbar, from *Lyrics of Love and Laughter* (1903)

When Dey 'Listed Colored Soldiers

Dey was talkin' in de cabin, dey was talkin' in de hall;
But I listened kin' o' keerless, not a-t'inkin' 'bout it all;
An' on Sunday, too, I noticed, dey was whisp'rin' mighty much,
Stan'in' all erroun' de roadside w'en dey let us out o' chu'ch.
But I didn't t'ink erbout it 'twell de middle of de week,
An' my 'Lias come to see me, an' somehow he couldn't speak.
Den I seed all in a minute whut he'd come to see me for; —
Dey had 'listed colo'ed sojers an' my 'Lias gwine to wah.

Oh, I hugged him, an' I kissed him, an' I baiged him not to go;
But he tol' me dat his conscience, hit was callin' to him so,
An' he could n't baih to lingah w'en he had a chanst to fight
For de freedom dey had gin him an' de glory of de right.
So he kissed me, an' he lef' me, w'en I'd p'omised to be true;
An' dey put a knapsack on him, an' a coat all colo'ed blue.
So I gin him pap's ol' Bible f'om de bottom of de draw', —
W'en dey 'listed colo'ed sojers an' my 'Lias went to wah.

But I t'ought of all de weary miles dat he would have to tramp,
An' I could n't be contented w'en dey tuk him to de camp.
W'y my hea't nigh broke wid grievin' 'twell I seed him on de street;

Den I felt lak I could go an' th'ow my body at his feet.
For his buttons was a-shinin', an' his face was shinin', too,
An' he looked so strong an' mighty in his coat o' sojer blue,
Dat I hollahed, "Step up, manny," dough my th'oat was so' an' raw, —
W'en dey 'listed colo'ed sojers an' my 'Lias went to wah.

Ol' Mis' cried w'en mastah lef' huh, young Miss mou'ned huh brothah Ned,
An' I did n't know dey feelin's is de ve'y wo'ds dey said
W'en I tol' 'em I was so'y. Dey had done gin up dey all;
But dey only seemed mo' proudah dat dey men had hyeahed de call.
Bofe my mastahs went in gray suits, an' I loved de Yankee blue,
But I t'ought dat I could sorrer for de losin' of 'em too;
But I could n't, for I did n't know de ha'f o' whut I saw,
'Twell dey 'listed colo'ed sojers an' my 'Lias went to wah.

Mastah Jack come home all sickly; he was broke for life, dey said;
An' dey lef' my po' young mastah some'r's on de roadside, — dead.
W'en de women cried an' mou'ned 'em, I could feel it thoo an' thoo,
For I had a loved un fightin' in de way o' dangah, too.
Den dey tol' me dey had laid him some'r's way down souf to res',
Wid de flag dat he had fit for shinin' daih acrost his breas'.
Well, I cried, but den I reckon dat 's whut Gawd had called him for,
W'en dey 'listed colo'ed sojers an' my 'Lias went to wah.

Notes

1 Jim Downs, *Sick from Freedom: African-American Illness and Suffering during the Civil War and Reconstruction* (New York: Oxford University Press, 2012), 4, 6.
2 Douglass refers to the 1st Louisiana Native Guard (later the 73rd U.S. Colored Infantry Regiment) and the 1st South Carolina Volunteers (later the 33rd U.S. Colored Infantry Regiment), both of which predated the 54th Massachusetts.
3 John A. Andrew (1818–1867), a lawyer of antislavery convictions, served as Governor of Massachusetts from 1861 to 1866; Charles Sumner (1811–1874) was the legendary senator from Massachusetts who devoted his life's energies to defeating slavery and, during Reconstruction, was one of the leaders of the Radical Republicans.
4 In 1822, Denmark Vesey helped plan a slave rebellion in Charleston, South Carolina. Although the conspiracy was discovered, and Vesey and dozens of other slaves and freedmen executed, the plot became a rallying cry for African American militancy.
5 Nat Turner, a slave in Southampton, Virginia, led a revolt in 1831 that killed dozens of whites, provoked a frenzy of reprisals against the local African American population, and became a mythic touchstone of militant resistance to slavery. Turner was convicted and hanged after going into hiding for more than two months.
6 Shields Green (1836?–1859), an ex-slave, and John Anthony Copeland, Jr. (1834–1859), a free black, were both hanged for participating in John Brown's raid on Harper's Ferry.
7 In *Notes on the State of Virginia* (1785), Thomas Jefferson, contemplating with dread the possibility of a war between whites and slaves, wrote that "Almighty has no attribute which can take side with us in such a contest."
8 The 54th Massachusetts trained at Camp Meigs in Readville, Mass.
9 Union Brig. Gen. John Potts Slough (1829–1867) served as military governor of Alexandria, Virginia, from 1862 through the end of the war.
10 Orator and politician Charles Sumner (1811–1874) was one of the preeminent antislavery voices in Massachusetts politics, leading the Radical Republicans in the U.S. Senate during the Civil War and Reconstruction. After delivering a particularly raw and impassioned speech to the Senate denouncing

the Kansas–Nebraska Act in 1856, Sumner was attacked on the Senate floor by South Carolina Congressman Preston Brooks, who beat Sumner with a cane until he was unconscious and nearly dead.

11 Formed in February of 1862, the Educational Commission for Freedmen was created in order to provide newly freed slaves with instruction in moral, religious, intellectual, and social matters. The commission first purchased land and established schools in South Carolina, later expanding to more Southern states and changing its name to the New England Freedmen's Aid Society.

12 Antislavery Fairs were often organized by the women of the antislavery movement to coincide with annual abolitionist conventions. These fairs raised money for the cause by selling handmade domestic goods and donated wares from Europe. The money was used to print newspapers and pamphlets, to fund antislavery organizations, and to provide assistance to free blacks.

13 On March 10, 1864, the Virginia Convention, called by the Unionist Restored Government of Virginia to form a new state constitution, voted 15–1 to abolish slavery.

14 Union officer Hugh Judson Kilpatrick (1836–1881) was a ruthless and ambitious leader in battle, known for exhausting his men and horses in aggressive, at times reckless, attacks on Confederate forces and civilians.

15 The Alexandria National Cemetery, established in 1862, primarily for soldiers who died in the Virginia theater of war, was nearly full by 1864.

16 In March, 1864, Stephen A. Swails (1832–1900) became the first African American soldier to receive a promotion in rank, rising to the position of second lieutenant.

17 Throughout the nineteenth century, the American Colonization Society worked toward "repatriation," removing African Americans from the United States and resettling them primarily in Africa, but also in the Caribbean. Here Jacobs most likely refers to the disastrous colonization effort in Isle a Vache, Haiti, where nearly 500 African Americans were sent in 1863. Faced with crippling hunger and ravaged by smallpox, nearly all of the emigrants in the infant colony perished. In March of 1864, a government ship brought the few survivors back to the U.S.

18 The Fifth Massachusetts Cavalry was an African American regiment formed in Readville in May, 1864.

19 Businessman George T. Downing (1819–1903) was one of the wealthiest African Americans in the country at the time; he worked tirelessly toward school desegregation and at recruiting efforts for the Fifth Massachusetts Cavalry. Charles Lenox Remond (1810–1873) was a black abolitionst and orator from Massachusetts, a prominent member of the American Anti-Slavery Society, and an active recruiter of black soldiers for the Union Army.

20 Nathaniel Lyon (1818–1861), the Union officer instrumental in the taking of the St. Louis Arsenal and the Camp Jackson affair (see note 21). He was killed in action at the Battle of Wilson's Creek.

21 In the "Camp Jackson Affair," as it has come to be known, Gen. Lyon led 6,000 soldiers in a march on Lindell's Grove (nicknamed Camp Jackson) just outside St. Louis, capturing nearly 700 members of the Missouri Volunteer Militia under Brig. Gen. Frost. The Union suspected the Militia of having designs on the St. Louis Arsenal, a major but lightly defended federal armory. After the militiamen refused an oath of allegiance to the Federal government, Lyon forced them to march through downtown St. Louis, angering the local population and provoking civil unrest, which resulted in at least 28 deaths and 100 injuries and, more importantly, contributed to the polarization of political sentiment in Missouri regarding the war.

22 Daniel Marsh Frost (1823–1900), a brigadier general who served in the Missouri Volunteer Militia and the Confederate States Army. John H. Kelly (1840–1864) was the youngest brigadier general in the Confederate States Army, killed during the Franklin–Nashville Campaign.

23 Union Major Robert Anderson (1805–1871), commander of Fort Sumter at the start of the Civil War.

24 During the last week of April, 1862, Union naval forces led by Flag Officer (later Admiral) David Farragut captured New Orleans, the largest Confederate city and an important port for trade and commerce, without significant resistance. Gen. Benjamin Butler oversaw the subsequent controversial occupation of the city.

25 This "famous Union song" appears not to have entered the historical record other than in Jackson's narrative.

26 I.e., obey.

27 A common nineteenth-century personification of the United States.

28 General Robert E. Lee's evacuation of Richmond, Virginia, and his surrender at the Appomattox Court House in April, 1865, effectively ended the Civil War.

29 After his assassination, Lincoln's body was transported by funeral train to Springfield, Illinois, for burial. At a dozen cities along the way, his body was exhibited for public viewing. The body lay in state at the Indiana State House in Indianapolis on April 30, 1865.

30 Adapted from Exodus 15:2–3.

31 Ron Powers, *Mark Twain: A Life* (New York: Free Press, 2005), 358.

32 This was the nickname of a Delaware regiment that fought in the American Revolution; "blue hen's chickens" later came to refer generally to natives or soldiers of Delaware, and the state adopted the blue hen chicken as its official bird in 1939.

33 William Henry Brisbane (1803?–1878) was a Baptist pastor and former planter from Beaufort County, South Carolina, who renounced slavery in the 1830s and moved to Wisconsin in 1853. During the war, Brisbane served as chaplain in the 2nd Wisconsin Cavalry and as a tax commissioner in South Carolina.

34 George Barrell Cheever (1807–1890) was the author of a number of books denouncing slavery, of which *God Against Slavery* (1857) is the best known.

35 Robert Gould Shaw (1837–1863), scion of Boston's elite, abolitionist, and skilled soldier, organized and commanded the 54th Massachusetts Infantry, the North's legendary African American regiment. He died on July 18, 1863 while leading the unsuccessful attack on Fort Wager, South Carolina.

36 Joseph Finegan (1810?–1885) started the Civil War as captain of the Fernandina Volunteers of Florida and rose to brigadier general commanding the District of East Florida in November 1862. During 1863–1864, his troops fought repeated engagements in northern Florida.

37 Thomas Wentworth Higginson (1823–1911), a minister, poet, feminist, abolitionist, politician, and author who had raised a white Massachusetts regiment earlier in 1862, took command of the 1st South Carolina Volunteers on November 10, 1862, when it was reorganized under Gen. Rufus Saxton. The regiment was renamed the 33rd United States Colored Troops in February 1864. Higginson led the regiment until May 1864, after being wounded during an expedition up the Edisto River. Out of this transformative experience he wrote *Army Life in a Black Regiment* (1869).

38 William Barnwell was a wealthy planter in Beaufort county.

39 The diminutive Clara Barton (1821–1912) earned a towering reputation during the war through her essentially freelance relief efforts on behalf of Union soldiers.

40 Folly Island and Morris Island lie along the South Carolina coast, just south of Charleston Harbor.

41 James Island lies inland from Morris Island, just south of Charleston.

42 After his "march to the sea" Union forces under Sherman attacked and captured Fort McAllister on December 13, 1864, preparing for the occupation of Savannah later that month.

43 The Fugitive Slave Act of 1850 prohibited the harboring of escaped slaves and created incentives for both federal and local officers to assist in their capture. To "prove property," as Smith puts it, required only a sworn statement of ownership.

44 Smith actually had three primary "masters" at different points—Richard ("Dick") Mitchell, Thomas Langsdon, and John Langsdon— although their precise relationships to him, and to each other, are not entirely clear.

45 As a young man in Heathsville, Va., Smith is hired out to a shoe-maker referred to earlier in the narrative as "Mr. Lacky."

46 Smith probably means the Israel Bethel Colored Methodist Episcopal Church, an independent African American church in Washington D.C. which played a prominent role in the antislavery movement and black civil rights.

47 Smith escaped with two friends in 1838 by stealing a boat from a plantation along the Coan River in Virginia, sailing to Frenchtown, Maryland, and then, "without a word being said to us" (47), buying tickets aboard a ship sailing from New Castle to Philadelphia.

48 After escaping by boat to Maryland, Smith heads overland by foot and is terrified when he sees a train for the first time: "I thought my last days had come; I shook from head to foot as the monster came rushing on towards me" (44).

49 When he was about six or seven years old, Smith suffered a terrible injury to his knee after a load of lumber was dropped on it. This injury, however, actually spared Smith from being used as an agricultural slave.

50 A "coach maker" who lived near Smith's family in Northern Neck, mentioned briefly early in the narrative.

51 A dredge—used, for example, in the construction and maintenance of harbors and canals.

52 In the first chapter of the narrative, this doctor helped cure Smith's father after an incident of poisoning.

53 These pine trees had grown up from the larger trees, (saplings as they are called,) and reminded me of past days, when the slaves had to fell them for fire-wood for our masters. The woodlands were owned by them, and nothing could induce them to buy fuel to burn as long as they had slaves to labor in felling trees [Smith's note].

54 On the Civil Rights Act of 1866, see p. 317, n. 2 (Pollard excerpt ch. 5).

55 On Smith's escape see note 47.

56 During the antebellum years, "[a]s the free black population grew in size, Delaware's legislature increasingly committed itself to denying it the same basic prerogatives that were considered sacrosanct for whites." The resulting "black codes" "could only be rationalized by . . . attacking the character,

honesty, and work ethic of free blacks" (William H. Williams, *Slavery and Freedom in Delaware, 1639–1865* [Wilmington, Del.: Scholarly Resources, 1996], 198, 189).

57 Major General John McAuley Palmer (1817–1900), an abolitionist and effective field commander, was appointed military governor of Kentucky in 1865, by Lincoln, in order to end slavery in the state and to suppress continued guerrilla warfare there. In that capacity, he imposed a series of initiatives aimed at providing legal and practical protections for Kentucky blacks. Smith refers to General Order no. 7, which, according to one newspaper report, came with "an invitation to the able-bodied to enlist, and get the three hundred dollars city bounty themselves" ("From Kentucky; Gen. Palmer Down on Guerrillas and Slave Pens . . ." *New York Times*, March 13, 1865).

58 Thomas James (1804–1891), an antislavery activist and traveling minister for the African Methodist Episcopal Church, assisted the Union Army in Louisville by helping take care of freedmen and contrabands, starting a Sunday school, conducting marriages, and releasing slaves from slave pens, among other activities.

59 In early August, 1865, as the Thirteenth Amendment was moving toward ratification, a convention of African American leaders met in Alexandria, Virginia, to implore the federal government not to back down from pursuing the cause of black civil rights in the face of Southern opposition and general postwar fatigue.

60 J. M. Langston (1829–1897), free black abolitionist, recruiter of African American troops, inspector general for the Freedmen's Bureau, and later law dean of Howard University.

61 Brig. Gen. Edward Augustus Wild (1825–1891), an abolitonist and physician, aggressively recruited newly liberated slaves to join the Union Army and commanded a group of black regiments known collectively as "Wild's African Brigade," which he led in a number of controversial raids, skirmishes, and battles in the Carolinas and Virginia.

62 The Excelsior Brigade, consisting of regiments from New York and Indiana, fought in the Peninsula Campaign of 1862, commanded by Gen. Daniel Edgar Sickles (1819–1914); the battle of Fair Oaks (or Seven Pines), fought to a bloody stand-off, marked the beginning of the end of the Peninsula Campaign.

63 Smith refers to the massive "Draft Riots" of July 13–16, 1863, in which working-class New Yorkers took to the streets to protest recent conscription laws passed by the U.S. Congress. The protests quickly spun out of control and for three days the city was wracked by running street battles and massive destruction of property. The mobs, driven largely by resentment of competition for jobs, also turned on African Americans, their homes and businesses; many—perhaps more than 100—were killed before local police, state militia, and federal troops could restore order.

64 This meeting of abolitionists, at which Frederick Douglass spoke, was broken up when "ruffians, hired by merchants engaged in the slave trade, invaded the hall, disrupted the proceedings, and singled out Douglass for attack" (*Frederick Douglass: Selected Speeches and Writings*, ed. Philip S. Foner and Yuval Taylor [Chicago: Lawrence Hill Books, 1999], 417).

65 The four-story Colored Orphan Asylum on Fifth Avenue, "an imposing symbol of white charity toward blacks and black upward mobility," was looted and burned to the ground on the first day of rioting; no children were hurt (Leslie M. Harris, *In the Shadow of Slavery: African Americans in New York City, 1626–1863* [Chicago: University of Chicago Press, 2003], 280).

66 Union Gen. William T. Sherman's "march to the sea," during which his troops systematically destroyed anything that could be used in the Southern war effort, including rail-lines, civilian crops, cotton gins, and much else, marked the conflict's most dramatic, and controversial, display of "total war." Although many slaves, as Smith describes, greeted the Union troops as liberators and trailed along after them, not all did; others felt victimized along with the rest of the Southern population.

67 As the war dragged on, the Confederate government faced growing difficulties in financing the war effort; hobbled by mounting debt, it printed more currency, which led to rampant inflation, and the measures enacted in 1863 and 1864—including a variety of new taxes—were inadequate to the problem. By 1865 the Confederacy was facing financial meltdown.

68 The Confederacy did not authorize the enlistment of black soldiers until March, 1865, when the war was effectively over.

69 "The war had successfully dismantled the institution of slavery, but it raised a whole new set of questions about how society should be reorganized, of which public health was just one aspect . . . . Due to the fact that there was no institutional structure to respond to the suffering and sickness of emancipated slaves, abolitionists initially attempted to fill the void" (Jim Downs, *Sick from Freedom: African-American Illness and Suffering during the Civil War and Reconstruction* [New York: Oxford University Press, 2012], 164).

70 Laura W. Stebbins (1821–1870) was an experienced educator from Springfield, Mass., who volunteered after the war as a freedmen's teacher in Washington D.C. and Virginia.

71 A former American colony on the western coast of Africa, established for the resettlement of free blacks, Liberia had a controversial and complex history in the nineteenth century, with emigration there

depending largely on circumstances in the United States. With the Southern backlash against Reconstruction, Liberia once again proved appealing to many Southern blacks seeking economic opportunity and political freedom.

72 This petition, drawn up by the black activist Henry Adams's Colonization Council in Louisiana, asked "for the government either to protect rights of black citizens or to give them a territory of their own. If Hayes could do neither, the petition asked for a federal appropriation of funds to send them back to their own land, Africa" (Kenneth C. Barnes, *Journey of Hope: The Back-to-Africa Movement in Arkansas in the Late 1800s* [Chapel Hill: University of North Carolina Press, 2004], 11).

73 The central and notorious phrase of the U.S. Supreme Court's proslavery decision in *Dred Scott* v. *Sandford* (1857), in which Chief Justice Roger B. Taney wrote that, when the Constitution was written, blacks "had for more than a century before been regarded as beings of an inferior order, and altogether unfit to associate with the white race, either in social or political relations; and so far inferior, that they had no rights which the white man was bound to respect; and that the negro might justly and lawfully be reduced to slavery for his benefit."

74 Elizabeth Comstock (1815–1891) was an English-born Quaker and reformer who lobbied actively in support of freedpeople seeking to move out of the South, particularly to Kansas.

The Texts

Abraham Lincoln, Final Emancipation Proclamation. Source: *Complete Works of Abraham Lincoln, Comprising his Speeches, Letters, State Papers, and Miscellaneous Writings*, ed. John G. Nicolay and John Hay. Vol. 2 (New York: The Century Company, 1920).

Frederick Douglass, "Men of Color, to Arms! A Call by Frederick Douglass." (Broadside). Rochester, New York: 1863. Source: Rare Books and Special Collections Division, Library of Congress. Douglass also published and circulated another recruiting broadside in 1863, headed "Men of Color, To Arms! To Arms! Now or Never!" and signed by a variety of African American activists, intellectuals, and preachers; the text differs but the message is essentially the same.

Frances Ellen Watkins Harper, "The Massachusetts Fifty-Fourth." Source: Donald Yacovone, *Freedom's Journey: African American Voices of the Civil War* (Chicago: Lawrence Hill Books, 2004). Originally published in the New York *Weekly Anglo-African*, October 10, 1863.

Harriet Jacobs and Louisa M. Jacobs, Letter to Lydia Maria Child. Source: *National Anti-Slavery Standard*, vol. 24 no. 49 (April 16, 1864), 2.

George Moses Horton, "The Use of Liberty." Source: *Naked Genius: By George Moses Horton, The Colored Bard of North Carolina* (Raleigh, N.C.: Wm. B. Smith & Co., Southern Field and Fireside Book Publishing House, 1865).

Mattie Jackson and L. S. Thompson, *The Story of Mattie J. Jackson*. Source: *The Story of Mattie J. Jackson; Her Parentage – Experience of Eighteen Years in Slavery – Incidents During the War – Her Escape from Slavery. A True Story. Written and arranged by Dr. L. S. Thompson (previously Mrs. Schuyler.) As given by Mattie* (Lawrence, Mass.: Printed at Sentinel Office, 123 Essex Street, 1866).

Mark Twain, "A True Story, Repeated Word for Word As I Heard It." Source: *The Atlantic Monthly* 34:205 (November 1874): 591–594.

Susie King Taylor, from *Reminiscences of My Life in Camp*. Source: *Reminiscences of My Life in Camp with the 33d United States Colored Troops Late 1st S. C. Volunteers* (Boston: The author, 1902).

James Lindsay Smith, from *Autobiography of James L. Smith*. Source: *Autobiography of James L. Smith, Including, Also, Reminiscences of Slave Life, Recollections of the War, Education of Freedmen, Causes of the Exodus, etc.* (Norwich, CT: The Bulletin, 1881).

Paul Laurence Dunbar, poems. Source: *The Complete Poems of Paul Laurence Dunbar*, ed. William Dean Howells (New York: Dodd, Mead & Co., 1922). "The Deserted Plantation" was originally published in *Lyrics of Lowly Life* (New York: Young People's Missionary Movement of the United States and Canada, 1895; New York: Dodd, Mead, and Co., 1896). "When Dey 'Listed Colored Soldiers" was originally published in the *New England Magazine* (August 1899), and subsequently included in *Lyrics of Love and Laughter* (New York: Dodd, Mead, and Co., 1903).

IV
The Home Front

Home again. Lithograph by Endicott & Co., 1866. Library of Congress Prints and Photographs Division, LC-DIG-pga-01172

Introduction

Because it was fought entirely on American soil, and because it absorbed the full energies of both North and South, the Civil War affected civilian life in far-reaching ways. Every state had an economic and political stake in the conflict; every state sent soldiers into the fray; and millions of families found their lives directly affected by events both near and far. In contrast to America's foreign wars, civilians participated and suffered in the Civil War in ways that few could have anticipated. The civilian experience in the Civil War entailed an array of changes—some minor and some major, some short-lived and some long-lasting—in both daily life and the broader framework of cultural attitudes that Americans had traditionally brought to their work, their homes, and their social relations.

Most directly, the war effort affected civilians by turning some of them into combatants—not always with their consent. As it became clear that the initial call-up of voluntary enlistments in 1861 would not suffice, both militaries turned to other means of recruitment, the most prominent being conscription (or the threat of conscription) and bounties (i.e., direct payments to new enlistees). By the end of the war, more than 3 million Americans, or about 10 percent of the total population, had fought. These soldiers represented a broad swath of the American public. The vast majority were native-born white men in their twenties and thirties, although immigrants made up about a quarter of the Union army and about 10 percent of the Confederate army. About half of the North's soldiers were farmers or farm laborers, compared to about two-thirds of Southern soldiers, while the rest hailed from a variety of social backgrounds, including a good number of skilled laborers and professionals.

What this meant was that very few families or towns could avoid the loss of sons, husbands, fathers, and productive workers. Maris Vinovskis has estimated—conservatively—that about 6 percent of Northern white males aged 13 to 43 in 1860 died in the Civil War, compared to about 18 percent of their Southern counterparts.[1] (Since the North had a much larger total population, it suffered a lower proportional rate of casualties.) Moreover, since many units were raised from the same geographic area, some communities could be particularly hard hit if a local regiment suffered high losses in combat.

By its very nature as a *civil* war, bound up and entangled with the general population, the conflict also produced a large number of civilian deaths, although historians have struggled to determine that toll with any certainty; estimates range from 50,000 to upwards of 250,000. What is certain is that non-combatants, even those far distant from the front, found their daily lives affected in profound ways. Inflation, stagnant wages, the disruption of commerce, and the destruction or diversion of necessary goods, took an economic toll on many families. Particularly vulnerable were civilians in the Southern border states, where much of the fighting took place, and in Georgia and South Carolina, where late in the war Gen. William T. Sherman waged a campaign against the Southern economic and military infrastructure. Meanwhile, both sides—the North more aggressively—instituted restrictions on free speech and political dissent, suspending the writ of habeas corpus and making arrests for activities deemed seditious or treasonous. And the war, in perhaps its most troubling legacy, affected children, both black and white; James Marten writes that "children were integrated and exposed to the conflict in previously unimaginable ways, contrary to developing notions of the nurturing and protection of children."[2] Many thousands, of course, were orphaned; others became politicized; some took on greater responsibilites, or even tried to enlist; and all, it is safe to say, grew up more quickly than they would have in peacetime.

In the midst of these difficulties, ordinary Americans worked to support the front-line militaries, raising money to purchase supplies, sending goods to soldiers in camp, and volunteering at hospitals and in benevolent organizations such as the Sanitary Commission or the Christian Commission. It is possible that this intensified public activity translated into various forms of postwar political activism, particularly on the part of women. Civilians also sustained a vital correspondence with soldiers at the front, and at times traveled to hospitals to find wounded family members or to encampments to get first-hand knowledge. Recounting their experiences enabled both civilians and soldiers to preserve intact a sense of community: "Keeping diaries, letters, and memoirs, and telling and re-telling the stories of the men and women who joined in the great cause sealed the union of home front and soldier after the war."[3]

Civilians also benefited from a roisterous press, getting news about the war from a rich variety of newspapers, magazines, and illustrated weeklies. This proved significant. The Civil War was, in a fundamental sense, an information war. Not only did a robust publishing industry and communications infrastructure bring the realities of war to the home front, but the information people took in affected public opinion, and public opinion in turn had a bearing on the military and political decisions that war leaders made. Behind many of these decisions—from Lincoln's timing of the Emancipation Proclamation to Robert E. Lee's decision to invade Pennsylvania—the pressure of the public mood could be felt, and that mood depended largely on what people read in the periodicals.

Tangible changes in daily life inevitably created intangible changes in cultural attitudes, but these are much more difficult to measure. Did shared military service, for instance, help to reduce class and ethnic tensions among soldiers from different backgrounds? Or might it have reinforced antagonism and prejudice? What about shared sacrifice by civilians? How did the war change public perceptions of political leaders? At a more personal level, how did the war affect Americans' thinking about mortality, and about the fragility of the human body? These are issues that cultural historians have only begun to address, but they promise to be a fruitful vein of study.

Much more work has looked at the Civil War's impact on gender roles and the family, and while a consensus has formed that the war challenged the traditional models, the extent to which it did so remains an open question. Since many women during the war had to move outside of their customary economic and social responsibilities, working on farms and in factories and hospitals, some scholars have suggested that the war brought about a "crisis in gender" and a "crisis of domesticity."[4] Joan E. Cashin, for instance, maintains that the war "unsettled, undermined, and sometimes destroyed traditional gender roles, in all regions, forcing people to reconsider their assumptions about appropriate behavior for men and women of both races."[5] But revolutions produce counter-revolutions, and—in the South particularly—the desire for pre-war stability may have led people to cling to familiar traditions in the face of upheaval. As George Rable observes, "the struggle for survival . . . provided the social context for both women and men to redefine—or, more accurately, re-establish—'proper' female roles."[6] In retrospect, what seems clear is that women's wartime and postwar experiences formed part of the complex, decades-long saga of their steadily increasing participation in the labor force and in American political culture.

As in any war, finally, veterans returned home to find a world changed, and they faced the challenge of reintegrating into civilian life. For many Southern veterans there was little left—except, perhaps, the sense of having fought honorably. Some veterans returned as heroes and some as deserters. All veterans found their relation to their communities and families changed, in subtle ways and dramatic ways. They were civilians again, and yet no longer civilians. The following writings, by and about both men and women, can only begin to convey just how difficult that transition was.

Harriet Beecher Stowe, "The Chimney-Corner" (1865)

From January 1865 to September 1866, Stowe published a series of essays in the *Atlantic Monthly* under the title of "The Chimney-Corner," on topics ranging from "How Shall We Entertain Our Company?" to "The Noble Army of Martyrs." In 1868, thirteen of the essays were gathered together and published by Ticknor & Fields as *The Chimney-Corner*, under the pseudonym Christopher Crowfield.

Here comes the First of January, Eighteen Hundred and Sixty-Five, and we are all settled comfortably into our winter places, with our winter surroundings and belongings; all cracks and openings are calked and listed, the double windows are in, the furnace dragon in the cellar is ruddy and in good liking, sending up his warming respirations through every pipe and register in the house; and yet, though an artificial summer reigns everywhere, like bees, we have our swarming-place, — in my library. There is my chimney-corner, and my table permanently established on one side of the hearth; and each of the female genus has, so to speak, pitched her own winter-tent within sight of the blaze of my camp-fire. I discerned to-day that Jennie had surreptitiously appropriated one of the drawers of my study-table to knitting-needles and worsted; and wicker work-baskets and stands of various heights and sizes seem to be planted here and there for permanence among the bookcases. The canary-bird has a sunny window, and the plants spread out their leaves and unfold their blossoms as if there were no ice and snow in the street, and Rover makes a hearth-rug of himself in winking satisfaction in front of my fire, except when Jennie is taken with a fit of discipline, when he beats a retreat, and secretes [sic] himself under my table.

Peaceable, ah, how peaceable, home and quiet and warmth in winter! And how, when we hear the wind whistle, we think of you, O our brave brothers, our saviours and defenders, who for our sake have no home but the muddy camp, the hard pillow of the barrack, the weary march, the uncertain fare, — you, the rank and file, the thousand unnoticed ones, who have left warm fires, dear wives, loving little children, without even the hope of glory or fame, — without even the hope of doing anything remarkable or perceptible for the cause you love, — resigned only to fill the ditch or bridge the chasm over which your country shall walk to peace and joy! Good men and true, brave unknown hearts, we salute you, and feel that we, in our soft peace and security, are not worthy of you! When we think of you, our simple comforts seem luxuries all too good for us, who give so little when you give all!

But there are others to whom from our bright homes, our cheerful firesides, we would fain say a word, if we dared.

Think of a mother receiving a letter with such a passage as this in it! It is extracted from one we have just seen, written by a private in the army of Sheridan, describing the death of a private. "He fell instantly, gave a peculiar smile and look, and then closed his eyes. We laid him down gently at the foot of a large tree. I crossed his hands over his breast, closed his eyelids down, but the smile was still on his face. I wrapped him in his tent, spread my pocket-handkerchief over his face, wrote his name on a piece of paper, and pinned it on his breast, and there we left him: we could not find pick or shovel to dig a grave." There it is! — a history that is multiplying itself by hundreds daily, the substance of what has come to so many homes, and must come to so many more before the great price of our ransom is paid!

What can we say to you, in those many, many homes where the light has gone out forever? — you, O fathers, mothers, wives, sisters, haunted by a name that has ceased to be spoken on earth, — you, for whom there is no more news from the camp, no more reading of lists, no more tracing of maps, no more letters, but only a blank, dead silence! The battle-cry goes on, but for you it is passed by! the victory comes, but, oh, never more to bring him back to you! your offering to this great cause has been made, and been taken; you have thrown into it *all* your living, even all that you had, and from henceforth your house is left unto you desolate! O ye watchers of the cross, ye waiters by the sepulchre, what can be said to you? We could almost extinguish our own home-fires, that seem too bright when we think of your darkness; the laugh dies on our lip, the lamp burns dim through our tears, and we seem scarcely worthy to speak words of comfort, lest we seem as those who mock a grief they cannot know.

But is there no consolation? Is it nothing to have had such a treasure to give, and to have given it freely for the noblest cause for which ever battle was set, — for the salvation of your country, for the freedom of all mankind? Had he died a fruitless death, in the track of common life, blasted by fever, smitten or rent by crushing accident, then might his most precious life seem to be as water spilled upon the ground; but now it has been given for a cause and a purpose worthy even the anguish of your loss and sacrifice. He has been counted worthy to be numbered with those who stood with precious incense between the living and the dead, that the plague which was consuming us might be stayed. The blood of these young martyrs shall be the seed of the future church of liberty, and from every drop shall spring up flowers of healing. O widow! O mother! blessed among bereaved women! there remains to you a treasure that belongs not to those who have lost in any other wise, — the power to say, "He died for his country." In all the good that comes of this anguish you shall have a right and share by virtue of this sacrifice. The joy of freedmen bursting from chains, the glory of a nation new-born, the assurance of a triumphant future for your country and the world, — all these become yours by the purchase-money of that precious blood.

Besides this, there are other treasures that come through sorrow, and sorrow alone. There are celestial plants of root so long and so deep that the land must be torn and furrowed, ploughed up from the very foundation, before they can strike and flourish; and when we see how God's plough is driving backward and forward and across this nation, rending, tearing up tender shoots, and burying soft wild-flowers, we ask ourselves, What is He going to plant?

Not the first year, nor the second, after the ground has been broken up, does the purpose of the husbandman appear. At first we see only what is uprooted and ploughed in, — the daisy drabbled, and the violet crushed, — and the first trees planted amid the unsightly furrows stand dumb and disconsolate, irresolute in leaf, and without flower or fruit. Their work is under the ground. In darkness and silence they are putting forth long fibres, searching hither and thither under the black soil for the strength that years hence shall burst into bloom and bearing.

What is true of nations is true of individuals. It may seem now winter and desolation with you. Your hearts have been ploughed and harrowed and are now frozen up. There is not a flower left, not a blade of grass, not a bird to sing, — and it is hard to believe that any brighter flowers, any greener herbage, shall spring up, than those which have been torn away: and yet there will. Nature herself teaches you to-day. Out-doors nothing but bare branches and shrouding snow; and yet you know that there is not a tree that is not patiently holding out at the end of its boughs next year's buds, frozen indeed, but unkilled. The rhododendron and the lilac have their blossoms all ready, wrapped in cere-cloth, waiting in patient faith. Under the frozen ground the crocus and the hyacinth and the tulip hide in their hearts the perfect forms of future flowers. And it is even so with you: your leaf-buds of the future are frozen, but not killed; the soil of your heart has many flowers under it cold and still now, but they will yet come up and bloom.

The dear old book of comfort tells of no present healing for sorrow. No chastening for the present seemeth joyous, but grievous, but *afterwards* it yieldeth peaceable fruits of righteousness. We, as individuals, as a nation, need to have faith in that AFTERWARDS. It is sure to come, — sure as spring and summer to follow winter.

There is a certain amount of suffering which must follow the rending of the great chords of life, suffering which is natural and inevitable; it cannot be argued down; it cannot be stilled; it can no more be soothed by any effort of faith and reason than the pain of a fractured limb, or the agony of fire on the living flesh. All that we can do is to brace ourselves to bear it, calling on God, as the martyrs did in the fire, and resigning ourselves to let it burn on. We must be willing to suffer, since God so wills. There are just so many waves to go over us, just so many arrows of stinging thought to be shot into our soul, just so many faintings and sinkings and revivings only to suffer again, belonging to and inherent in our portion of sorrow; and there is a work of healing that God has placed in the bands of Time alone.

Time heals all things at last; yet it depends much on us in our suffering, whether time shall send us forth healed, indeed, but maimed and crippled and callous, or whether, looking to the great Physician of sorrows, and coworking with him, we come forth stronger and fairer even for our wounds.

We call ourselves a Christian people, and the peculiarity of Christianity is that it is a worship and doctrine of sorrow. The five wounds of Jesus, the instruments of the passion, the cross, the sepulchre, — these are its emblems and watchwords. In thousands of churches, amid gold and gems and altars fragrant with perfume, are seen the crown of thorns, the nails, the spear, the cup of vinegar mingled with gall, the sponge that could not slake that burning death-thirst; and in a voice choked with anguish the Church in many lands and divers tongues prays from age to age, — "By thine agony and bloody sweat, by thy cross and passion, by thy precious death and burial!" — mighty words of comfort, whose meaning reveals itself only to souls fainting in the cold death-sweat of mortal anguish! They tell all Christians that by uttermost distress alone was the Captain of their salvation made perfect as a Saviour.

Sorrow brings us into the true unity of the Church, — that unity which underlies all external creeds, and unites all hearts that have suffered deeply enough to know that when sorrow is at its utmost there is but one kind of sorrow, and but one remedy. What matter, *in extremis*, whether we be called Romanist, or Protestant, or Greek, or Calvinist?

We suffer, and Christ suffered; we die, and Christ died; he conquered suffering and death, he rose and lives and reigns, — and we shall conquer, rise, live, and reign; the hours on the cross were long, the thirst was bitter, the darkness and horror real, — *but they ended*. After the wail, "My God, why hast thou forsaken me?" came the calm, "It is finished"; pledge to us all that our "It is finished" shall come also.

Christ arose, fresh, joyous, no more to die; and it is written, that, when the disciples were gathered together in fear and sorrow, he stood in the midst of them, and showed unto them his hands and his side; and then were they glad. Already had the healed wounds of Jesus become pledges of consolation to innumerable thousands; and those who, like Christ, have suffered the weary struggles, the dim horrors of the cross, — who have lain, like him, cold and chilled in the hopeless sepulchre, — if his spirit wakes them to life, shall come forth with healing power for others who have suffered and are suffering.

Count the good and beautiful ministrations that have been wrought in this world of need and labor, and how many of them have been wrought by hands wounded and scarred, by hearts that had scarcely ceased to bleed!

How many priests of consolation is God now ordaining by the fiery imposition of sorrow! how many Sisters of the Bleeding Heart, Daughters of Mercy, Sisters of Charity, are receiving their first vocation in tears and blood!

The report of every battle strikes into some home; and heads fall low, and hearts are shattered, and only God sees the joy that is set before them, and that shall come out of their sorrow. He sees our morning at the same moment that He sees our night, — sees us comforted, healed, risen to a higher life, at the same moment that He sees us crushed and broken in the dust; and so, though tenderer than we, He bears our great sorrows for the joy that is set before us.

After the Napoleonic wars had desolated Europe, the country was, like all countries after war, full of shattered households, of widows and orphans and homeless wanderers. A nobleman of Silesia, the Baron von Kottwitz, who had lost his wife and all his family in the reverses and sorrows of the times, found himself alone in the world, which looked more dreary and miserable through the multiplying lenses of his own tears. But he was one of those whose heart had been quickened in its death anguish by the resurrection voice of Christ; and he came forth to life and comfort. He bravely resolved to do all that one man could to lessen the great sum of misery. He sold his estates in Silesia, bought in Berlin a large building that had been used as barracks for the soldiers, and, fitting it up in plain, commodious apartments, formed there a great family-establishment, into which he received the wrecks and fragments of families that had been broken up by the war, — orphan children, widowed and helpless women, decrepit old people, disabled soldiers. These he made his family, and constituted himself their father and chief. He abode with them, and cared for them as a parent. He had schools for the children; the more advanced he put to trades and employments; he set up a hospital for the sick; and for all he had the priestly ministrations of his own Christ-like heart. The celebrated Professor Tholuck,[7] one of the most learned men of modern Germany, was an early _protégé_ of the old Baron's, who, discerning his talents, put him in the way of a liberal education. In his earlier years, like many others of the young who play with life, ignorant of its needs, Tholuck piqued himself on a lordly skepticism with regard to the commonly received Christianity, and even wrote an essay to prove the superiority of the Mohammedan to the Christian religion. In speaking of his conversion, he says, — "What moved me was no argument, nor any spoken reproof, but simply that divine image of the old Baron walking before my soul. That life was an argument always present to me, and which I never could answer; and so I became a Christian." In the life of this man we see the victory over sorrow. How many with means like his, when desolated by like bereavements, have lain coldly and idly gazing on the miseries of life, and weaving around themselves icy tissues of doubt and despair, — doubting the being of a God, doubting the reality of a Providence, doubting the divine love, embittered and rebellious against the power which they could not resist, yet to which they would not submit! In such a chill heart-freeze lies the danger of sorrow. And it is a mortal danger. It is a torpor that must be resisted, as the man in the whirling snows must bestir himself, or he will perish. The apathy of melancholy must be broken by an effort of religion and duty. The stagnant blood must be made to flow by active work, and the cold hand warmed by clasping the hands outstretched towards it in sympathy or supplication. One orphan child taken in, to be fed, clothed, and nurtured, may save a heart from freezing to death: and God knows this war is making but too many orphans!

It is easy to subscribe to an orphan asylum, and go on in one's despair and loneliness. Such ministries may do good to the children who are thereby saved from the street, but they impart little warmth and comfort to the giver. One destitute child housed, taught, cared for, and tended personally, will bring more solace to a suffering heart than a dozen maintained in an asylum. Not that the child will probably prove an angel, or even an uncommonly interesting mortal. It is a prosaic work, this bringing-up of children, and there can be little rosewater in it. The child may not appreciate what is done for him, may not be particularly grateful, may have disagreeable faults, and continue to have them after much pains on your part to eradicate them, — and yet it is a fact, that to redeem one human being from destitution and ruin, even in some homely every-day course of ministrations, is one of the best possible tonics and alteratives to a sick and wounded spirit.

But this is not the only avenue to beneficence which the war opens. We need but name the service of hospitals, the care and education of the freedmen, — for these are charities that have long been before the eyes of the community, and have employed thousands of busy hands: thousands of sick and dying beds to tend, a race to be educated, civilized, and Christianized, surely were work enough for one age; and yet this is not all. War shatters everything, and it is hard to say what in society will not need rebuilding and binding up and strengthening anew. Not the least of the evils of war are the vices which a great army engenders wherever it moves, — vices peculiar to military life, as others are peculiar to peace. The poor soldier perils for us not merely his body, but his soul. He leads a life of harassing and exhausting toil and privation, of violent strain on the nervous energies, alternating with sudden collapse, creating a craving for stimulants, and endangering the formation of fatal habits. What furies and harpies are those that follow the army, and that seek out the soldier in his tent, far from home, mother, wife, and sister, tired, disheartened, and tempt him to forget his troubles in a momentary exhilaration, that burns only to chill and to destroy! Evil angels are always active and indefatigable, and there must be good angels enlisted to face them; and here is employment for the slack hand of grief. Ah, we have known mothers bereft of sons in this war, who have seemed at once to open wide their hearts, and to become mothers to every brave soldier in the field. They have lived only to work, — and in place of one lost, their sons have been counted by thousands.

And not least of all the fields for exertion and Christian charity opened by this war is that presented by womanhood. The war is abstracting from the community its protecting and sheltering elements, and leaving the helpless and dependent in vast disproportion. For years to come, the average of lone women will be largely increased; and the demand, always great, for some means by which they may provide for themselves, in the rude jostle of the world, will become more urgent and imperative.

Will any one sit pining away in inert grief, when two streets off are the midnight dance-houses, where girls of twelve, thirteen, and fourteen are being lured into the way of swift destruction? How many of these are daughters of soldiers who have given their hearts' blood for us and our liberties!

Two noble women of the Society of Friends have lately been taking the gauge of suffering and misery in our land, visiting the hospitals at every accessible point, pausing in our great cities, and going in their purity to those midnight orgies where mere children are being trained for a life of vice and infamy. They have talked with these poor bewildered souls, entangled in toils as terrible and inexorable as those of the slave-market, and many of whom are frightened and distressed at the life they are beginning to lead, and earnestly looking for the means of escape. In the judgment of these holy women, at least one third of those with whom they have talked are children so recently entrapped, and so capable of reformation, that there would be the greatest hope in efforts for their salvation. While such things are to be done in our land, is there any reason why any one should die of grief? One soul redeemed will do more to lift the burden of sorrow than all the blandishments and diversions of art, all the alleviations of luxury, all the sympathy of friends.

In the Roman Catholic Church there is an order of women called the Sisters of the Good Shepherd, who have renounced the world to devote themselves, their talents and property, entirely to the work of seeking out and saving the fallen of their own sex; and the wonders worked by their self-denying love on the hearts and lives of even the most depraved are credible only to those who know that the Good Shepherd Himself ever lives and works with such spirits engaged in such a work. A similar order of women exists in New York, under the direction of the Episcopal Church, in connection with St. Luke's Hospital; and another in England, who tend the "House of Mercy" of Clewer.

Such benevolent associations offer objects of interest to that class which most needs something to fill the void made by bereavement. The wounds of grief are less apt to find a cure in that rank of life where the sufferer has wealth and leisure. The *poor* widow, whose husband was her all, *must* break the paralysis of grief. The hard necessities of life are her physicians; they send her out to unwelcome, yet friendly toil, which, hard as it seems, has yet its healing power. But the sufferer surrounded by the appliances of wealth and luxury may long indulge the baleful apathy, and remain in the damp shadows of the valley of death till strength and health are irrecoverably lost. How Christ-like is the thought of a woman, graceful, elegant, cultivated, refined, whose voice has been trained to melody, whose fingers can make sweet harmony with every touch, whose pencil and whose needle can awake the beautiful creations of art, devoting all these powers to the work of charming back to the sheepfold those wandering and bewildered lambs whom the Good Shepherd still calls his own! Jenny Lind, once, when she sang at a concert for destitute children, exclaimed in her enthusiasm, "Is it not beautiful that I can sing so?"[8] And so may not every woman feel, when her graces and accomplishments draw the wanderer, and charm away evil demons, and soothe the sore and sickened spirit, and make the Christian fold more attractive than the dizzy gardens of false pleasure?

In such associations, and others of kindred nature, how many of the stricken and bereaved women of our country might find at once a home and an object in life! Motherless hearts might be made glad in a better and higher motherhood; and the stock of earthly life that seemed cut off at the root, and dead past recovery, may be grafted upon with a shoot from the tree of life which is in the Paradise of God.

So the beginning of this eventful 1865, which finds us still treading the wine-press of our great conflict, should bring with it a serene and solemn hope, a joy such as those had with whom in the midst of the fiery furnace there walked one like unto the Son of God.

The great affliction that has come upon our country is so evidently the purifying chastening of a Father, rather than the avenging anger of a Destroyer, that all hearts may submit themselves in a solemn and holy calm still to bear the burning that shall make us clean from dross and bring us forth to a higher national life. Never, in the whole course of our history, have such teachings of the pure abstract Right been so commended and forced upon us by Providence. Never have public men been so constrained to humble themselves before God, and to acknowledge that there is a Judge that ruleth in the earth. Verily His inquisition for blood has been strict and awful; and for every stricken household of the poor and lowly, hundreds of households of the oppressor have been scattered. The land where the family of the slave was first annihilated, and the negro, with all the loves and hopes of a man, was proclaimed to be a beast to be bred and sold in market with the horse and the swine, — that land, with its fair name, Virginia, has been made a desolation so signal, so wonderful, that the blindest passer-by cannot but ask for what sin so awful a doom has been meted out. The prophetic visions of Nat Turner, who saw the leaves drop blood and the land darkened, have been fulfilled.[9] The work of justice which he predicted is being executed to the uttermost.

But when this strange work of judgment and justice is consummated, when our country, through a thousand battles and ten thousands of precious deaths, shall have come forth from this long agony, redeemed and regenerated, then God Himself shall return and dwell with us, and the Lord God shall wipe away all tears from all faces, and the rebuke of His people shall He utterly take away.

Walt Whitman, from *Drum-Taps* (1865)

"Come up from the Fields, Father"

Come up from the fields, father, here's a letter from our Pete;
And come to the front door, mother—here's a letter from thy dear son.

Lo, 'tis autumn;
Lo, where the trees, deeper green, yellower and redder,
Cool and sweeten Ohio's villages, with leaves fluttering in the moderate wind;
Where apples ripe in the orchards hang, and grapes on the trellis'd vines;
(Smell you the smell of the grapes on the vines?
Smell you the buckwheat, where the bees were lately buzzing?)

Above all, lo, the sky, so calm, so transparent after the rain, and with
    wondrous clouds;
Below, too, all calm, all vital and beautiful—and the farm prospers well.

Down in the fields all prospers well;
But now from the fields come, father—come at the daughter's call;
And come to the entry, mother—to the front door come, right away.
Fast as she can she hurries—something ominous—her steps trembling;
She does not tarry to smooth her white hair, nor adjust her cap.

Open the envelope quickly;
O this is not our son's writing, yet his name is sign'd;
O a strange hand writes for our dear son—O stricken mother's soul!
All swims before her eyes—flashes with black—she catches the main words only;
Sentences broken—*gun-shot wound in the breast, cavalry skirmish, taken
    to hospital,*
At present low, but will soon be better.

Ah, now the single figure to me,
Amid all teeming and wealthy Ohio, with all its cities and farms,

Sickly white in the face and dull in the head, very faint,
By the jamb of a door leans.

Grieve not so, dear mother, (the just-grown daughter speaks
    through her sobs;
The little sisters huddle around, speechless and dismay'd;)
See, dearest mother, the letter says Pete will soon be better.

Alas, poor boy, he will never be better, (nor may-be needs to be better,
    that brave and simple soul;)
While they stand at home at the door, he is dead already;
The only son is dead.

But the mother needs to be better;
She with thin form, presently drest in black;
By day her meals untouch'd—then at night fitfully sleeping,
    often waking,
In the midnight waking, weeping, longing with one deep
    longing,
O that she might withdraw unnoticed—silent from life, escape
    and withdraw,
To follow, to seek, to be with her dear dead son.

Julia Ward Howe, "Our Orders" (1865)

Weave no more silks, ye Lyons looms,[10]
    To deck our girls for gay delights!
The crimson flower of battle blooms,
    And solemn marches fill the nights.

Weave but the flag whose bars to-day
    Drooped heavy o'er our early dead,
And homely garments, coarse and gray,
    For orphans that must earn their bread!

Keep back your tunes, ye viols sweet,
    That poured delight from other lands!
Rouse there the dancer's restless feet:
    The trumpet leads our warrior bands.

And ye that wage the war of words
    With mystic fame and subtle power,
Go, chatter to the idle birds,
    Or teach the lesson of the hour!

Ye Sibyl Arts, in one stern knot
    Be all your offices combined!
Stand close, while Courage draws the lot,
    The destiny of human kind.

And if that destiny could fail,
    The sun should darken in the sky,
The eternal bloom of Nature pale,
    And God, and Truth, and Freedom die!

Sarah Morgan Bryan Piatt, "Giving Back the Flower" (1867)

So, because you chose to follow me into the subtle sadness of night,
    And to stand in the half-set moon with the weird fall-light on your
        glimmering hair,
Till your presence hid all of the earth and all of the sky from my sight,
    And to give me a little scarlet bud, that was dying of frost, to wear,

Say, must you taunt me forever, forever? You looked at my hand and
    you knew That I was the slave of the Ring, while you were as free as the wind is
        free.
When I saw your corpse in the coffin, I flung back your flower to you;
    It was all of yours that I ever had; you may keep it, and—keep from me.

Ah? so God is your witness. Has God, then, no world to look after but ours?
    May He not have been searching for that wild star, with the trailing plumage,
        that flew
Far over a part of our darkness while we were there by the freezing flowers,
    Or else brightening some planet's luminous rings, instead of thinking of you?

Or, if He was near us at all, do you think that He would sit listening there
    Because you sang "Hear me, Norma,"[11] to a woman in jewels and lace,
While, so close to us, down in another street, in the wet, unlighted air,
    There were children crying for bread and fire, and mothers who questioned
        His grace?

Or perhaps He had gone to the ghastly field where the fight had been that day,
    To number the bloody stabs that were there, to look at and judge the dead;
Or else to the place full of fever and moans where the wretched wounded lay;
    At least I do not believe that He cares to remember a word that you said.

So take back your flower, I tell you—of its sweetness I now have no need;
    Yes; take back your flower down into the stillness and mystery to keep;
When you wake I will take it, and God, then, perhaps will witness indeed,
    But go, now, and tell Death he must watch you, and not let you walk in
        your sleep.

Lucy Larcom, "Weaving" (1869)

All day she stands before her loom;
    The flying shuttles come and go:
By grassy fields, and trees in bloom,

She sees the winding river flow:
And fancy's shuttle flieth wide,
And faster than the waters glide.

Is she entangled in her dreams,
    Like that fair weaver of Shalott,
Who left her mystic mirror's gleams,
    To gaze on Sir Lancelot?[12]
Her heart, a mirror sadly true,
Brings gloomier visions into view.

"I weave, and weave, the livelong day:
    The woof is strong, the warp is good:
I weave, to be my mother's stay;
    I weave, to win my daily food:
But ever as I weave," saith she,
"The world of women haunteth me.

"The river glides along, one thread
    In nature's mesh, so beautiful!
The stars are woven in; the red
    Of sunrise; and the rain-cloud dull.
Each seems a separate wonder wrought;
Each blends with some more wondrous thought.

"So, at the loom of life, we weave
    Our separate shreds, that varying fall,
Some stained, some fair; and passing, leave
    To God the gathering up of all,
In that full pattern, wherein man
Works blindly out the eternal plan.

"In his vast work, for good or ill,
    The undone and the done he blends:
With whatsoever woof we fill,
    To our weak hands His might He lends,
And gives the threads beneath His eye
The texture of eternity.

"Wind on, by willow and by pine,
    Thou blue, untroubled Merrimack!
Afar, by sunnier streams than thine,
    My sisters toil, with foreheads black;
And water with their blood this root,
Whereof we gather bounteous fruit.

"I think of women sad and poor;
    Women who walk in garments soiled:
Their shame, their sorrow, I endure;

By their defect my hope is foiled:
The blot they bear is on my name;
Who sins, and I am not to blame?

"And how much of your wrong is mine,
    Dark women slaving at the South?
Of your stolen grapes I quaff the wine;
    The bread you starve for fills my mouth:
The beam unwinds, but every thread
With blood of strangled souls is red.

"If this be so, we win and wear
    A Nessus-robe of poisoned cloth;
Or weave them shrouds they may not wear, —
    Fathers and brothers falling both
On ghastly, death-sown fields, that lie
Beneath the tearless Southern sky.

"Alas! the weft has lost its white.
    It grows a hideous tapestry,
That pictures war's abhorrent sight:
    Unroll not, web of destiny!
Be the dark volume left unread,
The tale untold, the curse unsaid!"

So up and down before her loom
    She paces on, and to and fro,
Till sunset fills the dusty room,
    And makes the water redly glow,
As if the Merrimack's calm flood
Were changed into a stream of blood.

Too soon fulfilled, and all too true
    The words she murmured as she wrought:
But, weary weaver, not to you
    Alone was war's stern message brought:
"Woman!" it knelled from heart to heart,
"Thy sister's keeper know thou art!"

Lucy Larcom, "A Loyal Woman's No" (1890)

No! is my answer from this cold, bleak ridge,
    Down to your valley: you may rest you there:
The gulf is wide, and none can build a bridge
    That your gross weight would safely hither bear.

Pity me, if you will. I look at you
    With something that is kinder far than scorn,

And think, "Ah, well! I might have grovelled, too;
  I might have walked there, fettered and forsworn."

I am of nature weak as others are;
  I might have chosen comfortable ways;
Once from these heights I shrank, beheld afar,
  In the soft lap of quiet, easy days.

I might, — I will not hide it, — once I might
  Have lost, in the warm whirlpools of your voice,
The sense of Evil, the stern cry of Right;
  But Truth has steered me free, and I rejoice.

Not with the triumph that looks back to jeer
  At the poor herd that call their misery bliss;
But as a mortal speaks when God is near,
  I drop you down my answer: it is this:

I am not yours, because you prize in me
  What is the lowest in my own esteem:
Only my flowery levels can you see,
  Nor of my heaven-smit summits do you dream.

I am not yours, because you love yourself:
  Your heart has scarcely room for me beside.
I will not be shut in with name and pelf;
  I spurn the shelter of your narrow pride!

Not yours, — because you are not man enough
  To grasp your country's measure of a man.
If such as you, when Freedom's ways are rough,
  Cannot walk in them, learn that women can!

Not yours, — because, in this the nation's need,
  You stoop to bend her losses to your gain,
And do not feel the meanness of your deed:
  I touch no palm defiled with such a stain!

Whether man's thought can find too lofty steeps
  For woman's scaling, care not I to know;
But when he falters by her side, or creeps,
  She must not clog her soul with him to go.

Who weds me, must at least with equal pace
  Sometimes move with me at my being's height:
To follow him to his superior place,
  His rare atmosphere, were keen delight.

You lure me to the valley: men should call
    Up to the mountains, where the air is clear.
Win me and help me climbing, if at all!
    Beyond these peaks great harmonies I hear: —

The morning chant of Liberty and Law!
    The dawn pours in, to wash out Slavery's blot;
Fairer than aught the bright sun ever saw,
    Rises a Nation without stain or spot!

The men and women mated for that time
    Tread not the soothing mosses of the plain;
Their hands are joined in sacrifice sublime;
    Their feet firm set in upward paths of pain.

Sleep your thick sleep, and go your drowsy way!
    You cannot hear the voices in the air!
Ignoble souls will shrivel in that day;
    The brightness of its coming can you bear?

For me, I do not walk these hills alone:
    Heroes who poured their blood out for the truth,
Women whose hearts bled, martyrs all unknown,
    Here catch the sunrise of an immortal youth

On their pale cheeks and consecrated brows: —
    It charms me not, your call to rest below. I press their hands, my lips
      pronounce their vows:
    Take my life's silence for your answer: No!

Edward Bellamy, "An Echo of Antietam" (1889)

The air was tremulous with farewells. The regiment, recruited within sight of the steeples of Waterville, and for three months in camp just outside the city, was to march the next morning. A series of great battles had weakened the Federal armies, and the authorities at Washington had ordered all available men to the front.[13]

The camp was to be broken up at an early hour, after which the regiment would march through the city to the depot to take the cars. The streets along the route of the march were already being decorated with flags and garlands. The city that afternoon was full of soldiers enjoying their last leave of absence. The liquor shops were crowded with parties of them drinking with their friends, while others in threes and fours, with locked arms, paraded the streets singing patriotic songs, sometimes in rather maudlin voices, for to-day in every saloon a soldier might enter, citizens vied for the privilege of treating him to the best in the house. No man in a blue coat was suffered to pay for anything.

For the most part, however, the men were sober enough over their leave-taking. One saw everywhere soldiers and civilians, strolling in pairs, absorbed in earnest talk. They are brothers, maybe, who have come away from the house to be alone with each other, while they talk of family affairs and exchange last charges and promises as to what is to be done if anything happens. Or perhaps they are business partners, and the one who has put the country's business before his own is giving his last counsels as to how the store or the shop shall be managed in his absence. Many of the blue-clad men have women with them, and these are the couples that the people oftenest turn to look at. The girl who has a soldier lover is the envy of her companions to-day as she walks by his side. Her proud eyes challenge all who come, saying, "See, this is my hero. I am the one he loves."

You could easily tell when it was a wife and not a sweetheart whom the soldier had with him. There was no challenge in the eyes of the wife. Young romance shed none of its glamour on the sacrifice she was making for her native land. It was only because they could not bear to sit any longer looking at each other in the house that she and her husband had come out to walk.

In the residence parts of the town family groups were gathered on shady piazzas, a blue-coated figure the centre of each. They were trying to talk cheerfully, making an effort even to laugh a little.

Now and then one of the women stole unobserved from the circle, but her bravely smiling face as she presently returned gave no inkling of the flood of tears that had eased her heart in some place apart. The young soldier himself was looking a little pale and nervous with all his affected good spirits, and it was safe to guess that he was even then thinking how often this scene would come before him afterwards, by the camp-fire and on the eve of battle.

In the village of Upton, some four or five miles out of Waterville, on a broad piazza at the side of a house on the main street, a group of four persons were seated around a tea-table.

The centre of interest of this group, as of so many others that day, was a soldier. He looked not over twenty-five, with dark blue eyes, dark hair cut close to his head, and a mustache trimmed crisply in military fashion. His uniform set off to advantage an athletic figure of youthful slenderness, and his bronzed complexion told of long days of practice on the drill-ground in the school of the company and the battalion. He wore the shoulder-straps of a second lieutenant.

On one side of the soldier sat the Rev. Mr. Morton, his cousin, and on the other Miss Bertha Morton, a kindly faced, middle-aged lady, who was her brother's house-keeper and the hostess of this occasion.

The fourth member of the party was a girl of nineteen or twenty. She was a very pretty girl, and although to-day her pallid cheeks and red and swollen eyelids would to other eyes have detracted somewhat from her charms, it was certain that they did not make her seem less adorable to the young officer, for he was her lover, and was to march with the regiment in the morning.

Lieutenant Philip King was a lawyer, and by perseverance and native ability had worked up a fair practice for so young a man in and around Upton. When he volunteered, he had to make up his mind to leave this carefully gathered clientage to scatter, or to be filched from him by less patriotic rivals; but it may be well believed that this seemed to him a little thing compared with leaving Grace Roberts, with the chance of never returning to make her his wife. If, indeed, it had been for him to say, he would have placed his happiness beyond hazard by marrying her before the regiment marched; nor would she have been averse, but her mother, an invalid widow, took a sensible rather than a sentimental view of the case. If he were killed, she said, a wife would do him no good; and if he came home again, Grace would be waiting for him, and that ought to satisfy a reasonable man. It had to satisfy an unreasonable one. The Robertses had always lived just beyond the garden from the parsonage, and Grace, who from a little girl had been a great pet of the childless minister and his sister, was almost as much at home there as in her mother's house. When Philip fell in love with her, the Mortons were delighted. They could have wished nothing better for either. From the first Miss Morton had done all she could to make matters smooth for the lovers, and the present little farewell banquet was but the last of many meetings she had prepared for them at the parsonage.

Philip had come out from camp on a three-hours' leave that afternoon, and would have to report again at half-past seven. It was nearly that hour now, though still light, the season being midsummer. There had been an effort on the part of all to keep up a cheerful tone; but as the time of the inevitable separation drew near, the conversation had been more and more left to the minister and his sister, who, with observations sometimes a little forced, continued to fend off silence and the demoralization it would be likely to bring to their young friends. Grace had been the first to drop out of the talking, and Philip's answers, when he was addressed, grew more and more at random, as the meetings of his eyes with his sweetheart's became more frequent and lasted longer.

"He will be the handsomest officer in the regiment, that's one comfort. Won't he, Grace?" said Miss Morton cheerily.

The girl nodded and smiled faintly. Her eyes were brimming, and the twitching of her lips from time to time betrayed how great was the effort with which she kept her self-command.

"Yes," said Mr. Morton; "but though he looks very well now, it is nothing to the imposing appearance he will present when he comes back with a colonel's shoulder-straps. You should be thinking of that, Grace."

"I expect we shall hear from him every day," said Miss Morton. "He will have no excuse for not writing with all those envelopes stamped and addressed, with blank paper in them, which Grace has given him. You should always have three or four in your coat pocket, Phil."

The young man nodded.

"I suppose for the most part we shall learn of you through Grace; but you mustn't forget us entirely, my boy," said Mr. Morton. "We shall want to hear from you directly now and then."

"Yes; I'll be sure to write," Philip replied.

"I suppose it will be time enough to see the regiment pass if we are in our places by nine o'clock," suggested Miss Morton, after a silence.

"I think so," said her brother. "It is a great affair to break camp, and I don't believe the march will begin till after that time."

"James has got us one of the windows of Ray & Seymour's offices, you know, Philip," resumed Miss Morton; "which one did you say, James?"

"The north one."

"Yes, the north one," she resumed. "They say every window on Main Street along the route of the regiment is rented. Grace will be with us, you know. You mustn't forget to look up at us as you go by" — as if the young man were likely to!

He was evidently not now listening to her at all. His eyes were fastened upon the girl's opposite him, and they seemed to have quite forgotten the others. Miss Morton and her brother exchanged compassionate glances. Tears were in the lady's eyes. A clock in the sitting-room began to strike:

"One, two, three, four, five, six, seven."

Philip started.

"What time is that?" he asked, a little huskily. No one replied at once. Then Mr. Morton said:

"I am afraid it struck seven, my boy."

"I must leave in ten minutes then," said the young man, rising from the table. The rest followed his example.

"I wonder if the buggy will be in time?" said he.

"It is at the gate," replied Miss Morton. "I heard it drive up some time ago."

Unmindful of the others now, Philip put his arm about Grace's waist and drew her away to the end of the piazza and thence out into the garden.

"Poor young things," murmured Miss Morton, the tears running down her cheeks as she looked after them. "It is pitiful, James, to see how they suffer."

"Yes," said the minister; "and there are a great many just such scenes to-day. Ah, well, as St. Paul says, we see as yet but in part."[14]

Passing in and out among the shrubbery, and presently disappearing from the sympathetic eyes upon the piazza, the lovers came to a little summer-house, and there they entered. Taking her wrists in his hands, he held her away from him, and his eyes went slowly over her from head to foot, as if he would impress upon his mind an image that absence should not have power to dim.

"You are so beautiful," he said, "that in this moment, when I ought to have all my courage, you make me feel that I am a madman to leave you for the sake of any cause on earth. The future to most men is but a chance of happiness, and when they risk it they only risk a chance. In staking their lives, they only stake a lottery ticket, which would probably draw a blank. But my ticket has drawn a capital prize. I risk not the chance, but the certainty, of happiness. I believe I am a fool, and if I am killed, that will be the first thing they will say to me on the other side."

"Don't talk of that, Phil. Oh, don't talk of being killed!"

"No, no; of course not!" he exclaimed. "Don't fret about that; I shall not be killed. I've no notion of being killed. But what a fool I am to waste these last moments staring at you when I might be kissing you, my love, my love!" And clasping her in his arms, he covered her face with kisses.

She began to sob convulsively.

"Don't, darling; don't! Don't make it so hard for me," he whispered hoarsely.

"Oh, do let me cry," she wailed. "It was so hard for me to hold back all the time we were at table. I must cry, or my heart will break. Oh, my own dear Phil, what if I should never see you again! Oh! Oh!"

"Nonsense, darling," he said, crowding down the lump that seemed like iron in his throat, and making a desperate effort to keep his voice steady. "You will see me again, never doubt it. Don't I tell you I am coming back? The South cannot hold out much longer. Everybody says so. I shall be home in a year, and then you will be my wife, to be God's Grace to me all the rest of my life. Our happiness will be on interest till then; ten per cent. a month at least, compound interest, piling up every day. Just think of that, dear; don't let yourself think of anything else."

"Oh, Phil, how I love you!" she cried, throwing her arms around his neck in a passion of tenderness. "Nobody is like you. Nobody ever was. Surely God will not part us. Surely He will not. He is too good."

"No, dear, He will not. Some day I shall come back. It will not be long. Perhaps I shall find you waiting for me in this same little summer-house. Let us think of that. It was here, you know, we found out each other's secret that day."

"I had found out yours long before," she said, faintly smiling.

"Time's up, Phil." It was Mr. Morton's voice calling to them from the piazza.

"I must go, darling. Good-by."

"Oh, no, not yet; not quite yet," she wailed, clinging to him. "Why, we have been here but a few moments. It can't be ten minutes yet."

Under the influence of that close, passionate embrace, those clinging kisses and mingling tears, there began to come over Philip a feeling of weakness, of fainting courage, a disposition to cry out, "Nothing can be so terrible as this. I will not bear it; I will not go." By a tyrannical effort of will, against which his whole nature cried out, he unwound her arms from his neck and said in a choked voice: —

"Darling, this is harder than any battle I shall have to fight, but this is what I enlisted for. I must go."

He had reached the door of the summer-house, not daring for honor's sake to look back, when a heartbroken cry smote his ear.

"You haven't kissed me good-by!"

He had kissed her a hundred times, but these kisses she apparently distinguished from the good-by kiss. He came back, and taking her again in his embrace, kissed her lips, her throat, her bosom, and then once more their lips met, and in that kiss of parting which plucks the heart up by the roots.

How strong must be the barrier between one soul and another that they do not utterly merge in moments like that, turning the agony of parting to the bliss of blended being!

Pursued by the sound of her desolate sobbing, he fled away.

The stable-boy held the dancing horse at the gate, and Mr. Morton and his sister stood waiting there.

"Good-by, Phil, till we see you again," said Miss Morton, kissing him tenderly. "We'll take good care of her for you."

"Will you please go to her now?" he said huskily. "She is in the summer-house. For God's sake try to comfort her."

"Yes, poor boy, I will," she answered. He shook hands with Mr. Morton and jumped into the buggy.

"I 'll get a furlough and be back in a few months, maybe. Be sure to tell her that," he said.

The stable-boy stood aside; the mettlesome horse gave a plunge and started off at a three-minute gait. The boy drew out his watch and observed: "He hain't got but fifteen minutes to git to camp in, but he'll do it. The mare's a stepper, and Phil King knows how to handle the ribbons."

The buggy vanished in a cloud of dust around the next turn in the road. The stable-boy strode whistling down the street, the minister went to his study, and Miss Morton disappeared in the shrubbery in the direction of the summer-house.

II

Early next morning the country roads leading into Waterville were covered with carts and wagons and carriages loaded with people coming into town to see the regiment off. The streets were hung with flags and spanned with decorated arches bearing patriotic inscriptions. Red, white, and blue streamers hung in festoons from building to building and floated from cornices. The stores and places of business were all closed, the sidewalks were packed with people in their Sunday clothes, and the windows and balconies were lined with gazers long before it was time for the regiment to appear. Everybody — men, women, and children — wore the national colors in cockades or rosettes, while many young girls were dressed throughout in red, white, and blue. The city seemed tricked out for some rare gala-day, but the grave faces of the expectant throng, and the subdued and earnest manner which extended even to the older children, stamped this as no ordinary holiday.

After hours of patient waiting, at last the word passes from mouth to mouth, "They are coming!" Vehicles are quickly driven out of the way, and in a general hush all eyes are turned towards the head of the street. Presently there is a burst of martial music, and the regiment comes wheeling round the corner into view and fills the wide street from curb to curb with its broad front. As the blue river sweeps along, the rows of polished bayonets, rising and falling with the swinging tread of the men, are like interminable ranks of foam-crested waves rolling in upon the shore. The imposing mass, with its rhythmic movement, gives the impression of a single organism. One forgets to look for the individuals in it, forgets that there are individuals. Even those who have brothers, sons, lovers there, for a moment almost forget them in the impression of a mighty whole. The mind is slow to realize that this great dragon, so terrible in its beauty, emitting light as it moves from a thousand burnished scales, with flaming crest proudly waving in the van, is but an aggregation of men singly so feeble.

The hearts of the lookers-on as they gaze are swelling fast. An afflatus of heroism given forth by this host of self-devoted men communicates itself to the most stolid spectators. The booming of the drum fills the brain, and the blood in the veins leaps to its rhythm. The unearthly gayety of the fife, like the sweet, shrill song of a bird soaring above the battle, infects the nerves till the idea of death brings a scornful smile to the lips. Eyes glaze with rapturous tears as they rest upon the flag. There is a thrill of voluptuous sweetness in the thought of dying for it. Life seems of value only as it gives the poorest something to sacrifice. It is dying that makes the glory of the world, and all other employments seem but idle while the regiment passes.

The time for farewells is gone by. The lucky men at the ends of the ranks have indeed an opportunity without breaking step to exchange an occasional hand-shake with a friend on the sidewalk, or to snatch a kiss from wife or sweetheart, but those in the middle of the line can only look their farewells. Now and then a mother intrusts her baby to a file-leader to be passed along from hand to hand till it reaches the father, to be sent back with a kiss, or, maybe, perched aloft on his shoulder, to ride to the depot, crowing at the music and clutching at the gleaming bayonets. At every such touch of nature the people cheer wildly. From every window and balcony the ladies shower garlands upon the troops.

Where is Grace? for this is the Upton company which is passing now. Yonder she stands on a balcony, between Mr. Morton and his sister. She is very pale and the tears are streaming down her cheeks, but her face is radiant. She is smiling through her tears, as if there was no such thing on earth as fear or sorrow. She has looked forward to this ordeal with harrowing expectations, only to find herself at the trying moment seized upon and lifted above all sense of personal affliction by the passion of self-devotion with which the air is electric. Her face as she looks down upon her lover is that of a priestess in the ecstasy of sacrifice. He is saluting with his sword. Now he has passed. With a great sob she turns away. She does not care for the rest of the pageant. Her patriotism has suddenly gone. The ecstasy of sacrifice is over. She is no longer a priestess, but a broken-hearted girl, who only asks to be led away to some place where she can weep till her lover returns.

III

There was to be a great battle the next day. The two armies had been long manoeuvring for position, and now they stood like wrestlers who have selected their holds and, with body braced against body, knee against knee, wait for the signal to begin the struggle. There had been during the afternoon some brisk fighting, but a common desire to post-pone the decisive contest till the morrow had prevented the main forces from becoming involved. Philip's regiment had thus far only been engaged in a few trifling skirmishes, barely enough to stir the blood. This was to be its first battle, and the position to which it had been allotted promised a bloody baptism in the morning. The men were in excellent heart, but as night settled down, there was little or no merriment to be heard about the camp-fires. Most were gathered in groups, discussing in low tones the chances of the morrow. Some, knowing that every fibre of muscle would be needed for the work before them, had wisely gone to sleep, while here and there a man, heedless of the talk going on about him, was lying on his back staring up at the darkening sky, thinking.

As the twilight deepened, Philip strolled to the top of a little knoll just out of the camp and sat down, with a vague notion of casting up accounts a little in view of the final settlement which very possibly might come for him next day. But the inspiration of the scene around him soon diverted his mind from personal engrossments. Some distance down the lines he could see the occasional flash of a gun, where a battery was lazily shelling a piece of woods which it was desirable to keep the enemy from occupying during the night. A burning barn in that direction made a flare on the sky. Over behind the wooded hills where the Confederates lay, rockets were going up, indicating the exchange of signals and the perfecting of plans which might mean defeat and ruin to him and his the next day. Behind him, within the Federal lines, clouds of dust, dimly outlined against the glimmering landscape, betrayed the location of the roads along which artil-lery, cavalry, infantry were hurrying eagerly forward to take their assigned places for the morrow's work.

Who said that men fear death? Who concocted that fable for old wives? He should have stood that night with Philip in the midst of a host of one hundred and twenty-five thousand men in the full flush and vigor of life, calmly and deliberately making ready at dawn to receive death in its most horrid forms at one another's hands. It is in vain that Religion invests the tomb with terror, and Philosophy, shuddering, averts her face; the nations turn from these gloomy teachers to storm its portals in exultant hosts, battering them wide enough for thousands to charge through abreast. The heroic instinct of humanity with its high contempt of death is wiser and truer, never let us doubt, than superstitious terrors or philosophic doubts. It testifies to a conviction, deeper than reason, that man is greater than his seeming self; to an underlying consciousness that his mortal life is but an accident of his real existence, the fashion of a day, to be lightly worn and gayly doffed at duty's call.

What a pity it truly is that the tonic air of battlefields — the air that Philip breathed that night before Antietam — cannot be gathered up and preserved as a precious elixir to reinvigorate the atmosphere in times of peace, when men grow faint of heart and cowardly, and quake at thought of death.

The soldiers huddled in their blankets on the ground slept far more soundly that night before the battle than their men-folk and women-folk in their warm beds at home. For them it was a night of watching, a vigil of prayers and tears. The telegraph in those days made of the nation an intensely sensitive organism, with nerves a thousand miles long. Ere its echoes had died away, every shot fired at the front had sent a tremor to the anxious hearts at home. The newspapers and bulletin boards in all the towns and cities of the North had announced that a great battle would surely take place the next day, and, as the night closed in, a mighty cloud of prayer rose from innumerable firesides, the self-same prayer from each, that he who had gone from that home might survive the battle, whoever else must fall.

The wife, lest her own appeal might fail, taught her cooing baby to lisp the father's name, thinking that surely the Great Father's heart would not be able to resist a baby's prayer. The widowed mother prayed that if it were consistent with God's will he would spare her son. She laid her heart, pierced through with many sorrows, before Him. She had borne so much, life had been so hard, her boy was all she had to show for so much endured, — might not this cup pass? Pale, impassioned maids, kneeling by their virgin beds, wore out the night with an importunity that would not be put off. Sure in their great love and their little knowledge that no case could be like theirs, they beseeched God with bitter weeping for their lovers' lives, because, forsooth, they could not bear it if hurt came to them. The answers to many thousands of these agonizing appeals of maid and wife and mother were already in the enemy's cartridge-boxes.

IV

The day came. The dispatches in the morning papers stated that the armies would probably be engaged from an early hour.

Who that does not remember those battle-summers can realize from any telling how the fathers and mothers, the wives and sisters and sweethearts at home, lived through the days when it was known that a great battle was going on at the front in which their loved ones were engaged? It was very quiet in the house on those days of battle. All spoke in hushed voices and stepped lightly. The children, too small to understand the meaning of the shadow on the home, felt it and took their noisy sports elsewhere. There was little conversation, except as to when definite news might be expected. The household work dragged sadly, for though the women sought refuge from thought in occupation, they were constantly dropping whatever they had in hand to rush away to their chambers to face the presentiment, perhaps suddenly borne in upon them with the force of a conviction, that they might be called on to bear the worst. The table was set for the regular meals, but there was little pretense of eating. The eyes of all had a far-off expression, and they seemed barely to see one another. There was an intent, listening look upon their faces, as if they were hearkening to the roar of the battle a thousand miles away.

Many pictures of battles have been painted, but no true one yet, for the pictures contain only men. The women are unaccountably left out. We ought to see not alone the opposing lines of battle writhing and twisting in a death embrace, the batteries smoking and flaming, the hurricanes of cavalry, but innumerable women also, spectral forms of mothers, wives, sweethearts, clinging about the necks of the advancing soldiers, vainly trying to shield them with their bosoms, extending supplicating hands to the foe, raising eyes of anguish to Heaven. The soldiers, grim-faced, with battle-lighted eyes, do not see the ghostly forms that throng them, but shoot and cut and stab across and through them as if they were not there, — yes, through them, for few are the balls and bayonets that reach their marks without traversing some of these devoted breasts. Spectral, alas, is their guardianship, but real are their wounds and deadly as any the combatants receive.

Soon after breakfast on the day of the battle Grace came across to the parsonage, her swollen eyes and pallid face telling of a sleepless night. She could not bear her mother's company that day, for she knew that she had never greatly liked Philip. Miss Morton was very tender and sympathetic. Grace was a little comforted by Mr. Morton's saying that commonly great battles did not open much before noon. It was a respite to be able to think that probably up to that moment at least no harm had come to Philip. In the early afternoon the minister drove into Waterville to get the earliest bulletins at the "Banner" office, leaving the two women alone.

The latter part of the afternoon a neighbor who had been in Waterville drove by the house, and Miss Morton called to him to know if there were any news yet. He drew a piece of paper from his pocket, on which he had scribbled the latest bulletin before the "Banner" office, and read as follows: "The battle opened with a vigorous attack by our right. The enemy was forced back, stubbornly contesting every inch of ground. General ————'s division is now bearing the brunt of the fight and is suffering heavily. The result is yet uncertain."

The division mentioned was the one in which Philip's regiment was included. "Is suffering heavily," — those were the words. There was something fearful in the way the present tense brought home to Grace a sense of the battle as then actually in progress. It meant that while she sat there on the shady piazza with the drowsy hum of the bees in her ears, looking out on the quiet lawn where the house cat, stretched on the grass, kept a sleepy eye on the birds as they flitted in the branches of the apple-trees, Philip might be facing a storm of lead and iron, or, maybe, blent in some desperate hand-to-hand struggle, was defending his life — her life — against murderous cut and thrust.

To begin to pray for his safety was not to dare to cease, for to cease would be to withdraw a sort of protection — all, alas! she could give — and abandon him to his enemies. If she had been watching over him from above the battle, an actual witness of the carnage going on that afternoon on the far-off field, she could scarcely have endured a more harrowing suspense from moment to moment. Overcome with the agony, she threw herself on the sofa in the sitting-room and lay quivering, with her face buried in the pillow, while Miss Morton sat beside her, stroking her hair and saying such feeble, soothing words as she might.

It is always hard, and for ardent temperaments almost impossible, to hold the mind balanced in a state of suspense, yielding overmuch neither to hope nor to fear, under circumstances like these. As a relief to the torture which such a state of tension ends in causing, the mind at length, if it cannot abandon itself to hope, embraces even despair. About five o'clock Miss Morton was startled by an exceeding bitter cry. Grace was sitting upon the sofa. "Oh, Miss Morton!" she cried, bursting into tears which before she had not been able to shed, "he is dead!"

"Grace! Grace! what do you mean?"

"He is dead, I know he is dead!" wailed the girl; and then she explained that while from moment to moment she had sent up prayers for him, every breath a cry to God, she suddenly had been unable to pray more, and this she felt was a sign that petition for his life was now vain. Miss Morton strove to convince her that this was but an effect of overwrought nerves, but with slight success.

In the early evening Mr. Morton returned with the latest news the telegraph had brought. The full scope of the result was not yet known. The advantage had probably remained with the National forces, although the struggle had been one of those close and stubborn ones, with scanty laurels for the victors, to be expected when men of one race meet in battle. The losses on both sides had been enormous, and the report was confirmed that Philip's division had been badly cut up.

The parsonage was but one of thousands of homes in the land where no lamps were lighted that evening, the members of the household sitting together in the dark, — silent, or talking in low tones of the far-away star-lighted battlefield, the anguish of the wounded, the still heaps of the dead.

Nevertheless, when at last Grace went home she was less entirely despairing than in the afternoon. Mr. Morton, in his calm, convincing way, had shown her the groundlessness of her impression that Philip was certainly dead, and had enabled her again to entertain hope. It no longer rose, indeed, to the height of a belief that he had escaped wholly scathless. In face of the terrible tidings, that would have been too presumptuous. But perhaps he had been only wounded. Yesterday the thought would have been insupportable, but now she was eager to make this compromise with Providence. She was distinctly affected by the curious superstition that if we voluntarily concede something to fate, while yet the facts are not known, we gain a sort of equitable assurance against a worse thing. It was settled, she told herself, that she was not to be overcome or even surprised to hear that Philip was wounded, — slightly wounded. She was no better than other women, that he should be wholly spared.

The paper next morning gave many names of officers who had fallen, but Philip's was not among them. The list was confessedly incomplete; nevertheless, the absence of his name was reassuring. Grace went across the garden after breakfast to talk with Miss Morton about the news and the auspicious lack of news. Her friend's cheerful tone infused her with fresh courage. To one who has despaired, a very little hope goes to the head like wine to the brain of a faster, and, though still very tremulous, Grace could even smile a little now and was almost cheerful. Secretly already she was beginning to play false with fate, and, in flat repudiation of her last night's compact, to indulge the hope that her soldier had not been even wounded. But this was only at the bottom of her heart. She did not own to herself that she really did it. She felt a little safer not to break the bargain yet.

About eleven o'clock in the forenoon Mr. Morton came in. His start and look of dismay on seeing Grace indicated that he had expected to find his sister alone. He hastily attempted to conceal an open telegram which he held in his hand, but it was too late. Grace had already seen it, and whatever the tidings it might contain, there was no longer any question of holding them back or extenuating them. Miss Morton, after one look at her brother's face, silently came to the girl's side and put her arms around her waist. "Christ, our Saviour," she murmured, "for thy name's sake, help her now." Then the minister said: —

"Try to be brave, try to bear it worthily of him; for, my poor little girl, your sacrifice has been accepted. He fell in a charge at the head of his men."

V

Philip's body was brought home for burial, and the funeral was a great event in the village. Business of all kinds was suspended, and all the people united in making of the day a solemn patriotic festival. Mr. Morton preached the funeral sermon.

"Oh, talk about the country," sobbed Grace, when he asked her if there was anything in particular she would like him to speak of.

"For pity's sake don't let me feel sorry now that I gave him up for the Union. Don't leave me now to think it would have been better if I had not let him go."

So he preached of the country, as ministers sometimes did preach in those days, making it very plain that in a righteous cause men did well to die for their native land and their women did well to give them up. Expounding the lofty wisdom of self-sacrifice, he showed how truly it was said that "whosoever will save his life shall lose it: and whosoever will lose his life . . . shall find it,"[15] and how none make such rich profit out of their lives as the heroes who seem to throw them away.

They had come, he told the assembled people, to mourn no misadventure, no misfortune; this dead soldier was not pitiable. He was no victim of a tear-compelling fate. No broken shaft typified his career. He was rather one who had done well for himself, a wise young merchant of his blood, who having seen a way to barter his life at incredible advantage, at no less a rate indeed than a man's for a nation's, had not let slip so great an opportunity.

So he went on, still likening the life of a man to the wares of a shopkeeper, worth to him only what they can be sold for and a loss if overkept, till those who listened began to grow ill at ease in presence of that flag-draped coffin, and were vaguely troubled because they still lived.

Then he spoke of those who had been bereaved. This soldier, he said, like his comrades, had staked for his country not only his own life but the earthly happiness of others also, having been fully empowered by them to do so. Some had staked with their own lives the happiness of parents, some that of wives and children, others maybe the hopes of maidens pledged to them. In offering up their lives to their country they had laid with them upon the altar these other lives which were bound up with theirs, and the same fire of sacrifice had consumed them both. A few days before, in the storm of battle, those who had gone forth had fulfilled their share of the joint sacrifice. In a thousand homes, with tears and the anguish of breaking hearts, those who had sent them forth were that day fulfilling theirs. Let them now in their extremity seek support in the same spirit of patriotic devotion which had upheld their heroes in the hour of death. As they had been lifted above fear by the thought that it was for their country they were dying, not less should those who mourned them find inspiration in remembering it was for the nation's sake that their tears were shed, and for the country that their hearts were broken. It had been appointed that half in blood of men and half in women's tears the ransom of the people should be paid, so that their sorrow was not in vain, but for the healing of the nation.

It behooved these, therefore, to prove worthy of their high calling of martyrdom, and while they must needs weep, not to weep as other women wept, with hearts bowed down, but rather with uplifted faces, adopting and ratifying, though it might be with breaking hearts, this exchange they had made of earthly happiness for the life of their native land. So should they honor those they mourned, and be joined with them not only in sacrifice but in the spirit of sacrifice.

So it was in response to the appeal of this stricken girl before him that the minister talked of the country, and to such purpose was it that the piteous thing she had dreaded, the feeling, now when it was forever too late, that it would have been better if she had kept her lover back, found no place in her heart. There was, indeed, had she known it, no danger at all that she would be left to endure that, so long as she dreaded it, for the only prayer that never is unanswered is the prayer to be lifted above self. So to pray and so to wish is but to cease to resist the divine gravitations ever pulling at the soul. As the minister discoursed of the mystic gain of self-sacrifice, the mystery of which he spoke was fulfilled in her heart. She appeared to stand in some place overarching life and death, and there was made partaker of an exultation whereof if religion and philosophy might but catch and hold the secret, their ancient quest were over.

Gazing through streaming eyes upon the coffin of her lover, she was able freely to consent to the sacrifice of her own life which he had made in giving up his own.

Hamlin Garland, "The Return of a Private" (1891)

The nearer the train drew toward La Crosse, the soberer the little group of "vets" became. On the long way from New Orleans they had beguiled tedium with jokes and friendly chaff; or with planning with elaborate detail what they were going to do now, after the war. A long journey, slowly, irregularly, yet persistently pushing northward. When they entered on Wisconsin territory they gave a cheer, and another when they reached Madison, but after that they sank into a dumb expectancy. Comrades dropped off at one or two points beyond, until there were only four or five left who were bound for La Crosse County.

Three of them were gaunt and brown, the fourth was gaunt and pale, with signs of fever and ague upon him. One had a great scar down his temple, one limped, and they all had unnaturally large, bright eyes, showing emaciation. There were no bands greeting them at the station, no banks of gayly dressed ladies waving handkerchiefs and shouting "Bravo!" as they came in on the caboose of a freight train into the towns that had cheered and blared at them on their way to war. As they looked out or stepped upon the platform for a moment, while the train stood at the station, the loafers looked at them indifferently. Their blue coats, dusty and grimy, were too familiar now to excite notice, much less a friendly word. They were the last of the army to return, and the loafers were surfeited with such sights.

The train jogged forward so slowly that it seemed likely to be midnight before they should reach La Crosse. The little squad grumbled and swore, but it was no use; the train would not hurry, and, as a matter of fact, it was nearly two o'clock when the engine whistled "down brakes."

All of the group were farmers, living in districts several miles out of the town, and all were poor.

"Now, boys," said Private Smith, he of the fever and ague, "we are landed in La Crosse in the night. We've got to stay somewhere till mornin'. Now I ain't got no two dollars to waste on a hotel. I've got a wife and children, so I'm goin' to roost on a bench and take the cost of a bed out of my hide."

"Same here," put in one of the other men. "Hide'll grow on again, dollars'll come hard. It's goin' to be mighty hot skirmishin' to find a dollar these days."

"Don't think they'll be a deputation of citizens waitin' to 'scort us to a hotel, eh?" said another. His sarcasm was too obvious to require an answer.

Smith went on, "Then at daybreak we'll start for home — at least, I will."

"Well, I'll be dummed if I'll take two dollars out o' *my* hide," one of the younger men said. "I'm goin' to a hotel, ef I don't never lay up a cent."

"That'll do f'r you," said Smith; "but if you had a wife an' three young uns dependin' on yeh—"

"Which I ain't, thank the Lord! and don't intend havin' while the court knows itself."

The station was deserted, chill, and dark, as they came into it at exactly a quarter to two in the morning. Lit by the oil lamps that flared a dull red light over the dingy benches, the waiting room was not an inviting place. The younger man went off to look up a hotel, while the rest remained and prepared to camp down on the floor and benches. Smith was attended to tenderly by the other men, who spread their blankets on the bench for him, and, by robbing themselves, made quite a comfortable bed, though the narrowness of the bench made his sleeping precarious.

It was chill, though August, and the two men, sitting with bowed heads, grew stiff with cold and weariness, and were forced to rise now and again and walk about to warm their stiffened limbs. It did not occur to them, probably, to contrast their coming home with their going forth, or with the coming home of the generals, colonels, or even captains — but to Private Smith, at any rate, there came a sickness at heart almost deadly as he lay there on his hard bed and went over his situation.

In the deep of the night, lying on a board in the town where he had enlisted three years ago, all elation and enthusiasm gone out of him, he faced the fact that with the joy of home-coming was already mingled the bitter juice of care. He saw himself sick, worn out, taking up the work on his half-cleared farm, the inevitable mortgage standing ready with open jaw to swallow half his earnings. He had given three years of his life for a mere pittance of pay, and now! —

Morning dawned at last, slowly, with a pale yellow dome of light rising silently above the bluffs, which stand like some huge storm-devastated castle, just east of the city. Out to the left the great river swept on its massive yet silent way to the south. Bluejays called across the water from hillside to hillside through the clear, beautiful air, and hawks began to skim the tops of the hills. The older men were astir early, but Private Smith had fallen at last into a sleep, and they went out without waking him. He lay on his knapsack, his gaunt face turned toward the ceiling, his hands clasped on his breast, with a curious pathetic effect of weakness and appeal.

An engine switching near woke him at last, and he slowly sat up and stared about. He looked out of the window and saw that the sun was lightening the hills across the river. He rose and brushed his hair as well as he could, folded his blankets up, and went out to find his companions. They stood gazing silently at the river and at the hills.

"Looks natcher'l, don't it?" they said, as he came out.

"That's what it does," he replied. "An' it looks good. D' yeh see that peak?" He pointed at a beautiful symmetrical peak, rising like a slightly truncated cone, so high that it seemed the very highest of them all. It was touched by the morning sun and it glowed like a beacon, and a light scarf of gray morning fog was rolling up its shadowed side.

"My farm's just beyond that. Now, if I can only ketch a ride, we'll be home by dinner-time."

"I'm talkin' about breakfast," said one of the others.

"I guess it's one more meal o' hardtack f'r me," said Smith.

They foraged around, and finally found a restaurant with a sleepy old German behind the counter, and procured some coffee, which they drank to wash down their hardtack.

"Time'll come," said Smith, holding up a piece by the corner, "when this'll be a curiosity."

"I hope to God it will! I bet I've chawed hardtack enough to shingle every house in the coolly. I've chawed it when my lampers was down, and when they wasn't. I've took it dry, soaked, and mashed. I've had it wormy, musty, sour, and blue-mouldy. I've had it in little bits and big bits; 'fore coffee an' after coffee. I'm ready f'r a change. I'd like t' git holt jest about now o' some of the hot biscuits my wife c'n make when she lays herself out f'r company."

"Well, if you set there gabblin', you'll never *see* yer wife."

"Come on," said Private Smith. "Wait a moment, boys; less take suthin'. It's on me." He led them to the rusty tin dipper which hung on a nail beside the wooden water-pail, and they grinned and drank. Then shouldering their blankets and muskets, which they were "takin' home to the boys," they struck out on their last march.

"They called that coffee Jayvy," grumbled one of them, "but it never went by the road where government Jayvy resides. I reckon I know coffee from peas."

They kept together on the road along the turnpike, and up the winding road by the river, which they followed for some miles. The river was very lovely, curving down along its sandy beds, pausing now and then under broad basswood trees, or running in dark, swift, silent currents under tangles of wild grapevines, and drooping alders, and haw trees. At one of these lovely spots the three vets sat down on the thick green sward to rest, "on Smith's account." The leaves of the trees were as fresh and green as in June, the jays called cheery greetings to them, and kingfishers darted to and fro with swooping, noiseless flight.

"I tell yeh, boys, this knocks the swamps of Loueesiana into kingdom come."

"You bet. All they c'n raise down there is snakes, niggers, and p'rticler hell."

"An' fightin' men," put in the older man.

"An' fightin' men. If I had a good hook an' line I'd sneak a pick'rel out o' that pond. Say, remember that time I shot that alligator—"

"I guess we'd better be crawlin' along," interrupted Smith, rising and shouldering his knapsack, with considerable effort, which he tried to hide.

"Say, Smith, lemme give you a lift on that."

"I guess I c'n manage," said Smith, grimly.

"Course. But, yo' see, I may not have a chance right off to pay yeh back for the times you've carried my gun and hull caboodle. Say, now, gimme that gun, anyway."

"All right, if yeh feel like it, Jim," Smith replied, and they trudged along doggedly in the sun, which was getting higher and hotter each half-mile.

"Ain't it queer there ain't no teams comin' along," said Smith, after a long silence.

"Well, no, seein's it's Sunday."

"By jinks, that's a fact. It *is* Sunday. I'll git home in time f'r dinner, sure!" he exulted. "She don't hev dinner usually till about *one* on Sundays." And he fell into a muse, in which he smiled.

"Well, I'll git home jest about six o'clock, jest about when the boys are milkin' the cows," said old Jim Cranby. "I'll step into the barn, an' then I'll say: 'He*ah*! why ain't this milkin' done before this time o' day?' An' then won't they yell!" he added, slapping his thigh in great glee.

Smith went on. "I'll jest go up the path. Old Rover'll come down the road to meet me. He won't bark; he'll know me, an' he'll come down waggin' his tail an' showin' his teeth. That's his way of laughin'. An' so I'll walk up to the kitchen door, an' I'll say, '*Dinner* f'r a hungry man!' An' then she'll jump up, an'—"

He couldn't go on. His voice choked at the thought of it. Saunders, the third man, hardly uttered a word, but walked silently behind the others. He had lost his wife the first year he was in the army. She died of pneumonia, caught in the autumn rains while working in the fields in his place.

They plodded along till at last they came to a parting of the ways. To the right the road continued up the main valley; to the left it went over the big ridge.

"Well, boys," began Smith, as they grounded their muskets and looked away up the valley, "here's where we shake hands. We've marched together a good many miles, an' now I s'pose we're done."

"Yes, I don't think we'll do any more of it f'r a while. I don't want to, I know."

"I hope I'll see yeh once in a while, boys, to talk over old times."

"Of course," said Saunders, whose voice trembled a little, too. "It ain't *exactly* like dyin'." They all found it hard to look at each other.

"But we'd ought'r go home with you," said Cranby. "You'll never climb that ridge with all them things on yer back."

"Oh, I'm all right! Don't worry about me. Every step takes me nearer home, yeh see. Well, good-by, boys.

They shook hands. "Good-by. Good luck!"

"Same to you. Lemme know how you find things at home."

"Good-by."

"Good-by."

He turned once before they passed out of sight, and waved his cap, and they did the same, and all yelled. Then all marched away with their long, steady, loping, veteran step. The solitary climber in blue walked on for a time, with his mind filled with the kindness of his comrades, and musing upon the many wonderful days they had had together in camp and field.

He thought of his chum, Billy Tripp. Poor Billy! A "minie" ball[16] fell into his breast one day, fell wailing like a cat, and tore a great ragged hole in his heart. He looked forward to a sad scene with Billy's mother and sweetheart. They would want to know all about it. He tried to recall all that Billy had said, and the particulars of it, but there was little to remember, just that wild wailing sound high in the air, a dull slap, a short, quick, expulsive groan, and the boy lay with his face in the dirt in the ploughed field they were marching across.

That was all. But all the scenes he had since been through had not dimmed the horror, the terror of that moment, when his boy comrade fell, with only a breath between a laugh and a death-groan. Poor handsome Billy! Worth millions of dollars was his young life.

These sombre recollections gave way at length to more cheerful feelings as he began to approach his home coolly. The fields and houses grew familiar, and in one or two he was greeted by people seated in the doorways. But he was in no mood to talk, and pushed on steadily, though he stopped and accepted a drink of milk once at the well-side of a neighbor.

The sun was burning hot on that slope, and his step grew slower, in spite of his iron resolution. He sat down several times to rest. Slowly he crawled up the rough, reddish-brown road, which wound along the hillside, under great trees, through dense groves of jack oaks, with tree-tops far below him on his left hand, and the hills far above him on his right. He crawled along like some minute, wingless variety of fly.

He ate some hardtack, sauced with wild berries, when he reached the summit of the ridge, and sat there for some time, looking down into his home coolly.

Sombre, pathetic figure! His wide, round, gray eyes gazing down into the beautiful valley, seeing and not seeing, the splendid cloud-shadows sweeping over the western hills and across the green and yellow wheat far below. His head drooped forward on his palm, his shoulders took on a tired stoop, his cheek-bones showed painfully. An observer might have said, "He is looking down upon his own grave."

II

Sunday comes in a Western wheat harvest with such sweet and sudden relaxation to man and beast that it would be holy for that reason, if for no other, and Sundays are usually fair in harvest-time. As one goes out into the field in the hot morning sunshine, with no sound abroad save the crickets and the indescribably pleasant silken rustling of the ripened grain, the reaper and the very sheaves in the stubble seem to be resting, dreaming.

Around the house, in the shade of the trees, the men sit, smoking, dozing, or reading the papers, while the women, never resting, move about at the housework. The men eat on Sundays about the same as on other days, and breakfast is no sooner over and out of the way than dinner begins.

But at the Smith farm there were no men dozing or reading. Mrs. Smith was alone with her three children, Mary, nine, Tommy, six, and little Ted, just past four. Her farm, rented to a neighbor, lay at the head of a coolly or narrow gully, made at some far-off post-glacial period by the vast and angry floods of water which gullied these tremendous furrows in the level prairie—furrows so deep that undisturbed portions of the original level rose like hills on either side, rose to quite considerable mountains.

The chickens wakened her as usual that Sabbath morning from dreams of her absent husband, from whom she had not heard for weeks. The shadows drifted over the hills, down the slopes, across the wheat, and up the opposite wall in leisurely way, as if, being Sunday, they could take it easy also. The fowls clustered about the housewife as she went out into the yard. Fuzzy little chickens swarmed out from the coops, where their clucking and perpetually disgruntled mothers tramped about, petulantly thrusting their heads through the spaces between the slats.

A cow called in a deep, musical bass, and a calf answered from a little pen near by, and a pig scurried guiltily out of the cabbages. Seeing all this, seeing the pig in the cabbages, the tangle of grass in the garden, the broken fence which she had mended again and again—the little woman, hardly more than a girl, sat down and cried. The bright Sabbath morning was only a mockery without him!

A few years ago they had bought this farm, paying part, mortgaging the rest in the usual way. Edward Smith was a man of terrible energy. He worked "nights and Sundays," as the saying goes, to clear the farm of its brush and of its insatiate mortgage! In the midst of his Herculean struggle came the call for volunteers, and with the grim and unselfish devotion to his country which made the Eagle Brigade[17] able to "whip its weight in wild-cats," he threw down his scythe and grub-axe, turned his cattle loose, and became a bluecoated cog in a vast machine for killing men, and not thistles. While the million-aire sent his money to England for safe-keeping, this man, with his girl-wife and three babies, left them on a mortgaged farm, and went away to fight for an idea. It was foolish, but it was sublime for all that.

That was three years before, and the young wife, sitting on the well-curb on this bright Sabbath harvest morning, was righteously rebellious. It seemed to her that she had borne her share of the country's sorrow. Two brothers had been killed, the renter in whose hands her husband had left the farm had proved a villain; one year the farm had been without crops, and now the overripe grain was waiting the tardy hand of the neighbor who had rented it, and who was cutting his own grain first.

About six weeks before, she had received a letter saying, "We'll be discharged in a little while." But no other word had come from him. She had seen by the papers that his army was being discharged, and from day to day other soldiers slowly percolated in blue streams back into the State and county, but still *her* hero did not return.

Each week she had told the children that he was coming, and she had watched the road so long that it had become unconscious; and as she stood at the well, or by the kitchen door, her eyes were fixed unthinkingly on the road that wound down the coolly.

Nothing wears on the human soul like waiting. If the stranded mariner, searching the sun-bright seas, could once give up hope of a ship, that horrible grinding on his brain would cease. It was this waiting, hoping, on the edge of despair, that gave Emma Smith no rest.

Neighbors said, with kind intentions: "He's sick, maybe, an' can't start north just yet. He'll come along one o' these days."

"Why don't he write?" was her question, which silenced them all. This Sunday morning it seemed to her as if she could not stand it longer. The house seemed intolerably lonely. So she dressed the little ones in their best calico dresses and home-made jackets, and, closing up the house, set off down the coolly to old Mother Gray's.

"Old Widder Gray" lived at the "mouth of the coolly." She was a widow woman with a large family of stalwart boys and laughing girls. She was the visible incarnation of hospitality and optimistic poverty. With Western open-heartedness she fed every mouth that asked food of her, and worked herself to death as cheerfully as her girls danced in the neighborhood harvest dances.

She waddled down the path to meet Mrs. Smith with a broad smile on her face.

"Oh, you little dears! Come right to your granny. Gimme me a kiss! Come right in, Mis' Smith. How are yeh, anyway? Nice mornin', ain't it? Come in an' set down. Everything's in a clutter, but that won't scare you any."

She led the way into the best room, a sunny, square room, carpeted with a faded and patched rag carpet, and papered with white-and-green-striped wall-paper, where a few faded effigies of dead members of the family hung in variously sized oval walnut frames. The house resounded with singing, laughter, whistling, tramping of heavy boots, and riotous scufflings. Half-grown boys came to the door and crooked their fingers at the children, who ran out, and were soon heard in the midst of the fun.

"Don't s'pose you've heard from Ed?" Mrs. Smith shook her head. "He'll turn up some day, when you ain't lookin' for 'm." The good old soul had said that so many times that poor Mrs. Smith derived no comfort from it any longer.

"Liz heard from Al the other day. He's comin' some day this week. Anyhow, they expect him."

"Did he say anything of—"

"No, he didn't," Mrs. Gray admitted. "But then it was only a short letter, anyhow. Al ain't much for writin', anyhow.—But come out and see my new cheese. I tell yeh, I don't believe I ever had better luck in my life. If Ed should come, I want you should take him up a piece of this cheese."

It was beyond human nature to resist the influence of that noisy, hearty, loving household, and in the midst of the singing and laughing the wife forgot her anxiety, for the time at least, and laughed and sang with the rest.

About eleven o'clock a wagon-load more drove up to the door, and Bill Gray, the widow's oldest son, and his whole family, from Sand Lake Coolly, piled out amid a good-natured uproar. Every one talked at once, except Bill, who sat in the wagon with his wrists on his knees, a straw in his mouth, and an amused twinkle in his blue eyes.

"Ain't heard nothin' o' Ed, I s'pose?" he asked in a kind of bellow. Mrs. Smith shook her head. Bill, with a delicacy very striking in such a great giant, rolled his quid in his mouth, and said:

"Didn't know but you had. I hear two or three of the Sand Lake boys are comin'. Left New Orleenes some time this week. Didn't write nothin' about Ed, but no news is good news in such cases, mother always says."

"Well, go put out yer team," said Mrs. Gray, "an' go 'n bring me in some taters, an', Sim, you go see if you c'n find some corn. Sadie, you put on the water to bile. Come now, hustle yer boots, all o' yeh. If I feed this yer crowd, we've got to have some raw materials. If y' think I'm goin' to feed yeh on pie—you're jest mightily mistaken."

The children went off into the fields, the girls put dinner on to boil, and then went to change their dresses and fix their hair. "Somebody might come," they said.

"Land sakes, I *hope* not! I don't know where in time I'd set 'em, 'less they'd eat at the second table," Mrs. Gray laughed, in pretended dismay.

The two older boys, who had served their time in the army, lay out on the grass before the house, and whittled and talked desultorily about the war and the crops, and planned buying a threshing-machine. The older girls and Mrs. Smith helped enlarge the table and put on the dishes, talking all the time in that cheery, incoherent, and meaningful way a group of such women have,— a conversation to be taken for its spirit rather than for its letter, though Mrs. Gray at last got the ear of them all and dissertated at length on girls.

"Girls in love ain't no use in the whole blessed week," she said. "Sundays they're a-lookin' down the road, expectin' he'll *come*. Sunday afternoons they can't think o' nothin' else, 'cause he's *here*. Monday mornin's they're sleepy and kind o' dreamy and slimpsy, and good f'r nothin' on Tuesday and Wednesday. Thursday they git absent-minded, an' begin to look off toward Sunday agin, an' mope aroun' and let the dishwater git cold, right under their noses. Friday they break dishes, an' go off in the best room an' snivel, an' look out o' the winder. Saturdays they have queer spurts o' workin' like all p'ssessed, an' spurts o' frizzin' their hair. An' Sunday they begin it all over agin."

The girls giggled and blushed, all through this tirade from their mother, their broad faces and powerful frames anything but suggestive of lackadaisical sentiment. But Mrs. Smith said:

"Now, Mrs. Gray, I hadn't ought to stay to dinner. You've got—"

"Now you set right down! If any of them girls' beaus comes, they'll have to take what's left, that's all. They ain't s'posed to have much appetite, nohow. No, you're goin' to stay if they starve, an' they ain't no danger o' that."

At one o'clock the long table was piled with boiled potatoes, cords of boiled corn on the cob, squash and pumpkin pies, hot biscuit, sweet pickles, bread and butter, and honey. Then one of the girls took down a conch-shell from a nail, and going to the door, blew a long, fine, free blast, that showed there was no weakness of lungs in her ample chest.

Then the children came out of the forest of corn, out of the creek, out of the loft of the barn, and out of the garden.

"They come to their feed f'r all the world jest like the pigs when y' holler 'poo-ee!' See 'em scoot!" laughed Mrs. Gray, every wrinkle on her face shining with delight.

The men shut up their jack-knives, and surrounded the horse-trough to souse their faces in the cold, hard water, and in a few moments the table was filled with a merry crowd, and a row of wistful-eyed youngsters circled the kitchen wall, where they stood first on one leg and then on the other, in impatient hunger.

"Now pitch in, Mrs. Smith," said Mrs. Gray, presiding over the table. "You know these men critters. They'll eat every grain of it, if yeh give 'em a chance. I swan, they're made o' India-rubber, their stomachs is, I know it."

"Haf to eat to work," said Bill, gnawing a cob with a swift, circular motion that rivalled a corn-sheller in results.

"More like workin' to eat," put in one of the girls, with a giggle. "More eat 'n work with you."

"*You* needn't say anything, Net. Any one that'll eat seven ears—"

"I didn't, no such thing. You piled your cobs on my plate."

"That'll do to tell Ed Varney. It won't go down here where we know yeh."

"Good land! Eat all yeh want! They's plenty more in the fiel's, but I can't afford to give you young uns tea. The tea is for us women-folks, and 'specially f'r Mis' Smith an' Bill's wife. We're a-goin' to tell fortunes by it."

One by one the men filled up and shoved back, and one by one the children slipped into their places, and by two o'clock the women alone remained around the débris-covered table, sipping their tea and telling fortunes.

As they got well down to the grounds in the cup, they shook them with a circular motion in the hand, and then turned them bottom-side-up quickly in the saucer, then twirled them three or four times one way, and three or four times the other, during a breathless pause. Then Mrs. Gray lifted the cup, and, gazing into it with profound gravity, pronounced the impending fate.

It must be admitted that, to a critical observer, she had abundant preparation for hitting close to the mark, as when she told the girls that "somebody was comin'." "It's a man," she went on gravely. "He is cross-eyed—"

"Oh, you hush!" cried Nettie.

"He has red hair, and is death on b'iled corn and hot biscuit."

The others shrieked with delight.

"But he's goin' to get the mitten, that red-headed feller is, for I see another feller comin' up behind him."

"Oh, lemme see, lemme see!" cried Nettie.

"Keep off," said the priestess, with a lofty gesture. "His hair is black. He don't eat so much, and he works more."

The girls exploded in a shriek of laughter, and pounded their sister on the back.

At last came Mrs. Smith's turn, and she was trembling with excitement as Mrs. Gray again composed her jolly face to what she considered a proper solemnity of expression.

"Somebody is comin' to *you*," she said, after a long pause. "He's got a musket on his back. He's a soldier. He's almost here. See?"

She pointed at two little tea-stems, which really formed a faint suggestion of a man with a musket on his back. He had climbed nearly to the edge of the cup. Mrs. Smith grew pale with excitement. She trembled so she could hardly hold the cup in her hand as she gazed into it.

"It's Ed," cried the old woman. "He's on the way home. Heavens an' earth! There he is now!" She turned and waved her hand out toward the road. They rushed to the door to look where she pointed.

A man in a blue coat, with a musket on his back, was toiling slowly up the hill on the sun-bright, dusty road, toiling slowly, with bent head half hidden by a heavy knapsack. So tired it seemed that walking was indeed a process of falling. So eager to get home he would not stop, would not look aside, but plodded on, amid the cries of the locusts, the welcome of the crickets, and the rustle of the yellow wheat. Getting back to God's country, and his wife and babies!

Laughing, crying, trying to call him and the children at the same time, the little wife, almost hysterical, snatched her hat and ran out into the yard. But the soldier had disappeared over the hill into the hollow beyond, and, by the time she had found the children, he was too far away for her voice to reach him. And, besides, she was not sure it was her husband, for he had not turned his head at their shouts. This seemed so strange. Why didn't he stop to rest at his old neighbor's house? Tortured by hope and doubt, she hurried up the coolly as fast as she could push the baby wagon, the blue-coated figure just ahead pushing steadily, silently forward up the coolly.

When the excited, panting little group came in sight of the gate they saw the blue-coated figure standing, leaning upon the rough rail fence, his chin on his palms, gazing at the empty house. His knapsack, canteen, blankets, and musket lay upon the dusty grass at his feet.

He was like a man lost in a dream. His wide, hungry eyes devoured the scene. The rough lawn, the little unpainted house, the field of clear yellow wheat behind it, down across which streamed the sun, now almost ready to touch the high hill to the west, the crickets crying merrily, a cat on the fence near by, dreaming, unmindful of the stranger in blue—

How peaceful it all was. O God! How far removed from all camps, hospitals, battle lines. A little cabin in a Wisconsin coolly, but it was majestic in its peace. How did he ever leave it for those years of tramping, thirsting, killing?

Trembling, weak with emotion, her eyes on the silent figure, Mrs. Smith hurried up to the fence. Her feet made no noise in the dust and grass, and they were close upon him before he knew of them. The oldest boy ran a little ahead. He will never forget that figure, that face. It will always remain as something epic, that return of the private. He fixed his eyes on the pale face covered with a ragged beard.

"Who *are* you, sir?" asked the wife, or, rather, started to ask, for he turned, stood a moment, and then cried:

"Emma!"

"Edward!"

The children stood in a curious row to see their mother kiss this bearded, strange man, the elder girl sobbing sympathetically with her mother. Illness had left the soldier partly deaf, and this added to the strangeness of his manner.

But the youngest child stood away, even after the girl had recognized her father and kissed him. The man turned then to the baby, and said in a curiously unpaternal tone

"Come here, my little man; don't you know me?" But the baby backed away under the fence and stood peering at him critically.

"My little man!" What meaning, in those words! This baby seemed like some other woman's child, and not the infant he had left in his wife's arms. The war had come between him and his baby—he was only a strange man to him, with big eyes; a soldier, with mother hanging to his arm, and talking in a loud voice.

"And this is Tom," the private said, drawing the oldest boy to him. "*He'll* come and see me. *He* knows his poor old pap when he comes home from the war."

The mother heard the pain and reproach in his voice and hastened to apologize.

"You've changed so, Ed. He can't know yeh. This is papa, Teddy; come and kiss him—Tom and Mary do. Come, won't you?" But Teddy still peered through the fence with solemn eyes, well out of reach. He resembled a half-wild kitten that hesitates, studying the tones of one's voice.

"I'll fix him," said the soldier, and sat down to undo his knapsack, out of which he drew three enormous and very red apples. After giving one to each of the older children, he said:

"*Now* I guess he'll come. Eh, my little man? Now come see your pap."

Teddy crept slowly under the fence, assisted by the overzealous Tommy, and a moment later was kicking and squalling in his father's arms. Then they entered the house, into the sitting room, poor, bare, art-forsaken little room, too, with its rag carpet, its square clock, and its two or three chromos[18] and pictures from *Harper's Weekly* pinned about.

"Emma, I'm all tired out," said Private Smith, as he flung himself down on the carpet as he used to do, while his wife brought a pillow to put under his head, and the children stood about munching their apples.

"Tommy, you run and get me a pan of chips, and Mary, you get the tea-kettle on, and I'll go and make some biscuit."

And the soldier talked. Question after question he poured forth about the crops, the cattle, the renter, the neighbors. He slipped his heavy government brogan shoes off his poor, tired, blistered feet, and lay out with utter, sweet relaxation. He was a free man again, no longer a soldier under command. At supper he stopped once, listened and smiled. "That's old Spot. I know her voice. I s'pose that's her calf out there in the pen. I can't milk her to-night, though. I'm too tired. But I tell you, I'd like a drink o' her milk. What's become of old Rove?"

"He died last winter. Poisoned, I guess." There was a moment of sadness for them all. It was some time before the husband spoke again, in a voice that trembled a little.

"Poor old feller! He'd 'a' known me half a mile away. I expected him to come down the hill to meet me. It 'ud 'a' been more like comin' home if I could 'a' seen him comin' down the road an' waggin' his tail, an' laughin' that way he has. I tell yeh, it kind o' took hold o' me to see the blinds down an' the house shut up."

"But, yeh see, we—we expected you'd write again 'fore you started. And then we thought we'd see you if you *did* come," she hastened to explain.

"Well, I ain't worth a cent on writin'. Besides, it's just as well yeh didn't know when I was comin'. I tell you, it sounds good to hear them chickens out there, an' turkeys, an' the crickets. Do you know they don't have just the same kind o' crickets down South? Who's Sam hired t' help cut yer grain?"

"The Ramsey boys."

"Looks like a good crop; but I'm afraid I won't do much gettin' it cut. This cussed fever an' ague has got me down pretty low. I don't know when I'll get rid of it. I'll bet I've took twenty-five pounds of quinine if I've taken a bit. Gimme another biscuit. I tell yeh, they taste good, Emma. I ain't had anything like it— Say, if you'd 'a' hear'd me braggin' to th' boys about your butter 'n' biscuits I'll bet your ears 'ud 'a' burnt."

The private's wife colored with pleasure. "Oh, you're always a-braggin' about your things. Everybody makes good butter."

"Yes; old lady Snyder, for instance."

"Oh, well, she ain't to be mentioned. She's Dutch."

"Or old Mis' Snively. One more cup o' tea, Mary. That's my girl! I'm feeling better already. I just b'lieve the matter with me is, I'm *starved*."

This was a delicious hour, one long to be remembered. They were like lovers again. But their tenderness, like that of a typical American family, found utterance in tones, rather than in words. He was praising her when praising her biscuit, and she knew it. They grew soberer when he showed where he had been struck, one ball burning the back of his hand, one cutting away a lock of hair from his temple, and one passing through the calf of his leg. The wife shuddered to think how near she had come to being a soldier's widow. Her waiting no longer seemed hard. This sweet, glorious hour effaced it all.

Then they rose, and all went out into the garden and down to the barn. He stood beside her while she milked old Spot. They began to plan fields and crops for next year.

His farm was weedy and encumbered, a rascally renter had run away with his machinery (departing between two days), his children needed clothing, the years were coming upon him, he was sick and emaciated, but his heroic soul did not quail. With the same courage with which he had faced his Southern march he entered upon a still more hazardous future.

Oh, that mystic hour! The pale man with big eyes standing there by the well, with his young wife by his side. The vast moon swinging above the eastern peaks, the cattle winding down the pasture slopes with jangling bells, the crickets singing, the stars blooming out sweet and far and serene; the katydids rhythmically calling, the little turkeys crying querulously, as they settled to roost in the poplar tree near the open gate. The voices at the well drop lower, the little ones nestle in their father's arms at last, and Teddy falls asleep there.

The common soldier of the American volunteer army had returned. His war with the South was over, and his fight, his daily running fight with nature and against the injustice of his fellow-men, was begun again.

Kate Chopin, from *Bayou Folk* (1892)

"A Wizard from Gettysburg"

It was one afternoon in April, not long ago, only the other day, and the shadows had already begun to lengthen.

Bertrand Delmandé, a fine, bright-looking boy of fourteen years,—fifteen, perhaps,—was mounted, and riding along a pleasant country road, upon a little Creole pony, such as boys in Louisiana usually ride when they have nothing better at hand. He had hunted, and carried his gun before him.

It is unpleasant to state that Bertrand was not so depressed as he should have been, in view of recent events that had come about. Within the past week he had been recalled from the college of Grand Coteau to his home, the Bon-Accueil plantation.

He had found his father and his grandmother depressed over money matters, awaiting certain legal developments that might result in his permanent withdrawal from school. That very day, directly after the early dinner, the two had driven to town, on this very business, to be absent till the late afternoon. Bertrand, then, had saddled Picayune and gone for a long jaunt, such as his heart delighted in.

He was returning now, and had approached the beginning of the great tangled Cherokee hedge that marked the boundary line of Bon-Accueil, and that twinkled with multiple white roses.

The pony started suddenly and violently at something there in the turn of the road, and just under the hedge. It looked like a bundle of rags at first. But it was a tramp, seated upon a broad, flat stone.

Bertrand had no maudlin consideration for tramps as a species; he had only that morning driven from the place one who was making himself unpleasant at the kitchen window.

But this tramp was old and feeble. His beard was long, and as white as new-ginned cotton, and when Bertrand saw him he was engaged in stanching a wound in his bare heel with a fistful of matted grass.

"What's wrong, old man?" asked the boy, kindly.

The tramp looked up at him with a bewildered glance, but did not answer.

"Well," thought Bertrand, "since it's decided that I'm to be a physician some day, I can't begin to practice too early."

He dismounted, and examined the injured foot. It had an ugly gash. Bertrand acted mostly from impulse. Fortunately his impulses were not bad ones. So, nimbly, and as quickly as he could manage it, he had the old man astride Picayune, whilst he himself was leading the pony down the narrow lane.

The dark green hedge towered like a high and solid wall on one side. On the other was a broad, open field, where here and there appeared the flash and gleam of uplifted, polished hoes, that negroes were plying between the even rows of cotton and tender corn.

"This is the State of Louisiana," uttered the tramp, quaveringly.

"Yes, this is Louisiana," returned Bertrand cheerily.

"Yes, I know it is. I've been in all of them since Gettysburg. Sometimes it was too hot, and sometimes it was too cold; and with that bullet in my head—you don't remember? No, you don't remember Gettysburg."

"Well, no, not vividly," laughed Bertrand.

"Is it a hospital? It isn't a factory, is it?" the man questioned.

"Where we're going? Why, no, it 's the Delmandé plantation—Bon-Accueil. Here we are. Wait, I'll open the gate."

This singular group entered the yard from the rear, and not far from the house. A big black woman, who sat just without a cabin door, picking a pile of rusty-looking moss, called out at sight of them:—

"W'at's dat you's bringin' in dis yard, boy? top dat hoss?"

She received no reply. Bertrand, indeed, took no notice of her inquiry.

"Fu' a boy w'at goes to school like you does—whar's yo' sense?" she went on, with a fine show of indignation; then, muttering to herself, "Ma'ame Bertrand an' Marse St. Ange ain't gwine stan' dat, I knows dey ain't. Dah! ef he ain't done sot 'im on de gall'ry, plumb down in his pa's rockin'-cheer!"

Which the boy had done; seated the tramp in a pleasant corner of the veranda, while he went in search of bandages for his wound.

The servants showed high disapproval, the housemaid following Bertrand into his grandmother's room, whither he had carried his investigations.

"W'at you tearin' yo' gra'ma's closit to pieces dat away, boy?" she complained in her high soprano.

"I 'm looking for bandages."

"Den w'y you don't ax fu' ban'ges, an' lef yo' gra'ma's closit 'lone? You want to listen to me; you gwine git shed o' dat tramp settin' dah naxt to de dinin'-room! W'en de silva be missin', 'tain' you w'at gwine git blame, it 's me."

"The silver? Nonsense, 'Cindy; the man's wounded, and can't you see he's out of his head?"

"No mo' outen his head 'an I is. 'Tain' me w'at want to tres' [trust] 'im wid de sto'-room key, ef he is outen his head," she concluded with a disdainful shrug.

But Bertrand's protégé proved so unapproachable in his long-worn rags, that the boy concluded to leave him unmolested till his father's return, and then ask permission to turn the forlorn creature into the bath-house, and array him afterward in clean, fresh garments.

So there the old tramp sat in the veranda corner, stolidly content, when St. Ange Delmandé and his mother returned from town.

St. Ange was a dark, slender man of middle age, with a sensitive face, and a plentiful sprinkle of gray in his thick black hair; his mother, a portly woman, and an active one for her sixty-five years.

They were evidently in a despondent mood. Perhaps it was for the cheer of her sweet presence that they had brought with them from town a little girl, the child of Madame Delmandé's only daughter, who was married, and lived there.

Madame Delmandé and her son were astonished to find so uninviting an intruder in possession. But a few earnest words from Bertrand reassured them, and partly reconciled them to the man's presence; and it was with wholly indifferent though not unkindly glances that they passed him by when they entered. On any large plantation there are always nooks and corners where, for a night or more, even such a man as this tramp may be tolerated and given shelter.

When Bertrand went to bed that night, he lay long awake thinking of the man, and of what he had heard from his lips in the hushed starlight. The boy had heard of the awfulness of Gettysburg, till it was like something he could feel and quiver at.

On that field of battle this man had received a new and tragic birth. For all his existence that went before was a blank to him. There, in the black desolation of war, he was born again, without friends or kindred; without even a name he could know was his own. Then he had gone forth a wanderer; living more than half the time in hospitals; toiling when he could, starving when he had to.

Strangely enough, he had addressed Bertrand as "St. Ange," not once, but every time he had spoken to him. The boy wondered at this. Was it because he had heard Madame Delmandé address her son by that name, and fancied it?

So this nameless wanderer had drifted far down to the plantation of Bon-Accueil, and at last had found a human hand stretched out to him in kindness.

When the family assembled at breakfast on the following morning, the tramp was already settled in the chair, and in the corner which Bertrand's indulgence had made familiar to him.

If he had turned partly around, he would have faced the flower garden, with its graveled walks and trim parterres, where a tangle of color and perfume were holding high revelry this April morning; but he liked better to gaze into the back yard, where there was always movement: men and women coming and going, bearing implements of work; little negroes in scanty garments, darting here and there, and kicking up the dust in their exuberance.

Madame Delmandé could just catch a glimpse of him through the long window that opened to the floor, and near which he sat.

Mr. Delmandé had spoken to the man pleasantly; but he and his mother were wholly absorbed by their trouble, and talked constantly of that, while Bertrand went back and forth ministering to the old man's wants. The boy knew that the servants would have done the office with ill grace, and he chose to be cup-bearer himself to the unfortunate creature for whose presence he alone was responsible.

Once, when Bertrand went out to him with a second cup of coffee, steaming and fragrant, the old man whispered:—

"What are they saying in there?" pointing over his shoulder to the dining-room.

"Oh, money troubles that will force us to economize for a while," answered the boy. "What father and *mé-mère* feel worst about is that I shall have to leave college now."

"No, no! St. Ange must go to school. The war's over, the war's over! St. Ange and Florentine must go to school."

"But if there 's no money," the boy insisted, smiling like one who humors the vagaries of a child.

"Money! money!" murmured the tramp. "The war's over—money! money!"

His sleepy gaze had swept across the yard into the thick of the orchard beyond, and rested there.

Suddenly he pushed aside the light table that had been set before him, and rose, clutching Bertrand's arm.

"St. Ange, you must go to school!" he whispered. "The war's over," looking furtively around. "Come. Don't let them hear you. Don't let the negroes see us. Get a spade—the little spade that Buck Williams was digging his cistern with."

Still clutching the boy, he dragged him down the steps as he said this, and traversed the yard with long, limping strides, himself leading the way.

From under a shed where such things were to be found, Bertrand selected a spade, since the tramp's whim demanded that he should, and together they entered the orchard.

The grass was thick and tufted here, and wet with the morning dew. In long lines, forming pleasant avenues between, were peach-trees growing, and pear and apple and plum. Close against the fence was the pomegranate hedge, with its waxen blossoms, brick-red. Far down in the centre of the orchard stood a huge pecan-tree, twice the size of any other that was there, seeming to rule like an old-time king.

Here Bertrand and his guide stopped. The tramp had not once hesitated in his movements since grasping the arm of his young companion on the veranda. Now he went and leaned his back against the pecan-tree, where there was a deep knot, and looking steadily before him he took ten paces forward. Turning sharply to the right, he made five additional paces. Then pointing his finger downward, and looking at Bertrand, he commanded:—

"There, dig. I would do it myself, but for my wounded foot. For I've turned many a spade of earth since Gettysburg. Dig, St. Ange, dig! The war's over; you must go to school."

Is there a boy of fifteen under the sun who would not have dug, even knowing he was following the insane dictates of a demented man? Bertrand entered with all the zest of his years and his spirit into the curious adventure; and he dug and dug, throwing great spadefuls of the rich, fragrant earth from side to side.

The tramp, with body bent, and fingers like claws clasping his bony knees, stood watching with eager eyes, that never unfastened their steady gaze from the boy's rhythmic motions.

"That's it!" he muttered at intervals. "Dig, dig! The war's over. You must go to school, St. Ange."

Deep down in the earth, too deep for any ordinary turning of the soil with spade or plow to have reached it, was a box. It was of tin, apparently, something larger than a cigar box, and bound round and round with twine, rotted now and eaten away in places.

The tramp showed no surprise at seeing it there; he simply knelt upon the ground and lifted it from its long resting place.

Bertrand had let the spade fall from his hands, and was quivering with the awe of the thing he saw. Who could this wizard be that had come to him in the guise of a tramp, that walked in cabalistic paces upon his own father's ground, and pointed his finger like a divining-rod to the spot where boxes—may be [sic] treasures—lay? It was like a page from a wonder-book.

And walking behind this white-haired old man, who was again leading the way, something of childish superstition crept back into Bertrand's heart. It was the same feeling with which he had often sat, long ago, in the weird firelight of some negro's cabin, listening to tales of witches who came in the night to work uncanny spells at their will.

Madame Delmandé had never abandoned the custom of washing her own silver and dainty china. She sat, when the breakfast was over, with a pail of warm suds before her that 'Cindy had brought to her, with an abundance of soft linen cloths. Her little granddaughter stood beside her playing, as babies will, with the bright spoons and forks, and ranging them in rows on the polished mahogany. St. Ange was at the window making entries in a note-book, and frowning gloomily as he did so.

The group in the dining-room were so employed when the old tramp came staggering in, Bertrand close behind him.

He went and stood at the foot of the table, opposite to where Madame Delmandé sat, and let fall the box upon it.

The thing in falling shattered, and from its bursting sides gold came, clicking, spinning, gliding, some of it like oil; rolling along the table and off it to the floor, but heaped up, the bulk of it, before the tramp.

"Here's money!" he called out, plunging his old hand in the thick of it. "Who says St. Ange shall not go to school? The war's over—here's money! St. Ange, my boy," turning to Bertrand and speaking with quick authority, "tell Buck Williams to hitch Black Bess to the buggy, and go bring Judge Parkerson here."

Judge Parkerson, indeed, who had been dead for twenty years and more!

"Tell him that—that"—and the hand that was not in the gold went up to the withered forehead, "that—Bertrand Delmandé needs him!"

Madame Delmandé, at sight of the man with his box and his gold, had given a sharp cry, such as might follow the plunge of a knife. She lay now in her son's arms, panting hoarsely.

"Your father, St. Ange,—come back from the dead—your father!"

"Be calm, mother!" the man implored. "You had such sure proof of his death in that terrible battle, this *may* not be he."

"I know him! I know your father, my son!" and disengaging herself from the arms that held her, she dragged herself as a wounded serpent might to where the old man stood.

His hand was still in the gold, and on his face was yet the flush which had come there when he shouted out the name Bertrand Delmandé.

"Husband," she gasped, "do you know me—your wife?"

The little girl was playing gleefully with the yellow coin.

Bertrand stood, pulseless almost, like a young Actaeon cut in marble.

When the old man had looked long into the woman's imploring face, he made a courtly bow.

"Madame," he said, "an old soldier, wounded on the field of Gettysburg, craves for himself and his two little children your kind hospitality."

Charles Chesnutt, from *The Wife of his Youth* (1899)

"Cicely's Dream"

I

The old woman stood at the back door of the cabin, shading her eyes with her hand, and looking across the vegetable garden that ran up to the very door. Beyond the garden she saw, bathed in the sunlight, a field of corn, just in the ear, stretching for half a mile, its yellow, pollen-laden tassels over-topping the dark green mass of broad glistening blades; and in the distance, through the faint morning haze of evaporating dew, the line of the woods, of a still darker green, meeting the clear blue of the summer sky. Old Dinah saw, going down the path, a tall, brown girl, in a homespun frock, swinging a slat-bonnet in one hand and a splint basket in the other.

"Oh, Cicely!" she called.

The girl turned and answered in a resonant voice, vibrating with youth and life,—

"Yes, granny!"

"Be sho' and pick a good mess er peas, chile, fer yo' gran'daddy's gwine ter be home ter dinner ter-day."

The old woman stood a moment longer and then turned to go into the house. What she had not seen was that the girl was not only young, but lithe and shapely as a sculptor's model; that her bare feet seemed to spurn the earth as they struck it; that though brown, she was not so brown but that her cheek was darkly red with the blood of another race than that which gave her her name and station in life; and the old woman did not see that Cicely's face was as comely as her figure was superb, and that her eyes were dreamy with vague yearnings.

Cicely climbed the low fence between the garden and the cornfield, and started down one of the long rows leading directly away from the house. Old Needham was a good ploughman, and straight as an arrow ran the furrow between the rows of corn, until it vanished in the distant perspective. The peas were planted beside alternate hills of corn, the corn-stalks serving as supports for the climbing pea-vines. The vines nearest the house had been picked more or less clear of the long green pods, and Cicely walked down the row for a quarter of a mile, to where the peas were more plentiful. And as she walked she thought of her dream of the night before.

She had dreamed a beautiful dream. The fact that it was a beautiful dream, a delightful dream, her memory retained very vividly. She was troubled because she could not remember just what her dream had been about. Of one other fact she was certain, that in her dream she had found something, and that her happiness had been bound up with the thing she had found. As she walked down the corn-row she ran over in her mind the various things with which she had always associated happiness. Had she found a gold ring? No, it was not a gold ring—of that she felt sure. Was it a soft, curly plume for her hat? She had seen town people with them, and had indulged in day-dreams on the subject; but it was not a feather. Was it a bright-colored silk dress? No; as much as she had always wanted one, it was not a silk dress. For an instant, in a dream, she had tasted some great and novel happiness, and when she awoke it was dashed from her lips, and she could not even enjoy the memory of it, except in a vague, indefinite, and tantalizing way.

Cicely was troubled, too, because dreams were serious things. Dreams had certain meanings, most of them, and some dreams went by contraries. If her dream had been a prophecy of some good thing, she had by forgetting it lost the pleasure of anticipation. If her dream had been one of those that go by contraries, the warning would be in vain, because she would not know against what evil to provide. So, with a sigh, Cicely said to herself that it was a troubled world, more or less; and having come to a promising point, began to pick the tenderest pea-pods and throw them into her basket.

By the time she had reached the end of the line the basket was nearly full. Glancing toward the pine woods beyond the rail fence, she saw a brier bush loaded with large, luscious blackberries. Cicely was fond of blackberries, so she set her basket down, climbed the fence, and was soon busily engaged in gathering the fruit, delicious even in its wild state.

She had soon eaten all she cared for. But the berries were still numerous, and it occurred to her that her granddaddy would like a blackberry pudding for dinner. Catching up her apron, and using it as a receptacle for the berries, she had gathered scarcely more than a handful when she heard a groan.

Cicely was not timid, and her curiosity being aroused by the sound, she stood erect, and remained in a listening attitude. In a moment the sound was repeated, and, gauging the point from which it came, she plunged resolutely into the thick underbrush of the forest. She had gone but a few yards when she stopped short with an exclamation of surprise and concern.

Upon the ground, under the shadow of the towering pines, a man lay at full length,— a young man, several years under thirty, apparently, so far as his age could be guessed from a face that wore a short soft beard, and was so begrimed with dust and incrusted with blood that little could be seen of the underlying integument. What was visible showed a skin browned by nature or by exposure. His hands were of even a darker brown, almost as dark as Cicely's own. A tangled mass of very curly black hair, matted with burs, dank with dew, and clotted with blood, fell partly over his forehead, on the edge of which, extending back into the hair, an ugly scalp wound was gaping, and, though apparently not just inflicted, was still bleeding slowly, as though reluctant to stop, in spite of the coagulation that had almost closed it.

Cicely with a glance took in all this and more. But, first of all, she saw the man was wounded and bleeding, and the nurse latent in all womankind awoke in her to the requirements of the situation. She knew there was a spring a few rods away, and ran swiftly to it. There was usually a gourd at the spring, but now it was gone. Pouring out the blackberries in a little heap where they could be found again, she took off her apron, dipped one end of it into the spring, and ran back to the wounded man. The apron was clean, and she squeezed a little stream of water from it into the man's mouth. He swallowed it with avidity. Cicely then knelt by his side, and with the wet end of her apron washed the blood from the wound lightly, and the dust from the man's face. Then she looked at her apron a moment, debating whether she should tear it or not.

"I'm feared granny 'll be mad," she said to herself. "I reckon I'll jes' use de whole apron."

So she bound the apron around his head as well as she could, and then sat down a moment on a fallen tree trunk, to think what she should do next. The man already seemed more comfortable; he had ceased moaning, and lay quiet, though breathing heavily.

"What shall I do with that man?" she reflected. "I don' know whether he's a w'ite man or a black man. Ef he's a w'ite man, I oughter go an' tell de w'ite folks up at de big house, an' dey'd take keer of 'im. If he's a black man, I oughter go tell granny. He don' look lack a black man somehow er nuther, an' yet he don' look lack a w'ite man; he's too dahk, an' his hair's too curly. But I mus' do somethin' wid 'im. He can't be lef' here ter die in de woods all by hisse'f. Reckon I'll go an' tell granny."

She scaled the fence, caught up the basket of peas from where she had left it, and ran, lightly and swiftly as a deer, toward the house. Her short skirt did not impede her progress, and in a few minutes she had covered the half mile and was at the cabin door, a slight heaving of her full and yet youthful breast being the only sign of any unusual exertion.

Her story was told in a moment. The old woman took down a black bottle from a high shelf, and set out with Cicely across the cornfield, toward the wounded man.

As they went through the corn Cicely recalled part of her dream. She had dreamed that under some strange circumstances—what they had been was still obscure—she had met a young man—a young man whiter than she and yet not all white—and that he had loved her and courted her and married her. Her dream had been all the sweeter because in it she had first tasted the sweetness of love, and she had not recalled it before because only in her dream had she known or thought of love as something supremely desirable.

With the memory of her dream, however, her fears revived. Dreams were solemn things. To Cicely the fabric of a vision was by no means baseless. Her trouble arose from her not being able to recall, though she was well versed in dream-lore, just what event was foreshadowed by a dream of finding a wounded man. If the wounded man were of her own race, her dream would thus far have been realized, and having met the young man, the other joys might be expected to follow. If he should turn out to be a white man, then her dream was clearly one of the kind that go by contraries, and she could expect only sorrow and trouble and pain as the proper sequences of this fateful discovery.

II

The two women reached the fence that separated the cornfield from the pine woods.

"How is I gwine ter git ovuh dat fence, chile?" asked the old woman.

"Wait a minute, granny," said Cicely; "I'll take it down."

It was only an eight-rail fence, and it was a matter of but a few minutes for the girl to lift down and lay to either side the ends of the rails that formed one of the angles. This done, the old woman easily stepped across the remaining two or three rails. It was only a moment before they stood by the wounded man. He was lying still, breathing regularly, and seemingly asleep.

"What is he, granny," asked the girl anxiously, "a w'ite man, or not?"

Old Dinah pushed back the matted hair from the wounded man's brow, and looked at the skin beneath. It was fairer there, but yet of a decided brown. She raised his hand, pushed back the tattered sleeve from his wrist, and then she laid his hand down gently.

"Mos' lackly he 's a mulatter man f'om up de country somewhar. He don' look lack dese yer niggers roun' yere, ner yet lack a w'ite man. But de po' boy 's in a bad fix, w'ateber he is, an' I 'spec's we bettah do w'at we kin fer 'im, an' w'en he comes to he'll tell us w'at he is—er w'at he calls hisse'f. Hol' 'is head up, chile, an' I 'll po' a drop er dis yer liquor down his th'oat; dat 'll bring 'im to quicker 'n anything e'se I knows."

Cicely lifted the sick man's head, and Dinah poured a few drops of the whiskey between his teeth. He swallowed it readily enough. In a few minutes he opened his eyes and stared blankly at the two women. Cicely saw that his eyes were large and black, and glistening with fever.

"How you feelin', suh?" asked the old woman.

There was no answer.

"Is you feelin' bettah now?"

The wounded man kept on staring blankly. Suddenly he essayed to put his hand to his head, gave a deep groan, and fell back again unconscious.

"He 's gone ag'in," said Dinah. "I reckon we'll hafter tote 'im up ter de house and take keer er 'im dere. W'ite folks would n't want ter fool wid a nigger man, an' we doan know who his folks is. He 's outer his head an' will be fer some time yet, an' we can't tell nuthin' 'bout 'im tel he comes ter his senses."

Cicely lifted the wounded man by the arms and shoulders. She was strong, with the strength of youth and a sturdy race. The man was pitifully emaciated; how much, the two women had not suspected until they raised him. They had no difficulty whatever, except for the awkwardness of such a burden, in lifting him over the fence and carrying him through the cornfield to the cabin.

They laid him on Cicely's bed in the little lean-to shed that formed a room separate from the main apartment of the cabin. The old woman sent Cicely to cook the dinner, while she gave her own attention exclusively to the still unconscious man. She brought water and washed him as though he were a child.

"Po' boy," she said, "he doan feel lack he's be'n eatin' nuff to feed a sparrer. He 'pears ter be mos' starved ter def."

She washed his wound more carefully, made some lint,—the art was well known in the sixties,—and dressed his wound with a fair degree of skill.

"Somebody must 'a' be'n tryin' ter put yo' light out, chile," she muttered to herself as she adjusted the bandage around his head. "A little higher er a little lower, an' you would n' 'a' be'n yere ter tell de tale. Dem clo's," she argued, lifting the tattered garments she had removed from her patient, "don' b'long 'roun' yere. Dat kinder weavin' come f'om down to'ds Souf Ca'lina. I wish Needham 'u'd come erlong. He kin tell who dis man is, an' all erbout 'im."

She made a bowl of gruel, and fed it, drop by drop, to the sick man. This roused him somewhat from his stupor, but when Dinah thought he had enough of the gruel, and stopped feeding him, he closed his eyes again and relapsed into a heavy sleep that was so closely akin to unconsciousness as to be scarcely distinguishable from it.

When old Needham came home at noon, his wife, who had been anxiously awaiting his return, told him in a few words the story of Cicely's discovery and of the subsequent events.

Needham inspected the stranger with a professional eye. He had been something of a plantation doctor in his day, and was known far and wide for his knowledge of simple remedies. The negroes all around, as well as many of the poorer white people, came to him for the treatment of common ailments.

"He's got a fevuh," he said, after feeling the patient's pulse and laying his hand on his brow, "an' we'll hafter gib 'im some yarb tea an' nuss 'im tel de fevuh w'ars off. I 'spec',," he added, "dat I knows whar dis boy come f'om. He 's mos' lackly one er dem bright mulatters, f 'om Robeson County—some of 'em call deyse'ves Croatan Injins—w'at's been conscripted an' sent ter wu'k on de fo'tifications down at Wimbleton er some'er's er nuther, an' done 'scaped, and got mos' killed gittin' erway, an' wuz n' none too well fed befo', an' nigh 'bout starved ter def sence. We'll hafter hide dis man, er e'se we is lackly ter git inter trouble ou'se'ves by harb'rin' 'im. Ef dey ketch 'im yere, dey's liable ter take 'im out an' shoot 'im—an' des ez lackly us too."

Cicely was listening with bated breath.

"Oh, gran'daddy," she cried with trembling voice, "don' let 'em ketch 'im! Hide 'im somewhar."

"I reckon we'll leave 'im yere fer a day er so. Ef he had come f'om roun' yere I'd be skeered ter keep 'im, fer de w'ite folks 'u'd prob'ly be lookin' fer 'im. But I knows ev'ybody w'at's be'n conscripted fer ten miles 'roun', an' dis yere boy don' b'long in dis neighborhood. W'en 'e gits so 'e kin he'p 'isse'f we'll put 'im up in de lof' an' hide 'im till de Yankees come. Fer dey're comin' sho'. I dremp' las' night dey wuz close ter han', and I hears de w'ite folks talkin' ter deyse'ves 'bout it. An' de time is comin' w'en de good Lawd gwine ter set His people free, an' it ain' gwine ter be long, nuther."

Needham's prophecy proved true. In less than a week the Confederate garrison evacuated the arsenal in the neighboring town of Patesville,[19] blew up the buildings, destroyed the ordnance and stores, and retreated across the Cape Fear River, burning the river bridge behind them,—two acts of war afterwards unjustly attributed to General Sherman's army, which followed close upon the heels of the retreating Confederates.

When there was no longer any fear for the stranger's safety, no more pains were taken to conceal him. His wound had healed rapidly, and in a week he had been able with some help to climb up the ladder into the loft. In all this time, however, though apparently conscious, he had said no word to any one, nor had he seemed to comprehend a word that was spoken to him.

Cicely had been his constant attendant. After the first day, during which her granny had nursed him, she had sat by his bedside, had fanned his fevered brow, had held food and water and medicine to his lips. When it was safe for him to come down from the loft and sit in a chair under a spreading oak, Cicely supported him until he was strong enough to walk about the yard. When his strength had increased sufficiently to permit of greater exertion, she accompanied him on long rambles in the fields and woods.

In spite of his gain in physical strength, the newcomer changed very little in other respects. For a long time he neither spoke nor smiled. To questions put to him he simply gave no reply, but looked at his questioner with the blank unconsciousness of an infant. By and by he began to recognize Cicely, and to smile at her approach. The next step in returning consciousness was but another manifestation of the same sentiment. When Cicely would leave him he would look his regret, and be restless and uneasy until she returned.

The family were at a loss what to call him. To any inquiry as to his name he answered no more than to other questions.

"He come jes' befo' Sherman," said Needham, after a few weeks, "lack John de Baptis' befo' de Lawd. I reckon we bettah call 'im John."

So they called him John. He soon learned the name. As time went on Cicely found that he was quick at learning things. She taught him to speak her own negro English, which he pronounced with absolute fidelity to her intonations; so that barring the quality of his voice, his speech was an echo of Cicely's own.

The summer wore away and the autumn came. John and Cicely wandered in the woods together and gathered walnuts, and chinquapins and wild grapes. When harvest time came, they worked in the fields side by side,—plucked the corn, pulled the fodder, and gathered the dried peas from the yellow pea-vines. Cicely was a phenomenal cotton-picker, and John accompanied her to the fields and stayed by her hours at a time, though occasionally he would complain of his head, and sit under a tree and rest part of the day while Cicely worked, the two keeping one another always in sight.

They did not have a great deal of intercourse with other people. Young men came to the cabin sometimes to see Cicely, but when they found her entirely absorbed in the stranger they ceased their visits. For a time Cicely kept him away, as much as possible, from others, because she did not wish them to see that there was anything wrong about him. This was her motive at first, but after a while she kept him to herself simply because she was happier so. He was hers—hers alone. She had found him, as Pharaoh's daughter had found Moses in the bulrushes; she had taught him to speak, to think, to love. She had not taught him to remember; she would not have wished him to; she would have been jealous of any past to which he might have proved bound by other ties. Her dream so far had come true. She had found him; he loved her. The rest of it would as surely follow, and that before long. For dreams were serious things, and time had proved hers to have been not a presage of misfortune, but one of the beneficent visions that are sent, that we may enjoy by anticipation the good things that are in store for us.

III

But a short interval of time elapsed after the passage of the warlike host that swept through North Carolina, until there appeared upon the scene the vanguard of a second army, which came to bring light and the fruits of liberty to a land which slavery and the havoc of war had brought to ruin. It is fashionable to assume that those who undertook the political rehabilitation of the Southern States merely rounded out the ruin that the war had wrought—merely ploughed up the desolate land and sowed it with salt. Perhaps the gentler judgments of the future may recognize that their task was a difficult one, and that wiser and honester men might have failed as egregiously. It may even, in time, be conceded that some good came out of the carpet-bag governments, as, for instance, the establishment of a system of popular education in the former slave States. Where it had been a crime to teach people to read or write, a schoolhouse dotted every hillside, and the State provided education for rich and poor, for white and black alike. Let us lay at least this token upon the grave of the carpet-baggers. The evil they did lives after them, and the statute of limitations does not seem to run against it. It is but just that we should not forget the good.

Long, however, before the work of political reconstruction had begun, a brigade of Yankee schoolmasters and schoolma'ams had invaded Dixie, and one of the latter had opened a Freedman's Bureau School in the town of Patesville, about four miles from Needham Green's cabin on the neighboring sandhills.

It had been quite a surprise to Miss Chandler's Boston friends when she had announced her intention of going South to teach the freedmen. Rich, accomplished, beautiful, and a social favorite, she was giving up the comforts and luxuries of Northern life to go among hostile strangers, where her associates would be mostly ignorant negroes. Perhaps she might meet occasionally an officer of some Federal garrison, or a traveler from the North; but to all intents and purposes her friends considered her as going into voluntary exile. But heroism was not rare in those days, and Martha Chandler was only one of the great multitude whose hearts went out toward an oppressed race, and who freely poured out their talents, their money, their lives,—whatever God had given them,—in the sublime and not unfruitful effort to transform three millions of slaves into intelligent freemen. Miss Chandler's friends knew, too, that she had met a great sorrow, and more than suspected that out of it had grown her determination to go South.

When Cicely Green heard that a school for colored people had been opened at Patesville she combed her hair, put on her Sunday frock and such bits of finery as she possessed, and set out for town early the next Monday morning.

There were many who came to learn the new gospel of education, which was to be the cure for all the freedmen's ills. The old and gray-haired, the full-grown man and woman, the toddling infant,—they came to acquire the new and wonderful learning that was to make them the equals of the white people. It was the teacher's task, by no means an easy one, to select from this incongruous mass the most promising material, and to distribute among them the second-hand books and clothing that were sent, largely by her Boston friends, to aid her in her work; to find out what they knew, to classify them by their intelligence rather than by their knowledge, for they were all lamentably ignorant. Some among them were the children of parents who had been free before the war, and of these some few could read and one or two could write. One paragon, who could repeat the multiplication table, was immediately promoted to the position of pupil teacher.

Miss Chandler took a liking to the tall girl who had come so far to sit under her instruction. There was a fine, free air in her bearing, a lightness in her step, a sparkle in her eye, that spoke of good blood,—whether fused by nature in its own alembic, out of material despised and spurned of men, or whether some obscure ancestral strain, the teacher could not tell. The girl proved intelligent and learned rapidly, indeed seemed almost feverishly anxious to learn. She was quiet, and was, though utterly untrained, instinctively polite, and profited from the first day by the example of her teacher's quiet elegance. The teacher dressed in simple black. When Cicely came back to school the second day, she had left off her glass beads and her red ribbon, and had arranged her hair as nearly like the teacher's as her skill and its quality would permit.

The teacher was touched by these efforts at imitation, and by the intense devotion Cicely soon manifested toward her. It was not a sycophantic, troublesome devotion, that made itself a burden to its object. It found expression in little things done rather than in any words the girl said. To the degree that the attraction was mutual, Martha recognized in it a sort of freemasonry of temperament that drew them together in spite of the differences between them. Martha felt sometimes, in the vague way that one speculates about the impossible, that if she were brown, and had been brought up in North Carolina, she would be like Cicely; and that if Cicely's ancestors had come over in the *Mayflower*, and Cicely had been reared on Beacon Street, in the shadow of the State House dome, Cicely would have been very much like herself.

Miss Chandler was lonely sometimes. Her duties kept her occupied all day. On Sundays she taught a Bible class in the school-room. Correspondence with bureau officials and friends at home furnished her with additional occupation. At times, nevertheless, she felt a longing for the company of women of her own race; but the white ladies of the town did not call, even in the most formal way, upon the Yankee school-teacher. Miss Chandler was therefore fain to do the best she could with such companionship as was available. She took Cicely to her home occasionally, and asked her once to stay all night. Thinking, however, that she detected a reluctance on the girl's part to remain away from home, she did not repeat her invitation.

Cicely, indeed, was filling a double rôle. The learning acquired from Miss Chandler she imparted to John at home. Every evening, by the light of the pine-knots blazing on Needham's ample hearth, she taught John to read the simple words she had learned during the day. Why she did not take him to school she had never asked herself; there were several other pupils as old as he seemed to be. Perhaps she still thought it necessary to protect him from curious remark. He worked with Needham by day, and she could see him at night, and all of Saturdays and Sundays. Perhaps it was the jealous selfishness of love. She had found him; he was hers. In the spring, when school was over, her granny had said that she might marry him. Till then her dream would not yet have come true, and she must keep him to herself. And yet she did not wish him to lose this golden key to the avenues of opportunity. She would not take him to school, but she would teach him each day all that she herself had learned. He was not difficult to teach, but learned, indeed, with what seemed to Cicely marvelous ease,—always, however, by her lead, and never of his own initiative. For while he could do a man's work, he was in most things but a child, without a child's curiosity. His love for Cicely appeared the only thing for which he needed no suggestion; and even that possessed an element of childish dependence that would have seemed, to minds trained to thoughtful observation, infinitely pathetic.

The spring came and cotton-planting time. The children began to drop out of Miss Chandler's school one by one, as their services were required at home. Cicely was among those who intended to remain in school until the term closed with the "exhibition," in which she was assigned a leading part. She had selected her recitation, or "speech," from among half a dozen poems that her teacher had suggested, and to memorizing it she devoted considerable time and study. The exhibition, as the first of its kind, was sure to be a notable event. The parents and friends of the children were invited to attend, and a colored church, recently erected,—the largest available building,—was secured as the place where the exercises should take place.

On the morning of the eventful day, uncle Needham, assisted by John, harnessed the mule to the two-wheeled cart, on which a couple of splint-bottomed chairs were fastened to accommodate Dinah and Cicely. John put on his best clothes,—an ill-fitting suit of blue jeans,—a round wool hat, a pair of coarse brogans, a homespun shirt, and a bright blue necktie. Cicely wore her best frock, a red ribbon at her throat, another in her hair, and carried a bunch of flowers in her hand. Uncle Needham and aunt Dinah were also in holiday array. Needham and John took their seats on opposite sides of the cart-frame, with their feet dangling down, and thus the equipage set out leisurely for the town.

Cicely had long looked forward impatiently to this day. She was going to marry John the next week, and then her dream would have come entirely true. But even this anticipated happiness did not overshadow the importance of the present occasion, which would be an epoch in her life, a day of joy and triumph. She knew her speech perfectly, and timidity was not one of her weaknesses. She knew that the red ribbons set off her dark beauty effectively, and that her dress fitted neatly the curves of her shapely figure. She confidently expected to win the first prize, a large morocco-covered Bible, offered by Miss Chandler for the best exercise.

Cicely and her companions soon arrived at Patesville. Their entrance into the church made quite a sensation, for Cicely was not only an acknowledged belle, but a general favorite, and to John there attached a tinge of mystery which inspired a respect not bestowed upon those who had grown up in the neighborhood. Cicely secured a seat in the front part of the church, next to the aisle, in the place reserved for the pupils. As the house was already partly filled by townspeople when the party from the country arrived, Needham and his wife and John were forced to content themselves with places somewhat in the rear of the room, from which they could see and hear what took place on the platform, but where they were not at all conspicuously visible to those at the front of the church.

The schoolmistress had not yet arrived, and order was preserved in the audience by two of the elder pupils, adorned with large rosettes of red, white, and blue, who ushered the most important visitors to the seats reserved for them. A national flag was gracefully draped over the platform, and under it hung a lithograph of the Great Emancipator, for it was thus these people thought of him. He had saved the Union, but the Union had never meant anything good to them. He had proclaimed liberty to the captive, which meant all to them; and to them he was and would ever be the Great Emancipator.

The schoolmistress came in at a rear door and took her seat upon the platform. Martha was dressed in white; for once she had laid aside the sombre garb in which alone she had been seen since her arrival at Patesville. She wore a yellow rose at her throat, a bunch of jasmine in her belt. A sense of responsibility for the success of the exhibition had deepened the habitual seriousness of her face, yet she greeted the audience with a smile.

"Don' Miss Chan'ler look sweet," whispered the little girls to one another, devouring her beauty with sparkling eyes, their lips parted over a wealth of ivory.

"De Lawd will bress dat chile," said one old woman, in soliloquy. "I t'ank de good Marster I's libbed ter see dis day."

Even envy could not hide its noisome head: a pretty quadroon whispered to her neighbor:—

"I don't b'liebe she's natch'ly ez white ez dat. I 'spec' she's be'n powd'rin'! An' I know all dat hair can't be her'n; she's got on a switch, sho's you bawn."

"You knows dat ain' so, Ma'y 'Liza Smif," rejoined the other, with a look of stern disapproval; "you *knows* dat ain' so. You'd gib yo' everlastin' soul 'f you wuz ez white ez Miss Chan'ler, en yo' ha'r wuz ez long ez her'n."

"By Jove, Maxwell!" exclaimed a young officer, who belonged to the Federal garrison stationed in the town, "but that girl is a beauty." The speaker and a companion were in fatigue uniform, and had merely dropped in for an hour between garrison duty. The ushers had wished to give them seats on the platform, but they had declined, thinking that perhaps their presence there might embarrass the teacher. They sought rather to avoid observation by sitting behind a pillar in the rear of the room, around which they could see without attracting undue attention.

"To think," the lieutenant went on, "of that Junonian figure, those lustrous orbs, that golden coronal, that flower of Northern civilization, being wasted on these barbarians!" The speaker uttered an exaggerated but suppressed groan.

His companion, a young man of clean-shaven face and serious aspect, nodded assent, but whispered reprovingly,—

" 'Sh! some one will hear you. The exercises are going to begin."

When Miss Chandler stepped forward to announce the hymn to be sung by the school as the first exercise, every eye in the room was fixed upon her, except John's, which saw only Cicely. When the teacher had uttered a few words, he looked up to her, and from that moment did not take his eyes off Martha's face.

After the singing, a little girl, dressed in white, crossed by ribbons of red and blue, recited with much spirit a patriotic poem.

When Martha announced the third exercise, John's face took on a more than usually animated expression, and there was a perceptible deepening of the troubled look in his eyes, never entirely absent since Cicely had found him in the woods.

A little yellow boy, with long curls, and a frightened air, next ascended the platform.

"Now, Jimmie, be a man, and speak right out," whispered his teacher, tapping his arm reassuringly with her fan as he passed her.

Jimmie essayed to recite the lines so familiar to a past generation of schoolchildren:—

"I knew a widow very poor,
Who four small children had;
The eldest was but six years old,
A gentle, modest lad."

He ducked his head hurriedly in a futile attempt at a bow; then, following instructions previously given him, fixed his eyes upon a large cardboard motto hanging on the rear wall of the room, which admonished him in bright red letters to

"ALWAYS SPEAK THE TRUTH,"

and started off with assumed confidence—

"I knew a widow very poor,
Who"—

At this point, drawn by an irresistible impulse, his eyes sought the level of the audience. Ah, fatal blunder! He stammered, but with an effort raised his eyes and began again:

"I knew a widow very poor,
Who four"—

Again his treacherous eyes fell, and his little remaining self-possession utterly forsook him. He made one more despairing effort:—

"I knew a widow very poor,
Who four small"—

and then, bursting into tears, turned and fled amid a murmur of sympathy.

Jimmie's inglorious retreat was covered by the singing in chorus of "The Star-spangled Banner," after which Cicely Green came forward to recite her poem.

"By Jove, Maxwell!" whispered the young officer, who was evidently a connoisseur of female beauty, "that is n't bad for a bronze Venus. I'll tell you"—

" 'Sh!" said the other. "Keep still."

When Cicely finished her recitation, the young officers began to applaud, but stopped suddenly in some confusion as they realized that they were the only ones in the audience so engaged. The colored people had either not learned how to express their approval in orthodox fashion, or else their respect for the sacred character of the edifice forbade any such demonstration. Their enthusiasm found vent, however, in a subdued murmur, emphasized by numerous nods and winks and suppressed exclamations. During the singing that followed Cicely's recitation the two officers quietly withdrew, their duties calling them away at this hour.

At the close of the exercises, a committee on prizes met in the vestibule, and unanimously decided that Cicely Green was entitled to the first prize. Proudly erect, with sparkling eyes and cheeks flushed with victory, Cicely advanced to the platform to receive the coveted reward. As she turned away, her eyes, shining with gratified vanity, sought those of her lover.

John sat bent slightly forward in an attitude of strained attention; and Cicely's triumph lost half its value when she saw that it was not at her, but at Miss Chandler, that his look was directed. Though she watched him thenceforward, not one glance did he vouchsafe to his jealous sweetheart, and never for an instant withdrew his eyes from Martha, or relaxed the unnatural intentness of his gaze. The imprisoned mind, stirred to unwonted effort, was struggling for liberty; and from Martha had come the first ray of outer light that had penetrated its dungeon.

Before the audience was dismissed, the teacher rose to bid her school farewell. Her intention was to take a vacation of three months; but what might happen in that time she did not know, and there were duties at home of such apparent urgency as to render her return to North Carolina at least doubtful; so that in her own heart her *au revoir* sounded very much like a farewell.

She spoke to them of the hopeful progress they had made, and praised them for their eager desire to learn. She told them of the serious duties of life, and of the use they should make of their acquirements. With prophetic finger she pointed them to the upward way which they must climb with patient feet to raise themselves out of the depths.

Then, an unusual thing with her, she spoke of herself. Her heart was full; it was with difficulty that she maintained her composure; for the faces that confronted her were kindly faces, and not critical, and some of them she had learned to love right well.

"I am going away from you, my children," she said; "but before I go I want to tell you how I came to be in North Carolina; so that if I have been able to do anything here among you for which you might feel inclined, in your good nature, to thank me, you may thank not me alone, but another who came before me, and whose work I have but taken up where *he* laid it down. I had a friend,—a dear friend,—why should I be ashamed to say it?—a lover, to whom I was to be married,—as I hope all you girls may some day be happily married. His country needed him, and I gave him up. He came to fight for the Union and for Freedom, for he believed that all men are brothers. He did not come back again—he gave up his life for you. Could I do less than he? I came to the land that he sanctified by his death, and I have tried in my weak way to tend the plant he watered with his blood, and which, in the fullness of time, will blossom forth into the perfect flower of liberty."

She could say no more, and as the whole audience thrilled in sympathy with her emotion, there was a hoarse cry from the men's side of the room, and John forced his way to the aisle and rushed forward to the platform.

"Martha! Martha!"

"Arthur! O Arthur!"

Pent-up love burst the flood-gates of despair and oblivion, and caught these two young hearts in its torrent. Captain Arthur Carey, of the 1st Massachusetts,[20] long since reported missing, and mourned as dead, was restored to reason and to his world.

It seemed to him but yesterday that he had escaped from the Confederate prison at Salisbury;[21] that in an encounter with a guard he had received a wound in the head; that he had wandered on in the woods, keeping himself alive by means of wild berries, with now and then a piece of bread or a potato from a friendly negro. It seemed but the night before that he had laid himself down, tortured with fever, weak from loss of blood, and with no hope that he would ever rise again. From that moment his memory of the past was a blank until he recognized Martha on the platform and took up again the thread of his former existence where it had been broken off.

And Cicely? Well, there is often another woman, and Cicely, all unwittingly to Carey or to Martha, had been the other woman. For, after all, her beautiful dream had been one of the kind that go by contraries.

Notes

1 Maris A. Vinovskis, "Have Social Historians Lost the Civil War? Some Preliminary Demographic Speculations," in Vinovskis, ed., *Toward a Social History of the American Civil War* (Cambridge: Cambridge University Press, 1990), 1–30.

2 James Marten, ed., *Children and Youth During the Civil War Era* (New York: New York University Press, 2012), 2–3.

3 Paul A. Cimbala and Randall M. Miller, eds. *Union Soldiers and the Northern Home Front: Wartime Experiences, Postwar Adjustments* (New York: Fordham University Press, 2002), xii.

4 LeeAnn Whites, "The Civil War as a Crisis in Gender" and Jeanie Attie, "Warwork and the Crisis of Domesticity in the North," in Catherine Clinton and Nina Silber, eds., *Divided Houses: Gender and the Civil War* (New York: Oxford University Press, 1992).

5 Joan E. Cashin, ed., *The War Was You and Me: Civilians in the American Civil War* (Princeton, NJ: Princeton University Press, 2002), 3.

6 George C. Rable, *Civil Wars: Women and the Crisis of Southern Nationalism* (Urbana: University of Illinois Press, 1989), 241.

7 Friedrich August Gottreu Tholuck (1799–1877), Protestant theologian who emphasized the experience of faith rather than religious dogma.

8 Nicknamed the "Swedish Nightingale," the soprano Jenny Lind (1820–1887) became a celebrity after her singing tour of the United States in 1850–1852.

9 Nat Turner led the 1831 slave uprising at Southampton, Virginia. See Thomas Gray's *The Confessions of Nat Turner* (1831): "I saw white spirits and black spirits engaged in battle, and the sun was darkened—the thunder rolled in the Heavens, and blood flowed in streams" (10); "and shortly afterwards, while laboring in the field, I discovered drops of blood on the corn as though it were dew from heaven" (10).

10 The first viable mechanized loom, named after Joseph Marie Jacquard (1752–1834) of Lyons, France.

11 "The popular song 'Hear me, Norma' was based on Vincenzo Bellini's opera *Norma* (1832). Piatt may be suggesting that like the opera's Druidic heroine, secretly involved in a liaison with the Roman proconsul of Britain, the speaker took a lover from among the enemy" (Paula Bernat Bennett, ed., *Palace-Burner*, 163, n.5).

12 See Alfred Lord Tennyson's "The Lady of Shalott."

13 In July 1862, after a number of military setbacks in the Eastern theater, the Lincoln administration called for the enlistment of 300,000 three-month volunteers. Over the course of the war, Waterville, Maine, contributed more than its fair share of men—as many as 525, by one count—to the Union Army (see Isaac S. Bangs, *Military History of Waterville, Maine* [Augusta, Maine, 1902], 34).

14 See I Corinthians 13:12: "For now we see through a glass, darkly; but then face to face: now I know in part; but then shall I know even as also I am known."

15 See Matthew 16:25 ("For whosoever will save his life shall lose it: and whosoever will lose his life for my sake shall find it") and Luke 9:24 ("For whosoever will save his life shall lose it: but whosoever will lose his life for my sake, the same shall save it").

16 The Minié ball was a more accurate bullet, designed to expand and spin upon firing, introduced in the spring of 1863.

17 The 8th Wisconsin Infantry took its nickname from its mascot "Old Abe," a bald eagle. The regiment participated in battles and skirmishes at Corinth, Farmington, Vicksburg, and elsewhere in the Western theater.

18 Large portrait photographs.

19 "Patesville" is Chesnutt's fictionalized version of Fayeteville, N.C., which also appears in other of his works, including "The Goophered Grapevine" and *The House Behind the Cedars*. The massive federal arsenal at Fayetteville, seized by North Carolina troops in April 1861, became one of the Confederacy's military gems, specializing in the manufacture of rifles. Chesnutt's history is not quite accurate, however: Confederate troops did remove stores and destroy some equipment as Sherman advanced on Fayetteville, but it remains true that the Union general ordered its completed destruction in March, 1865.

20 The First Massachusetts Volunteer Cavalry. Its sharpest combat experience came at the battle of Aldie, Virginia, on June 17, 1863, where it suffered 66 casualties, including a Lt. Hugh Carey, and lost 88 prisoners.

21 Located in the small town of Salisbury, North Carolina, this prison camp, like its larger, more infamous counterpart at Andersonville, became a graveyard for thousands of Union troops. After the breakdown of prisoner exchanges in 1864, Salisbury was quickly overrun by inmates, many of whom escaped by tunneling out, but many more of whom succumbed to disease and malnourishment.

The Texts

Harriet Beecher Stowe, "The Chimney-Corner." Source: *The Atlantic Monthly*, vol. 15 no. 87 (January 1865), pp. 109–115.

Walt Whitman, "Come Up from the Fields, Father." Source: *Walt Whitman's Drum-Taps* (New York, s.n., 1865). Not substantially revised in subsequent editions of *Leaves of Grass*.

Julia Ward Howe, "Our Orders." Source: *From Sunset Ridge: Poems Old and New, by Julia Ward Howe* (Boston and New York: Houghton, Mifflin and Company; Cambridge: The Riverside Press, 1898).

Sarah Morgan Bryan Piatt, "Giving Back the Flower." Source: *Palace-Burner: The Selected Poetry of Sarah Piatt*, ed. Paula Bernat Bennett (Urbana: University of Illinois Press, 2001). Originally published in *The Galaxy* vol. 3, no. 4 (February 15, 1867), p. 409.

Lucy Larcom, "Weaving" and "A Loyal Woman's No." Source: *The Poetical Works of Lucy Larcom. Household Edition. With Illustrations* (Boston and New York: Houghton, Mifflin and Company, 1890).

Edward Bellamy, "An Echo of Antietam." Source: *The Blindman's World and Other Stories* (Boston: Houghton Mifflin, 1898). Originally published in *The Century Illustrated Monthly Magazine* (New York), vol. 38 (July 1889), 374–381.

Hamlin Garland, "The Return of a Private." Source: *Main-Travelled Roads* (New York: Harper & Brothers, 1899). Originally published as *Main-Travelled Roads: Six Mississippi Valley Stories* (Boston: Arena, 1891; New York: Harper & Row, 1891). Title-page epigraph: "On the road leading 'back to God's country' and wife and babies."

Kate Chopin, "A Wizard from Gettysburg." Source: *Bayou Folk* (Boston and New York: Houghton, Mifflin and Co.; Cambridge: The Riverside Press, 1894). Originally published in *Youth's Companion* (July 7, 1892).

Charles Chesnutt, "Cicely's Dream." Source: *The Wife of His Youth, and Other Stories of the Color Line* (Boston and New York: Houghton, Mifflin and Co., 1899).

V
Reconstructing

Charleston, S.C. The Mills House, with adjacent ruins. April 1865. Photographer: George Barnard. Library of Congress Prints and Photographs Division, LC-DIG-cwpb-02353

Introduction

In 1862, only a year into the conflict, the fire-breathing Richmond journalist Edward Pollard published a work titled *Southern History of the War: The First Year of the War*— which he later followed up with histories of the second, third, and fourth years. Pollard's choice of titles is intriguing, because it reveals an instinctive awareness that this war would have different histories written about it, and that he should get his into print, quickly. Pollard stands, in this sense, at the very head of a decades-long cultural effort, involving many actors and many agendas, to fix the place of the Civil War in American public memory. Indeed, that effort continues to this very day. New popular books and scholarly studies, though ranging widely in topic, disciplinary background, and ideological orientation, all enter into the struggle to influence how Americans understand the war, and therefore how our collective past will shape our modern cultural politics.

The theme of this section is reconstruction, in the fullest sense of the word. It refers both to the challenges of rebuilding the nation, particularly the South, in the aftermath of the war, and to the ways in which the war is reconstructed in memory, imagination, and representation. The former process, involving everything from the political reorganization of former Confederate states to the management of veterans' pensions to the belated interment of the remains of thousands of soldiers, was halting, violently controversial, frequently mismanaged, and often deemed a "failure," at least in the sense that the nation's racial wounds and pathologies were far from healed. Yet the United States did rebuild, and by the turn of the century its economic, political, and military consolidation enabled the country to assert itself forcefully in world affairs, most notably in the Spanish–American War of 1898 and soon after in the First World War. To get there, however, the United States also had to confront the psychosocial legacy of the Civil War, and while that often meant coming to terms with the war's causes and complexities, it also produced all manner of evasions and suppressions. Reconstructing the war for public memory (and consumption) proved to be an exercise not only of remembrance but of amnesia.

On April 15, 1865, a President lay dead in the Petersen House across from Ford's Theatre; the South lay literally in ruins; and at least 1.1 million Americans lay dead or wounded. At no other moment in its history has the United States confronted anything close to that kind of devastation, and the country's ability to move forward had much to do with explaining to itself the meaning of the ordeal through which it had passed. For what purpose had so many people suffered and died? What kind of place would the nation become, and what kind should it become, now that the violence had ceased? How should the war dead be remembered? Had the war fully resolved the conflicts that produced it, and if not, then what?

Such questions grew insistent in the late nineteenth century, and the writings collected in this section suggest how the meanings of the war, still unsettled, were interpreted and reinterpreted by people with very different ideas of American cultural identity. At the same time, they suggest that the desire for national reconciliation, for a release from the agonies of social conflict, made it more difficult to answer those questions honestly. Even for individuals, memory is not a straightforward transcription of the past, but an active process of magnifying certain experiences, distorting or suppressing others, and shaping the lot of them into some kind of coherent story. For an entire society, with many individual memories and interests at stake, the formation of historical memory, of a shared cultural narrative, becomes much more difficult. Rival versions of the past have to be sorted out, prioritized, officially recognized or officially discouraged. Agents of the state must figure out how to allocate limited resources toward commemorating the past and preserving its material traces. Cultural "authorities" in universities, museums, and historical institutions must decide what to emphasize and what to de-emphasize in representing the past. And all the while, every private actor with the means to do so—from a soapbox to a laptop—can seek to influence how the public perceives its own collective history.

The controversial meanings of the Civil War, like those of any other massive social trauma, have been framed by public monuments and memorials, by the activism of private interest groups, and by a torrent of literature and commentary. The main controversy, not surprisingly, concerns the racial dimension of the conflict, and the extent to which the war entailed upon a now unified nation the obligation to secure civil rights in practice as well as in theory. The problem of race did not simply disappear with the Reconstruction amendments. "What the war did not accomplish," Paul Shackel has observed, "was to change the racial ideologies that had developed in American culture over several centuries."[1] Particularly after the withdrawal of federal troops from the South in 1877, the dynamic between war remembrance and the politics of race grew more complex as the widespread desire for national harmony had to contend with racial violence and the resurgence of white supremacism.

Beginning immediately after the war, battlefields, graveyards, and statues became the principal sites of Civil War commemoration and reflection. The very landscape of the country has changed because of efforts to memorialize the war dead and to preserve intact the fields where they fell. From the National Cemetery at Arlington, to the Robert Gould Shaw Memorial on Boston Common, to the Shiloh National Military Park in Tennessee, these *lieux de mémoire* share certain common purposes and principles. They make memory visible, public, and grand. They serve as a link between past, present, and future, embodying the nation's sense of historical continuity. They imply permanence and coherence, in contrast to disorder and deterioration. They call upon us to invest them with emotional power, and to supply the missing context of the events they memorialize.

Similar purposes were served by the postbellum "reminiscence industry." Well into the twentieth century, veterans' groups (principally the Grand Army of the Republic), soldiers' memoirs, and observances of Decoration Day and Memorial Day gave Americans a way of celebrating their common national identity despite the cataclysm of civil war.

Against that background, a number of historians have argued that the processes of memorialization and cultural reconciliation inhibited serious attention to the unfinished business of emancipation. From this perspective, the aura of heroism and sacrifice conjured up by both monuments and retrospective literature can seem like an anaesthetic, serving to neutralize more critical evaluations of the war and its aftermath. In this critique, nostalgia is less an escape from ideology than a *form* of ideology. Other scholars, however, have emphasized the shifting, unruly meanings of memorial sites and texts, suggesting that the very act of remembering served to draw out the conflict. "To commemorate the dead," writes John R. Neff, "was to recall and honor the men themselves, the cause they championed, and especially the relationships between the dead, their cause, and the living."[2] Certainly, the highly ideological edge of both "Lost Cause" writings—offspring of Pollard's *The Lost Cause* (1867), which affirmed the principles of the defeated Confederacy—and the work of such writers as Albion Tourgée who cried out for racial justice, kept the controversy of the war ever simmering.

And finally there are the many authors who sought to explore the war in its broad social impact and its lingering power over the thoughts and lives of individuals. The literary struggle to come to terms with the Civil War meant different things to different people. At times it meant using the power of words to imagine, and help bring into being, a new social reality. At others, it provided a retreat from reality into a less difficult past, or a creative reinterpretation of the past to suit the needs of the present. Most commonly, the postbellum literary response to the Civil War—in scores of novels and hundreds of short stories and poems—focused on the individual experience of war, and the psychological and social consequences of organized destruction. Some memories would not be buried, and they resurfaced throughout the period as claimants to the nation's attention.

Abraham Lincoln, Second Inaugural Address (March 4, 1865)

Washington D.C. was a crowded place for Lincoln's second inauguration—thronged with out-of-town visitors, sick or wounded soliders, army patrols, Confederate deserters, political dignitaries, along with all its regular residents. The end of the war was in sight, and Lincoln recognized that the time for national healing and reconstruction was at hand; hundreds of thousands of Americans lay dead, and there would be calls for punitive policies toward the South. Lincoln, speaking in the Senate chamber because of the day's bad weather, once again turned his poetic and rhetorical skills to the task of defining the national moment, and directing both his listeners and posterity toward certain understandings of the meaning of the war.

Fellow-countrymen:

At this second appearing to take the oath of the presidential office, there is less occasion for an extended address than there was at the first. Then a statement, somewhat in detail, of a course to be pursued, seemed fitting and proper. Now, at the expiration of four years, during which public declarations have been constantly called forth on every point and phase of the great contest which still absorbs the attention and engrosses the energies of the nation, little that is new could be presented. The progress of our arms, upon which all else chiefly depends, is as well known to the public as to myself; and it is, I trust, reasonably satisfactory and encouraging to all. With high hope for the future, no prediction in regard to it is ventured.

On the occasion corresponding to this four years ago, all thoughts were anxiously directed to an impending civil war. All dreaded it – all sought to avert it. While the inaugural address was being delivered from this place, devoted altogether to saving the Union without war, insurgent agents were in the city seeking to destroy it without war – seeking to dissolve the Union, and divide effects, by negotiation. Both parties deprecated war; but one of them would make war rather than let the nation survive; and the other would accept war rather than let it perish. And the war came.

One-eighth of the whole population were colored slaves, not distributed generally over the Union, but localized in the Southern part of it. These slaves constituted a peculiar and powerful interest. All knew that this interest was, somehow, the cause of the war. To strengthen, perpetuate, and extend this interest was the object for which the insurgents would rend the Union, even by war; while the government claimed no right to do more than to restrict the territorial enlargement of it.

Neither party expected for the war the magnitude or the duration which it has already attained. Neither anticipated that the cause of the conflict might cease with, or even before, the conflict itself should cease. Each looked for an easier triumph, and a result less fundamental and astounding. Both read the same Bible, and pray to the same God; and each invokes his aid against the other. It may seem strange that any men should dare to ask a just God's assistance in wringing their bread from the sweat of other men's faces; but let us judge not, that we be not judged. The prayers of both could not be answered – that of neither has been answered fully.

The Almighty has his own purposes. "Woe unto the world because of offenses! for it must needs be that offenses come; but woe to that man by whom the offense cometh!" If we shall suppose that American slavery is one of those offenses which, in the providence of God, must needs come, but which, having continued through his appointed time, he now wills to remove, and that he gives to both North and South, this terrible war, as the woe due to those by whom the offense came, shall we discern therein any departure from those divine attributes which the believers in a living God always ascribe to him? Fondly do we hope – fervently do we pray – that this mighty scourge of war may speedily pass away. Yet, if God wills that it continue, until all the wealth piled by the bond-man's two hundred and fifty years of unrequited toil shall be sunk, and until every drop of blood drawn with the lash shall be paid by another drawn with the sword, as was said three thousand years ago, so still it must be said, "The judgments of the Lord are true and righteous altogether."

With malice toward none; with charity for all; with firmness in the right, as God gives us to see the right, let us strive on to finish the work we are in; to bind up the nation's wounds; to care for him who shall have borne the battle, and for his widow, and his orphan – to do all which may achieve and cherish a just and lasting peace among ourselves, and with all nations.

Elizabeth Keckley, from *Behind the Scenes; or, Thirty years a Slave, and Four Years in the White House* (1868)

Although most scholars agree that Keckley's memoir was to some extent edited by or ghost-written by James Redpath or Hamilton Busbey, two well-known journalists, it remains one of the major works by an African American woman of the nineteenth century. The narrative moves on fairly quickly from describing her childhood as a slave in Virginia, in order to focus on the war years, when Keckley worked as the personal seamstress to Mary Todd Lincoln. In that capacity, she enjoyed unusual access to the President and the First Lady, and particularly to the thoughts and feelings of the latter, during events ranging from the death of the Lincolns' son Willie, through the assassination of the President, to Mary Todd Lincoln's embarrassing attempt in 1867 to relieve her debts by selling her old clothing and jewelry. Here, in addition to the second inaugural, she recounts a remarkable passage in Lincoln's life: his journey to City Point, Virginia, in late March to meet with Ulysses S. Grant, followed by his tour of Richmond on April 4 and 5, 1865, one day after the fall of the Confederate capital and ten days before his assassination.

Chapter 10 – The Second Inauguration

Mrs. Lincoln came to my apartments one day towards the close of the summer of 1864, to consult me in relation to a dress. And here let me remark, I never approved of ladies, attached to the Presidential household, coming to my rooms. I always thought that it would be more consistent with their dignity to send for me, and let me come to them, instead of their coming to me. I may have peculiar notions about some things, and this may be regarded as one of them. No matter, I have recorded my opinion. I cannot forget the associations of my early life. Well, Mrs. Lincoln came to my rooms, and, as usual, she had much to say about the Presidential election.

After some conversation, she asked: "Lizzie, where do you think I will be this time next summer?"

"Why, in the White House, of course."

"I cannot believe so. I have no hope of the re-election of Mr. Lincoln. The canvass is a heated one, the people begin to murmur at the war, and every vile charge is brought against my husband."[3]

"No matter," I replied, "Mr. Lincoln will be re-elected. I am so confident of it, that I am tempted to ask a favor of you."

"A favor! Well, if we remain in the White House I shall be able to do you many favors. What is the special favor?"

"Simply this, Mrs. Lincoln – I should like for you to make me a present of the right-hand glove that the President wears at the first public reception after his second inaugural."

"You shall have it in welcome. It will be so filthy when he pulls it off, I shall be tempted to take the tongs and put it in the fire. I cannot imagine, Lizabeth, what you want with such a glove."

"I shall cherish it as a precious memento of the second inauguration of the man who has done so much for my race. He has been a Jehovah to my people – has lifted them out of bondage, and directed their footsteps from darkness into light. I shall keep the glove, and hand it down to posterity."

"You have some strange ideas, Lizabeth. Never mind, you shall have the glove; that is, if Mr. Lincoln continues President after the 4th of March next."

I held Mrs. Lincoln to her promise. That glove is now in my possession, bearing the marks of the thousands of hands that grasped the honest hand of Mr. Lincoln on that eventful night. Alas! it has become a prouder, sadder memento than I ever dreamed – prior to making the request – it would be.

In due time the election came off, and all of my predictions were verified. The loyal States decided that Mr. Lincoln should continue at the nation's helm. Autumn faded, winter dragged slowly by, and still the country resounded with the clash of arms. The South was suffering, yet suffering was borne with heroic determination, and the army continued to present a bold, defiant front. With the first early breath of spring, thousands of people gathered in Washington to witness the second inauguration of Abraham Lincoln as President of the United States. It was a stirring day in the National Capital, and one that will never fade from the memory of those who witnessed the imposing ceremonies. The morning was dark and gloomy; clouds hung like a pall in the sky, as if portending some great disaster. But when the President stepped forward to receive the oath of office, the clouds parted, and a ray of sunshine streamed from the heavens to fall upon and gild his face. It is also said that a brilliant star was seen at noon-day. It was the noon-day of life with Mr. Lincoln, and the star, as viewed in the light of subsequent events, was emblematic of a summons from on high. This was Saturday, and on Monday evening I went to the White House to dress Mrs. Lincoln for the first grand levee. While arranging Mrs. L.'s hair, the President came in. It was the first time I had seen him since the inauguration, and I went up to him, proffering my hand with words of congratulation.

He grasped my outstretched hand warmly, and held it while he spoke: "Thank you. Well, Madam Elizabeth" – he always called me Madam Elizabeth – "I don't know whether I should feel thankful or not. The position brings with it many trials. We do not know what we are destined to pass through. But God will be with us all. I put my trust in God." He dropped my hand, and with solemn face walked across the room and took his seat on the sofa. Prior to this I had congratulated Mrs. Lincoln, and she had answered with a sigh, "Thank you, Elizabeth; but now that we have won the position, I almost wish it were otherwise. Poor Mr. Lincoln is looking so broken-hearted, so completely worn out, I fear he will not get through the next four years." Was it a presentiment that made her take a sad view of the future? News from the front was never more cheering. On every side the Confederates were losing ground, and the lines of blue were advancing in triumph. As I would look out my window almost every day, I could see the artillery going past on its way to the open space of ground, to fire a salute in honor of some new victory. From every point came glorious news of the success of the soldiers that fought for the Union. And yet, in their private chamber, away from the curious eyes of the world, the President and his wife wore sad, anxious faces.

I finished dressing Mrs. Lincoln, and she took the President's arm and went below. It was one of the largest receptions ever held in Washington. Thousands crowded the halls and rooms of the White House, eager to shake Mr. Lincoln by his hand, and receive a gracious smile from his wife. The jam was terrible, and the enthusiasm great. The President's hand was well shaken, and the next day, on visiting Mrs. Lincoln, I received the soiled glove that Mr. Lincoln had worn on his right hand that night.

Many colored people were in Washington, and large numbers had desired to attend the levee, but orders were issued not to admit them. A gentleman, a member of Congress, on his way to the White House, recognized Mr. Frederick Douglass, the eloquent colored orator, on the outskirts of the crowd.

"How do you do, Mr. Douglass? A fearful jam to-night. You are going in, of course?"

"No, – that is, no to your last question."

"Not going in to shake the President by the hand! Why, pray?"

"The best reason in the world. Strict orders have been issued not to admit people of color."

"It is a shame, Mr. Douglass, that you should thus be placed under ban. Never mind; wait here, and I will see what can be done."

The gentleman entered the White House, and working his way to the President, asked permission to introduce Mr. Douglass to him.

"Certainly," said Mr. Lincoln. "Bring Mr. Douglass in, by all means. I shall be glad to meet him."

The gentleman returned, and soon Mr. Douglass stood face to face with the President. Mr. Lincoln pressed his hand warmly, saying: "Mr. Douglass, I am glad to meet you. I have long admired your course, and I value your opinions highly."[4]

Mr. Douglass was very proud of the manner in which Mr. Lincoln received him. On leaving the White House he came to a friend's house where a reception was being held, and he related the incident with great pleasure to myself and others.

On the Monday following the reception at the White House, everybody was busy preparing for the grand inaugural ball to come off that night. I was in Mrs. Lincoln's room the greater portion of the day. While dressing her that night, the President came in, and I remarked to him how much Mr. Douglass had been pleased on the night he was presented to Mr. Lincoln. Mrs. L. at once turned to her husband with the inquiry, "Father, why was not Mr. Douglass introduced to me?"

"I do not know. I thought he was presented."

"But he was not."

"It must have been an oversight then, mother; I am sorry you did not meet him."

I finished dressing her for the ball, and accompanied her to the door. She was dressed magnificently, and entered the ball-room leaning on the arm of Senator Sumner,[5] a gentleman that she very much admired. Mr. Lincoln walked into the ball-room accompanied by two gentlemen. This ball closed the season. It was the last time that the President and his wife ever appeared in public.[6]

Some days after, Mrs. Lincoln, with a party of friends, went to City Point[7] on a visit.

Mrs. Lincoln had returned to Washington prior to the 2d of April. On Monday, April 3d, Mrs. Secretary Harlan[8] came into my room with material for a dress. While conversing with her, I saw artillery pass the window; and as it was on its way to fire a salute, I inferred that good news had been received at the War Department. My reception-room was on one side of the street, and my work-room on the other side. Inquiring the cause of the demonstration, we were told that Richmond had fallen. Mrs. Harlan took one of my hands in each of her own, and we rejoiced together. I ran across to my work-room, and on entering it, discovered that the girls in my employ also had heard the good news. They were particularly elated, as it was reported that the rebel capital had surrendered to colored troops. I had promised my employees a holiday when Richmond should fall; and now that Richmond had fallen, they reminded me of my promise.

I recrossed to my reception-room, and Mrs. Harlan told me that the good news was enough for her – she could afford to wait for her dress, and to give the girls a holiday and a treat, by all means. She returned to her house, and I joined my girls in the joy of the long-promised holiday. We wandered about the streets of the city with happy faces, and hearts overflowing with joy.

The clerks in the various departments also enjoyed a holiday, and they improved it by getting gloriously fuddled. Towards evening I saw S., and many other usually clear-headed men, in the street, in a confused, uncertain state of mind.

Mrs. Lincoln had invited me to accompany her to City Point. I went to the White House, and told her that if she intended to return, I would regard it as a privilege to go with her, as City Point was near Petersburg, my old home. Mrs. L. said she designed returning, and would be delighted to take me with her; so it was arranged that I should accompany her.

A few days after we were on board the steamer, *en route* for City Point. Mrs. Lincoln was joined by Mrs. Secretary Harlan and daughter, Senator Sumner, and several other gentlemen.

Prior to this, Mr. Lincoln had started for City Point, and before we reached our destination he had visited Richmond, Petersburg, and other points. We arrived on Friday, and Mrs. Lincoln was much disappointed when she learned that the President had visited the late Confederate capital, as she had greatly desired to be with him when he entered the conquered stronghold. It was immediately arranged that the entire party on board the River Queen should visit Richmond, and other points, with the President. The next morning, after the arrangement was perfected, we were steaming up James River – the river that so long had been impassable, even to our gunboats. The air was balmy, and the banks of the river were beautiful, and fragrant with the first sweet blossoms of spring. For hours I stood on deck, breathing the pure air, and viewing the landscape on either side of the majestically flowing river. Here stretched fair fields, emblematic of peace – and here deserted camps and frowning forts, speaking of the stern vicissitudes of war. Alas! how many changes had taken place since my eye had wandered over the classic fields of dear old Virginia! A birthplace is always dear, no matter under what circumstances you were born, since it revives in memory the golden hours of childhood, free from philosophy, and the warm kiss of a mother. I wondered if I should catch a glimpse of a familiar face; I wondered what had become of those I once knew; had they fallen in battle, been scattered by the relentless tide of war, or were they still living as they lived when last I saw them? I wondered, now that Richmond had fallen, and Virginia been restored to the clustering stars of the Union, if the people would come together in the bonds of peace; and as I gazed and wondered, the River Queen rapidly carried us to our destination.

The Presidential party were all curiosity on entering Richmond. They drove about the streets of the city, and examined every object of interest. The Capitol presented a desolate appearance – desks broken, and papers scattered promiscuously in the hurried flight of the Confederate Congress. I picked up a number of papers, and, by curious coincidence, the resolution prohibiting all free colored people from entering the State of

Virginia. In the Senate chamber I sat in the chair that Jefferson Davis sometimes occupied; also in the chair of the Vice-President, Alexander H. Stephens. We paid a visit to the mansion occupied by Mr. Davis and family during the war,[9] and the ladies who were in charge of it scowled darkly upon our party as we passed through and inspected the different rooms. After a delightful visit we returned to City Point.

That night, in the cabin of the River Queen, smiling faces gathered around the dinner-table. One of the guests was a young officer attached to the Sanitary Commission. He was seated near Mrs. Lincoln, and, by way of pleasantry, remarked: "Mrs. Lincoln, you should have seen the President the other day, on his triumphal entry into Richmond. He was the cynosure of all eyes. The ladies kissed their hands to him, and greeted him with the waving of handkerchiefs. He is quite a hero when surrounded by pretty young ladies."

The young officer suddenly paused with a look of embarrassment. Mrs. Lincoln turned to him with flashing eyes, with the remark that his familiarity was offensive to her. Quite a scene followed, and I do not think that the Captain who incurred Mrs. Lincoln's displeasure will ever forget that memorable evening in the cabin of the River Queen, at City Point.

Saturday morning the whole party decided to visit Petersburg, and I was only too eager to accompany them.

When we arrived at the city, numbers crowded around the train, and a little ragged negro boy ventured timidly into the car occupied by Mr. Lincoln and immediate friends, and in replying to numerous questions, used the word "tote."

"Tote," remarked Mr. Lincoln; "what do you mean by tote?"

"Why, massa, to tote um on your back."

"Very definite, my son; I presume when you tote a thing, you carry it. By the way, Sumner," turning to the Senator, "what is the origin of tote?"

"Its origin is said to be African. The Latin word *totum*, from *totus*, means all – an entire body – the whole."

"But my young friend here did not mean an entire body, or anything of the kind, when he said he would tote my things for me," interrupted the President.

"Very true," continued the Senator. "He used the word tote in the African sense, to carry, to bear. Tote in this sense is defined in our standard dictionaries as a colloquial word of the Southern States, used especially by the negroes."[10]

"Then you regard the word as a good one?"

"Not elegant, certainly. For myself, I should prefer a better word; but since it has been established by usage, I cannot refuse to recognize it."

Thus the conversation proceeded in pleasant style.

Getting out of the car, the President and those with him went to visit the forts and other scenes, while I wandered off by myself in search of those whom I had known in other days. War, grim-visaged war, I soon discovered had brought many changes to the city so well known to me in the days of my youth. I found a number of old friends, but the greater portion of the population were strange to me. The scenes suggested painful memories, and I was not sorry to turn my back again upon the city. A large, peculiarly shaped oak tree, I well remember, attracted the particular attention of the President; it grew upon the outskirts of Petersburg, and as he had discovered it on his first visit, a few days previous to the second, he insisted that the party should go with him to take a look at the isolated and magnificent specimen of the stately grandeur of the forest. Every member of the party was only too willing to accede to the President's request, and the visit to the oak was made, and much enjoyed.

On our return to City Point from Petersburg the train moved slowly, and the President, observing a terrapin basking in the warm sunshine on the wayside, had the conductor stop the train, and one of the brakemen bring the terrapin in to him. The movements of the ungainly little animal seemed to delight him, and he amused himself with it until we reached James River, where our steamer lay. Tad[11] stood near, and joined in the happy laugh with his father.

For a week the River Queen remained in James River, anchored the greater portion of the time at City Point, and a pleasant and memorable week was it to all on board. During the whole of this time a yacht lay in the stream about a quarter of a mile distant, and its peculiar movements attracted the attention of all on board. General Grant and Mrs. Grant were on our steamer several times, and many distinguished officers of the army also were entertained by the President and his party.

Mr. Lincoln, when not off on an excursion of any kind, lounged about the boat, talking familiarly with every one that approached him.

The day before we started on our journey back to Washington, Mr. Lincoln was engaged in reviewing the troops in camp. He returned to the boat in the evening, with a tired, weary look.

"Mother," he said to his wife, "I have shaken so many hands to-day that my arms ache tonight. I almost wish that I could go to bed now."

As the twilight shadows deepened the lamps were lighted, and the boat was brilliantly illuminated; as it lay in the river, decked with many-colored lights, it looked like an enchanted floating palace. A military band was on board, and as the hours lengthened into night it discoursed sweet music. Many officers came on board to say good-by, and the scene was a brilliant one indeed. About 10 o'clock Mr. Lincoln was called upon to make a speech. Rising to his feet, he said:

"You must excuse me, ladies and gentlemen. I am too tired to speak to-night. On next Tuesday night I make a speech in Washington, at which time you will learn all I have to say. And now, by way of parting from the brave soldiers of our gallant army, I call upon the band to play Dixie. It has always been a favorite of mine, and since we have captured it, we have a perfect right to enjoy it." On taking his seat the band at once struck up with Dixie, that sweet, inspiring air; and when the music died away, there were clapping of hands and other manifestations of applause.[12]

At 11 o'clock the last good-by was spoken, the lights were taken down, the River Queen rounded out into the water and we were on our way back to Washington. We arrived at the Capital at 6 o'clock on Sunday evening, where the party separated, each going to his and her own home. This was one of the most delightful trips of my life, and I always revert to it with feelings of genuine pleasure.

Walt Whitman, from *Drum-Taps* (1865)

The Veteran's Vision

While my wife at my side lies slumbering, and the wars are over long,
And my head on the pillow rests at home, and the mystic midnight passes,
And through the stillness, through the dark, I hear, just hear, the breath of my infant,
There in the room, as I wake from sleep, this vision presses upon me;
The engagement opens there and then, in my busy brain unreal;
The skirmishers begin—they crawl cautiously ahead—I hear the irregular snap! snap!
I hear the sounds of the different missiles—the short *t-h-t! t-h-t!* of the rifle-balls;

I see the shells exploding, leaving small white clouds—I hear the great shells
shrieking as they pass;
The grape, like the hum and whirr of wind through the trees, (quick, tumultuous,
now the contest rages!)
All the scenes at the batteries themselves rise in detail before me again,
The crashing and smoking—the pride of the men in their pieces;
The chief gunner ranges and sights his piece, and selects a fuse of the right time;
After firing, I see him lean aside, and look eagerly off to note the effect;
—Elsewhere I hear the cry of a regiment charging—(the young colonel leads himself
this time, with brandish'd sword;)
I see the gaps cut by the enemy's volleys, (quickly fill'd up—no delay;)
I breathe the suffocating smoke—then the flat clouds hover low, concealing all;
Now a strange lull comes for a few seconds, not a shot fired on either side;
Then resumed, the chaos louder than ever, with eager calls, and orders of officers;
While from some distant part of the field the wind wafts to my ears a shout of
applause, (some special success;)
And ever the sound of the cannon, far or near, (rousing, even in dreams, a devilish
exultation, and all the old mad joy, in the depths of my soul;)
And ever the hastening of infantry shifting positions—batteries, cavalry, moving
hither and thither;
(The falling, dying, I heed not—the wounded, dripping and red, I heed not—some
to the rear are hobbling;)
Grime, heat, rush—aid-de-camps galloping by, or on a full run;
With the patter of small arms, the warning *s-s-t* of the rifles, (these in my vision I
hear or see,)
And bombs bursting in air, and at night the vari-color'd rockets.

Walt Whitman, from *Sequel to Drum-Taps* (1865–1866)

When Lilacs Last in the Door-Yard Bloom'd

Lincoln was shot and killed by Confederate sympathizer John Wilkes Booth on April 14, 1865, while attending an evening performance of *Our American Cousin* at Ford's Theatre in Washington D.C. Whitman wrote two poems about the event. This was the first, written in the summer of 1865, and published in October; the second was the regular verse "O Captain! My Captain!", published that November in the *Saturday Press*. After the assassination, Lincoln's body was transported by train to Springfield, Ill., for burial; the funeral cortege, or procession (described in sections 5 and 6 of "Lilacs"), was viewed by millions along the route.

1.

When lilacs last in the dooryard bloom'd,
And the great star early droop'd in the western sky in the night,
I mourn'd . . . and yet shall mourn with ever-returning spring.

O ever-returning spring! trinity sure to me you bring;
Lilac blooming perennial, and drooping star in the west,
And thought of him I love.

2.

O powerful, western, fallen star!
O shades of night! O moody, tearful night!
O great star disappear'd! O the black murk that hides the star!
O cruel hands that hold me powerless! O helpless soul of me!
O harsh surrounding cloud that will not free my soul.

3.

In the door-yard fronting an old farm-house near the white-wash'd palings,
Stands the lilac-bush, tall-growing, with heart-shaped leaves of rich green,
With many a pointed blossom, rising, delicate, with the perfume strong I love,
With every leaf a miracle . . . . . . and from this bush in the dooryard,
With delicate-color'd blossoms, and heart-shaped leaves of rich green,
A sprig, with its flower, I break.

4.

In the swamp, in secluded recesses,
A shy and hidden bird is warbling a song.

Solitary, the thrush,
The hermit, withdrawn to himself, avoiding the settlements,
Sings by himself a song.

Song of the bleeding throat!
Death's outlet song of life—(for well, dear brother, I know,
If thou wast not granted to sing, thou would'st surely die.)

5.

Over the breast of the spring, the land, amid cities,
Amid lanes, and through old woods, (where lately the violets peep'd from the
    ground, spotting the gray debris;)
Amid the grass in the fields each side of the lanes—passing the endless grass;
Passing the yellow-spear'd wheat, every grain from its shroud in the dark-brown
    fields uprising;
Passing the apple-tree blows of white and pink in the orchards;
Carrying a corpse to where it shall rest in the grave,
Night and day journeys a coffin.

6.

Coffin that passes through lanes and streets,
Through day and night, with the great cloud darkening the land,
With the pomp of the inloop'd flags, with the cities draped in black,
With the show of the States themselves, as of crape-veil'd women, standing,
With processions long and winding, and the flambeaus of the night,

With the countless torches lit—with the silent sea of faces, and the unbared heads,
With the waiting depot, the arriving coffin, and the sombre faces,
With dirges through the night, with the thousand voices rising strong and solemn;
With all the mournful voices of the dirges, pour'd around the coffin,
The dim-lit churches and the shuddering organs—Where amid these you journey,
With the tolling, tolling bells' perpetual clang;
Here! coffin that slowly passes,
I give you my sprig of lilac.

7.

(Nor for you, for one alone;
Blossoms and branches green to coffins all I bring:
For fresh as the morning—thus would I chant a song for you, O sane and
    sacred death.

All over bouquets of roses,
O death! I cover you over with roses and early lilies;
But mostly and now the lilac that blooms the first,
Copious, I break, I break the sprigs from the bushes:
With loaded arms I come, pouring for you,
For you and the coffins all of you, O death.)

8.

O western orb, sailing the heaven!
Now I know what you must have meant, as a month since we walk'd,
As we walk'd up and down in the dark blue so mystic,
As we walk'd in silence the transparent shadowy night,
As I saw you had something to tell, as you bent to me night after night,
As you droop'd from the sky low down, as if to my side, (while the other stars all
    look'd on;)
As we wander'd together the solemn night, (for something I know not what, kept me
    from sleep;)
As the night advanced, and I saw on the rim of the west, ere you went, how full you
    were of woe;
As I stood on the rising ground in the breeze, in the cool transparent night,
As I watch'd where you pass'd and was lost in the netherward black of the night,
As my soul in its trouble, dissatisfied, sank, as where you, sad orb,
Concluded, dropt in the night, and was gone.

9.

Sing on, there in the swamp!
O singer bashful and tender! I hear your notes—I hear your call;
I hear—I come presently—I understand you;
But a moment I linger—for the lustrous star has detain'd me;
The star, my comrade, departing, holds and detains me.

10.

O how shall I warble myself for the dead one there I loved?
And how shall I deck my song for the large sweet soul that has gone?
And what shall my perfume be, for the grave of him I love?

Sea-winds blown from east and west,
Blown from the eastern sea and blown from the western sea, till there on the
    prairies meeting:
These, and with these, and the breath of my chant,
I'll perfume the grave of him I love.

11.

O what shall I hang on the chamber walls?
And what shall the pictures be that I hang on the walls,
To adorn the burial-house of him I love?

Pictures of growing spring, and farms, and homes,
With the Fourth-month eve at sundown, and the gray-smoke lucid and bright,
With floods of the yellow gold of the gorgeous, indolent, sinking sun, burning,
    expanding the air;
With the fresh sweet herbage under foot, and the pale green leaves of the trees prolific;
In the distance the flowing glaze, the breast of the river, with a wind-dapple here and there;
With ranging hills on the banks, with many a line against the sky, and shadows;
And the city at hand, with dwellings so dense, and stacks of chimneys,
And all the scenes of life, and the workshops, and the workmen homeward returning.

12.

Lo! body and soul! this land!
Mighty Manhattan, with spires, and the sparkling and hurrying tides, and the ships;
The varied and ample land—the South and the North in the light—Ohio's shores,
    and flashing Missouri,
And ever the far-spreading prairies, cover'd with grass and corn.

Lo! the most excellent sun, so calm and haughty;
The violet and purple morn, with just-felt breezes;
The gentle, soft-born, measureless light;
The miracle, spreading, bathing all—the fulfill'd noon;
The coming eve, delicious—the welcome night, and the stars,
Over my cities shining all, enveloping man and land.

13.

Sing on! sing on, you gray-brown bird!
Sing from the swamps, the recesses—pour your chant from the bushes;
Limitless out of the dusk, out of the cedars and pines.

Sing on, dearest brother—warble your reedy song;
Loud human song, with voice of uttermost woe.
O liquid, and free, and tender!
O wild and loose to my soul! O wondrous singer!
You only I hear . . . . . . yet the star holds me, (but will soon depart;)
Yet the lilac, with mastering odor, holds me.

14.

Now while I sat in the day, and look'd forth,
In the close of the day, with its light, and the fields of spring, and the farmer
      preparing his crops,
In the large unconscious scenery of my land, with its lakes and forests,
In the heavenly aerial beauty, (after the perturb'd winds, and the storms;)
Under the arching heavens of the afternoon swift passing, and the voices
      of children and women,
The many-moving sea-tides,—and I saw the ships how they sail'd,
And the summer approaching with richness, and the fields all busy with
      labor,
And the infinite separate houses, how they all went on, each with its meals and
      minutia of daily usages;
And the streets how their throbbings throbb'd, and the cities pent,—lo! then
      and there,
Falling upon them all, and among them all, enveloping me with the rest,
Appear'd the cloud, appear'd the long black trail;
And I knew Death, its thought, and the sacred knowledge of death.

15.

Then with the knowledge of death as walking one side of me,
And the thought of death close-walking the other side of me,
And I in the middle, as with companions, and as holding the hands of
      companions,
I fled forth to the hiding receiving night, that talks not,
Down to the shores of the water, the path by the swamp in the
      dimness,
To the solemn shadowy cedars, and ghostly pines so still.

And the singer so shy to the rest receiv'd me;
The gray-brown bird I know, receiv'd us comrades three;
And he sang what seem'd the song of death, and a verse for him I love.

From deep secluded recesses,
From the fragrant cedars, and the ghostly pines so still,
Came the singing of the bird.

And the charm of the singing rapt me,
As I held, as if by their hands, my comrades in the night;
And the voice of my spirit tallied the song of the bird.

16.

Come, lovely and soothing Death,
Undulate round the world, serenely arriving, arriving,
In the day, in the night, to all, to each,
Sooner or later, delicate Death.

Prais'd be the fathomless universe,
For life and joy, and for objects and knowledge curious;
And for love, sweet love—But praise! O praise and praise,
For the sure-enwinding arms of cool-enfolding death.

Dark mother, always gliding near, with soft feet,
Have none chanted for thee a chant of fullest welcome?
Then I chant it for thee—I glorify thee above all;
I bring thee a song that when thou must indeed come, come unfalteringly.

Approach, encompassing Death—strong Deliveress!
When it is so—when thou hast taken them, I joyously sing the dead,
Lost in the loving, floating ocean of thee,
Laved in the flood of thy bliss, O Death.

From me to thee glad serenades,
Dances for thee I propose, saluting thee—adornments and feastings
    for thee;
And the sights of the open landscape, and the high-spread sky
    are fitting;
And life and the fields, and the huge and thoughtful night.

The night, in silence, under many a star;
The ocean shore, and the husky whispering wave, whose voice I know;
And the soul turning to thee, O vast and well-veil'd Death,
And the body gratefully nestling close to thee.

Over the tree-tops I float thee a song!
Over the rising and sinking waves—over the myriad fields, and the
    prairies wide;
Over the dense-pack'd cities all, and the teeming wharves and ways,
I float this carol with joy, with joy to thee, O death!

17.

To the tally of my soul,
Loud and strong kept up the gray-brown bird,
With pure, deliberate notes, spreading, filling the night.

Loud in the pines and cedars dim,
Clear in the freshness moist, and the swamp-perfume;
And I with my comrades there in the night.

While my sight that was bound in my eyes unclosed,
As to long panoramas of vision.

18.

I saw the vision of armies;
And I saw, as in noiseless dreams, hundreds of battle-flags;
Borne through the smoke of the battles, and pierc'd with missiles, I saw them,
And carried hither and yon through the smoke, and torn and bloody;
And at last but a few shreds left on the staffs, (and all in silence,)
And the staffs all splinter'd and broken.

I saw battle-corpses, myriads of them,
And the white skeletons of young men—I saw them;
I saw the debris and debris of all dead soldiers;
But I saw they were not as was thought;
They themselves were fully at rest—they suffer'd not;
The living remain'd and suffer'd—the mother suffer'd,
And the wife and the child, and the musing comrade suffer'd,
And the armies that remain'd suffer'd.

19.

Passing the visions, passing the night;
Passing, unloosing the hold of my comrades' hands;
Passing the song of the hermit bird, and the tallying song of my soul,
Victorious song, death's outlet song, (yet varying, ever-altering song,
As low and wailing, yet clear the notes, rising and falling, flooding
    the night,
Sadly sinking and fainting, as warning and warning, and yet again bursting
    with joy,)
Covering the earth, and filling the spread of the heaven,
As that powerful psalm in the night I heard from recesses.

Passing, I leave thee lilac with heart-shaped leaves,
I leave thee there in the door-yard, blooming, returning with spring.

20.

Must I leave thee, lilac with heart-shaped leaves?
Must I leave thee here in the door-yard, blooming, returning with spring?

Must I pass from my song for thee;
From my gaze on thee in the west, fronting the west, communing with thee,
O comrade lustrous, with silver face in the night?

I cease from my song for thee,
From my gaze on thee in the west, fronting the west, communing with thee,
O comrade lustrous with silver face in the night.

21.

Yet each to keep and all, retrievements out of the night,

Yet each I keep, and all;
The song, the wondrous chant of the gray-brown bird, I keep,
And the tallying chant, the echo arous'd in my soul, I keep,
With the lustrous and drooping star, with the countenance full of woe;
With the lilac tall, and its blossoms of mastering odor;
Comrades mine, and I in the midst, and their memory ever I keep—for the dead I
    loved so well;
For the sweetest, wisest soul of all my days and lands . . . and this for his dear sake;
Lilac and star and bird, twined with the chant of my soul,
With the holders holding my hand, nearing the call of the bird,
There in the fragrant pines, and the cedars dusk and dim.

Walt Whitman, from *Specimen Days* (1882)

The Million Dead, Too, Summ'd Up – The Unknown

The Dead in this war—there they lie, strewing the fields and woods and valleys and battle-fields of the south—Virginia, the Peninsula—Malvern Hill and Fair Oaks—the banks of the Chickahominy—the terraces of Fredericksburgh—Antietam bridge—the grisly ravines of Manassas—the bloody promenade of the Wilderness—the varieties of the *strayed* dead, (the estimate of the War department is 25,000 national soldiers kill'd in battle and never buried at all, 5,000 drown'd—15,000 inhumed by strangers, or on the march in haste, in hitherto unfound localities—2,000 graves cover'd by sand and mud by Mississippi freshets, 3,000 carried away by caving-in of banks, &c.,)—Gettysburgh, the West, Southwest—Vicksburgh—Chattanooga—the trenches of Petersburgh—the numberless battles, camps, hospitals everywhere—the crop reap'd by the mighty reapers, typhoid, dysentery, inflammations—and blackest and loathesomest of all, the dead and living burial-pits, the prison-pens of Andersonville, Salisbury, Belle-Isle, &c., (not Dante's pictured hell and all its woes, its degradations, filthy torments, excell'd those prisons)—the dead, the dead, the dead—*our* dead—or South or North, ours all, (all, all, all, finally dear to me)—or East or West—Atlantic coast or Mississippi valley—somewhere they crawl'd to die, alone, in bushes, low gullies, or on the sides of hill—(there, in secluded spots, their skeletons, bleach'd bones, tufts of hair, buttons, fragments of clothing, are occasionally found yet)—our young men once so handsome and so joyous, taken from us—the son from the mother, the husband from the wife, the dear friend from the dear friend—the clusters of camp graves, in Georgia, the Carolinas, and in Tennessee—the single graves left in the woods or by the road-side, (hundreds, thousands, obliterated)—the corpses floated down the rivers, and caught and lodged, (dozens, scores, floated down the upper Potomac, after the cavalry engagements, the pursuit of Lee, following Gettysburgh)—some lie at the bottom of the sea—the general million, and the special cemeteries in almost all the States—the infinite dead—(the land entire saturated, perfumed with their impalpable ashes' exhalation in Nature's chemistry distill'd, and shall be so forever, in every future grain of wheat and ear of corn, and every flower that grows, and every breath we draw)—not only Northern dead leavening

Southern soil—thousands, aye tens of thousands, of Southerners, crumble today in Northern earth.

And everywhere among these countless graves—everywhere in the many soldier Cemeteries of the Nation, (there are now, I believe, over seventy of them)—as at the time in the vast trenches, the depositories of slain, Northern and Southern, after the great battles—not only where the scathing trail passed those years, but radiating since in all the peaceful quarters of the land—we see, and ages yet may see, on monuments and gravestones, singly or in masses, to thousands or tens of thousands, the significant word Unknown.

(In some of the cemeteries nearly *all* the dead are unknown. At Salisbury, N.C., for instance, the known are only 85, while the unknown are 12,027, and 11,700 of these are buried in trenches. A national monument has been put up here, by order of Congress, to mark the spot—but what visible, material monument can ever fittingly commemorate that spot?)

The Real War Will Never Get in the Books

And so good-bye to the war. I know not how it may have been, or may be to others—to me the main interest I found, (and still, on recollection, find,) in the rank and file of the armies, both sides, and in those specimens amid the hospitals, and even the dead on the field. To me the points illustrating the latent personal character and eligibilities of these States, in the two or three millions of American young and middle-aged men, North and South embodied in those armies—and especially the one-third or one-fourth of their number, stricken by wounds or disease at some time in the course of the contest—were of more significance even than the political interests involved. (As so much of a race depends on how it faces death, and how it stands personal anguish and sickness. As, in the glints of emotions under emergencies, and the indirect traits and asides in Plutarch, we get far profounder clues to the antique world than all its more formal history.)

Future years will never know the seething hell and the black infernal background of countless minor scenes and interiors, (not the official surface-courteousness of the Generals, not the few great battles) of the Secession war; and it is best they should not—the real war will never get in the books. In the mushy influences of current times, too, the fervid atmosphere and typical events of those years are in danger of being totally forgotten. I have at night watch'd by the side of a sick man in the hospital, one who could not live many hours. I have seen his eyes flash and burn as he raised himself and recurr'd to the cruelties of his surrender'd brother, and mutilations of the corpse afterward. (See, in the preceding pages, the incident at Upperville—the seventeen kill'd as in the description, were left there on the ground. After they dropt dead, no one touch'd them—all were made sure of, however. The carcasses were left for the citizens to bury or not, as they chose.)

Such was the war. It was not a quadrille in a ball-room.[13] Its interior history will not only never be written—its practicality, minutiæ of deeds and passions, will never be even suggested. The actual soldier of 1862–'65, North and South, with all his ways, his incredible dauntlessness, habits, practices, tastes, language, his fierce friendship, his appetite, rankness, his superb strength and animality, lawless gait, and a hundred unnamed lights and shades of camp, I say, will never be written—perhaps must not and should not be.

The preceding notes may furnish a few stray glimpses into that life, and into those lurid interiors, never to be fully convey'd to the future. The hospital part of the drama from '61 to '65, deserves indeed to be recorded. Of that many-threaded drama, with its sudden and strange surprises, its confounding of prophecies, its moments of despair, the dread of foreign interference, the interminable campaigns, the bloody battles, the mighty and cumbrous and green armies, the drafts and bounties—the immense money expenditure, like a heavy-pouring constant rain—with, over the whole land, the last three years of the struggle, an unending, universal mourning-wail of women, parents, orphans—the marrow of the tragedy concentrated in those Army Hospitals—(it seem'd sometimes as if the whole interest of the land, North and South, was one vast central hospital, and all the rest of the affair but flanges)—those forming the untold and unwritten history of the war—infinitely greater (like life's) than the few scraps and distortions that are ever told or written. Think how much, and of importance, will be—how much, civic and military, has already been—buried in the grave, in eternal darkness.

Herman Melville, from *Battle-Pieces and Aspects of the War* (1866)

An Uninscribed Monument on One of the Battle-fields of the Wilderness

Silence and Solitude may hint
   (Whose home is in yon piney wood)
What I, though tableted, could never tell –
The din which here befell,
   And striving of the multitude.
The iron cones and spheres of death
   Set round me in their rust,
     These, too, if just,
Shall speak with more than animated breath.
   Thou who beholdest, if thy thought,
Not narrowed down to personal cheer,
Take in the import of the quiet here –
   The after-quiet – the calm full fraught;
Thou too wilt silent stand –
Silent as I, and lonesome as the land.

A Requiem for Soldiers Lost in Ocean Transports

When, after storms that woodlands rue,
   To valleys comes atoning dawn,
The robins blithe their orchard-sports renew;
   And meadow-larks, no more withdrawn,
Caroling fly in the languid blue;
The while, from many a hid recess,
Alert to partake the blessedness,
The pouring mites their air dance pursue.
   So, after ocean's ghastly gales,
When laughing light of hoyden morning breaks,
    Every finny hider wakes –
   From vaults profound swims up with glittering scales;
   Through the delightsome sea he sails,
With shoals of shining tiny things
Frolic on every wave that flings

Against the prow its showery spray;
All creatures joying in the morn,
Save them forever from joyance torn,
 Whose bark was lost where now the dolphins play;
Save them that by the fabled shore,
 Down the pale stream are washed away,
Far to the reef of bones are borne;
 And never revisits them the light,
Nor sight of long-sought land and pilot more;
 Nor heed they now the lone bird's flight
Round the lone spar where mid-sea surges pour.

On a Natural Monument in a Field of Georgia

No trophy this – a Stone unhewn,
 And stands where here the field immures
The nameless brave whose palms are won.
Outcast they sleep; yet fame is nigh –
 Pure fame of deeds, not doers;
Nor deeds of men who bleeding die
 In cheer of hymns that round them float:
In happy dreams such close the eye.
But withering famine slowly wore,
 And slowly fell disease did gloat.
Even Nature's self did aid deny;
They choked in horror the pensive sigh.
 Yea, off from home sad Memory bore
(Though anguished Yearning heaved that way),
Lest wreck of reason might befall.
 As men in gales shun the lee shore,
Though there the homestead be, and call,
And thitherward winds and waters sway –
As such lorn mariners, so fared they.
But naught shall now their peace molest.
 Their fame is this: they did endure –
Endure, when fortitude was vain
To kindle any approving strain
Which they might hear. To these who rest,
 This healing sleep alone was sure.

Frederick Douglass, "Reconstruction" (1866)

This essay appeared at a pivotal moment, when a divided federal government had to figure out what policies to pursue vis-à-vis the political reorganization of the South and the citizenship of African Americans. Douglass's immediate subject was the 39th Congress, dominated by Radical Republicans, who in the elections of 1866 had increased their share of the House of Representatives to a veto-proof 77 percent. This meant they could prevail in their chronic bitter fighting with President Andrew Johnson, a Democrat who favored leniency toward the South. Taking advantage of their numbers and the national mood, the Republicans pushed through a series of historic legislative achievements, including the Civil Rights Act of 1866, the Freedmen's Bureau Bill, and the Fourteenth Amendment (to be sent to the states for ratification). Douglass, who had argued in numerous speeches and essays for the strongest possible civil rights policies, wanted to keep the momentum going—against the power of inertia and the inevitability of white supremacist backlash. The urgent need now, he saw, was for the United States to guarantee the vote for blacks, a step which would come in the Fifteenth Amendment, ratified in 1870.

The assembling of the Second Session of the Thirty-ninth Congress may very properly be made the occasion of a few earnest words on the already much-worn topic of reconstruction.

Seldom has any legislative body been the subject of a solicitude more intense, or of aspirations more sincere and ardent. There are the best of reasons for this profound interest. Questions of vast moment, left undecided by the last session of Congress, must be manfully grappled with by this. No political skirmishing will avail. The occasion demands statesmanship.

Whether the tremendous war so heroically fought and so victoriously ended shall pass into history a miserable failure, barren of permanent results, — a scandalous and shocking waste of blood and treasure, — a strife for empire, as Earl Russell characterized it, of no value to liberty or civilization,[14] — an attempt to re-establish a Union by force, which must be the merest mockery of a Union, — an effort to bring under Federal authority States into which no loyal man from the North may safely enter, and to bring men into the national councils who deliberate with daggers and vote with revolvers, and who do not even conceal their deadly hate of the country that conquered them; or whether, on the other hand, we shall, as the rightful reward of victory over treason, have a solid nation, entirely delivered from all contradictions and social antagonisms, based upon loyalty, liberty, and equality, must be determined one way or the other by the present session of Congress. The last session really did nothing which can be considered final as to these questions. The Civil Rights Bill and the Freedmen's Bureau Bill and the proposed constitutional amendments, with the amendment already adopted and recognized as the law of the land, do not reach the difficulty, and cannot, unless the whole structure of the government is changed from a government by States to something like a despotic central government, with power to control even the municipal regulations of States, and to make them conform to its own despotic will. While there remains such an idea as the right of each State to control its own local affairs, — an idea, by the way, more deeply rooted in the minds of men of all sections of the country than perhaps any one other political idea, — no general assertion of human rights can be of any practical value. To change the character of the government at this point is neither possible nor desirable. All that is necessary to be done is to make the government consistent with itself, and render the rights of the States compatible with the sacred rights of human nature.

The arm of the Federal government is long, but it is far too short to protect the rights of individuals in the interior of distant States. They must have the power to protect themselves, or they will go unprotected, spite of all the laws the Federal Government can put upon the national statute-book.

Slavery, like all other great systems of wrong, founded in the depths of human selfishness, and existing for ages, has not neglected its own conservation. It has steadily exerted an influence upon all around it favorable to its own continuance. And to-day it is so strong that it could exist, not only without law, but even against law. Custom, manners, morals, religion, are all on its side everywhere in the South; and when you add the ignorance and servility of the ex-slave to the intelligence and accustomed authority of the master, you have the conditions, not out of which slavery will again grow, but under which it is impossible for the Federal government to wholly destroy it, unless the Federal government be armed with despotic power, to blot out State authority, and to station a Federal officer at every cross-road. This, of course, cannot be done, and ought not even if it could. The true way and the easiest way is to make our government entirely consistent with itself, and give to every loyal citizen the elective franchise, — a right and power which will be ever present, and will form a wall of fire for his protection.

One of the invaluable compensations of the late Rebellion is the highly instructive disclosure it made of the true source of danger to republican government. Whatever may be tolerated in monarchical and despotic governments, no republic is safe that tolerates a privileged class, or denies to any of its citizens equal rights and equal means to maintain them. What was theory before the war has been made fact by the war.

There is cause to be thankful even for rebellion. It is an impressive teacher, though a stern and terrible one. In both characters it has come to us, and it was perhaps needed in both. It is an instructor never a day before its time, for it comes only when all other means of progress and enlightenment have failed. Whether the oppressed and despairing bondman, no longer able to repress his deep yearnings for manhood, or the tyrant, in his pride and impatience, takes the initiative, and strikes the blow for a firmer hold and a longer lease of oppression, the result is the same, — society is instructed, or may be.

Such are the limitations of the common mind, and so thoroughly engrossing are the cares of common life, that only the few among men can discern through the glitter and dazzle of present prosperity the dark outlines of approaching disasters, even though they may have come up to our very gates, and are already within striking distance. The yawning seam and corroded bolt conceal their defects from the mariner until the storm calls all hands to the pumps. Prophets, indeed, were abundant before the war; but who cares for prophets while their predictions remain unfulfilled, and the calamities of which they tell are masked behind a blinding blaze of national prosperity?

It is asked, said Henry Clay, on a memorable occasion, will slavery never come to an end?[15] That question, said he, was asked fifty years ago, and it has been answered by fifty years of unprecedented prosperity. Spite of the eloquence of the earnest Abolitionists, — poured out against slavery during thirty years, — even they must confess, that, in all the probabilities of the case, that system of barbarism would have continued its horrors far beyond the limits of the nineteenth century but for the Rebellion, and perhaps only have disappeared at last in a fiery conflict, even more fierce and bloody than that which has now been suppressed.

It is no disparagement to truth, that it can only prevail where reason prevails. War begins where reason ends. The thing worse than rebellion is the thing that causes rebellion. What that thing is, we have been taught to our cost. It remains now to be seen whether we have the needed courage to have that cause entirely removed from the Republic. At any rate, to this grand work of national regeneration and entire purification Congress must now address itself, with full purpose that the work shall this time be thoroughly done. The deadly upas,[16] root and branch, leaf and fibre, body and sap, must be utterly destroyed. The country is evidently not in a condition to listen patiently to pleas for postponement, however, plausible, nor will it permit the responsibility to be shifted to other shoulders. Authority and power are here commensurate with the duty imposed. There are no cloud-flung shadows to obscure the way. Truth shines with brighter light and intenser heat at every moment, and a country torn and rent and bleeding implores relief from its distress and agony.

If time was at first needed, Congress has now had time. All the requisite materials from which to form an intelligent judgment are now before it. Whether its members look at the origin, the progress, the termination of the war, or at the mockery of a peace now existing, they will find only one unbroken chain of argument in favor of a radical policy of reconstruction. For the omissions of the last session, some excuses may be allowed. A treacherous President stood in the way; and it can be easily seen how reluctant good men might be to admit an apostasy which involved so much of baseness and ingratitude. It was natural that they should seek to save him by bending to him even when he leaned to the side of error. But all is changed now. Congress knows now that it must go on without his aid, and even against his machinations. The advantage of the present session over the last is immense. Where that investigated, this has the facts. Where that walked by faith, this may walk by sight. Where that halted, this must go forward, and where that failed, this must succeed, giving the country whole measures where that gave us half-measures, merely as a means of saving the elections in a few doubtful districts. That Congress saw what was right, but distrusted the enlightenment of the loyal masses; but what was forborne in distrust of the people must now be done with a full knowledge that the people expect and require it. The members go to Washington fresh from the inspiring presence of the people. In every considerable public meeting, and in almost every conceivable way, whether at court-house, school-house, or cross-roads, in doors and out, the subject has been discussed, and the people have emphatically pronounced in favor of a radical policy. Listening to the doctrines of expediency and compromise with pity, impatience, and disgust, they have everywhere broken into demonstrations of the wildest enthusiasm when a brave word has been spoken in favor of equal rights and impartial suffrage. Radicalism, so far from being odious, is now the popular passport to power. The men most bitterly charged with it go to Congress with the largest majorities, while the timid and doubtful are sent by lean majorities, or else left at home. The strange controversy between the President and Congress, at one time so threatening, is disposed of by the people. The high reconstructive powers which he so confidently, ostentatiously, and haughtily claimed, have been disallowed, denounced, and utterly repudiated; while those claimed by Congress have been confirmed.

Of the spirit and magnitude of the canvass nothing need be said. The appeal was to the people, and the verdict was worthy of the tribunal. Upon an occasion of his own selection, with the advice and approval of his astute Secretary, soon after the members of Congress had returned to their constituents, the President quitted the executive mansion, sandwiched himself between two recognized heroes, — men whom the whole country delighted to honor, — and, with all the advantage which such company could give him, stumped the country from the Atlantic to the Mississippi, advocating everywhere his policy as against that of Congress.[17] It was a strange sight, and perhaps the most disgraceful exhibition ever made by any President; but, as no evil is entirely unmixed, good has come of this, as from many others. Ambitious, unscrupulous, energetic, indefatigable, voluble, and plausible, — a political gladiator, ready for a "set-to" in any crowd, — he is beaten in his own chosen field, and stands to-day before the country as a convicted usurper, a political criminal, guilty of a bold and persistent attempt to possess himself of the legislative powers solemnly secured to Congress by the Constitution. No vindication could be more complete, no condemnation could be more absolute and humiliating. Unless reopened by the sword, as recklessly threatened in some circles, this question is now closed for all time.

Without attempting to settle here the metaphysical and somewhat theological question (about which so much has already been said and written), whether once in the Union means always in the Union, — agreeably to the formula, Once in grace always in grace,[18] — it is obvious to common sense that the rebellious States stand to-day, in point of law, precisely where they stood when, exhausted, beaten, conquered, they fell powerless at the feet of Federal authority. Their State governments were overthrown, and the lives and property of the leaders of the Rebellion were forfeited. In reconstructing the institutions of these shattered and overthrown States, Congress should begin with a clean slate, and make clean work of it. Let there be no hesitation. It would be a cowardly deference to a defeated and treacherous President, if any account were made of the illegitimate, one-sided, sham governments hurried into existence for a malign purpose in the absence of Congress. These pretended governments, which were never submitted to the people, and from participation in which four millions of the loyal people were excluded by Presidential order, should now be treated according to their true character, as shams and impositions, and supplanted by true and legitimate governments, in the formation of which loyal men, black and white, shall participate.[19]

It is not, however, within the scope of this paper to point out the precise steps to be taken, and the means to be employed. The people are less concerned about these than the grand end to be attained. They demand such a reconstruction as shall put an end to the present anarchical state of things in the late rebellious States, — where frightful murders and wholesale massacres are perpetrated in the very presence of Federal soldiers. This horrible business they require shall cease. They want a reconstruction such as will protect loyal men, black and white, in their persons and property; such a one as will cause Northern industry, Northern capital, and Northern civilization to flow into the South, and make a man from New England as much at home in Carolina as elsewhere in the Republic. No Chinese wall can now be tolerated. The South must be opened to the light of law and liberty, and this session of Congress is relied upon to accomplish this important work.

The plain, common-sense way of doing this work, as intimated at the beginning, is simply to establish in the South one law, one government, one administration of justice, one condition to the exercise of the elective franchise, for men of all races and colors alike. This great measure is sought as earnestly by loyal white men as by loyal blacks, and is needed alike by both. Let sound political prescience but take the place of an unreasoning prejudice, and this will be done.

Men denounce the negro for his prominence in this discussion; but it is no fault of his that in peace as in war, that in conquering Rebel armies as in reconstructing the rebellious States, the right of the negro is the true solution of our national troubles. The stern logic of events, which goes directly to the point, disdaining all concern for the color or features of men, has determined the interests of the country as identical with and inseparable from those of the negro.

The policy that emancipated and armed the negro — now seen to have been wise and proper by the dullest — was not certainly more sternly demanded than is now the policy of enfranchisement. If with the negro was success in war, and without him failure, so in peace it will be found that the nation must fall or flourish with the negro.

Fortunately, the Constitution of the United States knows no distinction between citizens on account of color. Neither does it know any difference between a citizen of a

State and a citizen of the United States. Citizenship evidently includes all the rights of citizens, whether State or national. If the Constitution knows none, it is clearly no part of the duty of a Republican Congress now to institute one. The mistake of the last session was the attempt to do this very thing, by a renunciation of its power to secure political rights to any class of citizens, with the obvious purpose to allow the rebellious States to disfranchise, if they should see fit, their colored citizens. This unfortunate blunder must now be retrieved, and the emasculated citizenship given to the negro supplanted by that contemplated in the Constitution of the United States, which declares that the citizens of each State shall enjoy all the rights and immunities of citizens of the several States, — so that a legal voter in any State shall be a legal voter in all the States.

Edward A. Pollard, from *The Lost Cause: A New Southern History of the War of the Confederates* (1866)

Like Douglass, Pollard wrote in reaction to the unfolding politics of Reconstruction, as Radical Republicans battled Andrew Johnson, Southern resistance, and Northern war fatigue. But whereas Douglass saw the need for consolidating civil rights gains and recommitting to the cause, Pollard argued that the war had only settled the narrow questions of secession and slavery, not obliterated the South's right to self-determination in political and cultural matters more generally. The South, that is, may have lost the military conflict but could and should still insist on a "war of ideas." Written when the South's devastation—economic, social, psychological—was everywhere abundant (and we have no better description of this than Pollard's own), *The Lost Cause* anticipates much of the tenor of Southern identity through the twentieth century and even to the present, when "neo-Confederate" revisionist history occupies a stubborn niche in American publishing. Pollard's rhetoric tends to the hyperbolic, but there is some sharp analysis here, and a prescient sense of the direction of Southern political culture.

Chapter 44

The record of the war closes exactly with the laying down of the Confederate arms. We do not design to transgress this limit of our narrative. But it will not be out of place to regard generally the political consequences of the war, so far as they have been developed in a formation of parties, involving the further destinies of the country, and in the light of whose actions will probably be read many future pages of American History.

The surrender of Gen. Lee's army was not the simple act of a defeated and over-powered General; it was not the misfortune of an individual. The public mind of the South was fully represented in that surrender. The people had become convinced that the Confederate cause was lost; they saw that the exertions of four years, misdirected and abused, had not availed, and they submitted to what they conceived now to be the determined fortune of the war.

That war closed on a spectacle of ruin, the greatest of modern times. There were eleven great States lying prostrate; their capital all absorbed; their fields desolate; their towns and cities ruined; their public works torn to pieces by armies; their system of labour overturned; the fruits of the toil of generations all swept into a chaos of destruction; their slave property taken away by a stroke of the pen; a pecuniary loss of two thousand millions of dollars involved in one single measure of spoliation—a penalty embraced in one edict, in magnitude such as had seldom been exacted unless in wars synonymous with robberies.

As an evidence of the poverty of the South, produced by the war, we may cite the case of the State of South Carolina. By the census of 1860, the property of the State was value[d] at $400,000,000. Of this, it has been estimated that the injury to the banks, private securities, railroads, cities, houses, plantations, stock, etc., amounted to $100,000,000. There were, by the same census, 400,000 slaves, valued at $200,000,000. This left only $100,000,000 for the value of all the property left in the State; and the principal portion of this consisted of lands, which had fallen in value immensely.

The close of the war presented the Government at Washington with the alternative of two distinct and opposite policies, with reference to the subdued Southern States. One was the policy of the restoration of the Union with reconciliation: the other the policy of restriction. The party that favoured the latter was not long in developing the full extent of its doctrine, which involved universal confiscation at the South, a general execution of prominent men, the disfranchisement of men who acted or sympathized with the Confederates, and the granting of the right of voting to the freed blacks.[20] This hideous programme was announced not only as a just punishment of "rebels," but as a security for the future, and the indispensable condition of the public peace.

But to men who had read the lessons of history it was clearly apparent that this policy would be destructive of the very ends it proposed; that it would increase the acerbity of feeling at the South; that it would deliver the two races over to the most violent discord; and that it would be the occasion of immeasurable chaos and interminable anarchy. It was the immortal BURKE who uttered the great philosophical truth of history: that "liberty, and not despotism, was the cure of anarchy;" and who proposed as the speedy and sovereign remedy for the disorders of the Colonies, that they should be "admitted to a share in the British Constitution."[21]

It was precisely this enlightened lesson which those who agreed in the sentiment of clemency, proposed to apply to the condition of the Southern States. It was this party[22] which took its instruction from exalted schools of statesmanship; which looked at the situation from the eminence of History; and which desired to bind up with the Federal authority the rights, peace, and prosperity of all parts of the country.

Obviously the policy of this party, with reference to what was called "Reconstruction," was to consider the Southern States as in the Union, without any ceremonies or conditions other than what might be found in the common Constitution of the country. What may be designated generally as the Conservative party in the North, had long held the doctrine that, as the Union was inviolable and permanent, secession was illegal, revolutionary, null, and void; that it had no legal validity or effect; that it was the act of seditious individuals, and did not affect the *status* of the States purporting to secede. This branch of their doctrine was accepted by a large number of the Republican party; among them Mr. Seward, the Secretary of State. President Lincoln had acted upon this theory when it became necessary to reorganize States overrun by Federal armies. It was held by the Conservative party, against all rational dispute, that the business of the Federal Government, with respect to the insurgent States, was simply to quell resistance, and to execute everywhere the Constitution and laws. Its contest was not with the States, but with the illegal powers within the States engaged in resisting its authority. When the resistance of these persons ceased, the work was done; and the States were *eo instante, ipso facto,*[23] as much within the Union as ever; no act of re-admission being necessary. It only remained for the judiciary to proceed by indictment and legal trial, under the forms of law, against the individuals who had resisted the authority of the Union to test the fact of treason, and to vindicate the reputation of the Government. And this was the whole extent to which the policy of penalties could be insisted upon.

On this opinion there was soon to be a sharp and desperate array of parties at Washington. When, by the tragical death of President Lincoln, in a public theatre, at the hands of one of the most indefensible but courageous assassins that history has ever produced, the Executive office passed to the Vice-President, Andrew Johnson, the Southern people ignorantly deplored the change as one to their disadvantage, and the world indulged but small expectations from the coming man. The new President was sprung from a low order of life, and was what Southern gentlemen called a "scrub." In qualities of mind it was generally considered that he had the shallowness and fluency of the demagogue; but in this there was a mistake. At any rate, it must be confessed, Mr. Johnson had no literature and but little education of any sort; in his agrarian speeches in the Senate, he quoted "the Lays of Ancient Rome" as "*translated* by Macaulay;"[24] and he was constantly making those mistakes in historical and literary allusions which never fail to characterize and betray self-educated men. Before his elevation to the Presidency, Mr. Johnson was considered a demagogue, who seldom ventured out of common-places, or attempted anything above the coarse sense of the multitude, successful, industrious, a clod-head, a "man of the people," that peculiar product of American politics. But there are familiar instances in history where characters apparently the most common-place and trifling, have been suddenly awakened and elevated as great responsibilities have been thrust upon them, and have risen to the demands of the new occasion. An example of such change was afforded by plain Andrew Johnson, when he stepped to the dignity of President of a restored Union, with all its great historical trusts for him to administer in sight of the world. From that hour the man changed. The eminence did not confound him; he saw before him a part in American history second only to that of George Washington; he left behind him the ambitions and resentments of mere party; he rose as the man who has been secretly, almost unconsciously, great—a common-place among his neighbour, the familiar fellow of the company—suddenly, completely to the full height and dignity of the new destiny that called him. The man who had been twitted as a tailor and condemned as a demagogue, proved a statesman, measuring his actions for the future, insensible to clamour and patient for results.

President Johnson belonged to an intermediate school of politics, standing between the doctrines of Mr. Calhoun and those of Alexander Hamilton.[25] He was never an extreme State-Rights man; he had never recognized the right of nullification, or that of secession; but he was always disposed to recognize, in a liberal degree, the rights of the States, and to combat the theory that the Federal Government absorbed powers and privileges, which, from the foundation of the republic, had been conceded to the States.

It was fortunate that the Chief Magistrate of the country, who was to administer its affairs and determine its course on the close of the war, occupied this medium ground in politics—the one that suggested the practicability of compromise, and assured a conservative disposition in a time of violent and critical dispute. It was natural that on the close of hostilities the tide of public opinion should have set strongly in favour of Consolidation; and that men should apply the precedent of powers used in the war, to the condition of peace. The great question which the war had left, was as to the form and spirit of the Government that ensued upon it—in short, the determination of the question whether the experience of the past four years had been a Constitutional Revolution, or the mere decision of certain special and limited questions. This was the great historical issue. The political controversies which figured in the newspapers were only its incidents; and the questions which agitated Congress all sounded in the great dispute, whether the war had merely accomplished its express and particular objects, or given the American people a change of polity, and dated a new era in their Constitutional history.

At the time these pages are committed to the press, a series of measures has already been accomplished or introduced by the Radical party in the Congress at Washington that would accomplish a revolution in the American system of government, the most thorough and violent of modern times. Propositions have been made so to amend the Constitution as to deprive the States of the power to define the qualifications of electors; propositions to regulate representation by the number of voters, and not of population; propositions to declare what obligations assumed by the States shall be binding on them, and what shall be the purposes of their taxation. What is known as the Civil Rights Bill (passed over the President's veto) has not only established negro equality, but has practically abolished, on one subject of jurisdiction at least, State laws and State courts.[26] In short, the extreme Black Republican party at Washington has sought to disfranchise the whole Southern people, to force negro suffrage upon the South, to prevent the South from being represented in Congress so as to perpetuate the power of the Radicals, and afford them the means of governing the Southern States as conquered and subjugated territories.

The practical fault of all Despotism is that it takes too little into account the sentimentalism which opposes it, and attempts to deal with men as inanimate objects, to which the application of a certain amount of force for a desired end is decisive. It never considers feelings and prejudices. It does not understand that in the science of government there are elements to conciliate as well as forces to compel. The Northern radicals look to the dragoon with his sword, the marshal with his process of confiscation, and the negro thrust into a false position as the pacificators of the country and the appropriate sentinels of the South. They never reflect on the results of such measures upon the feelings of the Southern people; they do not estimate the loss in that estrangement which makes unprofitable companions; they do not imagine the resentments they will kindle; they do not calculate the effect of a constant irritation that at last wears into the hearts of a people, and makes them ready for all desperate enterprises.

If on this subject the Northern people are best addressed in the language of their interests, they may be reminded that the policy of the Radicals is to detain and embarrass the South, not only in the restoration of her political rights, but in her return to that material prosperity, in which the North has a partnership interest, and the Government itself its most important financial stake. The Southern people must be relieved from the apprehension of confiscation, and other kindred measures of oppression, before they can be expected to go to work and improve their condition. They must be disabused of the idea that the new system of labour is to be demoralized by political theories, before giving it their confidence, and enlarging the experiment of it. The troubled sea of politics must be composed before the industry of the South can return to its wonted channels, and reach at last some point of approximation to former prosperity.

The financiers at Washington consider it of the utmost importance that the South should be able to bear its part of the burden of the national debt, and by its products for exchange contribute to the reduction of this debt to a specie basis. The whole edifice of Northern prosperity rests on the unstable foundation of paper credit. Every man in the North is intelligibly interested in the earliest development of the material prosperity of the South. It is not by political agitation that this interest is to be promoted; not under the hand of the Fanaticism that sows the wind that there are to grow up the fruits of industry. When the Southern people obtain political reassurance, and are able to lift the shield of the Constitution over their heads, they will be prepared for the fruitful works of peace; they will be ready then for the large and steady enterprises of industry. All history shows and all reason argues that where a people are threatened with political changes, and live in uncertainty of the future, capital will be timid, enterprise will be content with make-shifts, and labour itself, give but an unsteady hand to the common implements of industry.

He must be blind who does not perceive in the indications of Northern opinion and in the series of legislative measures consequent upon the war the sweeping and alarming tendency to Consolidation. It is not only the territorial unity of the States that is endangered by the fashionable dogma of the day, but the very cause of republican government itself. A war of opinions has ensued upon that of arms, far more dangerous to the American system of liberties than all the ordinances of Secession and all the armed hosts of the Confederates.

The State Rights put in question by the propositions we have referred to in Congress, are not those involved in the issue of Secession, and, therefore, decided against the South by the arbitration of the war. The Radical programme, which we have noted above, points the illustration that the war did not sacrifice the whole body of State Rights, and that there was an important *residuum* of them outside of the issue of Secession, which the people of the South were still entitled to assert, and to erect as new standards of party. It is precisely those rights of the States which a revolutionary party in Congress would deny, namely: to have their Constitutional representation, to decide their own obligations of debt, to have their own codes of crimes and penalties, and to deal with their own domestic concerns, that the Southern States claim have survived the war and are not subjects of surrender.

And it is just here that the people of the South challenge that medium doctrine of State Rights professed by President Johnson to make the necessary explanation, and to distribute the results of the war between North and South. They do not look at the propositions in Congress as involving a mere partisan dispute; they are not disposed to encounter them in a narrow circle of disputation, and make a particular question of what is one grand issue. They regard them in the broad and serious sense of a revolution against the Constitution; a rebellion against all the written and traditionary authority of American statesmanship; a war quite as distinct as that of bayonets and more comprehensive in its results than the armed contest that has just closed.

The following remarks of the President of the United States, do not magnify the occasion. They are historical:

> "The present is regarded as a most critical juncture in the affairs of the nation, scarcely less so than when an armed and organized force sought to overthrow the Government. To attack and attempt the disruption of the Government by armed Combination and military force, is no more dangerous to the life of the nation than an attempt to revolutionize and undermine it by a disregard and destruction of the safeguards thrown around the liberties of the people in the Constitution. My stand has been taken, my course is marked; I shall stand by and defend the Constitution against all who may attack it, from whatever quarter the attack may come. I shall take no step backward in this matter."[27]

An intelligent foreigner, making his observations at Washington at this time, would be puzzled to determine whether the Americans had a Government, or not. There are the names: The Executive, the Congress, the Judiciary; but what is the executive question, what the congressional question, what the judicial queston, it appears impossible to decide. It is a remarkable fact that at Washington to-day, there is not a single well-defined department of political power! There are the paraphernalia and decorations of a government; an elaborate anarchy; but the well-defined distribution of power and the order necessary to administer public affairs appear to have been wholly lost, the charter of the government almost obliterated, and the Constitution overlaid with amendments, which, carried into effect, would hardly leave a vestige of the old instrument or a feature in which could be recognized the work of our forefathers, and the ancient creation of 1789. The controversy thus engendered is something more than a mere question of parties where there are points of coincidence between the contestants sufficient to confine opposition, and where both argue from the common premises of a written constitution. It is something more than the temporary rack and excitement of those partisan difficulties in which the American people have had so much experience of exaggerated dangers and foolish alarms that they are likely to give them attention no longer, but as ephemeral sensations. It is something vastly more than the usual vapours of the political cauldron. When a Congress, representing not much more than a moiety of the American States, and, therefore, in the condition of an unconstitutional authority and factious party, undertakes to absorb the power of the government; to determine Executive questions by its close[d] "Committee of Reconstruction;"[28] to put down the judiciary of the Southern States and by a Freedmen's Bureau, and other devices, erect an *imperium in imperio*[29] in one part of the Union, it is obvious that the controversy is no narrow one of party, that it involves the traditions and spirit of the government, and goes to the ultimate contest of constitutional liberty in America. Regarding these issues, the question comes fearfully to the mind: *Has the past war merely laid the foundation of another?* The pregnant lesson of human experience is that few nations have had their first civil war without having their second; and that the only guaranty against the repetition is to be found in the policy of wise and liberal concessions gracefully made by the successful party. And such reconciliations have been rarest in the republican form of government; for, while generosity often resides in the breast of individual rulers, the history of mankind unhappily shows that it is a rare quality of political parties, where men act in feverish masses and under the dominion of peculiar passions.

To the division of parties in the North—Radicals and Conservatives—there has grown up to some extent a correspondent difference of opinions among the Southern people as to the consequences of the war. But only to a certain extent; for the party in the South that, corresponding to the theory of the Northern Radicals, account themselves entirely at the mercy of a conquering power and taking everything *ex gratia*,[30] is only the detestable faction of time-servers and the servile coterie that attends all great changes in history, and courts the new authority whatever it may be.

There is a better judgment already read by the Southern people of what the war has decided as against themselves. The last memorable remark of Ex-President Davis, when a fugitive, and before the doors of a prison closed upon him,[31] was: "The principle for which we contended is bound to reassert itself, though it may be at another time and in another form."[32] It was a wise and noble utterance, to be placed to the credit of an unfortunate ruler. And so, too, the man, marked above all others as the orator of the South—Henry A. Wise,[33] of Virginia, standing before his countrymen, with his gray hairs and luminous eyes, has recently proclaimed with trumpet-voice that all is not lost, that a great struggle of constitutional liberty yet remains, and that there are still missions of duty and glory for the South.

The people of the South have surrendered in the war what the war has conquered; but they cannot be expected to give up what was not involved in the war, and voluntarily abandon their political schools for the dogma of Consolidation. That dogma, the result has not properly imposed upon them; it has not "conquered ideas." The issues of the war were practical: the restoration of the Union and the abolition of slavery; and only so far as political formulas were necessarily involved in these have they been affected by the conclusion. The doctrine of secession was extinguished; and yet there is something left more than the shadow of State Rights, if we may believe President Johnson, who has recently and officially used these terms, and affirmed in them at least some substantial significance. Even if the States are to be firmly held in the Union; even if the authority of the Union is to be held supreme in *that respect*, it does not follow that it is to be supreme in all other respects; it does not follow that it is to legislate for the States; it does not follow that it is "a national Government over the States and people alike." It is for the South to preserve every remnant of her rights, and even, though parting with the doctrine of secession, to beware of the extremity of surrendering State Rights in gross, and consenting to a "National Government," with an unlimited power of legislation that will consider the States as divided only by imaginary lines of geography, and see in its subjects only "the one people of all the States."

But it is urged that the South should come to this understanding, so as to consolidate the peace of the country, and provide against a "war of ideas." Now a "war of ideas " is what the South wants and insists upon perpetrating. It may be a formidable phrase—"the war of ideas"—but after all, it is a harmless figure of rhetoric, and means only that we shall have parties in the country. We would not live in a country unless there were parties in it; for where there is no such combat, there is no liberty, no animation, no topics, no interest of the twenty-four hours, no theatres of intellectual activity, no objects of ambition. We do not desire the vacant unanimity of despotism. All that is left the South is "the war of ideas." She has thrown down the sword to take up the weapons of argument, not indeed under any banner of fanaticism, or to enforce a dogma, but simply to make the honourable conquest of reason and justice. In such a war there are noble victories to be won, memorable services to performed, and grand results to be achieved. The Southern people stand by their principles. There is no occasion for dogmatic assertion, or fanatical declamation, or inflammatory discourse as long as they have a text on which they can make a sober exposition of their rights, and claim the verdict of the intelligent.

Outside the domain of party politics, the war has left another consideration for the people of the South. It is a remarkable fact that States reduced by war are apt to experience the extinction of their literature, the decay of mind, and the loss of their distinctive forms of thought. Nor is such a condition inconsistent with a gross material prosperity that often grows upon the bloody crust of war. When Greece fell under the Roman yoke, she experienced a prosperity she had never known before. It was an era rank with wealth and material improvement. But her literature became extinct or emasculated; the distinctive forms of her art disappeared; and her mind, once the peerless light of the world, waned into an obscurity from which it never emerged.

It is to be feared that in the present condition of the Southern States, losses will be experienced greater than the immediate inflictions of fire and sword. The danger is that they will lose their literature, their former habits of thought, their intellectual self-asssertion, while they are too intent upon recovering the mere *material* prosperity, ravaged and impaired by the war. There are certain coarse advisers who tell the Southern people that the great ends of their lives now are to repair their stock of national wealth; to bring in Northern capital and labour; to build mills and factories and hotels and gilded caravansaries; and to make themselves rivals in the clattering and garish enterprise of the North. This advice has its proper place. But there are higher objects than the Yankee *magna bona* of money and display, and loftier aspirations than the civilization of material things. In the life of nations, as in that of the individual, there is something better than pelf, and the coarse prosperity of dollars and cents. The lacerated, but proud and ambitious heart of the South will scarcely respond to the mean aspiration of the recusant Governor of South Carolina—Mr. Orr: "I am tired of South Carolina as she was. I court for her the material prosperity of New England. I would have her acres teem with life and vigour and intelligence, as do those of Massachusetts."[34]

There are time-servers in every cause; there are men who fill their bellies with husks, and turn on their faces and die; but there are others who, in the midst of public calamities, and in their own scanty personal fortune, leave behind them the memory of noble deeds, and a deathless heritage of glory.

Defeat has not made "all our sacred things profane." The war has left the South its own memories, its own heroes, its own tears, its own dead. Under these traditions, sons will grow to manhood, and lessons sink deep that are learned from the lips of widowed mothers.

It would be immeasurably the worst consequence of defeat in this war that the South should lose its moral and intellectual distinctiveness as a people, and cease to assert its well-known superiority in civilization, in political scholarship, and in all the standards of individual character over the people of the North. That superiority has been recognized by every foreign observer, and by the intelligent everywhere; for it is the South that in the past produced four-fifths of the political literature of America, and presented in its public men that list of American names best known in the Christian world. That superiority the war has not conquered or lowered; and the South will do right to claim and to cherish it.

The war has not swallowed up everything. There are great interests which stand out of the pale of the contest, which it is for the South still to cultivate and maintain. She must submit fairly and truthfully to *what the war has properly decided*. But the war properly decided only what was put in issue: the restoration of the Union and the excision of slavery; and to these two conditions the South submits. But the war did not decide negro equality; it did not decide negro suffrage; it did not decide State Rights, although it might have exploded their abuse; it did not decide the orthodoxy of the Democratic party; it did not decide the right of a people to show dignity in misfortune, and to maintain self-respect in the face of adversity. And, these things which the war did not decide, the Southern people will still cling to, still claim, and still assert in them their rights and views.

This is not the language of insolence and faction. It is the stark letter of right, and the plain syllogism of common sense. It is not untimely or unreasonable to tell the South to cultivate her superiority as a people; to maintain her old schools of literature and scholarship; to assert, in the forms of her thought, and in the style of her manners, her peculiar civilization, and to convince the North that, instead of subjugating an inferiour country, she has obtained the alliance of a noble and cultivated people, and secured a bond of association with those she may be proud to call brethren!

In such a condition there may possibly be a solid and honourable peace; and one in which the South may still preserve many things dear to her in the past. There may not be a political South. Yet there may be a social and intellectual South. But if, on the other hand, the South, mistaking the consequences of the war, accepts the position of the inferiour, and gives up what was never claimed or conquered in the war; surrenders her schools of intellect and thought, and is left only with the brutal desire of the conquered for "bread and games;" then indeed to her people may be applied what Tacitus wrote of those who existed under the Roman Empire: "We cannot be said to have lived, but rather to have crawled in silence, the young towards the decrepitude of age and the old to dishonourable graves."[35]

Sidney Lanier, "The Dying Words of Stonewall Jackson" (1865)

"Order A. P. Hill to prepare for battle."
"Tell Major Hawks to advance the Commissary train."
"Let us cross the river and rest in the shade."[36]

> The stars of Night contain the glittering Day
> And rain his glory down with sweeter grace
> Upon the dark World's grand, enchanted face—
>   All loth to turn away.
>
> And so the Day, about to yield his breath,
> Utters the stars unto the listening Night,
> To stand for burning fare-thee-wells of light
>   Said on the verge of death.
>
> O hero-life that lit us like the sun!
> O hero-words that glittered like the stars
> And stood and shone above the gloomy wars
>   When the hero-life was done!
>
> The phantoms of a battle came to dwell
> I' the fitful vision of his dying eyes—
> Yet even in battle-dreams, he sends supplies
>   To those he loved so well.
>
> His army stands in battle-line arrayed:
> His couriers fly: all's done: now God decide!
> —And not till then saw he the Other Side
>   Or would accept the shade.
>
> Thou Land whose sun is gone, thy stars remain!
> Still shine the words that miniature his deeds.
> O thrice-beloved, where'er they great heart bleeds,
>   Solace has thou for pain!

Georgia, September, 1865.

Sidney Lanier, Laughter in the Senate (1868)

> In the South lies a lonesome, hungry Land;
> He huddles his rags with a cripple's hand;
> He mutters, prone on the barren sand,
>   What time his heart is breaking.
>
> He lifts his bare head from the ground;
> He listens through the gloom around:
> The winds have brought him a strange sound
>   Of distant merrymaking.

Comes now the Peace so long delayed?
Is it the cheerful voice of Aid?
Begins the time his heart has prayed,
    When men may reap and sow?

Ah, God! Back to the cold earth's breast!
The sages chuckle o'er their jest;
Must they, to give a people rest,
    Their dainty wit forego?

The tyrants sit in a stately hall;
They jibe at a wretched people's fall;
The tyrants forget how fresh is the pall
    Over their dead and ours.

Look how the senators ape the clown,
And don the motley and hide the gown,
But yonder a fast-rising frown
    On the people's forehead lowers.

1868.

Sidney Lanier, Resurrection (1868)

Sometimes in morning sunlights by the river
Where in the early fall long grasses wave,
Light winds from over the moorland sink and shiver
    And sighs as if just blown across a grave.

And then I pause and listen to this sighing.
    I look with strange eyes on the well-known stream.
I hear wild birth-cries uttered by the dying.
    I know men waking who appear to dream.

Then from the water-lilies slow uprises
    The still vast face of all the life I know,
Changed now, and full of wonders and surprises,
    With fire in eyes that once were glazed with snow.

Fair now the brows old Pain had erewhile wrinkled,
    And peace and strength about the calm mouth dwell.
Clean of the ashes that Repentance sprinkled,
    The meek head poises like a flower-bell.

All the old scars of wanton wars are vanished;
    And what blue bruises grappling Sense had left
And sad remains of redder stains are banished,
    And the dim blotch of heart-committed theft.

O still vast vision of transfigured features
    Unvisited by secret crimes or dooms,
Remain, remain amid these water-creatures,
    Stand, shine among yon water-lily blooms.

For eighteen centuries ripple down the river,
    And windy times the stalks of empires wave,
—Let the winds come from the moor and sigh and shiver,
    Fain, fain am I, O Christ, to pass the grave.

Sarah Morgan Bryan Piatt, Army of Occupation At Arlington (1866)

Arlington National Cemetery was established in 1864, on land formerly owned by Robert E. Lee, as Union losses required the acquisition of additional graveyard space. When this poem was published, in August 1866, the federal government was still gathering the bodies of unidentified soldiers who had died in the vicinity of Manassas and the Rappahannock River; their tomb was dedicated at Arlington in September 1866.

The summer blew its little drifts of sound—
    Tangled with wet leaf-shadows and the light
Small breath of scattered morning buds—around
The yellow path through which our footsteps wound.
    Below, the Capitol rose glittering white.

There stretched a sleeping army. One by one,
    They took their places until thousands met;
No leader's stars flashed on before, and none
Leaned on his sword or stagg[e]r'd with his gun—
    I wonder if their feet have rested yet!

They saw the dust, they joined the moving mass,
    They answer'd the fierce music's cry for blood,
Then straggled here and lay down in the grass:—
Wear flowers for such, shores whence their feet did pass;
    Sing tenderly; O river's haunted flood!

They had been sick, and worn, and weary, when
    They stopp'd on this calm hill beneath the trees:
Yet if, in some red-clouded dawn, again
The country should be calling to her men,
    Shall the r[e]veill[e] not remember these?

Around them underneath the mid-day skies
    The dreadful phantoms of the living walk,
And by low moons and darkness with their cries—
The mothers, sisters, wives with faded eyes,
    Who call still names amid their broken talk.

And there is one who comes alone and stands
    At his dim fireless hearth—chill'd and oppress'd
By Something he has summon'd to his lands,
While the weird pallor of its many hands
    Points to his rusted sword in his own breast!

Sarah Morgan Bryan Piatt, Another War (1872)

Yes, they are coming from the fort—
    Not weary they, nor dimm'd with dust;
Their march seems but a shining sport,
    Their swords too new for rust.

You think the captains look so fine,
    You like, I know, the long sharp flash,
The fair silk flags above the line,
    The pretty scarlet sash?

You like the horses when they neigh,
    You like the music most of all,
And, if they had to fight to-day,
    You'd like to see them fall.

I wisely think the uniform
    Was made for skeletons to wear,
But your young blood is quick and warm,
    And so—you do not care.

You lift your eager eyes and ask:
    "Could we not have another war?"
As I might give this fearful task
    To armies near and far.

Another war? Perhaps we could,
    Yet, child of mine with sunniest head,
I sometimes wonder if I would
    Bear then to see the dead!

But am I in a dream? For see,
    My pretty boy follows the men—
Surely he did not speak to me,
    Who could have spoken, then?

It was another child, less fair,
    Less young, less innocent, I know,
Who lost the light gold from its hair
    Most bitter years ago!

It was that restless, wavering child
   I call Myself. No other, dear.
Perhaps you knew it when you smiled
   Because none else was near.

Then not my boy, it seems, but I
   Would wage another war?—to see
The shining sights, to hear the cry
   Of ghastly victory?

No—for another war could bring
   No second bloom to wither'd flowers,
No second song to birds that sing,
   Lost tunes in other hours!

But, friend, since time is full of pain,
   Whether men fall by field or hearth,
I want the old war back again,
   And nothing new on earth!

Sarah Morgan Bryan Piatt, The Grave at Frankfort (1872)

I turned and threw my rose upon the mound
   Beneath whose grass my old, rude kinsman lies,
And thought had from his Dark and Bloody Ground
   The blood secured in the shape of flowers to rise.

I left his dust to dew and dimness then,
   Who did not need the glitter of mock stars
To show his homely generalship to men
   And light his shoulders through his troubled wars.

I passed his rustling wild-cane, reached the gate,
   And heard the city's noisy murmurings;
Forgot the simple hero of my State,
   Looked in the gaslight, thought of other things.

Ah, that was many withered springs ago;
   Yet once, last winter, in the whirl of snows,
A vague half-fever, or, for aught I know,
   A wish to touch the hand that gave my rose,

Showed me a hunter of the wooded West,
   With dog and gun, beside his cabin door;
And, in the strange fringed garments on his breast,
   I recognized at once the rose he wore!

Sarah Morgan Bryan Piatt, Over in Kentucky (1872)

"This is the smokiest city in the world,"
   A slight voice, wise and weary, said, "I know.

My sash is tied, and if my hair was curled,
   I'd like to have my prettiest hat and go
There where some violets had to stay, you said,
Before your torn-up butterflies were dead—
     Over in Kentucky."

Then one, whose half-sad face still wore the hue
   The North Star loved to light and linger on,
Before the war, looked slowly at me too,
   And darkly whispered: "What is gone is gone.
Yet, though it may be better to be free,
I'd rather have things as they used to be
     Over in Kentucky."

Perhaps I thought how fierce the master's hold,
   Spite of all armies, kept the slave within;
How iron chains, when broken, turned to gold,
   In empty cabins, where glad songs had been,
Before the Southern sword knew blood and rust,
Before wild cavalry sprang from the dust,
     Over in Kentucky.

Perhaps—but, since two eyes, half-full of tears,
   Half-full of sleep, would love to keep awake
With fairy pictures from my fairy years,
   I have a phantom pencile that can make
Shadows of moons, far back and faint, to rise
On dewier grass and in diviner skies,
     Over in Kentucky.

For yonder river, wider than the sea,
   Seems sometimes in the dusk a visible
   moan
Between two worlds—one fair, one dear to me.
   The fair has forms of ever-glimmering stone,
Weird-whispering ruin, graves where legends
   hide,
And lies in mist upon the charmèd side,
     Over in Kentucky.

The dear has restless, dimpled, pretty hands,
   Yearning toward unshaped steel, unfancied wars,
Unbuilded cities, and unbroken lands,
   With something sweeter than the faded stars
And dim, dead dews of my lost romance, found
In beauty that has vanished from the ground,
     Over in Kentucky.

Cincinatti, Ohio.

Frederick Douglass, Address at the Graves of the Unknown Dead (1871)

Arlington, Va., May 30, 1871

Friends and Fellow Citizens:

Tarry here for a moment. My words shall be few and simple. The solemn rites of this hour and place call for no lengthened speech. There is, in the very air of this resting-ground of the unknown dead, a silent, subtle, and all-pervading eloquence, far more touching, impressive, and thrilling than living lips have ever uttered. Into the measureless depths of every loyal soul it is now whispering lessons of all that is most precious and priceless; all that is holiest and most enduring, in human existence.

Dark and sad will be the hour to this nation, when it forgets to pay grateful homage to its greatest benefactors. The offering we bring today is due alike to the patriot soldiers dead and their noble comrades who still live; for, whether living or dead – whether in time or eternity – the loyal soldiers who perilled all for country and freedom, are one and inseparable.

Those unknown heroes whose whitened bones have been piously gathered here, and whose green graves we now strew with sweet and beautiful flowers, choice emblems alike of pure hearts and brave spirits, reached, in their glorious career, that last highest point of nobleness, beyond which human power cannot go. They died for their country.

No loftier tribute can be paid to the most illustrious of all the benefactors of mankind, than we pay to these unrecognized soldiers, when we write above their graves this shining epitaph.

When the dark and vengeful spirit of slavery, always ambitious, preferring to rule in hell than to serve in heaven, fired the Southern heart and stirred all the malign elements of discord; when our great Republic, the hope of freedom and self-government throughout the world, had reached the point of supreme peril; when the union of these states was torn and rent asunder at the center, and the armies of a gigantic rebellion came forth with broad blades and bloody hands to destroy the very foundation of American society, the unknown braves who slumber in these graves flung themselves into the yawning chasm where cannon roared and bullets whistled, fought and fell. They died for their country!

We are sometimes asked, in the name of patriotism, to forget the merits of this fearful struggle, and to remember with equal admiration those who struck at the nation's life, and those who struck to save it – those who fought for slavery, and those who fought for liberty and justice.

I am no minister of malice. I would not strike the fallen. I would not repel the repentant; but may my right hand forget its cunning, and my tongue cleave to the roof of my mouth, if I forget the difference between the parties to that terrible, protracted, and bloody conflict.

If we ought to forget a war which has filled our land with widows and orphans; which has made stumps of men of the very flower of our youth, and sent them on the journey of life armless, legless, maimed, and mutilated; which has piled up a debt heavier than a mountain of gold – swept uncounted thousands of men into bloody graves – and planted agony at a million hearthstones; I say, if this war is to be forgotten, I ask, in the name of all things sacred, what shall men remember?

The essence and significance of our devotions here today are not to be found in the fact that the men whose remains fill these graves were brave in battle. If we were met simply to show our sense of the worth of bravery, we should find enough to kindle admiration on both sides. In the raging storm of fire and blood, in the fierce torrent of shot and shell, of sword and bayonet, whether on foot or on horse, unflinching courage marked the rebel not less than the loyal soldier.

But we are here to applaud manly courage only as it has been displayed in a noble cause. We must never forget that victory to the rebellion meant death to the Republic. We must never forget that the loyal soldiers who rest beneath this sod flung themselves between the nation and the nation's destroyers. If today we have a country not boiling in an agony of blood, like France; if now we have a united country no longer cursed by the hell-black system of human bondage; if the American name is no longer a byword and a hissing to a mocking earth; if the star-spangled banner floats only over free American citizens in every quarter of the land, and our country has before it a long and glorious career of justice, liberty, and civilization, we are indebted to the unselfish devotion of the noble army which rests in these honored graves all around us.

Henry Timrod, "Ode" (to the Confederate Dead) (1866)

Sung on the Occasion of Decorating the Graves of the Confederate Dead, at Magnolia Cemetery, Charleston, S.C., 1866

I

Sleep sweetly in your humble graves,
   Sleep, martyrs of a fallen cause;
Though yet no marble column craves
   The pilgrim here to pause.

II

In seeds of laurel in the earth
   The blossom of your fame is blown,
And somewhere, waiting for its birth,
   The shaft is in the stone!

III

Meanwhile, behalf the tardy years
   Which keep in trust your storied tombs,
Behold! your sisters bring their tears,
   And these memorial blooms.

IV

Small tributes! but your shades will smile
   More proudly on these wreaths to-day,
Than when some cannon-moulded pile
   Shall overlook this bay.

V

Stoop, angels, hither from the skies!
   There is no holier spot of ground
Than where defeated valor lies,
   By mourning beauty crowned!

Samuel R. Watkins, from *Co. Aytch* (1882)

Chapter 1: Retrospective

"We Are One and Undivided"

About twenty years ago, I think it was—I won't be certain, though—a man whose name, if I remember correctly, was Wm. L. Yancy[37]—I write only from memory, and this was a long time ago—took a strange and peculiar notion that the sun rose in the east and set in the west, and that the compass pointed north and south. Now, everybody knew at the time that it was but the idiosyncrasy of an unbalanced mind, and that the United States of America had no north, no south, no east, no west. Well, he began to preach the strange doctrine of there being such a thing. He began to have followers. As you know, it matters not how absurd, ridiculous and preposterous doctrines may be preached, there will be some followers. Well, one man by the name of (I think it was) Rhett,[38] said it out loud. He was told to "s-h-e-e." Then another fellow by the name (I remember this one because it sounded like a graveyard) Toombs[39] said so, and he was told to "sh-sh-ee-ee." Then after a while whole heaps of people began to say that they thought that there was a north and a south; and after a while hundreds and thousands and millions said that there was a south. But they were the persons who lived in the direction that the water courses run. Now, the people who lived where the water courses started from came down to see about it, and they said, "Gents, you are very much mistaken. We came over in the Mayflower, and we used to burn witches for saying that the sun rose in the east and set in the west, because the sun neither rises nor sets, the earth simply turns on its axis, and we know, cause we are Pure(i)tans." The spokesman of the party was named (I think I remember his name because it always gave me the blues when I heard it) Horrors Greeley;[40] and another person by the name of Charles Sumner,[41] said there ain't any north or south, east or west, and you shan't say so, either. Now, the other people who lived in the direction that the water courses run, just raised their bristles and continued saying that there is a north and there is a south. When those at the head of the water courses come out furiously mad, to coerce those in the direction that water courses run, and to make them take it back. Well, they went to gouging and biting, to pulling and scratching at a furious rate. One side elected a captain by the name of Jeff Davis, and known as one-eyed Jeff, and a first lieutenant by the name of Aleck Stephens, commonly styled Smart Aleck. The other side selected as captain a son of Nancy Hanks, of Bowling Green, and a son of old Bob Lincoln, the rail-splitter, and whose name was Abe. Well, after he was elected captain, they elected as first lieutenant an individual of doubtful blood by the name of Hannibal Hamlin, being a descendant of the generation of Ham, the bad son of old Noah, who meant to curse him blue, but overdid the thing, and cursed him black.[42]

   Well, as I said before, they went to fighting, but old Abe's side got the best of the argument. But in getting the best of the argument they called in all the people and wise men of other nations of the earth, and they, too, said that America had no cardinal points, and that the sun did not rise in the east and set in the west, and that the compass did not point either north or south.

Well, then, Captain Jeff Davis' side gave it up and quit, and they, too, went to saying that there is no north, no south, no east, no west. Well, "us boys" all took a small part in the fracas, and Shep, the prophet, remarked that the day would come when those who once believed that the American continent had cardinal points would be ashamed to own it. That day has arrived. America has no north, no south, no east, no west; the sun rises over the hills and sets over the mountains, the compass just points up and down, and we can laugh now at the absurd notion of there being a north and a south.

Well, reader, let me whisper in your ear. I was in the row, and the following pages will tell what part I took in the little unpleasant misconception of there being such a thing as a north and south.

The Bloody Chasm

In these memoirs, after the lapse of twenty years, we propose to fight our "battles o'er again."

To do this is but a pastime and pleasure, as there is nothing that so much delights the old soldier as to revisit the scenes and battle-fields with which he was once so familiar, and to recall the incidents, though trifling they may have been at the time.

The histories of the Lost Cause are all written out by "big bugs," generals and renowned historians, and like the fellow who called a turtle a "cooter," being told that no such word as cooter was in Webster's dictionary, remarked that he had as much right to make a dictionary as Mr. Webster or any other man; so have I to write a history.

But in these pages I do not pretend to write the history of the war. I only give a few sketches and incidents that came under the observation of a "high private" in the rear ranks of the rebel army.[43] Of course, the histories are all correct. They tell of great achievements of great men, who wear the laurels of victory; have grand presents given them; high positions in civil life; presidents of corporations; governors of states; official positions, etc., and when they die, long obituaries are published, telling their many virtues, their distinguished victories, etc., and when they are buried, the whole country goes in mourning and is called upon to buy an elegant monument to erect over the remains of so distinguished and brave a general, etc. But in the following pages I propose to tell of the fellows who did the shooting and killing, the fortifying and ditching, the sweeping of the streets, the drilling, the standing guard, picket and videt, and who drew (or were to draw) eleven dollars per month and rations, and also drew the ramrod and tore the cartridge. Pardon me should I use the personal pronoun "I" too frequently, as I do not wish to be called egotistical, for I only write of what I saw as an humble private in the rear rank in an infantry regiment, commonly called "webfoot." Neither do I propose to make this a connected journal, for I write entirely from memory, and you must remember, kind reader, that these things happened twenty years ago, and twenty years is a long time in the life of any individual.

I was twenty-one years old then, and at that time I was not married. Now I have a house full of young "rebels," clustering around my knees and bumping against my elbow, while I write these reminiscences of the war of secession, rebellion, state rights, slavery, or our rights in the territories, or by whatever other name it may be called. These are all with the past now, and the North and South have long ago "shaken hands across the bloody chasm."[44] The flag of the Southern cause has been furled never to be again unfurled; gone like a dream of yesterday, and lives only in the memory of those who lived through those bloody days and times.

Eighteen Hundred and Sixty-one

Reader mine, did you live in that stormy period? In the year of our Lord eighteen hundred and sixty-one, do you remember those stirring times? Do you recollect in that year, for the first time in your life, of hearing Dixie and the Bonnie Blue Flag? Fort Sumter was fired upon from Charleston by troops under General Beauregard, and Major Anderson, of the Federal army, surrendered. The die was cast; war was declared; Lincoln called for troops from Tennessee and all the Southern states, but Tennessee, loyal to her Southern sister states, passed the ordinance of secession, and enlisted under the Stars and Bars. From that day on, every person, almost, was eager for the war, and we were all afraid it would be over and we not be in the fight. Companies were made up, regiments organized; left, left, left, was heard from morning till night. By the right flank, file left, march, were familiar sounds. Everywhere could be seen Southern cockades made by the ladies and our sweethearts. And some who afterwards became Union men made the most fiery secession speeches. Flags made by the ladies were presented to companies, and to hear the young orators tell of how they would protect that flag, and that they would come back with the flag or come not at all, and if they fell they would fall with their backs to the field and their feet to the foe, would fairly make our hair stand on end with intense patriotism, and we wanted to march right off and whip twenty Yankees. But we soon found out that the glory of war was at home among the ladies and not upon the field of blood and carnage of death, where our comrades were mutilated and torn by shot and shell. And to see the cheek blanch and to hear the fervent prayer, aye, I might say the agony of mind were very different indeed from the patriotic times at home.

Camp Cheatham

After being drilled and disciplined at Camp Cheatham, under the administrative ability of General R. C. Foster, 3rd, for two months, we, the First, Third and Eleventh Tennessee Regiments—Maney, Brown and Rains—learned of the advance of McClelland's [sic] army into Virginia, toward Harper's Ferry and Bull Run.[45]

The Federal army was advancing all along the line. They expected to march right into the heart of the South, set the negroes free, take our property, and whip the rebels back into the Union. But they soon found that secession was a bigger mouthful than they could swallow at one gobble. They found the people of the South in earnest.

Secession may have been wrong in the abstract, and has been tried and settled by the arbitrament of the sword and bayonet, but I am as firm in my convictions today of the right of secession as I was in 1861. The South is our country, the North is the country of those who live there. We are an agricultural people; they are a manufacturing people. They are the descendants of the good old Puritan Plymouth Rock stock, and we of the South from the proud and aristocratic stock of Cavaliers. We believe in the doctrine of State rights, they in the doctrine of centralization.

John C. Calhoun, Patrick Henry, and Randolph, of Roanoke, saw the venom under their wings, and warned the North of the consequences, but they laughed at them. We only fought for our State rights, they for Union and power. The South fell battling under the banner of State rights, but yet grand and glorious even in death. Now, reader, please pardon the digression. It is every word that we will say in behalf of the rights of secession in the following pages. The question has been long ago settled and is buried forever, never in this age or generation to be resurrected.

The vote of the regiment was taken, and we all voted to go to Virginia. The Southern Confederacy had established its capital at Richmond.

A man by the name of Jackson, who kept a hotel in Maryland, had raised the Stars and Bars, and a Federal officer by the name of Ellsworth tore it down, and Jackson had riddled his body with buckshot from a double-barreled shot-gun. First blood for the South.[46]

Everywhere the enemy were advancing; the red clouds of war were booming up everywhere, but as this particular epoch, I refer you to the history of that period.

A private soldier is but an automaton, a machine that works by the command of a good, bad, or indifferent engineer, and is presumed to know nothing of all these great events. His business is to load and shoot, stand picket, videt, etc., while the officers sleep, or perhaps die on the field of battle and glory, and his obituary and epitaph but "one" remembered among the slain, but to what company, regiment, brigade or corps he belongs, there is no account; he is soon forgotten.

A long line of box cars was drawn up at Camp Cheatham one morning in July, the bugle sounded to strike tents and to place everything on board the cars. We old comrades have gotten together and laughed a hundred times at the plunder and property that we had accumulated, compared with our subsequent scanty wardrobe. Every soldier had enough blankets, shirts, pants and old boots to last a year, and the empty bottles and jugs would have set up a first-class drug store. In addition, every one of us had his gun, cartridge-box, knapsack and three days' rations, a pistol on each side and a long Bowie knife, that had been presented to us by William Wood, of Columbia, Tenn. We got in and on top of the box cars, the whistle sounded, and amid the waving of hats, handkerchiefs and flags, we bid a long farewell and forever to old Camp Cheatham.

Arriving at Nashville, the citizens turned out *en masse* to receive us, and here again we were reminded of the good old times and the "gal we left behind us." Ah, it is worth soldiering to receive such welcomes as this.

The Rev. Mr. Elliott invited us to his college grove, where had been prepared enough of the good things of earth to gratify the tastes of the most fastidious epicure. And what was most novel, we were waited on by the most beautiful young ladies (pupils of his school). It was charming, I tell you. Rev. C. D. Elliott was our Brigade Chaplain all through the war, and Dr. C. T. Quintard the Chaplain of the First Tennessee Regiment—two of the best men who ever lived. (Quintard is the present Bishop of Tennessee).[47]

On the Road

Leaving Nashville, we went bowling along twenty or thirty miles an hour, as fast as steam could carry us. At every town and station citizens and ladies were waving their handkerchiefs and hurrahing for Jeff Davis and the Southern Confederacy. Magnificent banquets were prepared for us all along the entire route. It was one magnificent festival from one end of the line to the other. At Chattanooga, Knoxville, Bristol, Farmville, Lynchburg, everywhere, the same demonstrations of joy and welcome greeted us. Ah, those were glorious times; and you, reader, see why the old soldier loves to live over again that happy period.

But the Yankees are advancing on Manassas. July 21st finds us a hundred miles from that fierce day's battle. That night, after the battle is fought and won, our train draws up at Manassas Junction.

Well, what news? Everyone was wild, nay, frenzied with the excitement of victory, and we felt very much like the "boy the calf had run over." We felt that the war was over, and we would have to return home without even seeing a Yankee soldier. Ah, how we envied those that were wounded. We thought at that time that we would have given a thousand dollars to have been in the battle, and to have had our arm shot off, so we could have returned home with an empty sleeve. But the battle was over, and we left out.

Staunton

From Manassas our train moved on to Staunton, Virginia. Here we again went into camp, overhauled kettles, pots, buckets, jugs and tents, and found everything so tangled up and mixed that we could not tell tuther from which.

We stretched our tents, and the soldiers once again felt that restraint and discipline which we had almost forgotten en route to this place. But, as the war was over now, our captains, colonels and generals were not "hard on the boys;" in fact, had begun to electioneer a little for the Legislature and for Congress. In fact, some wanted, and were looking forward to the time, to run for Governor of Tennessee.

Staunton was a big place; whisky was cheap, and good Virginia tobacco was plentiful, and the currency of the country was gold and silver.

The State Asylums for the blind and insane were here, and we visited all the places of interest.

Here is where we first saw the game called "chuck-a-luck,"[48] afterwards so popular in the army. But, I always noticed that chuck won, and luck always lost.

Faro and roulette were in full blast; in fact, the skum had begun to come to the surface, and shoddy was the gentleman. By this, I mean that civil law had been suspended; the ermine of the judges had been overridden by the sword and bayonet. In other words, the military had absorbed the civil. Hence the gambler was in his glory.

Warm Springs, Virginia

One day while we were idling around camp, June Tucker sounded the assembly, and we were ordered aboard the cars. We pulled out for Millboro; from there we had to foot it to Bath Alum and Warm Springs. We went over the Allegheny Mountains.

I was on every march that was ever made by the First Tennessee Regiment during the whole war, and at this time I cannot remember of ever experiencing a harder or more fatiguing march. It seemed that mountain was piled upon mountain. No sooner would we arrive at a place that seemed to be the top than another view of a higher, and yet higher mountain would rise before us. From the foot to the top of the mountain the soldiers lined the road, broken down and exhausted. First one blanket was thrown away, and then another; now and then a good pair of pants, old boots and shoes, Sunday hats, pistols and Bowie knives strewed the road. Old bottles and jugs and various and sundry articles were lying pell-mell everywhere. Up and up, and onward and upward we pulled and toiled, until we reached the very top, when there burst upon our view one of the grandest and most beautiful landscapes we ever beheld.

Nestled in the valley right before us is Bath Alum and Warm Springs. It seemed to me at that time, and since, a glimpse of a better and brighter world beyond, to the weary Christian pilgrim who may have been toiling on his journey for years. A glad shout arose from those who had gained the top, which cheered and encouraged the others to persevere. At last we got to Warm Springs. Here they had a nice warm dinner waiting for us. They had a large bath-house at Warm Springs. A large pool of water arranged so that a person could go in any depth he might desire. It was a free thing, and we pitched in. We had no idea of the enervating effect it would have upon our physical systems, and as the water was but little past tepid, we stayed in a good long time. But when we came out we were as limp as dishrags. About this time the assembly sounded and we were ordered to march. But we couldn't march worth a cent. There we had to stay until our systems had

had sufficient recuperation. And we would wonder what all this marching was for, as the war was over anyhow.

The second day after leaving Warm Springs we came to Big Springs. It was in the month of August, and the biggest white frost fell that I ever saw in winter.

The Yankees were reported to be in close proximity to us, and Captain Field[49] with a detail of ten men was sent forward on the scout. I was on the detail, and when we left camp that evening, it was dark and dreary and drizzling rain. After a while the rain began to come down harder and harder, and every one of us was wet and drenched to the skin—guns, cartridges and powder. The next morning about daylight, while standing videt, I saw a body of twenty-five or thirty Yankees approaching, and I raised my gun for the purpose of shooting, and pulled down, but the cap popped. They discovered me and popped three or four caps at me; their powder was wet also. Before I could get on a fresh cap, Captain Field came running up with his seven-shooting rifle, and the first fire he killed a Yankee. They broke and run. Captain Field did all the firing, but every time he pulled down he brought a Yankee. I have forgotten the number that he did kill, but if I am not mistaken it was either twenty or twenty-one, for I remember the incident was in almost every Southern paper at that time, and the general comments were that one Southern man was equal to twenty Yankees. While we were in hot pursuit, one truly brave and magnanimous Yankee, who had been badly wounded, said, "Gentlemen, you have killed me, but not a hundred yards from here is the main line." We did not go any further, but halted right there, and after getting all the information that we could out of the wounded Yankee, we returned to camp.

One evening, General Robert E. Lee came to our camp. He was a fine-looking gentleman, and wore a moustache. He was dressed in blue cottonade and looked like some good boy's grandpa. I felt like going up to him and saying, good evening, Uncle Bob! I am not certain at this late day that I did not do so. I remember going up mighty close and sitting there and listening to his conversation with the officers of our regiment. He had a calm and collected air about him, his voice was kind and tender, and his eye was as gentle as a dove's. His whole make-up of form and person, looks and manner had a kind of gentle and soothing magnetism about it that drew every one to him and made them love, respect, and honor him. I fell in love with the old gentleman and felt like going home with him. I know I have never seen a finer looking man, nor one with more kind and gentle features and manners. His horse was standing nipping the grass, and when I saw that he was getting ready to start I ran and caught his horse and led him up to him. He took the reins of the bridle in his hand and said, "thank you, my son," rode off, and my heart went with him. There was none of his staff with him; he had on no sword or pistol, or anything to show his rank. The only thing that I remember he had was an opera-glass hung over his shoulder by a strap.

Leaving Big Springs, we marched on day by day, across Greenbrier and Gauley rivers to Huntersville, a little but sprightly town hid in the very fastnesses of the mountains. The people live exceedingly well in these mountains. They had plenty of honey and buckwheat cakes, and they called butter-milk "sour-milk," and sour-milk weren't fit for pigs; they couldn't see how folks drank sour-milk. But sourkraut was good. Everything seemed to grow in the mountains—potatoes, Irish and sweet; onions, snap beans, peas—though the country was very thinly populated. Deer, bear, and foxes, as well as wild turkeys, and rabbits and squirrels abounded everywhere. Apples and peaches were abundant, and everywhere the people had apple-butter for every meal; and occasionally we would come across a small-sized distillery, which we would at once start to doing duty. We drank the singlings[50] while they were hot, but like the old woman who could not eat corn bread until she heard that they made whisky out of corn, then she could manage to "worry a little of it down;" so it was with us and the singlings.

From this time forward, we were ever on the march—tramp, tramp, tramp—always on the march. Lee's corps, Stonewall Jackson's division—I refer you to the histories for the marches and tramps made by these commanders the first year of the war. Well, we followed them.

Cheat Mountain

One evening about 4 o'clock, the drummers of the regiment began to beat their drums as hard as they could stave, and I saw men running in every direction, and the camp soon became one scene of hurry and excitement. I asked some one what all this hubbub meant. He looked at me with utter astonishment. I saw soldiers running to their tents and grabbing their guns and cartridge-boxes and hurry out again, the drums still rolling and rattling. I asked several other fellows what in the dickens did all this mean? Finally one fellow, who seemed scared almost out of his wits, answered between a wail and a shriek, "Why, sir, they are beating the long roll." Says I, "What is the long roll for?" "The long roll, man, the long roll! Get your gun; they are beating the long roll!" This was all the information that I could get. It was the first, last, and only long roll that I ever heard. But, then everything was new, and Colonel Maney, ever prompt, ordered the assembly. Without any command or bugle sound, or anything, every soldier was in his place. Tents, knapsacks and everything was left indiscriminately.

We were soon on the march, and we marched on and on and on. About night it began to rain. All our blankets were back in camp, but we were expected every minute to be ordered into action. That night we came to Mingo Flats. The rain still poured. We had no rations to eat and nowhere to sleep. Some of us got some fence rails and piled them together and worried through the night as best we could. The next morning we were ordered to march again, but we soon began to get hungry, and we had about half halted and about not halted at all. Some of the boys were picking blackberries. The main body of the regiment was marching leisurely along the road, when bang, debang, debang, bang, and a volley of buck and ball came hurling right through the two advance companies of the regiment—companies H and K. We had marched into a Yankee ambuscade.

All at once everything was a scene of consternation and confusion; no one seemed equal to the emergency. We did not know whether to run or stand, when Captain Field gave the command to fire and charge the bushes. We charged the bushes and saw the Yankees running through them, and we fired on them as they retreated. I do not know how many Yankees were killed, if any. Our company (H) had one man killed, Pat Hanley, an Irishman, who had joined our company at Chattanooga. Hugh Padgett and Dr. Hooper, and perhaps one or two others, were wounded.

After the fighting was over, where, O where, was all the fine rigging heretofore on our officers? They could not be seen. Corporals, sergeants, lieutenants, captains, all had torn all the fine lace off their clothing. I noticed that at the time and was surprised and hurt. I asked several of them why they had torn off the insignia of their rank, and they always answered, "Humph, you think that I was going to be a target for the Yankees to shoot at?" You see, this was our first battle, and the officers had not found out that minnie as well as cannon balls were blind; that they had no eyes and could not see. They thought that the balls would hunt for them and not hurt the privates. I always shot at privates. It was they that did the shooting and killing, and if I could kill or wound a private, why, my chances were so much the better. I always looked upon officers as harmless personages. Colonel Field, I suppose, was about the only Colonel of the war that did as much shooting as the private soldier. If I shot at an officer, it was at long range, but when we got down to close quarters I always tried to kill those that were trying to kill me.

Sewell Mountain

From Cheat Mountain we went by forced marches day and night, over hill and everlasting mountains, and through lovely and smiling valleys, sometimes the country rich and productive, sometimes rough and broken, through towns and villages, the names of which I have forgotten, crossing streams and rivers, but continuing our never ceasing, unending march, passing through the Kanawha Valley and by the salt-works, and nearly back to the Ohio river, when we at last reached Sewell Mountain. Here we found General John B. Floyd,[51] strongly entrenched and fortified and facing the advance of the Federal army. Two days before our arrival he had charged and captured one line of the enemy's works. I know nothing of the battle. See the histories for that. I only write from memory, and that was twenty years ago, but I remember reading in the newspapers at that time of some distinguished man, whether he was captain, colonel or general, I have forgotten, but I know the papers said "he sought the bauble, reputation, at the cannon's mouth, and went to glory from the death-bed of fame." I remember it sounded gloriously in print. Now, reader, this is all I know of this grand battle. I only recollect what the newspapers said about it, and you know that a newspaper always tells the truth. I also know that beef livers sold for one dollar apiece in gold; and here is where we were first paid off in Confederate money. Remaining here a few days, we commenced our march again.

Sewell Mountain, Harrisonburg, Lewisburg, Kanawha Salt-works, first four, forward and back, seemed to be the programme of that day. Rosecrans, that wiley old fox, kept Lee and Jackson both busy trying to catch him, but Rosey would not be caught. March, march, march; tramp, tramp, tramp, back through the valley to Huntersville and Warm Springs, and up through the most beautiful valley—the Shenandoah—in the world, passing towns and elegant farms and beautiful residences, rich pastures and abundant harvests, which a Federal General (Fighting Joe Hooker), later in the war, ordered to be so sacked and destroyed that a "crow passing over this valley would have to carry his rations." Passing on, we arrived at Winchester. The first night we arrived at this place, the wind blew a perfect hurricane, and every tent and marquee in Lee's and Jackson's army was blown down. This is the first sight we had of Stonewall Jackson, riding upon his old sorrel horse, his feet drawn up as if his stirrups were much too short for him, and his old dingy military cap hanging well forward over his head, and his nose erected in the air, his old rusty sabre rattling by his side. This is the way the grand old hero of a hundred battles looked. His spirit is yonder with the blessed ones that have gone before, but his history is one that the country will ever be proud of, and his memory will be cherished and loved by the old soldiers who followed him through the war.

Romney

Our march to and from Romney was in midwinter in the month of January, 1862. It was the coldest winter known to the oldest inhabitant of these regions. Situated in the most mountainous country in Virginia, and away up near the Maryland and Pennsylvania line, the storm king seemed to rule in all of his majesty and power. Snow and rain and sleet and tempest seemed to ride and laugh and shriek and howl and moan and groan in all their fury and wrath. The soldiers on this march got very much discouraged and disheartened. As they marched along icicles hung from their clothing, guns, and knapsacks; many were badly frost bitten, and I heard of many freezing to death along the road side. My feet peeled off like a peeled onion on that march, and I have not recovered from its effects to this day. The snow and ice on the ground being packed by the soldiers tramping, the horses hitched to the artillery wagons were continually slipping and sliding and falling and wounding themselves and sometimes killing their riders. The wind whistling with a keen and piercing shriek, seemed as if they would freeze the marrow in our bones. The soldiers in the whole army got rebellious—almost mutinous— and would curse and abuse Stonewall Jackson; in fact, they called him "Fool Tom Jackson." They blamed him for the cold weather; they blamed him for everything, and when he would ride by a regiment they would take occasion, *sotto voce*, to abuse him, and call him "Fool Tom Jackson," and loud enough for him to hear. Soldiers from all commands would fall out of ranks and stop by the road side and swear that they would not follow such a leader any longer.

When Jackson got to Romney, and was ready to strike Banks and Meade in a vital point, and which would have changed, perhaps, the destiny of the war and the South, his troops refused to march any further, and he turned, marched back to Winchester and tendered his resignation to the authorities at Richmond.[52] But the great leader's resignation was not accepted. It was in store for him to do some of the hardest fighting and greatest generalship that was done during the war.

One night at this place (Romney), I was sent forward with two other soldiers across the wire bridge as picket. One of them was named Schwartz and the other Pfifer—he called it Fifer, but spelled it with a P—both full-blooded Dutchmen, and belonging to Company E, or the German Yagers, Captain Harsh, or, as he was more generally called, "God-for-dam."

When we had crossed the bridge and taken our station for the night, I saw another snow storm was coming. The zig-zag lightnings began to flare and flash, and sheet after sheet of wild flames seemed to burst right over our heads and were hissing around us. The very elements seemed to be one aurora borealis with continued lightning. Streak after streak of lightning seemed to be piercing each the other, the one from the north and the other from the south. The white clouds would roll up, looking like huge snow balls, encircled with living fires. The earth and hills and trees were covered with snow, and the lightnings seemed to be playing "King, King Canico" along its crusted surface. If it thundered at all, it seemed to be between a groaning and a rumbling sound. The trees and hills seemed white with livid fire. I can remember that storm now as the grandest picture that has ever made any impression on my memory. As soon as it quit lightning, the most blinding snow storm fell that I ever saw. It fell so thick and fast that I got hot. I felt like pulling off my coat. I was freezing. The winds sounded like sweet music. I felt grand, glorious, peculiar; beautiful things began to play and dance around my head, and I supposed I must have dropped to sleep or something, when I felt Schwartz grab me, and give me a shake, and at the same time raised his gun and fired, and yelled out at the top of his voice, "Here is your mule." The next instant a volley of minnie balls was scattering the snow all around us. I tried to walk, but my pants and boots were stiff and frozen, and the blood had ceased to circulate in my lower limbs. But Schwartz kept on firing, and at every fire he would yell out, "Yer is yer mool!" Pfifer could not speak English, and I reckon he said "Here is your mule" in Dutch. About the same time we were hailed from three Confederate officers, at full gallop right toward us, not to shoot. And as they galloped up to us and thundered right across the bridge, we discovered it was Stonewall Jackson and two of his staff. At the same time the Yankee cavalry charged us, and we, too, ran back across the bridge.

Standing Picket on the Potomac

Leaving Winchester, we continued up the valley.

The night before the attack on Bath or Berkly Springs, there fell the largest snow I ever saw.

Stonewall Jackson had seventeen thousand soldiers at his command. The Yankees were fortified at Bath. An attack was ordered, our regiment marched upon top of a mountain overlooking the movements of both armies in the valley below. About 4 o'clock one grand charge and rush was made, and the Yankees were routed and skedaddled.

By some circumstance or other, Lieutenant J. Lee Bullock came in command of the First Tennessee Regiment. But Lee was not a graduate of West Point, you see.

The Federals had left some spiked batteries on the hill side, as we were informed by an old citizen, and Lee, anxious to capture a battery, gave the new and peculiar command of, "Soldiers, you are ordered to go forward and capture a battery; just piroute up that hill; piroute, march. Forward, men; piroute carefully." The boys "pirouted" as best they could. It may have been a new command, and not laid down in Hardee's or Scott's tactics;[53] but Lee was speaking plain English, and we understood his meaning perfectly, and even at this late day I have no doubt that every soldier who heard the command thought it a legal and technical term used by military graduates to go forward and capture a battery.

At this place (Bath), a beautiful young lady ran across the street. I have seen many beautiful and pretty women in my life, but she was the prettiest one I ever saw. Were you to ask any member of the First Tennessee Regiment who was the prettiest woman he ever saw, he would unhesitatingly answer that he saw her at Berkly Springs during the war, and he would continue the tale, and tell you of Lee Bullock's piroute and Stonewall Jackson's charge.

We rushed down to the big spring bursting out of the mountain side, and it was hot enough to cook an egg. Never did I see soldiers more surprised. The water was so hot we could not drink it.

The snow covered the ground and was still falling.

That night I stood picket on the Potomac with a detail of the Third Arkansas Regiment. I remember how sorry I felt for the poor fellows, because they had enlisted for the war, and we for only twelve months. Before nightfall I took in every object and commenced my weary vigils. I had to stand all night. I could hear the rumblings of the Federal artillery and wagons, and hear the low shuffling sound made by troops on the march. The snow came pelting down as large as goose eggs. About midnight the snow ceased to fall, and became quiet. Now and then the snow would fall off the bushes and make a terrible noise. While I was peering through the darkness, my eyes suddenly fell upon the outlines of a man. The more I looked the more I was convinced that it was a Yankee picket. I could see his hat and coat—yes, see his gun. I was sure that it was a Yankee picket. What was I to do? The relief was several hundred yards in the rear. The more I looked the more sure I was. At last a cold sweat broke out all over my body. Turkey bumps rose. I summoned all the nerves and bravery that I could command, and said: "Halt! who goes there?" There being no response, I became resolute. I did not wish to fire and arouse the camp, but I marched right up to it and stuck my bayonet through and through it. It was a stump. I tell the above, because it illustrates a part of many a private's recollections of the war; in fact, a part of the hardships and suffering that they go through.

One secret of Stonewall Jackson's success was that he was such a strict disciplinarian. He did his duty himself and was ever at his post, and he expected and demanded of everybody to do the same thing. He would have a man shot at the drop of a hat, and drop it himself. The first army order that was ever read to us after being attached to his corps, was the shooting to death by musketry of two men who had stopped on the battlefield to carry off a wounded comrade. It was read to us in line of battle at Winchester.

Schwartz and Pfifer

At Valley Mountain the finest and fattest beef I ever saw was issued to the soldiers, and it was the custom to use tallow for lard. Tallow made good shortening if the biscuits were eaten hot, but if allowed to get cold they had a strong taste of tallow in their flavor that did not taste like the flavor of vanilla or lemon in ice cream and strawberries; and biscuits fried in tallow were something upon the principle of 'possum and sweet potatoes. Well, Pfifer had got the fat from the kidneys of two hindquarters and made a cake of tallow weighing about twenty-five pounds. He wrapped it up and put it carefully away in his knapsack. When the assembly sounded for the march, Pfifer strapped on his knapsack. It was pretty heavy, but Pfifer was "well heeled." He knew the good frying he would get out of that twenty-five pounds of nice fat tallow, and he was willing to tug and toil all day over a muddy and sloppy road for his anticipated hot tallow gravy for supper. We made a long and hard march that day, and about dark went into camp. Fires were made up and water brought, and the soldiers began to get supper. Pfifer was in a good humor. He went to get that twenty-five pounds of good, nice, fat tallow out of his knapsack, and on opening it, lo and behold! it was a rock that weighed about thirty pounds. Pfifer was struck dumb with amazement. He looked bewildered, yea, even silly. I do not think he cursed, because he could not do the subject justice. He looked at that rock with the death stare of a doomed man. But he suspected Schwartz. He went to Schwartz's knapsack, and there he found his cake of tallow. He went to Schwartz and would have killed him had not soldiers interfered and pulled him off by main force. His eyes blazed and looked like those of a tiger when he has just torn his victim limb from limb. I would not have been in Schwartz's shoes for all the tallow in every beef in Virginia. Captain Harsh made Schwartz carry that rock for two days to pacify Pfifer.

The Court-Martial

One incident came under my observation while in Virginia that made a deep impression on my mind. One morning, about daybreak, the new guard was relieving the old guard. It was a bitter cold morning, and on coming to our extreme outpost, I saw a soldier—he was but a mere boy—either dead or asleep at his post. The sergeant commanding the relief went up to him and shook him. He immediately woke up and seemed very much frightened. He was fast asleep at his post. The sergeant had him arrested and carried to the guard-house.

Two days afterwards I received notice to appear before a court-martial at nine. I was summoned to appear as a witness against him for being asleep at his post in the enemy's country. An example had to be made of some one. He had to be tried for his life. The court-martial was made up of seven or eight officers of a different regiment. The witnesses all testified against him, charges and specifications were read, and by the rules of war he had to be shot to death by musketry. The Advocate-General for the prosecution made the opening speech. He read the law in a plain, straightforward manner, and said that for a soldier to go to sleep at his post of duty, while so much depended upon him, was the most culpable of all crimes, and the most inexcusable. I trembled in my boots, for on several occasions I knew I had taken a short nap, even on the very outpost. The Advocate-General went on further to say, that the picket was the sentinel that held the lives of his countrymen and the liberty of his country in his hands, and it mattered not what may have been his record in the past. At one moment he had forfeited his life to his country. For discipline's sake, if for nothing else, you gentlemen that make up this court-martial find the prisoner guilty. It is necessary for you to be firm, gentlemen, for upon your decision depends the safety of our country. When he had finished, thinks I to myself, "Gone up the spout, sure; we will have a first-class funeral here before night."

Well, as to the lawyer who defended him, I cannot now remember his speeches; but he represented a fair-haired boy leaving his home and family, telling his father and aged mother and darling little sister farewell, and spoke of his proud step, though a mere boy, going to defend his country and his loved ones; but at one weak moment, when nature, tasked and taxed beyond the bounds of human endurance, could stand no longer, and upon the still and silent picket post, when the whole army was hushed in slumber, what wonder is it that he, too, may have fallen asleep while at his post of duty.

Some of you gentlemen of this court-martial may have sons, may have brothers; yes, even fathers, in the army. Where are they tonight? You love your children, or your brother or father. This mere youth has a father and mother and sister away back in Tennessee. They are willing to give him to his country. But oh! gentlemen, let the word go back to Tennessee that he died upon the battlefield, and not by the hands of his own comrades for being asleep at his post of duty. I cannot now remember the speeches, but one thing I do know, that he was acquitted, and I was glad of it.

"The Death Watch"

One more scene I can remember. Kind friends—you that know nothing of a soldier's life—I ask you in all candor not to doubt the following lines in this sketch. You have no doubt read of the old Roman soldier found amid the ruins of Pompeii, who had stood there for sixteen hundred years, and when he was excavated was found at his post with his gun clasped in his skeleton hands. You believe this because it is written in history. I have heard politicians tell it. I have heard it told from the sacred desk. It is true; no one doubts it.

Now, were I to tell something that happened in this nineteenth century exactly similar, you would hardly believe it. But whether you believe it or not, it is for you to say. At a little village called Hampshire Crossing, our regiment was ordered to go to a little stream called St. John's Run, to relieve the 14th Georgia Regiment and the 3rd Arkansas. I cannot tell the facts as I desire to. In fact, my hand trembles so, and my feelings are so overcome, that it is hard for me to write at all. But we went to the place that we were ordered to go to, and when we arrived there we found the guard sure enough. If I remember correctly, there were just eleven of them. Some were sitting down and some were laying down; but each and every one was as cold and as hard frozen as the icicles that hung from their hands and faces and clothing—dead! They had died at their post of duty. Two of them, a little in advance of the others, were standing with their guns in their hands, as cold and as hard frozen as a monument of marble—standing sentinel with loaded guns in their frozen hands! The tale is told. Were they true men? Does He who noteth the sparrow's fall, and numbers the hairs of our heads, have any interest in one like ourselves? Yes; He doeth all things well. Not a sparrow falls to the ground without His consent.

Virginia, Farewell

After having served through all the valley campaign, and marched through all the wonders of Northwest Virginia, and being associated with the army of Virginia, it was with sorrow and regret that we bade farewell to "Old Virginia's shore," to go to other fields of blood and carnage and death. We had learned to love Virginia; we love her now. The people were kind and good to us. They divided their last crust of bread and rasher of bacon with us. We loved Lee, we loved Jackson; we loved the name, association and people of Virginia. Hatton, Forbes, Anderson, Gilliam, Govan, Loring, Ashby and Schumaker[54] were names with which we had been long associated. We hated to leave all our old comrades behind us. We felt that we were proving recreant to the instincts of our own manhood, and that we were leaving those who had stood by us on the march and battlefield when they most needed our help. We knew the 7th and 14th Tennessee regiments; we knew the 3rd Arkansas, the 14th Georgia, and 42nd Virginia regiments. Their names were as familiar as household words. We were about to leave the bones of Joe Bynum and Gus Allen and Patrick Hanly. We were about to bid farewell to every tender association that we had formed with the good people of Virginia, and to our old associates among the soldiers of the Grand Army of Virginia. *Virginia, farewell!* Away back yonder, in good old Tennessee, our homes and loved ones are being robbed and insulted, our fields laid waste, our cities sacked, and our people slain. Duty as well as patriotism calls us back to our native home, to try and defend it, as best we can, against an invading army of our then enemies; and, Virginia, once more we bid you a long farewell!

Chapter 17: The Surrender

The Last Act of the Drama

On the 10th day of May, 1861, our regiment, the First Tennessee, left Nashville for the camp of instruction, with twelve hundred and fifty men, officers and line. Other recruits continually coming in swelled this number to fourteen hundred. In addition to this Major Fulcher's battalion of four companies, with four hundred men (originally), was afterwards attached to the regiment; and the Twenty-seventh Tennessee Regiment was afterwards consolidated with the First. And besides this, there were about two hundred conscripts added to the regiment from time to time. To recapitulate: The First Tennessee, numbering originally, 1,250; recruited from time to time, 150; Fulcher's battalion, 400; the Twenty-seventh Tennessee, 1,200; number of conscripts (at the lowest estimate), 200—making the sum total 3,200 men that belonged to our regiment during the war. The above I think a low estimate. Well, on the 26th day of April, 1865, General Joe E. Johnston surrendered his army at Greensboro, North Carolina. The day that we surrendered our regiment it was a pitiful sight to behold. If I remember correctly, there were just sixty-five men in all, including officers, that were paroled on that day. Now, what became of the original 3,200? A grand army, you may say. Three thousand two hundred men! Only sixty-five left! Now, reader, you may draw your own conclusions. It lacked just four days of four years from the day we were sworn in to the day of the surrender, and it was just four years and twenty-four days from the time that we left home for the army to the time that we got back again. It was indeed a sad sight to look at, the Old First Tennessee Regiment. A mere squad of noble and brave men, gathered around the tattered flag that they had followed in every battle through that long war. It was so bullet-riddled and torn that it was but a few blue and red shreds that hung drooping while it, too, was stacked with our guns forever.

Thermopylae[55] had one messenger of defeat, but when General Joe E. Johnston surrendered the Army of the South there were hundreds of regiments, yea, I might safely say thousands, that had not a representative on the 26th day of April, 1865.

Our cause was lost from the beginning. Our greatest victories—Chickamauga and Franklin—were our greatest defeats. Our people were divided upon the question of

Union and secession. Our generals were scrambling for "*Who ranked.*" The private soldier fought and starved and died for naught. Our hospitals were crowded with sick and wounded, but half provided with food and clothing to sustain life. Our money was depreciated to naught and our cause lost. We left our homes four years previous. Amid the waving of flags and handkerchiefs and the smiles of the ladies, while the fife and drum were playing Dixie and the Bonnie Blue Flag, we bid farewell to home and friends. The bones of our brave Southern boys lie scattered over our loved South. They fought for their "*country*," and gave their lives freely for that country's cause; and now they who survive sit, like Marius amid the wreck of Carthage, sublime even in ruins.[56] Other pens abler than mine will have to chronicle their glorious deeds of valor and devotion. In these sketches I have named but a few persons who fought side by side with me during that long and unholy war. In looking back over these pages, I ask, Where now are many whose names have appeared in these sketches? They are up yonder, and are no doubt waiting and watching for those of us who are left behind. And, my kind reader, the time is coming when we, too, will be called, while the archangel of death is beating the long roll of eternity, and with us it will be the last reveille. God Himself will sound the "assembly" on yonder beautiful and happy shore, where we will again have a grand "reconfederation." We shed a tear over their flower-strewn graves. We live after them. We love their memory yet. But one generation passes away and another generation follows. We know our loved and brave soldiers. We love them yet.

But when we pass away, the impartial historian will render a true verdict, and a history will then be written in justification and vindication of those brave and noble boys who gave their all in fighting the battles of their homes, their country, and their God.

"The United States has no North, no South, no East, no West." "*We are one and undivided.*"

Adieu

My kind friends—soldiers, comrades, brothers, all: The curtain is rung down, the footlights are put out, the audience has all left and gone home, the seats are vacant, and the cold walls are silent. The gaudy tinsel that appears before the footlights is exchanged for the dress of the citizen. Coming generations and historians will be the critics as to how we have acted our parts. The past is buried in oblivion. The blood-red flag, with its crescent and cross, that we followed for four long, bloody, and disastrous years, has been folded never again to be unfurled. We have no regrets for what we did, but we mourn the loss of so many brave and gallant men who perished on the field of battle and honor. I now bid you an affectionate adieu.

But in closing these memoirs, the scenes of my life pass in rapid review before me. In imagination, I am young again tonight. I feel the flush and vigor of my manhood—am just twenty-one years of age. I hear the fife and drum playing Dixie and Bonnie Blue Flag. I see and hear our fire-eating stump-orators tell of the right of secession and disunion. I see our fair and beautiful women waving their handkerchiefs and encouraging their sweethearts to go to the war. I see the marshaling of the hosts for "glorious war." I see the fine banners waving and hear the cry everywhere, "*To arms! to arms!*" And I also see our country at peace and prosperous, our fine cities look grand and gay, our fields rich in abundant harvests, our people happy and contented. All these pass in imagination before me. Then I look and see glorious war in all its splendor. I hear the shout and charge, the boom of artillery and the rattle of small arms. I see gaily-dressed officers charging backwards and forwards upon their mettled war horses, clothed in the panoply of war. I see victory and conquest upon flying banners. I see our arms triumph in every battle. And, O, my friends,

I see another scene. I see broken homes and broken hearts. I see war in all of its desolation. I see a country ruined and impoverished. I see a nation disfranchised and maltreated. I see a commonwealth forced to pay dishonest and fraudulent bonds that were issued to crush that people.[57] I see sycophants licking the boots of the country's oppressor. I see other and many wrongs perpetrated upon a conquered people. But maybe it is but the ghosts and phantoms of a dreamy mind, or the wind as it whistles around our lonely cabin-home. The past is buried in oblivion. The mantle of charity has long ago fallen upon those who think differently from us. We remember no longer wrongs and injustice done us by anyone on earth. We are willing to forget and forgive those who have wronged and falsified us. We look up above and beyond all these petty groveling things and shake hands and forget the past. And while my imagination is like the weaver's shuttle, playing back-ward and forward through these two decades of time, I ask myself, Are these things real? did they happen? are they being enacted today? or are they the fancies of the imagination in forgetful reverie? Is it true that I have seen all these things? that they are real incidents in my life's history? Did I see those brave and noble countrymen of mine laid low in death and weltering in their blood? Did I see our country laid waste and in ruins? Did I see soldiers marching, the earth trembling and jarring beneath their measured tread? Did I see the ruins of smouldering cities and deserted homes? Did I see my comrades buried and see the violet and wild flowers bloom over their graves? Did I see the flag of my country, that I had followed so long, furled to be no more unfurled forever? Surely they are but the vagaries of mine own imagination. Surely my fancies are running wild tonight. But, hush! I now hear the approach of battle. That low, rumbling sound in the west is the roar of cannon in the distance. That rushing sound is the tread of soldiers. That quick, lurid glare is the flash that precedes the cannon's roar. And listen! that loud report that makes the earth tremble and jar and sway, is but the bursting of a shell, as it screams through the dark, tempestuous night. That black, ebon cloud, where the lurid lightning flickers and flares, that is rolling through the heavens, is the smoke of battle; beneath is being enacted a carnage of blood and death. Listen! the soldiers are charging now. The flashes and roaring now are blended with the shouts of soldiers and confusion of battle.

But, reader, time has brought his changes since I, a young, ardent, and impetuous youth, burning with a lofty patriotism first shouldered my musket to defend the rights of my country.

Lifting the veil of the past, I see many manly forms, bright in youth and hope, standing in view by my side in Company H, First Tennessee Regiment. Again I look and half those forms are gone. Again, and gray locks and wrinkled faces and clouded brows stand before me.

Before me, too, I see, not in imagination, but in reality, my own loved Jennie, the partner of my joys and the sharer of my sorrows, sustaining, comforting, and cheering my pathway by her benignant smile; pouring the sunshine of domestic comfort and happiness upon our humble home; making life more worth the living as we toil on up the hill of time together, with the bright pledges of our early and constant love by our side while the sunlight of hope ever brightens our pathway, dispelling darkness and sorrow as we hand in hand approach the valley of the great shadow.

The tale is told. The world moves on, the sun shines as brightly as before, the flowers bloom as beautifully, the birds sing their carols as sweetly, the trees nod and bow their leafy tops as if slumbering in the breeze, the gentle winds fan our brow and kiss our cheek as they pass by, the pale moon sheds her silvery sheen, the blue dome of the sky sparkles with the trembling stars that twinkle and shine and make night beautiful, and the scene melts and gradually disappears forever.

Jefferson Davis, Speech Before Mississippi Legislature (March 10, 1884)

The 1880s were a busy time for the former President of the Confederacy. He published *The Rise and Fall of the Confederate Government* in 1881 and *A Short History of the Confederate States of America* in 1889. He also delivered a number of public addresses in which he grudgingly accepted the South's place in the Union while reiterating the principles of the Lost Cause. In 1884, the legislature of Mississippi, his home state, invited Davis to speak, and he returned to his characteristic theme. "When he had concluded he was seated in an easy chair, and for more than an hour extended his hand to the throng that crowded to meet him. The old Capitol took its last look of him when he left its halls at the end of that reception."[58]

March 10, 1884

Friends and Brethren of Mississippi: In briefest terms, but with deepest feeling, permit me to return my thanks for the unexpected honor you have conferred on me. Away from the political sea, I have in my secluded home observed with intense interest all passing events, affecting the interest or honor of Mississippi, and have rejoiced to see in the diversification of labor and the development of new sources of prosperity and the increased facilities of public education, reason to hope for a future to our State more prosperous than any preceding era. The safety and honor of a Republic must rest upon the morality, intelligence and patriotism of the community.

We are now in a transition state, which is always a bad one, both in society and in nature. What is to be the result of the changes which may be anticipated it is not possible to forecast, but our people have shown such fortitude and have risen so grandly from the deep depression inflicted upon them, that it is fair to entertain bright hopes for the future. Sectional hate concentrating itself upon my devoted head, deprives me of the privileges accorded to others in the sweeping expression of "without distinction of race, color or previous condition,"[59] but it cannot deprive me of that which is nearest and dearest to my heart, the right to be a Mississippian, and it is with great gratification that I received this emphatic recognition of that right by the representatives of our people. Reared on the soil of Mississippi, the ambition of my boyhood was to do something which would redound to the honor and welfare of the State. The weight of many years admonishes me that my day for actual service has passed, yet the desire remains undiminished to see the people of Mississippi prosperous and happy and her fame not unlike the past, but gradually growing wider and brighter as years roll away.

'Tis been said that I should apply to the United States for a pardon, but repentance must precede the right of pardon, and I have not repented. Remembering as I must all which has been suffered, all which has been lost, disappointed hopes and crushed aspirations, yet I deliberately say, if it were to do over again, I would again do just as I did in 1861. No one is the arbiter of his own fate. The people of the Confederate States did more in proportion to their numbers and mean than was ever achieved by any in the world's history. Fate decreed that they should be unsuccessful in the effort to maintain their claim to resume the grants made to the Federal Government. Our people have accepted the decree; it therefore behooves them, as they may, to promote the general welfare of the Union, to show to the world that hereafter, as heretofore, the patriotism of our people is not measured by lines of latitude and longitude, but is as broad as the obligations they have assumed and embraces the whole of our oceanbound domain. Let them leave to their children and children's children the grand example of never swerving from the path of duty, and preferring to return good for evil rather than to cherish the unmanly feeling of revenge. But never question or teach your children to desecrate the memory of the dead by admitting that their brothers were wrong in the effort to maintain the sovereignty, freedom and independence which was their inalienable birthright—remembering that the coming generations are the children of the heroic mothers whose devotion to our cause in its darkest hour sustained the strong and strengthened the weak, I cannot believe that the cause for which our sacrifices were made can ever be lost, but rather hope that those who now deny the justice of our asserted claims will learn from experience that the fathers builded wisely and the Constitution should be constructed according to the commentaries of the men who made it.

It having been previously understood that I would not attempt to do more than to return my thanks, which are far deeper than it would be possible for me to express, I will now, Senators and Representatives, and to you ladies and gentlemen, who have honored me by your attendance, bid you an affectionate, and it may be, a last farewell.

Timothy Thomas Fortune, "Bartow Black" (1886)

One of the consequences of Lost Cause ideology was to justify and encourage a backlash against Southern blacks during Reconstruction. After all, to the extent that the Confederacy fought to preserve slavery, Jefferson Davis's remark that "I cannot believe that the cause for which our sacrifices were made can ever be lost" invited a rearguard battle against the economic and political progress of African Americans. The violent dimension of Lost Cause ideology manifested itself in the rise of the Ku Klux Klan, which was organized by former Confederate officers soon after the war, and other white supremacist organizations, such as the Red Shirts and the Knights of the White Camelia. By terrorizing and committing violence against African Americans and Republican leaders, these groups played a vile but influential role in the larger movement to reassert control over Southern state and local governments and to roll back the gains of Reconstruction.

'Twas when the Proclamation came, —
    Far in the sixties back, —
He left his lord, and changed his name
    To "Mister Bartow Black."

He learned to think himself a man,
    And privileged, you know,
To adopt a new and different plan, —
    To lay aside the hoe.

He took the lead in politics,
    And handled all the "notes," —
For he was up to all the tricks
    That gather in the votes;

For when the war came to a close
    And negroes "took a stand,"
Young Bartow with the current rose,
    The foremost in command.

His voice upon the "stump" was heard;
    He "Yankeedom" did prate;
The "carpet-bagger" he revered;
    The Southerner did hate.

He now was greater than the lord
    Who used to call him slave,
For he was on the "County Board,"
    With every right to rave.

But this amazing run of luck
    Was far too good to stand;
And soon the chivalrous "Ku-Klux"
    Rose in the Southern land.

Then Bartow got a little note, —
    'Twas very queerly signed, —
It simply told him not to vote,
    Or be to death resigned.

Young Bartow thought this little game
    Was very fine and nice
To bring his courage rare to shame
    And knowledge of justice.

"What right have they to think I fear?"
    He to himself did say.
"Dare they presume that I do care
    How loudly they do bray?

"This is my home, and here I die,
    Contending for my right!
Then let them come! My colors fly!
    I'm ready now to fight!

"Let those who think that Bartow Black, —
    An office-holder, too! —
Will to the cowards show his back,
    Their vain presumption rue!"

Bartow pursued his office game,
    And made the money, too,
But home at nights he wisely came
    And played the husband true.

When they had got their subject tame,
   And well-matured their plan,
They at the hour of midnight came,
   And armed was every man!

They numbered fifty Southern sons,
   And masked was every face;
And Winfield rifles were their guns, —
   You could that plainly trace.

One Southern brave did have a key,
   An entrance quick to make;
They entered all; but meek, you see,
   Their victim not to wake!

They reached his room! He was in bed, —
   His wife was by his side!
They struck a match above his head, —
   His eyes he opened wide!

Poor Bartow could not reach his gun,
   Though quick his arm did stretch,
For twenty bullets through him spun,
   That stiffly laid the wretch.

And then they rolled his carcass o'er,
   And filled both sides with lead;
And then they turned it on the floor,
   And shot away his head!

Ere Black his bloody end did meet
   His wife had swooned away;
The Southern braves did now retreat, —
   There was no need to stay!

Charlotte L. Forten Grimké, "The Gathering of the Grand Army" (1890)

The Grand Army of the Republic was the largest and most influential of a number of veterans' organizations that arose in the wake of the Civil War. Composed predominantly of white Union Army veterans, the GAR was closely associated with the Republican Party and it advocated on behalf of veterans' pensions, organized memorial activities and charity drives, and provided a forum for fraternal camraderie and political activism. In 1890, membership in the GAR had reached about 410,000—a figure never to be regained[60]—and in August of that year, it held its 24th annual "national encampment" in Boston, an event which Grimké's poem celebrates.

Through all the city's streets there poured a flood,
   A flood of human souls, eager, intent;

One thought, one purpose stirred the people's blood,
    And through their veins its quickening current sent.

The flags waved gayly in the summer air,
    O'er patient watchers 'neath the clouded skies;
Old age, and youth, and infancy were there,
    The glad light shining in expectant eyes.

And when at last our county's saviors came, —
    In proud procession down the crowded street,
Still brighter burned the patriotic flame,
    And loud acclaims leaped forth their steps to greet.

And now the veterans scarred and maimed appear,
    And now the tattered battle-flags uprise;
A silence deep one moment fills the air,
    Then shout on shout ascends unto the skies.

Oh, brothers, ye have borne the battle strain,
    And ye have felt it through the ling'ring years;
For all your valiant deeds, your hours of pain,
    We can but give to you our grateful tears!

And now, with heads bowed low, and tear-filled eyes
    We see a Silent Army passing slow;
For it no music swells, no shouts arise,
    But silent blessings from our full hearts flow.

The dead, the living, — All, — a glorious host,
    A "cloud of witnesses," — around us press —
Shall we, like them, stand faithful at our post,
    Or weekly yield, unequal to the stress?

Shall it be said the land they fought to save,
    Ungrateful now, proves faithless to her trust?
Shall it be said the sons of sires so brave
    Now trail her sacred banner in the dust?

Ah, no! again shall rise the people's voice
    As once it rose in accents clear and high —
"Oh, outraged brother, lift your head, rejoice!
    Justice shall reign, — Insult and Wrong shall die!"

So shall this day the joyous promise be
    Of golden days for our fair land in store;
When Freedom's flag shall float above the free,
    And Love and Peace prevail from shore to shore.

            (August 12, 1890, Boston)

Albion Tourgée, "The South as a Field for Fiction" (1888)

By the late 1870s and early 1880s, it had become apparent to a perceptive few that while the South may have lost the war, it was succeeding in a promoting a revisionist account of its own history and a romantic self-image—in literature, educational materials, and religious and political rhetoric. For Tourgée—a lawyer, judge, former soldier, and newly popular author of *The Fool's Errand* (1879) and *Bricks Without Straw* (1880) —this development portended ill things for the republic (not to mention to its African American population), particularly since the myth was being adopted by Northern writers as well. Yet he also recognized the imaginative power of loss and suffering, and the rich if problematic artistry that lives at the juncture of history and fiction.

More than twenty years ago the writer ventured the prediction that the short but eventful lifetime of the Southern Confederacy, the downfall of slavery, and the resulting conditions of Southern life would furnish to the future American novelist his richest and most striking material. At that time he was entirely unknown as a writer of fiction, and it is probable that he is now generally supposed to have turned his attention in this direction more from political bias than from any literary or artistic attraction which it offered. The exact converse was in fact true; the romantic possibility of the situation appealed to him even more vividly than its political difficulty, though, as is always the case in great national crises, the one was unavoidably colored by the other. Slavery as a condition of society has not yet become separable, in the minds of our people, North or South, from slavery as a political idea, a factor of partisan strife. They do not realize that two centuries of bondage left an ineradicable impress on master and slave alike, or that the line of separation between the races, being marked by the fact of color, is as impassable since emancipation as it was before, and perhaps even more portentous. They esteem slavery as simply a dead, unpleasant fact of which they wish to hear nothing more, and regard any disparaging allusion to its results as an attempt to revive a defunct political sentiment.

It is not surprising, therefore, that the literary men of the North should have looked upon such a forecast with contempt and impatience. It seemed to them to be not only absurd, but inspired by a malicious desire to keep alive the memory of an epoch which it was the duty of every one to help bury in impenetrable oblivion. That was a foolish notion. A nation can never bury its past. A country's history may perish with it, but it can never outlive its history. Yet such was the force of the determination in the Northern mind to taboo all allusion to that social condition which had been the occasion of strife, that the editor of a leading magazine felt called upon to make emphatic protest against the obnoxious prediction. "However much of pathos there may have been in the slave's life," he said, with the positiveness of infallibility, "its relations can never constitute the groundwork of enjoyable fiction. The colored race themselves can never regard the estate of bondage as a romantic epoch, or desire to perpetuate its memories. Slavery and rebellion, therefore," he concludes, "with the conditions attendant upon and resulting from them, can never constitute a popular field for American fiction." Time is not always prompt in its refutation of bad logic, but in this case he is not chargeable with unnecessary delay. In obedience to a pronounced and undeniable popular demand, that very magazine has given a complete reversal of its own emphatic dictum, by publishing in a recent number a dialect story of Southern life written by one of the enslaved race.[61]

Under such circumstances, however, it is hardly surprising that the writer's farther prediction should have been regarded as too absurd for refutation. He himself is almost startled, as he looks at the dingy pages, to find himself averring, in the very glare of expiring conflict, that "within thirty years after the close of the war of rebellion popular sympathy will be with those who upheld the Confederate cause rather than with those by whom it was overthrown; our popular heroes will be Confederate leaders; our fiction will be Southern in its prevailing types and distinctively Southern in its character." There are yet seven years to elapse before the prescribed limit is reached, but the prediction is already almost literally fulfilled. Not only is the epoch of the war the favorite field of American fiction to-day, but the Confederate soldier is the popular hero. Our literature has become not only Southern in type, but distinctly Confederate in sympathy. The federal or Union soldier is not exactly depreciated, but subordinated; the Northern type is not decried, but the Southern is preferred. This is not because of any essential superiority of the one or lack of heroic attributes in the other, but because sentiment does not always follow the lead of conviction, and romantic sympathy is scarcely at all dependent upon merit. The writer makes no pretension to having foreseen the events that have occurred in the interval that has elapsed. Even the results he but perfectly comprehended, having no clear anticipation of the peculiar forms which Southern fiction would assume. The one thing he did perceive, and the causes of which he clearly outlined, was the almost unparalleled richness of Southern life of that period as a field for fictitious narrative.

But whatever the cause may be, it cannot be denied that American fiction of to-day, whatever may be its origin, is predominantly Southern in type and character. The East and the West had already been in turn the seat of romantic empire. American genius has traced with care each step in the mysterious process by which the "dude" was evolved from the Puritan and "cow-boy" from the pioneer. From Cooper to Hawthorne, colonial and Revolutionary life of the East was the favorite ground of the novelist. The slavery agitation gave a glimpse of one phase of Southern life. As soon as the war was over, as if to distract attention from that unpleasant fact, we were invited to contrast American crudeness with English culture. Then the Western type came boldly to the front and the world studied the assimilations of our early occidental life; its product has not yet been portrayed. For a time each of these overshadowed in American fiction all the others. Each was in turn worked out. The public relish for that particular diet palled, and popular taste, which is the tyrant of the realm of literature, demanded something else. To-day the South has unquestionably the preference. Hardly a novelist of prominence, except Mr. Howells and Mr. James, but has found it necessary to yield to the prevailing demand and identify himself with Southern types. Southern life does not lend itself readily to the methods of the former. It is earnest, intense, full of action, and careless to a remarkable degree of the trivialities which both these authors esteem the most important features of real life. Its types neither subsist upon soliloquy nor practice irrelevancy as a fine art; they are not affected by a chronic self-distrust nor devoted to anti-climax. Yet despite these imperfections the public appetite seems to crave their delineation.

A foreigner studying our current literature, without knowledge of our history, and judging our civilization by our fiction, would undoubtedly conclude that the South was the seat of intellectual empire in America, and the African the chief romantic element of our population. As an evidence of this, it may be noted that a few months ago every one of our great popular monthlies presented a "Southern story" as one of its most prominent features; and during the past year nearly two-thirds of the stories and sketches furnished to newspapers by various syndicates have been of this character.

To the Northern man, whose belief in averages is so profound, this flood of Southern fiction seems quite unaccountable. He recurs at once to the statistics of illiteracy, with an unfaltering belief that novels, poems, and all forms of literature are a natural and spontaneous product of the common-school system. He sees that twenty-eight out of every hundred of the white people of the South cannot read or write, and at once concludes that in literary production as well as in mechanical and financial achievement the North must of necessity excel, in about the same proportion that it does in capacity to assimilate the literary product.

Yet the fact ought not to surprise any one. One of the compensations of war is a swift ensuing excitation of the mental faculties, which almost always yields remarkable results. This is especially true when fortune turns against a spirited and ambitious people. The War of Rebellion was a far more terrible experience to the people of the South than to those of the North. The humiliation resulting from defeat was intense and universal. They had and can have no tide of immigration and no rush of business life greatly to lessen the force of these impressions, while the presence of the Negro in numbers almost equal to the whites prevents the possibility of forgetting the past. The generation which has grown up since the war not only has the birthmark of the hour of defeat upon it, but has been shaped and molded quite as much by regret for the old conditions as by the difficulties of the new. To the Southern man or woman, therefore, the past, present, and future of Southern life is the most interesting and important matter about which they can possibly concern themselves. It is their world. Their hopes and aspirations are bounded by its destiny, and their thought is not diluted by cosmopolitan ideas. Whether self-absorption is an essential requisite of literary production or not, it is unquestionably true that almost all the noted writers of fiction have been singularly enthusiastic lovers of the national life of which they have been a part. In this respect the Southern novelist has a vast advantage over his Northern contemporary. He has never any doubt. He loves the life he portrays and sincerely believes in its superlative excellence. He does not study it as a curiosity, but knows it by intuition. He never sneers at its imperfections, but worships even its defects.

The Southern writer, too, has a curiously varied life from which he may select his types, and this life is absolutely *terra incognita* to the Northern mind. The "Tyrant of Broomsedge Cove" may have a parallel on every hillside; Mrs. Burnett's miraculously transformed "poor-white" Cinderellas may still use the springs for pier-glasses; Joel Chandler Harris's quaintness, Chestnut's [sic] curious realism, or the dreamy idealism that still paints the master and the slave as complements of a remembered millennial state: any of these may be a true picture of this life so far as the Northern man's knowledge or conception is concerned.[62] He has a conventional "Southern man," a conventional "poor white," with a female counterpart of each already fitted out in his fancy; and as long as the author does not seriously disturb these preconceptions, the Northern reader likes the Southern story because it is full of life and fire and real feeling. And it is no wonder that he does, for it is getting to be quite a luxury to the novel reader to find a story in which the characters have any feeling beyond a self-conscious sensibility which seems to give them a deal of trouble without ever ripening into motive or resulting in achievement.

It is noteworthy in this revival that the Negro and the poor white are taking rank as by far the more interesting elements of Southern life. True, the dashing Confederate cavalier holds his place pretty well. It is rather odd that he was always a "cavalier"; but, so far as our fiction is concerned, there does not appear to have been any Confederate infantry. Still, even the "cavalier" has come to need a foil, just as Dives required a Lazarus,[63] and with like result—the beggar has overshadowed his patron. In literature as well as in politics, the poor white is having the best of the Southern *renaissance*. The sons of schoolmasters and overseers and even "crappers" have come to the fore in the "New

South," and the poor white is exalted not only in his offspring but in literature. There are infinite possibilities in the poor white of either sex; and as the supply is limited to the South, there seems to be no reason why he should not during the next half century become to the fiction of the United States what the Highlander is to Scottish literature— the only "interesting" white character in it.

But the Negro has of late developed a capacity as a stock character of fiction which no one ever dreamed that he possessed in the good old days when he was a merchantable commodity. It must be admitted, too, that the Southern writers are "working him for all he is worth," as a foil to the aristocratic types of the land of heroic possibilities. The Northern man, no matter what his prejudices, is apt to think of the Negro as having an individuality of his own. To the Southern mind, he is only a shadow—an incident of another's life. As such he is invariably assigned one of two roles. In one he figures as the devoted slave who serves and sacrifices for his master and mistress, and is content to live or die, do good or evil, for those to whom he feels himself under infinite obligation for the privilege of living and serving. There were such miracles no doubt, but they were so rare as never to have lost the miraculous character. The other favorite aspect of the Negro character from the point of view of the Southern fictionist, is that of the poor "nigger" to whom liberty has brought only misfortune, and who is relieved by the disinterested friendship of some white man whose property he once was. There are such cases, too, but they are not so numerous as to destroy the charm of novelty. About the Negro as a man, with hopes, fears, and aspirations like other men, our literature is very nearly silent. Much has been written of the slave and something of the freedman, but thus far no one has been found able to weld the new life to the old.

This indeed is the great difficulty to be overcome. As soon as the American Negro seeks to rise above the level of the former time, he finds himself confronted with the past of his race and the woes of his kindred. It is to him not only a record of subjection but of injustice and oppression. The "twice-told tales" of *his* childhood are animate with rankling memories of wrongs. Slavery colored not only the lives but the traditions of his race. With the father's and the mother's blood is transmitted the story, not merely of their individual wrongs but of a race's woe, which the impenetrable oblivion of the past makes even more terrible and which the sense of color will not permit him to forget. The white man traces his ancestry back for generations, knows whence they came, where they lived, and guesses what they did. To the American Negro the past is only darkness replete with unimaginable horrors. Ancestors he has none. Until within a quarter of a century he had no record of his kindred. He was simply one number of an infinite "no name series." He had no father, no mother; only a sire and dam. Being bred for market, he had no name, only a distinguishing appellative, like that of a horse or a dog. Even in comparison with these animals he was at a disadvantage; there was no "herdbook" of slaves. A well-bred horse may be traced back in his descent for a thousand years, and may show a hundred strains of noble blood ; but even this poor consolation is denied the eight millions of slave-descended men and women in our country.

The remembrance of this condition is not pleasant and can never become so. It is exasperating, galling, degrading. Every freedman's life is colored by this shadow. The farther he gets away from slavery, the more bitter and terrible will be his memory of it. The wrong that was done to his forebears is a continuing and self-magnifying evil. This is the inevitable consequence of the conditions of the past; no kindness can undo it; no success can blot it out. It is the sole inheritance the bondman left his issue, and it must grow heavier rather than lighter until the very suggestion of inequality has disappeared— if indeed such a time shall ever come.

The life of the Negro as a slave, freedman, and racial outcast offers undoubtedly the richest mine of romantic material that has opened to the English-speaking novelist since the Wizard of the North[64] discovered and depicted the common life of Scotland. The Negro as a man has an immense advantage over the Negro as a servant, being an altogether new character in fiction. The slave's devotion to the master was trite in the remote antiquity of letters; but the slave as a man, with his hopes, his fears, his faith, has been touched, and only touched, by the pen of the novelist. The traditions of the freedman's fireside are richer and far more tragic than the folk-lore which genius has recently put into his quaint vernacular. The freedman as a man—not as a "brother in black," with the curse of Cain yet upon him, but a man with hopes and aspirations, quick to suffer, patient to endure, full of hot passion, fervid imagination, desirous of being equal to the best—is sure to be a character of enduring interest.

The mere fact of having suffered or enjoyed does not imply the power to portray; but the Negro race in America has other attributes besides mere imagination. It has absorbed the best blood of the South, and it is quite within the possibilities that it may itself become a power in literature, of which even the descendants of the old regime shall be as proud as they now are of the dwellers in "Broomsedge Cove" and on the "Great Smoky."

Pathos lies at the bottom of all enduring fiction. Agony is the key of immortality. The ills of fate, irreparable misfortune, untoward but unavoidable destiny: these are the things that make for enduring fame. The "realists" profess to be truth-tellers, but are in fact the worst of falsifiers, since they tell only the weakest and meanest part of the grand truth which makes up the continued story of every life. As a rule, humanity is in serious earnest, and loves to have its sympathy moved with woes that are heavy enough to leave an impress of actuality on the heart. Sweetmeats may afford greater scope for the skill of the *chef*, but it is "the roast beef of old England" that "sticks to the ribs" and nourishes a race of giants. Dainties—peacocks' tongues and sparrows' brains—may bring delight to the epicure who loves to close his eyes and dream that he detects the hint of a flavor; but the strong man despises neutral things and a vigorous people demand a vigorous literature.

It is the poet of action whose clutch on the human soul is eternal, not the professor of analytics or the hierophant of doubt and uncertainty. In sincerity of passion and aspiration, as well as in the woefulness and humiliation that attended its downfall, the history of the Confederacy stands pre-eminent in human epochs. Everything about it was on a grand scale. Everything was real and sincere. The soldier fought in defense of his home, in vindication of what he deemed his right. There was a proud assumption of superiority, a regal contempt of their foe, which, like Rector's boastfulness, added wonderfully to the pathos of the result. Then, too, a civilization fell with it—a civilization full of wonderful contrasts, horrible beyond the power of imagination to conceive in its injustice, cruelty, and barbarous debasement of a subject race, yet exquisitely charming in its assumption of pastoral purity and immaculate excellence. It believed that the slave loved his chains and was all the better physically and morally for wearing them.

But then came the catastrophe, and all was changed. The man who fights and wins is only common in human esteem. The downfall of empire is always the epoch of romance. The brave but unfortunate reap always the richest measure of immortality. The roundheads are accounted base and common realities, but the cavaliers are glorified by disaster. In all history, no cause had so many of the elements of pathos as that which failed at Appomattox, and no people ever presented to the novelist such a marvelous array of curiously contrasted lives. Added to the various elements of the white race are those other exceptional and unparalleled conditions of this epoch, springing from "race, color, and previous condition of servitude." The dominant class itself presents the accumulated pathos of a million abdications. "We are all poor whites now," is the touching phrase in which the results of the conflict are expressed with instinctive accuracy by those to whom it meant social as well as political disaster. It is a truth as yet but half appreciated. The level of Caucasian life at the South must hereafter be run from the bench-line of the poor white, and there cannot be any leveling upward. The distance between its upper and lower strata cannot be maintained; indeed it is rapidly disappearing. To the woefulness of the conquered is added the pathos of a myriad of deposed sovereigns. Around them will cluster the halo of romantic glory, and the epoch of their overthrow will live again in American literature.

It matters not whence the great names of the literary epoch which is soon to dawn may derive their origin. No doubt there is something of truth in Herbert Spencer's suggestion, that the poets and novelists as well as the rulers of the future will come from the great plains and dwell in the shadows of the stern and silent mountains of the West. Greatness is rarely born where humanity swarms. Individual power is the product of a wide horizon. Inspiration visits men in solitude, and the Infinite comes nearer as the finite recedes from the mental vision; only solitude must not be filled with self. No solitary, self-imprisoned for his own salvation, ever sang an immortal strain; but he that taketh the woes of a people into the desert with him, sees God in the burning bush. Method is but half of art—its meaner half. Inspiration gives the better part of immortality. Homer's heroes made his song undying, not his sonorous measures; and the glow of English manfulness spreads its glamour over Shakespeare's lines, and makes him for all ages the poet from whom brave men will draw renewed strength and the unfortunate get unfailing consolation. Scott's loving faith in a chivalry which perhaps never existed, not only made his work imperishable, but inspires with healthful aspiration every reader of his shining pages.

Because of these things it is that the South is destined to be the Hesperides Garden of American literature. We cannot foretell the form its product will wear or even guess its character. It may be sorrowful, exultant, aspiring, or perhaps terrible, but it will certainly be great—greater than we have hitherto known, because its causative forces are mightier than those which have shaped the productive energy of the past. That its period of highest excellence will soon be attained there is little room to doubt. The history of literature shows that it is those who were cradled amid the smoke of battle, the sons and daughters of heroes yet red with slaughter, the inheritors of national woe or racial degradation, who have given utterance to the loftiest strains of genius. Because of the exceeding woefulness of a not too recent past, therefore, and the abiding horror of unavoidable conditions which are the sad inheritance of the present, we may confidently look for the children of soldiers and of slaves to advance American literature to the very front rank of that immortal procession whose song is the eternal refrain of remembered agony, before the birth-hour of the twentieth century shall strike.

Oliver Wendell Holmes, Jr., "The Soldier's Faith" (May 30, 1895)

An Address Delivered on Memorial Day, May 30, 1895, at a Meeting Called by the Graduating Class of Harvard University

The origins of Memorial Day lie in the many spontaneous gatherings of Americans, during and just after the Civil War, to remember their lost loved ones, neighbors, and friends. These events commonly involved decorating the graves of soldiers, and thus arose the term "Decoration Day," proposed in 1868 by the head of the Grand of Army of the Republic, Gen. John Logan, variously adopted by the states, and gradually changed to "Memorial Day" during the late nineteenth century. As the war receded into the past, commemorating the loss of life on both sides, with a focus on individual honor and valor, helped to depoliticize the conflict for Americans eager for a feeling of national unity. At the time of this address, Holmes, a Harvard graduate and Civil War veteran, served on the Massachusetts Supreme Court, and what he sought to do, writes G. Edward White, was to establish a "juxtaposition between the anarchic reality of experience and the ennobling quality of ideals."[65]

Any day in Washington Street, when the throng is greatest and busiest, you may see a blind man playing a flute. I suppose that some one hears him. Perhaps also my pipe may reach the heart of some passer in the crowd.

I once heard a man say, "Where Vanderbilt[66] sits, there is the head of the table. I teach my son to be rich." He said what many think. For although the generation born about 1840, and now governing the world, has fought two at least of the greatest wars in history, and has witnessed others, war is out of fashion, and the man who commands attention of his fellows is the man of wealth. Commerce is the great power. The aspirations of the world are those of commerce. Moralists and philosophers, following its lead, declare that war is wicked, foolish, and soon to disappear.

The society for which many philanthropists, labor reformers, and men of fashion unite in longing is one in which they may be comfortable and may shine without much trouble or any danger. The unfortunately growing hatred of the poor for the rich seems to me to rest on the belief that money is the main thing (a belief in which the poor have been encouraged by the rich), more than on any other grievance. Most of my hearers would rather that their daughters or their sisters should marry a son of one of the great rich families than a regular army officer, were he as beautiful, brave, and gifted as Sir William Napier.[67] I have heard the question asked whether our war was worth fighting, after all. There are many, poor and rich, who think that love of country is an old wife's tale, to be replaced by interest in a labor union, or, under the name of cosmopolitanism, by a rootless self-seeking search for a place where the most enjoyment may be had at the least cost.

Meantime we have learned the doctrine that evil means pain, and the revolt aginst pain in all its forms has grown more and more marked. From societies for the prevention of cruelty to animals up to socialism, we express in numberless ways the notion that suffering is a wrong which can be and ought to be prevented, and a whole literature of sympathy has sprung into being which points out in story and in verse how hard it is to be wounded in the battle of life, how terrible, how unjust it is that any one should fail.

Even science has had its part in the tendencies which we observe. It has shaken established religion in the minds of very many. It has pursued analysis until at last this thrilling world of colors and passions and sounds has seemed fatally to resolve itself into one vast network of vibrations endlessly weaving an aimless web, and the rainbow flush of cathedral windows, which once to enraptured eyes appeared the very smile of God, fades slowly out into the pale irony of the void.

And yet from vast orchestras still comes the music of mighty symphonies. Our painters even now are spreading along the walls of our Library glowing symbols of mysteries still real, and the hardly silenced cannon of the East proclaim once more that combat and pain still are the portion of man. For my own part, I believe that the struggle for life is the order of the world, at which it is vain to repine. I can imagine the burden changed in the way it is to be borne, but I cannot imagine that it ever will be lifted from men's backs. I can imagine a future in which science shall have passed from the combative to the dogmatic stage, and shall have gained such catholic acceptance that it shall take control of life, and condemn at once with instant execution what now is left for nature to destroy. But we are far from such a future, and we cannot stop to amuse or to terrify ourselves with dreams. Now, at least, and perhaps as long as man dwells upon the globe, his destiny is battle, and he has to take the chances of war. If it is our business to fight, the book for the army is a war-song, not a hospital-sketch. It is not well for soldiers to think much about wounds. Sooner or later we shall fall; but meantime it is for us to fix our eyes upon the point to be stormed, and to get there if we can.

Behind every scheme to make the world over, lies the question, What kind of world do you want? The ideals of the past for men have been drawn from war, as those for women have been drawn from motherhood. For all our prophecies, I doubt if we are ready to give up our inheritance. Who is there who would not like to be thought a gentleman? Yet what has that name been built on but the soldier's choice of honor rather than life? To be a soldier or descended from soldiers, in time of peace to be ready to give one's life rather than suffer disgrace, that is what the word has meant; and if we try to claim it at less cost than a splendid carelessness for life, we are trying to steal the good will without the responsibilities of the place. We will not dispute about tastes. The man of the future may want something different. But who of us could endure a world, although cut up into five-acre lots, and having no man upon it who was not well fed and well housed, without the divine folly of honor, without the senseless passion for knowledge outreaching the flaming bounds of the possible, without ideals the essence of which is that they can never be achieved? I do not know what is true. I do not know the meaning of the universe. But in the midst of doubt, in the collapse of creeds, there is one thing I do not doubt, that no man who lives in the same world with most of us can doubt, and that is that the faith is true and adorable which leads a soldier to throw away his life in obedience to a blindly accepted duty, in a cause which he little understands, in a plan of campaign of which he has little notion, under tactics of which he does not see the use.

Most men who know battle know the cynic force with which the thoughts of common sense will assail them in times of stress; but they know that in their greatest moments faith has trampled those thoughts under foot. If you wait in line, suppose on Tremont Street Mall, ordered simply to wait and do nothing, and have watched the enemy bring their guns to bear upon you down a gentle slope like that of Beacon Street, have seen the puff of the firing, have felt the burst of the spherical case-shot as it came toward you, have heard and seen the shrieking fragments go tearing through your company, and have known that the next or the next shot carries your fate; if you have advanced in line and have seen ahead of you the spot you must pass where the rifle bullets are striking; if you have ridden at night at a walk toward the blue line of fire at the dead angle of Spottsylvania, where for twenty-four hours the soldiers were fighting on the two sides of an earthwork, and in the morning the dead and dying lay piled in a row six deep, and as you rode you heard the bullets splashing in the mud and earth about you; if you have been in the picket-line at night in a black and unknown wood, have heard the splat of the bullets upon the trees, and as you moved have felt your foot slip upon a dead man's body; if you have had a blind fierce gallop against the enemy, with your blood up and a pace that left no time for fear—if, in short, as some, I hope many, who hear me, have known, you have known the vicissitudes of terror and triumph in war; you know that there is such a thing as the faith I spoke of. You know your own weakness and are modest; but you know that man has in him that unspeakable somewhat which makes him capable of miracle, able to lift himself by the might of his own soul, unaided, able to face annihilation for a blind belief.

From the beginning, to us, children of the North, life has seemed a place hung about by dark mists, out of which comes the pale shine of dragon's scales and the cry of fighting men, and the sound of swords. Beowulf, Milton, Durer, Rembrandt, Schopenhauer, Turner, Tennyson, from the first war song of the race to the stall-fed poetry of modern English drawing rooms, all have had the same vision, and all have had a glimpse of a light to be followed. "The end of wordly life awaits us all. Let him who may, gain honor ere death. That is best for a warrior when he is dead." So spoke Beowulf a thousand years ago.

> Not of the sunlight,
> Not of the moonlight,
> Not of the starlight!
> O Young Mariner,
> Down to the haven.
> Call your companions,
> Launch your vessel,
> And crowd your canvas,
> And, ere it vanishes
> Over the margin,
> After it, follow it,
> Follow The Gleam.

So sang Tennyson in the voice of the dying Merlin.[68]

When I went to the war I thought that soldiers were old men. I remembered a picture of the revolutionary soldier which some of you may have seen, representing a white-haired man with his flint-lock slung across his back. I remembered one or two examples of revolutionary soldiers whom I have met, and I took no account of the lapse of time. It was not long after, in winter quarters, as I was listening to some of the sentimental songs in vogue, such as—

> Farewell, Mother, you may never
> See your darling boy again,

that it came over me that the army was made up of what I should now call very young men. I dare say that my illusion has been shared by some of those now present, as they have looked at us upon whose heads the white shadows have begun to fall. But the truth is that war is the business of youth and early middle age. You who called this assemblage together, not we, would be the soldiers of another war, if we should have one, and we speak to you as the dying Merlin did in the verse which I have just quoted. Would that the blind man's pipe might be transformed by Merlin's magic, to make you hear the bugles as once we heard them beneath the morning stars! For you it is that now is sung the Song of the Sword:—

> The War-Thing, the Comrade,
> Father of Honor,
> And giver of kingship,
> The fame-smith, the song master.

> *Priest* (saith the Lord)
> *Of his marriage with victory*

Clear singing, clean slicing;
Sweet spoken, soft finishing;
Making death beautiful
Life but a coin
To be staked in a pastime
Whose playing is more
Than the transfer of being;
Arch-anarch, chief builder,
Prince and evangelist,
I am the Will of God:
I am the Sword.[69]

War, when you are at it, is horrible and dull. It is only when time has passed that you see that its message was divine. I hope it may be long before we are called again to sit at that master's feet. But some teacher of the kind we all need. In this snug, over-safe corner of the world we need it, that we may realize that our comfortable routine is no eternal necessity of things, but merely a little space of calm in the midst of the tempestuous untamed streaming of the world, and in order that we may be ready for danger. We need it in this time of individualist negations, with its literature of French and American humor, revolting at discipline, loving flesh-pots, and denying that anything is worthy of reverence—in order that we may remember all that buffoons forget. We need it every-where and at all times. For high and dangerous action teaches us to believe as right beyond dispute things for which our doubting minds are slow to find words of proof. Out of heroism grows faith in the worth of heroism. The proof comes later, and even may never come. Therefore I rejoice at every dangerous sport which I see pursued. The students at Heidelberg, with their sword-slashed faces, inspire me with sincere respect. I gaze with delight upon our polo players. If once in a while in our rough riding a neck is broken, I regard it, not as a waste, but as a price well paid for the breeding of a race fit for headship and command.

We do not save our traditions, in our country. The regiments whose battle-flags were not large enough to hold the names of the battles they had fought vanished with the surrender of Lee, although their memories inherited would have made heroes for a century. It is the more necessary to learn the lesson afresh from perils newly sought, and perhaps it is not vain for us to tell the new generation what we learned in our day, and what we still believe. That the joy of life is living, is to put out all one's powers as far as they will go; that the measure of power is obstacles overcome; to ride boldly at what is in front of you, be it fence or enemy; to pray, not for comfort, but for combat; to keep the soldier's faith against the doubts of civil life, more besetting and harder to over-come than all the misgivings of the battlefield, and to remember that duty is not to be proved in the evil day, but then to be obeyed unquestioning; to love glory more than the temptations of wallowing ease, but to know that one's final judge and only rival is oneself: with all our failures in act and thought, these things we learned from noble enemies in Virginia or Georgia or on the Mississippi, thirty years ago; these things we believe to be true.

"Life is not lost", said she, "for which is bought
Endlesse renown."[70]

We learned also, and we still believe, that love of country is not yet an idle name.

Deare countrey! O how dearly deare
Ought thy remembraunce, and perpetuall band
Be to thy foster-child, that from thy hand
Did commun breath and nouriture receave!
How brutish is it not to understand
How much to her we owe, that all us gave;
That gave unto us all, whatever good we have![71]

As for us, our days of combat are over. Our swords are rust. Our guns will thunder no more. The vultures that once wheeled over our heads must be buried with their prey. Whatever of glory must be won in the council or the closet, never again in the field. I do not repine. We have shared the incommunicable experience of war; we have felt, we still feel, the passion of life to its top.

Three years ago died the old colonel of my regiment, the Twentieth Massachusetts.[72] He gave the regiment its soul. No man could falter who heard his "Forward, Twentieth!" I went to his funeral. From a side door of the church a body of little choir-boys came in like a flight of careless doves. At the same time the doors opened at the front, and up the main aisle advanced his coffin, followed by the few grey heads who stood for the men of the Twentieth, the rank and file whom he had loved, and whom he led for the last time. The church was empty. No one remembered the old man whom we were burying, no one save those next to him, and us. And I said to myself, The Twentieth has shrunk to a skeleton, a ghost, a memory, a forgotten name which we other old men alone keep in our hearts. And then I thought: It is right. It is as the colonel would have it. This also is part of the soldier's faith: Having known great things, to be content with silence. Just then there fell into my hands a little song sung by a warlike people on the Danube, which seemed to me fit for a soldier's last word, another song of the sword, but a song of the sword in its scabbard, a song of oblivion and peace.

A soldier has been buried on the battlefield.

And when the wind in the tree-tops roared,
The soldier asked from the deep dark grave:
    "Did the banner flutter then?"
"Not so, my hero," the wind replied.
"The fight is done, but the banner won,
Thy comrades of old have borne it hence,
    Have borne it in triumph hence."
Then the soldier spake from the deep dark grave:
        "I am content."
Then he heareth the lovers laughing pass,
    And the soldier asks once more:
"Are these not the voices of them that love,
    That love—and remember me?"
"Not so, my hero," the lovers say,
"We are those that remember not;
For the spring has come and the earth has smiled,
    And the dead must be forgot."
Then the soldier spake from the deep dark grave:
        "I am content."

Rebecca Harding Davis, "The Mean Face of War" (1899)

In 1898, the United States won a short yet pivotal war against Spain, driven mainly by American economic interests in Cuba and by public outrage over the sinking of the USS *Maine* in Havana harbor. The conflict raged briefly in Spain's colonial possessions in the Pacific and the Caribbean, and when settled by treaty resulted in a long-term American military presence in the Philippines, Guam, Cuba, and Puerto Rico. Despite widespread support for the war, largely because it seemed to culminate the process of national reconciliation, many American progressives regarded the Spanish–American War as immoral expansionism. Davis, whose own son Richard Harding Davis was a dashing war correspondent who enthusiastically covered the fighting in Cuba, thought that the habit of celebrating the martial valor of Civil War veterans was leading to the glorification of war for its own sake —and in that light the following essay can be read as a kind of rejoinder to Holmes's "The Soldier's Faith."

Of all the gods on Olympus Mars is always the most popular figure. Especially is he heroic in the eyes of a nation which is just about to set the crown of Imperialism on its brows, to gird a sword on its thighs and drive another nation into civilization and Christianity — at the point of the bayonet.

By all means let us look this god of war closely in the face and see what he really is like. His features at a distance are noble and heroic, but seen at nearer range there are ugly smirches and meanings in them. Our campaign last summer,[73] for instance, loomed before us in June a glorious outburst of high chivalric purpose and individual courage. But when we looked back at it in September war had come to mean polluted camps, incompetent officers appointed by corrupt politicians, decayed meat and thousands of victims of disease and neglect.

I lived through the Civil War on the border States, and two or three facts which I remember may help young Americans to see this great god Mars, whom we are about to make our tutelary deity, just as he is. They are not the kind of facts which the historians of a campaign usually set down.

A sleepy old Southern town of which I knew was made by the Government, at an early date, the headquarters of a military department. Martial law was proclaimed; the two good-humored, leisurely constables were remanded into private life; sentinels patrolled the streets all day long; the body guard of the general in command galloped madly up and down; bugles sounded and flags waved from every house.

But the flag did not always indicate the real feeling of the owners of the house. Almost every family was divided against itself, the elders usually siding with the Government, the young people with the South. The young men, one by one, made their way across the lines and entered the Confederate army.

Before the war the drowsy old town had boasted a hall, the upper floor of a tobacco warehouse, which was used as a theater or concert room. The whole building was now converted by the Provost-Marshal into a military prison. He also, with difficulty, raised a Loyal Guard, in whose care it was placed. As all the fighting men of the town were already in one army or the other, this Loyal Guard necessarily was made up of material which no doubt furnished a good deal of amusement to the corps of regulars stationed in the place. No man in it was under sixty; they were quiet, honest mechanics and tradesmen; church-going fathers and grandfathers who had trodden the same secluded path since their birth, never once probably tempted to break a law of the land. Their ideas of military discipline were vague. For two or three weeks they guarded the empty warehouse by sitting in a row of chairs tilted back against the front wall, smoking their pipes and telling over their old stories, occasionally joining in a hymn sung with much fervor.

But at last one day after a skirmish in the hills some prisoners were brought in and led through the streets to the warehouse. Some of them were wounded. The sight of these limping, bloody men produced a strange effect upon the townspeople, who hitherto had really regarded the war as a passing disaster, the work of politicians, which might come to an end any day.

"To-morrow, perhaps," they would say, "we may waken and find the whole miserable business at an end, and comfort and peace come again."

But at the sight of these prisoners passing down the street a sudden passion of rage and malignancy semed to poison the air.

Some of the men were wounded, one, it was said, mortally; he was carried on a litter, and his hand, torn and red with dried blood, hung down limp, and swung to and fro. Other men, we were told, lay dead on the hill yonder, where we used to go to gather pink laurel and paw-paws in the spring.

This was — war.

Women cried out madly — gentle, delicate women — and ran from their houses shrieking into the street; men crowded together following the wounded with sharp, wordless yells of pity or of hate. That one sight of blood tore off the life-long mask of education or manners from each of us, and the natural brute showed itself.

When the prisoners were taken into the warehouse these kindly neighbors looked at each other with sudden suspicion and dislike. They hurried to their homes in silence. Who knew which man was his enemy? He might be next door — in the same house with him. The old friendships and affections of a life-time ended that morning, and gave place to an unreasoning distrust. Brother quarreled with brother, husband with wife, father with son. Very often neither man nor woman understood the cause of the war. But the contagion of hate was in the air. Men caught it from each other, as they take the poison of a disease. The old men of the Guard became suddenly possessed with a fury of zeal. They looked upon the prisoners as their personal enemies. The orderly, devout grandfathers raged like wild beasts outside of the prison, and fired at the prisoners when-ever they approached the windows. So bent were they upon their slaughter that it was found necessary at last to remove the old men from the post.

As time passed the bitterness deepened, the gentlest woman and most generous men in both factions often becoming the most unreasonable and malignant toward all who differed from them. Old lines of right and wrong were blurred in the sanest and most devout. There was no right and wrong to most people. Take a trifling example: Late in the summer one Sunday night, while the churches were still open, the bugles were suddenly sounded and cannon fired. The alarm spread that General Lee's army was advancing upon the town to burn it. There were no Federal troops in it at the time. So the staid citizens of the town mustered, and shouldering their muskets boarded a train to go forth, as they thought, to meet the Confederate army. I can see their stooped shoulders and gray heads now as they marched past peering into the darkness through their spectacles. Oh, such sorry warriors! But it was as fine a blaze of courage as any that illumined the war.

The courage blazed in vain. When the train reached the hills it was found that there was not a Confederate soldier within fifty miles. What happened then was told to me by the officer commanding the expedition.

The men alighted, formed in column, and boldly advanced into the sleeping village near which the train had halted. When no one appeared they held a brief council, and then, to the dismay of their leader, made a rush upon the village, firing their muskets, breaking into the houses and seizing upon whatever came first to hand — churns, rocking chairs, feather beds, sewing machines, etc. One man appeared with a huge copper kettle on his back. In vain their captain commanded them to give up their spoils, telling them that the people were harmless and poor, and most of them loyal to the Union.

They were crazed with excitement and rage, shouting: "Loot them! Loot them! Booty of war!"

He compelled some of them to leave their plunder behind them, but when the train arrived at home many of them marched away in triumph with their stolen goods, among them the conqueror of the copper kettle. Yet these men were class leaders, deacons and pious members of the Christian church.

I remember a company of young men, the sons of Scotch and Scotch-Irish families, honorable, devout, gentle folk, who enlisted in the Northern army to serve their country, and, as they thought (and it may be justly), their God. They went through the war gallantly. Whatever was best and highest in its discipline they took and assimilated; it became part of their character and life. Yet almost every one of those men brought home spoons, watches and jewelry which he had taken out of some Southern home.

It was the breath of war which had made them and the old men for the time heroes, murderers and thieves.

I remember another company recruited from the same class for the Confederate army. They fought bravely, remaining in the service during the full five years. Of those still alive at Lee's surrender every man sooner or later filled a drunkard's grave.

Since the close of that war I have read and listened to countless paeans in the South and in the North to the dauntless courage of the heroes who gave their lives for the cause which they held just.

All this is true. But I never yet have heard a word of the other side of the history of that great campaign, which is equally true, of the debilitating effect upon most men in mind and morals of years in camp, and the habits acquired of idleness, of drunkenness and of immorality.

The American is not used to idleness, nor to military discipline. Put a gun in his hand, and give him nothing to do but to wait for somebody to kill, and the monkey or beast in him will soon show itself.

After thirty years of peace, a sudden effort is now being made by interested politicians to induce the American people to make war its regular business.

The army is to be largely increased.[74] Many young men of all classes expect to find an opening in it to earn their livelihood — to make a career for life. The talk of glory and heroism and the service of the country is very tempting to these gallant immature boys.

What is really intended, of course, is the establishment of a uniformed guard to police the Philippine Islands in the interests of certain trusts.

But our brave young fellow sees only the waving of the flag.

Before he goes into camp for the rest of his days, let him look more closely into the life of it, to see what in time it will do to him — to his mind, his manners and the soul inside of them.

Mars, as I said, is just now the most popular figure among the gods. But there are ugly, mean features in his noble face when we come close to him.

Notes

1 Paul Shackel, *Memory in Black and White: Race, Commemoration, and the Post-Bellum Landscape* (Walnut Creek, CA: AltaMira Press, 2003), 1.

2 John R. Neff, *Honoring the Civil War Dead: Commemoration and the Problem of Reconciliation* (Lawrence: University Press of Kansas, 2005), 6–7.

3 During the close-fought Presidential campaign of 1864, Lincoln was routinely caricatured by Northern Copperheads, or anti-war Democrats— not to mention by Southerners and the pro-Southern elements of the British press—as a fanatical, murdering tyrant.

4 Historical accounts differ in the details of this meeting between Lincoln and Douglass, but generally agree that Douglass was the first African American to attend a Presidential inaugural reception; that Lincoln spotted him among the crowd of visitors and called to him; and that, when asked for his opinion, Douglass praised the inaugural address as a "sacred effort." This was not their first meeting, however; according to David Blight, Lincoln and Douglass first met at the White House in August, 1863 (*Frederick Douglass' Civil War: Keeping Faith in Jubilee* [Baton Rouge: Louisiana State University Press, 1991], 168).

5 See headnote in chapter 3 in Douglass's "Men of Color to Arms!"

6 This ignores the evening of April 14, 1865, when the President and Mary Todd Lincoln attended a play at Ford's Theatre in Washington D.C. together, where he was assassinated.

7 In 1864 and 1865, City Point, Virginia, served as an important Union port and supply hub, and as Grant's headquarters. In March, 1865, Lincoln, Grant, and Sherman met in the city to discuss the end of the war.

8 Ann Eliza Harlan (née Peck), wife of Iowa Senator James Harlan (1820–1899), who became Secretary of the Interior in April, 1865, after Lincoln's assassination.

9 This was the executive mansion of the Confederacy, rented from the city of Richmond; Jefferson Davis and his family lived there from 1861 until the fall of Richmond in April, 1865. The residence is now part of the Museum of the Confederacy.

10 The *Oxford English Dictionary* traces the word to 1677, but asserts that "[t]here is no foundation for an alleged origin in the black slave communities of the Southern States (and ultimately Africa). . . [L]ater the word is found well-established in the New England States; evidence for an Indian origin is also wanting."

11 Lincoln's fourth son, Thomas (1853–1871).

12 The song "Dixie," usually attributed to Daniel Decatur Emmett, imagined a liberated slave singing the praises of the plantation South. Keckley's anecdote is corroborated by other sources, and is generally taken as a moment of intended reconciliation between North and South.

13 Possibly a reference to a well-known political cartoon, "The Political Quadrille, Music by Dred Scott" published in 1860 by Rickey, Mallory & Company of Cincinnati. This cartoon parodies the candidates and issues of the 1860 presidential election by portraying the popular dance's four couples as John Breckinridge and James Buchanan; Abraham Lincoln and an African American woman; John Bell and a Native American; and Stephen Douglas and a dissolute Irishman.

14 John Russell, 1st Earl Russell (1792–1878), was the British Foreign Secretary from 1859 to 1860. In a speech in October, 1861, he is reported to have told the British public that North and South were "contending, as so many States in the old world have contended, the one for empire and the other for independence" (quoted in James Ford Rhodes, *History of the United States from the Compromise of 1850 to the Final Restoration of Home Rule at the South in 1877*, Vol. 3: 1860–1862 [New York: The Macmillan Co., 1906], 504).

15 Henry Clay of Kentucky (1777–1852) was one of the most powerful politicians in antebellum America, and his views on slavery among the most complex. Like Jefferson, he opposed it in principle yet could devise no practicable way to end it. As early as 1798, he advocated gradual emancipation and the reset-tlement of freed slaves to Africa, but he owned slaves himself and helped forge the major legislative compromises in the nineteenth century. Which "memorable occasion" Douglass refers to is unclear, since in a number of speeches, Clay raised the question of how long the institution of slavery could or should endure.

16 A deciduous tree native to Africa and southeast Asia that yields a poisonous sap.

17 In August and September of 1866, Johnson made a major campaign tour through the mid-Atlantic and Midwest that proved a major fiasco. Accompanied by Ulysses S. Grant and Admiral David Farragut, among others, his aim was to promote a moderate approach to Reconstruction, but he faced increas-ingly hostile crowds, gained a reputation for public drunkenness, argued with hecklers, and ultimately saw support for his policies and his Presidency diminish badly.

18 A reference to the Christian theological doctrine, central but not exclusive to traditional American Calvinism, that salvation by divine grace is eternal.

19 Before the imposition of stricter federal reconstruction policies by the Radical Republicans beginning in 1867, Southern state governments were still dominated by ex-Confederates and white supremacists, and many enacted "Black Codes" designed to limit or negate black political power and social opportunity. In response, in spring and summer of 1867, the 39th Congress declared the Confederate-era governments

illegitimate; placed the South effectively under martial law; expanded the state franchise to include African Americans; and made the readmission of rebellious states to the Union contingent upon their ratification of the Fourteenth Amendment.

20 The "universal confisciation" of Southern land and "general execution" of ex-Confederates were fringe views even within the Republican Party, not its "doctrine" or "programme."

21 Edmund Burke (1729–1797), member of the British Parliament, embraced a political philosophy that sought to balance individual liberty, national tradition, and social stability. He supported the American colonies during the Revolution, arguing before the House of Commons: "Let the colonies always keep the idea of their civil rights associated with your government,—they will cling and grapple to you, and no force under heaven will be of power to tear them from their allegiance."

22 I.e., the Democratic Party, which during the 1860 election split between Northern Democrats and Southern Democrats; during the war the Northern Democrats in turn faced divisions between the War Democrats and the Peace Democrats, or Copperheads. After the war, as the Democratic Party struggled to regain traction and power nationally, it appealed to white conservatives' resentment toward radical Reconstruction, particularly in the South and Midwest.

23 "At that moment, by the fact itself" (Latin).

24 Thomas Babington Macaulay (1800–1859) himself wrote the poems that make up the *Lays of Ancient Rome* (1842).

25 Hamilton, the first Secretary of the Treasury and co-author of the *Federalist*, was an advocate of strong centralized federal power.

26 The Civil Rights Act of 1866, introduced by Senator Lyman Trumbull, anticipated the Fourteenth Amendment by extending citizenship, with all its rights, to all persons born in the United States and giving federal authorities the final power to enforce civil rights. "In constitutional terms," writes Eric Foner, "the Civil Rights Bill represented the first attempt to give meaning to the Thirteenth Amendment, to define in legislative terms the essence of freedom" (*Reconstruction*, 244). The Republican-dominated Congress passed the bill over Andrew Johnson's veto in early April, 1866.

27 Slightly misquoted from Andrew Johnson's remarks to a delegation of Kentucky citizens, as reported in the *Washington Evening Star*, March 9, 1866.

28 The Congressional Joint Committee on Reconstruction, composed of 15 members representing both the House and the Senate, was formed in December, 1865; its report on conditions in the South, based on varied testimony, informed Radical Republican reconstruction policies during the 39th Congress.

29 I.e., a state within a state.

30 I.e., voluntarily.

31 In the first week of April 1865, Davis and a retinue of Confederate government holdouts evacuated Richmond, then travelled southward through North Carolina and South Carolina, into Georgia. Davis and his party were tracked down and arrested by federal cavalry outside Irwinville, Georgia, on May 10, 1865. Davis was held in Fort Monroe until May 13, 1867, when he was released on bail (with the help of Horace Greeley and abolitionist Gerrit Smith); the indictment of treason against him was dismissed in February 1869, after various delays and pre-trial motions. See William C. Davis, *An Honorable Defeat: The Last Days of the Confederate Government* (New York: Harcourt, 2001), ch. 10 and page 386.

32 This quote, probably apocryphal, appears to trace back to Frank H. Alfriend's biography *The Life of Jefferson Davis* (Cincinnati and Chicago, 1866), although Alfriend provides no information about his source.

33 Henry Alexander Wise (1806–1876) served Virginia variously as Representative, Senator, and Governor, and served the Confederacy as a competent general in the Eastern theater. Unlike many of his fellow confederates, Wise declined to request a pardon from the federal government after the war.

34 James Lawrence Orr (1822–1873) was elected the governor of South Carolina in 1865, as a Republican, and served until 1868.

35 From Tacitus, *The Life of Gnæus Julius Agricola* (c. 98 A.D.). Tacitus is actually describing the reign of Emperor Domitian, not the entire Roman Empire, and the quote begins, "A few of us, it is true, have survived the slaughter of our fellow citizens; I had almost said, we have survived ourselves; for in that chasm, which slavery made in our existence . . ."

36 On May 2, 1863, at the battle of Chancellorsville, Jackson was struck by friendly fire as he returned from a reconnaissance of the federal position. Despite the amputation of his left arm, Jackson developed pneumonia and died on May 10, at Guiney Station, where he reportedly said "Let us cross over the river and rest under the shade of the trees."

37 William Lowndes Yancey (1814–1863), U.S. Representative and Confederate Senator from Alabama.

38 Robert Barnwell Rhett, Sr. (1800–1876), fierce secessionist Congressman and journalist from South Carolina.

39 Robert Augustus Toombs (1810–1885), U.S. Senator from Georgia, Secretary of State and mediocre general of the Confederacy. Unrepentant to the end.

40 Horace Greeley (1811–1872), antislavery editor of the influential New York *Tribune*, and unsuccessful Presidential challenger to Ulysses S. Grant in 1872.

41 Sumner (1811–1874) was a long-serving abolitionist U.S. Senator from Massachusetts and champion of civil rights during Reconstruction.

42 Hamlin (1809–1891) was Lincoln's more radical, but not terribly influential, vice-president. Watkins's reference to Noah and Ham parodies the then-common Biblical "explanation" of the origins of black-ness. See Genesis 9:20–27 and Genesis 10:6–14.

43 Watkins served in the 1st Tennessee Infantry Volunteers, which was organized at Nashville in May 1861, composed of companies from Nashville and surrounding counties. Later merged with the 27th Tennessee, the regiment saw extensive service in Virginia, western Virginia, Tennessee, and Georgia. "At Perrville it lost 179 killed, wounded, or missing. The 1st/27th reported 8 killed and 75 wounded of the 457 at Murfreesboro, had 14 killed and 75 wounded at Chickamauga, and totalled 456 men and 290 arms in December, 1863. It surrendered with less than 125 effectives" (Joseph H. Crute, Jr., *Units of the Confederate States Army* [Midlothian, Va.: Derwent Books, 1987], 275).

44 This archetypally reconciliationist phrase is from Horace Greeley's letter accepting the Liberal Republican nomination in 1872, which Greeley concluded with a plea for the North and South "to clasp hands across the bloody chasm which has too long divided them. . ." Cartoonist Thomas Nast parodied the image in a series of cartoons during the summer and fall of that year.

45 Col. George Maney (1st Tennessee Infantry); Col. John Calvin Brown (3rd Tennessee Infantry); Col. James Edward Rains (11th Tennessee Infantry).

46 This incident actually took place in Virginia. Col. Elmer Ephraim Ellsworth (1837–1861) led the 44th New York regiment (the "Fire Zouaves"), which entered Alexandria on May 24, 1861. Here, after taking down a huge rebel flag flying above the Marshall House hotel, Ellsworth was shot and killed by the innkeeper, James William Jackson, who was himself then fatally shot by Corporal Francis Brownell. The episode quickly became a rallying cry in the North.

47 Charles Todd Quintard (1824–1898) was a physician and Episcopalian priest.

48 "A camp gambling game in which soldiers attempted to toss dice, rocks, or other small items into squares that contained different numbes" (John D. Wright, *The Language of the Civil War*).

49 Capt. Hume R. Field (the correct spelling), commanding officer of Company H, was later promoted to colonel of the 1st Tennessee regiment.

50 "The first crude spirit produced by distillation" (Wright).

51 Gen. Floyd (1806–1863) was a not terribly effective commander who had little success halting federal advances in western Virginia. He was transferred to Kentucky later that year.

52 Beginning in January 1862, Stonewall Jackson began a campaign against Union positions in the Shenandoah Valley. Although William Loring had occupied Romney, his complaints led Jefferson Davis to order Jackson to recall Loring to Winchester. Jackson threatened to resign in protest.

53 *Scott's Infantry Tactics* (1835), named for Major General Winfield Scott, focused on traditional infantry lines and movements; *Hardee's Rifle and Light Infantry Tactics* (1855), named for Lt. Col. William Joseph Hardee, emphasized speed and flexibility, in response to improvements in rifle technology.

54 Brig. Gen. Robert H. Hatton (1826–1862); Col. William A. Forbes (1824–1862); Lt. Col. Paul F. Anderson; Lt. Col. William A. Gilliam (1837–1903); Brig. Gen. Daniel Chevilette Govan (1829–1911); Gen. William Wing Loring (1818–1886); Col. Henry M. Ashby (1836–1868).

55 At the battle of Thermopylae, in the fifth century B.C., the greatly outnumbered Spartans, though finally killed to the last man, managed to hold off the Persian army long enough to allow the rest of the Greek army to withdraw, setting the stage for the Greek naval victory at the Battle of Salamis.

56 The Roman general and consul Caius Marius, uncle to Julius Caesar. After being arrested on orders of his rival Sulla, Marius was allowed to flee in exile to Carthage; he later returned to Rome and seized power in a violent uprising. The episode is the subject of the painting "Caius Marius Amid the Ruins of Carthage" (1807) by American painter John Vanderlyn.

57 During Reconstruction, cash-strapped Republican governments in the South issued bonds that not only frequently lost their value, but became common fodder for graft and fraudulent speculation.

58 Dunbar Rowland, *The Official and Statistical Register of the State of Mississippi* (Nashville, Tenn., 1908), 204.

59 This phrase is from Sec. 4 of the 1866 Civil Rights Act. Virtually identical language was subsequently included in the Fifteenth Amendment.

60 Stuart McConnell, *Glorious Contentment: The Grand Army of the Republic, 1865–1900* (Chapel Hill: University of North Carolina Press, 1992), 206.

61 Possibly Charles Chesnutt's "The Goophered Grapevine," which was published in *The Atlantic Monthly* in 1887. The editor of the *Atlantic* at that point was Thomas Bailey Aldrich.

62 The Tennessee native Mary Noailles Murfree's novel *The Despot of Broomsedge Cove* was serialized in the *Atlantic* in 1888 under the pseudonym Charles Egbert Craddock. Frances Hodgson Burnett's novel *Sara Crewe; or, What Happened at Miss Minchin's* (1888) is a variation on the Cinderella story; the Hodgson family had moved from England to Tennessee in 1865.

63 Luke 16:19–31.

64 The nickname for Sir Walter Scott.

65 G. Edward White, *Justice Oliver Wendell Holmes: Law and the Inner Self*, 82.

66 Cornelius Vanderbilt (1794–1877), the American shipping and railroads magnate.

67 William Napier (1785–1860) was a British general and historian.

68 Ninth and final stanza of Alfred Lord Tennyson's "Merlin and the Gleam" (1889).

69 From William Ernest Henley's "The Song of the Sword" (1892).

70 Britomart in Spenser's *Faerie Queene*.

71 *Faerie Queene*, Book II, canto X, stanza 69.

72 Col. William Raymond Lee (1807–1891) commanded the famous unit sometimes called the "Harvard regiment" because of the high number of officers connected to that university.

73 The Spanish–American War, though long in the making, lasted for just under four months, from late April to mid-August, 1898.

74 After the Spanish–American War, the McKinley administration began the process—to be continued over decades—of modernizing the military and expanding its international footprint; the aim was both to protect the United States's newly acquired territorial possessions and to position for potential geopolitical conflicts in the future.

The Texts

Abraham Lincoln, Second Inaugural Address. Source: *Complete Works of Abraham Lincoln, Comprising his Speeches, Letters, State Papers, and Miscellaneous Writings*, ed. John G. Nicolay and John Hay. Vol. 2 (New York: The Century Company, 1920).

Elizabeth Keckley, from *Behind the Scenes*. Source: *Behind the Scenes; or, Thirty Years a Slave, and Four Years in the White House* (New York: G. W. Carleton & Co., 1868).

Walt Whitman, "The Veteran's Vision." Source: *Walt Whitman's Drum-Taps* (New York, s.n., 1865). In *Leaves of Grass*, Whitman retitled this poem "The Artilleryman's Vision."

Walt Whitman, "When Lilacs Last in the Door-Yard Bloom'd." Source: *Sequel to Drum-Taps: When Lilacs Last in the Door-Yard Bloom'd, and Other Pieces* (Washington, s.n., 1865–1866). When Whitman revised this poem for inclusion in *Leaves of Grass*, he reduced the number of exclamation points, capitalized the word "death" less frequently, made substantive additions and deletions, and renumbered the poem's sections.

Walt Whitman, "The Million Dead, Too, Summ'd Up" and "The Real War Will Never Get in the Books." Source: *Specimen Days and Collect* (Philadelphia: D. McKay, 1882–1883). Originally published, in slightly different form, in *Memoranda During the War* (1875–1876).

Herman Melville, "An Uninscribed Monument," "A Requiem," and "On a Natural Monument." Source: *Battle-Pieces and Aspects of the War* (New York: Harper & Bros., 1866).

Frederick Douglass, "Reconstruction." Source: *Atlantic Monthly* 18 (December 1866), 761–765.

Edward A. Pollard, from *The Lost Cause*. Source: *The Lost Cause; A New Southern History of the War of the Confederates. Comprising a full and authhentic account of the rise and progress of the late Southern confederacy . . .* (New York: E. B. Treat & Co., 1866).

Sidney Lanier, selected poems. Source: *Poems of Sidney Lanier, Edited by His Wife*, ed. Mary D. Lanier (New York: Charles Scribner's Sons, 1884). "Resurrection" and "Laughter in the Senate" were originally published in the newspaper *The Round Table* in 1868. Mary Lanier includes "Dying Words of Stonewall Jackson" under the section "Unrevised Early Poems."

Sarah Morgan Bryan Piatt, selected poems. Source: *Palace-Burner: The Selected Poetry of Sarah Piatt*, ed. Paula Bernat Bennett (Urbana: University of Illinois Press, 2001). First publications: "Army of Occupation" in *Harper's Weekly* (1866); "The Grave at Frankfort" in *The Capital* (1872); "Another War" in *The Capital* (1872); "Over in Kentucky" in *The Independent* (1872).

Frederick Douglass, Address at the Graves of the Unknown Dead. Source: The Frederick Douglass Papers at the Library of Congress.

Henry Timrod, "Ode." Source: *Poems of Henry Timrod, with Memoir and Portrait* (Richmond, 1901). Although many editions of Timrod's poems give the date as 1867, the poem was first published in the Charleston *Daily Courier* on June 18, 1866. Another version, with slight but significant variations, appeared on July 23, 1866.

Samuel R. Watkins, from *Co. Aytch*. Source: *1861 vs. 1882, "Co. Aytch," Maury Grays, First Tennessee Regiment; or, A Side Show of the Big Show* (Nashville: Cumberland Presbyterian Pub. House, 1882). Originally serialized in the Columbia (Tenn.) *Herald*, 1881–1882.

Jefferson Davis, Speech Before Mississippi Legislature. Source: *Jefferson Davis: The Essential Writings*, ed. William J. Cooper, Jr. (New York: The Modern Library, 2003).

Timothy Thomas Fortune, "Bartow Black." Source: Joan R. Sherman, ed., *African American Poetry of the Nineteenth Century: An Anthology* (Urbana: University of Illinois Press, 1992). Originally published in the *A.M.E. Church Review* 3 (October 1886): 158–159.

Charlotte L. Forten Grimké, "The Gathering of the Grand Army." Source: Joan R. Sherman, ed., *African American Poetry of the Nineteenth Century: An Anthology* (Urbana: University of Illinois Press, 1992). Previously published in Anna J. Cooper, *Life and Writings of the Grimké Family*, vol. 2 (Washington, D.C., 1951).

Albion Tourgée, "The South as a Field for Fiction." Source: *The Forum*, vol. 6 (December 1888), pp. 404–413.

Oliver Wendell Holmes, Jr., "The Soldier's Faith." Source: *The Occasional Speches of Justice Oliver Wendell Holmes*, ed. Mark DeWolfe Howe (Cambridge: Harvard University Press, 1962).

Rebecca Harding Davis, "The Mean Face of War." Source: *The Independent* (New York), vol. 51 no. 2631 (May 4, 1899), 1931–1933.

The Writers

Alcott, Louisa May (1832–1888). As the daughter of Amos Bronson Alcott, the eccentric educational reformer and founder of the utopian community Fruitlands, Louisa May Alcott was probably destined to see the world in unconventional terms, and her fiction seems to bear out this assessment. Beginning in mid-December 1862, Alcott volunteered as a nurse at the Union Hotel Hospital in Georgetown, but returned to Concord in January 1863 after contracting typhoid fever. Her nursing experience formed the basis for Alcott's fictional alter ego Tribulation Periwinkle in *Hospital Sketches* (1863). She returned to the war in the story collection *On Picket Duty* (1864) and, indirectly, in the novel *Little Women* (1868). Alcott's antislavery and feminist politics inform all of this fiction, but so does her essentially apolitical compassion for both civilians and soldiers caught up in the gears of war.

Bellamy, Edward (1850–1898). Born into a family of Baptist ministers in Massachusetts, Edward Bellamy instead became a prominent socialist, author, and social reformer. After traveling in Europe and studying law in America, Bellamy turned to journalism and literature in order to articulate solutions to the economic injustices he witnessed both abroad and at home. His wildly popular utopian novel *Looking Backward: 2000–1887* (1887) imagined a futuristic socialism in the United States, which proved appealing to many Americans familiar with the abuses and inequalities of the Gilded Age. A full-fledged political movement grew out of *Looking Back*, which Bellamy called "Nationalism" and further developed through his magazines *The Nationalist* (1889–1891) and *The New Nation* (1891–1894). He continued publishing short fiction in the meantime, but his health declined rapidly, and he died from tuberculosis at the age of 48. Though his popularity was short-lived, Bellamy's writings influenced many twentieth-century authors, political activists, and social reformers alike.

Bierce, Ambrose (1842–1914?). In revisiting the Civil War, Bierce knew whereof he wrote. A veteran, with the Ninth Indiana Volunteers, of some of the bloodiest battles of the conflict, including Shiloh, Stones River, and Missionary Ridge, Bierce developed a grimly sardonic perspective on war and what it does to people. In the story collections *Tales of Soldiers and Civilians* (1891) and *Can Such Things Be?* (1893), and in the writings later collected as *Bits of Autobiography* (1909), Bierce returned almost obsessively to the war that had so colored his outlook on the world. Fascinated by the perceptual and experiential aspects of combat, in his fiction Bierce tends to hold at bay the broader ideological, and even military, contexts in which his characters operate, concentrating on situations and feelings that can seem abstracted from real history. Bierce disappeared during a sojourn into the state of Chihuahua to observe the Mexican Revolution.

Cavada, Federico Fernández (1831–1871). Before he even turned 40, Cavada had served as a military leader in two separate conflicts in the 1860s and 1870s: the American Civil War and the first war of Cuban liberation. Cuban by birth (to a Spanish father and American mother), Cavada grew up in Philadelphia, where his widowed mother moved with her three sons in 1838. When the Civil War erupted, Federico and his brother Adolfo enlisted in the 23rd Pennsylvania Infantry. His talent as an artist got him assigned to the Union Army Balloon Corps sketching the positions of the Confederate Army, and he was eventually promoted to the rank of Lieutenant Colonel. Captured at Gettysburg, Cavada was sent to Libby Prison in Richmond, Virginia, where he remained for over six months. After his release he published *Libby Life: Experiences of a Prisoner of War in Richmond, Virginia, 1863–64,* an illustrated text detailing the abusive treatment he was subjected to in the Confederate prison. When the war ended, Cavada was appointed U.S. Consul to Cuba, but he resigned his consulship in early 1869 to join the Cuban insurrection, where he once again rose through the ranks to become Commander-in-Chief of the Cuban forces, feared by the Spanish for his guerrilla tactics. In 1871, Cavada was captured by a Spanish gunboat and executed by firing squad. A *New York Times* correspondent and eyewitness to the execution reported his final words to be "Adios Cuba, para siempre": Goodbye, Cuba, forever.

Chesnut, Mary (1823–1886). Of the many forms of autobiography to come out of the Civil War, Chesnut's diary is perhaps the most remarkable. Born into privilege in Camden, South Carolina, Chesnut received an excellent education and grew into a high-spirited, independent-minded woman. Her marriage to James Chesnut, Jr., a wealthy and well-connected politician (a moderate-turned-secessionist), gave Mary entrée to the inner circles of South Carolina and Washington D.C. society. In 1859 and 1860, before James resigned from the U.S. Senate, they enjoyed a vibrant time in the capitol, where she became close friends with Varina Davis, the wife of Jefferson Davis. During the war, Mary Chesnut traveled between Richmond, Camden, Columbia, and the Chesnut plantation at Mulberry, and began her voluminous, rough-hewn, and riveting diary, an indispensable record of a Southern woman's perspective on the war and its participants. In the ruinous aftermath of war, Chesnut turned to other forms of writing, as she and her husband tried to rebuild their life, and began the long process of revising her diary for publication. It remained unpublished at her death, but the manuscript ended up in the hands of her friend Isabella D. Martin, who, with Myrta Lockett Avary, arranged for the publication of an edited version titled *A Diary from Dixie* (1905).

Chesnutt, Charles (1858–1932). During the darkest days of the post-Reconstruction South, Chesnutt sought, in three novels and two collections of short stories, to give full expression to the imaginative and cultural life of African Americans. A native of Fayetteville, North Carolina, who made his living as a legal stenographer in Cleveland, Chesnutt saw fiction as a means of shaping reality. His reimagining of plantation culture, his exploration of mixed-race experience, and his analysis of the springs of social history—all constituted a passionate rejoinder to the reduction and falsification of

African American life in the literary genres of dialect fiction and local color, not to mention the popular press. Though not without later critics of a more aggressive political bent, Chesnutt's lonely battle against the literary status quo helped make their emergence more likely.

Chopin, Kate (1851–1904). Chopin's two cities were St. Louis, where she was born and raised and did almost all of her writing, and New Orleans, where she lived for ten years while married to Oscar Chopin and where she set her most famous work, *The Awakening* (1899). The stories she submitted to various magazines during the 1880s and 1890s were less scandalous than that novel, and generally reflected her liberal-minded Catholicism and sense of personal reserve. Most of Chopin's fiction has an ironic quality to it, a sensuality, a vaguely European sensibility, and a gentle touch that still allowed for flashes of outrage. She returned time and again to the theme of women's expressive potential, and in *Bayou Folk* (1894), explored the complex racial, social, and economic culture of southern Louisiana. During the Civil War, Chopin's family sided with the South, and her half-brother George O'Flaherty died from typhoid fever during his imprisonment as a Confederate soldier.

Crane, Stephen (1871–1900). Arguably the finest writer on the Civil War, or, more precisely, on the individual soldier's complex experience of military service, Crane was not even born until six years after it ended. But the war gave Crane material for his signature themes: the human being under extreme pressure, the relation between the individual and the mass, the mechanization of war and society, the contrast between human ideals and universal indifference. His most important Civil War fiction includes *The Red Badge of Courage* (1895) and the stories collected in *The Little Regiment, and Other Episodes of the American Civil War* (1896). Based on his work as a war correspondent for the New York *World*, Crane also wrote a novel about the Greco–Turkish war, *Active Service* (1899), and he later drew on his reporting on the Spanish–American war for William Randolph Hearst's *Journal* for the collection *Wounds in the Rain* (1900). Crane's understanding of the Civil War, and of the society which emerged from it, cannot be separated from his experience covering these later conflicts, and his influence on the twentieth-century literary imagination is difficult to overstate. Crane died of a pulmonary hemorrhage brought on by tuberculosis.

Davis, Jefferson (1808–1889). He only reluctantly accepted the office of President of the Confederate States of America, but once the reins were in his hands, Davis saw it through to the bitter end and beyond. A Kentucky native, veteran of the annexation of Texas, and former cotton planter, Davis entered politics in the 1840s, and as a moderate states'-rights Senator from Mississippi tried to tamp down the forces of disunion—but ultimately cast his lot with his adopted state. His tactical and political leadership during the war was, and remains, controversial (could the South have won with a different President?), but his devotion to the cause is hard to question. After being imprisoned for two years, but never given the trial he would have welcomed, Davis became a popular and respected figure throughout the South, and showed no regret for his earlier course of action. In defeat, Davis found a poignant kind of personal victory.

Davis, Rebecca Harding (1831–1910). Raised in Washington, Pennsylvania, and Wheeling, Virginia, Davis gravitated toward literature at a young age, and practiced her hand at it, but it was not until she published "Life in the Iron Mills" in the *Atlantic* in

1861 that Davis put herself on the literary map. This story, an exposé of industrial capitalism, bears the hallmarks of her style and ethos: a compassion for the downtrodden; an eye for detail; an interest in social and economic forces; a passionate narratorial voice; a Christian faith in the redeemability of humankind. These qualities characterize her first novel, *Margaret Howth* (1862), and her novel of the Civil War, *Waiting for the Verdict* (1867), and mark Davis as an important figure in the emergence of American realism and naturalism. Throughout her long literary career, she explored racial and class disparities, the problems inherent in romanticizing war and violence, and what she saw as the American government's increasingly imperialist aims.

Douglass, Frederick (1818–1895). His years as an antislavery orator and his two ante-bellum autobiographies made Douglass the primary African American spokesman of the nineteenth century. From this position, he pushed for Northern victory in the war, which he regarded as an opportunity finally to defeat the scourge of slavery. In numerous essays and addresses, Douglass insisted that the war and its aftermath be understood as a struggle for freedom and civil rights, and sought to call his audience to a greater awareness of the racial issues at the heart of the conflict. In addition to active political employment, he devoted his postwar writing, including a third autobiography, to trying to diminish the power of American race hatred, and he "dearly hoped," writes David Blight, "that his own sense of self . . . would rest securely in new national traditions that he helped create" (*Frederick Douglass' Civil War*, 244).

Dunbar, Paul Laurence (1872–1906). His parents had been slaves in Kentucky before the war, and his father Joshua Dunbar served in the 55th Massachusetts—generating memories of violence and struggle that Dunbar absorbed as he developed his writing talents in Ohio's public schools. Like Charles Chesnutt, Dunbar struggled to give voice to African American experience while observing the rules of the late nineteenth-century American publishing industry. The result is a body of poetry and fiction expressing varying degrees of anger and accommodation. In *Oak and Ivy* (1893), *Majors and Minors* (1895), and other collections that combine dialect poetry and formal verse, Dunbar can seem ambiguously to celebrate the power of black folk traditions while pandering to the era's fascination with the antebellum plantation and its "picturesque" slaves. Other poems convey, in often subtle fashion, a stronger sense of cultural and political disfranchisement.

Edmonds, Sarah Emma (1841–1898). Born in New Brunswick, Canada, Edmonds made her way to the United States in 1860 and adopted the guise of "Franklin Thompson," a fictional identity she would use while selling Bibles for a Hartford publishing house and then retain after joining the 2nd Michigan Infantry at the beginning of the war. In this male guise, Edmonds worked as a nurse and mail carrier, but also saw combat at such battles as Fair Oaks and Fredericksburg. She apparently served with real soldierly competence, but deserted her regiment in 1863, possibly to avoid discovery. While working as a nurse for the United States Christian Commission in Ohio—having returned to her original female identity—Edmonds published a highly embellished memoir titled *Unsexed; or The Female Soldier* (1864), which claimed, rather dubiously, that she worked mainly as a spy. At a regimental reunion in 1884, Edmonds—now married, with two adopted children—outed herself to her former comrades, and later that year, Congress formally recognized her military service by approving a federal pension for "Franklin Thompson," which she received until her death in 1898.

Fortune, Timothy Thomas (1856–1928). A living embodiment of the opportunities created by emancipation, Thomas Fortune was born a slave and then rose to become the leading African American journalist of his generation. Growing up in Florida, Thomas had the opportunity to work as a page in the state senate and as a printer's apprentice for a Jacksonville newspaper, and this exposure to the worlds of both politics and publishing fired Fortune's intellectual curiosity, authorial ambitions, and civic-mindedness. After briefly studying law and journalism at Howard University, Fortune left school to work full-time for newspapers in Washington D.C., and, later, New York City, where he forged a literary and journalistic career dedicated to advancing racial equality and denouncing anti-black discrimination and violence. In 1890 Fortune co-founded the National Afro-American League, an organization that opened the door for later civil rights groups such as the NAACP, for he recognized that "[w]herever he turns [the black man] finds the strong arm of constituted authority powerless to protect him" (*Black and White: Land, Labor, and Politics in the South* [1884], 29).

Garland, Hamlin (1860–1940). Another author whose star has unfortunately dimmed, Garland, for half a century, was as prolific as Henry James, in a variety of genres: the novel, the short story, the memoir, the essay. Born in Wisconsin, he lived as a young man in the "middle border" states of Iowa and South Dakota before relocating to Boston and then Chicago. This experience sensitized Garland to the social dynamic between the urban and the rural, the young and the old, and in his fiction he returns time and again to the relation between place, character, and idea. In *Crumbling Idols* (1894), his collection of essays on art and literature, Garland expressed his belief in the essential power of regional identification: "art, to be vital, must be local in its subject; its universal appeal must be in its working out, – in the way it is done."

Grant, Ulysses Simpson (1822–1885). Forward-leaning in war, Grant was unassuming in prose, and both qualities made him surpassingly effective as both a warrior and a writer. His *Memoirs*, written while Grant was terminally ill and heavily in debt, represent the retrospective view of a man who had led the Union to victory and served as President for eight years, but had been humbled by personal and professional setbacks. Grant's defining assets as a general were a clear grasp of the importance of logistics, a tactical and strategic flexibility, and an unflagging determination to succeed. These qualities underlay his successes in the Western theater, particularly the capture of Vicksburg, which propelled him to the top of the military hierarchy, from where he led the final long and grinding campaign against Lee in Virginia. Grant's memoirs, tracing his rise from humble origins but stopping short of his pockmarked Presidency, are remarkably free of the self-vindication, competitiveness, or revisionism that marred the accounts of many other Civil War veterans. Combined with their clarity and straightforwardness, this modesty has led the *Memoirs* to be recognized as one of the masterpieces of American autobiography.

Grimké, Charlotte L. Forten (1837–1914). Hailing from an influential and affluent African American family, Grimké seems to have been predestined for her passionate antislavery and civil rights activism. Educated alongside white students in some of the best schools in the North, Charlotte also learned of the injustices done to African Americans through her family's social circle of intellectual abolitionists. A teacher by trade, Forten ("Grimké" came later) grew into a fervent abolitionist herself, giving public lectures and eventually moving south to teach freed slaves on St. Helena Island in South Carolina at the end of the Civil War. After falling too ill to continue teaching, she returned home and attained a position within the U.S. Treasury Department. In Washington, D.C., she met and married Presbyterian minister Francis J. Grimké and continued her literary pursuits up until her death in 1914. Throughout Grimké's life she wrote prolifically, journaling for herself but also publishing dozens of poems and essays in African American periodicals, most of which reflected her thoughtful dedication to social justice and racial equality.

Harper, Francis Ellen Watkins (1825–1911). As an orator, poet, and novelist, Harper broke new ground for African American women in the nineteenth century. Born in Baltimore to free black parents, Watkins was educated in a school run by her abolitionist uncle. When she entered the workforce as a housekeeper and seamstress, she continued to educate herself while also writing and contributing to the abolitionist cause. At just twenty years old, she published her first book of poetry, followed over the course of her long career by more volumes of poetry, short stories, essays, and a well-regarded novel, *Iola Leroy, or Shadows Uplifted* (1892). In the years leading up to the Civil War, Watkins toured the East and Midwest as a representative of the American Anti-Slavery Society, temporarily retiring in 1860 upon her marriage to Fenton Harper. After his death in 1864, she returned to the lecture circuit with her young daughter, speaking on abolitionism, education, civil rights, temperance, and women's suffrage. Harper's greatest legacy, perhaps, is her pioneering accomplishments as an author, regarded as one of the first African American women to be published in the United States.

Holmes, Oliver Wendell, Jr. (1841–1935). As a lawyer, legal theorist, and Supreme Court Justice, Holmes had an abiding distrust of ideological abstractions. His approach to the law emphasized behavior rather than inner states of mind, the pragmatics of policy rather than legal philosophy. Louis Menand has traced this outlook to Holmes's experience in the Civil War, which "made him lose his belief in beliefs" and taught him that "certitude leads to violence" (*The Metaphysical Club*, 4, 61). Holmes served in the 20th Massachusetts Volunteers for three years, and was wounded three times, twice severely at Ball's Bluff and Antietam. In the mind of the jurist, the memory of the soldier never faded.

Horton, George Moses (1798?–c.1883). Though a slave, the self-styled "colored bard of North Carolina" made a living for himself, and a name, by selling poems in and around the college town of Chapel Hill. In his two pre-war collections, *The Hope of Liberty* (1829) and *The Poetical Works* (1845), Horton found a measure of expressive freedom (within the limits of his time and place), but legal freedom would only come with Emancipation. At the end of the Civil War, Horton traveled through North Carolina with a Capt. William Banks of the Michigan Cavalry, gathering material and composing lyrics for a third volume, *Naked Genius* (1865). Only in this last collection did Horton not have to walk the razor's edge of trying to voice his discontent without alienating his white readers, benefactors, and masters.

Howe, Julia Ward (1819–1910). The overmastering fame of "The Battle Hymn of the Republic" has somewhat obscured Howe's other activities and accomplishments, including her prolific writings in a variety of genres and her decades-long work in the abolitionist, women's suffrage, and peace movements. Along with her husband, Samuel Gridley Howe, she edited the Boston *Commonwealth*, an antislavery newspaper; directed the Perkins Institute for the Blind in New York; and was the first woman elected to the American Academy of Arts and Letters. Howe's feminism coexisted with a belief in the sacredness of domestic life, and her religiosity coexisted with a sharp sense of humor, all of which are on display in her collections *Passion Flowers* (1854), *Words for the Hour* (1857) and *Later Lyrics* (1866).

Jackson, Mattie J. (1846?–?). As an historical figure, Mattie J. Jackson is something of a mystery, as the only known details of her life come from her own narrative. Born in Missouri around 1846 to slaves owned by different masters, Jackson watched her mother, Ellen Turner, sacrifice and struggle to keep her family together after Mattie's father and, later, her stepfather escaped to the North. Shuttled between different masters and subjected to cruel treatment, Jackson and her mother and siblings anxiously watched the events of the Civil War unfold in St. Louis. As the Union began gaining control of the border states, Jackson's spiteful master sold her family into Kentucky to profit while he still could, and there Mattie and her family were separated. In late 1864, Mattie escaped to freedom in Indianapolis on a steamer, returning to Missouri after the war to be reunited with her mother, though her sister was never heard from again. As Reconstruction commenced, Mattie's stepfather, George Brown, invited her and her half-brother to come to Lawrence, Massachusetts, where his new wife, Dr. L. S. Thompson, took an interest in Mattie and encouraged Mattie to let her record her story. What is known of Mattie ends in 1866, the date of her narrative's publication.

Jacobs, Harriet (1813–1897). Jacobs's importance as an African American writer rests squarely on her 1861 autobiography, *Incidents in the Life of a Slave Girl*, which focused on how a young woman navigated the particular challenges of sexuality and motherhood within a slave system. Yet her importance as a social activist, who had a direct and positive impact on real people's lives, extended well beyond that narrative. During and immediately after the Civil War, she worked toward the education and uplift of newly freed slaves or poor blacks in Virginia, Washington D.C., Boston, and Savannah, often in cooperation with her daughter Louisa. She subsequently operated a boarding house in Cambridge, Massachusetts, and then joined Louisa in Washington D.C. for the remaining years of her life. In his elegy to Jacobs, the Reverent Francis Grimké observed that she "was no reed shaken by the wind, vacillating, easily moved from a position. She did her own thinking; had opinions of her own, and held to them with great tenacity" (quoted in Jean Fagan Yellin, *Harriet Jacobs: A Life* [New York: Basic Civitas Books, 2004], 260).

Keckley, Elizabeth (1818–1907). Born a slave in Dinwiddie, Virginia, Keckley rose through talent and force of character to end up working as the personal dressmaker and fashion consultant for Mary Todd Lincoln during the war years. Having already earned enough money from her skills with cloth and needle to buy her freedom, Keckley moved to Washington D.C. in 1860, where she built a reputation and successful business for herself. Once hired by the Lincolns, she occupied a tricky position between white privilege and African American culture; to some extent this tension was resolved by her founding of the Contraband Relief Association in 1862, which drew funding from wealthy donors both black and white. After the war (in which her son George was killed in battle), Keckley published her memoir, which focuses on her time in the White House. Although scholars have questioned whether *Behind the Scenes* (1868) is fully her own text, the crafty, ironic, and talented woman we meet in its pages was very much her own creation.

Lanier, Sidney Clopton (1842–1881). A native son of Macon, Georgia, Lanier signed up enthusiastically at the beginning of war and fought for Southern independence for three years, before being captured aboard a blockade-running ship and imprisoned at Point Lookout, Maryland. After the war, he published *Tiger-Lilies* (1867), a rather labored and allegorical novel, and for several years practiced law with his father. In 1877, Lanier moved to Baltimore, where he lectured on literature at Johns Hopkins University, and began publishing poems, many of an agrarian or pastoral strain, in a variety of popular magazines. He died from tuberculosis.

Larcom, Lucy (1824–1893). Never privileged, Larcom's life was enriched by her love for nature and her sense of sisterhood with the working class. Having spent years working in the textile mills in Lowell, she attended the Monticello Female Seminary in Illinois before returning to Massachusetts and taking up work as a teacher, poet, and editor. She looked back fondly on her early life in *A New England Girlhood* (1889): "It still seems to me that in the Lowell mills, and in my log-cabin schoolhouse on the Western prairies, I received the best part of my early education." What she learned was the dignity of work and the vitality of ethics, and she put both into her studied, and steadied, poetry.

Lincoln, Abraham (1809–1865). The life and death of Lincoln are legendary almost to the point of myth: his days as a lawyer in Illinois, his rapid rise in Republican politics, his controversial leadership during the Civil War, his anguished grappling with the religious and spiritual implications of violence, his assassination at the hands of John Wilkes Booth. These matters alone fill volumes. What is especially important here is the impact of Lincoln's words, not just his ideas or decisions, on American political discourse and public attitudes. An unusually careful prose writer, simultaneously inventive and legal-istically precise, he helped fashion a new kind of civic language, one which eschewed ornateness, and in which metaphor worked organically with the literal meanings he wished to convey. Beyond his obvious importance as a political and military figure, Lincoln produced, on a number of critical occasions, some of the finest writing to come out of the Civil War—if by "fine" we mean something akin to what Whitman wrote of the President's physical appearance: "Of technical beauty it had nothing – but to the eye of a great artist it furnished a rare study, a feast and fascination."

Longfellow, Henry Wadsworth (1807–1882). Not many people read Longfellow anymore, but in the nineteenth century, the country's most famous poet—a central figure in the New England Renaissance—set the standard for what verse was supposed to do. His poems flowed easily, with natural-sounding rhythms, and presented little stylistic challenge for readers. Beneath the gracefulness of his meter, however, one can hear notes of sadness and tragedy. A professor at Bowdoin and later Harvard, Longfellow wrote on classical and mythological themes, but his most influential work—"Evangeline," "The Courtship of Miles Standish," "The Song of Hiawatha"—reflects his interest in local materials, and in helping a truly independent American literature take root.

Martineau, Harriet (1802–1876). Growing up in a middle-class Unitarian household in Norwich, England, Harriet expanded on her limited formal education by reading news-papers, taking lessons from her siblings, and studying independently. Harriet's physical adversities—she was deaf by age sixteen and later bedridden from a uterine tumor—seem to have fired her intellectual curiosity and her conviction to write about the social causes that were important to her. Having established herself in London as a daring writer, Martineau traveled in America from 1834 to 1836 and was courted by both pro- and anti-slavery advocates eager to seek her favor in print. In response, she wrote

Society in America, a fierce indictment of slavery and women's political subordination, and a pioneering work in the field of sociology. Throughout her long career (never derailed by getting married), Martineau remained deeply passionate about social injustice, writing essays and newspaper articles on women's rights and education, English politics, economic disparity, and military reform.

Melville, Herman (1819–1891). Melville made his reputation as the author of *Typee* (1846) and *Omoo* (1847), buoyant novels of South Sea adventure, and gradually squandered that reputation as the author of *Moby-Dick* (1851), *Pierre* (1852), and other works whose stylistic and philosophical complexities confounded a reading public more accustomed to the literary sensibilities of Longfellow or Stowe. Melville's politics were unionist and antislavery, but not partisan, and he followed the Civil War from Massachusetts, and then New York, with an eye toward its poetic possibilities. His volume *Battle-Pieces and Aspects of the War* (New York, 1866) sold poorly and impressed few critics, but has gained increasing respect for its poetic originality and its willingness to explore the psychological and social subtleties of the conflict. Rebelling against his era's conventions of imagery and meter, Melville tried to convey the fractured experience of war in poems that, for the most part, are less concerned with lamentation, celebration, or moral judgment than with the impossibility of ethical and cultural certitude. They respond powerfully to specific scenes, states of mind, and philosophical ironies, but reflect Melville's misgivings about the war's meaning for American history.

Mitchell, Silas Weir (1829–1914). His pioneering clinical research on neurological disorders laid the foundation not only for Mitchell's medical fame but for his surprisingly productive literary career. As a surgeon during the Civil War at the Army's Filbert Street Hospital in Philadelphia, Mitchell witnessed a terrible variety of physical and psychic trauma, and from this experience wrote two medical treatises, *Gunshot Wounds and Other Injuries of Nerves* (1864; with George R. Morehouse and William W. Keen) and *Injuries of Nerves and Their Consequences* (1872), along with his first novel, *In War Time* (1884). The relation between mind and body, and the dependence of identity on corporeal integrity, fascinated Mitchell, and although his fiction can seem contrived, it is the richer for his medical insights—and vice versa.

Piatt, Sarah Morgan Bryan (1836–1919). Though unfairly considered a "minor" poet by her readers in the twentieth century, and by some today, Piatt was actually one of the more interesting American writers of the Victorian era. Raised in the border state of Kentucky, Piatt and her husband moved to Washington D.C. at the outbreak of civil war, and then to Ohio in 1867. Over a career spanning decades, Piatt wrote on family life, culture, and politics with a skeptical eye and a psychological complexity that the sentimental veneer of her poetry can sometimes obscure. Contemporary reviewers had some trouble understanding Piatt's originality of vision, but she is now beginning to receive the more serious re-evaluation she deserves.

Pollard, Edward Alfred (1831–1872). Trained as a lawyer and journalist, this native son of Virginia became editor of the Richmond *Examiner* in 1861. From this post, his rabid advocacy of the Southern cause, combined with his public condemnations of Jefferson Davis, made Pollard an electrifying figure in Confederate politics. He published several books during the war, including *The Southern Spy* (1861), *The Rival Administrations* (1864), and the multi-part *Southern History of the War* (1862–1866). In *The Lost Cause*

(1866) and *The Lost Cause Regained* (1868), Pollard voiced an unrepentant, unrecon-structed commitment to the principles of the defeated Confederacy.

Smith, James L. (c. 1816–?). Much of the *Autobiography of James L. Smith* (1881) follows the standard arc of the nineteenth-century slave narrative. It opens with an account of his childhood (in Northern Neck, Virginia), describes his years of enslavement and his successful escape (by boat), and then relates his experience of life in the North (working at a shoe store in Springfield, Massachusetts, and then opening his own shop and serving as a minister in Norwich, Connecticut). What sets the memoir apart from many of its peers is Smith's interest in the Civil War, to which he devotes the second half of the book. Moving back and forth between personal experience and historical commentary, Smith sought to ensure that an African American rendition of the war—a counter-history—would take its place alongside the many retrospective works written by whites.

Stephens, Alexander Hamilton (1812–1883). From his humble background to his frail health, the future Vice-President of the Confederacy overcame much hardship to become a dominant presence in his nearly fifty-year career in Georgia state politics. Raised poor, orphaned by age fourteen, Stephens nonetheless graduated from Franklin College and went on to a successful law practice that led him into the Georgia state legis-lature and later into the U.S. House of Representatives. Stephens was a staunch supporter (and practitioner) of slavery, and he played a vital role in the passage of the Compromise of 1850, yet he opposed secession right up to the outbreak of the Civil War. After the war, Stephens was elected to the U.S. Senate, but his wartime role proved too controversial for many Northerners and he was refused the seat. On political hiatus, he took up writing but returned to politics as a senator in 1873. He was elected governor of Georgia in 1882, but his service was to be brief; he died four months into his term on March 4, 1883.

Stowe, Harriet Beecher (1811–1896). By any account, including Abraham Lincoln's, Stowe deserves some of the credit, or blame, for the outbreak of civil war. Her wildly popular abolitionist novel *Uncle Tom's Cabin* (1852) galvanized public opinion and contributed directly to the increasing animosity between North and South. Stowe's vision of the conflict over slavery was panoramic and apocalyptic, informed equally by her Christian piety, her belief in the redemptive power of domestic life, and her analytical approach toward social relations. Beginning in 1865, Stowe published a series of "Chimney-Corner" essays, some of which deal with the Civil War, but after the war she increasingly focused on religion, domesticity, and New England life rather than national politics.

Taylor, Susie King (1848–1912). Almost all of what we know about the life of Susie King Taylor—from her childhood as a slave and her escape at age fourteen, to her stint as a unofficial nurse and teacher for an early black regiment, the South Carolina Volunteers, and her work with the Woman's Relief Corps—she herself records in her autobiography, *Reminiscences of My Life in Camp* (1902). That memoir is remarkable not only in that it provides a woman's first-hand account of the business of war, but in that it creatively fuses two central genres of late nineteenth-century American literature, the slave narrative and the Civil War memoir. Doing so enabled her to focus on the war's emancipationist meaning from the perspective of direct experience rather than mere political theory.

Timrod, Henry (1828–1867). The *soi-disant* "poet laureate of the Confederacy," Timrod was neither particularly successful nor particularly long-lived, but in his short career he did manage to fuse classical lyricism and Southern pride in a number of enduring poems, the most important of which are connected to the Civil War. Born and raised in South Carolina, Timrod studied classics and the law, worked as a teacher on a plantation, and from the late 1840s, began publishing poems. He tried to participate in the Civil War as both a soldier and a correspondent, but had never been particularly healthy and was forced back to the home front. Timrod returned to newspaper work after the war, but reduced to poverty and sickness, it was was not long before he succumbed to tuberculosis. Timrod's war poetry was first collected in 1873 in *The Poems of Henry Timrod*, edited by his friend Paul Hamilton Hayne.

Tourgée, Albion Winegar (1838–1905). A latecomer to antislavery who became a tireless, if rather strident, advocate of civil rights during and after Reconstruction, Tourgée was less a writer of the Civil War itself than, in his own words, of "the causes that underlay the struggle and the results that followed from it" (*An Appeal to Caesar* [New York, 1884], 44). He undertook this effort in a series of novelistic histories of the war, beginning with *A Fool's Errand* (1879) and concluding with *Bricks Without Straw* (1886), which drew on his experience both as a soldier and as a lawyer in postwar North Carolina, along with plenty of secondary reading. He regarded the conflict as one between enlightenment and barbarity, and mourned what he saw as the North's retreat from its principles as race hatred flourished in the South.

Twain, Mark (1835–1910). Growing up in Hannibal, Missouri, with a father who was both a slave-owner and a judge, Samuel Langhorne Clemens gained first-hand insight into slavery, law, and the hypocrisy of American society, insight that would deeply inform his writings and his personality. After leaving home at the age of seventeen, Clemens worked as a typesetter, riverboat pilot, and gold miner—giving no indication of his future fame as an author. In 1861, he enlisted in the Missouri militia, but Missouri was a badly divided state, and although Twain's politics were mainly unionist, his unit effectively served the interests of the Confederacy. In any case, he abandoned his post after about two weeks and headed west—a decision born of both ambivalence and fear, which he sought on several occasions to explain and which provided fodder for his detractors. Though his "service" was brief, the Civil War left a great imprint upon Clemens and became a recurring subject in much of his work. Under the pseudonym of Mark Twain, Clemens wrote prolifically, from novels and short stories to essays and travel narratives, perfecting the art of the polemic against ruling-class hypocrisy, racism, religious fanaticism, and social injustice of all kinds. Twain left an indelible mark upon American literature, becoming the foremost voice in American realism and influencing generations of writers, humorists, and social critics in the twentieth century.

Velazquez, Loreta Janeta (1842–c. 1897). Who the "real" Loreta Velazquez was is a tricky thing to determine, because our main biographical source is *The Woman in Battle* (1876), a "memoir" which to some degree fictionalizes a life flamboyantly and implausibly filled with adventure (scholars continue to debate the creative license she took). Yet this is what we are told: Velazqez was born in Cuba and raised in Texas; her father moved the family back to Cuba after the U.S. annexed Texas; she was sent to school in New Orleans, where she married a Southern army officer, to her father's chagrin. She enlisted in the Confederate Army in 1861 and recruited troops in Arkansas; her husband (the first of four) died early in the war; she dressed as a man ("Lt. Harry T. Buford"), fought in various battles, conducted espionage missions, was exposed after being wounded. She traveled throughout Europe, South America, and the American West after the war; collected more husbands and had a baby; to help support that baby, published what she disingenuously calls a "plain and unpretentious account of my adventuresome career." Perhaps Velazquez is putting one over on us; if so, *The Woman in Battle* still provides a remarkable picture of nineteenth-century American life, as lived by a woman of striking independence.

Wallis, Severn Teackle (1816–1894). A native of Maryland, author and lawyer Wallis lived through the tricky politics of a slave state that stayed in the Union. After graduating from St. Mary's College in 1832, Wallis went on to study law and was admitted to the bar in 1837, beginning a legal career devoted to reform. A *Harper's Weekly* obituary described Wallis, a Whig-turned-Democrat, as "a sympathizer with the South," but he was also an ardent unionist. In 1861, serving one term in the Maryland state legislature, Wallis walked the line, arguing that the state should not secede—but also that the federal government had no rightful power to "coerce" her. On September 12, 1861, Wallis, suspected as a secessionist, was arrested by Union forces and imprisoned for over a year, without trial. Upon his release, he returned to a very active professional and civic life, including serving as provost of the University of Maryland. Throughout, Wallis maintained an avid literary career, publishing poetry and various items of literary and historical criticism. Though urged to return to politics, the lifelong bachelor preferred not to, keeping near to his home until his death in 1894.

Watkins, Samuel Rush (1839–1901). A regular guy from around Columbia, Tennessee, Watkins went on to become one of the finest, most distinctive Southern writers the Civil War produced. As a private in Company H (the "Maury Greys") of the First Tennessee Infantry, Watkins served for the entire war, from the earliest skirmishes through Joseph Johnston's surrender to William T. Sherman in April 1865. By the end of the war, both his company and regiment had suffered casualties in excess of 90 percent, but Watkins survived to return to Tennessee, earn a college degree, and start a family. What sets his memoir, *Co. Aytch*, apart from the pack of postwar retrospectives is its narrative voice: ironic, comic, outraged, modest, and perpetually fresh.

Whitman, Walt (1819–1892). His 1855 *Leaves of Grass* marks a watershed moment in American literature, when the polite verse of an age had to make room for the brash, earthy, and omnivorous poetry of a young rough from Brooklyn. Yet in Whitman's own words, the Civil War "completed" him. It gave him the raw material that, in *Drum-Taps* (1865), and in his prose works *Memoranda During the War* (1875–1876) and *Specimen Days and Collect* (1882), he worked and reworked, reaching for an understanding of the war's commanding significance for human beings and for the country. That material, however, was bought dear. After traveling to Washington D.C. to find his younger brother George, who had been wounded at the battle of Fredericksburg, and seeing there the war's wounded, Whitman began working as a volunteer nurse at army hospitals in Washington. In about three years of such work, according to biographer David Reynolds, Whitman tended to between 80,000 and 100,000 soldiers (*Walt Whitman's America*, 425). The physical trauma and emotional suffering he observed changed Whitman's imagination, even as the war itself seemed to be cleansing the nation, disencumbering it of a terrible burden, and even as he appreciated something of the romance of battle. His writings on the war—sketches, snapshots, reflections, essays—show Whitman to be one of the conflict's foremost interpreters.

Glossary

Andersonville (Camp Sumter). Following the breakdown of prisoner exchanges between North and South in 1863, both sides began building facilities to house enemy combatants, many of which facilities were inadequately provisioned and poorly managed. The camp at Andersonville in southern Georgia, however, was the worst: a wretched sink of disease, malnutrition, and overcrowding. Of the 45,000 federal prisoners held there between February 1864 and May 1865, almost 13,000 died. The commander of the camp, Captain Henry Wirz, was convicted and hanged after the war, but the bitter resentment generated by Andersonville was long in abating.

Antietam (Sharpsburg). September 17, 1862. This battle, near the Antietam Creek outside Sharpsburg, Maryland, produced in excess of 22,000 casualties, more than any other day in American history. The stakes could not have been higher. Lee had pushed north of the Potomac in the hope of reviving Southern morale, securing foreign diplomatic recognition, and putting the Union on the defensive. Lincoln, beyond the obvious need to reverse the advance, also sought a military victory that would give him political cover in issuing a proclamation of emancipation. The battle itself involved a complicated series of attacks and counter-attacks that yielded no clear advantage and that, in photographs by Alexander Gardner, produced some of the war's most startling images. Ultimately, Lee decided to withdraw his battered army across the Potomac, but the hypercautious McClellan refused a pursuit that could have greatly shortened the war.

Army of the Potomac. Organized, named, and commanded by George McClellan after the Union defeat at Bull Run, the Army of the Potomac would face the hardest duty of the war, along with morale problems in its early years, harassing congressional investigations, and a series of changes at the top as Lincoln tried to find the right general for the job. McClellan was replaced by Ambrose Burnside in November 1862, following Antietam; Burnside was replaced by Joseph Hooker in January 1863, following Fredericksburg; and Hooker was replaced by George Meade in June 1863, following Chancellorsville. Finally, Grant, promoted to lieutenant general in March 1864, assumed functional control of the Army while leaving Meade nominally in command, and began his long hard campaign against Lee's Army of Northern Virginia. From here to the end of the war, the Army of the

Potomac fought one bloody battle after another as Grant slowly wore down Lee and eventually trapped him near the Virginia town of Appomattox Court House.

Army of Northern Virginia. Originally the Confederate Army of the Potomac, the Army of Northern Virginia was renamed by Robert E. Lee, who took command in June 1862 after Gen. Joseph Johnston was wounded at the battle of Fair Oaks. Under Lee, James Longstreet, Stonewall Jackson, and Jeb Stuart, and later Richard Ewell and A. P. Hill, the army gained fame by proving that it could win battles even when outnumbered and outprovisioned. But after clever victories at the Seven Days' battles, Second Bull Run, Fredericksburg, and Chancellorsville, the army suffered a crushing defeat at Gettysburg, and retreated back into its own state. Throughout 1864, the Army found itself on the defensive against Grant, who undertook a relentless southward campaign intended to keep the strategic initiative and inflict casualties as much as to secure territory. After a series of battles that cost him men and officers he could ill afford to lose, Lee and the depleted, cornered Army of Northern Virginia surrendered on April 9, 1865, effectively ending the Civil War.

Ball's Bluff. October 21, 1861. This early battle had a low body count but important consequences. Federal forces under Gen. Charles P. Stone, commanded by Lincoln's personal friend Col. Edward D. Baker, crossed the Potomac River into Virginia, encountered sharp resistance from the Confederates, and were driven ignominiously back into the river. The defeat electrified both North and South, for different reasons, and resulted in the creation of the Congressional Joint Committee on the Conduct of the War.

Banks, Nathaniel Prentiss (1816–1894). A self-educated lawyer, journalist, and Congressman, the moderately antislavery Banks was appointed Union major general when the war began, but showed little aptitude for military command. After early defeats in the Shenandoah, Banks was reassigned to Louisiana, where he led a costly effort to capture Port Hudson and contributed to the debacle of the Red River expedition. His controversial reconstruction efforts in Louisiana, which included the conscription of free black laborers, proved politically divisive, leading to his recall to Washington in 1865, and Banks went on to lead a varied political career.

Beauregard, Pierre Gustave Toutant (1818–1893). One of the Civil War's more colorful and complex figures, the French-speaking, self-assured Gen. Beauregard served the Confederacy well throughout the war, yet quarreled bitterly about military strategy, and never really felt that he had received his due recognition. From ordering the firing on Fort Sumter, to redesigning the Confederate flag, to overseeing the defense of coastal areas, Beauregard contributed much to the Southern cause, but generally ended up serving under superiors who preferred a more defensive strategic vision.

Belmont. November 7, 1861. The battle of Belmont, in Missouri, was part of Grant's effort to capture the nearby Confederate bastion at Columbus, Kentucky, which was part of his larger campaign to control the Mississippi River. Initially successful, the assault on Belmont fell apart as green Union soldiers broke ranks, and as the Confederates reinforced and counter-attacked.

Bragg, Braxton (1817–1876). Commanding the Confederate Army of the Tennessee, but commanding it badly, and inspiring scant loyalty from either subordinates or superiors, in 1862 Gen. Bragg led an unproductive offensive through Tennessee and into Kentucky. Easily pushed back to Chattanooga, Bragg then made a successful stand at Chickamauga, but failed to follow through. After the breaking of his siege of Chattanooga in November 1863, Bragg tendered his resignation and served out the war as military adviser to Jefferson Davis.

Brown, John (1800–1859). Along with twenty-one other zealous abolitionists, on October 16, 1859 Brown led a raid on Harper's Ferry, Virginia, intending to spark an uprising by the local slave population. Although no uprising occurred, although U.S. Marines quickly repulsed the attack, and although Brown was hanged less than two months later, his violent approach to confronting slavery became a *cause célèbre* among radical Northerners and signaled the approach of civil war. "He was simple, exasperatingly simply; unlettered, plain, and homely," wrote W. E. B. Du Bois fifty years later, and yet he "grasped the very pith and kernel of the evil" of slavery (*John Brown* [1909], ed. John David Smith. Armonk, NY and London: M. E. Sharpe, 1997, pp. 173, 174).

Buchanan, James (1791–1868). Buchanan, the "Bachelor President," was nominated by the Democrats in 1856, and served as President until 1861. He was a unionist, but tilted politically toward slavery and compromise with the South.

Bull Run, First (First Manassas). July 21, 1861. The first major battle of the war, this clash near the Bull Run River in northeastern Virginia, was a harbinger of the larger engagements to come. It resulted from the over-eager Union effort, under Gen. Irvin McDowell, to grab the railway center of Manassas Junction, thereby securing territory around Washington D.C., and dividing two Confederate armies under Beauregard and Joseph Johnston. A series of missteps by federal forces, however, and timely reinforcements by the rebels, turned the battle into a stinging rout (almost 3,000 U.S. casualties to the rebels' 2,000) that dispelled the hopeful illusion that the war could be won quickly and easily.

Bull Run, Second (Second Manassas). August 28–30, 1862. The second battle of Bull Run closed an already auspicious summer for the South on a high note. This latest effort to move on Richmond, following the failure of McClellan's Peninsula campaign, was badly managed by U.S. Maj. Gen. John Pope, commanding the new Army of Virginia. After some early maneuvering, Lee, to prevent the Army of the Potomac from reinforcing Pope, moved Stonewall Jackson forward to destroy federal supplies at Manassas Junction. There, Jackson's men surprised and roughed up one of the marching federal columns. Pope counterattacked the next day, but in haphazard fashion and without adequate reinforcements, and several initially successful assaults fell through. A larger attack on the third day failed badly, and after Lee ordered Longstreet to follow up, Pope was forced to retreat toward Washington, having suffered in excess of 14,000 casualties, to approximately 9,000 for the South.

Burnside, Ambrose Everett (1824–1881). A capable soldier and a decent man, Burnside's unfortunate fate is to be known less for his achievements than for his muttonchop sideburns and his military failures. After leading successful operations along the Carolina coast in 1861–1862, Burnside returned to the Washington area to reinforce McClellan in the spring. After contributing to the Union effort at Antietam, Burnside found himself given command of the Army of the Potomac, though he did not particularly want it. His first major offensive resulted in the fiasco at Fredericksburg, and Burnside was transferred to the Department of the Ohio. Here he oversaw the capture of both Knoxville and of Clement Vallandigham, a fierce Ohio Peace Democrat, in 1863. Finally, Burnside returned to the East, but found his career swallowed up by the calamitous battle of the Crater during the siege of Petersburg. He resigned in April 1865.

Butler, Benjamin Franklin (1818–1893). The South despised Butler not for his military accomplishments, which were relatively few, but for his administrative style, which was fearsome. By 1860, Butler had established himself as a successful criminal lawyer with a thriving practice and a force to be reckoned with in Massachusetts Democratic politics. Reform-minded and fiercely unionist, Butler took his first commission as a brigadier general the 8th Massachusetts Militia and began cracking down on dissent in Maryland. Transferred to Fort Monroe, Virginia, Butler took a crucial step in designating as "contraband of war" slaves who had fled to Union lines and employing these contrabands in a military capacity. Given command of New Orleans in May 1862, Butler governed that occupied city with an iron fist before complaints led to his removal to the Eastern theater. After the war, Butler led a successful career in elective politics, pursuing civil rights and workers' rights legislation.

Calhoun, John Caldwell (1782–1850). South Carolina's preeminent politician during the first half of the nineteenth century, Calhoun served variously as Representative, Senator, Secretary of War, Secretary of State, and Vice-President. His political ideas centered on the distribution and balance of authority and on the importance of popular will. He became a staunch defender of the South against antislavery "interference," and yet worked to prevent tensions between North and South from spinning out of control.

Cameron, Simon (1799–1899). Cameron was Lincoln's first Secretary of War, serving from March 1861 to January 1862. He had built his career as an opportunistic businessman and key operator in Pennsylvania politics, and at one time or another had associated himself with the Democrats, the Whigs, the American Party, and the Republicans. He negotiated a cabinet post during the 1860 Republican Convention, but was not up to the task of first overhauling and then administering the War Department as it struggled to meet the Union's military needs. After angering Lincoln by prematurely and publicly recommending the arming of slaves, Cameron was made minister to Russia, where he served for less than a year before returning to the United States to work for Lincoln's re-election and reassert himself in Pennsylvania politics.

Chancellorsville. On May 2–3, 1863, at this small hamlet near Fredericksburg, Virginia, the military genius of Robert Lee and Stonewall Jackson gave the South one of its most spine-tingling victories. Outnumbered nearly two-to-one by Joseph Hooker's bristling Army of the Potomac, and badly hampered by a lack of supplies, Lee divided his army and sent Jackson on a daring flanking attack around the Union right, confusing Hooker and setting up a more concentrated attack the next day that prompted a northward Union retreat. Yet the battle's legacy was complicated. Although inflicting more than 17,000 casualties on the North (to 13,000 of its own), the South lost one of its premier generals (Jackson was hit by friendly fire and later succumbed to pneumonia), and Lee's confidence contributed to his overreaching at Gettysburg.

Chase, Salmon Portland (1808–1873). Chase served as Secretary of the Treasury from Lincoln's inauguration until June 1864. An Ohio attorney who had made his name defending fugitive slaves and had helped found the Free Soil Party, Chase was elected to the Senate in 1849 and spent the 1850s opposing slavery and trying to figure out how to become President. As Secretary of the Treasury, Chase instituted a variety of economic policies to help finance the war, principally the sale of government bonds and the levying of a federal income tax. He was ahead of the curve on issues of emancipation and civil rights, but his unsuccessful maneuvering for the Republican nomination in 1864 led to his resignation that summer. Lincoln nominated Chase for Chief Justice of the U.S. Supreme Court in December 1864, and from his seat on that court Chase fought for African American civil rights during the first years of Reconstruction.

Chickamauga. September 19–20, 1863. Fought in the dense woods around Chickamauga Creek, in northern Georgia, this bloody battle enabled the Army of the Tennessee temporarily to stop the Union's southward advance toward Georgia. Following a minor clash between federal infantry and rebel cavalry, the battle quickly mushroomed as each side sent reinforcements into the fray. On the second day, despite tactical delays, the Confederates managed to drive the Union forces back to Chattanooga. What one Confederate private described as "all this terrible thunder, blood, carnage, slaughter" produced in the order of 35,000 casualties (*The Civil War Letters of Joshua K. Callaway*, ed. Judith Lee Hallock, University of Georgia Press, 1997, p. 138).

Cold Harbor. June 3, 1864. Through May 1864, Grant had led the Army of the Potomac on a grinding campaign through Virginia in an effort to reach Richmond and defeat the wily Lee. After two days of inconclusive fighting around the Old Cold Harbor cross-roads, Grant, evidently eager for a showdown, ordered an assault against well-entrenched and well-reinforced Confederate positions. The poorly coordinated attack turned into a turkey-shoot, resulting in about 7,000 Union casualties, to the Confederates' 1,500.

Contrabands. In May 1861, three escaped slaves made their way to Fortress Monroe, Virginia, where they were designated "contrabands of war" by Union Gen. Benjamin Butler and employed in construction and picking cotton. This seemingly minor incident was actually a pivotal moment in the history of the war because it focused attention on the status of African Americans in the conflict and contributed to the gradually accelerating politics of emancipation. Although the legal status of contrabands was ambiguous—not technically free (until the Emancipation Proclamation), yet no longer property—former slaves understood that reaching federal lines was a route to freedom because, in practical terms, there would be no sending them back. Although the federal government wanted to move cautiously on the issue of emancipation so as not to alienate wavering border states or Northern Democrats, the ideological meaning of the war had its own momentum, and the use of contrabands by the Union Army contributed centrally to the eventual cause of abolishing slavery.

Copperheads. This term of opprobrium was applied to Northern Democrats who criticized or worked against the Lincoln administration's conduct of the war, even if they were not in engaged in serpentine sedition. Most Copperheads—many of whom were midwesterners and many of whom were of German or Irish extraction—strongly opposed emancipation measures and feared the ascendancy of Republican economic policies. Although the administration prosecuted some Democratic dissenters, the demise of the Copperheads came about primarily through the ultimate military success of the North.

Cumberland. See *Merrimack* and *Monitor*.

Douglas, Stephen Arnold (1813–1861). Born in Vermont, Douglas's political career as a Democrat took off in Illinois, which sent him to the House in 1843 and the Senate in 1847, where he played a central role in crafting the compromises on slavery of the 1850s. Guided by the principles of Jacksonian democracy and expansionist nationalism, Douglas thought that the status of slavery should be left to the people of a given territory, and in his 1858 Senatorial campaign debates with Lincoln rejected the idea that a house divided could not stand. He ran for President as one of two unsuccessful Democrats in 1860, and after the firing on Fort Sumter, after all efforts at compromise, fiercely rejected the doctrine of secession.

Fessenden, William Pitt (1806–1869). After rising through the ranks of Maine law and politics, Fessenden won a Senate seat in 1854 and emerged as an influential Republican leader. He became Secretary of the Treasury after Salmon P. Chase's resignation in July 1864, but served only for a year and then returned to the Senate, where he advocated a fairly aggressive Reconstruction policy.

First South Carolina Volunteer Infantry. The first black infantry unit of the war, the 1st South Carolina, of Hilton Head, started out inauspiciously as the "Hunter Experiment." Originally organized by General David Hunter in May 1862, in the Department of the South, the regiment ran into trouble quickly: Hunter had not obtained authorization from the War Department, and his policy of involuntary conscription worked to antagonize or alienate the very soldiers who would serve in it. Soon disbanded, the regiment was reorganized later that year by Gen. Rufus Saxton, and in November Sergeant C. T. Trowbridge was commisioned its Captain. In February 1864, the 1st South Carolina was redesignated the 33rd U.S. Colored Troops.

Forrest, Nathan Bedford (1821–1877). The great equestrian of the Confederacy, this Tennessee native and wealthy slave-owner became lieutenant colonel, then brigadier general, then major general, on the strength of his brilliant cavalry raids in the Western theater. Hot-tempered, independent-minded, and crafty, Forrest led cavalry attacks in Tennessee, Kentucky, and northern Mississippi that slowed the south-bound Grant and Sherman by disrupting supply lines and diverting federal resources. Although he cut a romantic figure, Forrest's reputation has suffered because of the 1864 Fort Pillow massacre, in which his men apparently murdered black troops who had surrendered, and because of his postwar leadership of the Ku Klux Klan.

Fort Monroe. The U.S. garrison at Fort Monroe, located at the southern end of the Chesapeake Bay near the mouth of the James River, played an important role in the Union war effort. It provided a base of operations for George McClellan during his 1862 campaign for Richmond and for Benjamin Butler during his support of Grant's 1864 campaign. It also served briefly as the prison for Jefferson Davis after the war.

Fort Pulaski. April 10–11, 1862. An island redoubt at the mouth of the Savannah River, Fort Pulaski was a state-of-the-art facility (seized by Georgia in January 1861) until it was bombarded into submission by Union forces. The bombardment, under Gen. Quincy Gillmore, demonstrated the great efficacy of rifled, as opposed to smoothbore, cannon, and the consequent vulnerability of masonry forts.

Fort Sumter. On April 12, 1861, South Carolina finally moved from rhetoric to war by firing on the federal garrison at Fort Sumter, commanded by U.S. Major Robert Anderson, and located at the entrance to Charleston Harbor. The attack, overseen by P. G. T. Beauregard, came after months of political and military maneuvering during which South Carolina Gov. Francis Pickens, the outgoing administration of James Buchanan, and the incoming administration of Lincoln struggled to resolve competing claims to the fort. As the state's siege of Fort Sumter took its toll, Anderson was prepared to surrender, but in order to prevent any possible reinforcement, the South opened fire. After a day and a half of bombardment, Anderson surrendered on April 14.

Fort Wagner. July 18, 1863. Located toward the northern end of Morris Island on the South Carolina coast, Fort Wagner figured into Union Gen. Quincy Gillmore's plans to control Charleston Harbor and besiege the city of Charleston. After a failed assault on July 11, and after an intense but fruitless morning bombardment a week later, Gillmore sent in the infantry across an unprotected stretch of beach. The lead regiment was the 54th Massachusetts Volunteers, the Union's premier African American unit. Although the attack failed badly, with over 1,500 Union casualties, it convinced many Northerners of the military prowess and determination of black troops.

Franklin. November 30, 1864. Another of the Civil War's poorly planned and disastrous frontal assaults, the battle at Franklin, Tennessee, saw John Bell Hood, commander of the Army of Tennessee, move against well-entrenched federal units commanded by John M. Schofield. Following his inability to protect Atlanta from Sherman, or to distract Sherman by harassing his supply lines, Hood reasoned that an expedition into Tennessee to capture federally occupied Nashville might shake things up. The plan went sideways at Franklin, where the Confederates' dramatic charge, intended to prevent Schofield from linking up with George Thomas in Nashville, instead resulted in about 7,300 Southern casualties in five hours.

Fredericksburg. December 13, 1862. One of the Union's most crushing defeats, the battle of Fredericksburg rocked Northern morale, derailed the career of Gen. Ambrose Burnside, and undermined Lincoln's political strength. Seeking to advance on Richmond, the Army of the Potomac faced unaccountable delays in crossing the Rappahannock River, allowing Robert E. Lee to establish a strong defensive position west of Fredericksburg, especially on the high ground of Marye's Heights. Burnside's decision to storm this position repeatedly, despite having wave after wave of men cut down in the open ground in front of it, ultimately cost almost 13,000 casualties. (A second battle at Fredericksburg occurred on May 3, 1863 as part of the Chancellorsville campaign.)

Frémont, John Charles (1813–1890). The brilliant yet unruly mathematician and cartographer made his name in the 1830s and 1840s as an explorer of the West. On the strength of this glamorous experience, Frémont accepted the 1856 Presidential nomination of the newly formed Republican Party, and although he lost this contest helped establish Republican political dominance in the North. During the Civil War, Gen. Frémont's commanded the Western Department poorly and angered Lincoln by issuing an unauthorized edict freeing the slaves and confiscating the property of Missouri rebels. Reassigned to West Virginia in March 1862, he found himself outmatched by Stonewall Jackson, and resigned that summer.

Gaines's Mill. June 27, 1862. Following immediately on the heels of Mechanicsville, this second, and largest, of the Seven Days' battles helped secure Lee's psychological advantage over his antagonist McClellan. After a pause following several hours of brutal but indecisive fighting, Lee ordered a full assault on Union positions and finally managed to break through against Fitz John Porter's V Corps. Although Southern casualties exceeded those of the North (about 8,700 to about 6,800), Gaines's Mill ranks as a Confederate victory because it contributed to driving the Army of the Potomac away from Richmond.

Gettysburg. If any single clash could be considered the turning point of the war, the three-day battle at Gettysburg, Pennsylvania (July 1–3, 1863), marked the moment when the South's ambitions—for foreign diplomatic recognition, for a major victory on Northern soil, and for moral recovery from the recent fall of Vicksburg—foundered and crumbled. The North, under Meade, suffered about 23,000 casualties, and the South, under Lee, about 28,000. Although Meade failed to pursue the retreating rebels and attempt a *coup de grâce*, and although the South would enjoy later military victories, Gettysburg galvanized the North, deterred England from recognizing the Confederacy, and became a grim omen of eventual Southern defeat.

Halleck, Henry Wager (1815–1872). Long before he became general-in-chief of Union forces in July 1862, Halleck had evidenced the academic and administrative bent that would define his Civil War leadership for good and ill. A former lawyer and the author of influential works on military science and international law, Halleck brought his scholarly and bureaucratic acumen first to the West, where he undertook a rapid reorganization of the Department of the Missouri, and then to Washington, where he helped coordinate the overall war effort. But Halleck's disinterest in field operations and his inability to manage subordinates effectively led to his reassignment to chief-of-staff in the spring of 1864, as Grant was promoted to commanding general. In the end, Halleck's primary contribution was less as a working general than as a smart desk-man who backed up Grant's offensive campaigns with good administrative support.

Harper's Ferry. This Virginia town had an importance far greater than its small size would suggest. Its strategic location at the meeting of the Potomac and Shenandoah rivers, and its national arsenal and armory, made Harper's Ferry a valuable asset to both sides. It gained notoriety in 1859 as the site of John Brown's raid, and then endured six years of back-and-forth warfare. In September 1862, the battle of Harper's Ferry, a major Confederate victory, encouraged Lee to continue his push into Maryland, and enabled the Army of Northern Virginia to reinforce once the going got rough at Antietam.

Hooker, Joseph (1814–1879). Ambitious, tough, and hard-drinking, Hooker began the war as brigadier general under George McClellan and, despite a rocky start, established himself at the battle of Antietam as a grizzled fighter. Given command of the Army of the Potomac after Burnside's defeat at Fredericksburg, Hooker worked wonders for morale by instituting an array of organizational and operational changes. But failure loomed. At Chancellorsville, Hooker was so outgeneralled by Lee that his career and reputation never really recovered (he was replaced by Meade in June 1863). Despite later helping to break the siege of Chattanooga and helping Sherman push south into Georgia, a greatly diminished Hooker served out the war as commander of reserve troops in Chicago.

Hunter, David (1802–1886). From the beginning of his career, Hunter was a bit of loose cannon, and by end of his career had become the South's favorite *bête noire*. As commander of Union forces along the Southern coast, Maj. Gen. Hunter in May 1862 issued his own order freeing Southern slaves, and then undertook to organize a black regiment, the 1st South Carolina Volunteers. Neither decision was authorized from above, and both were soon reversed. Nonetheless, in his efforts at emancipation and the employment of African Americans in a military capacity, Hunter anticipated the coming year's decisive change in federal policy.

Jackson, Thomas Jonathan (1824–1863). Next to Lee, "Stonewall" Jackson emerged during the Civil War as the South's most revered general. Deeply pious yet fierce in combat; introverted and asocial yet popular with his men; hard-driven yet given to periods of strange lassitude—Jackson's austere personality proved an almost mystical asset in his war career. Seeing the Confederate cause as a kind of holy crusade, Jackson brought his faith and his formidable military skill to many of the most important battles of the war: First Manassas, Winchester, Cedar Mountain, Antietam, Fredericksburg. At Chancellorsville, as he returned to camp from a reconnaissance of Union forces, Jackson was inadvertently shot by Confederate guards. His left arm was amputated that same night, but pneumonia had set in, and Jackson died eight days later, at the Chandler plantation outside Fredericksburg.

Johnston, Joseph Eggleston (1807–1891). For a variety of reasons both personal and circumstantial, the Virginia-born Gen. Johnston never managed to thrive in the Civil War. A highly developed ego led to a pattern of contending with superiors, particularly Jefferson Davis, and a defensive strategic vision too often seemed to inhibit him from committing to a fight. After being wounded at the battle of Seven Pines, and seeing Lee thereby promoted, Johnston was transferred to the West, where his molasses-like response to the siege of Vicksburg further strained relations with Davis. During his 1864 command of the Army of the Tennessee, Johnston pursued a campaign of what might be called strategic retreat as Sherman advanced toward Atlanta. Replaced by John Bell Hood, and then in 1865 given command over the remaining Confederate forces in the Carolinas, Johnston surrendered to Sherman on April 26, 1865 in North Carolina.

Kennesaw Mountain (June 27, 1864). As Sherman pushed Joseph Johnston back through Georgia during the late spring and early summer, the fighting had been sporadic but indecisive. At Kennesaw Mountain, where Johnston had entrenched along high ground, Sherman hoped that by extending the Confederate line and then attacking at its center, he could achieve a clear victory. But the assault, hampered by poor coordination, simply provided another lesson in the folly of attacking well-entrenched fortifications. Despite the repulse, Sherman had ample recourse: he withdrew and continued his steady maneuvering toward the prize of Atlanta.

Lee, Robert Edward (1807–1870). The Confederacy invested its hope, its identity, and its pride in Lee more than in any other single individual. The son of a Virginian Revolutionary War hero, a hero himself of the Mexican War, and a former superintendent of West Point, Lee felt divided loyalties to nation and to state at the onset of civil war—but in the end, Virginia and family came first, with fateful consequences. Having resigned from the U.S. Army in April 1861 and accepted the offer of major general commanding Virginian forces, Lee got off to a slow start. But once promoted to command of the Army of

Northern Virginia, on June 1, 1862, Lee quickly displayed an unequalled flair for the art of war: how to win against long odds, how to make the best of the available resources, how to seize the psychological advantage, how to keep morale high. Indeed, one of Lee's defining strengths as a general was his ability to inspire almost passionate loyalty from his men and from his society. This strength came from his qualities as a person: a sterling sense of honor and duty, and a graciousness in both victory and defeat. From his early success in keeping the Army of the Potomac away from Richmond, to his dubious forays into Maryland and Pennsylvania, to his long final defensive campaign against Grant, Lee kept the Confederacy alive beyond what could reasonably have been expected, given its relative weakness of men and materiel. When he resigned at Appomattox Court House on April 9, 1865, the South had no one else to turn to; the rebellion had faded. Unpardoned by Andrew Johnson, Lee assumed the presidency of Virginia's Washington College in August 1865, but died of a stroke five years later.

Longstreet, James (1821–1904). Though undistinguished at West Point, the Georgian Longstreet earned promotions during his service in the Mexican War and gained a reputation as a steady commander, well-liked and well-respected. His contributions at the Seven Days' battles gained him a place at Lee's side, and he went on to display his formidable tactical abilities at Second Bull Run and Fredericksburg. Gettysburg, however, remains the controversial event in Longstreet's career. Having advised Lee against an offensive campaign in Pennsylvania, and specifically against frontal assaults during Gettysburg, Longstreet performed reluctantly, delaying both a July 2 attack and the disastrous Pickett's charge on July 3. It may not have made any difference, but led to fierce criticism after the war by Jubal Early and other ex-Confederates, and second-guessing ever since.

Malvern Hill. July 1, 1862. The last of the Seven Days' Battles in Virginia, Malvern Hill was a tactical disaster for the South, but nonetheless contributed to Lee's successful effort to push McClellan back from Richmond. In a confused and controversial assault, Confederate forces stormed the heavily fortified and geographically secure Union positions around the high grounds of Malvern Hill. Although costing almost twice as many casualties as it inflicted (approx. 5,500 to 3,000), the assault prompted McClellan to withdraw—or in his view, reposition—to Harrison's Landing on the James River.

Manassas. See Bull Run.

McClellan, George Brinton (1826–1885). Seemingly destined for greatness, the Union's "Young Napoleon" found himself by the end of the war greatly decreased in stature and influence. As the commander, indeed creator, of the Army of the Potomac, McClellan showed a genius for military organization and preparation, but was cautious to a fault on the battlefield, where he preferred siege to confrontation, and conservative in his politics. After the failure of his long-delayed Peninsula campaign against Richmond in the spring of 1862, and his reluctance to pursue Lee after the battle of Antietam, McClellan was replaced by Ambrose Burnside in November 1862, amid questions about his political loyalty and his stomach for a fight. McClellan ran for President as a Democrat in 1864, losing badly to his former ally Lincoln.

Meade, George Gordon (1815–1872). A civil engineer by trade, and a veteran of both the Second Seminole War and the Mexican–American War, Meade proved himself a capable

Northern general in the early battles of the Civil War. On June 28, 1863, just days before the battle of Gettysburg, Meade was given command of the Army of the Potomac. Meade's defensive strategy at Gettysburg delivered success, but he would long regret his failure to follow up with a crushing blow. Eventually overshadowed by Grant and Sherman, Meade served out his time in the military competently but without great distinction.

***Merrimack* and *Monitor*.** Hampton Roads, the main federal blockade base at the entrance to the James River in Virginia, was the site of a battle that marked a new era in naval warfare. Here, on March 8, 1862, the Confederate ironclad *Virginia* (previously the USS *Merrimack*) rammed and sank the wood-sided *Cumberland* (temporarily commanded by Lt. George U. Morris), killing 121 of its crew, and shelled the *Congress* into submission, until being driven off, with minor damage, by the Union ironclad *Monitor*, commanded by John L. Worden. Lt. Joseph B. Smith, acting commander of the *Congress*, was killed.

Missionary Ridge. November 24–25, 1863. The battle of Missionary Ridge completed the Union's successful effort to break the poorly managed siege of the Army of the Cumberland in Chattanooga by Braxton Bragg's Army of the Tennessee. Grant, recently promoted to full command of Western forces, meant to break the Confederates' line along Missionary Ridge through concerted action by Gens. Hooker, Sherman, and Thomas. After Hooker's men took Lookout Mountain on the first day, Sherman's repeated assaults the next proved unsuccessful, and Grant's plan seemed to be in trouble. Thomas's troops saved the day, however, by following up an initial advance on Missionary Ridge with an unauthorized, risky, but dramatically successful charge up the steep ridge that routed the badly positioned Confederate defenders. The "miracle" of Missionary Ridge broke the siege of Chattanooga, ruined Bragg's career, and left the path open for Sherman's advance into Georgia.

Peace Democrats. These Northern critics of the Lincoln administration formed the conservative wing of the Democratic Party and sought to bring the war to a conclusion, and thus somehow save the Union, through a negotiated settlement rather than military victory. Peace Democrats accused the Republican Party of monopolizing power, of trampling civil liberties, of waging an unnecessarily cruel war, and of promoting elitist economic policies. Dubbed "Copperheads" by their detractors, these agitators occasionally faced both figurative and literal charges of treason as their dissent grew more vociferous. Their political fortunes waxed and waned with the progress of the war, however, and after Lincoln's victory in 1864 the Peace Democrats were effectively finished as a viable faction.

Petersburg. Grant's grand campaign for Petersburg, Virginia's second largest city, ran from June 1864 to April 1865, produced some of the highest body counts of the war, and eventually forced Lee to surrender. After a series of savage clashes during the Overland campaign in May and June, both armies dug in around Petersburg, a vital rail hub that linked Richmond to the rest of the Confederacy. Early direct assaults failed, so Grant moved around the city and settled in for a long siege, punctuated by a series of stabbing offensives designed to wear down the Confederates. Despite their numerically greater losses (in excess of 60,000), despite such embarrassing defeats as the battle of the Crater, and despite Lee's masterful generalling, Union forces eventually succeeded at dislodging and then pincering the Army of Northern Virginia.

Pickets. Pickets were individual soldiers, or small squads, charged with a variety of responsibilities, primarily reconnaissance, guard duty, and camp patrol. Beyond its military importance, picket duty—given its relatively unsupervised character—provided opportunities for soldiers to converse or trade with "enemy" pickets.

Rosecrans, William Starke (1819–1898). "Old Rosy," a Catholic Democrat from Ohio, participated in some of the Union's most important advances in the war, yet ultimately saw his military career fizzle out. He rose through the ranks by contributing to victories in western Virginia, Iuka and Corinth, Stones River, and—most of all—in Chattanooga, but ran into disaster at Chickamauga, where his stunned retreat stood in contrast to Gen. George Thomas's valiant stand. After Thomas replaced him as commander of the Army of the Cumberland, Rosecrans took charge of the Department of the Missouri, but had little further impact on the course of the war.

Sanitary Commission. The United States Sanitary Commission was a major charitable organization, staffed primarily by female volunteers that provided supplies, bureaucratic assistance, and medical care to thousands of Civil War soldiers at both camps and hospitals. In service of this work, it formed a slew of subsidiary relief organizations and advised the federal government on military medical policy. The Commission's approach to relief work was more pragmatic than philosophical, emphasizing workable strategies rather than lofty ideals.

Saxton, Rufus (1824–1908). After rising steadily through the military ranks, the Massachusetts-born Saxton was named brigadier general of volunteers in April 1862, and then given command of federal forces in the South Carolina Sea Islands in February 1863. His most important contribution to the Northern war effort was to organize, with authorization of the War Department, the training and deployment of freedmen and former slaves, or contrabands, whom the war had displaced. After the war, and until 1866, Saxton served as Freedmen's Bureau commissioner in South Carolina.

Scott, Winfield (1786–1866). A native of Virginia, Scott rose to the rank of general in the War of 1812 and then served as commanding general of the U.S. Army during the Mexican–American War of 1846–48. During this latter conflict, he commanded more than 100 officers who would go on to become Civil War generals, many of them applying the military lessons learned in Mexico. During the early months of the Civil War, Scott developed a far-reaching strategy to constrict the Confederacy with naval power, but this "Anaconda Plan," as it was dubbed, seemed too slow to many Northerners. Outpaced by George McClellan, and in poor health, Scott left office on November 1, 1861.

Sedgwick, John (1813–1864). "Uncle John" Sedgwick, brigadier general and major general in the Army of the Potomac, was a skillful, intrepid, and popular commander who made significant contributions to the Union war effort, at Antietam, Rappahannock Bridge, and even Fredericksburg. Wounded several times already, Sedgwick's luck ran out at the battle of Spotsylvania, where he was shot and killed while reviewing troop positions.

Seven Days' Battles. June 25–July 1, 1862. During April, May, and June, George McClellan had been preparing (in glacially slow fashion) a major assault on Richmond.

Though numerically superior, McClellan was unprepared for the inspired generalling of Lee, who had taken command of the Army of Northern Virginia after Joseph Johnston's wounding at the battle of Seven Pines. In a week-long series of battles—Oak Grove, Mechanicsville, Gaines' Mill, Savage's Station, Glendale/White Oak Swamp, Malvern Hill—Lee managed to thwart the Union advance, despite poor coordination, heavy casualties, and the repeated nonperformance of Stonewall Jackson. The battles spooked McClellan, protected Richmond, and helped to establish Lee as the South's leading military light.

Seward, William Henry (1830–1915). Ambitious, pragmatic, and complicated, Seward led one of the more colorful careers in American politics and as Secretary of State played a central role in the Civil War policies of the Lincoln administration. An antislavery Whig-turned-Republican, Seward tended to advise the moderate and publicly palatable course, in contrast to administration radicals, and he generally sought to soft-pedal the significance of emancipation and post-war reconstruction.

Sheridan, Philip Henry (1831–1888). Where some commanders had to learn aggression by experience, the North's Sheridan hit the ground running. He first proved his mettle in the West, at Perryville, Murfreesboro, Chickamauga, and Missionary Ridge, earning the opportunity to take command of cavalry in the Army of the Potomac. It was in this role that Sheridan wrote himself into history. After assisting in Grant's Overland campaign in 1864 by conducting raids around Richmond, he was sent to the fertile Shenandoah Valley to put down Jubal Early's marauding army. Here, Sheridan led his troops in a systematic scorched-earth campaign designed to deprive the Confederacy of resources and to sap its will to fight. His dramatic and unexpected victory at Cedar Creek, and then at Five Forks and Sayler's Creek in Virginia, allowed him to cut off Lee's retreat from Petersburg and thus precipitate the surrender of the Army of Northern Virginia.

Sherman, William Tecumseh (1820–1891). The early indications were not promising, despite his excellence at West Point. After a series of unsuccessful business ventures and financial problems, Sherman rejoined the Army, becoming colonel in 1861, but had a mixed record in his early battles in the Western theater. Two crucial turning points were his command of Memphis, during which he began developing his concept of total war, and his effective service under Grant during the grueling Vicksburg campaign. Named commander of Western forces after Grant's promotion to Lieutenant General, Sherman began pushing into Georgia against Joseph Johnston and then John Bell Hood. After subduing Atlanta, Sherman's army cut a wide swath to Savannah, then up into South Carolina, destroying as much property as possible in order to convince civilians of the futility of war. Having no particular animus toward Southerners, Sherman recommended lenient surrender terms and a nonvindictive Reconstruction policy. Sherman wrote his *Memoirs* while he served, rather unhappily, as commanding general of the United States Army, and they reflect the public personality of a man who had earned a profound understanding of both the details and the depths of war.

Shiloh. The battle of Shiloh, in Tennessee, took place on April 6–7, 1862, and it provided a horrifying spectacle of what kind of conflict the Civil War was becoming. In military terms, the primary significance of the battle—a costly strategic Union victory, achieved after a near-breakthrough by the South—lay in the Confederacy's failure to break increasing federal control of the Mississippi Valley, which would ultimately prove decisive in the Western theater. In psychological terms, the vast numbers of dead and wounded—at least 20,000, more than twice the total of all previous Civil War battles—revealed to both sides how intense and how long-lived the war would have to be.

Spotsylvania Court House. May 9–19, 1864. Just days after the battle of the Wilderness, the Army of Northern Virginia and the Army of the Potomac met again as Grant ground on with his Overland campaign, trying to get around Lee's right flank. After an unexpected day of fighting on May 8, the Confederates continued to strengthen their already redoubtable line of fieldworks north of the town of Spotsylvania Court House. Then came day after day of seesaw attacks and counterattacks, positioning and repositioning, as the Union forces struggled to get traction. Some of the most intense fighting of the war occurred on May 12 at a line of trenches known as the Bloody Angle, where the dead piled up for almost twenty hours of unrelenting close-quarters combat. By the nineteenth, another 18,000 Union soldiers had been killed, wounded, or captured; estimated Confederate losses range from 10,000 to 12,000.

Stanton, Edwin McMasters (1814–1869). As U.S. Secretary of War from January 1862 to May 1868, the hard-nosed former lawyer from Ohio played a central role in the Union's conduct of the war and, to a lesser extent, in the formulation of postwar reconstruction policies. He advised Lincoln on military appointments and strategy, usually pushing for the more aggressive option, such as removing McClellan or emancipating slaves and enlisting African American troops. His preeminent talent was logistics; Stanton's reorganization of the War Department and his efficiency in supplying and running the Union war machine were crucial factors in the North's eventual victory.

Stuart, James Ewell Brown (1833–1864). J. E. B. ("Jeb") Stuart embodied the spirit of dashing equestrian valor on which the South prided itself. Appointed colonel of the 1st Virginia Cavalry in July 1861, and then brigadier general after his performance at Bull Run, Stuart became a master of raiding and reconnaissance, blending caution and daring in his information-gathering forays around enemy positions and his sudden strikes against Union forces. Gettysburg was the black mark on his otherwise stellar career; otherwise occupied in Pennsylvania, Stuart did not show up until late on the second day, having unintentionally deprived Lee of crucial battlefield information. Stuart was shot on May 11, 1864, during an engagement against Sheridan at Yellow Tavern, and died the next day.

Vicksburg Campaign and Siege. March–July 1863. Located on the Mississippi River about 225 miles north of New Orleans, Vicksburg was one of the South's major military and economic hubs, with both strategic and psychological significance. Grant had early set his sights on this "Gibraltar of the Confederacy," and, after failing in direct efforts at capture, decided to circle around from the south. Landing at Bruinsburg, Mississippi, Grant's army marched northeast toward Jackson, Mississippi, living off the land and confiscating what they needed—a signature development in Civil War tactics. After Sherman took Jackson, Grant moved west toward Vicksburg, pushing Confederate Gen. John C. Pemberton back into Vicksburg. Two failed assaults convinced Grant to lay siege, and his men began the process of digging trenches, firing artillery, and cutting off food and supplies to the city. By early July, with no reinforcements forthcoming from the Eastern theater, the conditions inside the city had deteriorated to the point where

Pemberton saw the writing on the wall. He agreed to a surrender on July 4, turning over approximately 30,000 men and 60,000 firearms. The fall of Vicksburg was one of the major events—along with Gettysburg and the capture of Atlanta—that foretold the demise of the Confederacy.

Wilderness. The battle of the Wilderness (May 5–6, 1864) took its name from the thickly forested region of pine, scrub, and overgrowth near Chancellorsville, Virginia. It was the first confrontation between Lee and Grant, who had taken command of the Army of the Potomac in March, and had planned his Overland campaign to move south into Virginia in order to draw Lee into direct, open combat. Outnumbered nearly two to one, Lee preferred to hit the Northern army as it moved through the Wilderness, where the Union's advantage in artillery and troop strength would matter less. What followed was two days of savage but inconclusive fighting, a chaos of brushfires, blinding smoke, flying lead, hand-to-hand combat, and friendly fire. In the end, the North suffered about 18,000 casualties, the South about 11,000 (including James Longstreet) but this time, the Union commander, rather than turning back, determined to press on, toward Spotsylvania Court House.

Zouaves. Immediately before and during the Civil War, a number of military regiments, mostly Northern, adopted a colorful, exotic uniform inspired by the attire of French colonial forces in Algeria (whose Berber mercenaries were called "Zouaoua"). Zouave units enjoyed a dashing reputation probably in excess of their military performance, but they fought from start to finish in the war, and were undoubtedly good for morale.

Index